TECHNIQUES OF ECONOMIC
ANALYSIS WITH APPLICATIONS

TECHNIQUES OF ECONOMIC ANALYSIS WITH APPLICATIONS

Ashok Parikh and David Bailey

HARVESTER WHEATSHEAF

New York   London   Toronto   Sydney   Tokyo   Singapore

First published 1990 by
Harvester Wheatsheaf,
66 Wood Lane End, Hemel Hempstead,
Hertfordshire, HP2 4RG
A division of
Simon & Schuster International Group

© Parikh and Bailey, 1990

All rights reserved. No part of this publication may be
reproduced, stored in a retrieval system, or transmitted,
in any form, or by any means, electronic, mechanical,
photocopying, recording or otherwise, without the
prior permission, in writing, from the publisher.

Printed and bound in Great Britain at
the University Press, Cambridge

British Library Cataloguing in Publication Data

Bailey, David, *1943–*
Techniques of economic analysis with applications.
1. Economic analysis
I. Title   II. Parikh, Ashok, *1936–*
330

ISBN 0-7450-0375-3

1 2 3 4 5   94 93 92 91 90

CONTENTS

Acknowledgements vii

Chapter 1   **Introduction**   1

Chapter 2   **An introduction to regression analysis**   5
- 2.1   Multiple linear regression   5
- 2.2   Relaxation of the assumptions regarding the disturbance term   14
-       Appendix: the general linear model   25

Chapter 3   **Some applications of multiple linear regression**   35
- 3.1   Serial correlation   35
- 3.2   Heteroscedasticity   42
- 3.3   Specification error   45
- 3.4   Multicollinearity   48

Chapter 4   **Maximum likelihood methods**   56
- 4.1   The concept of maximum likelihood   56
- 4.2   Application of maximum likelihood in distributed lag models   70
- 4.3   Qualitative and limited dependent variables   77
- 4.4   Errors in variables   88

Chapter 5   **The generalised linear regression model**   101
- 5.1   Generalised linear regression model   101
- 5.2   Seemingly unrelated regressions   112

Chapter 6   **Estimation in simultaneous equation models**   131
- 6.1   Simultaneous equation models   131
- 6.2   The identification problem   135
- 6.3   Single-equation estimation methods in simultaneous equation models   141
- 6.4   System methods of estimation   154
- 6.5   Concluding remarks   160

Chapter 7	**An introduction to input–output analysis**		167
	7.1 The static Leontief open input–output model		168
	7.2 Backward and forward linkages		176
	7.3 Input–output analysis and foreign trade		179
	7.4 The dynamic Leontief input–output model		182
	7.5 Procedures for updating input–output matrices		188
Chapter 8	**Applied general equilibrium models**		195
	8.1 A model of general equilibrium		195
	8.2 The construction of an AGE model		201
	8.3 Some recent AGE models		204
	Appendix: social accounting matrix (SAM)		206
Chapter 9	**Linear programming**		210
	9.1 An introduction to linear programming		210
	9.2 The simplex method		214
	9.3 The dual of a linear program		221
	9.4 The dual simplex method		231
	9.5 The transportation problem		237
Chapter 10	**Integer and nonlinear programming**		247
	10.1 Integer programming		247
	10.2 Duality and integer programming		254
	10.3 An introduction to nonlinear programming		261
	10.4 Quadratic programming		271
	10.5 The peak load pricing problem		273
Chapter 11	**An introduction to dynamic optimisation**		282
	11.1 Optimal control theory		282
	11.2 Some economic applications of optimal control theory		287
	11.3 Dynamic programming		294
	11.4 Some economic applications of dynamic programming		298
Appendix 1:	**Summary of matrix algebra**		306
Appendix 2:	**Statistical results**		314
Appendix 3:	**Solutions and hints**		323
Appendix 4:	**Statistical tables**		338
Index			351

ACKNOWLEDGEMENTS

No book such as this one would have ever been written without the help, support and forbearance of family, friends and colleagues. The economics department at the University of East Anglia is a happy, congenial one, and we are indebted to our colleagues for many discussions over the years on matter pertaining to the subject material of this book. In particular, we are indebted to Richard Crum for his helpful comments and his contribution on the Social Accounting Matrix. Ros Pye deciphered our numerous drafts and typed the complete manuscript with her customary efficiency and good humour. Last but not least, thanks must be extended to Sue, Clare and Frances, Daksha and Ami, upon whom many of the costs, in the form of lost weekends, etc., of writing this book fell.

Chapter 1
INTRODUCTION

The book has evolved from undergraduate and graduate courses given by the authors at the University of East Anglia in the last ten years, and we are much indebted to our students for the stimulus provided by their enthusiasm for, and interest in, the subject matter of this book. The book aims at giving a simple but comprehensive treatment of both the econometric techniques and the optimisation methods which are widely used in economic analysis. The first half of the book is concerned with the exposition of econometric techniques, while in the second part we move away from stochastic models and embark upon a discussion of deterministic optimisation methods. We are both great believers in the old Chinese proverb: I hear and I forget, I see and I remember, I do and I understand. To this end throughout the book we seek to provide examples to illustrate the various techniques we have been discussing; as an aid to understanding, there is no substitute for working through such material, carefully following each step.

The reader of the book is assumed to have a sound understanding of the principles of economic theory, at least at a second-year undergraduate level, as well as a knowledge of the basic statistical and mathematical methods to which economics students are commonly exposed. On the statistical side we assume the student is familiar with the essential elements of hypothesis testing, while on the mathematical side we take it that students have followed an introductory course in mathematical methods which has covered the elements of calculus and matrix algebra. An important point we would like to make on the methodology we have utilised is that we have sought to adopt a relatively informal approach. Essential theorems are indeed proved but some purists might object that the book is not sufficiently rigorous. In our defence we would state that our main objective is to avoid bogging the reader down in a morass of algebraic detail but to motivate readers to acquire an understanding of the basic principles underlying the various techniques of economic analysis dealt with in the book.

The book, which is suitable for both undergraduate and beginning graduate students, can be used for two purposes: first, as an introductory text in econometrics which also has the advantage of having a considerable applied content; and second, as a text in optimisation theory in which linear, integer, nonlinear and dynamic programming are exposed from both a theoretical and empirical viewpoint. In

Chapters 2–6 single and simultaneous equation methods of estimation are discussed. Chapters 7 and 8 are concerned with input–output and applied general equilibrium models, while the final three chapters of the book outline mathematical programming methods.

In Chapter 2 we discuss the basic multiple linear regression model. Having stated the assumptions that are typically made about the stochastic disturbance term, we derive the least squares estimators and comment upon their properties. An illustrative numerical example with two explanatory variables is provided. We then go on to consider the consequences of relaxing the assumptions of the model. In particular, we are concerned with the implications of an assumption not holding for the properties of the estimators. In an appendix to the chapter the linear model is generalised and a presentation of the least squares procedure using matrix algebra is given.

Chapter 3 continues our discussion of the multiple linear regression model. In particular, we discuss some empirical studies in which the assumptions of the classical linear regression model are shown not to be satisfied. We estimate some money demand functions for the United Kingdom and discuss the problem of serial correlation which is found to be present in some of the estimated equations. The issue of heteroscedasticity in both cross-section and grouped data is then addressed, using as examples a study of productivity in Cypriot manufacturing industries and a cross-sectional consumption function for the United Kingdom. Specification errors are often made in econometric work and a discussion of simple specification error tests is provided. Finally, the chapter concludes with a section on multicollinearity, one of the most difficult problems that an investigator comes across in empirical investigation.

Chapter 4 contains an exposition of maximum likelihood methods. We commence the chapter by obtaining the ML estimators for both the simple and multiple linear regression models. We then go on to outline a number of asymptotic tests – the likelihood ratio test and other associated tests such as the Wald test and the Lagrange multiplier test – which can be employed for discriminating between alternative model specifications. An illustration of the use of these tests is provided in an empirical study of causality between money, prices and real output in Italy. Distributed lag models are very common in econometrics. Both adaptive expectations and partial adjustment models yield distributed lag forms and these models may be estimated using ML procedures; as an illustration we discuss the estimation of supply functions for coffee. Another important area where ML estimation procedures are to be recommended is in the estimation of models with a qualitative or limited dependent variable. Probit, logit and tobit models of estimation are discussed and examples are provided. In the final section of the chapter we turn to the problem of errors in variables and outline the instrumental variable estimation procedure for dealing with this problem.

In Chapter 5 we discuss the general linear regression model and consider the estimation of a regression equation where the variance–covariance matrix takes a very general form. We deal first with the case where the disturbances are heteroscedastic, and second where they follow a first-order autoregressive process; both kinds of disturbances are then allowed for in the estimation of a model in which time-series and cross-sectional observations have been pooled. The chapter concludes with a section on seemingly unrelated regression in which the stochastic disturbance term is correlated across equations. Zellner's procedure for estimating such a system of equations is presented and an illustration of the approach is provided by an empirical study on the demand for inputs in Indian agriculture.

Simultaneous equation models are discussed in Chapter 6. Having distinguished between endogenous and predetermined variables, we show how to derive the reduced form equations which enable us to solve for the endogenous variables in terms of the predetermined variables and disturbances of the model. We then go on to discuss the identification problem; here we are concerned with the conditions under which it will be possible to obtain the structural coefficients of the model given knowledge of the reduced form coefficients. Identification is one of the fundamental issues in econometrics and both the order and rank conditions are derived and applied. Having discussed identification we then turn to estimation; here we discuss both single-equation and system methods of estimation.

In Chapters 7 and 8 we deal, respectively, with input–output models and models of applied general equilibrium. Space considerations have precluded other than a brief introduction to these two techniques of economic analysis. One possibility would have been to delete the two chapters from the book; but finally we felt that, given the wide use of input–output analysis in developing countries and the growing popularity of applied general equilibrium models for policy analysis, it would be useful to include some discussion, however brief, of these techniques. The input–output model is a multisector equilibrium model which deals with the production side of the economy; it has wide applications in both developed and developing countries, including planning and the analysis of backward and forward linkages. In Chapter 7 we present both static and dynamic Leontief models in the context of both a closed and open economy.

While the input–output models assume exogenous demands, general equilibrium models treat demand and supply in an interdependent framework. In Chapter 8 we present the essential characteristics of applied general equilibrium models and provide a numerical example of a simple two-sector model. This example is then utilised to show the effects of a change in tax policy on output, prices and the distribution of income, welfare measures such as the compensating and equivalent variation being used to evaluate the gains and losses that stem from the change. A brief discussion of some recent studies on tax and trade policy is then presented and the chapter concludes with an outline of the social accounting matrix.

The final chapters, Chapters 9–11, are concerned with techniques of mathematical programming. In Chapter 9 we explain the basic principles of linear programming, starting with a diagrammatic analysis and then proceeding to the general case where we outline the simplex method. We discuss the dual of a linear program and show the connections between the original problem, the primal and its dual. Throughout the analysis we emphasise the economic significance of the results. The dual simplex method and sensitivity analysis are outlined with examples being given to illustrate the procedures. In the final section the transportation problem is discussed and the economic significance of the dual of the transportation problem is explained.

Chapter 10 is devoted to a consideration of both integer and nonlinear programming. In integer programming, one or more of the choice variables are restricted to take integer values. The features of the cutting method are presented for both the all-integer and the mixed integer problem. Problems associated with the interpretation of the dual of an integer programming problem are examined. In the second part of the chapter we turn to nonlinear programming and make clear the economic significance of the Kuhn–Tucker conditions; to this end we present an analysis of the optimal pricing and capacity decisions for a public enterprise producing, first a non-storable output and, second, a storable output.

In the final chapter of the book an introductory treatment of dynamic optimisation is provided in which time can be treated as a continuous or discrete variable. First we treat time as a continuous variable and outline the main elements of optimal control theory. The theory is then illustrated with reference to the problem of choosing an optimal consumption plan for an individual consumer and the optimal depletion path for an exhaustible resource. Turning to discrete time, we explain the significance of Bellman's optimality principle of dynamic programming. Associated with each dynamic programming problem is a fundamental recurrence relation which can be utilised to solve the problem. The chapter ends with some economic examples of the use of the technique.

Chapter 2
AN INTRODUCTION TO REGRESSION ANALYSIS

The basic purpose of this chapter is to explain the principles and procedures of regression analysis. We seek to make clear the meaning and significance of the assumptions underlying the regression model. We outline the computational procedures for obtaining estimators of the regression coefficients, and discuss the interpretation of the results along with an analysis of the econometric problems that investigators are likely to be faced with in their empirical work.

In Section 2.1 we discuss the (multiple) linear regression model: we derive the properties of the estimators and extend the discussion of hypothesis testing. In Section 2.2 we consider the consequences of relaxing the assumptions of the regression model. In particular, we are concerned with the implications of an assumption not holding for the properties of the estimators. A general linear model is presented in an appendix to the chapter.

2.1 MULTIPLE LINEAR REGRESSION

We postulate the existence of the following linear relationship between Y (the dependent) and X_2 and X_3 (the explanatory variables):

$$Y_i = \beta_1 + \beta_2 X_{2i} + \beta_3 X_{3i} + u_i \quad (i = 1, 2, \ldots, n) \tag{2.1}$$

where Y is the dependent variable, X_2 and X_3 are the explanatory variables and u is the stochastic disturbance term. Alternatively, equation (2.1) can be written in a slightly different notation:

$$Y_i = \beta_{1.23} + \beta_{12.3} X_{2i} + \beta_{13.2} X_{3i} + u_i \tag{2.2}$$

where $\beta_{1.23}$ is the constant or intercept term, measuring the average value of Y when X_2 and X_3 are set equal to zero, and $\beta_{12.3}$ and $\beta_{13.2}$ are called the partial regression coefficients, with $\beta_{12.3}$ ($\beta_{13.2}$) measuring the change in Y for a unit change in X_2 (X_3), given that X_3 (X_2) remains unchanged.

We make the following assumptions regarding the disturbance term:

1. $E(u_i) = 0$ $\quad (i = 1, \ldots, n)$ (2.3)
2. $E(u_i^2) = \sigma_u^2$ $\quad (i = 1, \ldots, n)$ (2.4)
3. $E(u_i u_j) = 0$ $\quad$ (when $i \neq j$) (2.5)
4. $E(X_{2i} u_j) = E(X_{3i} u_j) = 0$ $\quad$ (for all $i, j = 1, \ldots, n$) (2.6)

where E is the expectation operator.

In addition, we assume that there exists no exact linear relationship between the explanatory variables. There exists no set of numbers, $\lambda_2 \neq 0$ and $\lambda_3 \neq 0$, such that

$$\lambda_2 X_{2i} + \lambda_3 X_{3i} = 0 \tag{2.7}$$

If the above equation is only satisfied for $\lambda_2 = \lambda_3 = 0$, then X_2 and X_3 are said to be linearly independent.

Assumption (i) states that the mean value of the disturbance is zero. As a result of this assumption

$$\begin{aligned} E(Y_i) &= E(\beta_1 + \beta_2 X_{2i} + \beta_3 X_{3i} + u_i) \\ &= \beta_1 + \beta_2 X_{2i} + \beta_3 X_{3i} \end{aligned} \tag{2.8}$$

The second assumption implies that the u_i are drawn from the same population and their common variance is σ_u^2. We may also obtain the variance of Y_i:

$$\begin{aligned} \operatorname{Var}(Y_i) &= E[Y_i - e(Y_i)]^2 \\ &= E[Y_i - (\beta_1 + \beta_2 X_{2i} + \beta_3 X_{3i})]^2 \\ &= E(u_i^2) = \sigma_u^2 \end{aligned} \tag{2.9}$$

Given the random nature of the errors, they are independent of each other – this is the third assumption of zero covariance between successive disturbances. If two random variables are independent, their covariance is zero (see Kmenta, 1986, pp. 70–1). In the fourth assumption, the Xs are held constant from sample to sample and are independent of the random disturbance term. The significance of these assumptions and the implications of relaxing them will be developed in this chapter.

Using the model expressed in equation (2.1), we write the sample regression equation in which population parameters $(\beta_1, \beta_2, \beta_3)$ are replaced by sample parameters (b_1, b_2, b_3) as

$$Y_i = b_1 + b_2 X_{2i} + b_3 X_{3i} + e_i \tag{2.10}$$

The residual sum of squares we seek to minimise is given by

$$\Sigma e_i^2 = \Sigma (Y_i - b_1 - b_2 X_{2i} - b_3 X_{3i})^2 \tag{2.11}$$

Differentiating partially with respect to b_1, b_2 and b_3 and setting these partial derivatives equal to zero, we have

$$\left. \begin{aligned} \frac{\partial \Sigma e_i^2}{\partial b_1} &= -2\Sigma(Y_i - b_1 - b_2 X_{2i} - b_3 X_{3i}) = 0 \\ \frac{\partial \Sigma e_i^2}{\partial b_2} &= -2\Sigma X_{2i}(Y_i - b_1 - b_2 X_{2i} - b_3 X_{3i}) = 0 \\ \frac{\partial \Sigma e_i^2}{\partial b_3} &= -2\Sigma X_{3i}(Y_i - b_1 - b_2 X_{2i} - b_3 X_{3i}) = 0 \end{aligned} \right\} \tag{2.12}$$

Rearranging, we obtain the normal equations

$$\begin{aligned} \Sigma Y_i &= nb_1 + b_2 \Sigma X_{2i} + b_3 \Sigma X_{3i} \\ \Sigma Y_i X_{2i} &= b_1 \Sigma X_{2i} + b_2 \Sigma X_{2i}^2 + b_3 \Sigma X_{2i} X_{3i} \\ \Sigma Y_i X_{3i} &= b_1 \Sigma X_{3i} + b_2 \Sigma X_{2i} X_{3i} + b_3 \Sigma X_{3i}^2 \end{aligned} \quad (2.13)$$

From the first equation we have

$$b_1 = \bar{Y} - b_2 \bar{X}_2 - b_3 \bar{X}_3 \quad (2.14)$$

and substituting this expression for b_1 into the second and third equations yields

$$\Sigma Y_i X_{2i} = (\bar{Y} - b_2 \bar{X}_2 - b_3 \bar{X}_3) \Sigma X_{2i} + b_2 \Sigma X_{2i}^2 + b_3 \Sigma X_{2i} X_{3i}$$

$$\Sigma Y_i X_{3i} = (\bar{Y} - b_2 \bar{X}_2 - b_3 \bar{X}_3) \Sigma \bar{X}_{3i} + b_2 \Sigma X_{2i} X_{3i} + b_3 \Sigma X_{3i}^2$$

Rearranging the terms and using the result that

$$\Sigma X_i^2 - \bar{X} \Sigma X_i = \Sigma (X_i - \bar{X})^2$$

we obtain

$$\Sigma (X_{2i} - \bar{X}_2)(Y_i - \bar{Y}) = b_2 \Sigma (X_{2i} - \bar{X}_2)^2 + b_3 \Sigma (X_{2i} - \bar{X}_2)(X_{3i} - \bar{X}_3)$$

$$\Sigma (X_{3i} - \bar{X}_3)(Y_i - \bar{Y}) = b_2 \Sigma (X_{2i} - \bar{X}_2)(X_{3i} - \bar{X}_3) + b_3 \Sigma (X_{3i} - \bar{X}_3)^2$$

Using lower case letters for deviations from means, we can write

$$\begin{aligned} \Sigma x_{2i} y_i &= b_2 \Sigma x_{2i}^2 + b_3 \Sigma x_{2i} x_{3i} \\ \Sigma x_{3i} y_i &= b_2 \Sigma x_{2i} x_{3i} + b_3 \Sigma x_{3i}^2 \end{aligned} \quad (2.15)$$

Solving the above two equations for b_2 and b_3, we obtain

$$b_2 = \frac{\Sigma x_{2i} y_i \Sigma x_{3i}^2 - \Sigma x_{2i} x_{3i} \Sigma x_{3i} y_i}{\Sigma x_{2i}^2 \Sigma x_{3i}^2 - (\Sigma x_{2i} x_{3i})^2} \quad (2.16)$$

$$b_3 = \frac{\Sigma x_{3i} y_i \Sigma x_{2i}^2 - \Sigma x_{2i} x_{3i} \Sigma x_{2i} y_i}{\Sigma x_{2i}^2 \Sigma x_{3i}^2 - (\Sigma x_{2i} x_{3i})^2} \quad (2.17)$$

It can be shown that the least squares estimates are best linear unbiased estimates of the true regression coefficients. We will content ourselves with showing that b_2 is an unbiased estimator of β_2, and will derive its variance.

In terms of deviations from means, we have

$$y_i = \beta_2 x_{2i} + \beta_3 x_{3i} + u_i - \bar{u} \quad (2.18)$$

and substituting in equation (2.16) we obtain

$$b_2 = \frac{\Sigma x_{3i}^2 \Sigma x_{2i} [\beta_2 x_{2i} + \beta_3 x_{3i} + u_i - \bar{u}] - \Sigma x_{2i} x_{3i} \Sigma x_{3i} [\beta_2 x_{2i} + \beta_3 x_{3i} + u_i - \bar{u}]}{\Sigma x_{2i}^2 \Sigma x_{3i}^2 - (\Sigma x_{2i} x_{3i})^2} \quad (2.19)$$

Rearranging terms and noting that $\Sigma x_{2i} \bar{u} = \bar{u} \Sigma x_{2i} = 0$ since $\Sigma x_{2i} = 0$ and similarly $\Sigma x_{3i} \bar{u} = 0$, we have, after some simplification,

$$b_2 = \beta_2 + \frac{\Sigma x_{3i}^2 \Sigma x_{2i} u_i - \Sigma x_{2i} x_{3i} \Sigma x_{3i} u_i}{\Sigma x_{2i}^2 \Sigma x_{3i}^2 - (\Sigma x_{2i} x_{3i})^2} \qquad (2.20)$$

Taking expected values and remembering that x_{2i} and x_{3i} are fixed variables:

$$E(b_2) = \beta_2 + \frac{\Sigma x_{3i}^2 \Sigma x_{2i} E(u_i) - \Sigma x_{2i} x_{3i} \Sigma x_{3i} E(u_i)}{\Sigma x_{2i}^2 \Sigma x_{3i}^2 - (\Sigma x_{2i} x_{3i})^2}$$

$$= \beta_2 \text{ since } E(u_i) = 0 \qquad (2.21)$$

Thus b_2 is an unbiased estimator of β_2 and, given the symmetry, it obviously follows that b_3 is an unbiased estimator of β_3. In the appendix to this chapter, we show for the general linear model that all the estimators are best linear unbiased (BLUE).

Turning now to the variance of b_2, we have

$$\text{Var}(b_2) = E[(b_2 - \beta_2)^2] = E\left[\left(\frac{\Sigma x_{3i}^2 \Sigma x_{2i} u_i - \Sigma x_{2i} x_{3i} \Sigma x_{3i} u_i}{\Sigma x_{2i}^2 \Sigma x_{3i}^2 - (\Sigma x_{2i} x_{3i})^2}\right)^2\right] \qquad (2.22)$$

Consider the numerator of the expression on the right-hand side:

$$(\Sigma x_{3i}^2 \Sigma x_{2i} u_i - \Sigma x_{2i} x_{3i} \Sigma x_{3i} u_i)^2 = (\Sigma x_{3i}^2)^2 \left[\Sigma x_{2i}^2 u_i^2 + \sum_{i \neq j} x_{2i} x_{2j} u_i u_j\right]$$

$$+ (\Sigma x_{2i} x_{3i})^2 \left[\Sigma x_{3i}^2 u_i^2 + \sum_{i \neq j} x_{2i} x_{3j} u_i u_j\right]$$

$$- 2\Sigma x_{3i}^2 \Sigma x_{2i} x_{3i} \left[\Sigma x_{2i} x_{3i} u_i^2 + \sum_{i \neq j} x_{2i} x_{3j} u_i u_j\right] \qquad (2.23)$$

Now, taking expected values and remembering that $E(u_i^2) = \sigma_u^2$ and $E(u_i u_j) = 0$:

$$E[(\Sigma x_{3i}^2 \Sigma x_{2i} u_i - \Sigma x_{2i} x_{3i} \Sigma x_{3i} u_i)^2] = \sigma_u^2 [(\Sigma x_{3i}^2)^2 \Sigma x_{2i}^2 - 2\Sigma x_{3i}^2 (\Sigma x_{2i} x_{3i})^2$$

$$+ \Sigma x_{3i}^2 (\Sigma x_{2i} x_{3i})^2]$$

$$= \sigma_u^2 \Sigma x_{3i}^2 [\Sigma x_{2i}^2 \Sigma x_{3i}^2 - (\Sigma x_{2i} x_{3i})^2]$$

and hence

$$E[(b_2 - \beta_2)^2] = \frac{\sigma_u^2 \Sigma x_{3i}^2}{\Sigma x_{2i}^2 \Sigma x_{3i}^2 - (\Sigma x_{2i} x_{3i})^2} \qquad (2.24)$$

Similarly,

$$E[(b_3 - \beta_3)^2] = \frac{\sigma_u^2 \Sigma x_{2i}^2}{\Sigma x_{2i}^2 \Sigma x_{3i}^2 - (\Sigma x_{2i} x_{3i})^2} \qquad (2.25)$$

It can also be shown that

$$E[(b_1 - \beta_1)^2] = \frac{\sigma_u^2 [\Sigma x_{2i}^2 \Sigma x_{3i}^2 - (\Sigma x_{2i} x_{3i})^2]}{n [\Sigma x_{2i}^2 \Sigma x_{3i}^2 - (\Sigma x_{2i} x_{3i})^2]} \qquad (2.26)$$

and

Multiple linear regression

$$E[(b_2 - \beta_2)(b_3 - \beta_3)] = \frac{\sigma_u^2 \Sigma x_{2i} x_{3i}}{\Sigma x_{2i}^2 \Sigma x_{3i}^2 - (\Sigma x_{2i} x_{3i})^2} \quad (2.27)$$

The sampling variances and covariances are all functions of σ_u^2, the variance of the us and, generally, σ_u^2 is unknown. An unbiased estimator of σ_u^2 provided by

$$s^2 = \frac{\Sigma e_i^2}{n-3} \quad (2.28)$$

where Σe_i^2 is the sum of the squared residuals from the fitted relationship. The standard errors of the least squares estimators may then be calculated by substituting s^2 for the unknown σ^2. We have, for example,

$$se(b_2) = \sqrt{\left(\frac{s^2 \Sigma x_{3i}^2}{\Sigma x_{2i}^2 \Sigma x_{3i}^2 - (\Sigma x_{2i} x_{3i})^2}\right)} \quad (2.29)$$

The test of the null hypothesis $H_0: \beta_j = 0$ against the alternative hypothesis $H_1: \beta_j \neq 0$ assumes that the us are normally and independently distributed. This is based on the ratio

$$t = \frac{|b_j|}{se(b_j)} \quad (2.30)$$

If $t > t_{0.025}$ where $t_{0.025}$ is read off as the 2.5 per cent point of the t distribution with $n - 3$ degrees of freedom, we reject the null hypothesis in favour of the alternative. For testing the more general null hypothesis $H_0: \beta_j = \beta_j'$ against the alternative $H_1: \beta_j \neq \beta_j'$ t-test is based on the ratio

$$t = \frac{|b_j - \beta_j'|}{se(b_j)}$$

The test of the null hypothesis $H_0: \beta_2 + \beta_3 = C$ against the alternative hypothesis $H_1: \beta_2 + \beta_3 \neq C$ where C is a constant is based on the ratio

$$t = \frac{|b_2 + b_3 - C|}{se(b_2 + b_3)}$$

$$= \frac{|b_2 + b_3 - C|}{\sqrt{(\text{Var } b_2 + \text{Var } b_3 - 2 \text{ Cov } b_2 b_3)}} \quad (2.31)$$

which follows the t distribution with $n - 3$ degrees of freedom. In equation (2.31) estimated variances and covariances are to be used. They are obviously different from actual (true) variances and covariances.

The coefficient of determination (R^2) measures the proportion of the variation in the dependent variable which is explained by the behaviour of the independent variables:

$$R^2 = 1 - \frac{\Sigma e_i^2}{\Sigma y_i^2} \quad (2.32)$$

where Σe_i^2 is the sum of the squared residuals and

$$e_i = y_i - b_2 x_{2i} - b_3 x_{3i} \tag{2.33}$$

Multiplying by e_i and summing over the n observations, we have

$$\Sigma e_i^2 = \Sigma e_i y_i - b_2 \Sigma e_i x_{2i} - b_3 \Sigma e_i x_{3i} \tag{2.34}$$

However, in deriving b_2 and b_3, $\Sigma e_i x_{2i}$ and $\Sigma e_i x_{3i}$ were both set equal to zero in equation (2.12). Hence,

$$\begin{aligned}\Sigma e_i^2 &= \Sigma e_i y_i \\ &= \Sigma y_i (y_i - b_2 x_{2i} - b_3 x_{3i}) \\ &= \Sigma y_i^2 - b_2 \Sigma x_{2i} y_i - b_3 \Sigma x_{3i} y_i \end{aligned} \tag{2.35}$$

Rearranging, we have

$$\Sigma y_i^2 = b_2 \Sigma x_{2i} y_i + b_3 \Sigma x_{3i} y_i + \Sigma e_i^2 \tag{2.36}$$

total variation = explained variation + residual variation

The decomposition of the total variation into the explained and residual variation may also be expressed as

$$\Sigma y_i^2 = \Sigma (b_2 x_{2i} + b_3 x_{3i})^2 + \Sigma e_i^2 \tag{2.37}$$

We leave it as an exercise for the reader to derive the above result. Alternatively, the explained variation can be obtained by using $\Sigma(\hat{Y}_i - \bar{Y})^2$ where $\hat{Y}_i$ are the fitted values. This is more explicit than the one used in equation (2.37).

The coefficient of determination may therefore be expressed as either

$$\begin{aligned}R^2 &= \frac{\Sigma(b_2 x_{2i} + b_3 x_{3i})^2}{\Sigma y_i^2} \\ &= \frac{b_2^2 \Sigma x_{2i}^2 + b_3^2 \Sigma x_{3i}^2 + 2 b_2 b_3 \Sigma x_{2i} x_{3i}}{\Sigma y_i^2}\end{aligned} \tag{2.38}$$

or

$$R^2 = \frac{b_2 \Sigma x_{2i} y_i + b_3 \Sigma x_{3i} y_i}{\Sigma y_i^2} \tag{2.39}$$

and the F test of the null hypothesis $H_0: R^2 = 0$ against the alternative $H_1: R^2 > 0$ can be performed. The test for $H_0: R^2 = 0$ amounts to testing $\beta_2 = 0$ *and* $\beta_3 = 0$. Operationally speaking, the problem can be cast in an analysis of variance framework (see Table 2.1).

$$F = \frac{\text{mean explained sum of squares}}{\text{mean residual sum of squares}}$$

The ratio of the mean explained sum of squares to the mean residual sum of squares has the F distribution with 2 and $n - 3$ degrees of freedom, if H_0 is true. If the cal-

Multiple linear regression

Table 2.1 Analysis of variance

Source of variations	Sum of squares	Degrees of freedom	Mean sum of squares
Explained	$\Sigma(b_2 x_{2i} + b_3 x_{3i})^2$	2	$\Sigma(b_2 x_{2i} + b_3 x_{3i})^2/2$
Residual	Σe_i^2	$n-3$	$\Sigma e_i^2/n-3$
Total	Σy_i^2	$n-1$	

culated $F > F_{0.05}$, the null hypothesis is rejected at the five per cent significance level.

Although the addition of explanatory variables always increases R^2, this does not mean that the enlarged model is superior to the original one. The appropriate way to test this is to look at the estimator of the error variance. An equivalent measure is $\bar{R}^2$, the value of R^2 adjusted for the loss in degrees of freedom. It is defined as

$$1 - \bar{R}^2 = \frac{n-1}{n-k}(1 - R^2) \qquad (2.39a)$$

where k is the number of explanatory variables including the constant.

In the simple regression model, $Y_i = \alpha + \beta X_i + u_i$, the F test of the null hypothesis $H_0: R^2 = 0$ is equivalent to the t test of the null hypothesis $H_0: \beta = 0$. This equivalence does not directly carry over to the multiple regression model: if we find that R^2 is significantly different from zero, this does not imply necessarily that both β_2 and β_3 are statistically significantly different from zero. It is, however, possible to develop an equivalent F test to the t tests used for the separate null hypothesis that (i) $\beta_2 = 0$ and (ii) $\beta_3 = 0$. The procedure is, as follows, to test the null hypothesis $H_0: \beta_3 = 0$. Regress Y on X_2 and obtain the explained sum of squares from this regression; then regress Y on X_2 and X_3 and obtain the explained sum of squares and residual sum of squares from the multiple regression. The sum of squares explained by the addition of X_3 is the difference between the ESS of the second regression and those of the first. The ratio of the mean sum of squares explained by the addition of X_3 to the residual sum of squares from the multiple regression follows the F distribution with 1 and $n-3$ degrees of freedom and provides a test of significance for β_3, if H_0 is true. The identical procedure can be followed for testing the significance of β_2 by regressing Y on X_3 and subsequently obtaining the mean sum of squares explained by the addition of X_2, etc. The procedure is summarised in Table 2.2.

The test of significance of β_3 is based upon $F = S_2^2/S^2$ and the test of significance of R^2 is based upon $F = S_3^2/S^2$. In the F test of the significance of β_3, the calculated $F = t^2$ where $t = b_3/[\text{se}(b_3)]$.

We now provide a numerical example to illustrate the techniques discussed in this section.

The following imaginary data covering a twenty year period relate to the volume of Ambrosian exports (Y), an index of the competitiveness of Ambrosian exports (X_2), measured by the ratio of an index of Ambrosian export prices to an index of competitors' export prices, and an index of world industrial production (X_3). The equation to be estimated is

$$Y_t = \beta_1 + \beta_2 X_{2t} + \beta_3 X_{3t} + u_t$$

Table 2.2 Analysis of variance

Source of variation	Sum of squares	Degrees of freedom	Mean sum of squares
Explained by X_2	$b_2^s \Sigma x_{2i}^2$	1	$b_2^s \Sigma x_{2i}^2 = s_1^2$
Explained by addition of X_3	$\Sigma(b_2 x_{2i} + b_3 x_{3i})^2 - b_2^s \Sigma x_{2i}^2$	1	$\Sigma(b_2 x_{2i} + b_3 x_{3i})^2 = S_2^2 - b_2^s \Sigma x_{2i}^2$
Explained by X_2 and X_3	$\Sigma(b_2 x_{2i} + b_3 x_{3i})^2$	2	$\dfrac{\Sigma(b_2 x_{2i} + b_3 x_{3i})^2}{2} = S_3^2$
Residual	Σe_i^2	$n-3$	$\Sigma e_i^2/n-3 = S^2$
Total	Σy_i^2	$n-1$	

Note: b_2^s is the square of the simple regression coefficient of Y on X_2 while b_2 and b_3 are the partial regression coefficients of Y on X_2 and X_3 respectively.

and our *a priori* expectations are that $\beta_2 < 0$ and $\beta_3 > 0$. Since the data are time series, we have used the subscript t rather than i:

Exports (Y)	Index of competitiveness (X_2)	Index of world industrial production (X_3)
103.1	100	100
114.1	98	103
104.7	100	105
91.0	102	110
96.8	103	108
84.1	105	108
97.6	105	112
121.6	100	117
111.2	98	120
125.7	98	122
91.5	101	120
117.9	102	125
111.6	102	130
122.7	99	132
125.0	96	132
121.9	95	138
117.1	98	145
125.9	101	150
133.2	99	151
131.4	98	150

From the data the following have been calculated:

$\bar{Y} = 112.925 \qquad \Sigma Y^2 = 258\,524.79 \qquad \Sigma y^2 = 3483.6775$

$\bar{X}_2 = 100 \qquad \Sigma X_2^2 = 200\,136 \qquad \Sigma x_2^2 = 136$

$\bar{X}_3 = 123.9 \qquad \Sigma X_3^2 = 312\,222 \qquad \Sigma x_3^2 = 5197.8$

$\Sigma X_2 X_3 = 247\,443 \qquad \Sigma x_2 x_3 = -357$

$\Sigma X_2 Y = 225\,392.1 \qquad \Sigma x_2 y = -457.9$

$\Sigma X_3 Y = 282\,993.8 \qquad \Sigma x_3 y = 3165.65$

To obtain the least squares estimates, we have

$$b_2 = \frac{\Sigma x_2 y \Sigma x_3^2 - \Sigma x_3 y \Sigma x_2 x_3}{\Sigma x_2^2 \Sigma x_3^2 - (\Sigma x_2 x_3)^2} = \frac{-457.9(5197.8) + 3165.65(357)}{136(5197.8) - (357)^2} = -2.1571$$

$$b_3 = \frac{\Sigma x_3 y \Sigma x_2^2 - \Sigma x_2 y \Sigma x_2 x_3}{\Sigma x_2^2 \Sigma x_3^2 - (\Sigma x_2 x_3)^2} = \frac{3165.65(136) - 457.9(357)}{136(5197.8) - (357)^2} = 0.4609$$

$$b_1 = \bar{Y} - b_2 \bar{X}_2 - b_3 \bar{X}_3 = 112.952 + 2.1571(100) - 0.4609(123.9) = 271.5319$$

$$ESS = (b_2 \Sigma x_2^2 + b_3 \Sigma x_3^2)^2 = 2446.7227$$

$$R^2 = \frac{ESS}{TSS} = \frac{2446.7227}{3483.6775} = 0.7023$$

$$SEE = s = \sqrt{\left(\frac{RSS}{n-k}\right)} = \sqrt{\left(\frac{1941.9687}{17}\right)} = 10.386\,873$$

The standard errors of the regression coefficients are given by

$$se(b_1) = s\sqrt{\left(\frac{\Sigma X_2^2 \Sigma X_3^2 - (\Sigma X_2 X_3)^2}{n[\Sigma x_2^2 \Sigma x_3^2 - \Sigma x_2 x_3]^2}\right)} = 81.3981$$

$$se(b_2) = s\sqrt{\left(\frac{\Sigma x_3^2}{\Sigma x_2^2 \Sigma x_3^2 - (\Sigma x_2 x_3)^2}\right)} = 0.7398$$

$$se(b_3) = s\sqrt{\left(\frac{\Sigma x_2^2}{\Sigma x_2^2 \Sigma x_3^2 - (\Sigma x_2 x_3)^2}\right)} = 0.1197$$

To test the null hypothesis $H_0: \beta_i = 0$ against the alternative $H_1: \beta_i \neq 0$, we calculate the following test statistic:

$$t = \frac{|b_i|}{se(b_i)}$$

The calculated t ratios are presented in Table 2.3 and in each case the null hypothesis is rejected at the 1 per cent significance level, since $t_{0.025}$ with 17 degrees of freedom is

Table 2.3 Regression results for Ambrosian exports

	Constant	X_2	X_3	ESS	SEE	R^2
Eqn 1	449.6162 (89.097) (5.046)	−3.3669 (0.8907) (3.780)		1541.7088	10.3869	0.4426
Eqn 2	37.4654 (16.1113) (2.325)		0.6090 (0.1289) (4.723)	1927.9963	9.2966	0.5534
Eqn 3	271.5319 (81.3981) (3.336)	−2.1571 (0.7398) (2.916)	0.4609 (0.1197) (3.852)	2446.7227	7.8101	0.7023

Note: standard errors and t ratios appear in parentheses below the estimates of the regression coefficients.

Table 2.4 Analysis of variance

	Sum of squares	Degrees of freedom	Mean square squares	F
Explained by Y on X_2	1541.7088	1	1541.7088	
Addition of X_3	905.0139	1	905.0139	$F = \dfrac{905.0139}{60.9973}$
Residual	1036.9548	17	60.9973	$= 14.837$
Explained by Y on X_3	1927.9963	1	1927.9963	
Addition of X_2	518.7364	1	518.7264	$F = \dfrac{518.7264}{60.973}$
Residual	1036.9548	17		$= 8.504$
Explained by Y on X_2 and X_3	2446.7227	2	1223.3613	$F = \dfrac{1223.3613}{60.9973}$
Residual	1036.9548	17	60.9973	$= 20.056$

2.110. In the table the results are also given for the simple regressions of Y on X_2 and Y on X_3. The reader should verify the results presented there.

In Table 2.4 we present an analysis of variance. Since $F_{0.01}(1,17) = 8.40$, we may reject the null hypothesis that $\beta_2 = 0$ and similarly that $\beta_3 = 0$; since $F_{0.01}(2,17) = 6.11$, we may reject the null hypothesis that $R^2 = 0$.

2.2 RELAXATION OF THE ASSUMPTIONS REGARDING THE DISTURBANCE TERM

In the appendix to this chapter we will show that the assumptions we have made about the nature of the disturbance term in the linear regression model imply that the least squares estimators are best linear unbiased estimators. The assumption that the disturbance term is normally distributed, while not necessary for deriving the best linear unbiased property of the estimators, is required for hypothesis testing. In this section, we relax each of these assumptions in turn and consider the implications for the nature of the least squares estimators of a particular assumption being violated. Furthermore, we discuss how the available sample information can be utilised to test whether the particular assumption does or does not hold. Finally, we outline procedures to be adopted in cases where the assumption does not hold.

Violation of the assumption $E(u_i) = 0$

If the mean of the stochastic disturbance term is not zero, i.e. $E(u_i) \neq 0$, but is equal to a constant, say μ, then the estimator of the constant term in the regression model is biased but the estimators of the regression coefficients with respect to the explanatory variables are BLUE.

Relaxation of the assumptions for the disturbance term

However, if $E(u_i) = \mu_i \neq 0$ and μ_i varies from observation to observation, then all the estimators will be biased.

Consider the simple regression model (in which there is only one explanatory variable X) with

$$E(u_i) = \mu \quad (2.40)$$

$$Y_i = \alpha + \beta X_i + u_i \quad (2.41)$$

and

$$b = \beta + \Sigma k_i u_i \quad \left(\text{where } k_i = \frac{x_i}{\Sigma x_i^2}\right) \quad (2.42)$$

Taking expected values:

$$E(b) = \beta + \Sigma k_i E(u_i)$$
$$= \beta + \mu \Sigma k_i$$
$$= \beta \quad (\text{since } \Sigma k_i = 0) \quad (2.43)$$

On the other hand,

$$a = \alpha + \frac{1}{n}\Sigma u_i - \bar{X}\Sigma k_i u_i \quad (2.44)$$

Hence

$$E(a) = \alpha + \mu \neq \alpha \quad (2.45)$$

For the case where $E(u_i) = \mu_i$, we have

$$E(b) = \beta + \Sigma k_i \mu_i \neq \beta \quad (2.46)$$

and

$$E(a) = \alpha + \frac{1}{n}\Sigma \mu_i - \bar{X}\Sigma k_i \mu_i \neq \alpha \quad (2.47)$$

However, there is no way to test the assumption $E(u_i) = 0$ since the u_is are unobservable and no test can be devised from the residuals of the fitted equation for they sum to zero. In the first case it is impossible to obtain separate estimators of α and μ. In the second case the intercept becomes $\alpha + \mu_i$, varying from observation to observation; this means that $E(Y_i)$ changes not only as a result of changes in X_i but also for other reasons.

Serial correlation

Violation of the assumption $E(u_i u_j) = 0$ for $i \neq j$
Cases where this assumption is violated arise frequently in regression models using time-series data. Consider the following simple model:

$$Y_t = \alpha + \beta X_t + u_t \quad (t = 1, \ldots, T) \quad (2.48)$$

We replace the above assumption, $E(u_i u_j) = 0$, with the assumption $E(u_t, u_{t-s}) \neq 0$ for $s = 1, 2, \ldots$. This implies that the disturbance at time t is correlated with the disturbance at time $t - s$; this is known as autocorrelation or serial correlation. A common way to introduce serial correlation into the linear regression model is to assume the following first-order autoregressive scheme:

$$u_t = \rho u_{t-1} + \epsilon_t \tag{2.49}$$

where ρ is a parameter whose absolute value is less than 1 and ϵ_t is a normally and independently distributed random variable with mean zero and variance σ_ϵ^2, i.e. it is assumed to be independent of u_{t-1}:

$$\epsilon_t \sim N(0, \sigma_\epsilon^2) \quad \text{(for all } t\text{)} \tag{2.50}$$

$$E(\epsilon_t, \epsilon_{t-s}) = 0 \quad \text{(for all } s \neq 0\text{)} \tag{2.51}$$

$$E(\epsilon_t, u_{t-1}) = 0 \quad \text{(for all } t\text{)} \tag{2.52}$$

Lagging equation (2.49) by one period, we have

$$u_{t-1} = \rho u_{t-2} + \epsilon_{t-1} \tag{2.53}$$

Substituting for u_{t-1} in equation (2.49), we have

$$u_t = \rho^2 u_{t-2} + \rho \epsilon_{t-1} + \epsilon_t$$
$$= \rho^3 u_{t-3} + \rho^2 \epsilon_{t-2} + \rho \epsilon_{t-1} + \epsilon_t$$
$$\vdots$$
$$= \rho^t u_0 + \rho^{t-1} \epsilon_1 + \ldots + \rho \epsilon_{t-1} + \epsilon_t \tag{2.54}$$

Since $\rho^t \to 0$ as $t \to \infty$ we can write

$$u_t = \sum_{i=0}^{\infty} \rho^i \epsilon_{t-i} \tag{2.54a}$$

and

$$E(u_t) = 0 \tag{2.55}$$

$$E(u_t^2) = \text{Var}(u_t) = \frac{\sigma_\epsilon^2}{1 - \rho^2} \tag{2.56}$$

$$E(u_t, u_{t-s}) = \text{Cov}(u_t, u_{t-s}) = \rho^s \sigma_\epsilon^2 \tag{2.57}$$

If ρ is negative the covariance terms will alternate in sign but will become absolutely smaller as s increases; for positive ρ, the covariance terms will be positive but decreasing functions of s.

The main effect of autocorrelation is on the sampling variances of the estimators. The estimators are linear and unbiased but the variances obtained by the usual ordinary least squares, (OLS) approach are biased.

It can be shown that

$$\text{Var}(b) = \Sigma k_t^2 E(u_t^2) + 2 \sum_{s>0} k_t k_{t-s} E(u_t u_{t-s}) = \frac{\sigma_u^2}{\Sigma x_t^2}$$

if and only if $E(u_t u_{t-s}) = 0$ (for $s \neq 0$)   (2.58)

In the presence of positive autocorrelated disturbances, $E(u_t u_{t-s}) \neq 0$ and the true variance of b differs from that obtained by the usual OLS approach. The direction of bias depends upon the sign of the second term on the right-hand side of the above equation. If it is positive, which it certainly is for positive ρ and may be for negative ρ, $\sigma_u^2/\Sigma x_t^2$ is an underestimate of the true variance. In such circumstances, the standard error of b will also be biased downwards below its true value, the t ratio will be biased upwards and the test statistic will be biased towards rejecting the null hypothesis $H_0: \beta = 0$. In the presence of serial correlation, the OLS estimators do not have the minimum variance property. However, if ρ and σ_ϵ^2 are known the correct sampling variance for b can be derived.

In the presence of positive autocorrelation, the time path of the residuals will display more pronounced and longer runs of values having the same sign, while under negative autocorrelation sign changes will be frequent and the time series will appear spikier than with independent disturbances. A test for the presence of first-order autocorrelation is provided by the Durbin-Watson ratio statistic. Consider the following statistic:

$$\frac{\Sigma(u_t - u_{t-1})^2}{\Sigma(u_t - \bar{u})^2} \quad (2.59)$$

where $\bar{u}$ is the sample mean of disturbances. A small value for the above ratio would constitute *prima facie* evidence in favour of first-order positive serial correlation. However, a test based on the above statistic is nonoperational since the disturbances are not observable. We must use as proxies for these unobservable disturbances the residuals from the fitted regression line. Replacing u_t with e_t, we have the Durbin-Watson d statistic:

$$\begin{aligned}
d &= \frac{\Sigma_{t=2}^n (e_t - e_{t-1})^2}{\Sigma_{t=1}^n e_t^2} \\
&= \frac{\Sigma_{t=2}^n e_t^2 - 2\Sigma_{t=2}^n e_t e_{t-1} + \Sigma_{t=2}^n e_{t-1}^2}{\Sigma_{t=1}^n e_t^2} \\
&\simeq \frac{2(\Sigma_{t=2}^n e_t^2 - \Sigma_{t=2}^n e_t e_{t-1})}{\Sigma e_t^2} \quad \text{since } \Sigma e_t^2 \simeq \Sigma e_{t-1}^2 \\
&\simeq 2(1 - r)
\end{aligned}$$
(2.60)

where r is the correlation coefficient between e_t and e_{t-1} and is approximately equal to $\Sigma_{t=2}^n e_t e_{t-1}/\Sigma_{t=1}^n e_t^2$. The Durbin-Watson d statistic can be used to test for the presence of first-order autocorrelation. We test the null hypothesis $H_0: \rho = 0$ against the one-sided alternative $H_1: \rho > 0$. The probability of observing values of d depends on both the number of observations in the sample and the number of parameters being estimated. A complication arises since the residuals are functions of the Xs. Durbin and Watson were, however, able to tabulate lower (d_L) and upper (d_U) limits for the critical values of d at the 5 per cent and 1 per cent probability levels. If $d < d_L$, then the residuals indicate that the null hypothesis of no autocorrelation is rejected in favour of the alternative hypothesis $H_1 = \rho > 0$. If $d > d_U$, the null hypothesis is not rejected. If d lies between the two limits, the test is inconclusive. The procedure for testing for first-order negative autocorrelation is to calculate $4 - d$ and then to proceed as if one were testing for positive autocorrelation.

When the Durbin–Watson statistic suggests the presence of autocorrelation, careful examination of the residuals is recommended to see whether there is any obvious misspecification of the model arising from the omission of an explanatory variable.

The Durbin–Watson test is not applicable when the regression equation has been estimated without a constant term. Furthermore, if a lagged dependent variable is included among the regressors the test tends to be biased towards acceptance of the null hypothesis of no serial correlation. A number of procedures can be employed in this latter case and they will be discussed later.

Removing the effects of autocorrelation

If the Durbin–Watson test indicates the presence of first-order autocorrelation, then we respecify the simple regression model as follows:

$$Y_t = \alpha + \beta X_t + u_t \tag{2.61}$$

and

$$u_t = \rho u_{t-1} + \epsilon_t \tag{2.62}$$

If ρ is known, then lagging the first equation by one period and multiplying by ρ yields

$$\rho Y_{t-1} = \rho \alpha + \rho \beta X_{t-1} + \rho u_{t-1} \tag{2.63}$$

Subtracting this equation from the first equation yields

$$Y_t - \rho Y_{t-1} = \alpha(1 - \rho) + \beta(X_t - \rho X_{t-1}) + u_t - \rho u_{t-1} \quad (t = 2, \ldots, n) \tag{2.64}$$

We can rewrite the above equation in terms of newly defined variables when ρ is known:

$$W_t = \alpha(1 - \rho) + \beta Z_t + \epsilon_t \tag{2.65}$$

where $W_t = Y_t - \rho Y_{t-1}$ and $Z_t = X_t - \rho X_{t-1}$.

In general, however, ρ is not known; so we need to estimate it. A common procedure is to regress the residuals (e_t) from the first equation on the residuals lagged by one period (e_{t-1}). The obtained estimator is then substituted to estimate W_t and Z_t, and α and β are estimated. The obtained estimators are used to derive a new set of residuals and the procedure is repeated until the estimators converge subject to some preassigned criterion and the residuals from the regression provide no support for the hypothesis of serial correlation. This procedure is known as the Cochrane–Orcutt iterative procedure.

For other procedures to the problem of estimating a model with serially correlated disturbances, the reader is referred to such texts as Johnston (1984), Kmenta (1986) or Maddala (1977).

Heteroscedasticity

Violation of the assumption $E(u_i^2) = \sigma_u^2$

We now consider the consequences of the disturbances being nonhomoscedastic, i.e. $E(u_i^2) = \sigma_i^2 \neq \sigma_u^2$. This is known as the problem of heteroscedasticity and the applied econometrician is likely to come across its existence in investigations which employ cross-sectional data, e.g. in the estimation of a consumption function based on an expenditure survey of a sample of households. Households with low incomes have less scope to vary their expenditure than those with high incomes and we might, therefore, expect the variance of the disturbance term to increase as income increases rather than to remain constant.

What are the consequences for the properties of the least squares estimators of heteroscedasticity? The linear unbiased property of the OLS estimators remains unaltered by the replacement of the assumption of homoscedastic disturbances with one of the nonhomoscedastic disturbances. But when $E(u_i^2) = \sigma_i^2$:

$$\text{Var}(b) = \Sigma k_i^2 \sigma_i^2 \neq \sigma_u^2 \Sigma k_i^2 \tag{2.66}$$

and hence the preceding formula for the sampling variance of b is incorrect. Problems clearly arise in constructing confidence intervals for α and β and in drawing up significance tests of the regression coefficients since the sampling variances calculated on the assumption of homoscedastic variances are biased. If the variances σ_i^2 are known, then it is a straightforward matter to substitute them in the above expression to derive the sampling variance of b. Generally, however, the variances are not known and estimation of n variances from the data is unlikely since we have only n observations. We may use the residuals from the fitted regression line as proxies for the unobservable disturbances but with only one observation from each distribution no formal test for the difference between variances can be performed.

If we know *a priori* the specific form the heteroscedasticity takes, procedures are available to obtain estimators of the regression coefficients which will be BLUE. Consider the following model:

$$Y_i = \alpha + \beta X_i + u_i \text{ with } E(u_i^2) = \sigma_u^2 X_i^2 \tag{2.67}$$

then

$$\frac{Y_i}{X_i} = \frac{\alpha}{X_i} + \beta + \frac{u_i}{X_i} \tag{2.68}$$

and the redefined regression model is free of heteroscedasticity, since $E[(u_i/X_i)^2] = \sigma_u^2$ and the OLS estimators of α and β from the redefined model are BLUE.

In the absence of *a priori* information on whether heteroscedasticity is present, and, if so, what form it takes, White (1980) has suggested the following procedure for the k variable regression model. Estimate the model using OLS and derive the residuals from the fitted regression. Then regress the squared residuals on the explanatory variables and the squares and cross-products of the explanatory variables. For the three-variable case, we would estimate the following model:

$$e_i^2 = \text{constant} + \gamma_2 X_{2i} + \gamma_3 X_{3i} + \beta_{22} X_{2i}^2 + \beta_{23} X_{2i} X_{3i} + \beta_{33} X_{3i}^2 + w_i \quad (2.69)$$

and then test the null hypothesis that $R^2 = 0$. Rejection of the null hypothesis implies heteroscedastic disturbances. To obtain estimators with correction for heteroscedasticity we now calculate the predicted squared residuals from the above equation, $\hat{e}_i^2$, and then perform the following weighted regression:

$$\frac{Y_i}{\hat{e}_i} = \frac{\beta_1}{\hat{e}_i} + \beta_2 \frac{X_{2i}}{\hat{e}_i} + \frac{\beta_3 X_{3i}}{\hat{e}_i} + \frac{u_i}{\hat{e}_i} \quad (2.70)$$

Theoretically, weighted least squares estimators are BLUE, but because variances are estimated empirically they may not be BLUE.

Where the cause of heteroscedasticity is not known the suggestion is to make use of the estimated e_i^2 from the OLS regression in the computation of variances and covariances of regression coefficients. This is achieved by using the robust routine on TSP.

Violation of the assumption $E(X_i u_j) = 0$ for all i, j
Consider the model

$$Y_i = \alpha + \beta X_i + u_i \quad (2.71)$$

and assume that all the assumptions regarding the error term continue to hold except that $E(X_i u_j) \neq 0$ for all i, j. The least squares estimator of β is given by

$$b = \beta + \Sigma k_i u_i \quad \left(\text{where } k_i = \frac{x_i}{\Sigma x_i^2}\right) \quad (2.72)$$

so that

$$b = \beta + \frac{\Sigma x_i u_i}{\Sigma x_i^2} \quad (2.73)$$

and taking expectations:

$$E(b) = \beta + E\left(\frac{\Sigma x_i u_i}{\Sigma x_i^2}\right) \quad (2.74)$$

where the second term on the right-hand side involves the ratio of two random variables. Note also that if $Z = X/Y$ it is not necessarily true that

$$E(Z) = \frac{E(X)}{E(Y)} \quad (2.75)$$

Our estimators will thus not be unbiased. If, however, we make a less restrictive assumption that

$$\lim_{n \to \infty} \sum_{i=1}^{n} x_i^2 = \infty \quad (2.76)$$

Relaxation of the assumptions for the disturbance term

then probability limit, $\text{plim}_{n \to \infty} (\frac{1}{n} \sum_{i=1}^{n} x_i^2)$, is finite.

In the same way, we assume that there is a nonzero covariance between x and u, denoted by σ_{Xu}, and

$$\text{plim} \left(\frac{1}{n} \sum x_i u_i \right) = \sigma_{Xu} \tag{2.77}$$

We may write

$$\text{plim } Z = \frac{\text{plim } X}{\text{plim } Y} \tag{2.78}$$

and in evaluating the probability limit of b we obtain

$$\text{plim } b = \beta + \frac{\text{plim} \left(\frac{1}{n} \sum x_i u_i \right)}{\text{plim} \left(\frac{1}{n} \sum x_i^2 \right)} \tag{2.79}$$

$$= \beta + \frac{\sigma_{Xu}}{\sigma_X^2} \tag{2.80}$$

Since the second term on the right-hand side is nonzero we have

$$\text{plim } b \neq \beta$$

and b is an inconsistent estimator of β. If the assumption $E(X_i u_i) = 0$ is violated, the OLS estimators are biased. Consistent estimators can, however, be obtained under the weaker assumption that the errors and the explanatory variables are uncorrelated in the probability limit. To show this result, consider the following model with a lagged dependent variable:

$$Y_t = \alpha + \beta Y_{t-1} + u_t \tag{2.81}$$

and assume $|\beta| < 1$. By recursive substitution, we have

$$Y_t = \alpha(1 + \beta + \ldots + \beta^{t-1}) + \beta^t Y_0 + u_t + \beta u_{t-1} + \ldots + \beta^{t-1} u_1 \tag{2.82}$$

As $t \to \infty$, the right-hand side of equation (2.82) Y_t becomes

$$\frac{\alpha}{1 - \beta} + u_t + \beta u_{t-1} + \ldots \tag{2.83}$$

In the long run Y_t is the subject to random fluctuations around a fixed level. The explanatory variable, Y_{t-1}, is not correlated with the current disturbance, u_t, since Y_{t-1} depends on $Y_0, u_1, \ldots, u_{t-1}$ but not on u_t. The least squares estimators of β is

$$b = \beta + \frac{\sum y_{t-1} u_t}{\sum y_{t-1}^2} \tag{2.84}$$

and

$$\text{plim } b = \beta + \frac{\text{plim}\left(\frac{1}{n}\sum y_{t-1}u_t\right)}{\text{plim}\left(\frac{1}{n}\sum y_{t-1}^2\right)} = \beta \tag{2.85}$$

since $\frac{1}{n}\sum y_{t-1}u_t$ is a consistent estimator of the population covariance between Y_{t-1} and u_t, which is zero.

When the explanatory variable and the disturbance term are contemporaneously uncorrelated the OLS estimators are consistent and asymptotically efficient. However, in the presence of either errors in variables or simultaneity, the OLS estimators will not in general be consistent since the explanatory variables and the disturbance term will not be uncorrelated in the probability limit.

Multicollinearity

Multicollinearity is present when there exists a high degree of correlation between two or more explanatory variables. Let the model be

$$Y_i = \beta_1 + \beta_2 X_{2i} + \beta_3 X_{3i} + u_i \qquad (i = 1, \ldots, n) \tag{2.86}$$

First we discuss the extreme case of an exact linear relationship between X_{2i} and X_{3i}, say $X_{2i} = \lambda + \gamma X_{3i}$. Measuring the observations in terms of the deviation from the sample means, we obtain $x_{2i} = \gamma x_{3i}$ and substituting for x_{2i} in the expressions for b_2 and b_3 yields

$$b_2 = \frac{\gamma \sum y_i x_{3i} \sum x_{3i}^2 - \gamma \sum y_i x_{3i} \sum x_{3i}^2}{\gamma^2 (\sum x_{3i}^2)^2 - \gamma^2 (\sum x_{3i}^2)^2} = \frac{0}{0} \tag{2.87}$$

$$b_3 = \frac{\gamma^2 \sum y_i x_{3i} \sum x_{3i}^2 - \gamma^2 \sum y_i x_{3i} \sum x_{3i}^2}{\gamma^2 (\sum x_{3i}^2)^2 - \gamma^2 (\sum x_{3i}^2)^2} = \frac{0}{0} \tag{2.88}$$

Since it is not possible to evaluate the above ratios, the OLS procedure breaks down. The variances of b_2 and b_3 are defined by the following expressions:

$$\text{Var}(b_2) = \frac{\sigma_u^2 \sum x_{3i}^2}{\sum x_{2i}^2 \sum x_{3i}^2 - (\sum x_{2i} x_{3i})^2} = \frac{\sigma_u^2}{\sum x_{2i}^2 (1 - r_{23}^2)} \tag{2.89}$$

$$\text{Var}(b_3) = \frac{\sigma_u^2 \sum x_{2i}^2}{\sum x_{2i}^2 \sum x_{3i}^2 - (\sum x_{2i} x_{3i})^2} = \frac{\sigma_u^2}{\sum x_{3i}^2 (1 - r_{23}^2)} \tag{2.90}$$

where r_{23} is the simple correlation coefficient between X_2 and X_3. Clearly,

$$\lim \text{Var}(b_2) = \lim \text{Var}(b_3) = \infty \text{ as } r_{23}^2 \to 1. \tag{2.91}$$

The least squares procedure breaks down in the above circumstances because we are effectively trying to estimate a three-dimensional plane using a two-dimensional scatter of points. In practice, we do not observe an exact linear relationship between two explanatory variables, but multicollinearity is present whenever there is a high correlation between two or more explanatory variables. A simple procedure for the presence of multicollinearity in a multiple regression model is thereby suggested:

Regress each of the explanatory variables on all the remaining explanatory variables and calculate the coefficient of determination (R^2) in each case. If R^2 is close to unity, then the degree of multicollinearity is high.

In the general linear model, an alternative procedure for the presence of multicollinearity is provided by evaluating the determinant of sums of squares and cross-product matrix. A very low value for this determinant reveals the presence of multicollinearity. Note for the two-explanatory-variable case:

$$\text{Det} \begin{bmatrix} n & \Sigma X_{2i} & \Sigma X_{3i} \\ \Sigma X_{2i} & \Sigma X_{2i}^2 & \Sigma X_{2i} X_{3i} \\ X_{3i} & \Sigma X_{2i} X_{3i} & \Sigma X_{3i}^2 \end{bmatrix} = n \Sigma x_{2i}^2 \Sigma x_{3i}^2 (1 - r_{23}^2) \qquad (2.92)$$

and

$$\lim \text{Det} = 0 \text{ as } r_{23}^2 \rightarrow 1 \qquad (2.93)$$

In the presence of multicollinearity the standard errors of the estimated regression coefficients will be relatively large. If the estimated regression coefficients change markedly in value and their standard errors become very large when new variables are included in the regression model, the investigator should immediately suspect the presence of multicollinearity and check for it by examining the matrix of correlation coefficients between the explanatory variables. In some situations multicollinearity leads to an apparently paradoxical situation in which the coefficient of determination is high and statistically significantly different from zero, while none of the individual regression coefficients are significantly different from zero. The overall regression relationship is satisfactory, but the estimates of the individual parameters are unreliable.

Specification error

Model specification is one of the most important aspects of any applied econometric work. The researcher should always seek to ensure that the model specified has a sound economic–theoretic basis. When the correct specification of the model is assumed, the estimation and testing of the model become relatively straightforward. In practice, however, the investigator can never be certain that a given model is correctly specified. In attempting to find the specification which best describes the process under study, the investigator will typically examine a number of possible model specifications. Two common types of misspecification are likely to be committed: (i) the omission of relevant variables from the regression equation; and (ii) the inclusion of irrelevant variables in the regression equation. Misspecification arising from the nature of the disturbances has been discussed above.

(i) Absence of a relevant variable

Misspecification due to the absence of relevant variables can arise from a straightforward lack of data on some key variable or from the inherent impossibility of quantifying a variable which is essentially of a qualitative nature.

Consider a case in which a variable is unknowingly omitted from the 'true' or correct model specification. Let the correct model be

$$y_t = \beta_2 x_{2t} + \beta_3 x_{3t} + \epsilon_t \qquad (2.94)$$

while the estimated model is specified to be

$$y_t = \beta_2^* x_{2t} + \epsilon_t^* \qquad (2.95)$$

Note all the variables are expressed as deviations from their sample means.

The estimated slope parameter is given by

$$b_2^* = \frac{\Sigma x_{2t} y_t}{\Sigma x_{2t}^2} \qquad (2.96)$$

Substituting the true specification for y_t in the above expression, we have

$$b_2^* = \frac{\beta_2 \Sigma x_{2t}^2 + \beta_3 \Sigma x_{2t} x_{3t} + \Sigma x_{2t} \epsilon_t}{\Sigma x_{2t}^2} \qquad (2.97)$$

$$= \beta_2 + \beta_3 \frac{\Sigma x_{2t} x_{3t}}{\Sigma x_{2t}^2} + \frac{\Sigma x_{2t} \epsilon_t}{\Sigma x_{2t}^2} \qquad (2.98)$$

Taking expectations:

$$E(b_2^*) = \beta_2 + \beta_3 \frac{\text{Cov}(x_2 x_3)}{\text{Var}(x_2)} \qquad (2.99)$$

Hence the least squares slope estimator will yield a biased estimator of the true slope parameter. Only when the omitted variable is uncorrelated with all the included explanatory variables will the bias disappear. In the above example, when x_2 and x_3 are uncorrelated, the estimator b_2^* will be an unbiased estimator of β_2 and will have an identical variance with b_2, the least squares estimator of β_2. When x_2 and x_3 are correlated, the variance of b_2^* will not equal the variance of b_2: the usual estimate of the variance of b_2^* will be biased.

(ii) Presence of an irrelevant variable

Let the true regression model be

$$y_t = \beta_2 x_{2t} + \epsilon_t \qquad (2.100)$$

and the estimated model be

$$y_t = \beta_2^* x_{2t} + \beta_3^* x_{3t} + \epsilon_t^* \qquad (2.101)$$

We shall now see that the effects of adding an irrelevant variable are quite different from those of omitting a relevant variable. In this case, the estimated slope parameter is given by

$$b_2^* = \frac{\Sigma x_{3t}^2 \Sigma x_{2t} y_t - \Sigma x_{2t} x_{3t} \Sigma x_{3t} y_t}{\Sigma x_{2t}^2 \Sigma x_{3t}^2 - (\Sigma x_{2t} x_{3t})^2} \qquad (2.102)$$

Substituting the true specification for y_t in the above expression:

$$b_2^* = \beta_2 + \frac{\Sigma x_{3t}^2 \Sigma x_{2t}\epsilon_t - \Sigma x_{2t}\Sigma x_{3t}\epsilon_t}{\Sigma x_{2t}^2 \Sigma x_{3t}^2 - (\Sigma x_{2t}x_{3t})^2} \qquad (2.103)$$

from which it follows that

$$E(b_2^*) = \beta_2 \qquad (2.104)$$

Thus the inclusion of an irrelevant variable does not lead to a bias in the slope parameter estimates of any of the slope variables which appear in the correct model.

The inclusion of irrelevant variables, however, does affect the efficiency of the least squares estimators, since the variance of the least squares estimator b_2^* will be larger than the variance of b_2 unless x_{2t} and x_{3t} are uncorrelated; in this latter case there will be no loss of efficiency. This general loss of efficiency, i.e. the larger variance of b_2^*, makes it more difficult to reject the null hypothesis $H_0: \beta_2 = 0$.

(iii) Nonlinearities
Another specification error can occur if the researcher chooses to estimate a linear regression model that is linear in the explanatory variables when the true regression model is nonlinear in the explanatory variables. Assume the correct model is

$$y_t = \beta_2 x_{2t} + \beta_3 x_{2t}^2 + \epsilon_t \qquad (2.105)$$

and the estimated model is

$$y_t = \beta_2^* x_{2t} + \epsilon_t^* \qquad (2.106)$$

This case can be simply treated as a special case of an omitted variable; x_{2t}^2 is an omitted variable from the estimated model.

Other kinds of specification error arise due to:

(a) incorrect functional form;
(b) errors in variables; and
(c) the presence of simultaneity.

In all these cases the general problem is that both the estimators and their variances are biased if they are estimated from a misspecified model.

APPENDIX: THE GENERAL LINEAR MODEL

The k variable regression equation, linear in parameters and variables can be written in matrix–vector form as

$$y = X\beta + u \qquad (A2.1)$$

where

$$y = \begin{bmatrix} Y_1 \\ Y_2 \\ \vdots \\ Y_n \end{bmatrix} \quad X = \begin{bmatrix} 1 & X_{21} & \cdots & X_{k1} \\ 1 & X_{22} & & X_{k2} \\ \vdots & & & \\ 1 & X_{2n} & & X_{kn} \end{bmatrix}$$

$$\beta = \begin{bmatrix} \beta_1 \\ \beta_2 \\ \vdots \\ \beta_k \end{bmatrix} \quad u = \begin{bmatrix} u_1 \\ u_2 \\ \vdots \\ u_n \end{bmatrix}$$

We write the standard assumptions concerning the disturbance term as follows:

1. $E(u) = 0$.
2. $E(uu') = \sigma_u^2 I$ where I is an identity matrix.
3. X is a set of fixed regressors and is nonstochastic.
4. X has rank $k < n$ or, equivalently, $(X'X)^{-1}$ exists with full rank k.

For the sake of economy, interpretations are not repeated: they are similar to those presented for the two-explanatory-variable cases.

Turning to estimation, we define b as the estimated β vector of parameters and e as the vector of residuals. The least squares principle for choosing b involves minimising the sum of squared residuals, $e'e$:

$$e'e = (y - Xb)'(y - Xb)$$
$$= y'y - 2b'X'y + b'X'Xb \qquad (A2.2)$$

Differentiating with respect to b and setting equal to zero, we have

$$\frac{\partial e'e}{\partial b} = -2X'y + 2X'Xb = 0 \qquad (A2.3)$$

The second-order derivative is given by

$$\frac{\partial^2 e'e}{\partial b^2} = 2X'X$$

which is a positive definite matrix. Solving the first set of equations yields the OLS estimators

$$b = (X'X)^{-1} X'y \qquad (A2.4)$$

Proof that the OLS estimators are BLUE.

The fundamental theoretical underpinning for the OLS method is, of course, that the estimators are the best linear unbiased estimators. To show that b is unbiased, we write:

Appendix: the general linear model 27

$$E(b) = E[(X'X)^{-1}X'(X\beta + u)]$$
$$= \beta + (X'X)^{-1}X'E(u)$$
$$= \beta \text{ (since } E(u) = 0) \tag{A2.5}$$

To establish the best (minimum variance) property, we first derive the variance-covariance matrix of b:

$$\text{Var}(b) = E[(b - E(b))(b - E(b))']$$
$$= E[(b - \beta)(b - \beta)']$$
$$= E[(X'X)^{-1}X'uu'X(X'X)^{-1}]$$
$$= (X'X)^{-1}X'E(uu')X(X'X)^{-1}$$
$$= (X'X)^{-1}X'\sigma_u^2 I_n X(X'X)^{-1}$$
$$= \sigma_u^2 (X'X)^{-1} \tag{A2.6}$$

where the diagonal elements of this matrix denote the sampling variances of the corresponding elements of b and the off-diagonal elements the sampling covariances. Using the Gauss–Markov theorem, we can now show that the variances are the minimum possible, given unbiasedness.

Let $c'b$ be a scalar quantity in which c denotes a column vector. If we choose $c' = [1, 0, \ldots, 0]$, then $c'b = b_1$. Since c' is just a vector of constants, $E(c'b) = c'\beta$ and the variance of a linear unbiased estimator is

$$\text{Var}(c'b) = E[c'(b - \beta)(b - \beta)'c]$$
$$= c'\sigma_u^2 (X'X)^{-1} c$$
$$= \sigma_u^2 c'(X'X)^{-1} c \tag{A2.7}$$

Let us consider any other linear estimator, say d, where

$$d = a'y = a'(X\beta + u) \tag{A2.8}$$
$$E(d) = E(a'X\beta + a'u)$$
$$= a'X\beta \text{ (since } E(u) = 0) \tag{A2.9}$$

For d to be unbiased,

$$E(d) = c'\beta, \text{ which means that } a'X \text{ must equal } c' \tag{A2.10}$$
$$\text{Var}(d) = E[(d - c'\beta)(d - c'\beta)']$$
$$= E[a'uu'a] \text{ since } d - c'\beta = a'u$$
$$= a'E(uu')a$$
$$= \sigma^2 a'a \tag{A2.11}$$

We can now find the difference between the two variances:

$$\text{Var}(d) - \text{Var}(c'b) = \sigma_u^2 a'a - \sigma_u^2 c'(X'X)^{-1}c$$
$$= \sigma_u^2 a'a - \sigma_u^2 a'X(X'X)^{-1}X'a$$
$$= \sigma_u^2 a'[I - X(X'X)^{-1}X']a$$
$$= \sigma_u^2 a'Ma \qquad (A2.12)$$

where $M = [I - X(X'X)^{-1}X']$. Since M is an idempotent positive semidefinite matrix, $\sigma_u^2 a'Ma$ is non-negative and therefore $c'b$ has minimum variance.

In the above presentation it has been assumed that σ^2 is known. In practice, this is not the case and we seek an unbiased estimator from the observed residuals:

$$e = y - Xb$$
$$= y - X(X'X)^{-1}X'y$$
$$= [I - X(X'X)^{-1}X']y$$
$$= My = M(X\beta + u)$$
$$= Mu \text{ (since } MX = 0\text{)} \qquad (A2.13)$$

From the symmetric idempotentness of M, we have

$$e'e = u'Mu \qquad (A2.14)$$

and taking expectations:

$$E(e'e) = E(u'Mu) = E[\text{tr}(u'Mu)] \text{ since } u'Mu \text{ is a scalar}$$
$$= E[\text{tr } Muu']$$
$$= \text{tr } M\sigma_u^2 I_n = \sigma_u^2 \text{tr } M$$
$$= \sigma_u^2 (n - k) = (n - k)\sigma_u^2 \qquad (A2.15)$$

Thus $E(e'e/n - k) = \sigma_u^2$ and $e'e/(n - k)$ is an unbiased estimator of σ_u^2; $e'e$ can be obtained in the following ways:

$$e'e = y'y - b'X'y \qquad (A2.16)$$

or

$$e'e = y'y - b'x'x'b \qquad (A2.17)$$

s, the square root of $e'e/(n - k)$, is called the standard error of the estimate and measures the dispersion of the regression plane.

Exercises

1. Data on the variables Y_i, X_{2i} and X_{3i} ($i = 1, \ldots, n$) are supplied to two different investigators. The first investigator runs the regression

$$Y_i = \beta_1 + \beta_2 X_{2i} + \beta_3 X_{3i} + U_i$$

and obtains OLS estimates of its parameters, b_1, b_2 and b_3. The second investigator first runs the regression

$$X_{2i} = \alpha_2 + \alpha_3 X_{3i} + U_i'$$

and from this he calculates the residuals e_i, which are then used in the following OLS regression:

$$Y_i = \beta_1' + \beta_2' e_i + \beta_3' X_{3i} + U_i^*$$

to obtain the estimates b_1', b_2' and b_3'. Derive the relationship between b_2 and b_2' and interpret your findings.

2. Show that the total variation in y can be decomposed into explained and residual variation:

$$\Sigma y_i^2 = \Sigma(b_2 x_{2i} + b_3 x_{3i})^2 + \Sigma e_i^2$$

where y_i and x_{2i} and x_{3i} are deviations from means.

3. Consider the following models:

$$Y_t = \beta_1 + \beta_2 X_{1t} + U_t$$
$$Y_t = \theta_0 + \theta_1 X_{1t} + \theta_2 X_{2t} + V_t$$

where U_t and V_t are stochastic error terms.

(a) For either of these models show that after estimation by ordinary least squares, the total sum of squares may be expressed as the sum of an 'explained' and 'residual' sum of squares.
(b) Define the statistics 'R^2' and '$\bar{R}^2$'.
(c) What can be said about the relative size of R^2 and $\bar{R}^2$ for the two models above both within and between equations?

4. Explain what is meant by the sampling distribution of the ordinary least squares estimator $\hat{\beta}_2$ of the parameter β_2 in the model:

$$Y_t = \beta_1 + \beta_2 X_t + U_t$$

Discuss the effect on this sampling distribution of β_2 of

(a) the size of the variance of the stochastic term;
(b) the size of the variance of the data on X_2;
(c) the sample size;
(d) the introduction into this regression a further explanatory variable which is positively correlated with X_2 in the sample;
(e) the omission from the regression above of a variable which should be included in the regression equation.

5. Given the following information for a district in Andhra Pradesh (India) on groundnut production, irrigated area, unirrigated area, fertilisers and rainfall, estimate a log-linear production function. All variables are in logarithms.

Groundnuts

Year	Log Production	Log Irrigated Area	Log Unirrigated Area	Log Fertilisers	Log Rainfall
59–60	8.964 95	8.491 26	7.809 14	8.613 59	7.173 96
60–61	9.008 10	8.476 58	7.956 83	8.437 07	7.013 92
61–62	9.179 16	8.917 31	8.124 45	8.998 88	7.177 02
62–63	8.845 06	8.596 93	8.101 37	9.425 21	7.156 96
63–64	8.619 21	8.066 52	7.912 90	9.989 21	6.946 98
64–65	9.073 83	8.151 33	8.215 82	9.916 45	7.105 79
65–66	8.055 16	8.303 75	6.927 56	9.371 35	6.639 88
66–67	8.810 76	8.595 08	7.210 08	10.062 16	6.943 12
67–68	9.195 73	8.699 52	8.518 59	10.079 04	6.855 41
68–69	9.185 43	8.779 56	8.413 39	10.542 74	6.815 69
69–70	9.063 69	7.703 01	8.795 89	10.643 15	7.288 24
70–71	8.682 71	7.650 64	8.411 39	10.306 45	7.154 62
71–72	8.496 99	7.905 44	7.933 08	10.304 81	6.677 08
72–73	8.779 56	7.626 08	8.400 43	10.226 08	6.928 54
73–74	8.987 20	8.195 89	8.093 77	10.098 15	6.783 33
74–75	9.375 86	8.561 98	8.470 31	10.404 11	6.587 55

(a) Test the hypothesis that the elasticity of groundnut output with respect to irrigated area is not different from the elasticity of output with respect to unirrigated area.

(b) Estimate a log linear regression equation without fertilisers since fertilisers and irrigated area are highly correlated. Does this give an overestimate of the other parameters?

6. The table below contains annual data on aggregate saving and personal disposable income (both at current prices) for the United Kingdom:

Year	Saving (£m)	Personal disposable income (£m)
1964	2167	23859
1965	2442	25554
1966	2705	27166
1967	2581	28284
1968	2476	30155
1969	2737	32111
1970	3368	35331
1971	3069	38862
1972	4442	44908
1973	5877	51930
1974	7180	60260
1975	9503	74841
1976	10 276	86094
1977	11 150	97829
1978	14 314	114 187
1979	18 185	136 611
1980	24 338	161 572
1981	23 526	176 070
1982	24 670	192 032
1983	23 706	206 583
1984	25 929	221 640
1985	26 573	239 781

(a) Plot saving against personal disposable income.
(b) Estimate the marginal propensity to save by regressing saving on personal disposable income. Does your saving function correspond to economic theory?
(c) Calculate the residuals from your estimated saving function and plot these against time. Would you describe the plotted series as random?

7. After the least squares estimation (using annual data) of a linear model with three explanatory variables, the following residuals were obtained:

t	e_t	t	e_t
1	1.5	10	3.1
2	3.4	11	1.7
3	0.8	12	5.0
4	−2.7	13	4.0
5	−0.9	14	−0.3
6	−4.5	15	−2.2
7	−4.6	16	−2.3
8	−1.8		
9	−0.3		

$\Sigma e_t = 0$, $\Sigma e_t^2 = 131.82$.

(a) Test for first-order serial correlation by means of the Durbin–Watson statistic. Why is it important to carry out such a test?
(b) How would you alter your test if you were told that one of the explanatory variables was a lagged dependent variable? (To be attempted after Chapter 3.)

8. From the following data examine the relationship between poverty and economic development, where poverty is defined as the percentage of the population with income below $US 35 in 1975. In particular, estimate the following model:

$$P_i = \beta_1 + \beta_2 GNP_i + \beta_3 GNP_i^2 + \beta_4 SL_i + \beta_5 LE_i + \beta_6 GP_i + \beta_7 AL_i + u_i$$

and then test the following hypotheses:

(a) Poverty declines as *per capita* GNP increases.
(b) More rapid population growth leads to an increase in poverty.
(c) Increases in the adult literacy rate are associated with a reduction in poverty.

Income, poverty, literacy, life expectancy growth in GNP and population growth rates

Country	GNP*	P	LE	AL	GP	SL
Bangladesh	200	64	47	22	2.7	20.1
Ethiopia	213	68	39	10	2.1	16.8
Burma	237	65	52	67	2.2	15.7
Indonesia	280	59	48	62	2.1	16.1
Uganda	280	55	53	35	2.9	14.4
Zaire	281	53	46	31	2.6	14.6
Sudan	281	54	46	20	2.8	14.5

Income, poverty, literacy, life expectancy growth in GNP and population growth rates

Country	GNP*	P	LE	AL	GP	SL
Tanzania	297	51	51	66	2.9	14.3
Pakistan	299	43	51	21	3.2	16.5
India	300	46	51	36	2.3	17.0
Kenya	418	55	53	40	3.2	8.9
Nigeria	433	35	48	15	2.6	13.0
Philippines	469	33	60	87	3.0	11.6
Sri Lanka	471	14	69	75	2.4	19.3
Senegal	550	35	42	10	2.1	9.6
Egypt	561	20	54	44	2.5	13.9
Thailand	584	32	61	82	3.0	11.5
Ghana	628	25	48	30	2.6	11.2
Morocco	643	26	55	28	2.7	13.3
Ivory Coast	695	25	46	20	3.3	10.4
South Korea	797	8	63	91	2.1	16.9
Chile	798	11	67	88	2.2	13.1
Zambia	798	10	48	39	2.9	13.0
Colombia	851	19	62	81	3.1	9.9
Turkey	914	14	61	60	2.2	9.3
Tunisia	992	10	57	NA	2.5	11.1
Malaysia	1006	12	67	60	2.8	11.1
Taiwan	1075	5	72	82	2.8	22.3
Guatemala	1128	10	57	46	2.5	11.3
Brazil	1136	15	62	76	2.9	9.1
Peru	1183	18	56	72	2.8	7.3
Iran	1257	13	52	50	3.1	8.2
Mexico	1429	14	65	76	3.7	8.2

GNP* = GNP income *per capita* for 1975 with Kravis adjustment $US.
P = % of population with incomes below $US35 in 1975.
LE = expectation of life at birth (years).
AL = adult literacy rate (%).
GP = population growth rates 1960–75.
SL = share of lowest 40% in GNP (1975).

9. The model

$$Y_t = \beta_1 + \beta_2 X_{2t} + U_t$$

is to be estimated using forty-four quarterly time-series observations on Y and X_2:

(a) Given the following data, obtain the OLS estimate of β_2, and test the null hypothesis that $\beta_2 = 0$ at the 5 per cent level of significance outlining any assumptions necessary to conduct the test:

$$\Sigma(X_{2t} - \bar{X}_2)^2 = 50 \quad \Sigma(X_{2t} - \bar{X}_2)(Y_t - \bar{Y}) = 10 \quad \Sigma(Y_t - \bar{Y})^2 = 4$$

(b) When another variable, X_3, is included in this regression it is found to have an estimated coefficient value of 0.6. Given that

$$\Sigma(X_{2t} - \bar{X}_2)(X_{3t} - \bar{X}_3) = 25$$

Calculate what the estimated coefficient on X_2 in the multiple regression of Y on X_2 and X_3 will be.

Appendix: the general linear model

10. Estimate the parameters of the following model given the assumptions and data below. Justify your estimation technique explicitly.

MODEL

$$Y_t = \alpha + \beta X_t + U_t$$

with

$$E(U_t) = 0, E(U_t^2) = \sigma^2 X_t^2, E(U_t, U_{t+s}) = 0 \text{ for } s \neq 0$$

DATA

Y_t	X_t
12	6
18	11
19	10
12	8
23	14

11. The following data refer to the index of output in the manufacturing sector of the United Kingdom, the gross capital stock at 1975 replacement prices and numbers employed:

Year	Y Index no. of manufacturing output at constant factor cost (1975 = 100)	X_1 Gross capital stock at 1975 replacement cost (£ '000 million)	X_2 Number employed ('000)
1969	98.7	78.7	8923
1970	98.1	81.8	8341
1971	97.5	84.6	8058
1972	100.1	86.9	7779
1973	108.4	89.2	7830
1974	106.6	91.8	7873
1975	100.0	94.1	7490
1976	101.4	96.1	7246
1977	102.9	98.2	7292
1978	103.9	100.6	7257
1979	104.4	103.1	7176
1980	95.1	105.1	6819

Estimate the parameters of the following four equations and interpret the results:

$$\log Y_t = \alpha + \beta \log X_{1t} + \gamma \log X_{2t} + \log U_t$$
$$\log Y_t = \alpha' + \beta' \log X_{1t} + \gamma' \log X_{2t} + \sigma t + \log U_t'$$

$$\log \left(\frac{Y}{X_2}\right)_t = \alpha'' + \beta'' \log \left(\frac{X_1}{X_2}\right)_t + \log u_t''$$

$$\log \left(\frac{Y}{X_2}\right)_t = \alpha''' + \beta''' \log \left(\frac{X_1}{X_2}\right)_t + \sigma''' t + \log u_t'''$$

References

Cochrane, D. and Orcutt, G.H. (1949), 'Application of least squares regressions to relationships containing Autocorrelated Error Terms', *Journal of the American Statistical Association*, **44**, 32–61.

Durbin, J. and Watson, G.S. (1950), 'Testing for serial correlation in least squares regression', *Biometrica*, **37**, 409–28.

Durbin, J. and Watson, G.S. (1951), 'Testing for serial correlation in least squares regression', *Biometrica*, **38**, 159–78.

Johnston, J. (1984), *Econometric Methods*, 3rd edn, New York: McGraw–Hill.

Kmenta, J. (1986), *Elements of Econometrics*, 2nd edn, New York: MacMillan.

Maddala, G.S. (1977), *Econometrics*, International Student Edition, Tokyo: McGraw–Hill Kogakusha.

White, H. (1980), 'A heteroscedasticity consistent covariance matrix estimator and a direct test of heteroscedasticity', *Econometrica*, **48**, 817–38.

Chapter 3

SOME APPLICATIONS OF MULTIPLE LINEAR REGRESSION

The main objective of this chapter is to illustrate the use of multiple linear regression analysis in economics. Most investigators will come across the problems which we have discussed in Chapter 2; some simple remedies to these problems are provided in this chapter. The illustrations are drawn from both developing and developed economies. Much more applied econometric work has been carried out on advanced economies because of the availability of more extensive and higher quality data than is available for the less developed economies. Nevertheless, it is a key contention of ours that the techniques discussed in this book are of general applicability across a wide range of different economies and we are, accordingly, catholic in our choice of empirical examples.

In Section 3.1 we estimate some money demand functions for the United Kingdom and discuss the problem of serial correlation which is found to be present in some of the estimated equations. The presence of serial correlation suggests the possibility that the model has been misspecified and we consider alternative specifications and attempt to discriminate between them. In Section 3.2 the issue of heteroscedasticity in both cross-section and grouped data is addressed using as examples a study of productivity in Cypriot manufacturing industries and a cross-sectional consumption function for the United Kingdom. Some discussion of specification error is presented in Section 3.3 and a specification error test is performed using data on investment expenditures produced in the United States by General Motors. Finally, in Section 3.4 we deal with the problem of multicollinearity using as an example a study of Bangladesh agriculture, and show that remedies to this problem are not easy.

3.1 SERIAL CORRELATION

In the preceding chapter we demonstrated that in the presence of serially correlated errors the variances of the estimated coefficients of the OLS model are biased. The presence of such errors in time-series data is common and in this section we provide an empirical example where serial correlation is present. Tests are performed to test for the presence of various kinds of serial correlation, both in the absence and presence of a lagged dependent variable among the explanatory variables. Alternative model specifications are presented and a statistical evaluation of the different specifications is undertaken.

Employing data presented in M. Friedman and A. Schwartz's massive study, *Monetary Trends in the United States and the United Kingdom*, we estimate money demand functions for the United Kingdom for the period 1920–75. The data are given in Table 3.1. We commence by estimating a very simple model to explain the *per capita* demand for real money balances (M^d/P) as a function of real *per capita* income (y) and an opportunity cost variable in the form of a short-term interest rate (r). The proposed model is

$$\left(\frac{M^d}{P}\right)_t = B y_t^{\beta_2} r_t^{\beta_3} u_t \tag{3.1}$$

where t is time, B, β_2 and β_3 are parameters and u_t is a stochastic disturbance term. Taking natural logarithms of equation (3.1) we have

$$\ln\left(\frac{M^d}{P}\right)_t = \beta_1 + \beta_2 \ln y_t + \beta_3 \ln r_t + \epsilon_t \tag{3.2}$$

where $\beta_1 = \ln B$ and $\epsilon_t = \ln u_t$. We assume that ϵ_t is independently normally distributed: $\epsilon_t \sim \text{IN}(0, \sigma_\epsilon^2)$. The income elasticity of demand for real money balances, which we expect to be positive, is measured by β_2 and the interest elasticity of demand for real *per capita* money balances, which we expect to be negative, is measured by β_3. Equation (3.2) was estimated for the period 1920–75 by means of OLS and the results are presented below with the estimated t ratios given below the values of the estimated regression coefficients:

$$\begin{aligned}
\ln\left(\frac{M^d}{P}\right)_t &= -2.494\,43 + 0.7141 \ln y_t - 0.1423 \ln r_t \\
&\quad\;\;(7.9448)\quad\;(19.4129)\qquad(10.1759) \\
R^2 &= 0.8778 \quad n = 56 \quad \log L = 57.4918 \\
\bar{R}^2 &= 0.8732 \quad F(2,53) = 190.425 \quad SEE = 0.0891 \\
DW &= 0.4456
\end{aligned} \tag{3.3}$$

Table 3.1 Money demand functions for the United Kingdom for the period 1920–75

Year	Money stock (£M) M	Nominal income (£M) Y	Real income (1929 £M) y	Implicit price (1929 = 100) P	Population (M) POP	Short-term interest rate (annual percentage) r
1920	2 831	5 077	3 288	154.4	43.718	6.40
1921	2 768	4 249	3 099	137.1	44.072	5.16
1922	2 676	3 713	3 218	115.4	44.372	2.64
1923	2 561	3 542	3 342	106.0	44.596	2.72
1924	2 520	3 677	3 499	105.1	44.915	3.46
1925	2 500	3 959	3 742	105.8	45.059	4.14

Table 3.1–cont'd

Year	Money stock (£M) M	Nominal income (£M) Y	Real income (1929 £M) y	Implicit price (1929 = 100) P	Population (M) POP	Short-term interest rate (annual percentage) r
1926	2 509	3 747	3 599	104.1	45.232	4.48
1927	2 546	3 983	3 928	101.4	45.389	4.26
1928	2 600	3 996	3 980	100.4	45.578	4.16
1929	2 616	4 127	4 127	100.0	45.672	5.26
1930	2 638	4 065	4 098	99.2	45.866	2.57
1931	2 606	3 658	3 810	96.0	46.074	3.61
1932	2 666	3 550	3 838	92.5	46.335	1.86
1933	2 804	3 650	4 007	91.1	46.520	0.69
1934	2 812	3 910	4 325	90.4	46.666	0.82
1935	2 912	4 078	4 471	91.2	46.868	0.58
1936	3 100	4 308	4 703	91.6	47.081	0.61
1937	3 244	4 556	4 786	95.2	47.289	0.58
1938	3 228	4 754	4 876	97.5	47.494	0.64
1939	3 272	4 907	4 912	99.9	47.761	1.23
1940	3 607	5 530	4 834	114.4	48.226	1.04
1941	4 155	6 720	5 342	125.8	48.216	1.03
1942	4 788	7 449	5 584	133.4	48.400	1.03
1943	5 376	7 918	5 636	140.5	48.789	1.03
1944	6 082	8 114	5 611	144.6	49.016	1.03
1945	6 698	8 227	5 647	145.7	49.182	0.93
1946	7 396	8 165	5 447	149.9	49.217	0.53
1947	8 035	8 688	5 481	158.5	49.519	0.53
1948	8 173	9 621	5 633	170.8	50.014	0.56
1949	8 300	10 311	5 859	176.0	50.312	0.63
1950	8 382	10 823	6 091	177.7	50.565	0.69
1951	8 457	11 837	6 210	190.6	50.290	0.91
1952	8 584	12 729	6 170	206.3	50.431	2.71
1953	8 849	13 518	6 355	212.7	50.593	2.77
1954	9 189	14 437	6 629	217.8	50.765	1.84
1955	9 246	15 480	6 874	225.2	50.946	3.75
1956	9 175	16 606	6 939	239.3	51.184	5.05
1957	9 373	17 477	7 016	249.1	51.430	4.98
1958	9 704	18 222	6 987	260.8	51.652	4.74
1959	10 122	19 253	7 246	265.7	51.956	3.49
1960	10 495	20 959	7 745	270.6	52.372	5.05
1961	10 722	22 145	7 920	279.6	52.807	5.32
1962	10 925	23 203	8 029	289.0	53.274	4.41
1963	11 448	24 759	8 376	295.6	53.552	3.82
1964	12 010	26 772	8 836	303.0	53.885	4.81
1965	12 702	28 787	9 113	315.9	54.218	6.29
1966	13 219	30 385	9 195	330.5	54.500	6.43
1967	13 796	32 017	9 275	345.2	54.800	6.08
1968	14 780	34 201	9 377	364.7	55.049	5.42
1969	15 538	36 073	9 460	381.3	55.263	8.48
1970	16 528	39 600	9 607	412.2	55.421	8.26
1971	18 405	44 479	9 794	454.1	55.610	6.40
1972	22 002	49 696	9 976	498.1	55.793	6.11
1973	27 841	57 933	10 233	566.1	55.933	10.43
1974	33 175	66 512	10 470	635.2	55.965	13.06
1975	36 480	83 188	10 866	765.6	55.943	10.62

Source: Milton Friedman and Anna J. Schwartz (1982), *Monetary Trends in the United States and the United Kingdom*, Table 4.9, pp. 132–7. Chicago: The University of Chicago Press.

At first sight, the results appear promising; after correcting for degrees of freedom, almost 87 per cent of the variation in the dependent variable is explained. The coefficients on real income and the interest rate have the expected sign and the t ratios are high. However, the Durbin–Watson d statistic indicates the presence of first-order serial correlation; hence the variances of the estimators are biased and the standard tests of significance for both individual coefficients and for the overall regression are invalid.

Another very simple test for serial correlation can be conducted by regressing the residuals (e_t) from equation (3.3) on lagged values of the residuals (e_{t-1}):

$$\left.\begin{aligned} e_t &= 0.7634\, e_{t-1} \\ &\quad (8.9471) \\ R^2 &= 0.5981 \end{aligned}\right\} \tag{3.4}$$

The presence of serial correlation is confirmed by the high value of the t statistic for the coefficient on the lagged residual. Asymptotically, the autocorrelation coefficient must equal $1 - \frac{1}{2}d$, where d is the Durbin–Watson statistic; note for this particular case the above expression equals 0.7772, which is very close to the estimate in equation (3.4). To test for higher order autocorrelation, we can regress the residuals from the fitted regression on, say, both e_{t-1} and e_{t-2}. Since the test is an asymptotic one, the residuals for the periods preceding the sample periods are assigned a value of zero:

$$\left.\begin{aligned} e_t &= 0.9094\, e_{t-1} - 0.1618\, e_{t-2} \\ &\quad (6.5477) \quad\quad (1.1229) \\ R^2 &= 0.6225 \end{aligned}\right\} \tag{3.5}$$

The coefficient on e_{t-2} is not statistically significantly different from zero; tests for third- and fourth-order autocorrelation were also performed and the results revealed no such autocorrelation.

The money demand equation estimated above assumes implicitly that economic agents eliminate within the period any discrepancy between their desired and actual holdings of real money balances. To allow for the possibility that such adjustment may not be fully achieved within the period, the following partial adjustment mechanism is proposed:

$$\ln\left(\frac{M^d}{P}\right)_t - \ln\left(\frac{M^d}{P}\right)_{t-1} = \lambda\left(\ln\left(\frac{M^d}{P}\right)_t^* - \ln\left(\frac{M^d}{P}\right)_{t-1}\right) \tag{3.6}$$

where $(M^d/P)_t^*$ are desired real *per capita* money balances at time t and λ is a parameter whose value is expected to lie between 0 and 1 and

$$\ln\left(\frac{M^d}{P}\right)_t^* = \beta_1 + \beta_2 \ln y_t + \beta_3 \ln r_t + \epsilon_t \tag{3.7}$$

Hence the equation to be estimated is

Serial correlation

$$\ln\left(\frac{M^d}{P}\right)_t = \beta_1\lambda + \beta_2\lambda \ln y_t + \beta_3\lambda \ln r_t + (1-\lambda)\ln\left(\frac{M^d}{P}\right)_{t-1} + \lambda\epsilon_t \qquad (3.8)$$

Equation (3.8) has been estimated by OLS and the estimated equation is presented below:

$$\left.\begin{aligned}
\ln\left(\frac{M^d}{P}\right)_t &= \underset{(1.0967)}{-0.2438} + \underset{(2.5158)}{0.11864 \ln y_t} - \underset{(2.5173)}{0.02729 \ln r_t} + \underset{(13.3914)}{0.7910 \ln\left(\frac{M^d}{P}\right)_{t-1}} \\
R^2 &= 0.9698 \quad \log L = 98.2160 \quad SEE = 0.04213 \\
\bar{R}^2 &= 0.9680 \quad n = 55 \quad F(3,51) = 546.449 \\
DW &= 0.8744
\end{aligned}\right\} \qquad (3.9)$$

The computer program automatically calculates and presents the Durbin–Watson statistic; but in the presence of a lagged dependent variable it should not be used to test for the presence of first-order serial correlation. In such circumstances Durbin has shown for large samples that a test of the null hypothesis of no first-order autocorrelation is provided by the standard normal variate

$$h = r\sqrt{\left[\frac{n}{1 - n\,\text{Var}(b_4)}\right]}$$

where r is the estimate of the first-order autocorrelation coefficient, n is the number of observations in the sample and Var (b_4) is the estimate of the sampling variance of the coefficient on the lagged dependent variable $[\ln(M^d/P)_{t-1}]$ in the OLS regression of equation (3.8). If $h > 1.645$, then the null hypothesis of no first-order autocorrelation is to be rejected in favour of the alternative hypothesis of positive autocorrelation. The value of 1.645 is obtained from the normal distribution using the 5 per cent level of significance for a one-sided test of positive first-order autocorrelation.

If $n\,\text{Var}(b_4) \geq 1$, then, clearly the test cannot be applied. An alternative approach due to Breusch and Pagan (1979) is to regress the residuals from this original equation (3.9) on the residuals lagged by one period, $\ln y_t$ and $\ln r_t$. A significant coefficient on the lagged residual in this auxiliary equation suggests the presence of serial correlation. The same test, but with the alternative hypothesis confined to multiplicative heteroscedasticity, was proposed by Godfrey (1978a and b). More specifically, nR^2 follows the χ^2 distribution asymptotically if the null hypothesis is true with 1 degree of freedom: if $nR^2 > \chi^2_{0.05}(1)$, the null hypothesis of no first-order serial correlation is to be rejected. The results of the auxiliary regression reported in equation (3.10) lead us to reject the null hypothesis:

$$\left.\begin{aligned}
e_t &= \underset{(1.1360)}{0.01824 \ln y_t} - \underset{(0.5674)}{0.00337 \ln r_t} + \underset{(4.8502)}{0.6024\, e_{t-1}} - \underset{(1.1477)}{0.04388 \log\left(\frac{M}{P}\right)_{t-1}} \\
R^2 &= 0.3215 \quad n = 54 \\
nR^2 &= 18.00 \quad \chi^2_{0.05}(1) = 3.84
\end{aligned}\right\} \qquad (3.10)$$

In testing for the joint presence of first- and second-order autocorrelation, the following results were obtained:

$$e_t = -0.003\,78 \ln y_t - 0.001\,11 \ln r_t + 0.8267\,e_{t-1} - 0.4868\,e_{t-2}$$
$$\quad\quad (0.2304) \quad\quad (0.201\,67) \quad\quad (5.6884) \quad\quad (3.1326)$$

$$+ 0.008\,699 \log\left(\frac{M}{P}\right)_{t-1}$$
$$(0.2226) \tag{3.11}$$

$$R^2 = 0.4156 \quad n = 53$$
$$nR^2 = 22.026 \quad \chi^2_{0.05}(2) = 5.99$$

In this case, too, we reject the null hypothesis of no autocorrelation. Further investigations revealed no evidence of the presence of third- and fourth-order serial correlation; the latter is generally observed in time series where the data are available on a quarterly basis. The test presented above is an LM test and this is discussed in detail in Chapter 4.

In investigating the determinants of the demand for real money balances, we now consider alternative model specifications and attempt to discriminate between them. The three models we consider are generally very similar: namely the model we have already outlined with partial adjustment of actual balances towards the desired level; a model with a first-order serially correlated disturbance term; and a general dynamic model with lagged values of all the variables including the dependent variable among the regressors.

First we present the results of estimating a general dynamic model:

$$\ln\left(\frac{M^d}{P}\right)_t = -0.4619 - 0.002\,22 \ln y_t + 0.093\,04 \ln y_{t-1} - 0.047\,37 \ln r_t$$
$$\quad\quad (1.8100) \quad (0.0119) \quad\quad (0.4806) \quad\quad (2.5767)$$

$$+ 0.024\,23 \ln r_{t-1} + 0.811\,17 \ln\left(\frac{M^d}{P}\right)_{t-1}$$
$$(1.2751) \quad\quad (11.8390) \tag{3.12}$$

$$R^2 = 0.9489 \quad \log L = 97.6042 \quad SEE = 0.043\,46$$
$$\bar{R}^2 = 0.9437 \quad F(5,49) = 182.115$$

There are no restrictions in this model. For the model with first-order serial correlation, we have

$$\ln\left(\frac{M^d}{P}\right)_t = \beta_1 + \beta_2 \ln y_t + \beta_3 \ln r_t + u_t \tag{3.13}$$

where

$$u_t = \rho u_{t-1} + v_t$$

The model was estimated using a maximum likelihood iterative technique (discussed in Chapter 4) on TSP and the estimated equation is presented below:

$$\left.\begin{aligned}\ln\left(\frac{M^d}{P}\right)_t &= -2.3048 + 0.4176 \ln y_t - 0.047\,58 \ln r_t \\ &\quad (3.6460)\quad (3.1649) \quad\quad (2.6227) \\ \hat{u}_t &= \ 0.925\,18\, \hat{u}_{t-1} \\ &\quad (19.1668) \\ \log L &= 92.0006 \quad SEE = 0.109\,563 \\ n &= 55 \quad DW = 1.2298\end{aligned}\right\} \quad (3.14)$$

The estimated model yields a very high value of the autoregressive coefficient which is not significantly different from unity at the 5 per cent level. Given this finding one would, in fact, be tempted to estimate the demand for money function in terms of first differences, though we do not go down that road here.

In comparing the above model with the general model, we note that the former involves the estimation of fewer parameters than the general dynamic model where lags in all the variables are employed. In the model with the serially correlated disturbance term, we estimate four parameters, and in the general model we estimate six parameters. In order to discriminate between these two alternative specifications, the likelihood ratio (LR) test can be conducted. However, it does not necessarily follow that if a model equation has fewer parameters than another, the LR test can be used. The model may be non-nested, in which case the LR test cannot be applied. Letting $\log L_0$ represent the log of the likelihood for the restricted model (i.e. the one with serial correlation) and $\log L_1$ represent the log of the likelihood for the unrestricted model, then the likelihood ratio (LR) follows the χ^2 distribution, in this case with 2 degrees of freedom, and is given by $-2[\log L_0 - \log L_1]$. If LR is greater than χ^2 for the particular level of significance, then the restricted model is to be rejected in favour of the unrestricted model. For the particular case under consideration:

$$\begin{aligned}LR &= -2[92.0006 - 97.6042] \\ &= 11.2072 > \chi^2_{0.05}(2) = 5.991\end{aligned}$$

The model with the first-order serially correlated disturbance term is therefore rejected in favour of the more general model.

The same test may also be performed for the comparison between the general model of equation (3.12) and the model of equation (3.9) in which money balances adjust partially towards the desired level. In this case we have:

$$\begin{aligned}-2[\log L_0 - \log L_1] &= -2[96.5148 - 97.6042] \\ &= 2.1788\end{aligned}$$

For this comparison also, there are 2 degrees of freedom and employing the likelihood ratio test in this case will not lead us to reject the partial adjustment model. We have, however, shown earlier that the model with partial adjustment is unsatisfactory for other reasons: the presence of serially correlated residuals.

In this section we have discussed various tests for the presence of serially correlated disturbances as well as providing some discussions on model choice in the context of seeking to estimate a money demand function for the United Kingdom. The issue of model choice is of paramount importance in economics and when models based solely on economic–theoretic considerations fail to provide an adequate explanation of the data, the case for an empirical approach is strengthened. A systematic specification search to suit the data has recently been suggested by Hendry (1979). This approach starts with a general dynamic model which is overparametrised, i.e. it has more lags than is considered necessary. The model is then progressively simplified using a sequence of simplification tests. The sequential testing procedures are used to select a data coherent specification. It is asserted that until the model actually captures the data generation process, it is useless to test hypotheses of interest in economic theory.

3.2 HETEROSCEDASTICITY

In Chapter 2 it was shown that in the presence of heteroscedastic disturbances the variances of the estimators are biased and the conventional t and F tests are, accordingly, invalid. In this section we look at some empirical examples where heteroscedasticity is or may be present. First, we undertake an analysis to test the null hypothesis of homoscedastic disturbances. Then if the null hypothesis is rejected we consider how the data may be transformed so as to yield disturbances which are homoscedastic.

In our first example we consider a study by Episkopou (1988) of the determinants of interindustry labour productivity differentials in 1981 for the Greek Cypriot manufacturing sector. Data relating to forty-six manufacturing industries, each industry being a four-digit one under the Standard International Industrial Classification, were collected. The dependent variable was value added per labour employed (*LP*) in 1981. The explanatory variables were: total expenditure on fixed assets over the period 1978–81, divided by total labour employed in 1981 (*CAP*); technological opportunity (*UKLP*) measured by the level of labour productivity in the corresponding four-digit industry in the United Kingdom in 1968; capacity utilisation (*CUTIL*) measured by actual gross output as a percentage of the maximum possible gross output on an eight hour shift; female employment rate (*FEM*) measured by the ratio of female employees to total labour employed in 1981; non-production workers (*NPW*) measured by the number of employees not engaged directly in the production process divided by total labour employed in 1981; firm size (*TPS*) measured by the size of the median firm in each industry; small firms (*SMALL*) measured by the proportion of employment accounted for by firms with less than 5 employees; seller concentration (*CONC*) measured by the Herfindahl index applied to employment; market size (*MKTSZ*) measured by gross output plus imports less exports in 1981; employment in family plants (*FAM*) measured by the proportion of employees engaged in family owned plants in 1981; import penetration (*IMP*) defined as competitive imports as a proportion of market size; vertical integration *(VI)* measured by value added as a proportion of gross output in 1981; growth (*GROW*) defined as the rate of growth in the number of employees over the period 1978–81; advertising intensity (ADV) measured as advertising expenditure divided by gross output in 1981; and the nominal tariff rate (TAR) for the particular industry in 1981. The equation was then estimated by OLS to yield

$$LP = 0.009 + 0.056\,CAP + 0.013\,UKLP + 0.637\,CUTIL - 0.02\,FEM$$
$$(0.80)\quad(4.43)\qquad\quad(6.05)\qquad\qquad(6.50)\qquad\qquad(3.62)$$

$$-\,0.066\,NPW + 0.147\,TPS - 0.015\,SMALL - 0.021\,CONC + 0.033\,MKTSZ$$
$$\quad(4.89)\qquad\quad(6.01)\qquad\quad(3.85)\qquad\qquad(2.44)\qquad\qquad(3.34)\qquad(3.15)$$

$$-\,0.057\,VI - 0.036\,GROW + 0.697\,ADV - 0.009\,TAR$$
$$\quad(3.88)\qquad(2.93)\qquad\quad(3.79)\qquad\quad(2.29)$$

$$\bar{R}^2 = 0.943 \quad SEE = 0.13 \times 10^8$$

The coefficients of $UKLP$, $CUTIL$, TPS and $GROW$ have been multiplied by 10^{-2}; the coefficients of FEM, NPW, $SMALL$, $CONC$, VI, ADV, and the constant by 10^{-5}; the coefficient of $MKTSZ$ by 10^3; t values are reported in parentheses beneath the estimated regression coefficients.

At first sight, all the estimated coefficients apart from the constant appear to be significantly different from zero. However, in studies using cross-sectional data, it is not uncommon for the disturbances to be heteroscedastic and it is therefore appropriate to perform White's test for heteroscedastic disturbances on the Episkopou model. Since the equation estimated to explain interindustry differences in labour productivity contains thirteen explanatory variables and only forty-six observations, it is not possible to estimate an equation in which the squared residuals from the original equation are regressed on a constant, the original explanatory variables and the squares and cross-products of all the explanatory variables. As a second-best procedure the explanatory variables were divided into two groups and White's test was then performed separately for the regression of the squared residuals from the original equation on:
(i) a constant term plus the squares and cross-products of the following subset of explanatory variables: CAP, $UKLP$, $CUTIL$, FEM, NPW, TPS;
(ii) a constant term plus the squares and cross-products of the following subset of explanatory variables: $SMALL$, $CONC$, $MKTSZ$, VI, $GROW$, ADV, TAR.

$nR^2 \sim X^2(p)$ where n is the number of observations and R^2 is the coefficient of determination for the regression of the squared residuals on p explanatory variables. For the first regression we find $nR^2 = 10.53$, while $\chi^2_{0.05}$ with 21 degrees of freedom is 32.67; for the second regression we have $nR^2 = 12.13$, while $\chi^2_{0.05}$ with 28 degrees of freedom is 41.33. On the basis of this variant of White's test we cannot reject the null hypothesis of homoscedastic disturbances for the Episkopou model. The test is an LM test, which is discussed in Chapter 4.

For the second example, we consider the data given in Table 3.2 from the 1985 UK Family Expenditure Survey, where information on average weekly household expenditure and normal weekly disposable income is provided for groups of households where a household has been allocated to a group on the basis of its gross

Table 3.2 Expenditure of households at different levels of household income, UK 1985

Range of gross weekly income £ per week	Number of households	Normal weekly disposable household income (£)	Average weekly household expenditure (£)
Under 40	368	33.93	43.71
40– 50	362	44.11	46.43
50– 65	418	57.75	64.61
65– 80	428	70.78	78.01
80–100	429	86.46	94.69
100–125	430	102.89	113.15
125–150	456	120.32	127.20
150–175	464	137.40	139.64
175–200	449	155.16	154.31
200–225	392	172.52	170.43
225–250	417	190.29	173.72
250–300	681	216.28	197.24
300–350	551	252.66	226.45
350–400	354	292.01	249.38
400–500	445	338.01	297.62
500 +	368	502.82	383.96
All	7012	174.67	161.87

Source: Department of Employment (1986), *Family Expenditure Survey Report for 1985 Giving the Results for the United Kingdom*, Tables 5 and 22, London: HMSO.

normal weekly income. Say we wish to utilise this information on group means to estimate the regression of household expenditure on household disposable income. Let $\overline{HE}_g$ represent average household expenditure of group g, $\overline{DY}_g$ average household disposable income of group g and $\bar{u}_g$ the disturbance term for group g. Assume for individual households we have

$$HE_i = \beta_0 + \beta_1 DY_i + u_i \quad (3.16)$$

and

$$u_i \sim N(0, \sigma^2) \quad (3.17)$$

We seek to estimate

$$\overline{HE}_g = \beta_0 + \beta_1 \overline{DY}_g + \bar{u}_g \quad (3.18)$$

Notice that

$$E(\bar{u}_g) = 0 \quad (3.19)$$

and

$$\text{Var}(\bar{u}_g) = \frac{1}{n_g^2}[\sigma^2 + \ldots + \sigma^2] = \frac{n_g \sigma^2}{n_g^2} = \frac{\sigma^2}{n_g} \quad (3.20)$$

where n_g is the number of households in group g. Clearly, if we estimate equation (3.18) when the number of households in each group is not the same, then the disturbances will be heteroscedastic and the variances of the estimated regression coefficients will be biased.

In this case, however, a simple transformation can be employed to convert these heteroscedastic disturbances into homoscedastic ones. Multiply equation (3.18) by $\sqrt{n_g}$ to obtain

$$\overline{HE}_g \sqrt{n_g} = \beta_0 \sqrt{n_g} + \beta_1 \overline{DY}_g \sqrt{n_g} + \bar{u}_g \sqrt{n_g} \qquad (3.21)$$

with

$$\text{Var}(\bar{u}_g \sqrt{n_g}) = \sigma^2$$

Estimating equation (3.18) by OLS yields

$$\overline{HE}_g = 30.274 + 0.7486 \, \overline{DY}_g$$
$$(6.41) \quad (33.55) \qquad (3.22)$$
$$R^2 = 0.988 \quad SEE^* = 0.067\,61$$

We may compare this with the results of estimating equation (3.21) by OLS:

$$\left. \begin{array}{c} \overline{HE}_g \sqrt{n_g} = 30.493 \sqrt{n_g} + 0.7521 \, DY_g \sqrt{n_g} \\ (6.50) \qquad (33.52) \\ SEE^* = 0.064\,32 \end{array} \right\} \qquad (3.23)$$

where SEE^* is the standard error of the estimate normalised by dividing through by the mean value of the dependent variable, and t ratios are given in parentheses below the estimates of the regression coefficients. The normalised SEE is lower in the second equation where we have corrected for heteroscedasticity; but in this particular example there is not much difference between the respective variances of the regression coefficients for the two equations.

In estimating the equation using grouped data rather than the data relating to the individual households, information is necessarily lost and the variances of the estimators are greater, giving rise to a loss of efficiency. This is the case whether or not the disturbances in the grouped data specification have been corrected for heteroscedasticity.

3.3 SPECIFICATION ERROR

Consider the following true model:

$$y_i = \beta_1 x_{1i} + \beta_2 x_{2i} + u_i - \bar{u} \qquad (3.24)$$

where x_2 is an unobservable variable. If we regress y on x_1 alone, then, unless the covariance between x_1 and x_2 is zero, the OLS estimator of β_1 will be biased and, even with a zero covariance, the variance of the estimator will be overestimated.

If we did not know the true model, is it possible to test the null hypothesis $H_0: \beta_2 = 0$ when x_2 is unobservable? Ramsey (1969) has proposed a test for these circumstances known as the regression specification errors test (RESET). RESET involves approximating the unobservable variable, x_2, by a vector of regressors which are correlated with it. Regarding this vector of regressors, Thursby and Schmidt (1977) have shown that the most suitable variables to employ are the squares, cubes and fourth powers of the included variable(s). The test of whether the model has been wrongly specified by excluding x_2 is then simply an F test for the significance of the vector of regressors which are used to proxy x_2. The following statistic follows the F distribution with k_1 and $n - k$ degrees of freedom:

$$\frac{(RRSS - URSS)/k_1}{URSS/(n - k)}$$

where k_1 is the number of variables used to proxy x_2, n is the number of observations and k the number of parameters estimated in the unrestricted equation, $RRSS$ measures the sum of squared residuals for the equation which excludes the proxies for x_2 and $URSS$ the sum of squared residuals for the equation which includes all the variables.

We now consider an application of RESET, using data from Boot and De Wit (1960) on investment expenditure by General Motors during the period 1935–53. The data are presented in Table 3.3.

Assume a firm's desired capital stock (K^*) is a linear function of expected profitability:

Table 3.3 Gross investment, capital stock and stock market valuation of General Motors, 1935–1953

Year	I_t	K_{t-1}	V_{t-1}
1935	317.6	2.8	3078.5
1936	391.8	52.6	4661.7
1937	410.6	156.9	5387.1
1938	257.7	209.2	2792.2
1939	330.8	203.4	4313.3
1940	461.2	207.2	4643.9
1941	512.0	255.2	4551.2
1942	448.0	303.7	3244.1
1943	499.6	264.1	4053.7
1944	547.5	201.6	4379.3
1945	561.2	265.0	4840.9
1946	688.1	402.2	4900.9
1947	568.9	761.5	3526.5
1948	529.2	922.1	3254.7
1949	555.1	1020.1	3700.2
1950	642.9	1099.0	3755.6
1951	755.9	1207.7	4833.0
1952	891.2	1430.5	4924.9
1953	1304.4	1777.3	6241.7

Source: J.C.G. Boot and G.M. de Wit (1960), 'Investment demand: an empirical contribution to the aggregation problem', *International Economic Review*, **1**, 27.

All variables are in millions of dollars at constant (1947) prices. The capital stock figures are measured as deviations from the capital stock in a year prior to the sample period.

Specification error

$$K_t^* = \beta_0 + \beta_1 EP_t \tag{3.25}$$

Because of lags in adjustment, net investment (*NI*) during some period of time is taken to be proportional to the difference between the desired and actual capital stock (*K*) at the end of the preceding period:

$$NI_t = \lambda[K_{t-1}^* - K_{t-1}] \quad \text{(with } 1 \geqslant \lambda \geqslant 0) \tag{3.26}$$

Replacement investment, including repairs and maintenance (*RI*), is assumed to be proportional to the end of preceding period capital stock:

$$RI_t = \delta K_{t-1} \quad \text{(with } \delta > 0) \tag{3.27}$$

Using the above three equations, we obtain the following gross investment function (I):

$$I_t = \lambda\beta_0 + (\delta - \lambda)K_{t-1} + \lambda\beta_1 EP_{t-1} \tag{3.28}$$

Assume we have no information on expected profitability and regress I_t on K_{t-1} to obtain

$$I_t = 343.3236 + 0.3863 K_{t-1}$$
$$(7.901) \quad (6.765) \tag{3.29}$$
$$R^2 = 0.729 \quad SEE = 126.7376 \quad DW = 0.896 \quad n = 19$$

In order to test whether by excluding expected profitability from the regression the investment equation has been misspecified, we conduct the Ramsey test by regressing I_t on K_{t-1}, K_{t-1}^2, K_{t-1}^3 and K_{t-1}^4

$$I_t = 288.4402 + 1.1918 K_{t-1} - 2.033 \times 10^{-3} K_{t-1}^2 + 1.425 \times 10^{-6} K_{t-1}^3 - 2.68 \times 10^{-10} K_{t-1}^4$$
$$(3.982) \quad (2.011) \quad (1.364) \quad\quad\quad (1.028) \quad\quad\quad\quad (0.657) \tag{3.30}$$
$$R^2 = 0.887 \quad SEE = 90.319\,14 \quad DW = 1.028 \quad n = 19$$

and calculate

$$F = \frac{(RRSS - URSS)/k_1}{URSS/(n-k)}$$

$$= \frac{(273\,061.3 - 114\,205.6)/3}{114\,205.6/14}$$

$$= 6.491 \tag{3.31}$$

Since $F_{0.05}(3,14) = 3.34$, we reject the null hypothesis that there is no specification error by omitting expected profitability from the estimated equation.

If we now assume that the share price of the company reflects the present value of the expected future stream of dividend payments, then we may proxy expected profitability by the stock market valuation of the company (*V*) and include this variable along with the capital stock in the regression equation. The following results were obtained:

$$I_t = -109.7985 + 0.3261 K_{t-1} + 0.1142 V_{t-1}$$
$$(1.127) \quad (8.178) \quad\quad (4.862) \quad\quad\quad (3.32)$$
$$R^2 = 0.891 \quad SEE = 82.9937 \quad DW = 1.0907$$

The K_{t-1} and V_{t-1} are correlated with each other in this sample, the simple correlation coefficient between the two variables being 0.31. The inclusion of V_{t-1} in the regression reduces the standard error of the estimate, increases R^2 and reduces the estimate of the regression coefficient on K_{t-1} and its variance. On the basis of the t test, the null hypothesis that V_{t-1} is not a significant regressor is rejected, though note that the test is not strictly valid since the Durbin–Watson statistic for all equations (3.28, 3.29 and 3.31) falls into the inconclusive region.

In order to test the hypothesis whether any other variables have been wrongly omitted from the equation, a further equation was estimated by adding K_{t-1}^2, K_{t-1}^3, V_{t-1}^2 and V_{t-1}^3 to the regressors. In this case the RESET statistic was 2.278, whereas $F_{0.05}(4,12)$ was 3.26; hence the test does not support the hypothesis that the latter equation is misspecified.

The major problem with the Ramsey procedure is the inability of the test to discriminate between whether the specification error, if present, results from the omission of a relevant explanatory variable or from an inappropriate functional form for the estimated equation: a linear versus a non-linear specification. A more powerful test is proposed by Hausman (1978) and is discussed later in the book.

3.4 MULTICOLLINEARITY

In the extreme case where two or more explanatory variables of a regression model are perfectly correlated, the cross-products and sums of squares matrix, $X'X$, of the explanatory variables is singular and it is impossible to obtain estimates of the coefficients of the model. Singularity of $X'X$ occurs when the columns of X are not linearly independent. Consider the case where the x_1 column is equal to a times the x_2 column; then we may write:

$$\beta_1 x_1 + \beta_2 x_2 = \beta_1 x_1 + \beta_2 x_2 + \theta(x_1 - a x_2)$$
$$= (\beta_1 + \theta) x_1 + (\beta_2 - a\theta) x_2$$
$$= (a\beta_1 + \beta_2) x_2 \quad\quad (3.33)$$

It is clear that the coefficients β_1 and β_2 cannot be separately estimated. If β_1 and β_2 yield a good fit, then so will $\beta_1 + \theta$ and $\beta_2 - a\theta$ for any value of θ.

Associated with $X'X$ are sets of characteristic roots and vectors with

$$X'X = PDP' \quad\quad (3.34)$$

where D is a diagonal matrix whose elements are the characteristic roots, λ_i, $i = 1, \ldots, k$, of $X'X$ arranged in decreasing order and P is a matrix whose columns are the associated characteristic vectors. Note that $PP' = P'P = I$; this enables us to write the regression model $y = X\beta + u$ as

$$y = (XP)(P'\beta) + u$$
$$= Z\alpha + u \tag{3.35}$$

where $Z = XP$ is a matrix of new explanatory variables and $\alpha = P'\beta$ a vector of new coefficients. The new variables Z are called the principal components of X; note that Z_i, the ith column of Z, is a linear combination of the columns of X where the weights are the elements of P_i, the ith characteristic vector. An important property of the principal components is that they are pairwise orthogonal; hence the covariance between Z_i and Z_j is zero.

If the rank of X is $k - m$, m of the k characteristic roots are zero and the corresponding columns of P satisfy the condition:

$$X'XP_i = 0 \quad (\text{for } i = k - m + 1, \ldots, k) \tag{3.36}$$

implying $XP_i = 0$. If this condition were not met, then

$$P_i'X'XP_i = D_i \neq 0 \tag{3.37}$$

The last m coefficients of α disappear from $Z\alpha$ and cannot be estimated; naturally, it is possible to estimate the first $k - m$ coefficients of α.

If $X'X$ is not singular but there exists a high degree of collinearity between the explanatory variables, then all the characteristic roots are positive but some of the diagonal elements of $(X'X)^{-1}$ will be very large, with obvious implications for the size of the standard errors of the corresponding regression coefficients. In these circumstances, some of the characteristic roots will be very small and it is appropriate to treat m of the smallest roots as being zero. The last m principal components will, accordingly be zero. The model can then be estimated using $k - m$ principal components as explanatory variables and estimates of the first $k - m$ coefficients of α can then be obtained.

We now provide a discussion of an empirical study where multicollinearity among the explanatory variables vitiated any attempt to obtain precise estimates of the regression coefficients when the estimation technique was OLS; but some success was forthcoming with the use of principal components. In a study of the demand for fertiliser in Bangladesh during the period 1969-70 to 1983-4, Parikh (1990) sought to estimate the following log linear demand function:

$$\log QFERT_t = \text{constant} + b_1 \log HYA_t + b_2 \log INTEN_t + b_3 \log IA_t + b_4 TIME + b_5 \log PRATIO_t \tag{3.38}$$

where $QFERT$ is the quantity of fertiliser measured in tons; IA is the irrigated area as a proportion of the total cropped area; HYA is the high yielding variety rice acreage as a proportion of the total rice acreage; $INTEN$ is the intensity of cropping; $PRATIO$ is the ratio of the price of fertiliser to the growers' price of paddy.

The *a priori* expectations are for all the regression coefficients, except b_5, to be positive. There are strong complementarities between fertiliser use, high yielding varieties of rice and irrigation, and the time trend is hypothesised to be positive, reflecting, at least in part, technological diffusion. A rise in the relative price of fertiliser is expected to reduce demand for it.

Given a significant degree of collinearity between the explanatory variables, the author found it was not possible to include all the variables enumerated in equation (3.38) in the actual regression equations that were estimated. Rather, three separate equations were estimated in which subsets of the original explanatory variables were used. Some representative results are presented in Table 3.4. In some preliminary regressions the relative price variable always turned up with a positive but insignificant coefficient and was subsequently dropped from the analysis.

The multicollinearity that is present between high yielding variety rice area as a proportion of total rice cropped area, cropping intensity and irrigated area as a proportion of total cropped area makes it impossible, using OLS, to estimate unambiguously the contribution each of these factors makes to the demand for fertiliser. A possible solution to this problem is to employ the procedure suggested by Mundlak (1981) in which the significant principal components are separated from the nonsignificant ones. Regressions are then performed employing as regressors the significant principal components. The final stage in the procedure is to utilise these regression results to derive estimates of the regression coefficients and standard errors with respect to the original variables. The procedure adopted by Mundlak is to divide the k principal components into two subsets: k_1 is a subset of significant components and k_2 is a subset of insignificant components. The basis for the division into the two subsets is provided by regressing the dependent variable on all the principal components, obtaining the t statistic for each regressor and calculating the following statistic:

$$F = \frac{1}{k_2} \sum_{j \in k_2} t_j^2 \qquad (3.39)$$

which follows the F distribution with $(k_2, n - k)$ degrees of freedom. The k_2 principal components with the lowest t_j^2 statistics are then excluded from the regression model, with k_2 being determined by the following conditions:

$$F(k_2, n - k) < F_\alpha(k_2, n - k) \qquad (3.40)$$

$$F(k_2 + 1, n - k) > F_\alpha(k_2 + 1, n - k) \qquad (3.41)$$

where α represents the level of significance for the test and typically equals 0.01 or 0.05.

Table 3.4 Demand for fertiliser in Bangladesh

	Constant	LHYA	LINTEN	LIA	Time	R^2/SEE	F	DW
Eqn 1	−21.9357	0.4018	7.1988			0.83	30.07	1.46
	(2.936)	(3.803)	(4.860)			0.2351		
Eqn 2	−13.9368		6.1789	1.7049		0.82	27.07	1.27
	(1.543)		(3.658)	(3.502)		0.2455		
Eqn 3	−1.9456		2.8793		0.0906	0.91	59.12	1.91
	(0.266)		(1.942)		(5.981)	0.1750		

Notes: the dependent variable in each equation is *LQFERT*; *L* stands for logarithm in all cases.
t ratios appear in brackets below the estimated regression coefficients.

Consider the following model:
$$y_i = \beta_1 x_{1i} + \beta_2 x_{2i} + \beta_3 x_{3i} \tag{3.42}$$

Assume there is strong collinearity between the explanatory variables and that on the basis of the Mundlak test only the first two principal components are significant. Define these two significant principal components as

$$\left. \begin{array}{l} z_{1i} = p_{11} x_{1i} + p_{21} x_{2i} + p_{31} x_{3i} \\ z_{2i} = p_{12} x_{1i} + p_{22} x_{2i} + p_{32} x_{3i} \end{array} \right\} \tag{3.43}$$

and we now have the principal components model

$$y_i = \alpha_1 z_{1i} + \alpha_2 z_{2i} \tag{3.44}$$

Regress y on z_1 and z_2 to obtain the OLS estimators, a_1 and a_2, of the principal components regression parameters, α_1 and α_2. We can now derive estimators of the original regression parameters. These will be given by

$$\left. \begin{array}{l} b_1 = p_{11} a_1 + p_{12} a_2 \\ b_2 = p_{21} a_1 + p_{22} a_2 \\ b_3 = p_{31} a_1 + p_{32} a_2 \end{array} \right\} \tag{3.45}$$

and their variances will be given, respectively, by

$$\left. \begin{array}{l} \text{Var}(b_1) = p_{11}^2 \text{Var}(a_1) + p_{12}^2 \text{Var}(a_2) \\ \text{Var}(b_2) = p_{21}^2 \text{Var}(a_1) + p_{22}^2 \text{Var}(a_2) \\ \text{Var}(b_3) = p_{31}^2 \text{Var}(a_1) + p_{32}^2 \text{Var}(a_2) \end{array} \right\} \tag{3.46}$$

Note that since the principal components are pairwise orthogonal, $\text{Cov}(a_1, a_2)$ is zero and does not, therefore, appear in the expressions defining $\text{Var}(b_i)$. Furthermore, if z_1 is the only significant principal component, the t ratios for each b will be the same and will equal a_1/standard error of a_1.

What can we say about the principal component (PC) estimators? Whereas the OLS estimators are BLUE, these PC estimators are biased but have smaller variances, and the greater the covariance between the original explanatory variables, the better they tend to be relative to the OLS estimators (see McCallum, 1970).

The Mundlak approach was adopted by Parikh (1990) in his fertiliser study. For purposes of comparison, we present a pair of equations from his study, one equation estimated by OLS and the other by PC (see Table 3.5)

It is clear from Table 3.5 that there are large differences between the values of the OLS and PC estimators, particularly for LHYA and LIA. In all cases the variances of the PC estimators are considerably smaller than those of the OLS estimators and, in this sense, the former estimators, though biased, are more precise.

Multicollinearity is not uncommon in applied econometric work and the econometrician is often in the position of a surgeon treating the symptoms rather than the cause of a disease. By dispensing with some information and employing the method of principal components, we are able to obtain more precise but biased estimates of

Table 3.5 Ordinary least squares and principal component estimators

Method of examination	Constant	LHYA	LIA	LINTEN	R^2	SEE
OLS	2.5583	0.3400 (1.0193)	0.2884 (0.1959)	6.9935 (3.7474)	0.8342	0.245
PC	−16.6442	0.1766 (2.6433)	1.0175 (4.9384)	6.4923 (4.1238)	0.8304	0.247

Notes: the dependent variable in each equation is *LQFERT*. *t* ratios are given in brackets below the regression coefficients.

the parameters of the model. In general, what we require is more information, more and better data, and unfortunately they are rarely available.

Exercises

1. (a) What is the problem of autocorrelation and how might it arise?
   (b) Show that if the following model:
   $$Y_t = \beta_1 + \beta_2 X_t + u_t$$
   is estimated by ordinary least squares when autocorrelation is present that:
   (i) b_2 is unbiased.
   (ii) Var (b_2) is biased.
   (iii) s^2 = residual sum of squares/$n - k$ is biased where n is number of observations and k is number of explanatory variables.
   (iv) Are students' t and F statistics any longer appropriate?

2. In the model
   $$Y_t = \beta_1 + \beta_2 X_t + U_t$$
   where
   $$U_t = \lambda U_{t-1} + V_t$$
   and for all t,
   $$E(V_t) = 0 \text{ and } E(V_t, V_{t+s}) = \sigma_v^2 \quad \text{(for } s = 0\text{)}$$
   $$= 0 \quad \text{(for } s \neq 0\text{)}$$
   Show how the Cochrane–Orcutt method of estimation can be used to estimate the parameters β_1, β_2 and λ and discuss the properties of the estimators.

3. Apply the LM tests to test for first-, second-, third-, fourth- and twelfth-order serial correlation in errors for the estimation of a linear regression model on the data set of money supply and prices (Dhaka cost of living) presented in Chapter 4.

4. The following data were collected for twenty Bangladesh districts in 1976–7:

District	TNCAC	INTEN	HYA	IRGIP	PRAU (aus)	PRAM (aman)
Barisal	5.60	146.40	0.1400	0.0800	1379.3	1760.4
Bogra	10.22	153.24	0.1400	0.0500	1379.3	1787.6
Chittagong	23.25	156.79	0.3800	0.0800	1646.9	1914.4
Chittagong Hill Tracks	4.50	157.11	0.2400	0.0700	1646.9	1905.5
Comilla	15.02	158.44	0.2000	0.1200	1542.6	1842.0
Dhaka	12.14	145.73	0.1500	0.1300	1669.4	1950.9
Dinajpur	5.95	142.64	0.0700	0.0500	1270.4	1651.5
Faridpur	1.40	153.03	0.0200	0.0300	1533.3	1905.5
Jessore	4.44	133.90	0.0600	0.0400	1551.6	1851.0
Khulna	2.44	123.30	0.0800	0.0400	1451.7	1723.9
Kishoreganj	9.02	158.10	0.1700	0.2500	1506.1	1687.7
Kushtia	7.78	128.23	0.0700	0.0800	1569.8	1896.5
Mymensingh	5.20	170.63	0.1700	0.0800	1460.9	1651.5
Noakhali	7.74	154.13	0.2600	0.1200	1597.0	1914.4
Pabna	5.60	153.93	0.0500	0.0400	1551.6	1887.2
Pataukhali	3.31	124.81	0.0900	0.0700	1370.0	1832.8
Rajrampur	4.51	130.41	0.0700	0.0800	1397.2	1842.0
Rangpur	3.30	178.69	0.0800	0.0200	1379.3	1633.2
Sylhet	2.90	133.35	0.1100	0.2500	1429.1	1769.3
Tangail	6.59	167.49	0.1000	0.0800	1560.6	1851.0

TNCAC = nutrients (tons) per 1000 acres of cropped area.
INTEN = intensity of cropping.
HYA = proportion of high yielding variety area.
IRGIP = proportion of irrigated area.
PRAU (aus) = rice price per ton (taka).
PRAM (aman) = rice price per ton (taka).

It was decided to specify a general relationship for the above data for districts of Bangladesh on fertiliser consumption for 1976–7:

$$\log TNCAC_i = \text{constant} + k_1 \log IRGIP_i + k_2 \log HYA_i + k_3 \log (INTEN)_i + k_4 \log (PRAM)_i + k_5 \log (PRAU)_i$$

The inclusion of IRGIP and HYA led to significant collinearity and hence it was decided to estimate the model equation in two alternative forms (a) without log HYA, and (b) without log $IRGIP_i$. The price of nitrogen nutrient in Bangladesh was invariant across districts in 1976–7:

(a) Perform the LM test for heteroscedasticity.
(b) If significant heteroscedasticity is encountered use White's correction and indicate the differences in the variances of the OLS estimates and heteroscedasticity corrected estimates.

5. Define the term 'multicollinearity'. Explain how you would detect its presence in a multiple regression you have estimated.
6. In the model:

$$Y_t = \beta_1 + \beta_2 X_{2t} + \beta_3 X_{3t} + U_t$$

the coefficients are known to be related to a more basic economic parameter γ according to the equation

$$\beta_2 + \beta_3 = \gamma$$

Assuming that xs are nonrandom and that $u_t \sim IN(0, \sigma_u^2)$, find the best linear unbiased estimator of γ and its variance.

7. (a) Given the data below on UK net national product, estimate the following equation by OLS for the period 1920–38:

$$\log Q_t = \beta_1 + \beta_2 t + u_t$$

and then obtain $\log Q_t^*$ the predicted values of $\log Q_t$ from your estimated equation.

(b) Then use these predicted values to estimate the following equation to explain UK unemployment in the interwar period:

$$U_t = \gamma_1 + \gamma_2 \left(\frac{B}{W}\right) t + \gamma_3 (\log Q_t - \log Q_t^*) + \epsilon_t$$

   (i) Estimate the above equation for both the period 1920–38 and 1921–38. Are there significant differences in the two regressions?
   (ii) Would you suggest using a dummy variable for 1920?
   (iii) Use the LM test to test for first- and second-order autocorrelation.

Wages, benefits, unemployment and net national product: United Kingdom, 1920–38

Year	Weekly wage W (s)	Weekly benefits B (s)	Unemployment rate U %	Benefits/wages ratio	NNP (£m at 1938 factor cost)
1920	73.8	11.3	3.9	0.15	3426
1921	70.6	16.83	17.0	0.24	3242
1922	59.1	22.00	14.3	0.37	3384
1923	55.5	22.00	11.7	0.40	3514
1924	56.0	23.67	10.3	0.42	3622
1925	56.4	27.00	11.3	0.48	3840
1926	55.8	27.00	12.5	0.48	3656
1927	56.2	27.00	9.7	0.48	3937
1928	55.7	27.67	10.8	0.50	4003
1929	55.8	28.00	10.4	0.50	4097
1930	55.7	29.50	16.1	0.53	4082
1931	54.9	29.54	21.3	0.54	3832
1932	54.0	27.25	22.1	0.50	3828
1933	53.1	27.25	19.9	0.51	3899
1934	54.3	28.6	16.7	0.53	4196
1935	55.0	30.3	15.5	0.55	4365
1936	56.1	32.00	13.1	0.57	4498
1937	57.2	32.00	10.8	0.56	4665
1938	58.9	32.75	12.9	0.56	4807

s = shilling = £$\frac{1}{20}$.

Source: Benjamin, D.K. and Kochin L.A. (1979). Searching for an explanation of unemployment in interwar Britain, *Journal of Political Economy*, June 1979, pp. 441–78.

References

Breusch, T.S. and Pagan, A.R. (1979), 'A simple test for heteroscedasticity and random coefficient variation', *Econometrica*, **47** September, 1287-94.

Cochrane, D. and Orcutt, G.H. (1949), 'Application of least squares regressions to relationships containing autocorrelated error terms', *Journal of the American Statistical Association*, **44**, 32-61.

Durbin, J. (1970), 'Testing for serial correlation in least squares regression when some of the regressors are lagged dependent variables', *Econometrica*, **38**, 410-21.

Episkopou, S. (1988), 'Market structure and performance of a small open and developing economy: a case study for Cyprus', PhD thesis, Norwich: University of East Anglia.

Godfrey, L.G. (1978a), 'Testing against general autoregressive and moving average error models when the regressors include lagged dependent variables', *Econometrica*, **46**, 1293-302.

Godfrey, L.G. (1978b), 'Testing for multiplicative heteroscedasticity', *Journal of Econometrics*, **8**, October, 227-36.

Hendry, D.F. (1979), 'Predictive failure and econometric modelling in macroeconomics: the transactions demand for money', in P. Ormerod (ed.), *Economic Modelling*, pp. 217-42, London: Heinemann.

McCallum, B.T. (1970), 'Artificial orthogonalization in regression analysis', *Review of Economics and Statistics*, **52**, 110-13.

Mundlak, Y. (1981), 'On the concept of nonsignificant functions and its implications for regression analysis', *Journal of Econometrics*, **16**, 139-49.

Parikh, A. (1990), *The Economics of Fertiliser Use in Developing Countries: a Case Study of Bangladesh*, Chapter 2, Aldershot: Gower.

Ramsey, J.D. (1969), 'Test for specification errors in classical linear least squares regression analysis', *Journal of Royal Statistical Society*, Series B, **31**, 350-71.

Thursby, J.G. and Schmidt P. (1977), 'Some properties of tests for specification error in a linear regression model', *Journal of the American Statistical Association*, **72**, September, 635-41.

Chapter 4
MAXIMUM LIKELIHOOD METHODS

In this chapter we explain the basic procedures of maximum likelihood (ML) estimation. We first consider the linear regression model and obtain the ML estimators for both the simple and multiple linear regression models. These ML estimators, other than that of the variance of the disturbance term, are identical to the OLS estimators. We outline a number of asymptotic tests – the likelihood ratio test and other associated tests such as the Wald test and the Lagrange multiplier test – which can be employed for discriminating between alternative model specifications. We look at the application of maximum likelihood estimation in distributed lag models, since it is one of the procedures which yields consistent and asymptotically efficient estimates in models with lagged dependent variables. Other areas where the ML approach can be usefully applied are the estimation of models with qualitative or limited dependent variables.

In Section 4.1 the basic approach to maximum likelihood estimation is presented, along with a discussion of various test statistics. An empirical example of various specifications of a time-series consumption function is given and the results of applying the likelihood ratio, Wald and Lagrange multiplier tests are analysed. The same tests are also utilised in a discussion of causality between money and prices in Italy. In Section 4.2 the maximum likelihood estimation procedure is applied to distributed lag models and an illustration is provided using the estimation of supply functions for coffee. Section 4.3 is concerned with the application of the ML estimation procedure to models with qualitative or limited dependent variables. The linear probability, probit and logit models belong to the first set and the tobit model to the second set of models. Examples of both types of models are provided. Finally, in Section 4.4 the problem of measurement error – errors-in-variables – is addressed. Procedures for dealing with it, including instrumental variable estimation, are considered and an illustration is provided by Friedman's theory of consumption.

4.1 THE CONCEPT OF MAXIMUM LIKELIHOOD

Assume we have a random variable X with probability density function $f(x)$ characterised by a set of parameters $\theta_1, \theta_2, \ldots, \theta_k$. The probability distribution for a

The concept of maximum likelihood

continuous variable x (called the probability density function) is represented by a curve and the probability that x assumes a value in the interval from a to b is given by the area under this curve bounded by a and b. If we observe a sample $x_1, x_2, \ldots, x_n$, then we define the maximum likelihood (ML) estimators of the θ_is as those values of the parameters that would give rise to the sample observed most frequently. In employing the method of maximum likelihood, values are assigned to the parameters which maximise the likelihood of observing that particular set of sample observations.

We commence by illustrating the ML procedure in the context of the simple linear regression model:

$$Y_i = \alpha + \beta X_i + u_i \tag{4.1}$$

where $u_i \sim IN(0, \sigma^2)$ and all the other classical assumptions are assumed to hold. It can be demonstrated that $E(Y_i) = \alpha + \beta X_i$ and Var $(Y_i) = \sigma^2$, these results being similar to those we showed for a multiple linear regression model. Furthermore, a well-known theorem of mathematical statistics states that if for some variable X with probability density $f(x)$, another variable Z is a monotonic function of X, then the probability density $f(z)$ is given by:

$$f(z) = \left| \frac{dx}{dz} \right| f(x) \tag{4.2}$$

where $|dx/dz|$ is the absolute value of the derivative of x with respect to z. For the case of our regression model, the distribution of u_i is known; increases in u_i are clearly associated with increases in Y_i with $du_i/dy_i = 1$. Hence $f(y_i) = f(u_i)$ and Y_i is independently normally distributed with mean $(\alpha + \beta X_i)$ and variance σ^2.

The likelihood function is given by

$$l = \Pi_{i=1}^{n} f(y_i) \tag{4.3}$$

It is more convenient to take logarithms of equation (4.3) and write the log likelihood function L which we seek to maximise by appropriate choice of the estimators of α, β and σ^2:

$$L = \sum_{i=1}^{n} \log f(y_i) \tag{4.4}$$

where

$$f(y_i) = (2\Pi\sigma^2)^{-\frac{1}{2}} \exp\left[-\frac{1}{2} \left(\frac{Y_i - \alpha - \beta X_i}{\sigma} \right) \right]^2 \tag{4.5}$$

is the normal density function. Hence,

$$L = -\frac{n}{2} \log(2\pi) - \frac{n}{2} \log \sigma^2 - \frac{1}{2\sigma^2} \sum_{i=1}^{n} (Y_i - \alpha - \beta X_i)^2 \tag{4.6}$$

Differentiating with respect to α, β and σ^2 and setting these derivatives equal to zero, having let the maximum likelihood estimators be represented by $\hat{\alpha}$, $\hat{\beta}$ and $\hat{\sigma}^2$, respectively, we obtain

$$\frac{1}{2\hat{\sigma}^2} \sum_{i=1}^{n} (Y_i - \hat{\alpha} - \hat{\beta} X_i) = 0 \tag{4.7}$$

$$\frac{1}{2\hat{\sigma}^2} \sum_{i=1}^{n} X_i (Y_i - \hat{\alpha} - \hat{\beta} X_i) = 0 \tag{4.8}$$

$$-\frac{n}{2\hat{\sigma}^2} + \frac{1}{2\hat{\sigma}^4} \sum_{i=1}^{n} (Y_i - \hat{\alpha} - \hat{\beta} X_i)^2 = 0 \tag{4.9}$$

From the first two equations, we obtain

$$\Sigma Y_i = \hat{\alpha} n + \hat{\beta} \Sigma X_i \tag{4.10}$$

$$\Sigma X_i Y_i = \hat{\alpha} \Sigma X_i + \hat{\beta} \Sigma X_i^2 \tag{4.11}$$

which are called the normal equations and the maximum likelihood estimators of the regression coefficients are the same as the OLS estimators. The ML estimator of σ^2, however, differs from the OLS estimator: for the ML case, we have

$$\hat{\sigma}^2 = \frac{\sum_{i=1}^{n} (Y_i - \hat{\alpha} - \hat{\beta} X_i)^2}{n} = \frac{\sum_{i=1}^{n} e_i^2}{n} \tag{4.12}$$

Note the divisor is n and not $(n-2)$, so the ML estimator of the variance is just equal to the sample variance of the least squares residuals and no adjustment for degrees of freedom is made, as is the case with the unbiased estimator s^2.

In the k variable classical linear regression model, the above results stand. The ML estimators of the regression parameters are identical to the OLS estimators and the ML estimator of σ^2 is equal to $e'e/n$. For the general case, the log likelihood is given by

$$L = -\frac{n}{2} \log 2\pi - \frac{n}{2} \log \sigma^2 - \frac{1}{2\sigma^2} (y - X\beta)'(y - X\beta) \tag{4.13}$$

Differentiating partially with respect to β and σ^2 and setting these derivatives equal to zero, having let the ML estimators be represented by $\hat{\beta}$ and $\hat{\sigma}^2$, we obtain

$$-\frac{1}{2\hat{\sigma}^2} (-2X'y + 2X'X\hat{\beta}) = 0 \tag{4.14}$$

$$-\frac{1}{2\hat{\sigma}^2} + \frac{1}{2\hat{\sigma}^4} (y - X\hat{\beta})'(y - X\hat{\beta}) = 0 \tag{4.15}$$

solving these equations yields

$$\hat{\beta} = (X'X)^{-1} X'y \tag{4.16}$$

and

$$\hat{\sigma}^2 = \frac{e'e}{n} \qquad (4.17)$$

The second-order conditions for a maximum of L are satisfied. One of the most important properties of the ML estimators is that a minimum variance bound estimator, if it exists, is given by the ML method. The minimum variance bound establishes a lower limit below which the variance of an unbiased estimator cannot be reduced. Under very general conditions, maximum likelihood estimators are consistent. Let θ represent the parameters of the model and $I(\theta)$ the information matrix, i.e. minus the expectation of the matrix of the second-order partial derivatives of L with respect to $\theta = (\beta_1 \ldots \beta_k, \sigma^2)$:

$$I(\theta) = -E \begin{bmatrix} \frac{\partial^2 L}{\partial \beta_1^2} & \frac{\partial^2 L}{\partial \beta_1 \partial \beta_2} & \cdots & \frac{\partial^2 L}{\partial \beta_1 \partial \beta_k} & \frac{\partial^2 L}{\partial \beta_1 \partial \sigma^2} \\ \frac{\partial^2 L}{\partial \beta_1 \partial \beta_1} & \frac{\partial^2 L}{\partial \beta_2^2} & & \frac{\partial^2 L}{\partial \beta_1 \partial \beta_k} & \frac{\partial^2 L}{\partial \beta_1 \partial \sigma^2} \\ \vdots & & & & \\ \frac{\partial^2 L}{\partial \sigma^2 \partial \beta_1} & \frac{\partial^2 L}{\partial \sigma^2 \partial \beta_2} & & \frac{\partial^2 L}{\partial \sigma^2 \partial \beta_k} & \frac{\partial^2 L}{\sigma \sigma^4} \end{bmatrix} \qquad (4.18)$$

The inverse of the information matrix yields the variance–covariance matrix of the estimators and the ith diagonal element yields the minimum variance bound for each of the parameters. The lower limit specified is called the Cramer–Rao lower bound. It should be noted that the use of the Cramer–Rao inequality does not always work to our satisfaction because the lower bound need not be attainable by any unbiased estimator.

If we can find an unbiased estimator whose variance is equal to the Cramer–Rao lower bound, then we know that no other estimator can have a smaller variance and the estimator under consideration is efficient.

In the ML framework, three tests regarding the validity or otherwise of imposing restrictions on the parameters of the regression model have been discussed in the recent literature and much used in applied econometric work. The tests are: the likelihood ratio test (LR); the Wald test (W); and the Lagrange multiplier test (LM). The three tests are asymptotically equivalent and may be employed for testing either linear or nonlinear restrictions. Since they are only valid asymptotically, in small samples where the restrictions are linear, the conventional F test should be used since it is more reliable.

The LR test is based on the idea that if the restrictions are true, the value of the log likelihood function maximised with the restrictions imposed cannot differ too much from the value of the log likelihood function maximised in the absence of the restrictions. The restricted model is the null hypothesis H_0 and the obtained test statistic is asymptotic.

Let $L(\tilde{\beta}, \tilde{\sigma}^2)$ be the maximum of the log likelihood with the restrictions imposed and $L(\hat{\beta}, \hat{\sigma}^2)$ the maximum of the log likelihood in the absence of the restrictions; under H_0, asymptotically:

$$LR = -2[L(\tilde{\beta}, \tilde{\sigma}^2) - L(\hat{\beta}, \hat{\sigma}^2)] \sim \chi^2(m) \tag{4.19}$$

where m is the number of restrictions. If $LR > \chi^2(m)$ at the specified level of significance, we reject the restricted model in favour of the unrestricted model.

Since

$$L(\tilde{\beta}, \tilde{\sigma}^2) = -\frac{n}{2}\log(2\pi) - \frac{n}{2}\log\tilde{\sigma}^2 - \frac{1}{2\tilde{\sigma}^2}\sum_{i=1}^{n}\tilde{e}_i^2 \tag{4.20}$$

and

$$\tilde{\sigma}^2 = \frac{\sum_{i=1}^{n}\tilde{e}_i^2}{n} \tag{4.21}$$

where $\tilde{e}_i$ measures the residuals from the restricted equation and analogous expressions hold for $L(\hat{\beta}, \hat{\sigma}^2)$ and $\hat{\sigma}^2$, we may alternatively write:

$$LR = n[\log\tilde{\sigma}^2 - \log\hat{\sigma}^2] \sim \chi^2(m) \tag{4.22}$$

While both the restricted and unrestricted models have to be estimated for the investigator to be able to apply the LR test, the Wald test can be utilised when only the unrestricted model has been estimated. This test seeks to throw light on the extent to which the unrestricted estimates diverge from the values they would have taken in the restricted form of the model. Assume the restrictions take the form

$$g(\beta_1, \beta_2, \ldots, \beta_k) = 0 \tag{4.23}$$

then, though the equation obviously holds when we substitute in the restricted estimates $\tilde{\beta}$, it will not generally hold for the unrestricted estimates $\hat{\beta}$. The Wald test statistic is given by

$$W = \hat{g}'[\text{est. Var-Cov}(\hat{g})]^{-1}\hat{g} \sim \chi^2(m) \tag{4.24}$$

where the unrestricted estimates have been substituted into the restrictions to yield $\hat{g}$ and Var-Cov $(\hat{g})$ is given by:

$$\left(\frac{\partial\hat{g}}{\partial\hat{\beta}}\right)'[\text{est. Var-Cov}(\hat{\beta})]\left(\frac{\partial\hat{g}}{\partial\hat{\beta}}\right) \tag{4.25}$$

where $(\partial\hat{g}/\partial\hat{\beta})$ is the matrix of partial derivatives of the restrictions with respect to the unrestricted estimates, with the i,jth element being the partial derivative of the ith constraint with respect to the jth unrestricted estimate.

The discussion will become clearer with the following example. A model has been specified as follows:

$$y_i = \beta_1 x_{1i} + \beta_2 x_{2i} + \beta_3 x_{3i} + u_i \tag{4.26}$$

with one restriction, namely $\beta_1\beta_2 = 1$. Assume the model is estimated in the unrestricted form and the unrestricted estimates $\hat{\beta}_1$, $\hat{\beta}_2$ and $\hat{\beta}_3$ are obtained. For this particular example, the restriction is written as

$$g = \beta_1\beta_2 - 1 \qquad (4.27)$$

and

$$\left(\frac{\partial \hat{g}}{\partial \hat{\beta}}\right)' = [\hat{\beta}_2\ \hat{\beta}_1\ 0] \qquad (4.28)$$

Hence,

$$\text{est. Var}(\hat{g}) = [\hat{\beta}_2\ \hat{\beta}_1\ 0]\ \text{est.} \begin{bmatrix} \text{Var}(\hat{\beta}_1) & \text{Cov}(\hat{\beta}_1\hat{\beta}_2) & \text{Cov}(\hat{\beta}_1\hat{\beta}_3) \\ \text{Cov}(\hat{\beta}_1\hat{\beta}_2) & \text{Var}(\hat{\beta}_2) & \text{Cov}(\hat{\beta}_2\hat{\beta}_3) \\ \text{Cov}(\hat{\beta}_1\hat{\beta}_3) & \text{Cov}(\hat{\beta}_2\hat{\beta}_3) & \text{Var}(\hat{\beta}_3) \end{bmatrix} \begin{bmatrix} \hat{\beta}_2 \\ \hat{\beta}_1 \\ 0 \end{bmatrix}$$

$$= \hat{\beta}_2^2\ \text{Var}\ \hat{\beta}_1 + 2\hat{\beta}_1\hat{\beta}_2\ \text{Cov}\ \hat{\beta}_1\hat{\beta}_2 + \hat{\beta}_1^2\ \text{Var}\ \hat{\beta}_2 \qquad (4.29)$$

and

$$W = \frac{(\hat{\beta}_1\hat{\beta}_2 - 1)^2}{\hat{\beta}_2^2\ \text{est. Var}\ \hat{\beta}_1 + 2\hat{\beta}_1\hat{\beta}_2\ \text{est. Cov}\ \hat{\beta}_1\hat{\beta}_2 + \hat{\beta}_1^2\ \text{est. Var}\ \hat{\beta}_2} \sim \chi^2(1) \qquad (4.30)$$

As the restriction $\beta_1\beta_2 = 1$ is tested, it so happens that the full structure of information matrix is not reflected in the expression of variances.

The third test, the Lagrange multiplier test, can be utilised when only the restricted model has been estimated. Define $S(\beta)$ as the vector of derivatives of the log likelihood function with respect to the parameters of the model, β; $S(\beta) = \partial L/\partial \beta$ and is known as the score. When evaluated at $\beta = \hat{\beta}$ (the unrestricted estimates) the score will be zero. This will not normally be the case, however, when the score is evaluated at $\beta = \tilde{\beta}$. The LM test is then concerned with the extent to which $S(\tilde{\beta})$ differs from zero. The test statistic is given by

$$LM = S(\tilde{\beta})'\ I(\tilde{\beta})^{-1} S(\tilde{\beta}) \sim \chi^2(m) \qquad (4.31)$$

where $I(\tilde{\beta})^{-1}$ is the inverse of the information matrix and m is the number of restrictions.

In Figure 4.1 we depict the log likelihood as a function of a single parameter, β, and show for this simple case how the three tests relate to each other. The unrestricted estimate is given by $\hat{\beta}$ and the restricted one by $\tilde{\beta}$. The LR test is based on the vertical distance $L(\hat{\beta}) - L(\tilde{\beta})$, the W test on the horizontal distance $\hat{\beta} - \tilde{\beta}$ and the LM test on the slope of the log likelihood function, evaluated at $\beta = \tilde{\beta}$. Note that the three tests are asymptotically equivalent; in small samples with linear restrictions the following relationship holds between the three test statistics:

$$LM \leqslant LR \leqslant W \qquad (4.32)$$

with the clear implication that the investigator is likely to reject the null hypothesis by employing the Wald test statistic and least likely to reject it by utilising the LM test.

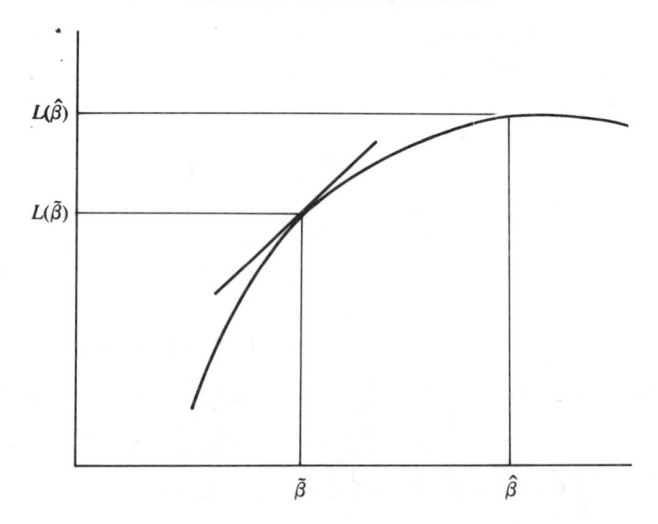

Figure 4.1 Likelihood ratio, LM and Wald test.

The equality holds only if the null hypothesis is exactly true in the sample; in practice there will always exist a significance level for which the asymptotic Wald, LR and LM tests will yield conflicting inference (Berndt and Savin, 1977).

In comparing the three classical test procedures, two issues are at stake. The first is computational convenience and the second is power. The issue of the power of the test cannot be resolved unambiguously since, in general, all three tests are asymptotic. When the sample size is large, all these tests have the distribution under the null hypothesis. However, this result does not support the notion that the three tests will have similar power in small samples.

When the restrictions are linear, it is preferable to use the F test because it is also valid in small samples.

We turn to consider an empirical study of the law of one price in which the likelihood ratio test was used to discriminate between alternative models. The absolute version of the law of one price implies that the domestic price of a tradeable good is equal to the corresponding world market price in domestic currency. The relative form of the law of one price states that changes in the prices of tradeable goods in a country will be equal to changes in other countries' prices of such goods expressed in a common currency.

The relationship between the prices of tradeable goods in different countries can be examined using models such as

$$\log P_{it} = a_0 + a_1 \log P_{jt} + U_{it} \quad (i = 1, \ldots, n \quad j = 1, \ldots, n \quad i \neq j) \tag{4.33}$$

and

$$\Delta \log P_{it} = b_0 + b_1 \Delta \log P_{jt} + \Delta U_{it} \tag{4.34}$$

where P_{it} measures the price in country i at time t. However, in this study more general forms of the above equations have been used, namely

$$\log P_{it} = \alpha + \beta \log P_{it-1} + \tau \log P_{jt} + \delta \log P_{jt-1} + W_{it} \qquad (4.35)$$

and

$$\Delta \log P_{it} = k + \lambda \Delta \log P_{jt} + \mu \log \left(\frac{P_{it-1}}{P_{jt-1}}\right) + V_{it} \qquad (4.36)$$

where $k = \alpha$, $\lambda = \tau$ and $\mu = -(\tau + \delta)$ if $\beta + \tau + \delta = 1$. It can be shown that if $\beta + \tau + \delta = 1$, then the long-run solution of equation (4.35) is

$$\log P_{it} = \frac{\alpha}{1-\beta} + \log P_{jt} + \text{stochastic disturbance} \qquad (4.36a)$$

In addition, if $\alpha = 0$, then the law of one price will hold in the long-run. If $\alpha \neq 0$ and $\beta + \tau + \delta = 1$, the long-run changes in the two countries price series are proportional. In the short-run, if $\alpha = 0$, $\beta = 0$, $\tau = 1$ and $\delta = 0$, the relative (log) version of the law of one price is valid, while if $\alpha \neq 0$, but $\beta = 0$, $\tau = 1$, $\delta = 0$ cannot be rejected, there is proportionality between the two sets of prices.

Equation (4.36) encompasses both long-run and short-run versions of the law of one price in relative form. The equation contains the error correction mechanism of Davidson, Hendry, Yeo and Srba (1978), with the change in the export price index of the ith country being a linear function of the change in the price index of the jth country, unless in the preceding period the ratio of the two prices deviated from its long-run value, in which case an additional adjustment is made in the ith country's price.

If $\mu = 0$ then equation (4.36) is equivalent to equation (4.34). Equation (4.36) is stable if $-2 < \mu < 0$. While $\mu > 0$ implies that, if in the preceding year the export price of the country under consideration was larger than that of the compared country, this divergence will be even greater in the current year.

Equation (4.36) incorporates the constraint $\beta + \tau + \delta = 1$, and can thus be treated as a restricted form of equation (4.35). Hence, it is possible to test between the restricted and unrestricted models using the likelihood ratio test.

Brenton and Parikh (1987) carried out a large number of tests of the law of one price on data, at different levels of aggregation, relating to a number of advanced industrialised countries. As an example of their approach, we consider the evidence obtained from the regression of the Italian producer price of pig iron on the German producer price of pig iron. The results for the general dynamic model (4.35) and the error correction model (4.36) are, respectively:

$$\log P_{it} = -0.1884 + 0.6357 \log P_{it-1} + 1.1065 \log P_{jt} - 0.7054 \log P_{jt-1} \qquad (4.37)$$
$$(0.196) \quad (1.460) \qquad (3.447) \qquad (1.375)$$
$$R^2 = 0.8080 \quad DW = 1.311 \quad SEE = 0.077\,43$$

log likelihood = 15.0199

$$\Delta \log P_{it} = -0.0305 + 1.0604 \Delta \log P_{jt} - 0.4156 \,[\log P_{it-1} - \log P_{jt-1}] \qquad (4.38)$$
$$(1.112) \quad (7.257) \qquad (1.458)$$
$$R^2 = 0.8785 \quad DW = 1.263 \quad SEE = 0.075\,27$$

log likelihood = 14.998 6.

Having estimated the general model we test, using the t- test, the null hypothesis that $\beta + \delta + \tau = 1$; it cannot be rejected with the calculated t ratio equalling 0.164. In comparing the restricted and the unrestricted models, the LR test statistic has a value of 0·0426, confirming in this case that the restricted model is as good as the unrestricted one. The error correction model cannot be rejected against a general dynamic model. Other features to note are that the constant term (α) in the first model is not significantly different from zero; evidence is thus provided for the law of one price holding in the long run. For a comprehensive discussion of a large amount of empirical material, the interested reader is referred to the original study.

Application of Wald, likelihood ratio and LM tests

Consider the following model which postulates that consumption expenditure (C) is a linear function of income (Y) and the disturbance term follows a first-order autoregressive process:

$$C_t = \alpha + \beta Y_t + \epsilon_t \tag{4.39}$$
$$\epsilon_t = \rho \epsilon_{t-1} + u_t \tag{4.40}$$

where u_t satisfies the usual assumptions made about the disturbance term in the classical linear regression model. Lagging equation (4.39) by one period, multiplying by ρ and rearranging we obtain

$$\rho \epsilon_{t-1} = \rho C_{t-1} - \alpha \rho - \beta \rho Y_{t-1} \tag{4.41}$$

Using this result, we may specify the consumption function as follows:

$$C_t = \alpha(1-\rho) + \rho C_{t-1} + \beta Y_t - \beta \rho Y_{t-1} + u_t \tag{4.42}$$

Alternatively, we may specify a general model of the form

$$C_t = \tau_0 + \tau_1 C_{t-1} + \tau_2 Y_t + \tau_3 Y_{t-1} + u_t \tag{4.43}$$

We may then estimate equation (4.42) and (4.43). To estimate the first equation is to impose the nonlinear restriction that $\tau_1 \tau_2 + \tau_3 = 0$ on the second equation. The restricted and unrestricted models were estimated using the data given in Table 4.1 and the results are presented in Table 4.2.

The likelihood ratio test statistic is given by

$$-2(L_0 - L_1) \tag{4.44}$$

where L_0 is the log likelihood for the restricted model and L_1 for the unrestricted model; in this case we have $LR = 1.298$ and since $\chi^2(1)_{0.05} = 3.841$ we cannot reject the model with first-order serial correlation. The Wald test statistic can also be calculated from the unrestricted equation.

Given the particular restriction being tested for, the Wald test statistic is given by equation (4.24):

$$\frac{(\hat{\tau}_1 \hat{\tau}_2 + \hat{\tau}_3)^2}{\text{est. Var}(\hat{\tau}_1 \hat{\tau}_2 + \hat{\tau}_3)}$$

Table 4.1 Data on consumption expenditure and disposable income: USA

Year	Consumption expenditure	Disposable income
1951	206.3	226.6
1952	216.7	238.3
1953	230.0	252.6
1954	236.5	257.4
1955	254.4	275.3
1956	266.7	293.2
1957	281.4	308.5
1958	290.1	318.8
1959	311.2	337.3
1960	325.2	350.0
1961	335.2	364.4
1962	355.1	385.5
1963	375.0	404.6
1964	401.2	438.1
1965	432.8	473.2
1966	466.3	511.9
1967	492.1	546.3
1968	536.2	591.0
1969	596.6	634.2

Note: data are in billions of current US dollars.

Source: Economic Report of the President, p. 212. (Washington, DC: US Government Printing Office, Jan. 1972).

Table 4.2 Parameter estimates for the restricted and unrestricted models

	Constant	C_{t-1}	Y_t	Y_{t-1}	R^2	log L
Restricted	2.123 54	0.4760	0.9049	−0.4308		−41.5039
	(0.925)	(2.113)	(96.179)	(n.c.)		
Unrestricted	0.1460	0.4538	0.7735	−0.2654	0.999	−40.855
	(0.049)	(2.008)	(6.006)	(1.021)		

Note: t ratios are presented below the estimated regression coefficients.

Note that the relevant estimated variance is the asymptotic variance. The test statistic takes on a value of 1.127, thereby suggesting that the restriction is not significantly violated when we estimate the unrestricted model. Finally, we report the value of the *LM* test statistic, which is derived from the restricted model. This takes on a value of 0.757, again providing support for the restricted model.

Tests of causality

Granger (1969) is the leading exponent of the concept of strict causality. The main principle of his definition of causality is that x causes y if taking account of past values of x leads to improved predictions of y. The variable x is said to cause y if the predictions of y based on all past information have a smaller mean square error than the predictions of y based on all past information excluding x. In order to test the hypothesis that x causes y, the investigator proceeds by regressing y_t on y_{t-1}, $y_{t-2}, \ldots y_{t-m}, x_{t-1}, x_{t-2}, \ldots, x_{t-n}$ and then performs a test for the joint significance of the lagged values of x. For the test to be valid, it is essential that the disturbance term in the regression is close to being 'white noise', i.e. there must be no serial correlation. To ensure this necessitates choosing suitable values for the lags m and n. Granger notes that the value of m is particularly important since the omission of relevant lagged values of the dependent variable could inflate the coefficients of the lagged xs.

Hsiao (1979) suggests detrending and deseasonalising both x and y values. Then, say, for y he determines the one-dimensional autoregressive process by using the Akaike final prediction error criterion (FPE).

Choose S to minimise

$$\left(\frac{T+S+1}{T-S-1}\right) \sum_{t=1}^{T} \frac{(y_t - \hat{y}_t)^2}{T} \tag{4.45}$$

where S is the order of the autoregressive process, T is the sample size, and $\hat{y}$ is the predicted value. Assume that the x variable controls the outcome of y and then use the FPE criterion to determine the lag order of x, say n, assuming that the order of the lag of y specified is S. In the third step, use the specified lag order of x as n and vary the order of the lag of y from 0 to S. We choose that value of $S = m$ which minimizes FPE:

$$\left[\frac{T+m+n+1}{T-m-n-1} \sum_{t=1}^{T} \frac{(y_t - \hat{y}_t)^2}{T}\right] \tag{4.46}$$

that is conditional on the lag order of x being n. The lag of y, m may or may not be equal to S. After this step, if the former $[FPE_y(S, 0)]$ is less than the latter $[FPE_y(m, n)]$ a one-dimensional autoregressive representation is to be used. If the converse is true, x causes y, and the optimal model for predicting y is the one which includes m lagged values of y and n lagged values of x. The same procedure is to be repeated, changing the roles of x and y.

Sims (1972) has suggested regressing y on both lagged and leading values of x:

$$y_t = \sum_{j=-m}^{n} \tau_j x_{t-j} + v_t \tag{4.47}$$

where v_t must be serially uncorrelated.

As before, one can test for x Granger causing y by testing for the joint significance of including the lagged values of x, while a test that y does not cause x is a test of the joint hypothesis $H_0: \tau_{-1} = \tau_{-2} = \ldots = \tau_{-m} = 0$. The disturbance must be serially uncorrelated for the F test of the null hypothesis to be valid. In order to ensure that the residuals from the fitted regression are white noise, appropriate filters have to be applied to the two time series. Sims himself used somewhat arbitrary filters, the same filter being applied to both variables, which gave rise to transformed variables of the following form:

$$y'_t = y_t - 1.50 y_{t-1} + 0.5625 y_{t-2}$$

upon which the actual regression was performed. There is no guarantee that such arbitrary filters will in fact eliminate the problem of serial correlation in the residuals.

An alternative approach which obviates the need to filter the data has been developed by Geweke (1982) in which a regression of y_t on $y_{t-1}, \ldots, y_{t-m}$ together with n lagged values of x and p leading values of x is performed. The choice of m and n must be such as to ensure random residuals. Contemporaneous causality can be allowed for by including the current period value of x as a regressor. The hypothesis that y does not cause x can then be evaluated by testing for the joint significance of the leading values of x.

Bailey (1984) has utilised the approaches of Granger and Geweke in an analysis of the relationship between the money supply and prices in Italy in the period since 1960. Data were collected on a quarterly basis for the period 1960(1)–1982(2) on the money supply (M) and the GDP deflator (P); the data are seasonally adjusted. To test for Granger causality, the following two sets of equations were estimated:

$$\log M_t = \text{constant} + \text{trend} + \sum_{j=1}^{m} \alpha_j \log M_{t-j} + u_{1t} \qquad (4.48)$$

$$\log M_t = \text{constant} + \text{trend} + \sum_{j=1}^{m} \alpha'_j \log M_{t-j} + \sum_{j=1}^{n} \beta'_j \log P_{t-j} + u_{2t} \qquad (4.49)$$

and

$$\log P_t = \text{constant} + \text{trend} + \sum_{j=1}^{m} \tau_j \log P_{t-j} + v_{1t} \qquad (4.50)$$

$$\log P_t = \text{constant} + \text{trend} + \sum_{j=1}^{m} \tau'_j \log P_{t-j} + \sum_{j=1}^{nn} \delta'_j \log M_{t-j} + v_{2t} \qquad (4.51)$$

When both the restricted and unrestricted models have been estimated for each set, the following formulations for the Wald, likelihood ratio and Lagrange multiplier test statistics (see Geweke et al., 1983) can be employed to test for Granger causality from prices to money and from money to prices:

$$W = \frac{T[\hat{\sigma}_r^2 - \hat{\sigma}_u^2]}{\hat{\sigma}_u^2} \qquad (4.52)$$

$$LR = T \log \left[\frac{\hat{\sigma}_r^2}{\hat{\sigma}_u^2} \right] \qquad (4.53)$$

$$LM = \frac{T[\hat{\sigma}_r^2 - \hat{\sigma}_u^2]}{\hat{\sigma}_r^2} \qquad (4.54)$$

where $\hat{\sigma}_r^2$ and $\hat{\sigma}_u^2$ are, respectively, the ML estimators of the variance of the disturbance term in the restricted and unrestricted models. As stated earlier, the above test statistics follow asymptotically the χ^2 distribution with degrees of freedom equal to the number of restrictions being tested.

Equations (4.48) through (4.51) were estimated with $m = 4$ and $n = 4$, 8 or 12 and some important features of the results are presented in Tables 4.3 and 4.4. The estimated equations fit extremely well with R^2 approaching unity. Of greater significance, there is no evidence of the presence of serial correlation in the residuals. The test statistics which have been employed to test for serial correlation are the Box–Pierce Q statistic and the LM test statistic; Q is measured by $T \sum_{k=1}^{P} \hat{r}_k^2$ where T is the size of the sample and $\hat{r}_k$ is the estimate of autocorrelation at lag k; $Q \sim \chi^2(p)$. The LM test, referred to in Chapter 3, is based on $TR^2 \sim \chi^2(p)$, where T is the number of observations and R^2 the coefficient of determination in

Table 4.3 Money and prices in Italy: tests for Granger causality (money on prices)

Lags of explanatory variable	Number of observations	Restricted residual sum of squares from eqn (4.48)	Unrestricted residual sum of squares from eqn (4.49)	F	W	LR	LM
4	86	0.002 033 40	0.001 943 04	0.884	3.997	3.907	3.819
8	82	0.001 792 20	0.001 648 21	0.786	7.164	6.868	6.588
12	78	0.001 666 97	0.001 230 95	1.771	27.629	23.651	20.402

Notes: each regression contains a constant, a time trend and four lags of the explanatory variable. The critical values of the test statistics at the 5 per cent significance level are: $F(4.76) = 2.49$, $F(8.68) = 2.08$ and $F(12.60) = 1.92$; $\chi^2(4) = 9.488$, $\chi^2(8) = 15.507$ and $\chi^2(12) = 26.217$:

$$F = \frac{(RRSS - URSS)/k_1}{URSS/(n - k)}$$

where k_1 measures the number of additional parameters estimated and $(n - k)$ the degrees of freedom in the unrestricted version.

Table 4.4 Money and prices in Italy: tests for Granger causality (prices on money)

Lags of explanatory variable	Number of observations	Restricted residual sum of squares from eqn (4.50)	Unrestricted residual sum of squares from eqn (4.51)	F	W	LR	LM
4	86	0.009 530 25	0.008 277 86	2.875	13.011	12.116	11.301
8	82	0.009 423 82	0.006 281 08	4.253	41.029	33.267	27.346
12	78	0.009 059 97	0.005 543 18	3.172	49.486	38.321	30.277

Notes: each regression contains a constant, a time trend and four lags of the explanatory variable. The critical values of the test statistics at the 5 per cent significance level are: $F(4.76) = 2.49$, $F(8.68) = 2.08$ and $F(12.60) = 1.92$; $\chi^2(4) = 9.488$, $\chi^2(8) = 15.507$ and $\chi^2(12) = 26.217$:

$$F = \frac{(RRSS - URSS)/k_1}{URSS/(n - k)}$$

where k_1 measures the number of additional parameters estimated and $(n - k)$ the degrees of freedom in the unrestricted version.

the regression of the current residual on p lagged values of the residual and all the explanatory variables of the original regression.

As far as the results of the regression of money on prices are concerned, only the Wald test statistic for the case of twelve lags of the price deflator provides any evidence for causality running from prices to money. In all other cases, the tests suggest that lagged values of the price deflator do not contribute to predicting the Italian money supply. Turning to the regression of prices on money, the tests reject conclusively the null hypothesis of there being no causal relationship running from money to prices; whatever the number of lags of the explanatory variable included and regardless of the particular test statistic employed, this result stands.

We now turn to consider the Geweke version of the Sims approach in which we include both the current and leading values of the explanatory variable. In a highly influential paper, Geweke (1982) has shown that dependence and feedback between two time series X and Y can be decomposed into the sum of linear feedback (causality) from X and Y, linear feedback from Y to X and instantaneous linear feedback (or contemporaneous causality). The decomposition which Geweke uses requires the estimation of the following four equations on our Italian data:

$$\log P_t = \text{constant} + \text{trend} + \sum_{j=1}^{m} \tau_j \log P_{t-j} + u_{1t} \tag{4.55}$$

$$\log P_t = \text{constant} + \text{trend} + \sum_{j=1}^{m} \tau'_j \log P_{t-j} + \sum_{j=1}^{n} \delta'_j \log M_{t-j} + u_{2t} \tag{4.56}$$

$$\log P_t = \text{constant} + \text{trend} + \sum_{j=1}^{m} \tau''_j \log P_{t-j} + \sum_{j=0}^{n} \delta''_j \log M_{t-j} + u_{3t} \tag{4.57}$$

$$\log P_t = \text{constant} + \text{trend} + \sum_{j=1}^{m} \tau'''_j \log P_{t-j} + \sum_{j=-p}^{n} \delta'''_j \log M_{t-j} + u_{4t} \tag{4.58}$$

Note that equation (4.55) contains lagged values of the dependent variable, equation (4.56) contains in addition lagged values of the explanatory variable, while equations (4.57) and (4.58) contain in addition the current and leading values of the explanatory variable respectively. We could likewise write a similar set of four equations, in which the dependent variable is $\log M_t$, though these equations are not shown here.

The measure of linear dependence ($F_{P \cdot M}$) is the sum of linear feedback from money to prices ($F_{M \to P}$), instantaneous linear feedback (F_{PXM}) and linear feedback from prices to money ($F_{P \to M}$):

$$F_{P \cdot M} = F_{M \to P} + F_{PXM} + F_{P \to M} \tag{4.59}$$

and the estimates of the relevant contributions of each of the components are given by

$$F_{P \cdot M} = \log \left(\frac{\hat{\sigma}_1^2}{\hat{\sigma}_4^2} \right) \tag{4.60}$$

$$F_{M \to P} = \log\left(\frac{\hat{\sigma}_1^2}{\hat{\sigma}_2^2}\right) \qquad (4.61)$$

$$F_{PXM} = \log\left(\frac{\hat{\sigma}_2^2}{\hat{\sigma}_3^2}\right) \qquad (4.62)$$

$$F_{P \to M} = \log\left(\frac{\hat{\sigma}_3^2}{\hat{\sigma}_4^2}\right) \qquad (4.63)$$

where $\hat{\sigma}_i^2$ is to be measured by the ML estimator of the variance of the disturbance term u_{it}.

We present estimates of Geweke's decomposition, based on estimating equations (4.55) through (4.58) on seventy-four observations of the Italian data with $m = 4$, $n = 8$, $p = 8$. The equivalent set of equations were also estimated with the money supply as the dependent variable and with the same lag structure. The results obtained were not sensitive to the choice of lag structure and serial correlation was not present in the residuals. The following decompositions were obtained:

$$F_{P \cdot M} = F_{M \to P} + F_{PXM} + F_{P \to M}$$

$$\begin{array}{cccc} \log 1.9214 = \log 1.6666 + \log 1.0139 + \log 1.1371 \\ (48.326^{**}) \quad (37.997^{**}) \quad (1.020) \quad (9.510) \end{array} \qquad (4.64)$$

and

$$F_{M \cdot P} = F_{P \to M} + F_{MXP} + F_{M \to P}$$

$$\begin{array}{cccc} \log 1.6061 = \log 1.0753 + \log 1.0117 + \log 1.4763 \\ (35.062^{**}) \quad (5.372) \quad (0.862) \quad (28.827^{**}) \end{array} \qquad (4.65)$$

For each element of the decomposition, it is a straightforward matter to apply the LR test for the significance of the particular type of feedback or causality. The corresponding value of the LR test statistic is provided in brackets beneath the Geweke decomposition measure, with ** signifying that the null hypothesis of no feedback can be rejected at the 1 per cent significance level. On the basis of the Geweke variant of the Sims test, we conclude that for Italy during the 1960s and 1970s there is evidence of causality in the sense of Granger running from the money supply to prices, but no evidence for either contemporaneous causality or for feedback from prices to money.

4.2 APPLICATION OF MAXIMUM LIKELIHOOD IN DISTRIBUTED LAG MODELS

A model with a distributed lag is one in which the influence of one or more of the explanatory variables on the dependent variable is distributed over a number of lagged values of the relevant explanatory variable(s). In the simple case where we

Distributed lag models

permit past values of X to affect Y, we may formulate the regression equation as follows:

$$Y_t = \alpha + \beta_0 X_t + \beta_1 X_{t-1} + \ldots + \beta_k X_{t-k} + \epsilon_t \qquad (4.66)$$

where k is the length of the lag. If k is large, then problems arise in that there may be insufficient observations available to enable estimates of all the parameters to be made; furthermore even if it is possible to obtain estimates of all the parameters, multicollinearity is likely to make precise estimation difficult, if not impossible. In practical applications, therefore, some restrictions are usually imposed on the form of the lag structure. Two common forms of restriction which the student will meet in the applied literature are: the geometric lag distribution where the coefficients on the lagged variables decline in geometric progression; and the Almon (polynomial) lag distribution which gives rise to coefficients on the lagged variables first increasing and then decreasing in value. We shall have some observations to make on the Almon lag distribution later in this section.

Where the βs follow the geometric lag distribution, we write equation (4.66) as

$$Y_t = \alpha + \beta_0 (X_t + \lambda X_{t-1} + \lambda^2 X_{t-2} + \ldots) + \epsilon_t \qquad (4.67)$$

where $0 < \lambda < 1$ and the effect of X on $E(Y_t)$ extends backwards indefinitely into the past. Define the average lag (AL) as the weighted average of all the lags; then

$$AL = \frac{\Sigma i \beta_i}{\Sigma \beta_i} \qquad (4.68)$$

which requires $\Sigma \beta_i$ to be finite and for the geometric lag distribution case it is a straightforward matter to show that

$$AL = \frac{\lambda}{1 - \lambda} \qquad (4.69)$$

Consider a model in which consumption at time t (C_t) is postulated to be proportional to permanent income at time t (Y_t^*). Changes in permanent income are assumed to be determined adaptively. We may thus write:

$$C_t = \beta Y_t^* + \epsilon_t \qquad (4.70)$$

and

$$(Y_t^* - Y_{t-1}^*) = (1 - \lambda)(Y_t - Y_{t-1}^*) \qquad (4.71)$$

where ϵ_t measures transitory consumption and $1 - \lambda$ is the adjustment parameter, showing how permanent income is revised in the light of discrepancies between actual income (Y) and previous permanent income. Rearranging equation (4.71) we have

$$Y_t^* = (1 - \lambda) Y_t + \lambda Y_{t-1}^* \qquad (4.72)$$

and substituting for Y_{t-1}^* in equation (4.72) we obtain

$$Y_t^* = (1 - \lambda) Y_t + \lambda (1 - \lambda) Y_{t-1} + \lambda^2 Y_{t-2}^* \qquad (4.73)$$

and finally, after successive substitutions, we end up with

$$Y_t^* = (1-\lambda)Y_t + \lambda(1-\lambda)Y_{t-1} + \lambda^2(1-\lambda)Y_{t-2} + \ldots \tag{4.74}$$

which then enables us to write the consumption function as

$$C_t = \beta(1-\lambda)[Y_t + \lambda Y_{t-1} + \lambda^2 Y_{t-2} + \ldots] + \epsilon_t \tag{4.75}$$

Lagging equation (4.75) by one period, multiplying through by λ and subtracting this new equation from the original one (this is known as the Koyck transformation), we obtain the following specification for the consumption function:

$$C_t = \beta(1-\lambda)Y_t + \lambda C_{t-1} + \eta_t \tag{4.76}$$

where $\eta_t = \epsilon_t - \lambda\epsilon_{t-1}$.

In models in which expectations are formed adaptively, expected variables are represented by a weighted average of the current value and the expected value in the preceding period. Such a formation of expectations is based on the idea that current expectations are derived by modifying previous expectations in the light of current experience.

The model above with adaptive expectations gives rise to an estimating equation which is similar in all but one important and highly significant respect to a model in which we have partial adjustment of the dependent variable towards its desired level. Consider the case where desired money holdings (M^*) are proportional to income (Y) and actual money holdings (M) change through time to eliminate part of the discrepancy between desired and actual holdings. For a variety of reasons, including technological constraints, human inertia, etc., adjustment is not instantaneous. Our partial adjustment model is:

$$M_t^* = \beta Y_t \tag{4.77}$$

and

$$M_t - M_{t-1} = (1-\gamma)(M_t^* - M_{t-1}) \tag{4.78}$$

After substituting for M_t^* and rearranging, we obtain

$$M_t = \beta(1-\gamma)Y_t + \gamma M_{t-1} + \epsilon_t \tag{4.79}$$

Note the only difference between these two specifications presented in equations (4.76) and (4.79) concerns the stochastic disturbance term; in the first case we have $\eta_t = \epsilon_t - \lambda\epsilon_{t-1}$ and in the second ϵ_t.

Turning to the adaptive expectations specification, OLS is not an appropriate estimation procedure for equation (4.76), for even if all the assumptions of the classical regression model hold for the disturbance term ϵ_t, this is not the case for the new disturbance term η_t. In particular, the new disturbance term and the lagged dependent variable will be correlated. Since

and
$$\left.\begin{array}{l}\eta_t = \epsilon_t - \lambda\epsilon_{t-1}\\ C_{t-1} = \beta(1-\lambda)Y_{t-1} + \lambda C_{t-2} + \eta_{t-1}\end{array}\right\} \tag{4.80}$$

then

$$E(\eta_\tau C_{t-1}) = E[(\epsilon_t - \lambda\epsilon_{t-1}) \\ (\beta(1-\lambda)Y_{t-1} + \lambda C_{t-2} - \epsilon_{t-1} - \lambda\epsilon_{t-2})] = -\lambda\sigma^2 \quad (4.81)$$

This means that the application of OLS will give rise to estimators which are inconsistent. There are two ways out of this problem: one is to employ the method of instrumental variables where we replace Y_{t-1} with variables which are correlated with it but not with the stochastic disturbance term; the second approach, which is of more significance given the subject material of this chapter, is to use the maximum likelihood method.

Note that we may write equation (4.76) as

$$\begin{aligned} C_t &= \beta(1-\lambda)(Y_t + \lambda Y_{t-1} + \ldots + \lambda^{t-1}Y_1) + \epsilon_t \\ &= \beta(1-\lambda)\lambda^t(Y_0 + \lambda Y_{-1} + \lambda^2 Y_{-2} + \ldots) + \epsilon_t \end{aligned} \quad (4.82)$$

Since $E(C_0) = \beta(1-\lambda)(Y_0 + \lambda Y_{-1} + \lambda^2 Y_{-2} + \ldots)$ and letting $E(C_0) = \phi_0$, we may write equation (4.82) as

$$C_t = \lambda^t \phi_0 + \beta_0 Y_t(\lambda) + \epsilon_t \quad (4.83)$$

where $\beta_0 = \beta(1-\lambda)$ and $Y_t(\lambda) = Y_t + \lambda Y_{t-1} + \ldots + \lambda^{t-1}Y_1$. The value of $E(C_0)$ is the expected value of consumption in period zero and can be treated as a parameter which we wish to estimate along with β_0 and λ. The logarithmic likelihood function for $C_1, C_2, \ldots, C_n$ is:

$$L = -\frac{n}{2}\log(2\pi\sigma^2) - \frac{1}{2\sigma^2}\sum_{t=1}^{n}[C_t - \lambda^t\phi_0 - \beta_0 Y_t(\lambda)]^2 \quad (4.84)$$

Maximising L with respect to β_0, λ and ϕ_0 is equivalent to minimising

$$S(\lambda) = \Sigma[C_t - \lambda^t\phi_0 - \beta_0 Y_t(\lambda)]^2 \quad (4.85)$$

with respect to the same set of parameters. The ML procedure can be implemented by setting a value for λ and then finding the values of $\hat{\beta}_0$ and ϕ_0 which minimise $S(\lambda)$ for that particular value of λ. One then changes the value of λ and repeats the procedure. We finally select that value of λ (from all those permissible values of λ which lie within the range $0 < \lambda < 1$) and the associated values of β_0 and ϕ_0 which give rise to the smallest value of $S(\lambda)$; hence the log likelihood will have been maximised.

Returning to the partial adjustment model as specified in equation (4.79), as long as the stochastic disturbance term is serially uncorrelated, estimation by OLS will give rise to consistent estimates. Problems only arise in the presence of serial correlation. Assume that the model to be estimated is:

$$M_t = \beta(1-\gamma)Y_t + \gamma M_{t-1} + \epsilon_t \quad (4.86)$$

$$\epsilon_t = \rho\epsilon_{t-1} + u_t \quad (4.87)$$

where $u_t \sim N(0, \sigma_u^2)$. Lagging the first equation by one period and multiplying by ρ

yields the expression for $\rho\epsilon_{t-1}$ which can then be used to eliminate ϵ_{t-1}, thus enabling us to write the function we seek to minimise:

$$S(\rho) = \sum_{t=2}^{n} [M_t(\rho) - \beta_0 Y_t(\rho) - \gamma M_{t-1}(\rho)]^2 \qquad (4.88)$$

where

$$\beta_0 = \beta(1-\gamma), \quad M_t(\rho) = M_t - \rho M_{t-1}, \quad Y_t(\rho) = Y_t - \rho Y_{t-1}$$

We allow ρ to vary between -1 and $+1$; for a given value of ρ, we find the values of β_0 and γ which minimise $S(\rho)$ and we end up choosing that value of ρ and the associated values of β_0 and γ which give rise to the smallest value of $S(\rho)$. These are the ML estimators of the parameters of the model.

If the original stochastic disturbance term of the model with adaptive expectations is serially correlated, then the procedure is more complicated but is in principle the same as that outlined above. For the case of first-order serial correlation, we can define the following function to be minimised by an appropriate choice of λ, ρ, β_0 and ϕ_0:

$$S(\lambda, \rho) = \Sigma[C_t(\rho) - \lambda^t \phi_0(\rho) - \beta_0 Y_t(\lambda, \rho)]^2 \qquad (4.89)$$

where $\phi_0(\rho) = \phi_0 - \rho\phi_{-1}$, $C_t(\rho) = C_t - \rho C_{t-1}$ and $Y_t(\lambda, \rho) = Y_t - \rho Y_{t-1} + \lambda(Y_{t-1} - \rho Y_{t-2}) + \ldots + \lambda^{t-1}(Y_1 - \rho Y_0)$. In this case, we must perform a two-dimensional search over values of λ ranging from 0 to 1 and ρ from -1 to $+1$.

Maximum likelihood estimation procedures were adopted by Zellner and Geisel (1970) to obtain estimates of the parameters of the consumption function discussed in this section. Assuming a first-order autoregressive scheme for the error term, they obtained the following ML estimates:

$$\hat{\lambda} = 0.66 \qquad \hat{\rho} = 0.69 \qquad \hat{\beta} = 0.94$$
$$(0.085) \qquad (0.321) \qquad (0.46)$$

$$\hat{\beta}_0 = 0.321$$
$$\text{(not calculated)}$$

where the standard errors of the regression coefficients are given in brackets. There is strong evidence of first-order serial correlation; the estimated propensity to consume out of permanent income is 0.94.

Variations in coffee production from year to year result from a number of different factors: changes in climatic conditions, particularly the incidence of frost; changes in cropping intensity; the biennial crop-bearing cycle which has been attributed to the strain suffered by the tree due to a heavy crop with the result that the next year's crop is a light one; and changes in the number of trees planted. There exists a substantial lag of the order of five or more years between planting a tree and that tree yielding a crop of beans; yields then tend to increase for a number of years before reaching a maximum. Increases in the current producer price of coffee are postulated to influence agents' expectations of future prices in the same direction and to encourage more intensive cultivation of the existing trees and an expansion of

Distributed lag models

plantings. The latter change will only affect production with a substantial time lag. These factors when taken together are likely to give rise to a situation in which supply responds to a distributed lag or prices, with the weights initially increasing and then decreasing (the Almon lag distribution referred to earlier).

Parikh (1979) has derived the following specification for the supply function for coffee of an individual coffee-producing country:

$$Y_t = \alpha_0 + \alpha_1 Y_{t-1} + \alpha_2 Y_{t-2} + \beta \sum_{i=0}^{k} w_i P_{t-i} + u_t \qquad (4.90)$$

$$w_i = \delta_0 + \delta_1 i + \delta_2 i^2 + \ldots + \delta_p i^p \quad (i = 0, 1, \ldots, p) \qquad (4.91)$$

where Y_t refers to output at time t, P_t is producer price at time t, k is the length of the lag, w_i the weight attached to the price at period $t - i$ and these weights are assumed to lie along a polynomial of degree p. Assume the polynomial is of degree 3, then we have

$$w_i = \delta_0 + \delta_1 i + \delta_2 i^2 + \delta_3 i^3 \qquad (4.92)$$

and we may write equation (4.90) as

$$Y_t = \alpha_0 + \alpha_1 Y_{t-1} + \alpha_2 Y_{t-2} + \beta [\delta_0 P_t + (\delta_0 + \delta_1 + \delta_2 + \delta_3) P_{t-1} \\ + (\delta_0 + 2\delta_1 + 2^2 \delta_2 + 2^3 \delta_3) P_{t-2} + \ldots + (\delta_0 + k\delta_1 + k^2 \delta_2 + k^3 \delta_3) P_{t-k})] + u_t \qquad (4.93)$$

or alternatively as

$$Y_t = \alpha_0 + \alpha_1 Y_{t-1} + \alpha_2 Y_{t-2} + \beta \delta_0 Z_{0t} + \beta \delta_1 Z_{1t} + \beta \delta_2 Z_{2t} + \beta \delta_3 Z_{3t} + u_t \qquad (4.94)$$

where

$$Z_{0t} = P_t + P_{t-1} + \ldots + P_{t-k}$$

$$Z_{1t} = P_{t-1} + 2P_{t-2} + \ldots + kP_{t-k}$$

$$Z_{2t} = P_{t-1} + 2^2 P_{t-2} + \ldots + k^2 P_{t-k}$$

$$Z_{3t} = P_{t-1} + 2^3 P_{t-2} + \ldots + k^3 P_{t-k}$$

In equation (4.94) β is not identified and, in practice, its value is usually taken to be unity.

Note that by adopting this specification we have replaced the $(k + 1)$ price variables with $(p + 1)$ constructed variables. If p, the degree of the polynomial, is substantially less than k, the length of the lag, we are left with more degrees of freedom and multicollinearity is also likely to be a less serious problem.

The applied econometrician, however, has the problem of choosing the appropriate values of k and p. The procedure to be adopted is as follows. Assume the maximum feasible length of lag is $\bar{k}$, then the unrestricted model will include among the regressors $P_t, P_{t-1}, \ldots, P_{t-\bar{k}}$ and the restricted model will have $P_t, P_{t-1}, \ldots, P_{t-\bar{k}+1}$. Use the standard F test to discriminate between the restricted and unrestricted model, i.e. test the null hypothesis that $w_{\bar{k}} = 0$. If we accept the null hypothesis, we then proceed in sequence to test the null hypothesis $w_{\bar{k}} = w_{\bar{k}-1} = 0$ and so on until we fail to accept the null hypothesis. This then determines the length of the lag k.

We then proceed to derive p, the degree of the polynomial. Assume the maximum degree is $\bar{p} \leqslant k$, then the regressors of the equation will include $Z_{0t}, Z_{1t}, \ldots, Z_{\bar{p}t}$. In this case we test the null hypothesis that $\delta_{\bar{p}} = 0$. If we accept the null hypothesis, we then proceed in sequence to test the null hypothesis $\delta_{\bar{p}} = \delta_{\bar{p}-1} = 0$ and so on until we fail to accept the null hypothesis. This then determines the degree of the polynomial p.

These procedures were employed by Parikh to estimate supply functions for eight major coffee producers with the following results: the optimal length of lag was usually found to be either eight or nine years and the degree of the polynomial to be three or four. Multicollinearity is a problem with individual regression coefficients being quite sensitive to changes in k and p and often not significant individually. The estimated mean lags were in the region of five years, similar to the maturation lag between planting and harvesting. For most producers there was supporting evidence for the biennial production cycle with Y_{t-2} having a positive significant effect on current output.

Serial correlation, however, is often present in distributed lag models and Parikh's study proves no exception to this as he discovered when he estimated the supply function with first-order serial correlation. The model equations now become

$$Y_t = \alpha_0 + \alpha_1 Y_{t-1} + \alpha_2 Y_{t-2} + \beta \sum_{i=0}^{k} w_i P_{t-i} + u_t \tag{4.95}$$

$$u_t = \rho u_{t-1} + \epsilon_t \tag{4.96}$$

and combining equations (4.95) and (4.96) yields

$$Y_t = \alpha_0 + \alpha_1 Y_{t-1} + \alpha_2 Y_{t-2} + \beta \sum_{i=0}^{k} w_i P_{t-1} + \rho u_{t-1} + \epsilon_t \tag{4.97}$$

or

$$Y_t = \alpha_0(1-\rho) + (\rho + \alpha_1) Y_{t-1} + (\alpha_2 - \alpha_1 \rho) Y_{t-2} - \alpha_2 \rho Y_{t-3}$$

$$+ \beta \sum_{i=0}^{k} w_i P_{t-i} - \rho \beta \sum_{i=0}^{k} w_i P_{t-i-1} + \epsilon_t \tag{4.97a}$$

or

$$Y_t - \rho Y_{t-1} = \alpha_0(1-\rho) + \alpha_1 (Y_{t-1} - \rho Y_{t-2}) + \alpha_2 (Y_{t-2} - \rho Y_{t-3})$$

$$+ \beta \sum_{i=0}^{k} w_i (P_{t-1} - \rho P_{t-i-1}) + \epsilon_t \tag{4.97b}$$

Parikh presented the results of estimation of the final version, using the Cochrane–

Orcutt procedure with eight or nine lags of the producer price and weights given by a third-degree polynomial. This procedure was devised for models with a first-order autoregressive transformation. The autoregressive parameter was estimated from the OLS residuals and then, in the subsequent stage, the transformed equation

$Y_t - \rho Y_{t-1} = \alpha(1-\rho) + \beta(x_t - \rho x_{t-1}) + V_t$ is estimated.

This transformation is for the model $Y_t = \alpha + \beta x_t + U_t$ where $U_t = \rho U_{t-1} + V_t$. The procedure can be iterated or it can be ended after two steps. We report as an illustration his results for Guatemala (see Table 4.5).

No individual regression coefficients on the price variables are significant, reflecting the presence of multicollinearity. The weights initially increase and then diminish in size, the mean lag is somewhat over four years and lagged output has a significant impact on current output. There is evidence of negative serial correlation. Since the paper was originally published, it is now known that employing the Cochrane–Orcutt procedure in such circumstances may give rise to inconsistent estimates of ρ (see Betancourt and Kelejian, 1981). The correct procedure when seeking to estimate a model with first-order serial correlation and lagged dependent variables is to employ maximum likelihood methods.

4.3 QUALITATIVE AND LIMITED DEPENDENT VARIABLES

In this section we consider the estimation of models in which the dependent variable is either a qualitative dependent variable or a limited dependent variable. We have a qualitative dependent variable in discrete choice models; this choice may involve a decision by a married woman or an older person whether or not to participate in the

Table 4.5 Estimates of supply function for coffee: Guatemala

	Estimate	t ratio
Constant	− 161.3109	0.8766
Y_{t-1}	0.7026	3.3440
Y_{t-2}	0.3431	1.5759
P_t	0.1385	0.3015
P_{t-1}	0.2669	0.4100
P_{t-2}	0.3774	0.5834
P_{t-3}	0.4622	0.8743
P_{t-4}	0.5137	1.2620
P_{t-5}	0.5241	1.2870
P_{t-6}	0.4856	0.9820
P_{t-7}	0.3906	0.7483
P_{t-8}	0.2313	0.6029
ρ	− 0.3142	1.7193
mean lag	4.301	
$\bar{R}^2$	0.848 66	
SEE	162.144	
n	27	

labour force, or a decision by a peasant farmer whether or not to purchase a particular chemical fertiliser. If the particular individual participates in the labour force or the peasant farmer buys the fertiliser, a value of unity is assigned to the dependent variable; otherwise it takes a value of zero. We would have a case of a limited dependent variable, for instance, in a model seeking to explain expenditure on some consumer durable, say a new car, during a particular time period. Many households in the sample would not have bought a new car and would, therefore, have spent nothing. Among the subset of the sample who have purchased a new car during the period under consideration there will be differences in the amount spent as some bought cheap family saloons, while others bought more luxurious vehicles. We consider each of these two models in turn.

For the case where the dependent variable is a binary or dichotomous 0,1 variable, we consider three alternative estimation procedures: (i) the linear probability model where the estimation procedure is OLS; (ii) the logit model; and (iii) the probit model. The latter two models involve the use of the maximum likelihood procedure. We will discuss the three procedures in the context of a simple model to explain the probability of ownership of a video cassette recorder (VCR) where this is just one explanatory variable: household weekly income.

The linear probability model

Our model is assumed to take the following form:

$$Y_i = \alpha + \beta X_i + \epsilon_i \tag{4.98}$$

where X_i is the weekly income of the ith household and Y_i is a binary variable which takes on a value of unity if the ith household owns a VCR, and zero otherwise. The explanatory variable is taken to be nonstochastic and the disturbance term ϵ_i is assumed to be random and to possess a finite variance. Given the binary nature of the dependent variable, its expected value $E(Y_i)$ is given by

$$E(Y_i) = 1 \times P_i + 0 \times (1 - P_i) = P_i \tag{4.99}$$

where P_i is the probability that a household with income X_i owns a VCR and, from equation (4.98),

$$E(Y_i) = \alpha + \beta X_i = P_i \tag{4.100}$$

We may state alternatively that $E(Y_i)$ measures the proportion of all households with income X_i who own the consumer durable in question. The fact that the dependent variable is a binary variable has an obvious implication for the distribution of the disturbance term ϵ_i. For a particular value of household income X_i, if $Y_i = 1$, $\epsilon_i = 1 - \alpha - \beta X_i$ and if $Y_i = 0$, $\epsilon_i = -\alpha - \beta X_i$. The former case will occur with probability P_i and the latter with probability $1 - P_i$. Since we have assumed that $E(\epsilon_i) = 0$, we must have

$$(1 - \alpha - \beta X_i)P_i + (-\alpha - \beta X_i)(1 - P_i) = 0 \tag{4.101}$$

Simplifying, we obtain

$$P_i = \alpha + \beta X_i \tag{4.102}$$

and it is then a straightforward matter to show that

$$\begin{aligned} E(\epsilon_i^2) &= (\alpha + \beta X_i)(1 - \alpha - \beta X_i) \\ &= E(Y_i)(1 - E(Y_i)) = P_i(1 - P_i) \end{aligned} \tag{4.103}$$

This leads to our first criticism of the linear probability model: since the variance of the error term depends upon $E(Y_i)$, the disturbances are heteroscedastic. One can easily correct for this heteroscedasticity by employing weighted least squares with the weights given by $1/\sqrt{(\hat{Y}_i(1 - \hat{Y}_i))}$ in which $\hat{Y}_i$ are the least squares fitted value of Y_i.

Secondly, since the expected value of the dependent variable measures the probability that a household with income X_i will own a VCR, $\hat{Y}_i$ ought to lie between 0 and 1, but in practice it may not be confined within this range. Finally, both the intercept and slope are not constant for all values of X but switch in value as X changes. If $X_i < -\alpha/\beta$, then both intercept and slope are zero; and if $X_i > (1 - \alpha)/\beta$, the intercept takes a value of unity and the slope is zero. Only within the range $(-\alpha/\beta \leq X_i \leq (1 - \alpha)/\beta$ do we have the intercept given by α and the slope by β. If, in estimating α and β, we include observations on X which lie outside the above range, such estimators are both biased and inconsistent and we cannot exclude such observations *a priori* since we do not know the values of α and β in advance.

Given the above problems with the linear probability model, it is preferable to turn to an alternative estimation procedure. We first consider the logit model.

The logit model

We wish to specify a model in which the probability of ownership of a VCR rises with income, but in a nonlinear manner with the rate of change of this probability first rising and then falling as income increases. Furthermore, we wish to confine the predicted probability within the interval 0, 1. A specification which fits these requirements is based on the logistic S-shaped curve and gives rise to the logit model in which the expected value of Y_i is given by

$$E(Y_i) = \frac{1}{1 + \exp(-\alpha - \beta X_i)} = \frac{\exp(\alpha + \beta X_i)}{1 + \exp(\alpha + \beta X_i)} = \Pi_i \tag{4.104}$$

where Π_i is the probability that a household with income X_i will own a VCR. Having defined Π_i in this way, after some manipulation, we obtain the following expression for the natural log of the ratio of the odds of $Y_i = 1$ against $Y_i = 0$:

$$\log \frac{\Pi_i}{1 - \Pi_i} = \alpha + \beta X_i \tag{4.105}$$

Note that this transformation does not confine the left-hand side variable to the interval 0,1: the left-hand side of equation (4.105) can range from $-\infty$ to ∞.

The procedure for estimating the logit model depends upon whether or not there exist replicated observations on Y for each different value of X. Let us deal first with the case where replication is absent. Our sample data contains no households with the same income level as any other households in the sample: for each income level there is only one observation on Y. The method of estimation to apply in these circumstances or where there are only a small number of replicated observations is that of maximum likelihood.

Given that Y_i is a binomial variable which takes a value of 1 with probability Π_i and a value of 0 with probability $1 - \Pi_i$, the log likelihood function for n independent observations is

$$L = \sum_{i=1}^{n} [Y_i \log \Pi_i + (1 - Y_i) \log (1 - \Pi_i)] \qquad (4.106)$$

Substituting equation (4.104) into (4.106) we obtain

$$L = \sum_{i=1}^{n} \{Y_i(\alpha + \beta X_i) - \log [1 + \exp(\alpha + \beta X_i)]\} \qquad (4.107)$$

Differentiating the log likelihood function with respect to α and β we obtain the following first-order conditions for a maximum:

$$\frac{\partial L}{\partial \alpha} = \sum_{i=1}^{n} \{Y_i - 1/[1 + \exp(-\alpha - \beta X_i)]\} = 0 \qquad (4.108)$$

$$\frac{\partial L}{\partial \beta} = \sum_{i=1}^{n} \{Y_i - 1/[1 + \exp(-\alpha - \beta X_i)]\} X_i = 0 \qquad (4.109)$$

These two equations can be solved numerically to obtain the ML estimators, and the associated asymptotic standard errors can be derived from the inverse of the information matrix.

A more straightforward estimation procedure can be utilised when for each income level there is more than one observation on Y. If we let P_i (replacing Π_i) represent the proportion of households with income X_i who own a VCR, then we may apply the least squares method once we have applied weights to the observations to correct for the heteroscedastic nature of the disturbances. The equation to be estimated is

$$\frac{1}{S_i} \log \left(\frac{P_i}{1 - P_i}\right) = \alpha \left(\frac{1}{S_i}\right) + \beta \left(\frac{X_i}{S_i}\right) + u_i \qquad (4.110)$$

where $1/S_i$ is equal to $\sqrt{[n_i P_i(1 - P_i)]}$ with n_i being the number of households receiving an income of X_i. For the derivation of this result, the interested reader is referred to Maddala (1983).

The probit model

An alternative procedure which can be applied to obtain estimates of the parameters of a discrete choice model is the probit model in which the relevant distribution function is the cumulative distribution of the standard normal.

Assume the true model is given by

$$Y_i^* = \alpha + \beta X_i + \epsilon_i \qquad (4.111)$$

where Y_i^* is an unobservable or latent variable and $\epsilon_i \sim IN(0, 1)$ and is independent. Note that in this case the standard deviation of the normal distribution is assumed to be 1 rather than σ. In general σ remains underidentified in such models. The postulated relationship between the latent variable, Y_i^* and the observed binary variable, Y_i is as follows

$$Y_i = 1 \text{ if } Y_i^* > 0 \qquad (4.112)$$

$$= 0 \text{ if } Y_i^* \leq 0 \qquad (4.113)$$

The probability that a household with income X_i owns a VCR is given by

$$\begin{aligned} E(Y_i) = \Pi_i &= P(Y_i^* > 0) \\ &= P(-\epsilon_i < \alpha + \beta X_i) \\ &= F(\alpha + \beta X_i) \end{aligned} \qquad (4.114)$$

where $F(\cdot)$ represents the cumulative distribution of the standard normal distribution and is given by

$$F(\alpha + \beta X_i) = \int_{-\infty}^{\alpha + \beta X_i} f(z) dz \qquad (4.115)$$

with $f(z)$ representing the density function of $z \sim N(0, 1)$. This result follows from the fact the disturbance term in the true model is a standard normal variate.

In the probit case, the log likelihood function for the n observations is, therefore, given by

$$L = \sum_{i=1}^{n} \{Y_i \log F(\alpha + \beta X_i) + (1 - Y_i) \log [1 - F(\alpha + \beta X_i)]\} \qquad (4.116)$$

The log likelihood can then be maximised to obtain the maximum likelihood estimators of α and β. Fortunately, given the complicated nature of the log likelihood function, computer packages are available to provide estimates of the parameters α and β which give rise to a maximum of equation (4.116).

Inverting equation (4.114) we have

$$Z_i = F^{-1}(\Pi_i) = \alpha + \beta X_i \qquad (4.117)$$

where Z_i is assumed to be a linear function of the individual's attribute X_i and $F^{-1}(\cdot)$ is the inverse of the cumulative standard normal distribution. Let us now consider the probit model for the case where we have a number of observations at each level of household income, X_i. Define P_i as the proportion of households with income X_i who own a VCR. We have

$$P_i = \Pi_i + \epsilon_i \qquad (4.118)$$

and taking a first-order Taylor series expansion of $F^{-1}(P_i)$ around Π_i, we obtain

$$F^{-1}(P_i) = \alpha + \beta X_i + \frac{\epsilon_i}{f(\alpha + \beta X_i)} \qquad (4.119)$$

where $f(\cdot)$ is a standard normal density function. The disturbance term in the above equation has an expected value of zero and its variance is given by

$$\frac{\Pi_i(1 - \Pi_i)}{n_i[f(\alpha + \beta X_i)]^2}$$

where n_i measures the number of households with income equal to X_i.

The following procedure can then be employed to obtain estimates of the parameters of the probit model for the case of replicated observations: estimate equation (4.119) by OLS and utilise the estimates of α and β so derived along with the sample proportions P_i as a substitute for the unobservable Π_i to obtain a consistent estimator of the variance of the disturbance term; the second stage then involves estimating the model by least squares, having corrected for heteroscedasticity.

A measure of how well the logit or probit model fits the given data is provided by the likelihood ratio index (LRI) which is measured by

$$LRI = 1 - \frac{L(UR)}{L(R)} \qquad (4.120)$$

where $L(UR)$ is the maximum value of the log likelihood obtained by maximising either equation (4.107) in the logit case or equation (4.116) in the probit case and $L(R)$ is the maximum value of the respective log likelihood when β is constrained to equal zero. It is a straightforward matter to show that for the logit model the restricted log likelihood is given by

$$L(R) = s \log r - n \log (1 + e^{\log r}) \qquad (4.121)$$

and for the probit model by

$$L(R) = s \log P + (n - s) \log (1 - P) \qquad (4.122)$$

where P is the probability of success, $r = P/1 - P$, s the number of successes and n the number of observations.

The likelihood ratio index lies between 0 and 1; the closer to unity, the better is the fit. The likelihood ratio test can be utilised to test for the significance of β. If $-2(L(R) - L(UR)) > \chi^2_{0.05}(1)$, then we reject the null hypothesis that $\beta = 0$. The degree of freedom for the test is equal to the number of explanatory variables of the model, not including the constant.

After estimating the model, we would like to know the effects of changes in the explanatory variable on the probabilities of any observation belonging to either of the two groups. These effects are given by

$$\frac{\partial P_i}{\partial X_i} = \begin{cases} \beta & \text{for the linear probit model} \\ \beta P_i(1 - P_i) & \text{for the logit model} \\ \beta \phi(Z_i) & \text{for the probit model} \end{cases}$$

where $\phi(\cdot)$ is the density function of the standard normal. In the case of the linear probability model, these derivatives are constant, while in logit and probit models we need to calculate them at different levels of the explanatory variable to get the range of variation of the resulting changes in probabilities.

Traditionally, probit analysis has been used less widely in econometric work than in the biological sciences where the technique was first developed by Finney (1971) for use in biological assay. Given the greater analytical tractability of the logit approach, econometricians have tended to resort to the logit method more frequently than to probit. In comparing the logit and probit models, one finds that the logistic and cumulative normal functions are vary close in the mid-range, but the logistic function has slightly heavier tails than the cumulative normal. The differences between the two approaches are much greater when the dependent variable is not simply a dichotomous one.

Multinomial logit and probit models can be formulated for cases where the dependent variable is not simply a dichotomous variable. Estimation by maximum likelihood is complicated but, again, readily available computer packages can be utilised.

In the final part of this section we employ the three procedures discussed above to some sample data on ownership of VCRs and household income. The data are presented in Table 4.6 and estimates of the parameters obtained using the three different methods are presented in Table 4.7.

If the household owns a VCR, the dependent variable takes a value of one, otherwise it is zero.

Because of the problems associated with the linear probability model, our preferences are to utilise either the probit or logit models. In comparing the estimated parameters from these two models, Amemiya (1981) has suggested multiplying the estimates obtained using the probit model by 1.6 and then comparing them with the estimates from the logit model. The reader will notice that when this scaling is performed on the estimates presented in Table 4.7, the scaled probit estimates are very similar to the logit ones. For both models, the $L(R)$ takes the value of -36.0436; this results from the fact that in the sample the proportion of successes is one-half. For both models, the likelihood ratio test leads to the rejection of the null hypothesis that $\beta = 0$.

Tobit models

We now turn to a consideration of the case where we have a limited dependent variable. Examples where such cases arise are expenditure on a particular consumer durable and hours of work supplied by members of a group whose participation rate

Table 4.6 Video cassette recorder ownership and household income (£ per week)

VCR	Household income	VCR	Household income
0	40	0	230
0	42	1	238
1	45	1	250
0	48	0	259
0	50	0	270
0	55	1	295
0	57	1	310
0	60	0	320
1	65	0	325
0	70	1	332
0	85	1	340
0	90	1	351
1	98	1	360
0	110	1	375
1	118	1	388
0	125	0	400
0	150	1	420
0	162	1	428
1	168	1	440
0	175	0	455
0	190	1	460
0	195	1	470
0	210	1	475
1	212	1	486
0	215	1	490
1	220	1	495

Table 4.7 Parameter estimates for three models

Model	$\hat{\alpha}$	$\hat{\beta}$	Log likelihood	LRI	LR test statistic
Linear probability	0.0712 (0.0605)	0.001 75 (4.254)			
Logit	−2.0482 (3.016)	0.008 47 (3.367)	−28.4878	0.210	15.112
Probit	−1.232 (3.196)	0.005 11 (3.612)	−28.4830	0.210	15.121

Note: *t* ratios are provided below the estimated regression coefficients.

is relatively low. In both these cases many observations on the dependent variable are likely to be zero but assigning a zero value to each observation where an individual household does not purchase the consumer durable, or the married woman does not supply any hours of market work, fails to distinguish any differences in intensity of preference. A married woman who places a value on her time in nonmarket production only marginally above the wage rate she could have received in employment is very close to supplying hours of work in comparison with her sister surrounded by a number of small children whose shadow price of time is considerably in excess of her potential market wage. A similar argument also applies in the case of the consumer durable.

It was Tobin (1958) who made the first contribution to the literature on estimating functions in which the dependent variable takes the above form. Consider the following model applied to the case of expenditure on a consumer durable:

$$Y_i^* = \alpha + \beta X_i + \epsilon_i^* \tag{4.123}$$

where X_i represents income of the ith household and ϵ_i^* is the disturbance term assumed to satisfy all the usual properties of the disturbance term in the classical linear regression model. More importantly for our purposes, Y_i^* measures the strength of the ith household's desire for the consumer durable. If the household actually buys the good we assign a value to Y_i^* equal to actual expenditure on the good Y_i ($Y_i = Y_i^*$ if $Y_i^* > 0$), whereas if the household does not purchase the good, then Y_i^* is unobservable and Y_i is given a value of zero ($Y_i = 0$ if $Y_i^* \leq 0$). The significance of this procedure is that in the model now written as

$$Y_i = \alpha + \beta X_i + \epsilon_i \tag{4.124}$$

the lower tails of the distribution of both Y_i and ϵ_i have been chopped off and, consequently, the mean of the disturbance term ϵ_i is no longer equal to zero.

The above model is known as the tobit model and we shall discuss two alternative procedures for estimating it, both of which involve maximum likelihood estimation. The first approach is estimation by maximum likelihood, while the second, due to Heckman (1979), adopts a two-stage procedure in which ML estimation is employed in the first stage to be followed by OLS in the second stage.

Note that equation (4.123) implies that $Y_i^* \leq 0$ if $\epsilon_i^* < -\alpha - \beta X_i$ and since Y_i^* is a random, independent, normally distributed variable with mean $\alpha + \beta X_i$ and variance σ^2, we have

$$P(Y_i^* \leq 0) = F\left(\frac{-\alpha - \beta X_i}{\sigma}\right) \tag{4.125}$$

where $F(\cdot)$ is a cumulative distribution function of a standard normal variate. For those observations where actual expenditure on the consumer durable is zero, the log likelihood function only differs from the probit version, presented earlier in this section, by the fact that the variance of the disturbance term is equal to σ^2 rather than unity. For those observations where Y_i is positive, the log likelihood function is the standard one for the classical linear regression model (see equation (4.6)).

Letting $Z_i = 1$ if $Y_i > 0$ and 0 if $Y_i = 0$, we have

$$L = \sum_{i=1}^{n} \left\{ (1 - Z_i) \log F\left(\frac{-\alpha - \beta X_i}{\sigma}\right) + Z_i \left[-\frac{1}{2} \log(2\pi\sigma^2) - \frac{1}{2\sigma^2}(Y_i - \alpha - \beta X_i)^2 \right] \right\} \tag{4.126}$$

Maximum likelihood estimates of the parameters of the model can then be obtained by maximising the above function with respect to α, β and σ^2.

The Heckman approach is to consider, first, the subset of the sample observations for which Y_i^* and hence actual expenditure Y_i is positive. For these observations the regression model is

$$Y_i = \alpha + \beta X_i + \epsilon_i \qquad (4.127)$$

and, taking expected values, we obtain

$$E(Y_i) = \alpha + \beta X_i + E(\epsilon_i | \epsilon_i^* > -(\alpha + \beta X_i)) \qquad (4.128)$$

Note that if ϵ_i did not exceed $-(\alpha + \beta X_i)$, then Y_i^* would be non-positive and Y_i would be correspondingly assigned a value of 0. Since $\epsilon_i^* \sim N(0, \sigma^2)$, then the truncated variable ϵ_i has a positive expected value which is given by

$$E(\epsilon_i | \epsilon_i^* > -(\alpha + \beta X_i)) = \frac{\sigma f(\alpha + \beta X_i/\sigma)}{F(\alpha + \beta X_i/\sigma)} = \sigma \lambda_i \qquad (4.129)$$

where $f(\cdot)$ and $F(\cdot)$ are, respectively, the density and cumulative distribution functions of the standard normal distribution. Letting the ratio of the density to the cumulative distribution for given X_i be represented by λ_i, the regression model for positive expenditure observations may now be expressed as

$$Y_i = \alpha + \beta X_i + \sigma \lambda_i + \epsilon_i^* \qquad (4.130)$$

in which the disturbance term now has a zero expected value. If information were available on λ_i, then equation (4.130) could be estimated by OLS. However, such information is not available and we need to obtain a consistent estimator of λ_i. How can this be done? To investigate this equation, we must return to the complete sample.

Introduce a binary variable Z_i (as in the Probit model) such that $Z_i = 1$ if $Y_i^* > 0$ and is otherwise equal to zero. Hence we have

$$P(Z_i = 0) = P(\epsilon_i^* \leq -\alpha - \beta X_i) \qquad (4.131)$$

$$P(Z_i = 1) = P(\epsilon_i^* > -\alpha - \beta X_i) \qquad (4.132)$$

The log likelihood function for this new variable Z_i defined over the complete sample is then given by

$$L = \sum_{i=1}^{n} \left[(1 - Z_i) \log F\left(\frac{-\alpha - \beta X_i}{\sigma}\right) + Z_i \log F\left(\frac{\alpha + \beta X_i}{\sigma}\right) \right] \qquad (4.133)$$

Maximising equation (4.132) yields the consistent estimates of $(\alpha + \beta X_i)/\sigma$ and, therefore, of λ_i. Once this has been performed, the second stage of the procedure can proceed with the estimation of equation (4.130) by OLS. The problem with this procedure, however, is that using this consistent estimator of λ_i leads to heteroscedastic disturbance. The maximum likelihood approach is to be preferred.

An example of the use of the maximum likelihood tobit procedure is provided in a study by Parikh (1990) of fertiliser use by farmers in Bangladesh. Data were collected in sixteen villages spread throughout the country on the use of fertiliser and other inputs; information on the price of fertiliser, crop type and cropping patterns, and infrastructural characteristics of the villages was also obtained. Due to gaps in the data, a full set of observations was available for 461 farmers, of whom forty-nine used no fertiliser. A number of different equations were estimated to explain fertiliser demand, using two estimation procedures: OLS and tobit. A typical specification is

$$FQB_i = \text{constant} + b_1 FPRICE_i + b_2 FLB_i + b_3 HLB_i \\ + b_4 DINF_i + b_5 CROPIN_i + b_6 HYVA_i + b_7 B_i + \epsilon_i \qquad (4.134)$$

where FQB_i represents the quantity of fertiliser per acre of sown area used by the ith farmer; $FPRICE$ is the unit price of fertiliser; FLB is hours of employment of family labour (per sown acre); HLB is hours of employment of hired labour (per sown acre); $DINF$ is an index of the infrastructural characteristics of the village in which the farmer is located and is based on such factors as proximity to market and distribution centres, access to financial institutions, etc.; $CROPIN$ is a measure of cropping intensity; $HYVA$ is the proportion of total cropped area sown with high yielding varieties of seed; and B is the total area sown by the farmer. Given the greater need for weed control when fertilisers are applied, fertiliser use and labour are expected to be complementary inputs. Strong complementarities also exist between fertiliser use and the planting of high yielding varieties; positive coefficients are expected on $HYVA$, and on $CROPIN$, and b also. The coefficient on $FPRICE$ is hypothesised to be negative, as is the coefficient on $DINF$, the index being defined in such a way that a fall in its value is associated with an infrastructure more favourable to fertiliser use.

The results of estimating equation (4.134) by OLS and tobit are presented in Table 4.8. The estimated coefficients have the expected signs and most have high t ratios, though the OLS estimates are not consistent. Greene (1981) has demonstrated that a consistent estimator is provided by multiplying the OLS coefficients by n/m, where n measures the number of observations and m the number of nonzero observations. In this case the scaling factor is 1.119 and, when such a scaling is performed, the OLS estimates so adjusted do not differ all that much from the maximum likelihood tobit estimates.

Table 4.8 Fertiliser demand in Bangladesh agriculture, ordinary least squares and tobit estimates

	OLS	t ratio	Tobit	t ratio
Constant	126.956	6.807	101.077	6.773
FPRICE	−25.2434	5.226	−25.6201	6.811
FLB	0.4772	6.331	0.6004	9.667
HLB	1.0277	9.785	1.1119	15.907
DINF	−8.219	9.424	−8.8312	8.237
CROPIN	0.9197	0.813	1.2657	0.749
HYVA	142.544	13.529	163.271	17.731
B	2.3534	1.466	3.9792	1.595
σ			66.537	55.048
R^2	0.5377			
SEE	62.985			
F	75.26			
log L			−2362.0	

4.4 ERRORS IN VARIABLES

In the final section to this chapter we consider the problems which arise when the explanatory variable in a regression model is measured with error; this is the problem of errors in variables. We show that in this case the OLS estimators are not generally consistent and we consider alternative estimation procedures to obtain consistent estimators. Note that here we are discussing the case where the explanatory variable is measured with error. Errors in the measurement of the dependent variable are of no great significance, as long as we assume that they possess the same properties as the disturbance term of the classical linear regression model and that they are not correlated with it. If this is the case we may simply allow for these measurement errors in the normal stochastic disturbance term. Problems, however, may arise in time-series data if improvements have been made through time in the collection of data such that measurement errors in the dependent variable tend to be smaller in the more recent observations, this will give rise to heteroscedastic disturbances. In such circumstances the usual procedures for dealing with heteroscedasticity can be employed. In what follows we shall assume that Y_i is measured without error.

Consider the following model:

$$Y_i = \alpha + \beta X_i + \epsilon_i \tag{4.135}$$

where $\epsilon_i \sim N(0, \sigma^2)$, $E(\epsilon_i \epsilon_j) = 0$ for $i \neq j$, and X_i is the true value of the explanatory variable, assumed to be unobservable. We observe X_i^0 where

$$X_i^0 = X_i + w_i \tag{4.136}$$

with $w_i \sim N(0, \sigma_w^2)$, $E(w_i w_j) = 0$ for $i \neq j$, and $E(w_i \epsilon_j) = 0$ for all i, j.

Eliminating the unobservable variable X_i in equation (4.135) by using equation (4.136), we have

$$Y_i = \alpha + \beta(X_i^0 - w_i) + \epsilon_i$$
$$= \alpha + \beta X_i^0 + \epsilon_i^0 \tag{4.137}$$

where $\epsilon_i^0 = \epsilon_i - \beta w_i$; X_i^0 is a stochastic variable and can easily be shown to be correlated with ϵ_i^0:

$$\text{Cov}(X_i^0 \epsilon_i^0) = E[X_i^0 - E(X_i^0)][\epsilon_i^0 - E(\epsilon_i^0)]$$
$$= E[w_i(\epsilon_i - \beta w_i)]$$
$$= -\beta \sigma_w^2 \tag{4.138}$$

The implication of this nonzero covariance is that the OLS estimator of β is no longer consistent.

Consider the model in deviation form:

$$y_i = \beta x_i^0 + \epsilon_i^{0'} = \beta x_i^0 + \epsilon_i' - \beta w_i' \tag{4.139}$$

where $\epsilon_i^{0'} = \epsilon_i^0 - \bar{\epsilon}^0$, etc. The OLS estimator of β is given by

$$\hat{\beta} = \frac{\Sigma x_i^0 y_i}{\Sigma (x_i^0)^2} = \frac{\Sigma x_i^0 (\beta x_i^0 + \epsilon_i^{0'})}{\Sigma (x_i^0)^2}$$

Errors in variables

$$= \beta + \frac{\Sigma x_i^0 \epsilon_i^{0\prime}}{\Sigma (x_i^0)^2} = \beta + \frac{\Sigma (x_i + w_i^\prime)(\epsilon_i^\prime - \beta w_i^\prime)}{\Sigma (x_i + w_i^\prime)^2} \quad (4.140)$$

Given the assumptions we have made about the nature of the disturbance terms, we have

$$\text{plim } \hat{\beta} = \beta - \frac{\beta \sigma_w^2}{\sigma_x^2 + \sigma_w^2} = \beta \left[\frac{\sigma_x^2}{\sigma_x^2 + \sigma_w^2} \right] \quad (4.141)$$

where $\sigma_x^2 = \lim_{n \to \infty} \Sigma x_i^2/n$.

For $\beta \neq 0$ and finite σ_x^2, the OLS estimator is asymptotically biased towards zero whenever errors of measurement are present in X_i. The OLS estimator of α is also inconsistent.

Since $Y_i \sim N(\alpha + \beta X_i, \sigma^2)$ and $X_i^0 \sim N(X_i, \sigma_w^2)$, then the likelihood function for the n observations on $(Y_1, X_1^0), (Y_2, X_2^0), \ldots, (Y_n, X_n^0)$, is given by

$$\prod_{n=1}^{n} \frac{1}{\sqrt{(2\pi\sigma^2)}} \exp\left[-\tfrac{1}{2}\left(\frac{Y_i - \alpha - \beta X_i}{\sigma} \right)^2 \right] \frac{1}{\sqrt{(2\pi\sigma_w^2)}} \exp[-\tfrac{1}{2}(X_i^0 - X_i/\sigma_w)^2] \quad (4.142)$$

and the log likelihood is therefore given by

$$L = -\frac{n}{2} \log 2\pi\sigma^2 - \frac{n}{2} \log 2\pi\sigma_w^2 - \frac{1}{2\sigma^2} \sum_{i=1}^{n} (Y_i - \alpha - \beta X_i)^2$$

$$- \frac{1}{2\sigma_w^2} \sum_{i=1}^{n} (X_i^0 - X_i)^2 \quad (4.143)$$

In this case we must find values for $(n + 4)$ parameters – α, β, σ^2, σ_w^2, $X_1, X_2, \ldots, X_n$ – which give rise to a maximum of L.

An additional observation in the sample requires the estimation of an additional parameter: the corresponding value of X_{n+1}. In these circumstances the ML estimators are no longer consistent.

If the investigator possesses knowledge of the magnitude of σ_w^2, then a consistent estimator of $\hat{\beta}$ is provided by

$$\hat{\beta} = \frac{\Sigma x_i^0 y_i / n}{(\Sigma (x_i^0)^2 / n) - \sigma_w^2} \quad (4.144)$$

$$\text{plim } \hat{\beta} = \text{plim} \left[\frac{\Sigma x_i^0 (\beta x_i^0 + \epsilon_i^\prime - \beta w_i^\prime)/n}{\frac{\Sigma (x_i^0)^2}{n} - \sigma_w^2} \right]$$

$$= \text{plim} \left[\frac{(\beta \Sigma x_i^{02} + \Sigma \epsilon_i^\prime x_i^0 - \beta \Sigma w_i x_i - \beta \Sigma w_i^2)/n}{\frac{\Sigma (x_i^0)^2}{n} - \sigma_w^2} \right]$$

$$= \beta \quad (4.145)$$

since $x_i^0 = x_i + w_i^\prime$.

Alternatively, if the dependent variable is measured without error and there are no other disturbances in the regression, then $\sigma^2 = 0$, a consistent estimator of β can be obtained by regressing X^0 on Y and then taking the reciprocal of the estimated coefficient on Y as the estimate of β. If the numerical values $\Sigma x_i^0 y_i / \Sigma x_i^{02}$ and $\Sigma y_i^2 / \Sigma x_i^0 y_i$ do not differ very much, we may conclude that measurement error is not a serious problem.

In the general case, however, the investigator does not possess information on σ^2, σ_w^2 or even their relative magnitude. In order, therefore, to obtain consistent estimators, instrumental variable estimation is to be applied. We replace X_i^0 with a new variable Z_i which must possess two important properties: (i) it must be uncorrelated in the probability limit with the error term ϵ^0; and (ii) it must be correlated in the probability limit with X_i^0. Hence we must have

$$\text{plim}\left(\frac{\Sigma z_i \epsilon_i^{0'}}{n}\right) = 0 \qquad (4.146)$$

and

$$\text{plim}\left(\frac{\Sigma z_i x_i^0}{n}\right) \neq 0 \qquad (4.147)$$

where $z_i = Z_i - \bar{Z}$. The instrumental variable estimator of β is given by

$$\beta^{IV} = \frac{\Sigma y_i z_i}{\Sigma x_i^0 z_i} = \frac{\Sigma(\beta x_i^0 + \epsilon_i^{0'}) z_i}{\Sigma x_i^0 z_i}$$

$$= \beta + \frac{\Sigma \epsilon_i^{0'} z_i}{\Sigma x_i^0 z_i} \qquad (4.148)$$

Note that the term in the denominator is $\Sigma x_i^0 z_i$ and not Σz_i^2. Taking the limit in probability, we obtain

$$\text{plim } \beta^{IV} = \beta \qquad (4.149)$$

The instrumental variable estimator of α is given by

$$\alpha^{IV} = \bar{Y} - \beta^{IV} \bar{X}^0$$

and

$$\begin{aligned} \text{plim } \alpha^{IV} &= \text{plim } (\bar{Y} - \beta^{IV} \bar{X}^0) \\ &= \text{plim } (\alpha + \beta \bar{X}^0 + \epsilon^0 - \beta^{IV} \bar{X}^0) \\ &= \alpha \end{aligned} \qquad (4.150)$$

The estimated variances of α^{IV} and β^{IV} are obtained from equations (4.148) and (4.149), respectively, as

$$\text{est. Var}(\alpha^{IV}) = s^2 \left[\frac{1}{n} + \frac{(\bar{X}^0)^2 \Sigma z_i^2}{(\Sigma x_i^0 z_i)^2}\right] \qquad (4.151)$$

$$\text{est. Var}(\beta^{IV}) = s^2 \frac{\Sigma z_i^2}{(\Sigma x_i^0 z_i)^2} \qquad (4.152)$$

where

$$s^2 = \frac{\Sigma(Y_i - \alpha^{IV} - \beta^{IV}X_i^0)^2}{n-2} \qquad (4.153)$$

Example

Now, we illustrate the problem of errors in variables. A true model, unknown to the investigator, is given by

$$Y_i = 2X_i \qquad (4.154)$$

$$X_i^0 = X_i + w_i \qquad (4.155)$$

where X_i^0 is the observed value of X_i and $w_i \sim N(0, 100)$.

Consider the data given in Table 4.9. We suspect the presence of measurement error in observed X_0 and we are fortunate to have available an instrumental variable Z which is strongly correlated with X^0 but is assumed not to be correlated with ϵ^0. The results of estimating the regressions of Y on X^0, X^0 on Y and instrumental variable estimation of Y on Z are presented in Table 4.10.

It will be noted from Table 4.10 that, using both the first and third equations, the investigator would reject the null hypothesis $H_0: \beta = 2$. Instrumental variable estimation is not very successful in this case. However, the inverse least squares estimate of 1.890 (1/0.529) derived from the second equation does give us a value which is not too different from 2.

A formal test for the absence of measurement error has been proposed by Hausman (1978). This test can be employed when an instrumental variable for

Table 4.9 Sample data on Y_i, X_i^0 and Z_i

Y_i	X_i^0	Z_i
104	41.6	18.98
112	72.7	33.63
116	49.5	19.60
122	56.6	23.84
124	52.1	19.58
134	86.8	39.96
140	75.7	32.38
144	58.8	26.71
160	81.9	40.21
170	72.1	31.08
172	97.6	46.53
174	65.3	33.83
180	85.7	36.23
184	88.5	42.43
190	101.8	51.33
190	77.7	35.71
196	103.9	41.52
208	102.0	46.42
220	112.7	50.87
220	125.0	55.10

92   Maximum likelihood methods

Table 4.10 Ordinary least squares and instrumental variable estimation

OLS	$Y_i = 51.290 + 1.389 \, X_i^0$	$R^2 = 0.7346$
	(16.403) (0.197)	$SEE = 19.3065$
OLS	$X_i^0 = -5.784 + 0.529 \, Y_i$	$R^2 = 0.7346$
	(12.496) (0.075)	$SEE = 11.910$
IV	$Y_i = 50.115 + 1.404 \, X_i^0$	
	(16.894) (0.203)	$SEE = 19.309$

Note: standard errors of the regression coefficients are given in parentheses.

X^0 is available. Assume such a variable, Z_i, exists and consider the following auxiliary regression:

$$X_i^0 = \gamma + \delta Z_i + u_i \qquad (4.156)$$

Estimate equation (4.156) by OLS and obtain the predicted values of X_i^0; they are given by

$$\hat{X}_i^0 = \hat{\gamma} + \hat{\delta} Z_i \qquad (4.157)$$

where $\hat{\gamma}$ and $\hat{\delta}$ are the OLS estimators of γ and δ. The least squares residuals from the fitted regression are given by

$$\hat{u}_i = X_i^0 - \hat{X}_i^0 \qquad (4.158)$$

In order to test the null hypothesis of no measurement error $H_0: \sigma_w^2 = 0$ against the alternative hypothesis, $H_a: \sigma_w^2 > 0$, consider the following regression:

$$Y_i = \alpha + \beta \hat{X}_i^0 + \beta \hat{u}_i + \epsilon_i^0 \qquad (4.159)$$

As we have seen above in discussing the instrumental variable approach, the least squares estimator of the coefficient of $\hat{X}_i^0$ is consistent under both the null and alternative hypotheses. Note that since $\hat{x}_i^0 = \hat{\delta} z_i$ and $\text{Cov}(\hat{X}_i^0 \hat{u}_i) = 0$ the OLS estimator of the coefficient of $\hat{X}_i^0$ is given by $\Sigma z_i y_i / \Sigma x_i^0 z_i$. However, it is not generally true that the OLS estimator of $\hat{u}_i$ is consistent since

$$\text{plim}\left(\frac{\Sigma \hat{u}_i \epsilon_i^{0\prime}}{n}\right) = \text{plim}\left(\frac{\Sigma (x_i^0 - \hat{\delta} z_i)(\epsilon_i' - \beta w_i')}{n}\right)$$

$$= -\beta \sigma_w^2 \qquad (4.160)$$

Let the coefficient on $\hat{u}_i$ in equation (4.159) be θ rather than β and substitute $X_i^0 - \hat{u}_i = \hat{X}_i^0$ in the same equation to obtain

$$Y_i = \alpha + \beta X_i^0 + (\theta - \beta)\hat{u}_i + \epsilon_i^0$$

Define $\phi = \theta - \beta$ and let $\hat{\phi}$ be its OLS estimator. It can be shown that plim $\hat{\phi} = -\beta \sigma_w^2 [\sigma_{X^0}^2 - \sigma_{\hat{u}}^2]$, and since $\sigma_{X^0}^2 > \sigma_{\hat{u}}^2$, provided that $\beta \neq 0$, then plim $\hat{\phi} = 0$ if $\sigma_w^2 = 0$. We may therefore test the null hypothesis $H_0: \phi = 0$ by applying the t test. Acceptance of the null hypothesis means that there is no evidence of measurement error in X; note, however, that the test is only valid in large samples.

The results of applying the Hausman test to the data presented earlier in this

Errors in variables

Table 4.11 Testing for measurement error

OLS	$X_i^0 = 7.733 + 2.002\, Z_i$	$R^2 = 0.9390$
	(4.550) (0.120)	$SEE = 5.7122$
OLS	$Y_i = 50.115 + 1.404\, X_i^0 - 0.239\, RES_i$	$R^2 = 0.7359$
	(17.341) (0.209) (0.844)	$SEE = 19.8194$

Note: standard errors of the regression coefficients are given in brackets.

section are presented in Table 4.11. Standard errors of the regression coefficients are given in brackets.

There is a high degree of correlation between X and its instrument Z; but when the residuals from the first equation are included as an explanatory variable in the second equation, they are insignificant. On the basis of the Hausman test we would therefore accept the null hypothesis of no measurement error in X, despite the fact that it is actually present by construction in the data. Note, however, that we have only a small number of observations, twenty in all, and the OLS and IV equations in Table 4.11 yield very similar estimates for the coefficient on X.

An example of an unobservable variable is provided in Friedman's (1957) theory of consumption in which permanent consumption (C_p) is specified to be proportional to permanent income (Y_p):

$$C_p = \beta Y_p \qquad (4.161)$$

However C_p and Y_p are both unobservable variables and Friedman assumed that both observed consumption (C) and observed income (Y) could be decomposed into a permanent and transitory component such that

$$C = C_p + C_T \qquad (4.162)$$

and

$$Y = Y_p + Y_T \qquad (4.163)$$

where C_T represents transitory consumption and Y_t transitory income. The relationship between the observed variables is therefore given by

$$C = \beta(Y - Y_T) + C_T \qquad (4.164)$$

$$= \beta Y + v_t \qquad (4.165)$$

where $v_t = -\beta Y_T + C_T$. This is an example of an errors-in-variables problem. One possible solution to this problem is to postulate a relationship between the unobservable variable, permanent income, and a set of observable variables such as educational attainment, age, value of home, etc. Let these observable variables be represented by $Z_1, Z_2, \ldots, Z_m$ and assume that permanent income is related to these variables in the following way:

$$Y_p = \delta_1 Z_1 + \delta_2 Z_2 + \ldots + \delta_m Z_m \qquad (4.166)$$

Substituting equation (4.166) in equation (4.164) we obtain

$$C = \beta\delta_1 Z_1 + \beta\delta_2 Z_2 + \ldots + \beta\delta_m Z_m + C_T \qquad (4.167)$$

Assuming that transitory consumption possesses the usual properties of the disturbance term in the classical linear regression model and in particular that it is not correlated with the Zs, equation (4.167) can be estimated by OLS. However, such a procedure will not enable us to identify β. In order for this to be possible, a two-step procedure can be adopted. First, the following equation is estimated and in this case transitory income is assumed to possess the usual properties of a stochastic disturbance term:

$$Y = \delta_1 Z_1 + \delta_2 Z_2 + \ldots + \delta_m Z_m + Y_T \qquad (4.168)$$

The predicted values of income, $\hat{Y}$, from the above equation are then substituted for actual income in equation (4.165) to obtain

$$C = \beta\hat{Y} + v_t \qquad (4.169)$$

This equation can then be estimated by OLS and an estimate of β be thereby obtained.

Exercises

1. Comment on the following, either correcting any errors you find or justifying the statement by use of the appropriate theory:

   (a) The Durbin–Watson test for serial correlation is especially useful in a distributed-lag model;
   (b) Instrumental variable estimation is a method of estimation used to give consistent estimates of parameters.

2. What effect on the ordinary least squares estimators does a correlation between an explanatory variable and the disturbance term have in a regression equation?
   Outline the circumstances in which such a correlation might arise and show how the model could be estimated so as to deal with the effects of the correlation.

3. Consider the Koyck (adaptive expectation model) namely:

   $$Y_t = \alpha(1 - \lambda) + \beta_0 X_t + \lambda Y_{t-1} + U_t - \lambda U_{t-1}$$

   Suppose in the original model that U_t follows the first-order autoregressive scheme $U_t - \rho U_{t-1} = \epsilon_t$, where ρ is the coefficient of autocorrelation and where ϵ_t satisfies all the classical assumptions:

   (a) If $\rho = \lambda$, can the Koyck model be estimated by OLS?
   (b) Will the estimates thus obtained be inconsistent? Consistent? Why? Why not?
   (c) How reasonable is it to assume that $\rho = \lambda$?

4. In studying the farm demand for tractors, Griliches used the following model:

   $$T_t^* = X_{1t-1}^{\beta_1} X_{2t-1}^{\beta_2}$$

   where T^* = desired stock of tractors; X_1 = relative price of tractors; X_2 = interest rate. Using the stock-adjustment model, he obtained the following results for the period 1921–57:

$$\log T_t = \text{constant} - 0.218 \log X_{1t-t} - 0.855 \log X_{2t-1} + 0.864 \log T_{t-1}$$
$$\qquad\qquad\qquad (0.051) \qquad\qquad (0.170) \qquad\qquad (0.035)$$

$$R^2 = 0.987$$

where the figures in parentheses are the estimated standard errors.

(a) What is the estimated coefficient of adjustment? Give reasons for the particular value taken by the adjustment coefficient.
(b) What are the short-run and long-run price elasticities?
(c) What are the corresponding interest elasticities?

5. Consider the following errors in the variables model:

$$Y_t = \alpha + \beta X_t + U_t$$

where the measured value of the X_t variable is denoted by X_t^* and

$$X_t^* = X_t + w_t$$

(a) Show how the instrumental variable technique can be used to derive consistent estimators of the parameters of this model?
(b) Consider the reverse OLS regression:

$$X_t^* = \Theta + \tau Y_t + V_t$$

and show that

$$\text{plim } \hat{\tau} = \frac{\beta \sigma_x^2}{\beta^2 \sigma_x^2 + \sigma_u^2}$$

where $\hat{\tau}$ denotes the OLS slope estimate and where σ_x^2 and σ_u^2 denote the variances of X_t and U_t respectively. Discuss the importance of this result.

6. For the monthly data on the Bangladesh money supply and the Dhaka cost of living index, obtain the optimum lags for 'Granger' and 'Geweke' causality tests.

(a) Estimate equations (4.48)–(4.51) to obtain m and n in the respective equations using Hsiao's procedure.
(b) Estimate equations (4.55)–(4.58) to determine m, n and p.
(c) Apply Wald, LR and LM tests to test for 'Granger' and 'Geweke' causality.

	MS1	PDAK
1973:11	7714.89990	240.00000
1973:12	8083.70020	244.30000
1974:1	8101.50000	249.60001
1974:2	8086.00000	259.20001
1974:3	8287.20020	267.20001
1974:4	8273.90039	278.20001
1974:5	8218.59961	284.39999

	MS1	PDAK
1974:6	8167.79980	303.70001
1974:7	8115.39990	316.10001
1974:8	8133.70020	352.39999
1974:9	8208.59961	384.60001
1974:10	8745.59961	416.50000
1974:11	9114.09961	422.60001
1974:12	9576.70020	430.29999
1975:1	9263.59961	458.50000
1975:2	8832.29980	448.00000
1975:3	8916.90039	427.70001
1975:4	7683.29980	416.89999
1975:5	8294.29980	407.79999
1975:6	8408.90039	409.70001
1975:7	7804.39990	414.79999
1975:8	7732.39990	405.89999
1975:9	7923.20020	393.50000
1975:10	8389.09961	391.10001
1975:11	8407.70020	382.10001
1975:12	9661.79980	376.10001
1976:1	9240.79980	374.60001
1976:2	9246.20020	372.00000
1976:3	9060.59961	358.29999
1976:4	8883.20020	360.29999
1976:5	8924.70020	366.79999
1976:6	9526.40039	366.10001
1976:7	9149.09961	371.50000
1976:8	6063.20020	377.89999
1976:9	9798.90039	380.70001
1976:10	9581.09961	380.00000
1976:11	10028.00000	375.39999
1976:12	10722.20020	375.89999
1977:1	9766.20020	373.10001
1977:2	9832.70020	377.89999
1977:3	10092.09961	378.60001
1977:4	10600.79980	391.20001
1977:5	9875.40039	400.00000
1977:6	10262.20020	407.50000
1977:7	10047.79980	420.20001
1977:8	10342.09961	428.89999
1977:9	10865.59961	430.60001
1977:10	10866.29980	430.89999
1977:11	11417.70020	441.29999
1977:12	12562.70020	440.20001
1978:1	12231.70020	447.20001
1978:2	12422.70020	448.00000
1978:3	12081.70020	442.29999
1978:4	11896.40039	452.10001
1978:5	12080.40039	448.70001
1978:6	12759.00000	457.29999
1978:7	12652.59961	461.39999
1978:8	13101.70020	475.39999
1978:9	13753.70020	478.60001
1978:10	13918.09961	489.89999
1978:11	14917.09961	485.79999
1978:12	15847.29980	482.39999
1979:1	14885.90039	479.29999
1979:2	15006.09961	476.39999

	MS1	PDAK
1979:3	14924.20020	480.89999
1979:4	14528.59961	494.20001
1979:5	14485.70020	494.20001
1979:6	15536.40039	522.70001
1979:7	14944.09961	539.29999
1979:8	15673.29980	555.20001
1979:9	15705.90039	561.50000
1979:10	16771.50000	562.40002
1979:11	17013.40039	549.90002
1979:12	17772.69922	549.79999
1980:1	17265.80078	556.90002
1980:2	17135.80078	564.00000
1980:3	17245.69922	571.09998
1980:4	17103.09961	578.29999
1980:5	16995.30078	585.40002
1980:6	18247.09961	592.50000
1980:7	17356.00000	599.59998
1980:8	18010.69922	607.00000
1980:9	18263.00000	617.20001
1980:10	18242.80078	616.59998
1980:11	17991.19922	625.59998
1980:12	19831.90039	622.09998
1981:1	19892.69922	624.09998
1981:2	19245.30078	619.40002
1981:3	19373.80078	621.40002
1981:4	19520.80078	621.40002
1981:5	19590.40039	670.20001
1981:6	20791.80078	670.59998
1981:7	20519.90039	680.90002
1981:8	19932.09961	691.29999
1981:9	20464.19922	692.09998
1981:10	20543.80078	700.79999
1981:11	20690.50000	715.40002
1981:12	22019.90039	710.90002
1982:1	20601.80078	714.79999
1982:2	20672.80078	715.50000
1982:3	20814.90039	722.09998
1982:4	20399.90039	729.09998
1982:5	19319.90039	724.29999
1982:6	21092.40039	709.00000
1982:7	20790.09961	724.50000
1982:8	20367.19922	739.00000
1982:9	21647.19922	757.29999
1982:10	21175.90039	757.20001
1982:11	21937.80078	751.09998
1982:12	24538.59961	746.00000
1983:1	23492.40039	755.79999
1983:2	24117.90039	761.40002
1983:3	23747.30078	759.59998
1983:4	26797.69922	772.20001
1983:5	25438.30078	779.40002
1983:6	27568.19922	791.59998
1983:7	27692.80078	788.50000
1983:8	27904.19922	799.50000
1983:9	29560.40039	808.40002
1983:10	29885.90039	818.09998
1983:11	30380.19922	835.29999

	MS1	PDAK
1983:12	33467.60156	824.70001
1984:1	32501.59961	836.29999
1984:2	32550.09961	832.09998
1984:3	33109.30078	831.79999
1984:4	32949.89844	849.20001
1984:5	31764.80078	873.59998
1984:6	34191.00000	897.70001
1984:7	34669.30078	920.29999
1984:8	35565.00000	918.90002
1984:9	38038.60156	919.09998
1984:10	38609.60156	920.79999
1984:11	39919.60156	920.79999
1984:12	43552.89844	921.00000
1985:1	42904.80078	926.90002
1985:2	41359.69922	934.79999
1985:3	44797.30078	939.59998
1985:4	40126.50000	946.59998
1985:5	38457.69922	953.50000
1985:6	45955.89844	955.90002
1985:7	41447.50000	974.20001
1985:8	43450.00000	973.20001
1985:9	41277.00000	979.40002
1985:10	41244.00000	991.40002
1985:11	43986.00000	1007.79999
1985:12	45951.00000	1020.70001
1986:1	44777.00000	1007.40002
1986:2	45085.00000	1001.70001
1986:3	45863.00000	1013.59998
1986:4	46151.00000	1045.40002
1986:5	46249.00000	1075.19995
1986:6	49274.00000	1082.09998
1986:7	46897.00000	1104.09998
1986:8	49174.00000	1103.19995
1986:9	46600.00000	1104.59998
1986:10	45850.00000	1134.30005
1986:11	45634.00000	1150.90002

7. It was decided to estimate Cagan's hyperinflation demand for the money model using the Bangladesh data on money supply (narrow money) and the Dhaka cost of living index given in question 6. According to this model, the demand for real money balances is inversely related to the expected rate of inflation:

$$\log NM_t - \log P_t = a + b(\log P^*_{t+1} - \log P_t) + \epsilon_t \quad (b < 0) \qquad \text{(A)}$$

Rewritting $\log NM_t - \log P_t = Y_t$ and $\log P^*_{t+1} - \log P_t = \Pi^*_{t+1}$, we obtain

$$Y_t = a + b\Pi^*_{t+1} + U_t$$

Using the adaptive expectation scheme on Π^*_{t+1}, i.e.

$$\Pi^*_{t+1} = \sum_{i=0}^{\infty} (1 - \lambda)\lambda^i \Pi_{t-i},$$

we obtain the estimable equation

where
$$Y_t = a(1 - \lambda) + \lambda Y_{t-1} + b(1 - \lambda)\Pi_t + v_t$$
$$v_t = \epsilon_t - \lambda \epsilon_{t-1}$$
(B)

(a) Estimate (B) using the Zellner–Geisel procedure. If log P_t is an endogenous and log NM_t an exogenous variable, the estimation of (B) by OLS yields biased estimates. This would require normalization of the equation with respect to log P_t. Normalize with respect to log P_t and then estimate the equation.

(b) If

and
$$Y_t = \alpha_0 \Pi_t + \alpha_1 \Pi_{t-1} + \ldots + \alpha_k \Pi_{t-k} + U_t$$
$$\alpha_i = \beta_0 + \beta_1 i + \beta_2 i^2 + \beta_3 i^3$$
(C)

estimate the parameters $\alpha_0, \alpha_1, \ldots, \alpha_k$ and $\beta_0, \beta_1, \beta_2$ and β_3 using the lag length of twelve periods ($k = 12$).

8. Apply the logit model to the information on the poverty and economic development variables of Chapter 2. The dependent variable would be log $[P_i/(1 - P_i)]$ where P_i is poverty index.

   (a) Analyse these results and test for heteroscedasticity.
   (b) Make use of weighted least squares and test various hypotheses between poverty and income growth.

References

Almon, S. (1965), 'The distributed lag between capital appropriations and expenditures', *Econometrica*, **33**, January, 178–96.

Amemiya, T. (1981), 'Qualitative response models: a survey', *Journal of Economic Literature*, **19**, December, 1488–1536.

Bailey, D. (1984), '*Money, Prices and Real Output in Italy: testing for causality*, mimeo.

Brenton, P. and Parikh, A. (1987), 'Price behaviour in European countries: testing the law of one price in the short and long-run at various levels of aggregation', *Applied Economics*, **19**, (11), 1533–59.

Berndt, E.R. and Savin, N.E. (1977), 'Conflict among criteria for testing hypotheses in multivariate regression model', *Econometrica*, **45**, July, 1263–78.

Betancourt, R. and Kelejian, H. (1981), 'Lagged endogenous variables and the Cochrane–Orcutt procedure', *Econometrica*, **49**, 1073–8.

Davidson, J.E.H., Hendry, D.F., Srba, F. and Yeo, S. (1978), 'Econometric modelling of the aggregate time series relationship between consumers' expenditure and income in the United Kingdom', *Economic Journal*, **88**, 661–92.

Finney, D.J. (1971), *Probit Analysis*, 3rd edn Cambridge: Cambridge University Press.

Friedman, M. (1957), *A Theory of the Consumption Function*, Princeton, NJ: Princeton University Press for NBER.

Geweke, J. (1982), 'Measurement of linear dependence and feedback between multiple time series', *Journal of the American Statistical Association*, **77**, (378), 304–13.

Geweke, J., Meese, R. and Dent, W. (1983) 'Comparing alternate tests of causality in temporal systems: analytic results and experimental evidence', *Journal of Econometrics*, **21**, 161–94.

Granger, C.W.J. (1969), 'Investigating causal relations by econometric models and spectral methods,' *Econometrica*, **37**, 24–36.

Greene, W.H. (1981), 'On the asymptotic bias of the ordinary least squares estimator of the tobit model', *Econometrica*, **49**, 505–13.

Hausman, J.A. (1978), 'Specification tests in econometrics', *Econometrica*, **46**, November, 1251–71.

Heckman, J.J. (1979), 'Sample selection bias as a specification error' *Econometrica*, **47**, January, 153–61.

Hsiao, C., (1979), 'Autoregressive modelling of Canadian money and income data', *Journal of American Statistical Association*, **74**, 395–402.

Koyck, L.M. (1954), *Distributed Lags and Investment Analysis*, Amsterdam: North-Holland.

Maddala, G.S. (1983), *Limited Dependent and Qualitative Variables in Econometrics*, Cambridge: Cambridge University Press.

Parikh, A. (1979), 'Estimation of supply functions for coffee', *Applied Economics*, **11**, 43–54.

Parikh, A. (1990), *The Economics of Fertiliser Use in Developing Countries: A Case Study of Bangladesh*, Aldershot: Gower.

Sims, C.A. (1972), 'Money income and causality', *American Economic Review*, **62**, September, 540–52.

Tobin, J., (1958), 'Estimation of relationship for limited dependent variables', *Econometrica*, **26**, January, 24–36.

Zellner, A. and Geisel, M.S. (1970), 'Analysis of distributed lag models with application to consumption function estimation,' *Econometrica*, **38**, 865–88.

Chapter 5
THE GENERALISED LINEAR REGRESSION MODEL

Introduction

In this chapter we relax the assumptions made about the stochastic disturbance term in the classical linear regression model and consider the estimation of a regression equation where the variance–covariance matrix of the disturbances takes a very general form. In Section 5.1 we outline the procedure for estimating the generalised linear regression model. First, we briefly consider the cases where the disturbances are heteroscedastic and, second, where they follow a first-order autoregressive procedure, showing in both cases how the generalised least squares estimators can be derived. We then move on to apply the approach to the estimation of a model in which time-series and cross-sectional observations have been pooled. An example is presented in which generalised least square estimation has been used to obtain estimates of the parameters of a demand function for fertilisers in Bangladesh.

In Section 5.2 we turn to the subject of seemingly unrelated regression in which the stochastic disturbance term is correlated across equations. We discuss Zellner's procedure for estimating such a system of equations and deal, in addition, with the question of imposing cross-equation restrictions on certain parameter values. An illustration of the approach is provided by an empirical study on the demand for inputs in Indian agriculture. Cost-share equations are estimated for a number of different inputs using Zellner's method of seemingly unrelated regression equations (SURE) with cross-equation restrictions.

5.1 GENERALISED LINEAR REGRESSION MODEL

In this section we present a linear regression model for which the assumptions made in the classical linear regression model regarding the disturbance term have been relaxed. Let the model under consideration be

$$Y_i = \beta_1 + \beta_2 X_{2i} + \beta_3 X_{3i} + \ldots \beta_k X_{ki} + u_i$$

for which the following assumptions regarding the disturbance term and the explanatory variables are postulated as follows:

1. The joint distribution of the disturbances is multivariate normal with $E(u_j) = 0$ for all $i = 1, 2, \ldots, n$, and $E(u_i u_j) = \sigma_{ij}$ for all $i, j = 1, 2, \ldots, n$; σ_{ij} is assumed to be finite in all cases.
2. Each explanatory variable is nonstochastic and possesses a finite nonzero variance for any sample size n.
3. The number of observations (n) is greater than the number of explanatory variables including the constant (K).
4. The rank of $X'X$ is K, i.e. we rule out the possibility of perfect collinearity between two or more variables.

In matrix notation we have

$$y = X\beta + u \qquad (5.1)$$

and, given the assumption we have made about $E(u_i u_j)$,

$$E(uu') = \Omega = \begin{bmatrix} \sigma_{11} & \sigma_{12} & \cdots & \sigma_{1n} \\ \sigma_{21} & \sigma_{22} & & \sigma_{2n} \\ \vdots & & & \\ \sigma_{n1} & \sigma_{n2} & & \sigma_{nn} \end{bmatrix} = \text{symmetric} \qquad (5.2)$$

The OLS estimator of β is given by

$$\hat{\beta} = (X'X)^{-1}X'y = \beta + (X'X)^{-1}X'u \qquad (5.3)$$

and is still unbiased since

$$E(\hat{\beta}) = \beta \qquad (5.4)$$

given that $E(X'u) = 0$. Regarding the variance–covariance matrix of $\hat{\beta}$ we have

$$E(\hat{\beta} - \beta)(\hat{\beta} - \beta)' = E(X'X)^{-1}X'uu'X(X'X)^{-1}$$
$$= (X'X)^{-1}X'\Omega X(X'X)^{-1}$$
$$= \sigma^2(X'X)^{-1} \text{ iff } \Omega = \sigma^2 I \qquad (5.5)$$

Hence, invalid inferences will be made in hypotheses testing if the usual formula for the estimated variance–covariance matrix is employed when $\Omega \neq \sigma^2 I$.

It can, however, be shown that (Aitken, 1934–5), for the case where $\Omega \neq \sigma^2 I$, and Ω is known, the best linear unbiased estimator is given by

$$\tilde{\beta} = (X'\Omega^{-1}X)^{-1}(X'\Omega^{-1}y) \qquad (5.6)$$

and the variance–covariance matrix of $\tilde{\beta}$ is given by

$$E(\tilde{\beta} - \beta)(\tilde{\beta} - \beta)' = (X'\Omega^{-1}X)^{-1} \qquad (5.7)$$

The estimator $\tilde{\beta}$ is known as the generalised least squares or Aitken estimator and is in fact equivalent to the maximum likelihood estimator of the generalised linear regression model. For this model the log likelihood function for the y vector is given by

$$L = -\frac{n}{2} \log(2\pi) - \frac{1}{2} \log|\Omega| - \frac{1}{2} (y - X\beta)'\Omega^{-1}(y - X\beta) \qquad (5.8)$$

Differentiating equation (5.8) with respect to β we obtain

$$\frac{\partial L}{\partial \beta} = -\frac{1}{2} (-2X'\Omega^{-1}y + 2X'\Omega^{-1}X\beta) \qquad (5.9)$$

Setting the derivative equal to zero and letting the ML estimator be represented by β^{ML}, after some rearrangement we have

$$\beta^{ML} = (X'\Omega^{-1}X)^{-1}(X'\Omega^{-1}y) \qquad (5.10)$$

Note that the right-hand side of equation (5.10) is identical with that of equation (5.6). In order to be able to apply this formula, the investigator must know the variance–covariance matrix Ω. However, this will rarely, if ever, be the case and the investigator must therefore have to rely on there being available a consistent estimator $\hat{\Omega}$ of Ω which can then be substituted for Ω in equations (5.6) or (5.10), thus enabling the investigator to obtain a consistent estimator of β. This feasible generalised least squares estimator is given by

$$\tilde{\tilde{\beta}} = (X' \hat{\Omega}^{-1} X)^{-1}(X' \hat{\Omega}^{-1} y) \qquad (5.11)$$

and its asymptotic variance–covariance matrix by

$$\text{asympt. Var-Cov}(\tilde{\tilde{\beta}}) = (X' \hat{\Omega}^{-1} X)^{-1} \qquad (5.12)$$

The above estimator possesses the desirable properties of consistency, asymptotic efficiency and of being asymptotically normal. There is, however, one very serious problem: the availability of a consistent estimator of Ω. It is clearly impossible to obtain ML estimators of β and Ω by maximising L of equation (5.8) since this would require us to estimate $k + [n(n + 1)]/2$ unknown parameters from only n observations. The only way forward is to impose some restrictions *ab initio* on the form that Ω can take. It is this question to which we now turn.

Premultiplying equation (5.1) by a transformation matrix T we obtain

$$Ty = TX\beta + Tu \qquad (5.13)$$

and the OLS estimator of β in the above equation is given by

$$\hat{\beta} = [(TX)'TX]^{-1}(TX)'Ty$$
$$= (X'T'TX)^{-1}X'T'Ty \qquad (5.14)$$

Hence, if $T'T = \Omega^{-1}$, then $\hat{\beta}$ is the generalised least squares estimator.

Consider the estimation of a model using observations relating to a sample of firms or households: in this cross-sectional study assume the disturbances are heteroscedastic. Then we have

$$\Omega = \begin{bmatrix} \sigma_1^2 & 0 & \cdots & 0 \\ 0 & \sigma_2^2 & & 0 \\ \vdots & & & \\ 0 & 0 & & \sigma_n^2 \end{bmatrix}$$

If we let

$$T = \begin{bmatrix} \dfrac{1}{\sigma_1} & 0 & \cdots & 0 \\ 0 & \dfrac{1}{\sigma_2} & & 0 \\ \vdots & & & \\ 0 & 0 & & \dfrac{1}{\sigma_n} \end{bmatrix}$$

then $T'T = \Omega^{-1}$.

In order to obtain a consistent estimator of Ω in this case, the procedure is to estimate the model by OLS and then calculate the squared residuals from this regression, $\hat{u}_i^2$. A consistent estimator of σ_i^2 is then provided by s_i^2 where $s_i^2 = \hat{u}_i^2 = (y_i - \hat{\alpha} - \hat{\beta} X_i)^2$ in the simple two-variable case. The generalised least squares estimators can then be obtained by estimating the transformed equation

$$\frac{Y_i}{S_i} = \alpha \frac{1}{S_i} + \beta \frac{X_i}{S_i} + u_i^* \tag{5.15}$$

We now turn to consider a model with first-order serial correlation:

$$Y_t = \alpha + \beta X_t + u_t \tag{5.16}$$

$$u_t = \rho u_{t-1} + \epsilon_t \tag{5.17}$$

with $\epsilon_t \sim IN(0, \sigma^2)$, $E(\epsilon_t u_{t-1}) = 0$, $E(\epsilon_t \epsilon_{t-j}) = 0$ for $j \neq 0$. For this model the variance–covariance matrix of the disturbances is given by

$$\Omega = \frac{\sigma_\epsilon^2}{1-\rho^2} \begin{bmatrix} 1 & \rho & \rho^2 & \cdots & \rho^{n-1} \\ \rho & 1 & \rho & & \rho^{n-2} \\ \rho^2 & \rho & 1 & & \rho^{n-3} \\ \vdots & & & & \\ \rho^{n-1} & \rho^{n-2} & \rho^{n-3} & & 1 \end{bmatrix} \tag{5.18}$$

It can easily be checked that

$$\Omega^{-1} = \frac{1}{\sigma_\epsilon^2} \begin{bmatrix} 1 & -\rho & 0 & \cdots & 0 & 0 & 0 \\ -\rho & 1+\rho^2 & -\rho & & 0 & 0 & 0 \\ 0 & -\rho & 1+\rho^2 & & 0 & 0 & 0 \\ \vdots & & & & & & \\ 0 & 0 & 0 & & -\rho & 1+\rho^2 & -\rho \\ 0 & 0 & 0 & & 0 & -\rho & 1 \end{bmatrix} \quad (5.19)$$

We now define a transformation matrix T_0 which has dimensions $(n-1)$ by n:

$$T_0 = \begin{bmatrix} -\rho & 1 & 0 & \cdots & 0 & 0 & 0 \\ 0 & -\rho & 1 & & 0 & 0 & 0 \\ \vdots & & & & & & \\ 0 & 0 & 0 & & -\rho & 1 & 0 \\ 0 & 0 & 0 & & 0 & -\rho & 1 \end{bmatrix} \quad (5.20)$$

$$T_0' T_0 = \begin{bmatrix} \rho^2 & -\rho & 0 & \cdots & 0 & 0 & 0 \\ -\rho & 1+\rho^2 & -\rho & & 0 & 0 & 0 \\ 0 & -\rho & 1+\rho^2 & & 0 & 0 & 0 \\ \vdots & & & & & & \\ 0 & 0 & 0 & & -\rho & 1+\rho^2 & -\rho \\ 0 & 0 & 0 & & 0 & -\rho & 1 \end{bmatrix} \quad (5.21)$$

Note that there are two minor differences between $T_0'T_0$ and Ω^{-1}; the first element of the former is ρ^2 rather than unity and the latter contains the scalar $1/\sigma_\epsilon^2$; otherwise the two matrices are the same. Using the matrix T_0 to transform the original variables, one obtains the following equation:

$$Y_t - \rho Y_{t-1} = \alpha(1-\rho) + \beta(X_t - \rho X_{t-1}) + \epsilon_t \quad \text{(for } t=2,\ldots,n\text{)} \quad (5.22)$$

with one observation having been lost. A transformation which avoids this is provided by T which differs from T_0 in that it contains an additional first row, the first element of which is $(1-\rho^2)^{1/2}$ and all other elements zero:

$$t = \begin{bmatrix} \sqrt{(1-\rho^2)} & 0 & 0 & \cdots & 0 & 0 & 0 \\ -\rho & 1 & 0 & & 0 & 0 & 0 \\ 0 & -\rho & 1 & & 0 & 0 & 0 \\ \vdots & & & & & & \\ 0 & 0 & 0 & & -\rho & 1 & 0 \\ 0 & 0 & 0 & & 0 & -\rho & 1 \end{bmatrix} \quad (5.23)$$

and
$$T'T = \sigma_\epsilon^2 \Omega^{-1} \tag{5.24}$$

Using this new transformation matrix the original model now becomes

$$\sqrt{(1-\rho^2)}Y_t = \alpha\sqrt{(1-\rho^2)} + \beta\sqrt{(1-\rho^2)}X_t + \sqrt{(1-\rho^2)}u_t \quad \text{(for } t=1\text{)} \tag{5.25}$$

$$Y_t - \rho Y_{t-1} = \alpha(1-\rho) + \beta(X_t - \rho X_{t-1}) + \epsilon_t \quad \text{for } (t=2,\ldots,n) \tag{5.26}$$

with all n observations being utilised.

Employing the transformation T_0, we may write

$$Y_t - \rho Y_{t-1} = \alpha(1-\rho) + \beta(X_t - \rho X_{t-1}) + \epsilon_t \tag{5.27}$$

$$Y_t - \alpha - \beta X_t = \rho(Y_{t-1} - \alpha - \beta X_{t-1}) + \epsilon_t \tag{5.28}$$

The Cochrane-Orcutt procedure for estimating the model with first-order serial correlation is to assume initially that $\rho = 0$ and estimate equation (5.16)' by OLS to obtain estimates of the parameters α and β. These estimates are then used in the second stage to obtain an estimate of ρ by regressing the current residual from the first equation on its lagged value (i.e. equation (5.17) where residuals are used in place of disturbances). The variables are then transformed using this estimate of ρ and new estimates of α and β are obtained. The procedure continues untill the estimates converge. Alternatively, the second transformation, i.e. equations (5.25) and (5.26), may be employed; this is the Prais-Winsten (1954) approach and is more efficient, particularly in small samples, since it uses all the information. The Prais-Winsten approach uses all observations and no information is lost. Since the explanatory variables are nonstochastic and since ϵ_t satisfies all the basic assumptions, the least squares estimators are best linear unbiased estimators.

A particularly rich application of the generalised least squares approach is provided in the estimation of a multiple linear regression model where observations are available for a sample of units, say firms, households or districts, over a number of different time periods, the number of periods being the same for each unit. We have here a pooling of cross-sectional and time-series observations for which we are likely to find a different pattern to the disturbances in the cross-section as compared to the pattern of the disturbances through time for a given unit. For a very general case we could assume not only that the disturbances relating to a particular unit over the whole period under consideration were heteroscedastic and followed a first-order autoregressive process, but also that in the cross-section the disturbances were correlated.

Assume we have data on N units over T time periods, giving us NT observations in total, to enable us to estimate the following model:

$$y = X\beta + u \tag{5.29}$$

where

$$y = \begin{bmatrix} y_{11} \\ y_{12} \\ \vdots \\ y_{1T} \\ y_{21} \\ y_{NT} \end{bmatrix} \quad X = \begin{bmatrix} X_{11,1} & X_{11,2} & \cdots & X_{11,K} \\ X_{12,1} & X_{12,2} & & X_{12,K} \\ \vdots \\ X_{1T,1} & X_{1T,2} & & X_{1T,K} \\ X_{21,1} & X_{21,2} & & X_{21,K} \\ X_{NT,1} & X_{NT,2} & & X_{NT,K} \end{bmatrix}$$

$$\beta = \begin{bmatrix} \beta_1 \\ \beta_2 \\ \vdots \\ \beta_K \end{bmatrix} \quad u = \begin{bmatrix} u_{11} \\ u_{12} \\ \vdots \\ u_{1T} \\ u_{21} \\ \vdots \\ u_{NT} \end{bmatrix} \tag{5.30}$$

Note that $X_{it,j}$ is the value of the jth explanatory variable for the ith unit in time period t and in the usual case $X_{it,1}$ is taken to be unity for all i, t; y_{it} and u_{it} are, respectively, the values of the dependent variable and disturbance term for the ith unit in period t.

Regarding the nature of the variance–covariance matrix Ω, we shall deal with a very general case in which we shall assume that between units the disturbances are heteroscedastic and mutually correlated, while in the time series for a particular unit they follow a first-order autoregressive process. Hence, we assume

$$E(u_{it}^2) = \sigma_{ii} \tag{5.31}$$

$$E(u_{it}u_{jt}) = \sigma_{ij} \tag{5.32}$$

$$u_{it} = \rho_i u_{it-1} + \epsilon_{it} \quad |\rho_i| < 1 \quad \text{(for all } i\text{)} \tag{5.33}$$

where

$$\epsilon_{it} \sim N(0, \phi_{ii})$$

$$E(u_{it-1}\epsilon_{it}) = 0 \tag{5.34}$$

$$E(\epsilon_{it}\epsilon_{jt}) = \phi_{ij} \tag{5.35}$$

$$E(\epsilon_{it}, \epsilon_{js}) = 0 \quad \text{(for } t \neq s\text{)} \tag{5.36}$$

Given the above assumptions, it follows that

$$\sigma_{ii} = \frac{\phi_{ii}}{1 - \rho_i^2} \tag{5.37}$$

and

$$\sigma_{ij} = \frac{\phi_{ij}}{1 - \rho_i \rho_j} \qquad (5.38)$$

If we further assume that $u_i \sim N(0, \sigma_{ii})$, then the variance–covariance matrix Ω, which is of order $NT \times NT$, is given by

$$\Omega = \begin{bmatrix} \sigma_{11} V_{11} & \sigma_{12} V_{12} & \cdots & \sigma_{1N} V_{1N} \\ \sigma_{21} V_{21} & \sigma_{22} V_{22} & & \sigma_{2N} V_{2N} \\ \vdots & & & \\ \sigma_{N1} V_{N1} & \sigma_{N2} V_{N2} & & \sigma_{NN} V_{NN} \end{bmatrix} \qquad (5.39)$$

where

$$V_{ij} = \begin{bmatrix} 1 & \rho_j & \rho_j^2 & \cdots & \rho_j^{T-1} \\ \rho_i & 1 & \rho_j & & \rho_j^{T-2} \\ \rho_i^2 & \rho_i & 1 & & \rho_j^{T-3} \\ \vdots & & & & \\ \rho_i^{T-1} & \rho_i^{T-1} & \rho_i^{T-3} & & 1 \end{bmatrix} \qquad (5.40)$$

In order to obtain the generalised least squares estimators the procedure is first to apply the OLS method to the complete set of observations. The residuals from this regression can then be utilised to obtain consistent estimators of $\rho_1, \rho_2, \ldots, \rho_n$. Note that a consistent estimator of ρ_i is given by

$$\hat{\rho}_i = \frac{\sum_{t=2}^{T} \hat{u}_{it} \hat{u}_{it-1}}{\sum_{t=2}^{T} \hat{u}_{it-1}^2} \quad (i = 1, 2, \ldots, n) \qquad (5.41)$$

where the $\hat{u}_{it}$s are the residuals from the original regression. An alternative consistent estimator is provided by the sample correlation coefficient between $\hat{u}_{it}$ and $\hat{u}_{it-1}$ and, with a small number of observations in the time series, it may be necessary to use this alternative estimator to ensure that the absolute value of $\hat{\rho}_i$ is less than unity. These $\hat{\rho}_i$s can then be employed to transform the original variables in order to enable us to perform a further OLS regression from which the residuals $\hat{\varepsilon}_{it}$ can be obtained. The particular transformations to be adopted are the Prais–Winsten ones and are as follows:

$$Y_{it}^* = \sqrt{(1 - \hat{\rho}_i^2)}\, Y_{it} \quad (\text{for } t = 1) \qquad (5.42)$$

$$Y_{it}^* = Y_{it} - \hat{\rho}_i Y_{it-1} \quad (\text{for } t = 2, 3, \ldots, T) \qquad (5.43)$$

$$X_{it,k}^* = \sqrt{(1 - \hat{\rho}_i^2)} X_{it,k} \quad \left(\text{for } \begin{cases} t = 1 \\ k = 1, 2, \ldots, K \end{cases}\right) \qquad (5.44)$$

$$X_{it,k}^* = X_{it,k} - \hat{\rho}_i X_{it-1,k} \quad \left(\text{for } \begin{cases} t = 2, 3, \ldots, T \\ k = 1, 2, \ldots, K \end{cases}\right) \qquad (5.45)$$

for all four transformations $i = 1, 2, \ldots, N$.

We then estimate

$$y^* = X^*\beta + u^* \tag{5.46}$$

from which consistent estimators of the ϕ_{ij}s can be derived. They are given by

$$\hat{\phi}_{ij} = \frac{\sum_{t=1}^{T} \hat{u}_{it}^* \hat{u}_{jt}^*}{T - K} \tag{5.47}$$

Having thus derived consistent estimators of the ρ_is and ϕ_{ij}s, we have now available all the elements of $\hat{\Omega}$, and equations (5.11) and (5.12) can then be used to obtain the Aitken estimators and the associated asymptotic variance–covariance matrix. Maximum likelihood estimates can be obtained by iteration of the above procedure.

The model we have outlined above is a particularly rich one as far as the specification of Ω is concerned. More straightforward cases would arise, for instance, if we assumed that: the autoregressive parameter was constant across units; the disturbances between units were not correlated; or there was no heteroscedasticity in the cross-section. The degree of generality in the specification of Ω will depend in part on *a priori* information; for instance, mutual correlation of the disturbances is more likely to be present when the units relate to contiguous geographical areas within a particular nation state than to randomly selected firms or households.

If we assume the autoregressive parameter is constant across units, then the estimator $\hat{\rho}$ would be given by

$$\hat{\rho} = \frac{\sum_{i=1}^{N} \sum_{t=2}^{T} \hat{u}_{it} \hat{u}_{it-1}}{\sum_{i=1}^{N} \sum_{t=2}^{T} \hat{u}_{it-1}^2} \tag{5.48}$$

while absence of mutual correlation would imply that the submatrices of Ω equal to $\sigma_{ij} V_{ij}$ $(i \neq j)$ were all null matrices of order $T \times T$. The estimator of Ω is simpler with these restrictions, but the basic approach to obtaining the Aitken estimators is not fundamentally altered.

Example

In a recent study by Parikh (1988), data covering twenty districts in Bangladesh and six years of observations were pooled in order to estimate a demand equation for fertiliser, one of the major objectives of the study being to assess the responsiveness of the demand to changes in the price of fertilisers. Regarding the nature of Ω, it was assumed that the disturbances in the cross-section were heteroscedastic and mutually correlated, but a common serial correlation coefficient for each district was imposed.

The following equation was estimated using the generalised least squares procedure:

$$\log TNCAC_{it} = 0.828\,06 + 0.273\,68 \log ZT4_{it} - 0.016\,06 \log AVY_{i,t-1}$$
$$\qquad\qquad (1.2748) \quad (4.1210) \qquad\qquad (0.1658)$$

$$\qquad - 0.000\,37\, INTEN_{it} + 0.538\,13 \log PRAV_{i,t-1}$$
$$\qquad\qquad (0.2439) \qquad\qquad (5.507\,2)$$

$$+ 0.686\,31 \; \log PRAM_{i,t-1} - 0.886\,18 \; \log FERTPT_t$$
$$(4.0785) \qquad\qquad\qquad (4.6319)$$

$$\hat{\rho} = 0.8572 \tag{5.49}$$

where *TNCAC* represents total nutrients in tons per 1000 acres of cropped area; *ZT4* is high yielding rice acreage as a proportion of total cropped acreage; *INTEN* is an index of cropping intensity; *AVY* is average yield per acre used as a proxy for capital and liquidity constraint; *PRAV* is rice price in aus (monsoon) season in takas per ton; *PRAM* is rice price in aman season in takas per ton; and *FERTPT* is the fertiliser price in takes per ton. Asymptotic *t*- ratios are given in brackets beneath the parameter estimates.

Lagged rice prices in both the aus and aman seasons have a positive significant impact on the demand for fertilisers, as does the area under high yielding rice varieties. The own price elasticity of demand for fertiliser is significantly different from zero and equals -0.886.

Error component and covariance models

Two other approaches to the estimation of models using pooled cross-sectional and time-series data are: (i) the error component model, and (ii) the covariance model. In the error component model the stochastic disturbance term is assumed to consist of three components: one component is associated with a particular cross-sectional unit, the second with time and the final one varies with both unit and time. Each separate component is assumed to possess the properties of the disturbance term in the classical linear regression model, nor are the components correlated with each other. Letting u_{it} represent the disturbance for the *i*th unit at time *t*, we have

$$u_{it} = v_i + w_t + z_{it} \quad (i = 1, 2, \ldots, N; t = 1, 2, \ldots, T). \tag{5.50}$$

with

$$v_i \sim N(0, \sigma_v^2) \tag{5.51}$$

$$w_t \sim N(0, \sigma_w^2) \tag{5.52}$$

$$z_{it} \sim N(0, \sigma_z^2) \tag{5.53}$$

and

$$E(v_i w_t) = E(v_i z_{it}) = E(w_t z_{it}) = 0 \tag{5.54}$$

$$E(v_i v_j) = 0 \quad (i \neq j) \tag{5.55}$$

$$E(w_t w_s) = 0 \quad (t \neq s) \tag{5.56}$$

$$E(z_{it} z_{is}) = E(z_{it} z_{jt}) = E(z_{it} z_{js}) = 0 \quad (i \neq j, t \neq s) \tag{5.57}$$

Given the above assumptions, the disturbance u_{it} is homoscedastic and its variance is given by

$$\text{Var}(u_{it}) = \sigma^2 = \sigma_v^2 + \sigma_w^2 + \sigma_z^2 \tag{5.58}$$

The covariance between the disturbances of two different cross-sectional units at a given point in time, Cov($u_{it}u_{jt}$), is given by σ_w^2, while the covariance between the disturbances of two different points in time for a given cross-sectional unit, Cov($u_{it}u_{is}$), is given by σ_v^2, which is clearly independent of the difference in time between the two observations. Finally, the covariance between the disturbances of two different cross-sectional units at two different points in time, Cov($u_{it}u_{js}$), is zero.

It thus follows that the variance–covariance matrix of the disturbances for the error component model is given by

$$\Omega = \begin{bmatrix} \sigma_v^2 A_T & \sigma_w^2 I_T & \cdots & \sigma_w^2 I_T \\ \sigma_w^2 I_T & \sigma_v^2 A_T & & \sigma_w^2 I_T \\ \vdots & & & \\ \sigma_w^2 I_T & \sigma_w^2 I_T & & \sigma_v^2 A_T \end{bmatrix} \quad (5.59)$$

where

$$A_t = \begin{bmatrix} \frac{\sigma^2}{\sigma_v^2} & 1 & \cdots & 1 \\ 1 & \frac{\sigma^2}{\sigma_v^2} & & 1 \\ \vdots & & & \\ 1 & 1 & & \frac{\sigma^2}{\sigma_v^2} \end{bmatrix} \quad (5.60)$$

where Ω is a matrix of dimensions $NT \times NT$ and A_T a matrix of dimensions $T \times T$.

An alternative version of the error component model suppresses the second component and leads to a simpler Ω in which null submatrices replaces $\sigma_w^2 I_T$ of the three component model, the submatrices along the principal diagonal remaining unchanged at $\sigma_v^2 A_T$. For both cases, consistent estimators of the variances of the separate components of the disturbance term can be derived and the generalised least squares estimators can then be obtained (see Fomby, Hill and Johnson, 1984, pp. 333–6).

In the covariance model, differences between cross-sectional units and between different time periods are allowed for by assuming a separate intercept term for each unit and for each time period. The regression equation thus takes the following form:

$$Y_{it} = \beta_1 + \beta_2 X_{it,2} + \beta_3 X_{it,3} + \ldots + \beta_k X_{it,k} + \gamma_2 D_2 + \gamma_3 D_3 + \ldots + \gamma_N D_N + \delta_2 D_2' \\ + \delta_3 D_3' + \ldots + \delta_t D_t' + u_{it} \quad (5.61)$$

where $D_2, D_3, \ldots, D_N$ are cross-sectional dummies with D_i taking a value of unity for the ith unit and zero for all other units, and $D_2', D_3', \ldots, D_T'$ are time-series dummies with D_T' taking a value of unity for the ith period and zero for all other periods.

In the error component model, the effects of time cross-sectional unit are treated as random, whereas in the covariance model, these effects are fixed by employing time period and cross-sectional dummies (Mundlak, 1978). The disadvantage of the latter approach is the loss of a potentially significant number of degrees of freedom as a result of estimating $N + T - 2$ coefficients on the dummy variables. The alternative approach, however, is not without its problems either; for example, if the disturbance term is correlated with any of the explanatory variables, then the estimated coefficients in the error component model will be biased and inconsistent. In deciding which of the two approaches to adopt, the crucial question to bear in mind is the likelihood of the presence of such a correlation and that will clearly depend upon the particular case under consideration.

Assume we seek to estimate a production function for some industrial good based on observations covering a number of different firms over a period of years. Small firms are less likely to be unionised than large firms and thereby face somewhat lower labour costs; on the other hand, the cost of capital to them is probably higher. In these circumstances it is not implausible that there will be a situation in which a cross-sectional characteristic (firm size) is correlated with one or more explanatory variables (the input of labour services and/or the input of capital services). In chosing which approach to adopt, the investigator may be in the position of having to trade off loss of efficiency against the possibility of biased, inconsistent estimates. It should be noted, however, that specification tests such as the Hausman test, discussed in Chapter 4, are available to test for the existence of correlation between the explanatory variables and the disturbance term.

5.2 SEEMINGLY UNRELATED REGRESSIONS

Assume we seek to estimate the coefficients of a set of M regression equations, where each equation represents the supply function of a particular agricultural product. Observations are available for a particular economy over a number of years. The effects of variations in climatic conditions are reflected in the stochastic disturbance term of each equation. These disturbances are assumed to possess all the properties assumed in the classical linear regression model; in addition, however, we allow for the disturbances to be correlated across equations. These M equations make up a system of seemingly unrelated regression equations (SURE) and the purpose of this section is to consider how to estimate such a system of equations.

We assume that the same number of observations, T, is available for each equation, though we allow the number of explanatory variables including the constant, K_m, to differ between equations. In matrix notation the system of equations can be written as

$$y_m = X_m \beta_m + u_m \quad (m = 1, 2, \ldots, M) \tag{5.62}$$

Regarding the disturbance term we assume

$$E(u_m) = 0 \left.\vphantom{\begin{matrix}a\\b\end{matrix}}\right\} \quad (5.63)$$
$$E(u_m u'_m) = \sigma_m I_T$$

and we also allow for mutual correlation of the disturbance term across equations by assuming

$$E(u_m u'_p) = \sigma_{mp} I_T \quad (5.64)$$

where σ_{mp} measures the covariance of the disturbances of the mth and pth equations and is taken to be constant across all observations.

In the general case the variance–covariance matrix of the disturbances is not known. In his seminal paper on seemingly unrelated regression Zellner (1962) suggested the following procedure for obtaining a consistent estimator of the variance–covariance matrix of the disturbances: estimate each equation by OLS and then calculate the residuals from each equation. An estimator of σ_{mp} is then provided by

$$s_{mp} = \frac{1}{T - K_m} \sum_{t=1}^{T} \hat{u}_{mt} \hat{u}_{pt} \quad (m, p = 1, 2, \ldots M) \quad (5.65)$$

where $K_m \geqslant K_p$. An alternative procedure for obtaining an estimator of s_{mp} is to use T rather than $T - K_m$ as the divisor; this can be justified by appealing to the fact that this change will have no effect on the asymptotic properties of the estimator of β. The estimated variance–covariance matrix of the disturbances is then given by

$$\hat{\Omega} = \begin{bmatrix} s_{11} I_T & s_{12} I_T & \cdots & s_{1M} I_T \\ s_{21} I_T & s_{22} I_T & & s_{2M} I_T \\ \vdots & & & \\ s_{M1} I_T & s_{M2} I_T & & s_{MM} I_T \end{bmatrix} \quad (5.66)$$

The two-stage Aitken estimator is now obtainable as

$$\tilde{\tilde{\beta}} = (X' \hat{\Omega}^{-1} X)^{-1} X' \hat{\Omega}^{-1} y \quad (5.67)$$

with

$$\text{asympt. Var-Cov}(\tilde{\tilde{\beta}}) = (X' \hat{\Omega}^{-1} X)^{-1} \quad (5.68)$$

where X is a matrix of dimensions $MT \times \sum_{m=1}^{M} K_m$ and y is a column vector containing MT elements. The two-stage Aitken estimator of β is asymptotically equivalent to the generalised least squares estimator and therefore to the ML estimator which possesses all the desirable asymptotic properties.

For the case of a system of M seemingly unrelated regressions, McElroy (1977) has shown that a measure of goodness of fit is provided by the following statistic:

$$R^2_{\text{SURE}} = 1 - \frac{\tilde{u}' \hat{\Omega}^{-1} \tilde{u}}{y' \Delta^{-1} y} \quad (5.69)$$

where $\hat{u}$ is the vector of two-stage Aitken residuals

$$\Delta^{-1} = \begin{bmatrix} s_{11}A_T & s_{12}A_T & \cdots & s_{1M}A_T \\ s_{21}A_T & s_{22}A_T & & s_{2M}A_T \\ \vdots & & & \\ s_{M1}A_T & s_{M2}A_T & & s_{MM}A_T \end{bmatrix} \quad (5.70)$$

$$A_T = I_T - (i'i)\frac{1}{T} \quad (5.71)$$

i is a unit column with T elements.

To test for the significance of the goodness of fit for the system of equations the following F test statistic may be calculated:

$$F_{\text{SURE}} = \frac{R^2_{\text{SURE}}}{1 - R^2_{\text{SURE}}} \left(\frac{MT - \sum_{m=1}^{M} K_m}{\sum_{m=1}^{m} K_m - M} \right) \quad (5.72)$$

There will be equivalence between the OLS estimators and the SURE estimators under two sets of circumstances: (i) if $X_m = X_p$ for $m, p = 1, 2, \ldots, M$, and (ii) if $\hat{\Omega}$ of (5.66) is a diagonal matrix. The second possibility can be tested for by performing a likelihood ratio test, having obtained the log likelihood for the cases where $\hat{\Omega}$ is restricted and unrestricted.

Estimation of a system with cross-equation restrictions

We now turn to consider estimation of a system of equations where, in addition to allowing for contemporaneous correlation of the stochastic disturbances across equations, we impose some cross-equation restrictions on the values that can be taken by particular parameters of the model. The rationale for such restrictions will usually be an economic–theoretic one. To clarify the discussion, consider the case of a firm which is a price taker in its input markets and which seeks to minimise the costs of producing a given level of output $\overline{Q}$. Let its production function be given by

$$Q = F(X_1, X_2, \ldots, X_n) \quad (5.73)$$

where Q is output per period and X_i the productive services flowing during the period of the ith factor of production. By minimising

$$\sum_{i=1}^{n} P_i X_i \text{ subject to } \overline{Q} = F(X_1, X_2, \ldots, X_n) \quad (5.74)$$

where P_i is the price of the ith productive service, we obtain the firm's set of input demand functions:

$$X_i = F_i(P_1, P_2, \ldots, P_n, \overline{Q}) \quad (i = 1, 2, \ldots, n) \quad (5.75)$$

Substituting the input demand functions into $\sum_{i=1}^{n} P_i X_i$, we obtain the firm's cost function

Seemingly unrelated regressions

$$C = C(P_1, P_2, \ldots, P_n, \overline{Q}) \tag{5.76}$$

The cost function shows the minimum cost of producing a level of output $\overline{Q}$ for a given set of input prices. A well-known property of the cost function is that its partial derivative with respect to P_i yields the demand function for the ith input (see Shephard, 1970):

$$\frac{\partial C}{\partial P_i} = X_i \tag{5.77}$$

and

$$\frac{\partial C}{\partial P_i} \cdot \frac{P_i}{C} = \frac{P_i X_i}{C} = S_i \tag{5.78}$$

where S_i is the relative share in total cost of the ith input. Naturally, the cost share equations will be functions of the same set of variables as the cost function.

The particular forms taken by the cost function and the associated cost share equations depend crucially upon the form of the underlying production function. Because of its generality, recent work has relied heavily on the transcendental logarithmic production function and the associated translog cost function (see, for example, Christensen, Jorgenson and Lau, 1973). The latter is a second-order approximation to an arbitrary cost function and has the following form:

$$\log C = \alpha_0 + \alpha_Q \log Q + \sum_{i=1}^{n} \alpha_i \log P_i + \frac{1}{2} \gamma_{QQ} (\log Q)^2$$

$$+ \frac{1}{2} \sum_{i=1}^{n} \sum_{j=1}^{n} \gamma_{ij} \log P_i \log P_j + \sum_{i=1}^{n} \gamma_{iQ} \log P_i \log Q + u_i \tag{5.79}$$

This is a nonhomothetic cost function; in a homothetic specification all the terms which are products of output and prices and the square of log Q (i.e. $\gamma_{iQ} = 0$ and $\gamma_{QQ} = 0$) would be suppressed. Differentiating equation (5.79) partially with respect to $\log P_i$ we obtain the cost share equations, assuming that $\gamma_{ij} = \gamma_{ji}$:

$$\frac{\partial \log C}{\partial \log P_i} = S_i = \alpha_i + \sum_{j=1}^{n} \gamma_{ij} \log P_j + \gamma_{iQ} \log Q \quad (i = 1, 2, \ldots, n) \tag{5.80}$$

We now turn to the cross-equation restrictions. Since the cost shares must sum to unity, the following additivity restrictions must be imposed:

$$\sum_{i=1}^{n} \alpha_i = 1, \ \sum_{i=1}^{n} \gamma_{ij} = 0 \quad (j = 1, 2, \ldots, n) \tag{5.81}$$

$$\sum_{i=1}^{n} \gamma_{iQ} = 0 \tag{5.82}$$

Furthermore, since an equiproportional change in all input prices should not affect the cost shares, we also have the homogeneity restrictions

$$\sum_{j=1}^{n} \gamma_{ij} = 0 \quad (i = 1, 2, \ldots, n) \tag{5.83}$$

The final set of restrictions is necessary to ensure symmetry. Note that in the cost-share equation for X_i, the coefficient on log P_j is γ_{ij} and in the cost-share equation for X_j, the coefficient on log P_i is also γ_{ij}. Hence we have a set of restrictions of the form

$$\gamma_{ij} = \gamma_{ji} \tag{5.84}$$

We have a set of n cost-share equations with each equation containing $(n + 2)$ parameters. The imposition of the additivity and homogeneity restrictions reduces the number of equations in the set to $(n - 1)$, with each equation now containing $(n + 1)$ parameters. The cost-share equations with these restrictions now take the form

$$S_i = \alpha_i + \sum_{j=1}^{n-1} \gamma_{ij} \log\left(\frac{P_j}{P_n}\right) + \gamma_{iQ} \log Q \quad (i = 1, 2, \ldots, n - 1) \tag{5.85}$$

The imposition of the symmetry restrictions yields an additional $(n^2 - 3n + 2)/2$ restrictions of the form $\gamma_{ij} = \gamma_{ji}$. In total, when all the above restrictions are taken into account, there will be $(n^2 + 3n - 4)/2$ independent parameters to be estimated. Furthermore, there will be contemporaneous correlation of the disturbances across the cost-share equations. In order to identify the parameters α_0, α_Q and γ_{QQ}, it is necessary to estimate the cost function also; this necessitates the imposition of further cross-equation restrictions. Having applied all the cross-equation restrictions, the above set of equations can then be estimated by applying Zellner's iterative SURE procedure (Zellner, 1963), which is available on many regression packages.

Example

The above procedure was utilised by Parikh (1985) to estimate the parameters of a nonhomothetic translog cost function for Indian agriculture, employing data collected for a stratified random sample of 150 farms in the Muzaffarnagar district of Uttar Pradesh for the year 1968–9. Variability on input prices across farms was large enough to make cross-sectional estimation of the system feasible. The measure of output utilised was the value in rupees of the major crops produced and price data were obtained for eight different inputs; family labour, hired labour, animal labour, major implements, minor implements, fertilisers, manures, and land. Farms were allocated to one of three size categories–(i) small, under 5 hectares; (ii) medium, 5–10 hectares; and (iii) large, over 10 hectares–with estimation of the system of equations performed for each size group.

The result of estimating individual cost-share equations separately, not part of a system, in both an unrestricted form and with the restriction of homogeneity of degree zero in prices imposed, was to support the null hypothesis of zero homogeneity. The additivity and homogeneity restrictions were thus imposed and the cost-share equation for land was taken to be the residual equation. The system was then estimated for the other seven cost-share equations with and without the symmetry restrictions, using the Zellner SURE procedure. To test the validity of the symmetry restrictions, the procedure is to calculate the following statistic which follows a χ^2 distribution:

$$-2 \log \lambda = N[\log |\hat{\Omega}_r| - \log |\hat{\Omega}_u|] \qquad (5.86)$$

where $|\hat{\Omega}_r|$ and $|\hat{\Omega}_u|$ are the absolute values of the determinants of the estimated variance–covariance matrix of the residuals for the restricted and unrestricted models and N is the number of observations of a cross-section sample which is 73 for small farms. The degrees of freedom for the test is the number of parametric restrictions. If the computed χ^2 falls short of the theoretical value, the null hypothesis that the restricted model is the true model is accepted. This is another application of the likelihood ratio test we have discussed in Chapter 4.

The computed χ^2 values for small, medium and large farms were 25.7982, 29.0146 and 59.047 respectively. Since $\chi^2_{0.05}$ for 21 degrees of freedom (the number of symmetry restrictions in the model) is 32.6705, these results suggest that the symmetry restrictions cannot be rejected for the small and medium farms. For the large farms, however, the computed χ^2 exceeds the theoretical value, leading us to reject the null hypothesis that the restricted model is the true model.

The results of estimating the seven cost-share equations for the seventy-three small farms with additivity, homogeneity and symmetry restrictions imposed are presented in Table 5.1. The table also contains the derived coefficients for the land cost-share equation.

We reject the null hypothesis of a homothetic cost function since on the basis of the t-test some of the γ_{iQ} values are significantly different from zero, as is α_Q in the case of the small farms: γ_{QQ} is not significant for either category. A joint test would be better and would reject the null hypothesis in this example. The translog production function collapses on the Cobb–Douglas production function if all $\gamma_{ij} = 0$, $\gamma_{iQ} = 0$ and $\gamma_{QQ} = 0$; hence the estimated results lead us to reject the null hypothesis that the underlying production technology is Cobb–Douglas.

Estimates of the Allen partial elasticities of substitution between pairs of inputs for small- and medium-size firms can be computed from the following formulae, positive values indicating that pairs of inputs are substitutes and negative ones that they are complements:

$$\hat{\sigma}_{ii} = \frac{\hat{\gamma}_{ii} + \hat{S}_i(\hat{S}_i - 1)}{\hat{S}_i^2} \qquad (5.87)$$

$$\hat{\sigma}_{ij} = \frac{\hat{\gamma}_{ij} + \hat{S}_i \hat{S}_j}{\hat{S}_i \hat{S}_j} \quad \text{(for } i \neq j\text{)} \qquad (5.88)$$

where $\hat{S}_i$ measures the estimated mean share of the ith input. Their asymptotic variances are given by

$$\text{Var}(\hat{\sigma}_{ij}) = \frac{\text{Var}(\hat{\gamma}_{ij})}{\hat{S}_i^2 \hat{S}_j^2}$$

Table 5.1 Small farms: estimation of cost shares and cost equation using Zellner's seemingly unrelated procedure with symmetry and cross-equation restrictions (73 observations)

Cost shares	Constant α_i	γ_{i1}	γ_{i2}	γ_{i3}	γ_{i4}	γ_{i5}	γ_{i6}	γ_{i7}	Derived coefficient γ_{i8}	γ_{iQ}
Share of family labour	0.505 20* (0.125 20)	0.06 091* (0.02 59)	−0.001 62 (0.001 00)	−0.052 71* (0.008 12)	0.001 77 (0.001 17)	0.000 48 (0.005 99)	−0.000 39 (0.001 02)	0.000 96 (0.000 59)	−0.009 40	−0.022 36* (0.009 01)
Share of hired labour	−0.082 51 (0.073 13)	−0.001 62 (0.001 00)	0.000 47 (0.000 75)	−0.001 83 (0.002 20)	0.000 66 (0.000 93)	0.000 29 (0.000 78)	−0.000 31 (0.000 80)	0.000 04 (0.000 45)	−0.002 34	0.012 11 (0.007 87)
Share of animal labour	0.878 90* (0.124 00)	−0.052 71* (0.008 12)	−0.001 83 (0.002 20)	0.078 58* (0.018 13)	−0.002 14 (0.001 53)	0.011 75* (0.005 85)	−0.000 58 (0.001 41)	0.000 96 (0.000 83)	−0.034 05	−0.059 22* (0.013 57)
Share of major implements	0.101 79* (0.051 24)	0.001 77 (0.001 17)	0.000 66 (0.000 93)	−0.002 14 (0.001 53)	0.002 91* (0.000 77)	−0.000 12 (0.000 64)	−0.000 54 (0.000 56)	−0.000 58 (0.000 35)	−0.000 19	−0.006 66 (0.005 38)
Share of minor implements	0.100 72 (0.056 03)	0.000 48 (0.005 98)	0.000 29 (0.000 78)	0.011 75* (0.005 85)	−0.000 12 (0.000 64)	0.002 28 (0.005 87)	0.000 07 (0.000 59)	−0.000 42 (0.000 35)	−0.014 34	−0.003 21 (0.004 78)
Share of fertilisers	−0.006 66 (0.048 93)	−0.000 39 (0.001 02)	−0.000 31 (0.000 80)	−0.000 58 (0.001 41)	−0.000 54 (0.000 56)	0.000 07 (0.000 59)	0.002 10* (0.000 62)	−0.000 36 (0.000 30)	−0.000 02	0.005 51 (0.005 16)
Share of manures	0.008 54 (0.027 38)	0.000 96 (0.000 59)	0.000 04 (0.000 45)	0.000 96 (0.000 83)	−0.000 58 (0.000 35)	−0.000 42 (0.000 35)	−0.000 36 (0.000 30)	0.001 59* (0.000 24)	−0.002 19	0.003 32 (0.002 95)
Derived coefficients of share of land	−0.505 95	−0.009 40	−0.002 34	−0.034 05	−0.000 19	−0.014 34	−0.000 02	−0.002 19	+0.060 33	0.070 51

Notes: *Significant at 5% level.
Bracketed figures are standard errors.
Constant of cost equations $\alpha_0 = 2.597\ 79^*$ (1.018 37); $\alpha_Q = 0.506\ 29^*$ (0.103 12).

Table 5.2 Substitutes and complements in Indian agriculture

	Substitutes	Complements
Small farms	Family labour and hired labour Family labour and fertilisers Family labour and manures Hired labour and animal labour Hired labour and major implements Animal labour and major implements Animal labour and minor implements Animal labour and fertilisers Animal labour and manures	
Medium farms	Family labour and animal labour Family labour and fertilisers Hired labour and manures Animal labour and fertilisers Animal labour and manures	Family labour and major implements

The significant findings are summarised in Table 5.2, which shows that complementarities in Indian agriculture are virtually nonexistent.

Own and cross-price elasticities of demand for inputs can be derived using the following formulae:

$$\hat{\eta}_{ii} = \hat{\sigma}_{ii} S_i \quad \text{and} \quad \eta_{ij} = \hat{\sigma}_{ij} S_j$$

and their asymptotic variances are given by

$$\text{Var}(\hat{\eta}_{ii}) = \frac{\text{Var}(\hat{\gamma}_{ii})}{\hat{S}_i^2} \quad \text{and} \quad \text{Var}(\hat{\eta}_{ij}) = \frac{\text{Var}(\hat{\gamma}_{ij})}{\hat{S}_i^2}$$

The demand elasticities naturally have the same sign as the Allen partial elasticities of substitution and many of them are significant, particularly in the small farm category. For a more comprehensive discussion of the results the interested reader is referred to the original paper.

Exercises

1. Consider the model

$$Y_t = \alpha_1 + \alpha_2 X_{2t} + \alpha_3 X_{3t} + U_{1t} \quad \text{in region 1}$$
$$Y_t = \beta_1 + \beta_2 X_{2t} + \beta_3 X_{3t} + U_{2t} \quad \text{in region 2}$$
$$Y_t = \tau_1 + \tau_2 X_{2t} + \tau_3 X_{3t} + U_{3t} \quad \text{in region 3}$$

   where α_i, β_i and τ_i ($i = 1, 2, 3$) are parameters and U_{it} are stochastic disturbances.

   (a) Show how you would test the null hypothesis that $\alpha_3 = \beta_3 = \tau_3$
   (b) Show how you would test the null hypothesis that $\alpha_2 = \alpha_3$.

2. Berndt and Christensen (1973) derived the following cost share equations for equipment, structures and labour inputs from the translog production function:

$$\left.\begin{array}{l}M_1 = \alpha_1 + \tau_{11}\log X_1 + \tau_{12}\log X_2 + \tau_{13}\log X_3 \\ M_2 = \alpha_2 + \tau_{12}\log X_1 + \tau_{22}\log X_2 + \tau_{23}\log X_3 \\ M_3 = \alpha_3 + \tau_{13}\log X_1 + \tau_{23}\log X_2 + \tau_{33}\log X_3\end{array}\right\} \quad (1)$$

where M_1 is the cost share of equipment, M_2 of structures and M_3 of labour, X_1 is an input quantity index of equipment, X_2 of structures and X_3 of labour with 1949 = 1.00 in all three cases.

The cost shares sum to unity at each observation. The estimates of the α_is and τ_{ij}s are denoted by a_i and c_{ij}. Estimation equation-by-equation can yield two different values of some of the parameters. The additivity constraints on the parameters are:

$$\left.\begin{array}{l}a_1 + a_2 + a_3 = 1 \\ c_{11} + c_{12}^2 + c_{13}^3 = 0 \\ c_{12}^1 + c_{22} + c_{23}^3 = 0 \\ c_{13}^1 + c_{23}^2 + c_{33} = 0\end{array}\right\} \quad (2)$$

where the superscript indicates the equation in the system (1) from which the estimate was obtained.

The symmetry restrictions for the problem are:

$$\left.\begin{array}{l}c_{12}^1 = c_{12}^2 \\ c_{13}^1 = c_{13}^3 \\ c_{23}^2 = c_{23}^3\end{array}\right\} \quad (3)$$

Cost shares and input quantity indices

Equipment M_1	Cost shares of Structures M_2	Labour M_3	Equipment X_1	Input quantity indices Structures X_2	Labour X_3
0.0762	0.1114	0.8124	0.6143	1.0365	0.8977
0.0915	0.1034	0.8051	0.6279	1.1010	0.8129
0.0822	0.0947	0.8231	0.6167	1.1056	0.6686
0.0879	0.0837	0.8284	0.5869	1.0642	0.5228
0.1225	0.1055	0.7720	0.5401	1.0016	0.5129
0.0592	0.0618	0.8790	0.5020	0.9634	0.5073
0.0961	0.1032	0.8007	0.4769	0.9277	0.5827
0.0858	0.1037	0.8105	0.4701	0.8885	0.6835
0.0710	0.0970	0.8320	0.4856	0.8681	0.7667
0.0757	0.0918	0.8325	0.5097	0.8744	0.6692
0.0849	0.0892	0.8259	0.5026	0.8486	0.7298
0.0725	0.0852	0.8423	0.5073	0.8320	0.7922
0.0903	0.0712	0.8385	0.5337	0.8381	0.8796
0.0958	0.0563	0.8479	0.5688	0.8734	0.8406
0.0875	0.0690	0.8435	0.5676	0.8460	0.8432
0.0771	0.0731	0.8498	0.5632	0.7990	1.1020
0.0706	0.0593	0.8701	0.5770	0.7603	1.1070
0.1193	0.0421	0.8386	0.6300	0.7661	1.0407
0.1139	0.0677	0.8184	0.7310	0.8888	1.0779

Equipment M_1	Cost shares of Structures M_2	Labour M_3	Equipment X_1	Input quantity indices Structures X_2	Labour X_3
0.0738	0.1019	0.8243	0.8813	0.9530	0.9299
0.0734	0.0850	0.8416	1.0000	1.0000	1.0000
0.1106	0.0565	0.8279	1.0517	1.0170	0.9746
0.1000	0.0722	0.8278	1.0999	1.0163	1.1048
0.1020	0.0595	0.8385	1.1869	1.0494	1.2500
0.0926	0.0622	0.8452	1.2626	1.0747	1.3812
0.0961	0.0786	0.8253	1.3307	1.0967	1.4052
0.0952	0.0725	0.8323	1.3983	1.1142	1.4473
0.0933	0.0580	0.8487	1.4505	1.1374	1.5479
0.0974	0.0622	0.8404	1.5507	1.1789	1.6036
0.1078	0.0745	0.8177	1.6369	1.2258	1.6036
0.1089	0.0756	0.8155	1.6370	1.2499	1.6811
0.1066	0.0651	0.8283	1.6326	1.2456	1.7311
0.1128	0.0623	0.8249	1.6580	1.2535	1.7214
0.1090	0.0580	0.8330	1.6713	1.2582	1.7808
0.1095	0.0594	0.8311	1.7043	1.2594	1.8181
0.0992	0.0625	0.8383	1.7520	1.2688	1.8562
0.1016	0.0642	0.8342	1.8437	1.2827	1.9423
0.1016	0.0630	0.8354	1.9958	1.3215	2.0699
0.1017	0.0571	0.8412	2.1976	1.3846	2.1378
0.1092	0.0586	0.8322	2.3529	1.4398	2.2000

Year	(1)	(2)	(3)	Exogenous variables (4)	(5)	(6)	(7)	(8)	(9)	(10)
1929	121.767	1277.527	0.017 823 3	0.014 726 2	4.512	0.064	11.998	3.522	8.299	887.583
1930	123.077	1306.332	0.019 588 5	0.015 012 6	5.496	0.474	12.597	2.825	7.592	902.591
1931	124.040	1330.199	0.021 381 1	0.015 458 1	5.599	1.228	13.224	1.995	6.884	898.816
1932	124.840	1353.262	0.029 099 1	0.017 002 2	4.397	1.729	12.932	1.275	5.863	882.261
1933	125.579	1376.680	0.042 602 7	0.018 121 6	3.340	2.564	15.126	1.338	5.792	850.107
1934	126.374	1401.461	0.052 602 2	0.018 224 1	4.415	3.312	19.277	1.900	5.432	822.402
1935	127.250	1426.614	0.048 667 2	0.018 455 8	3.934	2.422	20.438	2.060	5.666	804.038
1936	128.053	1452.509	0.047 412 0	0.018 869 2	5.541	2.473	25.182	2.381	5.778	799.169
1937	128.825	1476.617	0.045 715 3	0.019 112 5	4.906	3.134	22.153	3.444	6.356	804.296
1938	129.825	1503.587	0.048 619 1	0.018 132 3	5.469	4.203	25.211	3.315	6.575	816.353
1939	130.870	1530.790	0.046 014 0	0.018 805 5	5.942	4.172	25.041	3.717	6.333	808.577
1940	132.122	1561.180	0.046 557 7	0.019 497 3	5.996	4.605	25.554	5.147	5.868	812.868
1941	133.402	1594.685	0.046 573 5	0.019 420 6	16.970	7.218	30.297	5.420	5.750	828.975
1942	134.860	1628.425	0.040 282 4	0.017 826 9	51.429	19.725	41.945	3.768	4.016	856.479
1943	136.739	1662.762	0.038 658 6	0.016 392 8	77.989	20.335	70.441	3.077	3.695	849.792
1944	138.397	1697.406	0.043 959 2	0.015 707 0	83.435	23.240	81.459	3.421	4.162	832.929
1945	139.928	1729.538	0.051 589 3	0.015 387 0	66.256	17.490	76.427	3.950	6.196	817.655
1946	141.389	1760.075	0.055 507 9	0.014 907 7	6.908	3.455	36.460	6.249	13.303	810.791
1947	144.126	1794.566	0.051 155 6	0.014 207 9	7.356	3.353	28.660	8.966	13.634	849.977
1948	146.631	1830.195	0.050 580 8	0.013 047 1	10.654	6.590	29.390	6.516	11.603	887.333
1949	149.188	1862.762	0.052 830 8	0.013 122 7	14.354	7.616	31.014	6.436	11.683	933.570
1950	152.271	1898.882	0.051 118 2	0.013 891 8	14.988	4.824	32.446	5.559	10.699	963.672
1951	154.878	1930.389	0.048 378 2	0.013 532 9	27.219	8.081	40.823	6.323	13.010	1020.540
1952	157.553	1961.421	0.050 349 4	0.013 039 8	37.097	12.050	44.849	6.641	11.569	1067.793
1953	160.184	1990.193	0.050 843 5	0.013 441 9	38.356	18.032	45.072	6.722	11.088	1099.507
1954	163.026	2022.765	0.047 558 6	0.013 788 3	34.234	12.002	44.578	7.040	11.798	1134.034
1955	165.931	2056.082	0.047 964 3	0.014 447 0	30.933	11.301	44.148	8.031	12.842	1162.602
1956	168.901	2090.245	0.048 223 9	0.014 923 0	32.292	9.586	44.740	9.244	14.949	1213.500
1957	171.984	2126.352	0.047 797 3	0.014 769 3	33.355	11.944	45.882	9.953	16.200	1255.497

					Exogenous variables					
Year	(1)	(2)	(3)	(4)	(5)	(6)	(7)	(8)	(9)	(10)
1958	174.882	2176.213	0.047 222 5	0.014 723 4	35.611	14.377	46.885	8.263	14.804	1287.920
1959	177.820	2234.486	0.048 574 8	0.015 222 1	34.623	15.415	47.785	8.052	15.708	1305.766
1960	180.684	2280.622	0.050 983 1	0.015 792 9	33.410	15.440	49.327	9.803	17.461	1341.361
1961	183.756	2327.080	0.049 541 6	0.016 393 3	36.113	16.746	51.469	9.700	18.322	1373.958
1962	186.656	2372.149	0.049 532 5	0.017 023 0	37.560	20.046	54.005	10.162	19.862	1399.188
1963	189.417	2433.075	0.050 073 7	0.017 258 0	38.958	20.053	55.401	10.778	21.360	1436.691
1964	192.120	2490.964	0.049 395 7	0.017 558 9	37.965	21.298	57.096	12.410	24.139	1477.827
1965	194.593	2548.773	0.047 993 2	0.017 893 9	37.353	23.723	59.101	12.414	25.024	1524.475
1966	196.920	2611.734	0.044 927 3	0.017 711 5	40.343	29.297	64.729	13.592	26.652	1582.329
1967	199.114	2677.764	0.045 504 2	0.017 768 2	45.429	34.624	69.783	14.488	27.608	1646.243
1968	201.152	2745.537	0.048 322 6	0.017 860 1	46.885	39.516	72.765	16.226	29.394	1696.546

(1) US population.
(2) US population of working age.
(3) Effective rate of sales and excise taxation.
(4) Effective rate of property taxation.
(5) Government purchases of durable goods.
(6) Government purchases of nondurable goods and services.
(7) Government purchases of labour services.
(8) Real exports of durable goods.
(9) Real exports of nondurable goods and services.
(10) US tangible capital stock at the end of the previous year.
Source: Berndt, E.R. and L.R. Christensen (1973). The Translog function and the substitution of equipment, structures and labour in US manufacturing, 1926-68, *Journal of Econometrics*, **1** (1), pp. 81-113.

ANSWER THE FOLLOWING:

(a) Do the OLS estimates of (1) differ from the SURE estimates of (1) in the case where there are only additivity restrictions which are satisfied by the data on shares?

(b) Since price data are not available, estimate $\log X_1$, $\log X_2$ and $\log X_3$ by regressing each on the ten exogenous variables which are given above. Having then obtained the predicted values of $\log X_1$, $\log X_2$ and $\log X_3$, use these predicted values to obtain the estimates a_i and c_i by using (i) OLS, and (ii) SURE.

(c) Use the SURE iterative procedure to estimate the model with the symmetry restrictions specified on (3). Then use the likelihood ratio statistic to test the restricted against the unrestricted model.

(d) What advantages, if any, result from just estimating the restricted model and then using the Lagrange multiplier test for the appropriateness of the symmetry restrictions?

3. The data shown below for nineteen districts of Andhra Pradesh over the years 1959-60 to 1974-5 for the groundnut crop were obtained from the Ministry of Food and Agriculture in India.

The specified time-series and cross-sectional relationships are given below:

$$Y_{it} = A_t I_{it}^{\alpha_t} UI_{it}^{\beta_t} F_{it}^{\gamma_t} R_{it}^{\lambda_t} \epsilon_{it} \quad \text{(cross-section, time-specific parameters)} \quad (1)$$

$$i = 1, 2, \ldots, 19$$

$$t = 1, 2, \ldots, 16$$

$$Y_{it} = A_i I_{it}^{\alpha_i} UI_{it}^{\beta_i} F_{it}^{\tau_i} R_{it}^{\lambda_i} V_{it} \quad \text{(time-series, district-specific parameters)} \quad (2)$$

$$i = 1, 2, \ldots, 19$$

$$t = 1, 2, \ldots, 16$$

where

Y_{it} = output of the groundnut crop in district i at time t (in metric tonnes);
A_t = constant at each point of time t;
A_i = constant for each district;
I_{it} = irrigated area under crop ('000 acres);
UI_{it} = unirrigated area in district i at time t derived as a difference between total cropped area for groundnut and the irrigated area for that crop ('000 acres);
F_{it} = chemical fertilisers used in district i at time t defined as total nutrients of nitrogen, phosphorus and potash in tonnes;
R_{it} = rainfall for district i at time t (in millimeters);
ϵ_{it}, V_{it} = unobserved error terms, one for each cross-section and the other for time-series model;
A_t, α_t, β_t, τ_t, λ_t and A_i, α_i, β_i and λ_i are, respectively, time- and district-specific parameters.

District	Year	Production	Irrigated area ('000 acres)	Unirrigated area ('000 acres)	Chemical fertilisers (tonnes)	Rainfall (mms)
Srikakulam	59–60	30 041.35	2305.08	28 389.66	1464.06	1063.96
	60–61	30 102.39	5908.22	24 850.43	793.03	1065.96
	61–62	34 387.55	395.02	37 416.62	1750.07	876.97
	62–63	39 881.98	1.00	38 606.67	2738.10	1487.94
	63–64	40 278.77	25.00	50 114.74	2962.12	955.96
	64–65	65 500.95	11.00	58 571.90	4292.18	1089.95
	65–66	39 710.06	12.00	45 960.63	2654.10	716.97
	66–67	73 223.37	1.00	51 962.65	7476.28	877.97
	67–68	57 583.99	1.00	66 693.34	4123.18	838.97
	68–69	60 528.52	1.00	65 559.96	3762.17	1193.95
	69–70	74 442.32	349.01	68 368.02	5575.24	1191.95
	70–71	83 162.34	335.01	66 866.30	7464.32	994.96
	71–72	81 663.29	126.00	70 074.93	5772.21	782.97
	72–73	60 172.45	56.00	68 945.42	6731.28	995.96
	73–74	75 865.70	1002.03	57 698.73	8456.33	675.97
	74–75	84 461.40	2043.07	77 157.99	10 042.39	789.97
Vishakhapatnam	59–60	41 191.64	9479.71	32 591.26	1395.06	1037.03
	60–61	31 030.65	496.98	34 811.37	1152.05	815.02
	61–62	23 044.46	510.98	30 900.24	1549.05	1117.03
	62–63	22 312.46	260.99	27 740.24	2819.12	1183.03
	63–64	32 971.56	1243.97	39 782.38	1617.07	1165.03
	64–65	38 997.80	1188.97	40 629.08	5384.23	1011.03
	65–66	26 824.49	234.99	33 354.21	3708.15	849.02
	66–67	46 027.79	255.99	44 543.40	4826.18	825.02
	67–68	29 160.51	249.99	48 029.44	3587.14	783.02
	68–69	24 690.42	249.99	47 260.46	3366.13	852.02
	69–70	36 273.42	5.00	55 518.38	5015.21	1055.03

District	Year	Production	Irrigated area ('000 acres)	Unirrigated area ('000 acres)	Chemical fertilisers (tonnes)	Rainfall (mms)
E. Godavari	70-71	43 200.64	1.00	55 000.05	8154.29	1281.04
	71-72	59 501.13	281.99	56 318.56	6107.24	774.02
	72-73	54 600.62	65.00	58 635.13	4364.15	754.02
	73-74	68 001.20	126.00	60 174.22	7424.27	605.02
	74-75	62 601.25	988.97	61 811.17	7570.31	877.02
	59-60	2845.03	1621.07	1212.95	3892.18	1640.99
	60-61	5314.50	1262.05	4029.83	3104.15	801.00
	61-62	3282.04	1819.07	3106.87	6969.34	1157.99
	62-63	3810.06	2164.08	2891.87	7480.36	1498.99
	63-64	5771.05	1308.05	4878.83	9316.44	933.00
	64-65	6673.10	1217.04	6405.74	10 953.52	1144.00
	65-66	6503.07	590.02	7341.73	11 119.50	648.99
	66-67	7722.08	1111.05	6739.76	17 568.91	1080.00
	67-68	13 919.13	1000.04	15 914.41	17 950.91	677.00
	68-69	8230.06	1000.04	8387.69	24 576.25	713.99
	69-70	10 161.07	210.01	12 658.45	25 521.23	1092.99
	70-71	6300.09	206.01	7893.70	19 678.97	1388.99
	71-72	9700.08	399.02	10 600.54	19 439.96	796.99
	72-73	6900.09	319.01	8680.64	24 170.20	1014.99
	73-74	9300.09	1355.06	7644.72	23 738.08	949.00
	74-75	11 200.11	1373.05	9726.60	11 396.55	1025.99
W. Godavari	59-60	7823.91	4872.24	2463.04	5505.86	1305.00
	60-61	8168.90	4801.24	2855.04	4614.91	1112.00
	61-62	9692.90	7460.36	3376.04	8093.83	1309.00
	62-63	6939.95	5415.28	3299.02	12 396.73	1283.00
	63-64	5536.95	3186.15	2757.03	21 789.59	1040.00
	64-65	8723.88	3468.16	3699.04	20 260.49	1219.00
	65-66	3149.97	4039.19	1020.01	11 746.70	765.00
	66-67	6705.94	5405.27	1353.01	23 438.56	1035.99
	67-68	9854.85	6000.33	5007.04	23 837.56	949.00
	68-69	9753.87	6500.34	4507.06	37 900.81	912.00
	69-70	8635.87	2215.11	6607.10	41 904.05	1462.99
	70-71	5899.95	2102.09	4498.05	29 924.35	1280.00
	71-72	4899.95	2712.13	2788.03	29 875.31	793.99
	72-73	6499.95	2051.10	4449.02	27 613.44	1021.00
	73-74	7999.94	3626.19	3274.04	23 112.47	883.00
	74-75	11 799.94	5229.28	4771.04	32 994.22	726.00
Krishna	59-60	28 156.40	4820.87	21 565.29	6170.16	1164.30
	60-61	17 222.81	3474.89	12 668.71	8734.27	921.03
	61-62	17 923.89	6403.81	15 566.71	7611.22	1273.03
	62-63	21 877.19	6126.81	25 894.61	12 236.39	1600.05
	63-64	21 694.19	5283.90	19 880.61	15 047.38	782.02
	64-65	21 213.01	5529.81	22 218.49	15 492.47	1079.03
	65-66	15 139.01	5942.88	20 725.71	11 553.33	760.02
	66-67	19 305.97	8360.80	22 435.51	15 422.45	1207.03
	67-68	26 621.38	7999.78	26 640.56	29 316.02	677.02
	68-69	20 525.02	7999.78	21 217.68	39 476.05	1147.04
	69-70	21 541.14	4297.89	27 226.34	45 576.13	544.02
	70-71	29 101.35	4724.84	29 874.49	28 127.96	1006.03
	71-72	26 101.29	7033.85	25 765.46	30 913.84	578.01
	72-73	17 000.87	4534.90	23 164.59	32 442.01	787.02
	73-74	38 001.84	7575.84	23 123.63	20 460.66	959.03
	74-75	31 201.45	7274.85	29 224.43	16 455.57	748.02
Guntur	59-60	32 189.33	2856.01	29 193.43	5767.87	634.00
	60-61	33 835.31	2856.01	30 833.56	5610.86	753.01
	61-62	29 436.20	3427.00	29 507.47	9675.76	879.00

District	Year	Production	Irrigated area ('000 acres)	Unirrigated area ('000 acres)	Chemical fertilisers (tonnes)	Rainfall (mms)
	62-63	36 721.23	599.00	43 020.79	20 162.48	740.00
	63-64	18 167.70	516.00	32 046.68	23 685.51	829.00
	64-65	23 008.99	85.00	27 656.30	19 777.67	757.00
	65-66	6096.26	378.00	30 298.36	12 939.74	496.00
	66-67	26 215.09	1175.00	26 992.35	19 465.49	581.00
	67-68	24 690.91	1000.01	40 926.74	28 559.32	535.00
	68-69	40 541.46	1000.01	39 064.87	42 204.78	565.00
	69-70	45 622.69	32 829.11	14 641.70	53 578.80	544.00
	70-71	55 201.77	36 526.05	15 674.79	50 819.67	786.01
	71-72	57 802.10	37 494.93	22 006.19	43 234.70	530.00
	72-73	24 000.99	10 774.00	16 326.73	37 407.96	595.00
	73-74	39 701.35	13 286.99	24 614.20	25 668.47	612.00
	74-75	40 801.35	20 485.06	20 316.10	41 656.75	615.00
Nellore	59-60	8240.21	3025.07	5175.80	1271.97	658.99
	60-61	9642.17	2962.06	6637.76	1462.95	1480.98
	61-62	14 824.28	3099.05	13 468.50	1864.95	1384.99
	62-63	14 672.37	2161.05	16 661.39	3075.92	1275.99
	63-64	9439.25	2406.05	9165.66	5561.81	992.99
	64-65	6459.14	1334.03	10 771.61	5444.82	886.99
	65-66	1727.04	4619.08	4092.86	3027.92	939.99
	66-67	13 209.24	13 395.32	1.00	4616.86	1557.99
	67-68	19 914.47	13 000.21	11 603.58	8763.75	855.99
	68-69	6096.14	6000.15	3063.89	9014.77	724.99
	69-70	16 257.37	8343.19	6670.76	10 169.72	1596.98
	70-71	9500.23	143.00	9656.62	15 194.51	725.99
	71-72	18 800.37	9915.16	6784.73	12 476.59	953.99
	72-73	12 100.25	7585.17	3214.86	11 372.68	1275.99
	73-74	19 800.48	14 341.33	658.97	13 084.58	717.99
	74-75	31 000.59	14 001.23	10 498.62	12 373.59	507.99
Kurnool	59-60	138 760.29	5266.87	132 894.02	1212.03	607.03
	60-61	155 393.08	13 258.59	151 781.50	1428.04	718.03
	61-62	54 235.62	19 007.54	120 336.50	1891.04	864.04
	62-63	88 841.86	16 173.53	121 989.14	3146.07	732.03
	63-64	110 840.02	17 541.44	124 334.06	5973.09	679.03
	64-65	158 432.39	18 342.41	164 273.38	6491.12	944.05
	65-66	103 126.66	25 924.18	172 809.87	5157.10	701.03
	66-67	154 843.96	45 895.45	167 890.50	5447.11	607.03
	67-68	166 528.74	49 998.15	209 839.30	13 321.31	476.02
	68-69	136 351.75	39 998.66	162 294.40	29 828.52	627.03
	69-70	122 330.69	29 859.29	182 064.68	22 600.57	670.03
	70-71	137 096.89	43 393.34	191 095.25	26 419.57	740.03
	71-72	153 797.67	37 139.68	203 751.68	16 506.35	587.02
	72-73	125 998.24	31 429.15	197 860.45	22 641.51	347.02
	73-74	158 898.86	39 222.71	148 071.01	21 390.46	542.03
	74-75	177 297.29	38 826.61	168 863.72	17 820.42	710.03
Cudappa	59-60	67 667.41	2629.92	69 245.97	1137.02	499.98
	60-61	58 604.69	4965.85	57 282.49	1250.03	930.97
	61-62	44 907.94	2814.92	74 475.11	1943.04	783.97
	62-63	53 666.81	6834.78	85 835.69	2568.04	908.97
	63-64	81 424.38	5017.86	97 018.82	2922.05	738.97
	64-65	66 554.07	4001.88	109 102.19	2746.05	822.97
	65-66	211 229.40	4892.85	99 554.47	2354.04	528.98
	66-67	93 270.58	9021.71	90 407.29	2377.03	983.97
	67-68	137 265.19	9999.69	135 360.95	6400.10	994.96
	68-69	93 371.37	9999.69	102 824.63	18 078.33	611.98
	69-70	107 190.19	8526.72	134 730.29	8220.19	824.97

District	Year	Production	Irrigated area ('000 acres)	Unirrigated area ('000 acres)	Chemical fertilisers (tonnes)	Rainfall (mms)
Chitoor	70–71	90 097.71	11 824.63	139 026.55	9716.19	853.97
	71–72	77 698.40	10 219.67	133 973.89	11 298.20	540.98
	72–73	57 098.32	6796.82	79 302.13	8979.14	725.97
	73–74	133 696.82	12 032.66	119 765.41	10 515.22	781.97
	74–75	135 396.12	8077.76	128 720.70	7771.12	689.97
	59–60	97 935.99	8417.18	95 602.34	1025.01	480.01
	60–61	105 079.17	12 193.28	99 407.48	969.01	611.02
	61–62	106 348.78	11 468.28	95 777.46	1233.02	654.02
	62–63	106 258.42	11 049.28	114 168.72	1850.02	910.03
	63–64	149 876.87	17 539.31	138 130.28	2471.03	611.02
	64–65	179 044.45	13 453.31	134 865.41	3575.03	796.02
	65–66	82 197.43	16 687.42	121 833.74	2773.01	441.01
	66–67	149 661.20	21 682.49	105 469.03	6288.07	1208.03
	67–68	201 480.80	25 000.48	146 827.34	6776.05	808.02
	68–69	146 614.12	25 000.48	120 683.01	6819.08	474.01
	69–70	186 746.88	20 624.40	161 279.25	7740.10	750.02
	70–71	248 395.96	29 534.67	173 463.52	9346.06	859.02
	71–72	261 696.15	30 837.60	179 161.44	6012.04	833.02
	72–73	247 399.41	28 522.55	174 278.98	10 762.15	897.03
	73–74	295 797.20	32 983.74	198 712.16	10 667.11	739.02
	74–75	275 694.70	25 688.54	211 206.71	10 141.08	638.02
Hyderabad	59–60	1818.92	1.00	4425.99	541.01	998.96
	60–61	1442.94	2.00	3389.00	474.01	726.98
	61–62	3575.86	126.00	2962.00	366.00	863.97
	62–63	2407.90	93.00	3644.99	1615.02	1152.96
	63–64	3037.90	94.00	3916.99	2094.02	849.97
	64–65	3721.87	184.00	5044.99	1031.01	647.98
	65–66	4063.87	249.00	6265.98	1587.01	793.97
	66–67	2641.89	505.01	6375.00	1853.02	965.96
	67–68	4368.83	600.01	6643.01	5895.06	838.97
	68–69	3859.84	600.01	6643.01	9281.14	713.97
	69–70	4978.83	345.00	7100.99	7630.05	646.98
	70–71	5199.77	1325.02	5975.00	9638.10	1122.96
	71–72	5699.77	296.00	10 904.05	9269.08	538.98
	72–73	5999.79	188.00	9011.98	8642.09	467.98
	73–74	4999.79	1620.02	5080.02	8254.05	908.97
	74–75	7999.71	2386.02	7214.01	4142.02	792.97
Nizamabad	59–60	3607.03	76.00	5414.25	3455.87	1124.03
	60–61	4217.04	72.00	6298.33	3909.83	976.03
	61–62	7935.08	208.00	9305.49	4391.82	1136.04
	62–63	9663.10	524.00	8528.42	8778.67	1192.04
	63–64	5192.03	561.00	6279.34	8084.71	1194.03
	64–65	6067.06	1404.01	5616.31	1400.94	864.02
	65–66	4752.04	186.00	7098.36	8027.99	1088.04
	66–67	3455.04	1358.01	7545.37	9537.63	966.03
	67–68	5791.05	1500.01	7726.41	14 924.36	781.02
	68–69	4673.06	1500.01	6755.35	18 188.23	721.02
	69–70	5283.05	580.00	7473.36	19 814.12	1053.03
	70–71	6800.08	1765.02	7735.38	22 474.13	1287.04
	71–72	5800.04	2093.01	9607.50	19 316.21	482.01
	72–73	5200.03	69.00	12 831.64	13 355.45	641.02
	73–74	7900.09	556.00	9444.52	7458.73	1241.03
	74–75	9100.09	1.00	12 000.57	12 358.51	977.03
Medak	59–60	1788.03	1.00	3500.08	692.99	1203.94
	60–61	1595.05	1.00	3094.06	468.99	718.97
	61–62	4471.14	1.00	3857.14	697.99	1093.96

District	Year	Production	Irrigated area ('000 acres)	Unirrigated area ('000 acres)	Chemical fertilisers (tonnes)	Rainfall (mms)
	62–63	2011.06	1.00	4319.09	1171.99	1258.94
	63–64	2652.08	4.00	5207.11	1579.98	986.96
	64–65	3012.09	7.00	4224.10	1850.98	902.96
	65–66	3251.10	47.00	5214.09	2251.97	1003.96
	66–67	1930.06	199.01	4900.10	3542.97	864.96
	67–68	4572.10	200.01	7489.15	4069.96	982.96
	68–69	3962.10	200.01	7286.15	4399.95	692.97
	69–70	6300.21	47.00	9463.15	5799.92	775.97
	70–71	6600.22	369.01	8831.24	5435.95	1156.96
	71–72	4300.12	170.01	9230.15	3475.97	698.97
	72–73	3100.10	25.00	8175.20	1568.98	468.98
	73–74	6300.21	278.01	7522.17	2552.99	1168.95
	74–75	4600.12	596.02	5604.14	5303.96	983.96
Mehbob-nagar	59–60	29 740.66	472.02	109 044.35	776.99	1005.01
	60–61	25 472.64	1350.05	97 047.90	955.99	893.01
	61–62	35 480.57	3560.15	100 291.87	574.99	1258.01
	62–63	47 663.94	7024.29	121 039.22	1276.99	840.01
	63–64	41 231.61	3169.12	106 961.04	1454.98	864.01
	64–65	61 001.30	6031.25	104 285.74	6109.92	1299.01
	65–66	558 846.64	9559.39	86 416.16	1747.99	722.01
	66–67	30 075.63	14 968.59	86 523.38	2452.98	842.01
	67–68	66 653.34	15 000.66	89 800.87	7163.90	902.01
	68–69	53 953.10	12 000.45	83 975.46	6838.95	703.01
	69–70	76 306.27	13 991.56	102 720.80	5824.91	842.01
	70–71	91 601.27	73 645.57	75 657.36	8259.91	990.01
	71–72	57 200.64	19 010.74	137 090.96	5793.95	586.01
	72–73	43 300.54	16 342.58	131 359.08	8773.92	517.00
	73–74	78 101.17	25 858.10	80 343.78	7111.93	882.01
	74–75	113 301.80	22 815.82	108 285.87	9748.90	911.01
Nalgonda	59–60	13 320.36	33.00	41 038.21	189.00	703.01
	60–61	11 359.38	383.01	34 556.77	351.00	702.00
	61–62	29 577.80	1649.01	33 443.71	363.00	827.00
	62–63	19 203.53	530.01	40 764.17	881.00	876.01
	63–64	37 524.12	556.01	51 344.28	1276.01	715.01
	64–65	45 957.36	2096.03	60 216.33	1858.01	770.01
	65–66	37 289.96	2504.01	66 373.22	1822.00	532.00
	66–67	39 322.00	3310.02	62 693.24	2729.00	658.01
	67–68	44 097.10	3500.04	66 306.88	4548.99	691.01
	68–69	35 257.00	4000.04	69 893.57	4944.01	754.01
	69–70	43 284.91	7090.06	72 025.02	7350.04	761.01
	70–71	77 702.24	23 273.22	66 625.91	8957.00	736.01
	71–72	55 701.33	25 590.30	68 508.90	6225.02	549.01
	72–73	35 501.11	9194.11	73 405.11	8595.05	470.00
	73–74	40 300.91	15 639.09	36 360.52	11 831.98	796.01
	74–75	43 001.03	25 486.10	31 913.64	11 554.97	722.01
Warangal	59–60	9490.14	462.99	16 873.30	479.00	1418.98
	60–61	4948.10	229.99	8784.18	1192.05	777.99
	61–62	9348.20	91.00	8399.17	782.03	1384.98
	62–63	9124.14	1850.94	10 786.25	1245.05	1039.98
	63–64	12 589.25	1868.94	16 267.23	2081.08	715.99
	64–65	18 911.37	5278.83	20 518.41	3692.14	944.98
	65–66	14 936.28	4881.85	18 994.37	2977.12	751.99
	66–67	8738.19	9371.69	15 031.27	3140.13	1205.97
	67–68	28 144.54	9999.69	28 566.44	6323.26	881.98
	68–69	26 518.52	9999.69	26 907.43	8305.31	819.98
	69–70	27 129.55	14 074.64	25 584.39	10 630.48	1254.98

District	Year	Production	Irrigated area ('000 acres)	Unirrigated area ('000 acres)	Chemical fertilisers (tonnes)	Rainfall (mms)
	70–71	41 000.46	16 193.56	32 106.63	13 166.49	912.99
	71–72	33 700.52	12 663.62	37 936.45	11 818.46	721.99
	72–73	38 900.75	8619.73	39 980.52	7870.29	547.99
	73–74	41 100.63	19 539.41	21 260.32	7718.31	883.99
	74–75	49 000.64	12 819.58	36 180.58	7698.34	716.99
Khamman	59–60	2884.94	261.01	4647.25	371.01	1284.97
	60–61	3037.96	323.01	4792.23	672.01	851.98
	61–62	13 594.77	2893.06	8830.46	450.01	1279.98
	62–63	9977.82	1872.04	11 942.66	759.01	1258.97
	63–64	14 549.77	4128.10	16 034.88	969.01	985.98
	64–65	20 198.63	6925.13	21 456.05	2045.03	982.98
	65–66	16 865.75	1595.04	23 092.24	2022.03	914.98
	66–67	8839.81	2461.05	20 000.09	2203.05	941.98
	67–68	26 924.45	3000.07	27 028.36	2543.05	1044.98
	68–69	22 860.60	3000.07	26 664.33	3463.06	1206.97
	69–70	32 208.32	9994.21	30 799.75	4700.10	1489.97
	70–71	19 699.53	3458.09	25 443.41	8060.16	1292.97
	71–72	27 099.49	3730.07	30 871.60	7925.16	759.98
	72–73	18 599.69	1704.03	31 897.79	6767.10	728.98
	73–74	27 099.49	5542.12	23 459.29	7461.18	968.97
	74–75	20 799.62	8652.22	23 349.29	7811.16	1030.97
Karimnagar	59–60	6481.80	2.00	13 475.78	660.97	1126.03
	60–61	4175.89	5.00	8668.83	904.96	764.02
	61–62	6075.83	1.00	7784.81	887.96	1445.02
	62–63	7802.76	155.00	8928.82	1736.94	1324.02
	63–64	6888.81	486.99	9022.79	2283.90	1196.03
	64–65	9070.78	1060.98	12 844.74	4724.80	681.01
	65–66	10 566.70	1780.97	14 163.72	2268.90	997.02
	66–67	14 833.64	2428.94	21 042.50	4584.84	1321.02
	67–68	20 320.45	2799.96	25 486.38	6941.76	1064.02
	68–69	16 662.62	2499.96	20 485.64	8154.70	755.02
	69–70	15 646.67	2804.95	22 042.54	6114.76	1207.02
	70–71	23 599.32	1.00	29 299.31	12 412.51	1003.02
	71–72	20 599.52	4600.92	23 898.46	8873.64	582.01
	72–73	14 999.66	2651.95	24 247.51	5895.77	691.01
	73–74	29 199.10	7489.83	21 509.49	8990.65	1653.04
	74–75	33 599.05	3616.93	387 371.46	16 418.27	1037.05
Adilabad	59–60	1209.04	1.00	3426.11	167.01	1326.02
	60–61	894.03	7.00	2579.00	244.01	932.01
	61–62	1870.10	1.00	5750.20	190.01	1231.02
	62–63	3211.10	1.00	6900.23	172.01	1044.02
	63–64	3546.12	8.00	6940.23	419.02	1316.02
	64–65	4217.12	16.99	5907.16	695.03	974.02
	65–66	4471.14	17.99	5890.17	1075.06	842.01
	66–67	4877.16	17.99	12 608.42	830.05	1043.02
	67–68	6502.22	19.99	11 027.31	2122.10	1052.02
	68–69	5791.16	19.99	11 149.39	2751.14	722.02
	69–70	7417.21	18.99	11 069.29	1930.11	960.01
	70–71	10 100.28	32.98	14 167.42	2583.14	970.02
	71–72	7200.23	1.00	15 700.54	652.03	577.01
	72–73	5600.15	1.00	15 200.45	1667.09	615.01
	73–74	15 000.50	24.99	19 075.50	2538.13	1223.02
	74–75	13 100.41	8.00	18 292.57	4047.21	931.02

ANSWER THE FOLLOWING QUESTIONS:
(a) For each time period, using the data on nineteen districts, estimate a cross-sectional relationship, i.e. sixteen regression equations.
(b) For each district, using sixteen years' data, estimate a time-series relationship, i.e. nineteen regression equations.
(c) Obtain the averaged data over sixteen years for each district and estimate a long-run relationship using the averaged data.
(d) Pool the entire set of data ($19 \times 16 = 304$) and estimate a regression equation by ordinary least squares (a) without district and time dummies; (b) with district dummies; (c) with time dummies; and (d) with both district and time dummies, and test the hypothesis that district and time effects are not significant.
(e) Arrange the data by time, i.e. nineteen districts in period 1, nineteen districts in period 2, and similarly for period 16, and apply the SURE procedure for estimating the parameters of the model. If the data are stacked in an alternative form, i.e. by districts, can the SURE procedure be used?
(f) It is suggested that the data can be pooled over time and districts and stacked up by districts (i.e. district 1, sixteen observations, and so on). Assuming equations (5.31)–(5.36) and (5.48), estimate the parameters using the pooled data.
(g) What are the advantages and disadvantages of the pooled estimates obtained in your answer to (6) compared to the OLS estimates using the pooled data in (3) and (4)?

References

Aitken, A.C. (1934–5), 'On least squares and linear combinations of observations', *Proceedings of the Royal Society of Edinburgh*, **55**, 42–8.

Berndt, E.R. and Christensen, L.R. (1973) 'The translog function and the substitution of equipment structures and labor in U.S. manufacturing, 1929–68', *Journal of Econometrics*, **1**, 81–113.

Christensen, L.R., Jorgenson, D.W., and Lau, L.M. (1973), 'Transcendental logarithmic production frontiers', *Review of Economics and Statistics*, **55**(1), 28–45.

Cochrane, D. and Orcutt, G.H. (1949), 'Application of least squares regressions to relationships containing autocorrelated error terms', *Journal of the American Statistical Association*, **44**, 32–61.

Fomby, T.B., Hill, R.C. and Johnson, S.R. (1984), *Advanced Econometric Methods*, New York: Springer-Verlag.

McElroy, M.B. (1977), 'Goodness of fit for seemingly unrelated regression', *Journal of Econometrics*, **6**, 381–7.

Mundlak, Y. (1978), 'On the pooling of time series and cross-section data', *Econometrica*, **46**, 69–85.

Parikh, A. (1985), 'Some aspects of employment in Indian agriculture', *World Development*, **13** (6), 691–704.

Parikh, A. (1988), 'An econometric analysis of fertilizer demand in Bangladesh using cross-section and time series data', *Journal of Quantitative Economics*, **4**, 157–71.

Prais, S.J. and Winsten, C.B. (1954), 'Trend estimators and serial correlation', Cowles Commission Discussion Paper No 383, Chicago.

Shephard, R. (1970), *Theory of Cost and Production Functions*, Princeton NJ: Princeton University Press.
Zellner, A. (1962) 'An efficient method of estimating seemingly unrelated regressions and tests of aggregation bias', *Journal of the American Statistical Association*, **57**, 348–68.
Zellner, A. (1963), 'Estimators of seemingly unrelated regressions: some exact finite sample results', *Journal of the American Statistical Association*, **58**, 977–92.

Chapter 6
ESTIMATION IN SIMULTANEOUS EQUATION MODELS

This chapter is devoted to a consideration of simultaneous equation models. In Section 6.1 we set the scene, distinguishing between endogenous and predetermined variables and showing how to derive the reduced form equations which enable us to solve for the endogenous variables in terms of the predetermined variables and disturbances of the model. In Section 6.2 we discuss the identification problem; here we are concerned with the conditions under which it will be possible to identify the structural coefficients of the model given knowledge of the reduced form coefficients. In considering the restrictions that it is necessary to impose on an equation for it to be identifiable, we deal first with the simpler case of exclusion restrictions, i.e. whether or not a particular variable is present in the structural equation under consideration. We then go on to consider more general restrictions. In the following two sections, we discuss estimation methods in simultaneous equation models. In Section 6.3 we outline single-equation methods of estimation, presenting the main features of the following procedures: indirect least squares, instrumental variable estimation, two-stage least squares and limited information maximum likelihood. Section 6.4 briefly explores system methods of estimation: here we look at the three-stage least squares and full information maximum likelihood methods of estimation. The chapter ends with a short concluding section.

6.1 SIMULTANEOUS EQUATION MODELS

In the preceding chapter we considered the case where the stochastic disturbance term of one equation was correlated with that of another equation; this gave rise to our discussion of seemingly unrelated regression. We now turn to a discussion of the econometric issues pertaining to simultaneous equation models. In such a model we seek to determine simultaneously the values of certain variables whose behaviour is explained by the structural equations of the model. Such variables are called endogenous variables, while the variables which tend to explain the behaviour of these endogenous variables are called predetermined variables and these can be divided into two groups: exogenous variables and lagged endogenous variables. The former are variables whose values are determined completely outside the system under consideration, while the latter's values are given by past values of the endogenous variables of the model. For the system to be a simultaneous one, all the relationships specified in the system must be necessary to determine the value of at least one of the endogenous variables.

Of key significance in such models is the question of whether a variable is endogenous or predetermined, since in order for the model to be capable of being estimated, one condition which must be satisfied is that the number of endogenous variables in the model must equal the number of independent equations. Statisticians such as Granger (see the discussion of causality in Chapter 4) have proposed procedures for ascertaining whether causality runs from one variable to another by considering whether past values of some variable X help to predict current values of some other variable Y. If they do, then X is said to Granger cause Y. Though causality and exogeneity are not identical concepts, they are closely related econometrically (see Engle, Hendry and Richard, 1983) and some econometricians (e.g. Sargent, 1976) have used causality tests in order to establish the exogeneity status or otherwise of the variables to be utilised in an econometric model. This procedure, however, is adopted relatively infrequently; more generally econometricians use *a priori* considerations based on the relevant economic theory to classify the variables under consideration as either exogenous or endogenous. Economic theory often provides qualitative guidance in the form of the sign of a derivative on the likely impact of a predetermined variable on an endogenous one, but it is usually much more silent on such matters as the functional form, length of lag, etc. Hence the econometrician has considerable discretion in the specification of his model, including the form of the stochastic disturbances, economic models being normally deterministic ones.

Consider the following economic model:

$$Q^d = f_1(P, Y) \tag{6.1}$$

$$Q^s = f_2(P, W) \tag{6.2}$$

$$Q^d = Q^s \tag{6.3}$$

where Q^d is quantity demanded of some agricultural product, Q^s is quantity supplied, P is the price of the product, Y is disposable income and W is an index of weather conditions. The endogenous variables are Q^d, Q^s and P, while the exogenous variables are Y and W. Specifying a linear relationship for the demand and supply functions, making the model stochastic and setting demand equal to supply, we obtain the following econometric model:

$$Q_t = \alpha_1 + \alpha_2 P_t + \alpha_3 Y_t + u_{1t} \tag{6.4}$$

$$Q_t = \beta_1 + \beta_2 P_t + \beta_3 W_t + u_{2t} \tag{6.5}$$

where Q_t represents the equilibrium amount traded at time t, the αs and βs are the parameters of the model, and the us are the random disturbances about which we make the following assumptions:

$$\left.\begin{array}{ll} E(u_{1t}) = 0 & E(u_{1t}^2) = \sigma_{11} \\ E(u_{2t}) = 0 & E(u_{2t}^2) = \sigma_{22} \\ E(u_{1t} u_{2t}) = \sigma_{12} & \end{array}\right\} \quad (6.5a)$$

Solving the structural equations (6.4) and (6.5) for the endogenous variables we obtain the so-called reduced form equations for the endogenous variables, q_t and P_t:

$$Q_t = \frac{\alpha_1 \beta_2 - \alpha_2 \beta_1}{\beta_2 - \alpha_2} + \frac{\alpha_3 \beta_2}{\beta_2 - \alpha_2} \cdot Y_t - \frac{\alpha_2 \beta_3}{\beta_2 - \alpha_2} \cdot W_t + \frac{\beta_2 u_{1t} - \alpha_2 u_{2t}}{\beta_2 - \alpha_2} \quad (6.6)$$

$$P_t = \frac{\alpha_1 - \beta_1}{\beta_2 - \alpha_2} + \frac{\alpha_3}{\beta_2 - \alpha_2} \cdot Y_t - \frac{\beta_3}{\beta_2 - \alpha_2} \cdot W_t + \frac{u_{1t} - u_{2t}}{\beta_2 - \alpha_2} \quad (6.7)$$

Equations (6.6) and (6.7) show how the two endogenous variables depend jointly upon the predetermined variables and are fully explained by Y_t, W_t and the disturbance terms, u_{1t} and u_{2t}. The total effect of a change in income on quantity traded is given by the coefficient on Y_t in equation (6.6). This can be decomposed into the direct effect of a change in Y on Q and an indirect effect through the effect the change in Y has on P and hence on Q:

$$\frac{\alpha_3 \beta_2}{\beta_2 - \alpha_2} \text{ (total effect)} = \alpha_3 \text{ (direct effect)} + \frac{\alpha_2 \alpha_3}{\beta_2 - \alpha_2} \text{ (indirect effect)} \quad (6.8)$$

A similar decomposition can be applied to the other reduced form coefficients in equations (6.6) and (6.7). In circumstances where the total and direct effects are known, the decomposition can be used to obtain the indirect effect.

Note from the above two equations that

$$E(P_t u_{1t}) = \frac{\sigma_{11} - \sigma_{12}}{\beta_2 - \alpha_2} \quad (6.9)$$

and

$$E(P_t u_{2t}) = \frac{\sigma_{12} - \sigma_{22}}{\beta_2 - \alpha_2} \quad (6.10)$$

In other words, P_t is correlated with both the disturbances with the obvious implication that OLS estimation of the structural equations (6.4) and (6.5), in both of which P_t appears as an explanatory variable, would lead to biased and inconsistent estimates of the regression coefficients. Estimation in simultaneous equation models is a matter we take up in great detail later in the chapter.

We move away from our specific supply and demand example to consider the general case of a system of G simultaneous equations (and, correspondingly,

G endogenous variables). We assume that there are K predetermined variables in total, with T observations for each equation. We write the system of equations as follows:

$$\left.\begin{aligned}\beta_{11}y_{1t}+\beta_{12}y_{2t}+\ldots+\beta_{1G}y_{Gt}+\gamma_{11}x_{1t}+\gamma_{12}x_{2t}+\ldots+\gamma_{1K}x_{Kt}&=u_{1t}\\ \beta_{21}y_{1t}+\beta_{22}y_{2t}+\ldots+\beta_{2G}y_{Gt}+\gamma_{21}x_{1t}+\gamma_{22}x_{2t}+\ldots+\gamma_{2K}x_{Kt}&=u_{2t}\\ \vdots&\\ \beta_{G1}y_{1t}+\beta_{G2}y_{2t}+\ldots+\beta_{GG}y_{Gt}+\gamma_{G1}x_{1t}+\gamma_{G2}x_{2t}+\ldots+\gamma_{GK}x_{Kt}&=u_{Gt}\end{aligned}\right\} \quad (6.11)$$

Not all the endogenous and predetermined variables appear in each equation. In each equation, one of the endogenous variables acts as a dependent variable with the corresponding β coefficient taking a value of unity. A constant term can be allowed for in each equation by letting one of the xs equal unity for all $t = 1, 2, \ldots, T$. The system can also accommodate the inclusion of identities for which cases the coefficients are known and the stochastic disturbance term is zero.

The system of equations may also be written more economically in matrix notation as

$$By_t + \Gamma x_t = u_t \qquad (6.12)$$

where y_t is a column vector of G endogenous variables, x_t is a column vector of K predetermined variables, u_t is a column vector of G stochastic disturbances, B is a $G \times G$ matrix of structural coefficients on the G endogenous variables and Γ a $G \times K$ matrix of structural coefficients on the K exogenous variables. Each stochastic disturbance is assumed to possess the usual properties

$$u_{gt} \sim N(0, \sigma_{gg}) \quad (g = 1, 2, \ldots, G)$$
$$E(u_{gt}u_{gs}) = 0 \quad (t, s = 1, 2, \ldots, T)$$
$$(t \neq s)$$

though allowing for the disturbances to be correlated across equations, we also have

$$E(u_{gt}u_{ht}) = \sigma_{gh} \quad (g, h = 1, 2, \ldots, G)$$

The variance–covariance matrix of the disturbances is therefore given by

$$\Omega = \begin{bmatrix} \sigma_{11} & \sigma_{12} & \ldots & \sigma_{1G} \\ \sigma_{21} & \sigma_{22} & & \sigma_{2G} \\ \vdots & & & \\ \sigma_{G1} & \sigma_{G2} & \ldots & \sigma_{GG} \end{bmatrix} \qquad (6.13)$$

If there are no identities in the system, Ω is of order $G \times G$; more generally if there are M identities in the G equations, it will be of order $G \times G$ but of rank $G - M \times G - M$.

From equation (6.11) we may solve for the endogenous variables in terms of the predetermined variables and the disturbances. This gives rise to the following set of reduced form equations:

$$\left.\begin{array}{l}y_{1t} = \pi_{11}x_{1t} + \pi_{12}x_{2t} + \ldots + \pi_{1K}x_{Kt} + v_{1t} \\ y_{2t} = \pi_{21}x_{1t} + \pi_{22}x_{2t} + \ldots + \pi_{2K}x_{Kt} + v_{2t} \\ \vdots \\ y_{Gt} = \pi_{G1}x_{1t} + \pi_{G2}x_{2t} + \ldots + \pi_{GK}x_{Kt} + v_{Gt}\end{array}\right\} \quad (6.14)$$

where the πs represent the reduced form coefficients and the vs the reduced form disturbances.

We may alternatively write the reduced form equations in matrix notation:

$$y_t = \Pi x_t + v_t \quad (6.15)$$

where Π is a $G \times K$ matrix of reduced form coefficients and v_t a column of G reduced form disturbances. Note that since

$$By_t + \Gamma x_t = u_t$$

then

$$y_t = -B^{-1}\Gamma x_t + B^{-1}u_t$$

Hence,

$$\Pi = -B^{-1}\Gamma \text{ OR } B\Pi + \Gamma = 0 \quad (6.16)$$

$$v_t = B^{-1}u_t \quad (6.17)$$

The variance–covariance matrix of the reduced form disturbances is given by

$$E(v_t v_t') = E(B^{-1}u_t u_t'(B^{-1})')$$
$$= B^{-1}\Omega(B^{-1})' \quad (6.18)$$

6.2 THE IDENTIFICATION PROBLEM

For any set of simultaneous equations, we can obtain the reduced form equations and by applying OLS to these equations obtain estimates of the reduced form coefficients. What we are interested in primarily, however, is obtaining estimates of the structural coefficients of the model. In this section of the chapter we concern ourselves with the conditions under which it will be possible to identify the structural coefficients of the model from the reduced form coefficients. We consider the restrictions that it is necessary to impose on an equation for it to be identifiable. We commence by considering exclusion restrictions only, i.e. whether or not a particular variable is present in the structural equation under consideration.

Returning to the matrices of structural coefficients, B and Γ, rearrange the columns of B and Γ such that the first G_1 elements in the first row of B and the first K_1 elements in the first row of Γ are all nonzero, with the remaining $G_2 = G - G_1$ elements in the first row of B and the remaining $K_2 = K - K_1$ elements in the first row of Γ being all zero. The G_2 endogenous variables and K_2 predetermined variables are, therefore, excluded from the first structural equation. Letting the first rows of B and Γ be represented respectively, by β' and γ' we have

$$\beta' = [\beta_1' \quad 0] \quad \gamma' = [\gamma_1' \quad 0] \tag{6.19}$$

where the row vectors β_1' and γ_1' contain G_1 and K_1 elements respectively.

Rearrange Π, the $G \times K$ matrix of reduced form coefficients so that it is conformable for premultiplication by the rearranged b and partition it in the following way:

$$\Pi = \begin{bmatrix} \Pi_{11} & \Pi_{12} \\ \Pi_{21} & \Pi_{22} \end{bmatrix} \tag{6.20}$$

where Π_{11} is of order $G_1 \times K_1$, Π_{12} of order $G_1 \times K_2$, Π_{21} of order $G_2 \times K_1$ and Π_{22} of order $G_2 \times K_2$.

Since $B\Pi = -\Gamma$, premultiplying Π by β' we have

$$[\beta_1' \quad 0] \begin{bmatrix} \Pi_{11} & \Pi_{12} \\ \Pi_{21} & \Pi_{22} \end{bmatrix} = [-\gamma_1' \quad 0] \tag{6.21}$$

Hence,

$$\beta_1' \Pi_{11} = -\gamma_1' \tag{6.22}$$

and

$$\beta_1' \Pi_{12} = 0 \tag{6.23}$$

Equation (6.23) contains K_2 equations in G_1 unknowns; however, in each structural equation one of the βs is equal to unity, so we only need to solve for $G_1 - 1$ unknown βs. The γs do not enter into the second set of equations; if we can solve equation (6.23) for the unknown βs, the K_1 unknown γs can then easily be derived from equation (6.22). A necessary condition to be able to solve for the $G_1 - 1$ unknown βs is that the number of equations in model (6.23) is at least as large as the number of unknowns. This condition is known as the order condition of identification and for the first equation to be identified we must have (Hood and Koopmans, 1953)

$$K_2 \geqslant G_1 - 1 \text{ or, equivalently, } G_2 + K_2 \geqslant G_1 + G_2 - 1 \tag{6.24}$$

In order to be able to identify a particular structural equation, the order condition states that the number of predetermined variables excluded from the equation must be at least as large as the number of endogenous variables included, less 1. This condition, however, is a necessary though not sufficient condition for the parameters of the particular structural equation to be identified, since the K_2 equations may contain less than $G_1 - 1$ different pieces of information about the relationship between the structural and reduced form parameters. Provided that the number of independent equations is equal to $G_1 - 1$, it will be possible to identify the structural parameters. There will be exist $G_1 - 1$ independent equations if and only if the order of the largest nonzero determinant that can be formed from all the square submatrices of Π_{12} is $G_1 - 1$. We may therefore state the rank condition for identifiability:

The identification problem 137

$$\text{Rank } (\Pi_{12}) = G_1 - 1 \tag{6.25}$$

Taking the order and rank conditions together, we consider the following set of possibilities:

1. If $K_2 > G_1 - 1$ and rank $(\Pi_{12}) = G_1 - 1$, then the equation is overidentified;
2. If $K_2 = G_1 - 1$ and rank $(\Pi_{12}) = G_1 - 1$, then the equation is just identified;
3. If $K_2 \geqslant G_1 - 1$ and rank $(\Pi_{12}) < G_1 - 1$, then the equation is underidentified;
4. If $K_2 < G_1 - 1$, then the equation is underidentified.

To find the rank of Π_{12} is not always a straightforward matter and there exists an alternative rank condition, the application of which does not require the investigator to solve for the reduced form of the set of equations. We proceed to outline this alternative approach by first writing B and Γ in the following partitioned forms:

$$B = \begin{bmatrix} \beta_1' & 0 \\ B_1 & B_2 \end{bmatrix} \quad \Gamma = \begin{bmatrix} \gamma_1' & 0 \\ \Gamma_1 & \Gamma_2 \end{bmatrix} \tag{6.26}$$

Define a new matrix C of order $G \times (G_2 + K_2)$

$$C = \begin{bmatrix} -\Pi_{12} & 0 \\ -\Pi_{22} & I_{G_2} \end{bmatrix} \tag{6.27}$$

Premultiplying C by B, we obtain

$$BC = \begin{bmatrix} -\beta_1'\Pi_{12} & 0 \\ -(B_1\Pi_{12} + B_2\Pi_{22}) & B_2 \end{bmatrix} \tag{6.28}$$

Since $B\Pi = -\Gamma$, we have $-\beta_1'\Pi_{12} = 0$ and $-(B_1\Pi_{12} + B_2\Pi_{22}) = \Gamma_2$. Hence,

$$BC = \begin{bmatrix} 0 & 0 \\ \Gamma_2 & B_2 \end{bmatrix} = P \tag{6.29}$$

Note that P is a matrix whose elements are the coefficients on those predetermined and endogenous variables which are excluded from the structural equation whose parameters we are seeking to identify.

Since B is a nonsingular matrix, the rank of BC and hence of P is the same as the rank of C. In order to determine the rank of C, postmultiply C by the following nonsingular matrix D; this gives a matrix with the same rank as C.

$$D = \begin{bmatrix} I_{K_2} & 0 \\ \Pi_{22} & I_{G_2} \end{bmatrix} \tag{6.30}$$

Hence

$$\text{Rank } C = \text{Rank } \begin{bmatrix} -\Pi_{12} & 0 \\ -\Pi_{22} & I_{G_2} \end{bmatrix} \begin{bmatrix} I_{K_2} & 0 \\ \Pi_{22} & I_{G_2} \end{bmatrix}$$

$$= \text{Rank } \begin{bmatrix} -\Pi_{12} & 0 \\ 0 & I_{G_2} \end{bmatrix}$$

$$= \text{Rank } (\Pi_{12}) + G_2 \tag{6.31}$$

For the rank condition of identifiability to be satisfied we saw above that the rank of Π_{12} must be equal to $G_1 - 1$. Hence if the rank of C, and hence of P, is $G - 1$, Π_{12} will have rank $G_1 - 1$. The alternative formulation for the rank condition may now be stated; the rank of the matrix P whose elements are the coefficients of the variables, both predetermined and endogenous, excluded from the equation we are seeking to identify should be equal to the number of equations in the system, less one.

Let us examine whether the following model is identified equation-by-equation:

$$\left.\begin{array}{l} y_{1t} + \beta_{12} y_{2t} + \gamma_{11} x_{1t} + \gamma_{12} x_{2t} + \gamma_{14} x_{4t} = u_{1t} \\ \phantom{y_{1t} +} y_{2t} + \beta_{23} y_{3t} + \gamma_{21} x_{1t} + \phantom{\gamma_{12} x_{2t}} \gamma_{23} x_{3t} \phantom{+ \gamma_{14} x_{4t}} = u_{2t} \\ \phantom{y_{1t} +} \beta_{32} y_{2t} + \phantom{\beta_{23}} y_{3t} + \gamma_{31} x_{1t} \phantom{+ \gamma_{12} x_{2t} + \gamma_{14} x_{4t}} = u_{3t} \end{array}\right\} \quad (6.32)$$

where y_{1t}, y_{2t} and y_{3t} are endogenous variables: x_{1t}, x_{2t}, x_{3t} and x_{4t} are exogenous variables; and u_{1t}, u_{2t} and u_{3t} are stochastic disturbances.

Regarding the first equation of (6.32), there are two endogenous variables (y_{1t}, y_{2t}) included in the equation and one predetermined variable (x_{2t}) excluded from the equation. Hence, by the order condition, the first equation is identified. We now turn to the rank condition. The matrix of structural coefficients on the endogenous and predetermined variables excluded from the first equation in the other equations of the system is

$$\begin{bmatrix} \beta_{23} & \gamma_{23} \\ 1 & 0 \end{bmatrix}$$

The largest nonzero determinant that can be formed from this matrix is of order 2×2, hence the matrix has rank 2 which is one less than the number of equations in the model and the rank condition for identifiability is, accordingly, satisfied. Since $K_2 = G_1 - 1$, the equation is exactly identified.

Turning to the second equation of the model, there are two endogenous variables (y_{2t}, y_{3t}) included in the equation and two predetermined variables (x_{2t}, x_{4t}) excluded from the equation. Hence, by the order condition, the second equation is identified. To see whether the rank condition is satisfied we must evaluate the rank of the following matrix:

$$\begin{bmatrix} 1 & \gamma_{12} & \gamma_{14} \\ 0 & 0 & 0 \end{bmatrix}$$

Since it is only of rank 1, the rank condition for identification is not satisfied; the second equation remains underidentified and we will not be able to obtain estimates of its structural coefficients.

Lastly, the third equation contains two endogenous variables (y_{2t}, y_{3t}) and only one of the four predetermined variables of the system (x_{1t}); by the order condition the equation is identified. The rank condition will be satisfied if the rank of the following matrix is 2:

$$\begin{bmatrix} 1 & \gamma_{12} & 0 & \gamma_{14} \\ 0 & 0 & \gamma_{23} & 0 \end{bmatrix}$$

The identification problem 139

The largest nonzero determinant is of order 2 × 2; hence the necessary and sufficient conditions for identification of this third equation are satisfied. Since $K_2 > G_1 - 1$, the equation is overidentified.

The *a priori* restrictions we have considered so far in our discussion of identification have been simple exclusion restrictions; either a particular parameter in a structural equation is assigned a value of zero or not, so that the associated variable is excluded from that structural equation or not. More generally, we can impose other homogeneous *a priori* restrictions of the form

$$\gamma_{ij} - \gamma_{ik} = 0 \tag{6.33}$$

This means that in the ith structural equation we are constraining the coefficients on the variables x_j and x_k to be equal. It may also be possible to accommodate some nonhomogeneous restrictions. Assume that we wish to restrict the sum of two coefficients in the ith structural equation to equal unity, say $\gamma_{ij} + \gamma_{ik} = 1$. Assume, further, that in this equation we have normalised on the variable y_g by setting its coefficient $\beta_{ig} = 1$. Then we may convert the original nonhomogeneous restriction into a homogeneous one by combining the two restrictions to obtain

$$\beta_{ig} - \gamma_{ij} - \gamma_{ik} = 0 \tag{6.34}$$

What modifications are necessary to our conditions for identification in the presence of the above type of restrictions? In principle, the order condition is unaltered other than it must now be expressed in terms of the number of *a priori* restrictions rather than in terms of the number of predetermined variables. It now becomes a necessary condition for identification that the number of *a priori* restrictions (R) be at least as large as the number of endogenous variables in the model, less 1, i.e. $R \geqslant G - 1$.

Regarding the rank condition, we first introduce the following notation: A is a $G \times (G + K)$ matrix of structural coefficients and Φ_i is a $(G + K) \times R$ matrix of restrictions for the ith equation where R is the number of restrictions:

$$A = [B \quad \Gamma] \tag{6.35}$$

and the restrictions take the form

$$a_i \Phi_i = 0 \tag{6.36}$$

where a_i is the ith row of A.

The rank condition for identification, stated here without proof, is that rank $[A\Phi_i] = G - 1$. If all the *a priori* restrictions are simple exclusion ones, then $A\Phi_i = P$. For a detailed treatment of the identification problem, the reader is referred to Fisher (1966).

Consider the following two-equation model:

$$\beta_{11} y_{1t} + \beta_{12} y_{2t} + \gamma_{11} x_{1t} + \gamma_{12} x_{2t} + \gamma_{13} x_{3t} = u_{1t}$$
$$\beta_{21} y_{1t} + \beta_{22} y_{2t} + \gamma_{21} x_{1t} + \gamma_{22} x_{2t} + \gamma_{23} x_{3t} = u_{2t}$$

in which we impose the following *a priori* restrictions:

$$\gamma_{12} - \gamma_{13} = 0$$
$$\beta_{22} = 1, \gamma_{21} + \gamma_{22} = 1, \gamma_{23} = 0$$

For the first equation there is one *a priori* restriction and

$$\Phi_1 = \begin{bmatrix} 0 \\ 0 \\ 0 \\ 1 \\ -1 \end{bmatrix}$$

Note that $a_1 \Phi_1 = \gamma_{12} - \gamma_{13} = 0$. For the first equation there is one restriction and two included endogenous variables, so the order condition suggests that the equation is exactly identified. Turning to the rank condition, we have

$$A\Phi_1 = \begin{bmatrix} \gamma_{12} - \gamma_{13} \\ \gamma_{22} - \gamma_{23} \end{bmatrix} = \begin{bmatrix} 0 \\ \gamma_{22} \end{bmatrix}$$

Now, $A\Phi_1$ has rank 1 provided that $\gamma_{22} \neq 0$ and the first equation is just identified since there is one restriction. Had γ_{22} been restricted to equal zero, the first equation would not have been identified, even though it satisfies the order condition for identification.

For the second equation of the model there are two *a priori* restrictions since the restrictions $\beta_{22} = 1$ and $\gamma_{21} + \gamma_{22} = 1$ collapse into the single homogeneous restriction $\beta_{22} - \gamma_{21} - \gamma_{22} = 0$. Hence,

$$\Phi_2 = \begin{bmatrix} 0 & 0 \\ 1 & 0 \\ -1 & 0 \\ -1 & 0 \\ 0 & 1 \end{bmatrix}$$

and

$$A\Phi_2 = \begin{bmatrix} \beta_{12} - \gamma_{11} - \gamma_{12} & \gamma_{13} \\ 0 & 0 \end{bmatrix}$$

which has rank 1 provided that $\gamma_{13} \neq 0$ or $\beta_{12} - \gamma_{11} - \gamma_{12} \neq 0$ or both. The second equation of the model is overidentified since $R > 1$, and the first is exactly identified.

Let us consider the following model:

$$\left. \begin{array}{l} y_{1t} = \beta_{12} y_{2t} + \gamma_{11} x_{1t} + \gamma_{12} x_{2t} + u_{1t} \\ y_{1t} = \beta_{22} y_{2t} + \gamma_{21} x_{1t} + u_{2t} \end{array} \right\} \quad (6.37)$$

It is straightforward to show that the first equation is underidentified and the second equation is exactly identified. Without imposing some further restrictions it will not be possible to estimate the structural parameters of the first equation. One way out of this impasse is to assume that the covariance between the disturbance terms of the two structural equations is zero (i.e. $E(u_{1t} u_{2t}) = 0$).

Solving for the reduced form equations from the structural equations, we find that the reduced form parameters of the model are

$$\left.\begin{array}{ll} \Pi_{11} = \dfrac{\beta_{12}\gamma_{21} - \beta_{22}\gamma_{11}}{\beta_{12} - \beta_{22}} & \Pi_{12} = \dfrac{-\beta_{22}\gamma_{12}}{\beta_{12} - \beta_{22}} \\[2ex] \Pi_{21} = \dfrac{\gamma_{21} - \gamma_{11}}{\beta_{12} - \beta_{22}} & \Pi_{22} = \dfrac{-\gamma_{12}}{\beta_{12} - \beta_{22}} \end{array}\right\} \quad (6.38)$$

The above equations can be rearranged to yield the following relationships between the reduced form and structural parameters of the model:

$$\left.\begin{array}{ll} \Pi_{11} = \gamma_{11} + \beta_{12}\Pi_{21} & \Pi_{11} = \gamma_{21} + \beta_{22}\Pi_{21} \\ \Pi_{12} = \beta_{12}\Pi_{21} + \gamma_{12} & \Pi_{12} = \beta_{22}\Pi_{22} \end{array}\right\} \quad (6.39)$$

These equations can be solved to find the parameters of the second equation, but not those of the first.

The reduced form disturbances of the model are given, respectively, by

$$v_{1t} = \frac{\beta_{12} u_{2t} - \beta_{22} u_{1t}}{\beta_{12} - \beta_{22}} \quad \text{and} \quad v_{2t} = \frac{u_{2t} - u_{1t}}{\beta_{12} - \beta_{22}} \quad (6.40)$$

Rearranging these equations we can obtain the disturbances of the structural equations as functions of the reduced form disturbances:

$$u_{1t} = v_{1t} - \beta_{12} v_{2t} \quad \text{and} \quad u_{2t} = v_{1t} - \beta_{22} v_{2t} \quad (6.41)$$

We now make use of the restriction $E(u_{1t} u_{2t}) = 0$; this implies

$$E(v_{1t} - \beta_{12} v_{2t})(v_{1t} - \beta_{22} v_{2t}) = 0$$

or

$$\left.\begin{array}{c} E(v_{1t} - \beta_{12} v_{2t})(v_{1t} - \beta_{22} v_{2t}) = 0 \\[1ex] \text{Var}(v_{1t}) - (\beta_{12} + \beta_{22})\,\text{Cov}(v_{1t} v_{2t}) + \beta_{12}\beta_{22}\,\text{Var}(v_{2t}) = 0 \end{array}\right\} \quad (6.42)$$

The introduction of this further restriction now enables us to solve for the structural parameters of the first equation. Substituting $\beta_{22} = \Pi_{12}/\Pi_{22}$ in equation (6.42) we can find β_{12}. Having found β_{12}, we can then solve for γ_{11} and γ_{12} using the relationship given in equation (6.39).

6.3 SINGLE-EQUATION ESTIMATION METHODS IN SIMULTANEOUS EQUATION MODELS

In order to estimate the structural parameters of a particular equation of a simultaneous equation model, that equation must be either just identified or overidentified. In this section we consider single-equation methods of estimation (Anderson and Rubin, 1949). There are a number of such estimation methods available to the investigator and the purpose of this section is to outline the main features of each approach and to comment on the relative advantages and disadvantages of the various approaches. The methods we shall discuss are: indirect least squares estimation (ILS); instrumental variable estimation (IV); two-stage least squares estimation (2SLS); and limited information maximum likelihood estimation (LIML). In the following section we go on to consider system methods of estimation.

Indirect least squares

When an equation of a simultaneous equation model is exactly identified, the method of indirect least squares may be employed in order to obtain estimates of the parameters of that particular structural equation. The ILS method involves estimating the reduced form coefficients of the model and then utilises this information in order to obtain estimates of the underlying structural parameters.

Consider the following model in which both structural equations are exactly identified:

$$\left. \begin{array}{l} y_{1t} = \beta_{12} y_{2t} + \gamma_{11} x_{1t} + u_{1t} \\ y_{2t} = \beta_{21} y_{1t} + \gamma_{22} x_{2t} + u_{2t} \end{array} \right\} \quad (6.43)$$

The reduced form equations are

$$\left. \begin{array}{l} y_{1t} = \dfrac{\gamma_{11}}{1 - \beta_{12}\beta_{21}} x_{1t} + \dfrac{\beta_{12}\gamma_{22}}{1 - \beta_{12}\beta_{21}} x_{2t} + v_{1t} \\ y_{2t} = \dfrac{\beta_{21}\gamma_{11}}{1 - \beta_{12}\beta_{21}} x_{1t} + \dfrac{\gamma_{22}}{1 - \beta_{12}\beta_{21}} x_{2t} + v_{2t} \end{array} \right\} \quad (6.44)$$

where

$$v_{1t} = \frac{u_{1t} + \beta_{12} u_{2t}}{1 - \beta_{12}\beta_{21}} \quad \text{and} \quad v_{2t} = \frac{\beta_{21} u_{1t} + u_{2t}}{1 - \beta_{12}\beta_{21}}$$

Let the estimators of the reduced form coefficients be given by $\hat{\Pi}_{ij}$ with $i, j = 1, 2$. The estimators of the structural coefficients are therefore given by

$$\left. \begin{array}{l} \hat{\beta}_{12} = \dfrac{\hat{\Pi}_{12}}{\hat{\Pi}_{22}}, \quad \hat{\beta}_{21} = \dfrac{\hat{\Pi}_{21}}{\hat{\Pi}_{11}} \\ \hat{\gamma}_{11} = \hat{\Pi}_{11}[1 - \hat{\beta}_{12}\hat{\beta}_{21}], \quad \hat{\gamma}_{22} = \hat{\Pi}_{22}[1 - \hat{\beta}_{12}\hat{\beta}_{21}] \end{array} \right\} \quad (6.45)$$

Let us, however, consider the following model in which the stochastic disturbance terms have been suppressed for reasons of convenience:

$$\left. \begin{array}{l} y_{1t} = \beta_{12} y_{2t} + \gamma_{11} x_{1t} + \gamma_{12} x_{2t} \\ y_{2t} = \beta_{21} y_{1t} \end{array} \right\} \quad (6.46)$$

The reduced form equations are

$$\left. \begin{array}{l} y_{1t} = \dfrac{\gamma_{11}}{1 - \beta_{12}\beta_{21}} \cdot x_{1t} + \dfrac{\gamma_{12}}{1 - \beta_{12}\beta_{21}} \cdot x_{2t} \\ y_{2t} = \dfrac{\beta_{21}\gamma_{11}}{1 - \beta_{12}\beta_{21}} \cdot x_{1t} + \dfrac{\beta_{21}\gamma_{12}}{1 - \beta_{12}\beta_{21}} \cdot x_{2t} \end{array} \right\} \quad (6.47)$$

Single-equation estimation methods

The first equation of (6.46) is underidentified and it is impossible to obtain estimates of the structural coefficients from the estimates of the reduced form coefficients. On the other hand, the second equation of (6.46) is overidentified and we cannot obtain a unique estimate of β_{21} since it is clear that

$$\hat{\beta}_{21} = \frac{\hat{\Pi}_{21}}{\hat{\Pi}_{11}} \text{ or } \frac{\hat{\Pi}_{22}}{\hat{\Pi}_{11}} \tag{6.48}$$

with the second expression not being the same as the first. Finally, let us deal with a simple model where the first structural equation is exactly identified and the second equation overidentified:

$$\left.\begin{aligned} y_{1t} &= \beta_{12} y_{2t} + \gamma_{11} x_{1t} + \gamma_{13} x_{3t} \\ y_{2t} &= \beta_{21} y_{1t} + \gamma_{22} x_{2t} \end{aligned}\right\} \tag{6.49}$$

The reduced form equations are

$$\left.\begin{aligned} y_{1t} &= \frac{\gamma_{11}}{1 - \beta_{12}\beta_{21}} \cdot x_{1t} + \frac{\beta_{12}\gamma_{22}}{1 - \beta_{12}\beta_{21}} \cdot x_{2t} + \frac{\gamma_{13}}{1 - \beta_{12}\beta_{21}} \cdot x_{3t} \\ y_{2t} &= \frac{\beta_{21}\gamma_{11}}{1 - \beta_{12}\beta_{21}} \cdot x_{1t} + \frac{\gamma_{22}}{1 - \beta_{12}\beta_{21}} \cdot x_{2t} + \frac{\beta_{21}\gamma_{13}}{1 - \beta_{12}\beta_{21}} \cdot x_{3t} \end{aligned}\right\} \tag{6.50}$$

Estimators of the structural coefficients of the first equation can be derived from the estimators of the reduced form coefficients and are given by the following set of equations:

$$\left.\begin{aligned} \hat{\beta}_{12} &= \frac{\hat{\Pi}_{12}}{\hat{\Pi}_{22}} \\ \hat{\gamma}_{11} &= \hat{\Pi}_{11} - \hat{\beta}_{12}\hat{\Pi}_{21} \\ \hat{\gamma}_{13} &= \hat{\Pi}_{13} - \hat{\beta}_{12}\hat{\Pi}_{23} \end{aligned}\right\} \tag{6.51}$$

Since the second structural equation is overidentified we do not obtain a unique result using the ILS method:

$$\hat{\beta}_{21} = \frac{\hat{\Pi}_{21}}{\hat{\Pi}_{11}} \text{ or } \frac{\hat{\Pi}_{23}}{\hat{\Pi}_{13}} \tag{6.52}$$

Indirect least squares estimation, when it can be applied, has the advantage over OLS for the estimation of the equations of a simultaneous equation model in that the estimators are consistent. The major problem with this method of estimation, however, is that it can only be applied to the estimation of equations that are exactly identified. Other estimation procedures have to be utilised for estimating the parameters of overidentified equations and in applied work equations are much more likely to be overidentified than just identified. When the equation is just identified, there is a unique relationship between the reduced form and the structural parameters, but when it is overidentified, as in the second equation of (6.49), there is more than one relationship between reduced form and structural parameters, i.e. equation (6.52).

Instrumental variable estimation (IV)

Return to the model given in equation (6.49) where the first equation was exactly identified and the second equation overidentified. Let us consider using IV estimation on the second equation:

$$\left.\begin{array}{l} y_{1t} = \beta_{12}y_{2t} + \gamma_{11}x_{1t} + \gamma_{13}x_{3t} + u_{1t} \\ y_{2t} = \beta_{21}y_{1t} + \gamma_{22}x_{2t} + u_{2t} \end{array}\right\} \quad (6.53)$$

We need to choose as our instrument for y_{1t} a variable which is correlated with y_{1t} but is uncorrelated with the stochastic disturbance term u_{2t}. An obvious instrument to choose is one of the predetermined variables which does not appear in the second equation; we have, therefore, a choice of either x_{1t} or x_{3t} as the instrument for y_{1t}. Say we choose x_{1t} as the instrument. Using the conditions $\Sigma x_{1t}u_{2t} = \Sigma x_{2t}u_{2t} = 0$, we derive the following equations:

$$\left.\begin{array}{l} \Sigma x_1 y_2 = \beta_{21} \Sigma x_1 y_1 + \gamma_{22} \Sigma x_1 x_2 \\ \Sigma x_2 y_2 = \beta_{21} \Sigma x_2 y_1 + \gamma_{22} \Sigma x_2^2 \end{array}\right\} \quad (6.54)$$

Solving equation (6.54) for the IV estimators of β_{21} and γ_{22}, we obtain

$$\left.\begin{array}{l} \hat{\beta}_{21}^{IV} = \dfrac{\Sigma x_2^2 \Sigma x_1 y_2 - \Sigma x_1 x_2 \Sigma x_2 y_2}{\Sigma x_2^2 \Sigma x_1 y_1 - \Sigma x_1 x_2 \Sigma x_2 y_1} \\[2ex] \hat{\gamma}_{22}^{IV} = \dfrac{\Sigma x_1 y_1 \Sigma x_2 y_2 - \Sigma x_2 y_1 \Sigma x_1 y_2}{\Sigma x_2^2 \Sigma x_1 y_1 - \Sigma x_1 x_2 \Sigma x_2 y_1} \end{array}\right\} \quad (6.55)$$

Note, however, that had we chosen x_3 rather than x_1 as our instrument we would have obtained the following IV estimators:

$$\hat{\beta}_{21}^{IV} = \frac{\Sigma x_2^2 \Sigma x_3 y_2 - \Sigma x_2 x_3 \Sigma x_2 y_2}{\Sigma x_2^2 \Sigma x_3 y_1 - \Sigma x_2 x_3 \Sigma x_2 y_1}$$

$$\hat{\gamma}_{22}^{IV} = \frac{\Sigma x_3 y_1 \Sigma x_2 y_2 - \Sigma x_2 y_1 \Sigma x_3 y_2}{\Sigma x_2^2 \Sigma x_3 y_1 - \Sigma x_2 x_3 \Sigma x_2 y_1} \quad (6.56)$$

Hence, the IV estimators are not unique when the equation is overidentified.

Let us now consider the estimation of an exactly identified structural equation of a general model using the instrumental variable approach. The equation we seek to estimate is the first structural equation of a system of G equations; $G_1 - 1$ right-hand-side endogenous variables are included in the equation with $K - K_1 = K_2$ predetermined variables excluded from the equation. Given that the equation is assumed to be exactly identified, $K_2 = G_1 - 1$. The equation to be estimated is

$$y_{1t} + \beta_{12}y_{2t} + \beta_{13}y_{3t} + \ldots + \beta_{1G_1}y_{G_1t} + \gamma_{11}x_{1t} + \gamma_{12}x_{2t} + \ldots + \gamma_{1K_1}x_{K_1t} = u_{1t} \quad (6.57)$$

or, in matrix notation,

$$y_1 = Y_1(-\beta_1) + X_1(-\gamma_1) + u_1 \quad (6.58)$$

where y_1 is a $T \times 1$ vector of the endogenous variable whose coefficient in the first equation is 1, Y_1 is a $T \times (G_1 - 1)$ matrix of the remaining endogenous variables included in the first equation, X_1 is a $T \times K_1$ matrix of the predetermined variables included in the first equation, $-\beta_1$ and $-\gamma_1$ are, respectively, $G_1 - 1 \times 1$ and $K_1 \times 1$ vectors of coefficients on the endogenous and predetermined variables, respectively (and u_1 is a $T \times 1$ vector of stochastic disturbances).

If we define

$$Z_1 = [Y_1 \quad X_1] \text{ and } \delta_1 = \begin{bmatrix} -\beta_1 \\ -\gamma_1 \end{bmatrix} \tag{6.59}$$

then we may rewrite equation (6.58) as

$$y_1 = Z_1 \delta_1 + u_1 \tag{6.60}$$

An instrumental variable estimator of the structural coefficients is then

$$\delta_1^{IV} = (W_1' Z_1)^{-1} W_1' y_1 \tag{6.61}$$

and its estimated variance-covariance matrix is

$$\text{est. Var-Cov}(\delta_1^{IV}) = s_{11}(W_1' Z_1)^{-1}(W_1' W_1)(Z_1' W_1)^{-1} \tag{6.62}$$

where W_1 is a $T \times (G_1 - 1 + K_1)$ matrix of the observed values of the chosen instrumental variables. The estimator s_{11} can be obtained from the formula

$$s_{11} = \frac{(y_1 - Z_1 \delta_1^{IV})'(y_1 - Z_1 \delta_1^{IV})}{T - G_1 - K_1 + 1} \tag{6.63}$$

Alternatively, one may divide by T rather than by $T - G_1 - K_1 + 1$; this also yields a consistent estimator.

In IV estimation, the set of $(G_1 - 1)$ right-hand-side endogenous variables is replaced by a set of instrumental variables; the most natural candidates for these instruments are those predetermined variables which appear in the system of equations but which are excluded from the particular equation to be estimated. The number of such predetermined variables is $K_2 = K - K_1$ which, for the exactly identified equation, is equal to the number of included right-hand-side endogenous variables.

Let X_0 be the $T \times (K - K_1)$ matrix of the observed values of the instruments for Y_1; then define

$$W_1 = [X_0 \quad X_1] \tag{6.64}$$

Hence,

$$W_1' Z_1 = \begin{bmatrix} X_0' \\ X_1' \end{bmatrix} [Y_1 \quad X_1]$$

$$= \begin{bmatrix} X_0' Y_1 & X_0' X_1 \\ X_1' Y_1 & X_1' X_1 \end{bmatrix} \tag{6.65}$$

and

$$W_1'y_1 = \begin{bmatrix} X_0'y_1 \\ X_1'y_1 \end{bmatrix} \tag{6.66}$$

The instrumental variable estimator is therefore

$$\delta_1^{IV} = \begin{bmatrix} -\beta_1^{IV} \\ -\gamma_1^{IV} \end{bmatrix} = \begin{bmatrix} X_0'Y_1 & X_0'X_1 \\ X_1'Y_1 & X_1'X_1 \end{bmatrix}^{-1} \begin{bmatrix} X_0'y_1 \\ X_1'y_1 \end{bmatrix} \tag{6.67}$$

and its estimated variance–covariance matrix is

$$\text{est. Var-Cov}(\delta_1^{IV}) = s_{11} \begin{bmatrix} X_0'Y_1 & X_0'X_1 \\ X_1'Y_1 & X_1'X_1 \end{bmatrix}^{-1} \begin{bmatrix} X_0'X_0 & X_0'X_1 \\ X_1'X_0 & X_1'X_1 \end{bmatrix}$$

$$\begin{bmatrix} Y_1'X_0 & Y_1'X_1 \\ X_1'X_0 & X_1'X_1 \end{bmatrix}^{-1} \tag{6.68}$$

For an exactly identified equation, the IV estimator is identical to the ILS estimator and use of the above formula for the estimated variance–covariance matrix of the estimator is recommended rather than the complicated calculation of the standard errors of the ILS estimators from the variance–covariance matrix of the reduced form coefficients.

Two-stage least squares

A special kind of IV estimation arises in the two-stage least squares procedure (2SLS); this is the most commonly used single-equation estimation procedure in simultaneous equation models and is particularly useful for estimating equations which are overidentified. In our discussion of 2SLS we start out with a simple specific case before moving on to consider the general case of an overidentified equation.

To outline the 2SLS procedure, we first discuss its application to the model given in equation (6.43) where both equations are exactly identified:

$$\left. \begin{array}{l} y_{1t} = \beta_{12}y_{2t} + \gamma_{11}x_{1t} + u_{1t} \\ y_{2t} = \beta_{21}y_{1t} + \gamma_{22}x_{2t} + u_{2t} \end{array} \right\} \tag{6.69}$$

To obtain the 2SLS estimators of the parameters of the second structural equation of (6.69) we first apply (OLS) to the reduced form equation for y_{1t} and then calculate the predicted value of $\hat{y}_{1t}$, i.e. we regress y_{1t} on all the predetermined variables of the model to obtain

$$\hat{y}_{1t} = \hat{\Pi}_{11}x_{1t} + \hat{\Pi}_{12}x_{2t} \tag{6.70}$$

In the second stage of the procedure we perform the OLS regression of y_{2t} on $\hat{y}_{1t}$ and x_{2t}. Since $\hat{y}_{1t}$ is uncorrelated with the stochastic disturbance term u_{2t}, i.e. plim $(\Sigma \hat{y}_{1t}u_{2t}/n) = 0$, this two-stage procedure gives rise to consistent estimators of the parameters of the second structural equation. In a similar manner, consistent estimators of the parameters of the first structural equation can also be obtained.

For the above model, the reduced form estimators are, respectively,

$$\left.\begin{aligned}\hat{\Pi}_{11} &= (\Sigma x_2^2 \Sigma x_1 y_1 - \Sigma x_1 x_2 \Sigma x_2 y_1)/D \\ \hat{\Pi}_{12} &= (\Sigma x_1^2 \Sigma x_2 y_1 - \Sigma x_1 x_2 \Sigma x_1 y_1)/D \\ \hat{\Pi}_{21} &= (\Sigma x_2^2 \Sigma x_1 y_2 - \Sigma x_1 x_2 \Sigma x_2 y_2)/D \\ \hat{\Pi}_{22} &= (\Sigma x_1^2 \Sigma x_2 y_2 - \Sigma x_1 x_2 \Sigma x_1 y_2)/D\end{aligned}\right\} \quad (6.71)$$

where
$$D = \Sigma x_1^2 \Sigma x_2^2 - (\Sigma x_1 x_2)^2$$

Carrying out the second stage of the estimation procedure for the second structural equation we have

$$\left.\begin{aligned}\beta_{21}^{2\text{SLS}} &= \frac{\Sigma x_2^2 \Sigma \hat{y}_1 y_2 - \Sigma \hat{y}_1 x_2 \Sigma x_2 y_2}{\Sigma \hat{y}_1^2 \Sigma x_2^2 - (\Sigma \hat{y}_1 x_2)^2} \\ \gamma_{22}^{2\text{SLS}} &= \frac{\Sigma \hat{y}_1^2 \Sigma x_2 y_2 - \Sigma \hat{y}_1 x_2 \Sigma \hat{y}_1 y_2}{\Sigma \hat{y}_1^2 \Sigma x_2^2 - (\Sigma \hat{y}_1 x_2)^2}\end{aligned}\right\} \quad (6.72)$$

Substituting $\hat{y}_{1t} = \hat{\Pi}_{11} x_{1t} + \hat{\Pi}_{12} x_{2t}$ in the expression for $\beta_{21}^{2\text{SLS}}$, we obtain after some manipulation,

$$\begin{aligned}\beta_{21}^{2\text{SLS}} &= \frac{\hat{\Pi}_{11}(\Sigma x_2^2 \Sigma x_1 y_2 - \Sigma x_1 x_2 \Sigma x_2 y_2)}{\hat{\Pi}_{11}^2(\Sigma x_1^2 \Sigma x_2^2 - (\Sigma x_1 x_2)^2)} = \frac{\hat{\Pi}_{21}}{\hat{\Pi}_{11}} \\ &= \frac{\Sigma x_2^2 \Sigma x_1 y_2 - \Sigma x_1 x_2 \Sigma x_2 y_2}{\Sigma x_2^2 \Sigma x_1 y_1 - \Sigma x_1 x_2 \Sigma x_2 y_1}\end{aligned} \quad (6.73)$$

Similarly, it can be shown for our particular model that

$$\gamma_{22}^{2\text{SLS}} = \frac{\Sigma x_1 y_1 \Sigma x_2 y_2 - \Sigma x_2 y_1 \Sigma x_1 y_2}{\Sigma x_2^2 \Sigma x_1 y_1 - \Sigma x_1 x_2 \Sigma x_2 y_1} \quad (6.74)$$

2SLS estimation of the second equation is IV estimation where the instrument for y_{1t} is $\hat{y}_{1t}$. In the case where the equation is exactly identified, as applies in this case, the 2SLS estimators are equal to the IV estimators, where the instruments for y_{1t} are the predetermined variables not included in the particular structural equation. Using x_{1t} as an instrument for y_{1t} and x_{2t} as an instrument for itself in the IV estimation of our second structural equation, we have

$$\left.\begin{aligned}\Sigma x_1 y_2 &= \beta_{21} \Sigma x_1 y_1 + \gamma_{22} \Sigma x_1 x_2 \\ \Sigma x_2 y_2 &= \beta_{21} \Sigma x_2 y_1 + \gamma_{22} \Sigma x_2^2\end{aligned}\right\} \quad (6.75)$$

Solving for the IV estimators, we obtain

$$\beta_{21}^{\text{IV}} = \frac{\Sigma x_2^2 \Sigma x_1 y_2 - \Sigma x_1 x_2 \Sigma x_2 y_2}{\Sigma x_2^2 \Sigma x_1 y_1 - \Sigma x_1 x_2 \Sigma x_2 y_1} \quad (6.76)$$

$$\gamma_{22}^{\text{IV}} = \frac{\Sigma x_1 y_1 \Sigma x_2 y_2 - \Sigma x_2 y_1 \Sigma x_1 y_2}{\Sigma x_2^2 \Sigma x_1 y_1 - \Sigma x_1 x_2 \Sigma x_2 y_1} \quad (6.77)$$

Comparing equations (6.73) with (6.76) and equation (6.74) with (6.77) we see that the 2SLS estimators and IV estimators are equivalent when the equation is exactly identified. It is also the case that, for an exactly identified equation, they are both equal to the ILS estimators.

We now consider the general case of the estimation of an overidentified equation by means of 2SLS.

Assume that the first structural equation of the system is overidentified as in equation (6.58):

$$y_1 = Y_1\beta_1 + X_1\gamma_1 + u_1 \qquad (6.78)$$

where y_1 is a $T \times 1$ vector of the endogenous variable whose coefficient in the first equation is 1, Y_1 is a $T \times G_1 - 1$ matrix of the remaining endogenous variables included in the first equation, X_1 is a $T \times K_1$ matrix of the predetermined variables included in the first equation and u_1 is a $T \times 1$ vector of stochastic disturbances. Rewrite equation (6.78) as

$$y_1 = Z_1\delta_1 + u_1$$

where

$$Z_1 = [Y_1 \ X_1] \text{ and } \delta_1 = \begin{bmatrix} \beta_1 \\ \gamma_1 \end{bmatrix} \qquad (6.79)$$

The reduced form equations for the $G_1 - 1$ right-hand-side endogenous variables of this equation are given by

$$\left. \begin{aligned} y_2 &= X\Pi_2 + v_2 \\ y_3 &= X\Pi_3 + v_3 \\ &\vdots \\ y_{G_1} &= X\Pi_{G_1} + v_{G_1} \end{aligned} \right\} \qquad (6.80)$$

where X is a $T \times K$ matrix of all the predetermined variables of the system, Π_i is a $K \times 1$ vector of reduced form coefficients and v_i is a $T \times 1$ vector of reduced form disturbances. Since the first structural equation is overidentified by assumption, the number of predetermined variables excluded from the equation, $K - K_1$, is greater than $G_1 - 1$ and, accordingly, there are more instruments available than are actually required in the instrumental variable estimation. As our set of instruments for Y_1 we therefore utilise $\hat{Y}_1$, namely $\hat{Y}_1 = [\hat{y}_2, \ldots, \hat{y}_{G_1}]$:

$$\left. \begin{aligned} \hat{y}_2 &= X\hat{\Pi}_2 \\ \hat{y}_3 &= X\hat{\Pi}_3 \\ &\vdots \\ \hat{y}_{G_1} &= X\hat{\Pi}_{G_1} \end{aligned} \right\} \qquad (6.81)$$

where $\hat{\Pi}_i$ is a vector of estimated reduced form coefficients. Let

$$W_1 = [\hat{Y}_1 \ X_1]$$

Hence

$$W_1'Z_1 = \begin{bmatrix} \hat{Y}_1' \\ X_1' \end{bmatrix} [Y_1 \ X_1] = \begin{bmatrix} \hat{Y}_1'Y_1 & \hat{Y}_1'X_1 \\ X_1'Y_1 & X_1'X_1 \end{bmatrix} \quad (6.82)$$

and

$$W_1'y_1 = \begin{bmatrix} \hat{Y}_1'y_1 \\ X_1'y_1 \end{bmatrix} \quad (6.83)$$

The instrumental estimator, δ^{IV}, is then given by

$$\delta^{IV} = \begin{bmatrix} \hat{Y}_1'Y_1 & \hat{Y}_1'X_1 \\ X_1'Y_1 & X_1'X_1 \end{bmatrix}^{-1} \begin{bmatrix} \hat{Y}_1'y_1 \\ X_1'y_1 \end{bmatrix} \quad (6.84)$$

Note that

$$\hat{Y}_1'Y_1 = (Y_1 - \hat{V}_1)'Y_1 = Y_1'Y_1 - \hat{V}_1'(\hat{Y}_1 + \hat{V}_1)$$
$$= Y_1'Y_1 - \hat{V}_1'\hat{V}_1 \quad (6.85)$$

where $\hat{V}_1$ is the $T \times G_1 - 1$ matrix of estimated reduced form disturbances which are uncorrelated with $\hat{Y}_1$. Also

$$\hat{Y}_1'X_1 = (Y_1 - \hat{V}_1)'X_1 = Y_1'X_1 \quad (6.86)$$

and

$$\hat{Y}_1'y_1 = (Y_1 - \hat{V}_1)'y_1 = Y_1'y_1 - \hat{V}_1'y_1 \quad (6.87)$$

Utilising equations (6.85) through (6.87) we may write the IV estimator as

$$\delta^{IV} = \begin{bmatrix} Y_1'Y_1 - \hat{V}_1'\hat{V}_1 & Y_1'X_1 \\ X_1'Y_1 & X_1'X_1 \end{bmatrix}^{-1} \begin{bmatrix} Y_1'y_1 - \hat{V}_1'y_1 \\ X_1'y_1 \end{bmatrix} \quad (6.88)$$

The above IV estimator in equation (6.88) is the two-stage least squares estimator. We may rewrite the first structural equation of our simultaneous equation model as

$$y_1 = (Y_1 - V_1)\beta_1 + X_1\gamma_1 + (u_1 + V_1\beta_1) \quad (6.89)$$

Since $Y_1 - V_1$ depends only on X and does not involve any disturbance, it is uncorrelated with $u_1 + V_1\beta_1$. Estimation of equation (6.89) by OLS will, therefore, give rise to consistent estimates. However, V_1 is unobservable and must accordingly be replaced by $\hat{V}_1$, the reduced form least squares residuals from the regressions of each of the right-hand-side endogenous variables of the structural equation on all the predetermined variables of the model:

$$Y_1 - \hat{V}_1 = \hat{Y}_1 = [X\hat{\Pi}_2, X\hat{\Pi}_3, \ldots, X\hat{\Pi}_{G-1}] \quad (6.90)$$

Since plim $(Y_1 - \hat{V}_1) = Y_1 - V_1$, $(Y_1 - \hat{V}_1)$ and $(u_1 + \hat{V}_1\beta_1)$ are asymptotically uncorrelated with each other. Consistent estimates of β_1 and γ_1 can therefore be obtained by estimating the following equation by OLS:

$$y_1 = \hat{Y}_1\beta_1 + X_1\gamma_1 + u_1^* \quad (6.91)$$

where $u_1^* = u_1 + \hat{V}_1\beta_1$.

These estimators are two-stage least squares estimators. In the first stage, we apply OLS to estimate the reduced form equations for each right-hand-side endogenous variable of the structural equation. In the second stage, the structural equation is then estimated also by OLS but with the right-hand-side endogenous variables having been replaced by their fitted values from the reduced form equations.

Equation (6.91) may be written as

$$y_1 = \hat{Z}_1 \delta_1 + u_1^* \tag{6.92}$$

where $\hat{Z}_1 = [\hat{Y}_1 \ X_1]$. The 2SLS estimator is then given by

$$\delta_1^{2SLS} = \begin{bmatrix} \beta_1^{2SLS} \\ \gamma_1^{2SLS} \end{bmatrix} = (\hat{Z}_1'\hat{Z}_1)^{-1}\hat{Z}_1'y_1$$

$$= \begin{bmatrix} \hat{Y}_1'\hat{Y}_1 & \hat{Y}_1'X_1 \\ X_1'\hat{Y}_1 & X_1'X_1 \end{bmatrix}^{-1} \begin{bmatrix} \hat{Y}_1'y_1 \\ X_1'y_1 \end{bmatrix} \tag{6.93}$$

Since $\hat{Y}_1 = X\hat{\Pi}_1 = X(X'X)^{-1}X'Y_1$, where $\hat{\Pi}_1$ is a $K \times G_1 - 1$ matrix of estimated reduced form coefficients, and $\hat{Y}_1'X_1 = Y_1'X_1$, an alternative formulation is

$$\delta_1^{2SLS} = \begin{bmatrix} Y_1'X(X'X)^{-1}X'Y_1 & Y_1'X_1 \\ X_1'Y_1 & X_1'X_1 \end{bmatrix}^{-1} \begin{bmatrix} Y_1'X(X'X)^{-1}X'y_1 \\ X_1'y_1 \end{bmatrix} \tag{6.94}$$

Furthermore, since $\hat{V}_1'\hat{Y}_1 = 0$ and $\hat{Y}_1'\hat{Y}_1 = Y_1'Y_1 - \hat{V}_1'\hat{V}_1$, we also have

$$\delta_1^{2SLS} = \begin{bmatrix} Y_1'Y_1 - \hat{V}_1'\hat{V}_1 & Y_1'X_1 \\ X_1'Y_1 & X_1'X_1 \end{bmatrix}^{-1} \begin{bmatrix} Y_1'y_1 - \hat{V}_1'y_1 \\ X_1'y_1 \end{bmatrix} \tag{6.95}$$

which is exactly equivalent to the IV estimator given in equation (6.88). Equation (6.93) brings out the two-stage nature of the estimation procedure, while equation (6.94) is computationally convenient.

The estimated variance–covariance matrix of the two-stage least squares estimators is given by

$$\text{est. Var–Cov}(\delta_1^{2SLS}) = s_{11} \begin{bmatrix} Y_1'Y_1 - \hat{V}_1'\hat{V}_1 & Y_1'X_1 \\ X_1'Y_1 & X_1'X_1 \end{bmatrix}^{-1} \tag{6.96}$$

where a consistent estimator of $\text{Var}(u_{1t})$ is provided by

$$s_{11} = \frac{(y_1 - Y_1\beta_1^{2SLS} - x_1\gamma_1^{2SLS})'(y_1 - Y_1\beta_1^{2SLS} - x_1\gamma_1^{2SLS})}{T} \tag{6.97}$$

Note that in the formula for s_{11}, we have Y_1 rather than $\hat{Y}_1$. Our model equation is with respect to Y_1 and not $\hat{Y}_1$ and therefore s_{11} should be based on Y_1 rather than $\hat{Y}_1$. The 2SLS estimator, though consistent, is not asymptotically efficient since no account has been taken in the construction of the estimators of the correlation across the model equations of the stochastic disturbances. However, the approach does have the advantage that complete knowledge of the whole system is not required. It is sufficient to have a listing of the predetermined variables of the complete model.

Limited information maximum likelihood

For completeness we mention briefly another single-equation estimation procedure known as limited information maximum likelihood (LIML). Given the following structural equation of a simultaneous equation model which is assumed to be identified:

$$y_1 = \beta_{12}y_2 + \gamma_{11}x_1 + \gamma_{12}x_2 + u_1 \qquad (6.98)$$

let $y_1^* = y_1 - \beta_{12}y_2$; if β_{12} were known, then the investigator could regress y_1^* on the predetermined variables of the structural equation and obtain the residual sum of squares (RSS_1) from this regression. A further regression of y_1^* on all the predetermined variables of the model could also be performed and the associated residual sum of squares (RSS) be obtained. Form the ratio of RSS_1 to RSS, noting that it cannot fall below unity since the addition of new regressors can never lead to an increase in the residual sum of squares:

$$l = \frac{RSS_1}{RSS} \qquad (6.99)$$

In the LIML approach, we minimise l by choosing appropriate values of the coefficients on the endogenous variables included on the right-hand side of the particular structural equation. Having obtained estimates of these parameters, estimates of the coefficients on the predetermined variables appearing in the structural equation can then be obtained by performing the OLS regression of estimated y_1^* on the relevant predetermined variables. If the structural equation is exactly identified, the LIML gives the same results as the other single-equation estimation techniques we have discussed in this section.

A desirable feature of LIML is that the estimates are invariant to the particular normalisation adopted. Consider the following equation of a simultaneous equation model:

$$\beta_{11}y_{1t} + \beta_{12}y_{2t} + \gamma_{11}x_{1t} + \gamma_{12}x_{2t} + \gamma_{13}x_{3t} = u_{1t} \qquad (6.100)$$

If we normalise on y_1 by setting β_{11} equal to unity, i.e. we let y_1 be the left-hand-side 'dependent' variable, then the first structural equation of the model becomes

$$y_{1t} = -\beta_{12}y_{2t} - \gamma_{11}x_{1t} - \gamma_{12}x_{2t} - \gamma_{13}x_{3t} + u_{1t} \qquad (6.101)$$

Assuming this equation is identified, we can then employ either 2SLS or LIML to obtain estimates of the parameters of this equation.

Consider the case where we normalise on y_2 by setting β_{12} equal to unity, in this case we would now have

$$y_{2t} = -\beta_{11}y_{1t} - \gamma_{11}x_{1t} - \gamma_{12}x_{2t} - \gamma_{13}x_{3t} + u_{1t} \qquad (6.102)$$

This equation can then be estimated, for example by either 2SLS or LIML. However, employing the method of 2SLS, it will not generally be the case that

$$\beta_{11}^{2SLS} = \frac{1}{\beta_{12}^{2SLS}} \qquad (6.103)$$

whereas with LIML it will always be the case that the estimators will be invariant to normalisation in the sense that

$$\beta_{11}^{LIML} = \frac{1}{\beta_{12}^{LIML}} \tag{6.104}$$

The other LIML estimators γ_{11}, γ_{12} and γ_{13} are related with β_{12} (LIML) and the values of γ_{11}, γ_{12} and γ_{13} depend upon the obtained estimator β_{12}.

This invariance property is a highly desirable property for the LIML estimator to possess. Since in a simultaneous equation model the endogenous variables are all jointly determined, it is accordingly somewhat arbitrary which variable is chosen as the left-hand-side variable for a particular equation. In order to estimate the parameters of a particular equation it is obviously necessary to set one of the parameters equal to unity. With 2SLS the estimates will be influenced by which variable is used for normalisation unless the equation is exactly identified. Despite this advantage of LIML over 2SLS, because of its greater computational complexity, the former approach is used less frequently in empirical work.

An example

Assume that we wish to obtain estimates of the parameters of the following model in which both equations are exactly identified:

$$\left. \begin{array}{l} y_{1t} = \beta_{12} y_{2t} + \gamma_{11} x_{1t} + u_{1t} \\ y_{2t} = \beta_{21} y_{1t} + \gamma_{22} x_{2t} + u_{2t} \end{array} \right\} \tag{6.105}$$

The sample consists of 100 observations and the sample matrices are as follows:

$$X'X = \begin{bmatrix} 50 & 0 \\ 0 & 100 \end{bmatrix} \quad X'Y = \begin{bmatrix} 10 & 25 \\ -50 & 70 \end{bmatrix}$$

$$Y'Y = \begin{bmatrix} 100 & 35 \\ 35 & 80 \end{bmatrix}$$

First we estimate the reduced form coefficients for the two reduced form equations:

$$\hat{\Pi}_1 = \begin{bmatrix} 50 & 0 \\ 0 & 100 \end{bmatrix}^{-1} \begin{bmatrix} 10 \\ -50 \end{bmatrix}$$

$$= \begin{bmatrix} 0.02 & 0 \\ 0 & 0.01 \end{bmatrix} \begin{bmatrix} 10 \\ -50 \end{bmatrix} = \begin{bmatrix} 0.2 \\ -0.5 \end{bmatrix}$$

$$\hat{\Pi}_2 = \begin{bmatrix} 0.02 & 0 \\ 0 & 0.01 \end{bmatrix} \begin{bmatrix} 25 \\ 70 \end{bmatrix} = \begin{bmatrix} 0.5 \\ 0.7 \end{bmatrix}$$

From the reduced form coefficients, equation (6.45), it is a straightforward matter to obtain estimates of the structural coefficients:

$$\hat{\beta}_{12} = \frac{\hat{\Pi}_{12}}{\hat{\Pi}_{22}} = \frac{-0.5}{0.7} = -0.714\,285\,7$$

$$\hat{\beta}_{21} = \frac{\hat{\Pi}_{21}}{\hat{\Pi}_{11}} = \frac{0.5}{0.2} = 2.5$$

$$\hat{\gamma}_{11} = \hat{\Pi}_{11}[1 - \hat{\beta}_{12}\hat{\beta}_{21}] = 0.557\,142\,8$$

$$\hat{\gamma}_{22} = \hat{\Pi}_{22}[1 - \hat{\beta}_{12}\hat{\beta}_{21}] = 1.95$$

We now turn to consider the 2SLS approach. Since we have already obtained estimates of the reduced form coefficients, we can move on quickly to the second stage:

$$\hat{y}_{1t} = 0.2x_{1t} - 0.5x_{2t}$$

Hence,

$$\Sigma \hat{y}_{1t}^2 = 0.04 \Sigma x_{1t}^2 - 0.2 \Sigma x_{1t}x_{2t} + 0.25 \Sigma x_{2t}^2$$

$$= 27$$

$$\Sigma \hat{y}_{1t} x_{2t} = 0.2 \Sigma x_{1t}x_{2t} - 0.5 \Sigma x_{2t}^2$$

$$= -50$$

and

$$\Sigma \hat{y}_{1t} y_{2t} = 0.2 \Sigma x_{1t} y_{2t} - 0.5 \Sigma x_t y_{2t}$$

$$= -30$$

Since $\hat{y}_{2t} = 0.5\,x_{1t} + 0.7\,x_{2t}$, it follows that

$$\Sigma \hat{y}_{2t}^2 = 61.5 \quad \Sigma \hat{y}_{2t} x_{1t} = 25$$

and

$$\Sigma \hat{y}_{2t} y_{1t} = -30$$

The TSLS estimates for the first structural equation are, therefore, given by:

$$\delta_1^{\text{2SLS}} = \begin{bmatrix} 61.5 & 25 \\ 25 & 50 \end{bmatrix}^{-1} \begin{bmatrix} -30 \\ 10 \end{bmatrix}$$

$$= \begin{bmatrix} 0.020\,408 & -0.010\,204 \\ -0.010\,204 & 0.025\,102 \end{bmatrix} \begin{bmatrix} -30 \\ 10 \end{bmatrix} = \begin{bmatrix} -0.714\,285\,7 \\ 0.557\,142\,8 \end{bmatrix}$$

and for the second structural equation by:

$$\delta_2^{\text{2SLS}} = \begin{bmatrix} 27 & -50 \\ -50 & 100 \end{bmatrix}^{-1} \begin{bmatrix} -30 \\ 70 \end{bmatrix}$$

$$= \begin{bmatrix} 0.5 & 0.25 \\ 0.25 & 0.135 \end{bmatrix} \begin{bmatrix} -30 \\ 70 \end{bmatrix} = \begin{bmatrix} 2.5 \\ 1.95 \end{bmatrix}$$

Note that these estimates are identical to the indirect least squares estimates. We may also obtain the asymptotic standard errors of the 2SLS estimates.

$$s_{11} = \frac{\Sigma(y_{1t} + 0.714\,285\,7y_{2t} - 0.557\,142\,8x_{1t})^2}{100}$$

$$= 2.349\,897\,7$$

and
$$s_{22} = \frac{\Sigma(y_{2t} - 2.5y_{1t} - 1.95x_{2t})^2}{100}$$

$$= 1.707\,5$$

The standard error of the estimate of the first equation is, therefore, 1.532 937 6, and of the second equation it is 1.306 713 4.

Hence, the asymptotic standard errors of the estimated parameters are as follows:

$$se(\hat{\beta}_{12}) = 1.532\,937\,6\,\sqrt{(0.020\,408)} = 0.218\,991$$

$$se(\hat{\gamma}_{11}) = 1.532\,937\,6\,\sqrt{(0.025\,102)} = 0.242\,872\,6$$

$$se(\hat{\beta}_{11}) = 1.306\,713\,4\,\sqrt{(0.5)} = 0.923\,986$$

$$se(\hat{\gamma}_{22}) = 1.306\,713\,4\,\sqrt{(0.135)} = 0.480\,117$$

In all four cases, the asymptotic t ratio is absolutely greater than 2 and we would reject the null hypothesis of a zero coefficient in every case.

6.4 SYSTEM METHODS OF ESTIMATION

The single-equation estimation procedures that have been discussed in the preceding section yield consistent estimators of the parameters of the model, but since they do not take account of the contemporaneous correlation of the stochastic disturbances of different equations of the model, the estimators are not, in general, asymptotically efficient. System-wide methods of estimation – three-stage least squares (3SLS) (Zellner and Theil, 1962) and full information maximum likelihood (FIML) – allow for the disturbances across equations to be correlated; FIML estimators are also invariant to normalisation (Hood and Koopmans, 1953). We provide a brief introduction to these system methods of estimation.

Three-stage least squares estimation

Let us normalise the first equation of the model with respect to y_1, i.e. we set $\beta_{11} = 1$, the second equation of the model with respect to y_2, i.e. $\beta_{22} = 1$, and so on. Then in matrix notation we have, for the ith equation,

$$y_i = Y_i\beta_i + X_i\gamma_i + u_i \quad (i = 1, 2, \ldots, G) \tag{6.106}$$

where $[y_i \quad Y_i]$ is a $T \times G_i$ matrix of observations on the G_i endogenous variables occurring in the ith equation, β_i is a $(G_i - 1) \times 1$ vector of parameters on the right-

System methods of estimation 155

hand-side-endogenous variables, X_i is a $T \times K_i$ matrix of observations on the K_i predetermined variables of the ith equation, γ_i is a $K_i \times 1$ vector of parameters on the predetermined variables, and u_i is a $T \times 1$ vector of disturbances in this equation. We assume that the order condition for identification is satisfied for each of the G equations of the model.

Let

$$Z_i = [Y_i \quad X_i] \text{ and } \delta_i = \begin{bmatrix} \beta_i \\ \gamma_i \end{bmatrix}$$

then we may rewrite equation (6.106) as

$$y_i = Z_i \delta_i + u_i \quad (i = 1, 2, \ldots, G) \tag{6.107}$$

We now assume that the disturbances in different equations are contemporaneously correlated but are independent over time:

$$E(u_i u_j') = \sigma_{ij} I \tag{6.108}$$

Premultiply equation (6.107) by X':

$$X' y_i = X' Z_i \delta_i + X' u_i \quad (i = 1, 2, \ldots, G) \tag{6.109}$$

which may be written as

$$\begin{bmatrix} X'y_1 \\ X'y_2 \\ \vdots \\ X'y_G \end{bmatrix} = \begin{bmatrix} X'Z_1 & 0 & \ldots & 0 \\ 0 & X'Z_2 & & 0 \\ \vdots & & & \\ 0 & 0 & & X'Z_G \end{bmatrix} \begin{bmatrix} \delta_1 \\ \delta_2 \\ \vdots \\ \delta_G \end{bmatrix} + \begin{bmatrix} X'u_1 \\ X'u_2 \\ \vdots \\ X'u_G \end{bmatrix} \tag{6.110}$$

The variance–covariance matrix of the stochastic disturbances of the above system is given by

$$E(X' u_i u_j' X) = \begin{bmatrix} \sigma_{11}(X'X) & \sigma_{12}(X'X) & \ldots & \sigma_{1G}(X'X) \\ \sigma_{21}(X'X) & \sigma_{22}(X'X) & & \sigma_{2G}(X'X) \\ \vdots & & & \\ \sigma_{G1}(X'X) & \sigma_{G2}(X'X) & & \sigma_{GG}(X'X) \end{bmatrix} \tag{6.111}$$

In order to estimate the parameters of this system of equations, in absence of a a priori information on the σ_{ij}s, we need consistent estimates of the variances and covariances of the stochastic disturbance terms. Such estimates are available by estimating each individual equation by 2SLS and then by calculating

$$s_{ij} = \frac{(y_i - Z_i \delta_i^{2SLS})'(y_j - Z_j \delta_j^{2SLS})}{T} \quad (i, j = 1, 2, \ldots, G) \tag{6.112}$$

The 3SLS estimator is then given by

$$\delta^{3SLS} = \begin{bmatrix} s^{11}Z'_1X(X'X)^{-1}X'Z_1 & s^{12}Z'_1X(X'X)^{-1}X'Z_2 \cdots & s^{1G}Z'_1(X'X)^{-1}X'Z_G \\ s^{21}Z'_2X(X'X)^{-1}X'Z_1 & s^{21}Z'_2X(X'X)^{-1}X'Z_2 & s^{2G}Z'_2(X'X)^{-1}X'Z_G \\ \vdots & & \\ s^{G1}Z'_GX(X'X)^{-1}X'Z_i & s^{G2}Z'_GX(X'X)^{-1}X'Z_2 & s^{GG}Z'_G(X'X)^{-1}X'Z_G \end{bmatrix}$$

$$\times \begin{bmatrix} \sum_{j=1}^{G} s^{1j} \; Z'_1X(X'X)^{-1} \; X'y_j \\ \sum_{j=1}^{G} s^{2j} \; Z'_2X(X'X)^{-1} \; X'y_j \\ \vdots \\ \sum_{j=1}^{G} s^{Gj} \; Z'_GX(X'X)^{-1} \; X'y_j \end{bmatrix} \quad (6.113)$$

where s^{ij} denotes the ijth element of the inverse of the estimated variance–covariance matrix of the stochastic disturbances. The estimated variance–covariance matrix of δ^{3SLS} is given by the first matrix on the right-hand side of equation (6.113).

Three stage least squares estimates of the structural parameters are both consistent and asymptotically efficient. They are, in fact, identical to 2SLS estimates under two sets of circumstances: first when $E(u_i u'_j) = \sigma_{ij} = 0$ for $i \neq j$, i.e. when the contemporaneous correlations between the stochastic disturbances are zero and, second, when each equation in the system is exactly identified regardless of whether or not the stochastic disturbances are correlated. Another interesting feature of this approach is that exactly identified equations add nothing to the estimation of the other equations of the system and their exclusion from the 3SLS estimation will not affect the estimates of the parameters of the remaining equations. An iterative 3SLS procedure may also be utilised in which a second estimate of the variance–covariance matrix of the disturbances is obtained from the 3SLS residuals. This second estimate of the variance–covariance matrix can then be used to derive a second-round 3SLS estimate of the coefficients and the procedure can be repeated until the estimates converge.

Full information maximum likelihood estimation

The second system method of estimation for a simultaneous equation model is full information maximum likelihood. Repeating equation (6.11) we write the complete system of equations of the model. Recalling equation (6.12), we have

$$By_t + \Gamma x_t = u_t \quad (6.114)$$

and the variance–covariance matrix of u_t is

$$E(u_t u'_t) = \Sigma \quad (6.115)$$

The joint distribution of the elements of $u_t \sim N(0, \Sigma)$ is

System methods of estimation   157

$$f(u_t) = (2\Pi)^{-G/2} \Sigma^{-\frac{1}{2}} \exp[(u_t' \Sigma^{-1} u_t)/2] \qquad (6.116)$$

The probability transformation from the unobservable u_t to the observable y_t is

$$f(y_t | x_t) = f(u_t) \left| \frac{\partial u_t}{\partial y_t} \right| = f(u_t) \left| \frac{\partial (By_t + \Gamma x_t)}{\partial y_t} \right|$$

$$= f(u_t) |B| \qquad (6.117)$$

where $|B|$ is the absolute value of the determinant of B, the matrix of coefficients on the jointly endogenous variables of the system. The log likelihood function for the T observations on y_t conditional on the values of x_t which we seek to maximise is, accordingly, given by

$$L = -\frac{GT}{2} \log(2\Pi) - \frac{T}{2} \log |\Sigma| + T \log |B|$$

$$- \frac{1}{2} \sum_{t=1}^{T} (By_t + \Gamma x_t)' \Sigma^{-1} (By_t + \Gamma x_t) \qquad (6.118)$$

We obtain FIML estimators of B, Γ and Σ by maximising the above expression numerically with respect to these parameters. The estimators thereby obtained are consistent, asymptotically efficient, and their asymptotic distribution is normal. In fact the FIML and 3SLS estimators share the same asymptotic variance–covariance matrix which can be obtained in the usual way from the information matrix. An advantage of the FIML procedure is that, as with its single-equation counterpart LIML, the estimators are invariant to the particular normalisation adopted for a given equation. Set against this advantage is the greater computational complexity of the method which arises out of the need to numerically solve a set of nonlinear equations. For a unified treatment of all simultaneous equations estimators, the reader is referred to Hendry (1976).

A simulation exercise
In order to compare the estimates of the parameters of a simultaneous equation model derived from alternative single equation and system methods of estimation, the following simulation exercise was performed. The following true model was first specified in which both equations of the model are overidentified:

$$\left. \begin{array}{l} Y_{1t} = 7.5 + 5Y_{2t} - 4X_{2t} + 8X_{3t} + u_{1t} \\ Y_{2t} = 50.5 - 0.6Y_{1t} + 0.5X_{4t} + 10X_{5t} + u_{2t} \end{array} \right\} \qquad (6.119)$$

We specified the sample values of the predetermined variables and obtained values for the disturbances from a table of standard normal deviates. Using the reduced form equations, we were then able to generate values for the endogenous variables. The data for this exercise are presented in Table 6.1. The model was estimated using three single-equation estimation methods (OLS, 2SLS and LIML) and the two system methods (3SLS and FIML). The results are presented in Table 6.2.

Estimation in simultaneous equation models

Table 6.1 Data for simulation exercise

Y_1	Y_2	X_2	X_3	X_4	X_5	u_1	u_2
166.5100	88.7940	74	1	35	12	3.04	0.70
535.8000	126.8200	30	2	74	36	1.80	0.80
601.3175	148.3295	43	3	20	45	0.17	−1.38
779.3475	167.2115	24	4	46	56	−0.21	1.32
222.8675	70.2495	44	5	26	14	0.12	0.47
1120.8450	261.7030	61	6	48	86	0.83	−0.29
1215.9100	261.5940	39	7	21	93	0.44	0.14
1011.0025	222.2385	43	8	59	75	0.31	−1.16
1211.1700	275.8780	62	9	80	91	0.28	2.08
431.4050	96.0570	34	10	29	29	−0.38	−0.10
769.3425	181.1545	58	11	67	56	0.07	−1.24
1122.5625	271.7025	85	12	88	85	0.55	0.74
740.0100	193.6940	85	13	37	57	0.04	−1.30
280.0900	63.3960	39	14	23	17	−0.39	−0.55
1016.4025	244.9285	84	15	25	79	0.26	1.77
1118.6300	254.6720	72	16	14	87	−2.23	−1.65
427.2925	86.4345	37	17	82	25	−0.38	1.31
832.6375	150.0675	18	18	97	55	2.80	0.65
1009.8150	183.9610	17	19	19	73	−1.49	−0.15
630.6225	168.6965	95	20	93	45	−0.36	0.07
1217.2125	277.0925	86	21	32	94	0.25	0.92
273.6175	41.1995	29	22	49	13	0.12	0.37
564.6075	109.0855	43	23	73	36	−0.32	0.85
566.5700	140.8980	84	24	23	42	−1.42	−1.16
598.6950	139.6730	77	25	75	41	0.83	0.89
508.9875	73.7875	19	26	77	29	0.55	0.18
826.5475	162.1515	52	27	36	59	0.29	−0.42
833.8350	159.5290	49	28	17	60	0.69	0.83
1170.1650	254.2210	85	29	54	88	−0.44	−1.18
1171.0325	200.7605	20	30	25	84	−0.27	0.38

Table 6.2 Results of the simulation exercise

Equation 1 Method of estimation	Constant	Y_2	X_2	X_3	SEE
OLS	7.932 573 (0.6888)	4.998 302 (0.0033)	−3.996 724 (0.0096)	7.983 638 (0.0237)	1.119 95
2SLS	7.930 004 (0.6888)	4.998 326 (0.0033)	−3.996 756 (0.0096)	7.983 651 (0.0237)	1.119 96
LIML	7.584 779 (0.6536)	5.001 588 (0.0031)	−4.001 147 (0.0091)	7.985 309 (0.0225)	1.062 65
3SLS	7.930 004 (0.6338)	4.998 326 (0.0030)	−3.996 756 (0.0088)	7.983 651 (0.0217)	1.042 62
FIML	7.865 294 (1.3131)	4.998 209 (0.0061)	−3.995 942 (0.0093)	7.986 315 (0.0320)	1.043 05
True values	7.5	5	−4	8	

Equation 2 Method of estimation	Constant	Y_1	X_4	X_5	SEE
OLS	49.822 03 (0.6549)	−0.595 57 (0.0063)	0.509 751 (0.0080)	9.944 954 (0.0780)	0.980 942

Equation 2 Method of estimation	Constant	Y_1	X_4	X_5	SEE
2SLS	49.894 45 (0.6556)	−0.596 929 (0.0063)	0.510 602 (0.0080)	9.961 608 (0.0781)	0.981 808
LIML	49.8928 (0.6103)	−0.596 898 (0.0059)	0.510 583 (0.0075)	9.961 227 (0.0727)	0.913 977
3SLS	49.894 45 (0.6051)	−0.596 929 (0.0059)	0.510 602 (0.0073)	9.961 608 (0.0727)	0.914 013
FIML	50.007 13 (0.8558)	−0.596 948 (0.0108)	0.508 417 (0.0115)	9.961 731 (0.1325)	0.915 774
True values	50.5	−0.6	0.5	10	

Note: Figures in parentheses are standard errors of regression coefficients.

Whatever the method of estimation employed, the estimates do not differ much from the true values of the parameters; this is even the case for the OLS estimates. For the first equation the system methods of estimation give rise to a smaller standard error of the estimate, but this is not the case for the second equation where LIML has the smallest SEE.

All the simultaneous equation methods of estimation, both single-equation and system-wide procedures, produce estimators with some desirable asymptotic properties. However, such properties are only going to be present in large sample estimators, while typically the applied econometrician has a restricted number of observations available to him. We possess much less information about the properties of the various estimators in small samples. The evidence we have from Monte Carlo simulation studies suggests that the OLS estimator tends to have a smaller variance but larger bias than either the 2SLS or LIML estimator. Using the minimum square error (MSE) as the criterion for evaluating different estimators, then in some cases the OLS estimator will be superior and in other cases inferior to the 2SLS or LIML estimator. In comparing the 2SLS and LIML estimators, the former tend to score higher on the MSE criterion. The advantages of the system methods of estimation usually continue to hold in small samples, though FIML appears to be particularly sensitive to specification error in comparison to, say, 2SLS. Using the *t* test for hypothesis testing in small samples in simultaneous equation models is not strictly valid since the asymptotic distribution of the estimator is normal, but no great harm results from employing the test in such samples. Certainly, as far as hypothesis testing is concerned, consistent methods of estimation are to be preferred to OLS.

Estimating a structural equation of a simultaneous equation model by OLS may give rise to highly misleading results. Many labour economists, for example, have sought to estimate the impact that trades unions have on the relative pay of their members. Typically, they have found that the earnings of trades unionists are some 10–15 per cent above the level paid to nonunion members with similar skills and qualifications; for a survey of this literature see Parsley (1980). In a large number of these studies, OLS was the chosen estimation technique; however, there are good reasons for thinking that earnings and being a union member are likely to be jointly determined. Unions may push up pay above the competitive level, but at the same time the demand for union services may, in turn, be positively influenced by income and hence by earnings. Furthermore, higher earnings may be associated, in part, with greater quantities of specific human capital in the sense of Becker (1964). Workers with large endowments of such capital are more likely to seek to improve their position by taking collective rather than individual action. This preference for 'voice' over 'exit' will increase the probability that such workers are union members and enhance the likelihood that wages and unionism are jointly determined variables.

This issue of the endogeneity of unionism was addressed in a well-known paper by Ashenfelter and Johnson (1972). In their basic model, the log of the wage rate (hourly earnings) was held to depend upon labour quality, the proportion of the workforce unionised and the proportion of the workforce who were female, while the unionism variable was postulated to depend upon the log of the wage rate and the degree of concentration within the industry. The study was based on a cross-section of two digit US manufacturing industries for the year 1960. In a further development of the basic model, a third equation defining labour quality as dependent upon a skill index and urbanisation was explicitly introduced and the whole system was then estimated by 3SLS. In Table 6.3 we present the results for the basic model. It is particularly instructive to compare the OLS and 2SLS estimates of the impact of unionism on earnings; the 2SLS estimate is less than half the OLS estimate and it is not significantly different from zero. For the unionism equation, however, there is little difference in the two sets of estimates.

In the more general model estimated by 3SLS, the coefficient on the unionism variable in the wage equation, was actually negative, though it was not significantly different from zero.

6.5 CONCLUDING REMARKS

Prior to estimating the parameters of a structural equation of a simultaneous equation model, as we have discussed earlier in the chapter, identifying restrictions must be imposed. Following estimation, however, it may transpire that the nonzero

Table 6.3 Unionsm and wages

	Log of wage rate	Labour quality	Unionism	Proportion female	Concentration	Constant	SEE
OLS	1	0.077	0.382	− 0.473		− 0.172	0.053
		(0.013)	(0.093)	(0.082)		(0.127)	
2SLS	1	0.090	0.176	− 0.521			0.059
		(0.021)	(0.267)	(0.108)			
OLS	0.576		1		0.280	0.109	0.098
	(0.122)				(0.142)	(0.100)	
2SLS	0.534		1		0.290	0.139	0.098
	(0.131)				(0.143)	(0.10)	

Note: standard errors appear in brackets below the parameter estimates.

restrictions on the structural parameters are not fulfilled, with the result that one or more equations of the model will, *ex post*, remain underidentified. An example will help to clarify the point.

In his inaugural lecture, Kaldor (1966) proposed the hypothesis that the growth rate in certain mature economies was constrained by a shortage of labour. As an economy developed, differences in productivity levels between different sectors of the economy tended to narrow and the scope for rapid growth of output as a result of resource reallocation became attenuated. According to Kaldor a more rapid rate of growth of overall output was associated with a more rapid rate of growth of manufacturing output. The more rapid manufacturing output grew, the greater the increase in productivity growth due to both economies of scale and learning effects; but this growth of manufacturing output could be constrained by a shortage of labour. Kaldor's work generated substantial interest and controversy as well as one new tax: selective employment tax. One line of development was to allow explicitly for simultaneity in the model.

Consider the following model proposed by Parikh (1978):

$$\mathring{E}_m = a + b\mathring{Q}_m + c\mathring{G}_w + dI + u_1 \tag{6.120}$$

$$\mathring{Q}_m = e + f\mathring{E}_m + g\mathring{X} + u_2 \tag{6.121}$$

$$\mathring{G}_w = \lambda \mathring{E}_m + (1-\lambda)N\mathring{M}E \tag{6.122}$$

$$\mathring{P}_m + \mathring{Q}_m = \mathring{E}_m \tag{6.123}$$

The endogenous variables are the rate of growth of manufacturing employment ($\mathring{E}_m$), the rate of growth of manufacturing output ($\mathring{Q}_m$), the rate of growth of the workforce ($\mathring{G}_w$) and the rate of growth of productivity in the manufacturing sector ($\mathring{P}_m$). The exogenous variables are the investment output ratio in the manufacturing sector (I), the rate of growth of exports ($\mathring{X}$), the rate of growth of the nonmanufacturing workforce ($N\mathring{M}E$) and manufacturing employment as a proportion of the labour force in the first year of the period (λ). Pooled cross-section and time-series data for a sample of OECD countries including Japan were utilised, giving 41 observations in total. The definitional equation for $\mathring{G}_w$ was used to eliminate this variable from the first equation of the model. The first equation is just identified, while the second is overidentified. The estimated equations, using 2SLS, are

$$\mathring{E}_m = -0.6921 + 0.4003\mathring{Q}_m + 0.265\,N\mathring{M}E - 0.0086I$$
$$\quad\quad (1.2540)\;(2.7670)\quad\;\;(1.3270)\quad\quad\;(0.1410)$$

SEE = 1.0806

$$\mathring{Q}_m = 1.5364 + 0.1322\mathring{X} + 1.9907\mathring{E}_m$$
$$\quad\quad (1.9370)\;(0.7840)\quad\;(2.5870)$$

SEE = 2.0910

Using the asymptotic t test we are unable to reject the null hypothesis that the coefficients on the exogenous variables are zero. A joint test would also lead to the same conclusion. This means that $\mathring{E}_m$ is determined by $\mathring{Q}_m$ and $\mathring{Q}_m$ is determined by $\dot{E}_m$. Without a significant influence of a different exogenous variable in each of the equations, both equations remain underidentified.

Problems may arise if the investigator seeks to estimate a large-scale econometric model using 2SLS when the number of exogenous variables of the model is large in relation to the total number of observations. In extreme cases, the former may indeed exceed the latter and the technique cannot be applied. In such circumstances, one solution would be to utilise the first few principal components of the full set of exogenous variables as the right-hand-side variables in the first stage of the estimation procedure. Many large-scale models have, in practice, been estimated using OLS rather than by using the consistent methods of estimation we have discussed in this chapter.

The econometric issues we have discussed earlier in the book in the context of a single-equation model – heteroscedasticity, autocorrelation, multicollinearity and specification error – also arise in simultaneous equation models. Discussion, however, of these issues in the framework of a simultaneous equation model is beyond the scope of this book. For a treatment of these issues, the interested reader is referred to Griliches and Intriligator (1983), Judge et al. (1985), Kmenta (1986).

Exercises

1. Use the order and rank conditions to assess the identifiability of each equation in the structure:

$$y_{1t} + \beta_{12}y_{2t} + \gamma_{11}x_{1t} + \gamma_{13}x_{3t} = \epsilon_{1t}$$

$$\beta_{21}y_{1t} + y_{2t} + \beta_{23}y_{3t} + \gamma_{21}x_{1t} + \gamma_{22}x_{2t} = \epsilon_{2t}$$

$$\beta_{32}y_{2t} + y_{3t} + \gamma_{31}x_{1t} = \epsilon_{3t}$$

2. Let the model be

$$y_{1t} + \beta_{12}y_{2t} + \gamma_{11}x_{1t} + \gamma_{13}x_{3t} = \epsilon_{1t}$$

$$\beta_{21}y_{1t} + y_{2t} + \gamma_{22}x_{2t} + \gamma_{23}x_{3t} = \epsilon_{2t}$$

Suppose the observations on the variables are

y_1	y_2	x_1	x_2	x_3
4	3	1	4	2
7	6	2	4	2
8	2	3	8	4
9	5	4	10	5
10	7	5	12	6
11	9	6	20	10

(a) Examine whether the rank and order conditions for identification are satisfied by each equation and suggest a suitable estimation procedure for each equation.
(b) Use the above data and a suitable estimation procedure to obtain estimates of the parameters of the model. In the light of your numerical results, discuss whether the model needs modification and if so in what way.

3. Let the model be

$$y_{1t} + \beta_{12}y_{2t} + \gamma_{12}x_{2t} + \gamma_{13}x_{3t} = \epsilon_{1t}$$
$$\beta_{21}y_{1t} + y_{2t} + \gamma_{21}x_{1t} + \gamma_{24}x_{4t} = \epsilon_{2t}$$

If the second-moment matrices of a sample of 100 observations are

$$y'y = \begin{bmatrix} 80.0 & -4.0 \\ -4.0 & 5.0 \end{bmatrix} \quad y'x = \begin{bmatrix} 2.0 & 1.0 & -3.0 & -5.0 \\ -0.5 & 1.5 & 0.5 & -1.0 \end{bmatrix}$$

$$x'x = \begin{bmatrix} 3.0 & 0 & 0 & 0 \\ 0 & 2.0 & 0 & 0 \\ 0 & 0 & 1.0 & 0 \\ 0 & 0 & 0 & 0.5 \end{bmatrix}$$

Find the 2SLS estimates of the coefficients of the first equation and their standard errors.

4 (a) Using the data below, estimate by the method of indirect least squares the coefficients of the consumption function of the following model

$$C_t = \alpha + \beta Y_t + \epsilon_t$$
$$Y_t = C_t + Z_t$$

C_t	Y_t	Z_t
34.9	45.2	9.2
35.9	47.0	10.5
37.9	50.3	12.1
41.1	55.7	14.4
43.5	59.9	16.1
46.7	65.2	16.4
48.9	68.9	17.3
52.0	74.3	18.0
56.1	81.2	19.3
62.6	92.2	21.0

(b) Compare these ILS estimates to the OLS estimates of the model

$$C_t = \alpha + \beta Y_t + \epsilon_t$$

5. Study the identifiability of each equation in the structural model equations (6.120)–(6.123). Using the data given below, estimate the parameters of the model by:
   (a) two-stage least squares;
   (b) three-stage least squares;
   (c) full information maximum likelihood.

Analyse and intrepret the results. Assess the identification of each equation after estimation of the model.

Data on endogenous and exogenous variables

Country	Period	$\dot{E}_m$	$\dot{Q}_m$	I	$\dot{G}_w$
Austria	1957–61	1.83	4.27	13.67	0.05
	1961–66	0.27	4.31	14.18	−0.13
	1966–70	−0.71	6.65	12.62	−2.75
Canada	1951–56	1.49	5.32	12.90	2.05
	1956–66	2.70	5.20	13.81	2.23
	1966–69	1.47	3.46	16.89	3.07
Norway	1951–56	0.74	3.87	19.12	0.25
	1956–60	0.00	3.57	16.51	0.13
	1960–65	1.29	5.44	20.30	−0.07
	1965–70	1.37	4.43	19.04	0.79
Belgium	1951–57	0.42	3.64	13.86	−0.06
	1957–64	0.82	5.77	17.52	0.58
	1964–70	0.16	4.89	20.08	0.59
United States of America	1951–56	1.01	2.86	11.59	0.89
	1956–66	1.08	4.28	11.12	1.24
	1966–69	1.62	3.36	13.42	2.15
United Kingdom	1951–55	1.17	3.76	11.48	0.73
	1955–60	0.73	2.81	12.77	0.30
	1960–65	0.49	3.28	13.14	0.80
	1965–69	−0.93	2.78	12.81	−0.30
Japan	1953–57	6.27	13.81	22.14	2.30
	1957–61	5.63	14.59	31.70	1.30
	1961–64	4.19	11.46	35.17	1.04
	1964–69	2.74	13.14	27.67	1.66
W. Germany	1951–56	5.82	11.30	13.46	1.79
	1956–61	2.93	7.99	14.95	0.93
	1961–64	1.75	6.12	16.72	0.89
	1964–69	0.65	5.53	15.20	−0.26
Italy	1955–59	1.52	6.61	22.05b	1.35
	1959–63	5.28	9.59	24.35	−0.19
	1963–70	1.18	6.81	22.81	−0.62
France	1957–60	0.37	4.40	13.11	0.06
	1960–64	2.19	6.87	17.22	0.98
	1964–69	0.44	5.86	17.49	0.69
Netherlands	1951–56	1.92	6.24	13.96	1.48
	1956–60	1.29	5.94	16.13	0.81
	1960–65	1.69	5.63	18.64	0.61
	1965–70	−0.13	7.06	18.86	0.91
Denmark	1957–62	4.02	5.66	9.26	1.13
	1962–65	1.09	5.71	11.08	0.69
	1965–69	0.97	4.02	9.82	0.67

(a) Definitions of variables:

$\dot{E}_m$ = rate of growth in manufacturing employment;

$\dot{Q}_m$ = rate of growth in manufacturing output;

$\dot{X}$ = rate of growth in exports;

$\dot{G}_w$ = rate of growth in workforce;

I = investment: output ratios in manufacturing;

$NM\dot{E}_m = \dot{G}_w - \lambda\dot{E}_m$.

(b) All investment–output ratios refer to the whole economy.

Concluding remarks

(c) Rates of growth of output in manufacturing, employment and investment ratio are taken from Cripps and Tarling (1973). Cripps and Tarling divide the time period covered for each country into subperiods, each period beginning and ending at a cyclical peak.

(d) *Per capita* figures are derived from OECD national accounts for the first year of the subperiod.

(e) Rate of growth in the workforce is derived by fitting an exponential curve to the data on the workforce collected from *Labour Force Statistics* (OECD, Paris). For the same subperiods, rates of growth in exports are again derived on the same basis from *International Financial Statistics*.

6. Given the data on X_2, X_3, X_4 and X_5 in Table 6.1 and the following values for the disturbances u_1 and u_2, use the equations given in (6.119) to obtain the true values of Y_1 and Y_2

u_1	u_2
− 1.34	− 0.98
0.13	0.10
0.02	− 0.88
0.63	− 1.02
0.70	− 0.98
0.12	− 0.90
0.55	0.63
− 0.59	0.49
− 0.43	0.56
0.31	0.04
0.48	1.62
− 1.51	− 1.27
0.27	0.89
− 0.01	0.12
− 1.40	0.55
0.63	− 0.48
0.24	− 1.08
0.95	− 1.16
− 1.70	1.02
− 0.03	− 0.35
− 0.84	1.74
− 0.74	2.58
0.87	0.18
0.94	0.81
0.76	0.19
− 0.08	− 0.47
0.42	− 0.85
0.49	− 0.65
0.23	− 0.87
0.40	− 1.22

Then perform your own simulation exercise and obtain OLS, 2SLS, LIML, 3SLS and FIML estimates of the parameters of the model. Compare your results to those given in Table 6.2.

References

Anderson, T.W. and Rubin, H. (1949). 'Estimation of the parameters of a single equation in a complete system of stochastic equations', *Annals of Mathematical Statistics,* **20**(1), 46–63.

Ashenfelter, O. and Johnson, G.E. (1972), 'Unionism, relative wages and labor quality in US manufacturing industries', *International Economic Review*, **13**(3), 488–508.

Becker, G. (1964), *Human Capital: a theoretical and empirical analysis with special reference to education*, Princeton NJ: Princeton University Press for NBER.

Cripps, T.F. and Tarling, R.J. (1973) *Growth in Advanced Capitalist Economies, 1950–1970*, Department of Applied Economics, Occasional Paper (40), Cambridge: Cambridge University Press.

Engle, R.F., Hendry, D.F. and Richard, J.F. (1983), 'Exogeneity', *Econometrica*, **51**, 277–304.

Fisher, F.M. (1966), *The Identification Problem in Econometrics*, New York: McGraw-Hill.

Griliches, Z. and Intriligator, M. (eds.) (1983), *Handbook of Econometrics*, Volume 1, Amsterdam: North-Holland.

Hendry, D.F. (1976). 'The structure of simultaneous equation estimators', *Journal of Econometrics*, **4**, 51–88.

Hood, W.C. and Koopmans, T.C. (eds.) (1953), *Studies in Econometric Method*, New York: Wiley.

Judge, G. Griffiths, W.E., Carter Hill, R., Lutkepohl, H. and Lee, T.C. (1985), *The Theory and Practice of Econometrics*, New York: Wiley.

Kaldor, N. (1966), *Causes of the Slow Rate of Economic Growth of the United Kingdom*, Cambridge: Cambridge University Press.

Kmenta, J. (1986), *Elements of Econometrics*, New York: MacMillan.

Parikh, A. (1978), 'Differences in growth and Kaldor's laws', *Economica*, **45**, 83–91.

Parsley, C.J. (1980), 'Labor unions and wages: a survey', *Journal of Economic Literature*, **XVIII** (1), 1–31.

Sargent, T.J. (1976) 'A classical macroeconometric model of the United States', *Journal of Political Economy*, **84** (2) 207–37.

Zellner, A. and Theil, H. (1962), 'Three stage least squares: simultaneous estimation of simultaneous equations', *Econometrica*, **30**, 63–8.

Chapter 7

AN INTRODUCTION TO INPUT–OUTPUT ANALYSIS

In this chapter we provide an introduction to input–output analysis. In Section 7.1 we discuss the main features of the open Leontief input–output model (Leontief, 1986). We state the conditions which must be satisfied by the matrix of technical input–output coefficients for the Leontief system to be a viable one in the sense of being able to satisfy any arbitrary final demand vector subject only to there being sufficient primary inputs available. An economic interpretation of the elements of the Leontief inverse is provided. The determination of equilibrium prices for this static input–output model is then elucidated.

In Section 7.2 we discuss the repercussions which occur throughout the economy as the output of a particular good changes. We are concerned here with both backward and forward linkages and we discuss ways of measuring the extent of such linkages.

In Section 7.3 we introduce foreign trade into the static input–output model and show how the enlarged model can be utilised to examine the structure of an economy's international trade. In particular, we show that the technique enables one to determine whether an economy's exports are more or less capital intensive than its import substitutes.

In Section 7.4 we touch upon the Leontief dynamic input–output model. We deal with the question of whether an economy is capable of balanced growth in which all sectors of the economy expand in proportion. We deal initially with the polar case in which there is no consumption, but we later adopt a more general approach.

In Section 7.5 the procedures for updating input–output tables are discussed. First, we consider the mechanical procedure of RAS which is used to update the table when relevant full census data are not available. Thereafter, we suggest other procedures for updating input–output matrices.

Throughout the chapter we provide numerical examples to aid the reader's understanding of the material.

7.1 THE STATIC LEONTIEF OPEN INPUT–OUTPUT MODEL

In this section we outline the basic features of Leontief's open input–output model. The economy is made up of a number of different industries, each of which will be assumed to produce a single good; ruling out joint production or production of many different goods by the industry is clearly a substantial oversimplification but it is made for reasons of pedagogy. In order to produce its output, an industry utilises certain primary inputs, e.g. labour of various skill types, capital equipment, etc., and in addition requires a number of the goods produced elsewhere in the economy as intermediate inputs. Unlike the capital equipment at the disposal of the industry, these intermediate inputs are totally used up during the production process. To produce beet sugar, the manufacturer must purchase inputs from other industries, such as sugar beet, limestone, coal, electricity, paper and packaging, and transportation services in addition to the primary inputs necessary for the production process. In turn, these demands for intermediate inputs give rise to demands by other industries for intermediate inputs to produce the intermediate inputs required in the original industry, and so on. Such repercussions will in many instances impinge on the original industry; to mine more coal, more electricity is required to power the mining machinery, while to generate more electricity requires more coal for the power stations, etc. The Leontief system is thus a highly interdependent one. The technology underlying the system is one of fixed production coefficients; to produce a ton of steel requires a given amount of coal, electricity, iron ore, etc. Constant returns to scale prevail; a doubling of output requires a doubling in the employment of the intermediate inputs. The output of a particular industry can be decomposed into two parts: that part which is used as an intermediate input in its own and other industries; and that part allocated to final demand which includes consumption, investment including changes in physical stocks, government expenditure and net exports. We assume that the final demands for each good are exogenously given.

Mathematically, the system takes the following form:

$$\left.\begin{aligned} a_{11}x_1 + a_{12}x_2 + \ldots + a_{1n}x_n + d_1 &= x_1 \\ a_{21}x_1 + a_{22}x_2 + \ldots + a_{2n}x_n + d_2 &= x_2 \\ &\vdots \\ a_{n1}x_1 + a_{n2}x_2 + \ldots + a_{nn}x_n + d_n &= x_n \end{aligned}\right\} \quad (7.1)$$

where a_{ij} represents the amount of the ith good necessary to produce a unit of the jth good, x_j is the gross output of the jth good and d_j the final demand for good j. Each equation of the system states that the gross output of good i is equal to the sum of the intermediate demands for good i ($\sum_{j=1}^{n} a_{ij}x_j$) and the final demand d_i.

More compactly we may write the system of equations in matrix notation:

$$Ax + d = x \quad (7.2)$$

where A is a $(n \times n)$ matrix of technical input–output coefficients, the a_{ij}s, x and d

are, respectively ($n \times 1$) column vectors of gross outputs of and final demands for the n goods. Rearranging equation (7.2) we have

$$(I - A)x = d \tag{7.3}$$

where I is an identity matrix. Premultiplying equation (7.3) by $(I - A)^{-1}$, we obtain

$$x = (I - A)^{-1} d \tag{7.4}$$

Equation (7.4) gives us the gross output vector that it will be necessary to produce in order to satisfy some exogenously given set of final demands.

In Table 7.1 we present information for an economy with three industries on the allocation of each industry's gross output between intermediate and final demand. We assume there is only one primary input: labour. All the data are in physical units. Of the agricultural gross output of 600 units, 150 units were used as an intermediate input in the production of the agricultural output; 320 units were used as an intermediate input in the production of the manufacturing output; there was no direct input into services; and 130 units were consumed by the household sector, who also supplied 147 units of labour of agriculture. A similar interpretation can be given to the remainder of the table for the manufacturing and service industries. From the above information on interindustry flows, given our assumption of constant returns to scale, we may obtain the matrix of technical input–output coefficients. Letting x_{ij} represent the flow of output from industry i to industry j and x_j, as before, be the gross output of industry j, we have

$$a_{ij} = \frac{x_{ij}}{x_j} \tag{7.5}$$

For example, let manufacturing be indexed by i and services by j, then

$$a_{ij} = \frac{100}{500} = 0.2$$

In order to produce one unit of the service, we require 0.2 units of the manufactured good.

In this way, we may build up the A matrix. For the above hypothetical economy, we have

Table 7.1 Interindustry transactions

Input from	Agriculture	Manufacturing	Services	Final demand	Gross output
Agriculture	150	320	0	130	600
Manufacturing	60	80	100	560	800
Services	30	160	100	210	500
Labour	147	256	320		

$$A = \begin{bmatrix} 0.25 & 0.4 & 0 \\ 0.1 & 0.1 & 0.2 \\ 0.05 & 0.2 & 0.2 \end{bmatrix} \quad (7.6)$$

Hence,

$$(I - A) = \begin{bmatrix} 0.75 & -0.4 & 0 \\ -0.1 & 0.9 & -0.2 \\ -0.05 & -0.2 & 0.8 \end{bmatrix} \quad (7.7)$$

The matrix formed from the cofactors of $(I - A)$ is given by

$$C = \begin{bmatrix} 0.68 & 0.09 & 0.65 \\ 0.32 & 0.6 & 0.17 \\ 0.08 & 0.15 & 0.635 \end{bmatrix} \quad (7.8)$$

and since the determinant of $(I - A)$ is 0.474, we have

$$(I - A)^{-1} = \frac{1}{0.474} \begin{bmatrix} 0.68 & 0.32 & 0.08 \\ 0.09 & 0.6 & 0.15 \\ 0.065 & 0.17 & 0.635 \end{bmatrix}$$

$$= \begin{bmatrix} 1.4346 & 0.6751 & 0.1688 \\ 0.1899 & 1.2658 & 0.3165 \\ 0.1371 & 0.3586 & 1.3397 \end{bmatrix} \quad (7.9)$$

On the assumption that there exists a linear relationship between the demand for the primary input (L_j) by industry j and its gross output of the form

$$L_j = l_j x_j \quad (7.10)$$

then the labour input coefficients vector l is easily derived:

$$l' = \begin{bmatrix} \dfrac{147}{600} & \dfrac{256}{800} & \dfrac{320}{500} \end{bmatrix}$$

$$= [0.245 \quad 0.32 \quad 0.64] \quad (7.11)$$

In order to produce a unit of gross output of the agricultural good, 0.245 units of labour must be employed; a similar interpretation can be given to the remaining elements of the l vector.

Now what interpretation can be given to the elements of the Leontief inverse? Let us assume we wish to produce a consumption bundle which simply contains one unit of good j; in other words, the final demand vector d contains 1 in the jth row and 0s everywhere else. Under these circumstances, the gross output vector it will be necessary to produce in order to meet the final demand is given by the jth column of

$(I-A)^{-1}$. If we let $R = (I-A)^{-1}$ and a typical element of R be given by r_{ij}, then r_{ij} measures the total amount of good i that it is necessary to produce in order to make available a unit of net output of good j for consumption or any other final demand purposes. Hence, for our hypothetical economy, in order to make available one unit of the agricultural good for consumption purposes, we must produce 1.4346 units of the agricultural good, 0.1899 units of the manufactured good and 0.1371 units of the service. These are the sums of the direct and indirect requirements for each good. 0.4346 units of the agricultural good are used up in the production of the agricultural good itself and in the production of the other goods which are necessary to produce the agricultural good, and so on. A similar interpretation applies to the remaining columns of the Leontief inverse. Given this interpretation of the elements of R, it is clear that each r_{ij} must be non-negative; it would be economically nonsensical for any of them to be negative. At most, the gross output of some good can be zero when we satisfy a particular final demand requirement; it cannot be negative.

In the light of the above interpretation of the elements of the Leontief inverse, let us now briefly consider the interpretation to be given to the elements of the row vector $l'(I-A)^{-1}$. The first element of this vector is

$$l_1 r_{11} + l_2 r_{21} + \ldots + l_n r_{n1}$$

which tells us the total amount of labour which must be employed in the production of the n goods in order to make available one unit of the first good for final demand. More generally, we have that the ith element of $l'(I-A)^{-1}$ measures the direct and indirect labour requirements for unit net output of good i. For our three-sector hypothetical economy, we have

$$l'(I-A)^{-1} = [0.245 \quad 0.32 \quad 0.64] \begin{bmatrix} 1.4346 & 0.6751 & 0.1688 \\ 0.1899 & 1.2658 & 0.3165 \\ 0.1371 & 0.3586 & 1.3397 \end{bmatrix}$$

$$= [0.5 \quad 0.8 \quad 1] \qquad (7.12)$$

In this particular economy, the service sector is the most labour intensive and agriculture the least labour intensive.

In order to meet a given bill of final demands d, there must be available a sufficient supply of any primary inputs which are required in the production process. Assuming only one primary input – labour – whose total supply is L, then we must have, in order to meet a given final demand vector,

$$l'(I-A)^{-1} d \leq L \qquad (7.13)$$

What restrictions need to be imposed on the technical input-output coefficients for all the r_{ij}s to be non-negative and for any net output bundle to be producible provided the economy has available a sufficient quantity of the primary inputs? Conditions for the non-negativity of the r_{ij}s have been derived by Hawkins and Simon (1949). These conditions are commonly referred to as the Hawkins-Simon conditions and a neat economic interpretation can be given to them. They are defined with respect to the $(I-A)$ matrix and they require that all the principal minors of $(I-A)$ be positive.

For the general case of a system containing n industries, we must therefore have that:

(1) $1 - a_{jj} > 0$ (for $j = 1, 2, \ldots, n$);
(2) all the second-order principal minors of $(I - A)$ be positive;
$\vdots$
($n - 1$) all the $(n - 1)$th order principal minors of $(I - A)$ positive;
(n) $|I - A| > 0$.

The above conditions are complex, with the degree of complexity clearly increasing rapidly as the number of sectors in the model increases. Despite this complexity the basic economic rationale for the conditions is easily understood. Since a_{jj} measures the amount of good j used as a direct intermediate input in the production of one unit of good j, the first part of the condition simply requires that less than one unit of good j is used directly to produce a unit of good j. Furthermore, once a part of a unit of a good has been allocated to its own production, there must be sufficient remaining of that good to be allocated to those other sectors that require this good as an input and whose output is itself required as an input into the original good.

To illustrate: consider a particularly simple system of a two-sector input–output model in which neither sector uses its own output directly as an intermediate input. Then

$$(I - A) = \begin{bmatrix} 1 & -a_{12} \\ -a_{21} & 1 \end{bmatrix} \tag{7.14}$$

and

$$|I - A| = 1 - a_{12}a_{21} \tag{7.15}$$

which, by the Hawkins–Simons conditions, must be positive. Writing the equations of this model out in full, we have

$$x_1 = a_{12}x_2 + d_1 \tag{7.16}$$

$$x_2 = a_{21}x_1 + d_2 \tag{7.17}$$

Now assume the final demand for good 1 is zero and substitute equation (7.16) in equation (7.17) to obtain

$$x_2 = a_{21}a_{12}x_2 + d_2 \tag{7.18}$$

The gross output of good 2 is the sum of the amount allocated to final demand, d_2, and the amount of good 2 which is used as an intermediate input in the production of good 1, which is itself required to produce good 2. To produce x_2 units of good 2 we require $a_{12}x_2$ units of good 1 which, in turn, require $a_{21}a_{12}x_2$ units of good 2. If the Hawkins–Simon conditions are violated, then $a_{21}a_{12}$ is greater than 1. In other words, more than a unit of good 2 is used up in producing a unit of good 2. Hence the system is not productive.

The above interpretation is of general applicability. In order for the technology to be viable, the production of one unit of a good must require less than one unit of itself as an input into its own production when all the repercussions throughout the system, both direct and indirect, have been taken into account. The satisfaction of the Hawkins–Simon conditions guarantees that this will indeed be the case.

Light can be thrown on this matter from a slightly different angle. We wish to meet a final bill of goods d; then the gross output bundle that must be produced is given by

$$x = d + AD + A^2 d + \ldots$$
$$= (I + A + A^2 + \ldots)d \qquad (7.19)$$

In order to produce the final bill of goods, d, the vector of direct intermediate inputs, Ad, must be available: but to meet these direct intermediate input demands there is a need for further intermediate inputs which is given by $A^2 d$, and so on *ad infinitum*.

Letting

$$S = I + A + A^2 + \ldots \qquad (7.20)$$

and postmultiplying by A, we have

$$SA = A + A^2 + A^3 + \ldots \qquad (7.21)$$

Subtracting equation (7.21) from equation (7.20), we obtain

$$S(I - A) = I - \lim_{n \to \infty} A^n$$

Hence if $\lim_{n \to \infty} A^n = 0$, which it will be provided that each column sum of A is less than 1:

$$S = (I - A)^{-1} \qquad (7.22)$$

and

$$x = (I - A)^{-1} d \qquad (7.23)$$

Consider the case where the Leontief technical input–output coefficients matrix A is decomposable such that by permuting rows and columns it may be partitioned in the following way:

$$A = \begin{bmatrix} A_{11} & A_{12} \\ 0 & A_{22} \end{bmatrix} \begin{matrix} \text{rows} \\ n - m \\ m \end{matrix} \qquad (7.24)$$

$$\text{columns} \quad n - m \quad m$$

where A_{11} and A_{22} are square, nonsingular matrices and 0 and A_{12} are rectangular matrices. Then

$$I - A = \begin{bmatrix} \hat{A}_{11} & \hat{A}_{12} \\ 0 & \hat{A}_{22} \end{bmatrix} \qquad (7.25)$$

where $\hat{A}_{11} = I - A_{11}$, $\hat{A}_{22} = I - A_{22}$ and $\hat{A}_{12} = -A_{12}$.

From the inverse of a partitioned matrix, we have

$$(I - A)^{-1} = \begin{bmatrix} \hat{A}_{11}^{-1} & -\hat{A}_{11}^{-1} \hat{A}_{12} \hat{A}_{22}^{-1} \\ 0 & \hat{A}_{22}^{-1} \end{bmatrix} \qquad (7.26)$$

Assume we wish to produce a bill of final goods d in which $d_i = 0$ for $i = n - m + 1, \ldots, n$, then the gross output vector x will only contain positive quantities of the first $(n - m)$ goods. None of the other goods will be produced, being needed neither for final demand nor as an input into the production of the first $(n - m)$ goods. A necessary condition, therefore, for the production of any final bill of goods to require positive quantities of all goods to be produced is that A be indecomposable. More generally, for a non-negative, square, indecomposable matrix A, then $(I - A)^{-1}$ is positive provided that the dominant eigenvalue of A, λ^*, is less than 1. This dominant eigenvalue will be necessarily positive and associated with it is a positive eigenvector (see Debreu and Herstein, 1953). This result is of great significance for the analysis of a dynamic input–output model which we discuss below in Section 7.4.

There exists a number of alternative ways of expressing the necessary and sufficient conditions for any arbitrary non-negative final demand vector to be associated with a non-negative gross output vector. We state them here for convenience. Given a vector of final demands, d, the associated vector of gross outputs will be non-negative iff:

(a) $\lim_{n \to \infty} A^n = 0$;
(b) the principal minors of $(I - A)$ are all positive;
(c) the dominant eigenvalue of A is less than 1;
(d) $(I - A)$ has a positive dominant diagonal.

The fourth alternative is just given for completeness; for a discussion of dominant diagonal matrices the interested reader is referred to McKenzie (1960). The above four conditions are all equivalent; if one is satisfied, so will be the other three. Given that A is a non-negative square matrix, the above conditions will all be satisfied iff the column sums of A or the row sums of A, or both, are all less than unity. Whenever the A matrix is constructed from industry flow data in value terms, which is the usual procedure for the construction of input–output tables for actual economies, the column sums of A will be necessarily less than unity. Each element in the jth column measures the cost share of the ith intermediate input in the production of good j and, assuming each good requires at least one primary input for its production, the profitable production of each good clearly requires the sum of the cost shares of the intermediate inputs to be less than unity. The technology that is utilised is naturally an economically viable one.

Now our discussion to date has run in terms of physical quantities. Assume there is only one primary input – labour – and let w represent the wage rate and p_i the price of good i. In a competitive economy zero profits are earned and we have

$$\left. \begin{array}{l} a_{11}p_1 + a_{21}p_2 + \ldots + a_{n1}p_n + wl_1 = p_1 \\ a_{12}p_1 + a_{22}p_2 + \ldots + a_{n2}p_n + wl_2 = p_2 \\ \vdots \\ a_{1n}p_1 + a_{2n}p_2 + \ldots + a_{nn}p_n + wl_n = p_n \end{array} \right\} \quad (7.27)$$

More compactly, the above system of equations may be written in matrix notation as

$$p'A + wl' = p' \tag{7.28}$$

Rearranging we have

$$p'(I - A) = wl' \tag{7.29}$$

and postmultiplying by $(I - A)^{-1}$, we obtain

$$p' = wl'(I - A)^{-1} \tag{7.30}$$

Since the elements of $l'(I - A)^{-1}$ yield the direct and indirect labour requirements for unit net output of each good, these prices simply reflect the value of the labour embodied directly and indirectly in a unit of each good. If we let labour be the numeraire, then with $w = 1$ we can easily find the equilibrium prices for each good. As we have seen earlier for our hypothetical economy:

$$l'(I - A)^{-1} = [0.5 \quad 0.8 \quad 1] \tag{7.31}$$

In this special case, with labour the only primary input, the prices of the goods equal the value of the labour embodied in each good; the labour theory of value holds in this instance.

Using the above prices, we may convert our original table (Table 7.1) where all the information was presented in physical units into one in which all the flows are given in value terms (Table 7.2), which is the form in which input–output tables for actual economies are always presented. Total value added in the economy is 723 which is paid out in full to the household sector for the provision of labour services.

Real world interindustry transactions tables are invariably given in value terms. From the data given in value terms in Table 7.2 we may calculate the associated A matrix and then derive the Leontief $(I - A)^{-1}$ matrix:

$$A = \begin{bmatrix} 0.25 & 0.25 & 0 \\ 0.16 & 0.1 & 0.16 \\ 0.1 & 0.25 & 0.2 \end{bmatrix}$$

Table 7.2 Interindustry transactions using wage rate = 1

Input from	Agriculture	Manufacturing	Services	Final demand	Gross output
Agriculture	75	160	0	65	300
Manufacturing	48	64	80	448	640
Services	30	160	100	210	500
Labour	147	256	320	723	1440

and

$$(I-A)^{-1} = \begin{bmatrix} 1.4346 & 0.4219 & 0.0844 \\ 0.3038 & 1.2658 & 0.2532 \\ 0.2743 & 0.4483 & 1.3397 \end{bmatrix}$$

We shall use the above Leontief inverse in deriving our measures of the strength of backward linkages in the next section.

7.2 BACKWARD AND FORWARD LINKAGES

When the final demand for a particular good changes, this has repercussions backwards throughout the economy as the demand for intermediate inputs changes. In tracing through those backward linkages, we may measure the direct, immediate impact on the demand for intermediate inputs of a unit increase in the final demand for good j by adding the elements in the jth column of the A matrix ($\Sigma_{i=1}^{n} a_{ij}$). Of more significance, however, are the direct and indirect effects on the demand for intermediate inputs of the postulated change; these are to be measured by adding the elements in the jth column of $(I-A)^{-1}$, i.e. $\Sigma_{i=1}^{n} r_{ij}$. In evaluating the extent of these backward linkages and in particular for purposes of comparing the relative effects of different final demand increases, it makes sense to normalise the measure of the strength of the backward linkages. The measure then becomes

$$bL_j = \frac{1/n \Sigma_{i=1}^{n} r_{ij}}{1/n^2 \Sigma_{i=1}^{n} \Sigma_{j=1}^{n} r_{ij}} \tag{7.32}$$

where the numerator measures the average impact on the n industries of a unit change in the final demand for good j and the denominator measures the average impact on the n industries of a unit change in the final demand for all n goods.

If for a particular good j, the above measure has a value in excess of unity, then a unit increase in the final demand for good j gives rise to a greater than average impact on the supplying sectors, and conversely for bL_j less than unity. We are also interested in the extent to which these backward linkages are concentrated on one or a small number of sectors or are more evenly spread across the economy. The extent to which the backward effects are dispersed can be measured by the coefficient of variation:

$$CV_j^b = \frac{\sqrt{\{(1/n-1)\Sigma_{i=1}^{n}[r_{ij} - (1/n)\Sigma_{i=1}^{n} r_{ij}]^2\}}}{(1/n)\Sigma_{i=1}^{n} r_{ij}} \tag{7.33}$$

with a lower value of CV_j^b being associated with a more even distribution of the effects on the supplying industries.

For our particular numerical example, we have the following measures of the extent and dispersion of the backward linkages associated with our three industries:

	bL_j	CV_j^b
Agriculture	1.0364	0.9861
Manufacturing	1.0999	0.6739
Services	0.8637	1.6603

It will be noted from the above tableau that the backward linkages from manufacturing are not only more extensive but are also more evenly spread between the different sectors than those from either agriculture or services.

In addition to the above backward linkages, cognizance should also be taken of forward linkages. The increased availability of, say, good j makes possible an increased production of those goods which use good j as an intermediate input. At first sight it might appear by symmetry with our measure of backward linkages that the extent of these forward linkages can be assessed by taking the row sums of A for the direct impact and the row sums of $(I-A)^{-1}$ for the combined direct and indirect impacts. The demands made on the output of sector i when the final demand for each good in the economy increases by one unit is measured by $\Sigma_{j=1}^n r_{ij}$. This latter assumption is unusual and it is not really helpful to devise a measure of forward linkages based on an assumption that demand increases in each industry by one unit, regardless of the fact that there are significant differences in the sizes of the individual industries. Let the production of good j be highly intensive in the use of good i; *ceteris paribus*, this fact would lead to a high estimate of forward linkages stemming from the sector producing good i despite the fact that sector j might be very small relative to the size of the overall economy. To overcome this problem it has been suggested that the r_{ij}s should be weighted according to the overall structure of demand in the economy: each r_{ij} would be multiplied by s_j, value added in sector j as a proportion of total value added. However, this, too, is not a satisfactory way of measuring forward linkages since $\Sigma_{j=1}^n s_j r_{ij}$ measures the demands made on the output of sector i if final demand expands by one pound with the relative size of each sector in terms of value added remaining unchanged. These measures – $\Sigma_{j=1}^n r_{ij}$ and $\Sigma_{j=1}^n s_j r_{ij}$ – or normalised versions of them, are telling us nothing about forward linkages.

In order to develop an appropriate measure of such effects, it is necessary to utilise what is known as the Leontief output inverse rather than the Leontief (input) inverse. To form the latter as we have seen above, it is first necessary to obtain the A matrix, whose elements (the a_{ij}s) measure intermediate inputs as a share of total inputs including value added. Then, $(I-A)^{-1}$ can easily be obtained. To obtain the former inverse, we work with a matrix b, whose elements (the b_{ij}s) measure intermediate sales as a share of total sales including final demand.

Whereas

$$a_{ij} = \frac{x_{ij}}{x_j} \tag{7.34}$$

we have

$$b_{ij} = \frac{x_{ij}}{x_i} \tag{7.35}$$

Given our definition of the B matrix, it follows that

$$x' = x'B + v' \qquad (7.36)$$

where x' is a row vector of gross outputs in value terms and v' is a row vector of value added in each sector. From equation (7.36) it follows that

$$x' = v'(I - B)^{-1} \qquad (7.37)$$

where $(I - B)^{-1}$ is the Leontief output inverse. Let $P = (I - B)^{-1}$, then

$$x' = v'P \qquad (7.38)$$

Writing out this system of equations in full, we obtain

$$\left.\begin{array}{l} x_1 = p_{11}v_1 + p_{21}v_2 + \ldots + p_{n1}v_n \\ x_2 = p_{12}v_1 + p_{22}v_2 + \ldots + p_{n2}v_n \\ \vdots \\ x_n = p_{1n}v_1 + p_{2n}v_2 + \ldots + p_{nn}v_n \end{array}\right\} \qquad (7.39)$$

If value added in sector i increases by one unit, then the sum of the forward repercussions of this change throughout the economy is given by the sum of the n elements in the ith row of P (i.e. $\Sigma_{j=1}^{n} p_{ij}$). As before with our measure of backward linkages, we may normalise to obtain

$$fL_i = \frac{1/n \Sigma_{j=1}^{n} p_{ij}}{1/n^2 \Sigma_{i=1}^{n} \Sigma_{j=1}^{n} p_{ij}} \qquad (7.40)$$

As a measure of the degree of dispersion of the forward linkages, we have

$$CV_i^f = \frac{\sqrt{\{1/(n-1) \Sigma_{j=1}^{n} [p_{ij} - (1/n) \Sigma_{j=1}^{n} p_{ij}]^2\}}}{1/n \Sigma_{j=1}^{n} p_{ij}} \qquad (7.41)$$

An initial increase of value added of one unit in sector i is associated with an expansion of gross output in this same sector. Subsequently, this increase of gross output in sector i is made available to the using sectors in line with the b_{ij} coefficients. These sectors then increase their gross outputs which, in turn, are distributed to the using sectors and so on in this forward progression.

In order to measure the extent of the forward linkages for our hypothetical economy, we must first construct the Leontief output inverse:

$$B = \begin{bmatrix} 75/300 & 160/300 & 0/300 \\ 48/640 & 64/640 & 80/640 \\ 30/500 & 160/500 & 100/500 \end{bmatrix} = \begin{bmatrix} 0.25 & 0.53\ldots & 0 \\ 0.075 & 0.1 & 0.125 \\ 0.06 & 0.32 & 0.2 \end{bmatrix} \qquad (7.42)$$

Hence,

$$I - B = \begin{bmatrix} 0.75 & -0.53\ldots & 0 \\ -0.075 & 0.9 & -0.125 \\ -0.06 & -0.32 & 0.8 \end{bmatrix} \qquad (7.43)$$

and

$$P = (I - B)^{-1} = \begin{bmatrix} 1.4346 & 0.9001 & 0.1398 \\ 0.1424 & 1.2658 & 0.1978 \\ 0.1646 & 0.5738 & 1.3397 \end{bmatrix} \quad (7.44)$$

Having obtained the Leontief output inverse, we may now measure the extent and dispersion of the forward linkages for our hypothetical economy.

	fL_i	CV_i^f
Agriculture	1.2054	0.7889
Manufacturing	0.7823	1.1828
Services	1.0123	0.8611

In contrast with our results on backward linkages, it is the manufacturing sector that has the weakest and most dispersed forward linkages of the three sectors.

7.3 INPUT–OUTPUT ANALYSIS AND FOREIGN TRADE

To date, we have made no allowance for part of the final demand for a particular good to be met by imports, nor have we considered the possibility that the production of some goods might require as intermediate inputs goods which are not available domestically and which have thus to be imported. We may refer to the former category of imports as 'competitive imports' and the latter as 'noncompetitive imports'. We shall assume that the total value of both exports (E) and competitive imports (M) is given; furthermore we postulate that exports of good j are a constant proportion of total exports (e_j) and, similarly, that competitive imports of good j are a constant proportion of total competitive imports (c_j). Regarding noncompetitive imports, we assume that constant returns to scale prevail here also, with m_j noncompetitive imports being required to produce £1 worth of gross output of good j. Finally, the value of exports equals the value of total imports, both competitive and noncompetitive.

Our system of equations may thus be written as

$$\left.\begin{aligned} a_{11}x_1 + a_{12}x_2 + \ldots + a_{1n}x_n + d_1 + e_1E - c_1M &= x_1 \\ a_{21}x_1 + a_{22}x_2 + \ldots + a_{2n}x_n + d_2 + e_2E - c_2M &= x_2 \\ &\vdots \\ a_{n1}x_1 + a_{n2}x_2 + \ldots + a_{nn}x_n + d_n + e_nE - c_nM &= x_n \\ m_1x_1 + m_2x_2 + \ldots + m_nx_n + M + M_{NC} &= E \end{aligned}\right\} \quad (7.45)$$

The first n equations are of the form that the gross output of good i must be allocated to intermediate use ($\sum_{j=1}^{n} a_{ij}x_j$), final demand except exports (d_i) and net exports ($e_iE - c_iM$). With M_{NC} representing the value of noncompetitive imports allocated to final demand, the final equation expresses the requirement that the balance of trade be in equilibrium.

Rearranging the above system of equations and expressing them in matrix notation, we have

$$\begin{bmatrix} I-A & -e \\ -m' & 1 \end{bmatrix} \begin{bmatrix} x \\ E \end{bmatrix} + \begin{bmatrix} c \\ -1 \end{bmatrix} M = \begin{bmatrix} d \\ M_{NC} \end{bmatrix} \qquad (7.46)$$

from which it follows that

$$\begin{bmatrix} x \\ E \end{bmatrix} = H \left\{ - \begin{bmatrix} c \\ -1 \end{bmatrix} M + \begin{bmatrix} d \\ M_{NC} \end{bmatrix} \right\} \qquad (7.47)$$

where

$$H = \begin{bmatrix} I-A & -e \\ -m' & 1 \end{bmatrix}^{-1} \qquad (7.48)$$

Equation (7.47) informs the planners of the vector of gross outputs and the value of exports which must be produced in order to satisfy a given set of final domestic demands and to ensure equilibrium in the balance of trade, where M and M_{NC} are both exogenously given.

Letting k' and l' represent, respectively, row vectors of capital and labour input coefficients, the associated demands for the primary inputs, capital and labour, will be given by

$$[k' \quad 0] \begin{bmatrix} x \\ E \end{bmatrix} \qquad (7.49)$$

and

$$[l' \quad 0] \begin{bmatrix} x \\ E \end{bmatrix} \qquad (7.50)$$

On the other hand, if the planners drop the requirement that trade must balance, the system of equations now becomes

$$(I-A)x - eE + cM = d \qquad (7.51)$$

Hence, after some manipulation, we have

$$x = (I-A)^{-1}[d + eE - cM] \qquad (7.52)$$

The demand for the primary inputs would then be given by

$$k'x \qquad (7.53)$$

and

$$l'x \qquad (7.54)$$

while the associated demand for noncompetitive imports would be

$$m'x \qquad (7.55)$$

A model of the above type was utilised by Leontief (1956) to test the propositions of the factor proportions theory of international trade developed by Heckscher and Ohlin. The Heckscher-Ohlin theorem states that countries will export commodities which are intensive in their abundant factor and import commodities which are intensive in their scarce factor. Leontief surmised that, in comparison to the rest of the world, the United States was capital rich and therefore, according to the theorem, exports from the United States should be capital intensive and import substitutes labour intensive. Leontief was able to calculate the changes in the demand for the primary inputs – capital and labour – which would result from varying the level of competitive imports and exports. Two approaches were adopted: one approach drops the requirement that the balance of trade be in equilibrium, whereas the second approach maintains this equilibrium.

Using the first approach, if competitive imports and exports are both reduced by a million dollars with a corresponding increase in the output of domestic industries to replace the competitive imports, the net increases in the demand for capital and labour will be given, respectively, by

$$k'(I-A)^{-1}(c-e) \qquad (7.56)$$

and

$$l'(I-A)^{-1}(c-e) \qquad (7.57)$$

On the basis of the 1947 input–output table, Leontief obtained the following domestic capital and labour requirements per million dollars of US exports and competitive import replacements:

	Exports	Import replacements	Net change
Capital (dollars, in 1947 prices)	2 550 780	3 091 339	540 559
Labour (man years)	182 313	170 004	– 12 309

Hence, if exports were reduced and import replacements increased by a million dollars, the demand for capital would rise and that for labour would fall. The capital–labour ratio is higher in the production of import replacements than in exports. Contrary to Leontief's initial hypothesis, US exports are labour and not capital intensive; this is the well-known Leontief paradox.

The above empirical estimates were based on the first approach, which neglects the balance of trade equation. However, as we expand domestic production of import substitutes and reduce the production of exports, there are consequential changes in the demand for imported noncompetitive inputs. Depending upon the actual structure of production, it is clearly not necessary if trade is to remain balanced that exports be reduced by an amount equivalent to the increase in value of the increased production of import replacements. More imported inputs are now required, directly and indirectly, to produce the increased output of import replacements, but correspondingly less of such imports are needed to produce the smaller quantity of exports required to ensure balance of trade equilibrium. Whether exports are required to fall by more or less than competitive imports depends upon differences in the non-competitive import intensity of export and import replacement production. If the increased use of imported inputs by the industries producing import replacements is greater (less) than the reduced use of these same inputs in the exporting industries, then exports will fall by less (more) than competitive imports to keep trade balanced. The change in exports will be smaller than the change in competitive imports when the production of import replacements is more intensive in noncompetitive imports than is the production of exports.

Turning to equation (7.47), we can see that the required change in exports for a given change in competitive imports is given by the product of the last row of H, which we shall label H_{n+1}, and $[^c_{-1}]$. Hence,

$$\Delta E = -H_{n+1} \begin{bmatrix} c \\ -1 \end{bmatrix} \Delta M = \mu \Delta M \qquad (7.58)$$

Furthermore, using the second approach, net capital requirements per million dollars of competitive import replacements (i.e. after the neccesary change in export production has been effected in order to keep trade balanced) are given by

$$[k \quad 0] \; H \begin{bmatrix} c \\ -1 \end{bmatrix} \qquad (7.59)$$

The corresponding figure for net labour requirements is given by

$$[l \quad 0] \; H \begin{bmatrix} c \\ -1 \end{bmatrix} \qquad (7.60)$$

Using this second approach, Leontief found for the United States that μ was typically slightly higher than 1 and that import substitutes were again relatively more capital intensive than exports.

7.4 THE DYNAMIC LEONTIEF INPUT–OUTPUT MODEL

In this section we outline a dynamic Leontief input–output model (Leontief, 1970). To produce a unit of good j requires, in addition to current intermediate inputs where the input coefficients are given by the relevant elements in the A matrix, capital inputs. We define the following capital input coefficients matrix:

$$C = \begin{bmatrix} c_{11} & c_{12} & \cdots & c_{1n} \\ c_{21} & c_{22} & & c_{2n} \\ \vdots & & & \\ c_{n1} & c_{n2} & & c_{nn} \end{bmatrix} \qquad (7.61)$$

The dynamic Leontief input–output model

where c_{ij} measures the amount of good i required as a capital input to produce a unit of good j. Letting the vector of capital goods be given by k, then full employment of capital at time t requires

$$k_t = Cx_t \tag{7.62}$$

The capital goods are all assumed to have an infinite life and the same gestation period, with investment in period t satisfying the following condition:

$$k_{t+1} - k_t = C(x_{t+1} - x_t) \tag{7.63}$$

We shall assume initially that part of the current output of each good is used as an intermediate input in the production of all goods and that the remainder is allocated to increasing the stock of capital goods in the economy. We shall later allow for part of the economy's output to be allocated to consumption purposes. We neglect the role of labour in this economy, but we are implicitly assuming that there exists an unlimited supply of labour such that no constraint on the growth rate achievable within this economy arises from the side of labour.

Given our assumption that current output is allocated only to intermediate demand and investment demand, we have

$$x_t = Ax_t + C(x_{t+1} - x_t) \tag{7.64}$$

This can be rearranged to yield the following first-order difference equation:

$$x_{t+1} = [I + C^{-1}(I - A)]x_t \tag{7.65}$$

or, equivalently,

$$x_{t+1} = [I + C^{-1}(I - A)]^{t+1}x_0 \tag{7.66}$$

We may now consider the question as to whether there exists a balanced growth path such that the vector of gross outputs increases through time but with its composition remaining unchanged:

$$x_{t+1} = \lambda^{t+1}x_0 \quad (\text{with } \lambda > 1) \tag{7.67}$$

Defining $G = I + C^{-1}(I - A)$, we may rewrite equation (7.65) as

$$x_{t+1} = Gx_t \tag{7.68}$$

If the above growth path for x_t is balanced, then it must be the case that

$$Gx_t = \lambda x_t \tag{7.69}$$

or, equivalently, that

$$(G - \lambda I)x_t = 0 \tag{7.70}$$

Were the matrix G to have a positive eigenvector x^* and an associated eigenvalue λ^* greater than unity, then it would be the case that

$$Gx^* = \lambda^* x^* \tag{7.71}$$

Furthermore if $x_0 = x^*$, then we would also have a balanced growth path since

$$\left.\begin{aligned} x_1 &= \lambda^* x_0 \\ x_2 &= (\lambda^*)^2 x_0 \\ &\vdots \\ x_{t+1} &= G x_t = (\lambda^*)^{t+1} x_0 \end{aligned}\right\} \quad (7.72)$$

Now it can be shown that a sufficient condition for this system to be capable of balanced growth is that the matrix of technical input–output coefficients, A, be indecomposable and that its dominant eigenvalue be less than 1 in absolute value. If A is indecomposable, then all the elements of $(I-A)^{-1}$ will be positive. Furthermore, since the inverse of the capital input coefficients matrix C was assumed to exist, then each row and column of C must contain at least one nonzero entry. Thus $(I-A)^{-1}C$ will be a positive, and hence an indecomposable, matrix because $(I-A)^{-1}$ is indecomposable and positive. Given its indecomposability, it will possess a dominant eigenvalue μ and an associated positive eigenvector x^*. Hence

$$(I-A)^{-1}Cx^* = \mu x^* \quad (7.73)$$

Premultiplying equation (7.73) by $(1/\mu) C^{-1}(I-A)$, we obtain

$$C^{-1}(I-A)x^* = \frac{1}{\mu} x^* \quad (7.74)$$

and by adding x^* to both sides of equation (7.74), we have

$$[I + C^{-1}(I-A)]x^* = \left(1 + \frac{1}{\mu}\right) x^* \quad (7.75)$$

Hence G has an eigenvalue greater than 1 and a unique positive eigenvector associated with this eigenvalue. Starting out from an initial vector of positive gross outputs given by x^*, the dynamic Leontief input–output model is capable of balanced growth at a rate of expansion $\lambda^* = [1 + (1/\mu)]$.

At this stage we may make two comments. First there is the practical question of the nonsingularity of the matrix of capital input coefficients C. This requires as a necessary though not sufficient condition that each good of the system is required as a capital input somewhere in the system; this is a condition that rarely holds in multisectoral models since only a small number of sectors contribute to capital formation. Second, there is no obvious reason why the capital stock in existence at some time $t = 0$ would permit the production of the gross output vector x^*. Some of the initial capital stocks inherited from past decisions would have to remain unutilised to permit balanced growth at the rate $1/\mu$. For discussion of singularity of the C matrix and consistency with the initial conditions, the reader is referred to Leontief (1970) and Kendrick (1972).

The above discussion has been based on the assumption that the only source of final demand for goods came from investment demand. We can easily allow for other elements of final demand such as consumption, and again we may find a balanced growth path in which all the elements of both consumption and gross output grow at

The dynamic Leontief input–output model

the same rate. The precise form which will be taken by the system once we allow for consumption depends upon whether we assume a constant fraction of gross output or of net output going to consumption in each period. In the former case, with the fraction of the gross output of good i going to the consumption demand given by d_i, the system would take the following form:

$$x_t = Ax_t + C[x_{t+1} - x_t] + Dx_t \tag{7.76}$$

where

$$D = \begin{bmatrix} d_1 & 0 & \cdots & 0 \\ 0 & d_2 & & 0 \\ \vdots & & & \\ 0 & 0 & & d_n \end{bmatrix} \tag{7.77}$$

Hence, the first-order difference equation takes the following form:

$$x_{t+1} = [I + C^{-1}(I - A - D)]x_t \tag{7.78}$$

The system will be capable of balanced growth provided that the matrix $A + D$ is indecomposable with its dominant eigenvalue less than 1 in absolute value.

On the other hand, if consumption demand for good i is a constant proportion d_i of net output of good i, we would have instead

$$x_t = Ax_t + C[x_{t+1} - x_t] + D(I - A)x_t \tag{7.79}$$

After some manipulation, we obtain

$$x_{t+1} = [I + C^{-1}(I - D)(I - A)]x_t \tag{7.80}$$

This system would be capable of balanced growth provided that $A + D(I - A)$ was indecomposable with its dominant eigenvalue less than 1 in absolute value.

Returning to the case where the only source of final demand is investment demand, when an economy is capable of balanced growth at some rate $\tau = 1/\mu$, then we have

$$x_t = Ax_t + \tau Cx_t \tag{7.81}$$

which, upon rearrangement, yields

$$[I - A - \tau C]x_t = 0 \tag{7.82}$$

Now consider briefly the role of prices in the dynamic Leontief model. Assume that in order to produce goods in period $t + 1$, capital goods must be held in the preceding period, while current inputs are simply supplied during period $t + 1$. Allowing for the opportunity costs of holding capital goods, the zero profits condition requires

$$p_{t+1} = p_{t+1}A + rp_tC - (p_{t+1} - p_t)C \tag{7.83}$$

where r is the rate of interest. The price of a good must be such that it just covers the variable cost of production of the good plus the interest foregone in investing in its production less the capital gains on its capital inputs. We now ask whether there exists a particular value of the rate of interest such that the price vector is constant through time. Setting $p = p_t = p_{t+1}$, we obtain, after some rearrangement

$$p[I - A - rC] = 0 \tag{7.84}$$

Note, immediately, the similarity with equation (7.82). If the economy is capable of balanced growth at rate τ, then there will exist an unchanging non-negative price vector consistent with zero profits throughout the economy, provided that the rate of interest is equal to the balanced rate of growth.

Some numerical examples
We deal first of all with the case where the only final demand is investment demand:

$$A = \begin{bmatrix} 0.2 & 0.1 \\ 0.2 & 0.1 \end{bmatrix} \text{ and } C = \begin{bmatrix} 2 & 0 \\ 0 & 4 \end{bmatrix}$$

Since A is an indecomposable matrix whose dominant eigenvalue is less than 1 in absolute value, the system is capable of balanced growth. The balanced rate of growth is given by $1/\mu_{max}$ where μ_{max} is the dominant eigenvalue of $(I - A)^{-1}C$:

$$I - A = \begin{bmatrix} 0.8 & -0.1 \\ -0.2 & 0.9 \end{bmatrix}$$

Hence,

$$(I - A)^{-1} = \begin{bmatrix} 1.2857 & 0.1429 \\ 0.2857 & 1.1429 \end{bmatrix}$$

and

$$(I - A)^{-1}C = \begin{bmatrix} 2.5714 & 0.5716 \\ 0.5716 & 4.5716 \end{bmatrix}$$

To find the eigenvalues of $(I - A)^{-1}C$ we solve the following quadratic equation:

$$\mu^2 - 7.143\mu + 11.4287 = 0$$

The solution is $\mu = 4.7235$ or 2.4195, hence the balanced rate of growth for this system is $\frac{1}{4.7235}$, i.e. 21.2 per cent.

In our second example, we assume that consumption demand is a constant proportion of gross output with the D matrix being given by

$$D = \begin{bmatrix} 0.5 & 0 \\ 0 & 0.2 \end{bmatrix}$$

We maintain the same A and C matrices as in the case above. For balanced growth in this case $A + D$ must be indecomposable and have a dominant eigenvalue less than 1 in absolute value. The reader should check that this is indeed the case. The balanced rate of growth is given by $1/\mu_{max}$ where μ_{max} is the dominant eigenvalue of $(I - A - D)^{-1}C$:

$$I - A - D = \begin{bmatrix} 0.3 & -0.1 \\ -0.2 & 0.7 \end{bmatrix}$$

Hence

$$(I - A - D)^{-1} = \begin{bmatrix} 3.6842 & 0.5263 \\ 1.0526 & 1.5789 \end{bmatrix}$$

and

$$(I - A - D)^{-1}C = \begin{bmatrix} 7.3684 & 2.1052 \\ 2.1052 & 6.3156 \end{bmatrix}$$

Solving the following quadratic:

$$\mu^2 - 13.684\mu + 42.104 = 0$$

we find $\mu = 4.672$ or 9.012. Hence the balanced rate of growth in this case is $\frac{1}{9.012}$, i.e. 11.1 per cent.

Finally, we consider an example where consumption demand is a constant proportion of net output, with the D matrix being given by

$$D = \begin{bmatrix} 0.8 & 0 \\ 0 & 0.5 \end{bmatrix}$$

The A and C matrices are as before. In this case, for balanced growth to be possible, $A + D(I - A)$ must be indecomposable, with its dominant eigenvalue less than 1 in absolute value. This can easily be shown to be satisfied. To find the balanced rate of growth for this system, we find the dominant eigenvalue of $[(I - D)(I - A)]^{-1}C$:

$$(I - D)(I - A) = \begin{bmatrix} 0.2 & 0 \\ 0 & 0.5 \end{bmatrix} \begin{bmatrix} 0.8 & -0.1 \\ -0.2 & 0.9 \end{bmatrix}$$

$$= \begin{bmatrix} 0.16 & -0.02 \\ -0.1 & 0.45 \end{bmatrix}$$

Hence,

$$[(I - D)(I - A)]^{-1} = \begin{bmatrix} 6.4286 & 0.2857 \\ 1.4286 & 2.2857 \end{bmatrix}$$

and

$$[(I - D)(I - A)]^{-1}C = \begin{bmatrix} 12.8572 & 1.1428 \\ 2.8572 & 9.1428 \end{bmatrix}$$

The eigenvalues are given by the solution to the following quadratic:

$$\mu^2 - 22\mu + 114.2856 = 0$$

The roots are 13.5912 or 8.4088; hence the balanced rate of growth in this case is $\frac{1}{13.5912} = 7.4$ per cent.

7.5 PROCEDURES FOR UPDATING INPUT–OUTPUT MATRICES

It is widely accepted that predictions of such key quantities as imports, final demands, gross domestic output and employment depend crucially on a knowledge of the input coefficients of the technology matrix. However, many investigators have pointed out that these coefficients change over time owing to alterations in the product mix at a sectoral level, changes in production techniques, relative price changes, and economies of scale. The impact of relative price effects has been analysed by econometricians such as Theil and Tilanus (1964), but little attention has been paid in the literature to analysing the significance of either product mix changes or economies of scale.

It is well known that input–output tables are based on census data but, due to the expense of collection, these data are frequently not available. However, a procedure known as the RAS method has been developed to update the input–output matrix between the census years.

The RAS method

The basic method is outlined in the Department of Applied Economies, Cambridge, *Programme for Growth* series, Vol. 3 (1963, pp. 27-30) and in O'Connor and Henry (1975). If we denote the base year technology matrix by $A_0 = (a_{ij})$, then each coefficient A_{ij} is subject to two intertemporal effects:
(a) the substitution effect which is measured by the extent to which the output of the ith sector has been replaced by, or used as a substitute for, other sectoral outputs in intermediate production, and may be largely induced by relative price changes as, for example, the substitution of gas for oil in many UK industries after 1973;
(b) the fabrication effect which is measured by the extent to which the ratio of intermediate to total inputs decreased or increased in the jth sector.

It is assumed that each effect works uniformly. The substitution multipliers which operate along the rows are denoted by the vector r, and the fabrication multipliers operating on the columns are denoted by the vector s. Each cell in the base matrix A_0 will be subject to these effects and the new coefficient matrix A_1 can thus be written as

$$A_1 = \hat{r} A_0 \hat{s} \qquad (7.85)$$

where $\hat{r}$ and $\hat{s}$ are matrices with the vectors r and s in the main diagonals and zeros elsewhere. These matrices, r and s may be obtained from a knowledge of the base year flow (absorption) matrix (X_0) and the row and column totals of the new flow matrix (X_1) by an iterative solution of the two-equation system:

$$\hat{r} X_0 s = u \qquad (7.86)$$

$$r' X_0^{\hat{s}} = v' \qquad (7.87)$$

where u is the column vector of the row sum of the updated year's flow matrix, v' is the row vector of its column totals, s is the column vector of the diagonal elements of $\hat{s}$ and r is the column vector of the diagonal elements of $\hat{r}$. This method amounts to a successive biproportional adjustment of the rows and columns on the base matrix, until convergence is reached. Each row of A_0 in equation (7.85) is multiplied by the r_i (substitution) factor. Notice that since each element of a column of A_0 is multiplied by a different element of r, this will bring about changes in the proportion in which different intermediate inputs are used, but compensating increases or decreases could leave the primary inputs virtually unchanged. Obviously, the fabrication factors must (if different from unity) alter the primary input coefficient since each element of a column A_0 is multiplied by the same element of s, with consequently no compensating variations. A relative substitution multiplier with value greater than unity indicates that the product of the compensating industry has been substituted for other products in intermediate production, while a relative fabrication multiplier with value greater than unity indicates that production in a certain industry has come to absorb a greater amount of intermediate inputs per unit value added. The method of solution yields a matrix in which all original zero entries remain the same.

The matrices $\hat{s}$ and $\hat{r}$ can be determined only up to a factor of proportionality, since if $\hat{s}_1$ and $\hat{r}_1$ satisfy equations (7.86) and (7.87), then so will $\lambda \hat{r}_1$ and $\lambda^{-1}\hat{s}_1$ where λ is a constant.

The RAS method can be modified to incorporate exogenous information into selected rows, columns or individual cells of the updated matrix. This simply involves setting such cells equal to zero, and applying the normal RAS procedure to the modified matrix after subtracting the exogenously determined new value of the cells from the appropriate row and column totals for the forecast year.

Lynch (1986) has shown that an RAS update of the 1963 absorption flow matrix resulted in large percentage errors. He improved the estimate by the incorporation of six exogenously fixed rows and columns, though errors still remained large. In fact, it has been suggested that the direct application of the original 1963 UK table to the 1968 final demand matrix is as effective as the use of the updated version of the matrix for 1968. Lynch (1986, p. 283) concludes that: 'The RAS method may be used as a convenient means of constraining matrices to given row and column totals, but forecasts of the absorption matrix at a high level of disaggregation are unlikely to be appropriate.' Parikh (1979) has compared the RAS forecasts with actual outcomes for nine European countries and his evidence confirms large errors in the RAS predictions.

Updating input–output tables for price changes

The key assumption in input–output analysis is that there exists a fixed relationship between input and output in physical quantities. As physical coefficients are rarely available in detail, we assume that there is a fixed relationship between input and output at constant prices when the coefficients are expressed in values. In the base year (0) we observe

$$a_{ij}^0 = \frac{x_{ij}^0}{x_j^0} \qquad (7.88)$$

where units i and j have been chosen such that their price is equal to one. In the current year (1) we would observe

$$a_{ij}^1 = \frac{x_{ij}^1}{x_j^1} \qquad (7.89)$$

and, in general, $a_{ij}^1 \neq a_{ij}^0$ because of changes in relative prices. The numerator and denominator of equation (7.89) can differ because prices and quantities change. If quantity change is absent, we can relate

$$\hat{A}_{ij}^1 = a_{ij}^0 \left(\frac{P_i}{P_j}\right) \qquad (7.90)$$

or, in matrix terms,

$$\hat{A}^1 = \hat{P}(A^0)\hat{P}^{-1} \qquad (7.91)$$

where $\hat{P}$ is a diagonal matrix whose jth element is P_j so that we can approximate the input–output coefficient matrix of the current year $\hat{A}^1$ by combining the vector of price relatives with the base year matrix A^0.

Large changes in prices raise problems regarding the stability of the input–output matrix (Bulmer-Thomas, 1982). When large price changes take place it is very unlikely that the assumption of constant physical input coefficients can be sustained.

If there are time series available for the row and column totals of the input–output absorption matrix, we can modify the r and s multipliers. Theoretically, the most attractive procedure is to use relative prices (i.e. relative to base year) to explain the changes on the row sums of intermediate purchases and the column sums of intermediate sales over time:

$$\log r = \log \hat{\Pi} \lambda + e \qquad (7.92)$$

$$\log s = \log \hat{\Pi} \mu + \epsilon \qquad (7.93)$$

where e and ϵ are stochastic vectors, while $\hat{\Pi}$ is a diagonal matrix of relative prices. The jth element of $\hat{\Pi}$ is the relative price of the jth commodity; λ and μ are unknown vectors which are to be derived through regression analysis. The estimated λ and μ can be incorporated in a model which reflects the impact of relative price changes on the technological coefficients, i.e.

$$a_{ij}(t) = a_{ij}^0 [\Pi_i(t)^{\lambda_i}] [\Pi_j(t)]^{\mu_i} u_{ij}(t)$$

where $u_{ij}(t)$ is the disturbance term. Thus the base year a_{ij}^0 is modified through price effects.

Exercises

1. In a simple three-industry economy, the matrix of current input coefficients is given by

$$A = \begin{bmatrix} 0.1 & 0.2 & 0.3 \\ 0 & 0.2 & 0.2 \\ 0.2 & 0 & 0.1 \end{bmatrix}$$

   There is one scarce factor, labour, and the labour requirements vector is given by

   $$l = [0.2 \quad 0.4 \quad 0.3]$$

   (a) Calculate the gross output vector necessary to meet the final demand vector:

   $$d = \begin{bmatrix} 100 \\ 150 \\ 200 \end{bmatrix}$$

   (b) Which industry is the most labour intensive?
   (c) How much labour is required to meet the final demands?

2. Given the input–output current input coefficients matrix a, the final demand vector d, and the labour input requirements vector l, where

   $$A = \begin{bmatrix} 0 & 0.2 & 0.1 \\ 0.25 & 0.2 & 0.2 \\ 0 & 0 & 0.1 \end{bmatrix} \quad d = \begin{bmatrix} 100 \\ 250 \\ 200 \end{bmatrix}$$

   $$l = [0.5 \quad 0.25 \quad 1]$$

   (a) Obtain the gross output vector x
   (b) On the assumption that the wage rate is unity, derive the price vector p.
   (c) What is distinctive about the technology as embodied in the a matrix above?

3. Given

   $$A = \begin{bmatrix} 0.2 & 0.2 \\ 0.2 & 0.1 \end{bmatrix} \quad l = [0.5 \quad 1]$$

   $$k = [2 \quad 0.8] \quad L = 250 \quad K = 500$$

   where A is the current input coefficients matrix, l the labour input vector, k the capital input vector, L and K the respective endowments of labour and capital, obtain the net output vector compatible with full employment of both resources.

4. The following table is a summary interindustry transactions table for Ambrosia

£ million

From \ To	Agriculture	Industry	Services	Total intermediate sales	Consumption	Investment	Exports	Total final sales	Total
Agriculture	–	5	–	5	30	5	10	45	50
Industry	10	–	20	30	43	20	7	70	100
Services	5	20	–	25	50	–	5	55	80
Total intermediate purchases	15	25	20						60
Imports	5	10	5						20
Indirect taxes	–	15	–						15
Wages and salaries	20	35	40						95
Gross profits	10	15	15						40
Total	50	100	80	60	123	25	22	170	230

(a) Construct a set of summary national accounts for Ambrosia showing:
 (i) GDP at market prices from expenditure data;
 (ii) GDP at factor cost by factor income;
 (iii) GDP at factor cost by industry of origin.
(b) Calculate the Leontief inverse.
(c) Suppose that final demand increases by a total of £30 million made up as follows: final demand for agriculture increases by £5 million, that for industry by £10 million, and that for services by £15 million:
 (i) Compute the increases in total output required from each of the three industries.
 (ii) By how much will imports and indirect taxes increase?
 (iii) By how much will GDP at factor cost increase?
(d) Does £1 million added to the exports of agriculture increase the export surplus by more or less than £1 million added to the exports of industry?
(e) Do you consider that an input–output table serves much useful purpose at this level of aggregation?

5. Data on interindustry flows and final demands are given in value terms in the following table (all values are in £ million):

Output to \ Input from	Agriculture	Manufactures	Services	Final demand	Gross output
Agricultures	80	150	0	170	400
Manufacturers	100	225	75	350	750
Services	40	75	105	530	750

(a) Use the above data to analyse the strength and nature of the backward linkages in this economy by calculating bL_j and CV_j^b for each sector.

(b) Calculate fL_i and CV_i^f for each sector and comment upon the strength and nature of the forward linkages.

6. Consider the case of the following two-sector open economy:

$$A = \begin{bmatrix} 0.1 & 0.2 \\ 0.15 & 0.2 \end{bmatrix} \quad b = \begin{bmatrix} 0.8 \\ 0.2 \end{bmatrix} \quad c = \begin{bmatrix} 0.1 \\ 0.9 \end{bmatrix}$$

$$d = [0.25 \quad 0.3] \quad k = [9 \quad 5] \quad l = [1 \quad 2]$$

where A is a matrix of current input coefficients;
b is a column of export coefficients;
c is a column of competitive import coefficients;
d is a row of non-competitive import input coefficients;
k is a row of capital coefficients;
l is a row of labour coefficients.

Calculate net capital requirements (direct and indirect) per million pounds of competitive import replacements. Repeat the calculation for net labour requirements.

7. If the current input coefficients matrix A is given by

$$A = \begin{bmatrix} a_{11} & 0 & a_{13} \\ a_{12} & a_{22} & a_{23} \\ a_{31} & a_{32} & a_{33} \end{bmatrix}$$

(a) Is this an indecomposable system?
(b) What would you conclude about the indecomposability of the system if $a_{32} = 0$?
(c) What is the significance of indecomposability?

8. Given

$$A = \begin{bmatrix} 0.1 & 0.2 \\ 0.25 & 0 \end{bmatrix} \quad \text{and} \quad C = \begin{bmatrix} 5 & 0 \\ 0 & 8 \end{bmatrix}$$

where A is the current input coefficients matrix and C the capital input requirements matrix:
(a) Calculate the maximum balanced rate of growth for this closed model.
(b) Allow for consumption and assume that consumption is 75 per cent of net output in each industry; what will be the maximum balanced rate of growth now?

References

Bulmer-Thomas, V. (1982), *Input-Output Analysis in Developing Countries: sources, methods and applications*, London: Wiley.

Debreu, G. and Herstein, I.N. (1953), 'Non-negative square matrices', *Econometrica*, **21**, 597-606.
Department of Applied Economics, University of Cambridge (1963), *Input-Output Relationships, 1954-66*, London: Chapman and Hall.
Hawkins, D. and Simon, H.A. (1949), 'Note: some conditions of macroeconomic stability', *Econometrica*, **17**, 245-8.
Kendrick, D. (1972), 'On the Leontief dynamic inverse' *Quarterly Journal of Economics*, **86**, 693-6.
Leontief, W.W. (1956), 'Factor proportions and the structure of American trade: further theoretical and empirical analysis', *Review of Economics and Statistics*, **38**, 386-407.
Leontief, W.W. (1970), 'The dynamic inverse', in A. Carter and A. Brody (eds.), *Contributions to Input-Output Analysis*, Vol. 1, Amsterdam: North-Holland.
Leontief, W.W. (1986), *Input-Output Economics*, Oxford: Oxford University Press.
Lynch, R. (1986), 'An assessment of the RAS method for updating input-output tables,' in I. Sohn (ed.), *Readings in Input-Output Analysis*, Oxford: Oxford University Press.
McKenzie, L. (1960), 'Matrices with dominant diagonals and economic theory', in K.J. Arrow, S. Karlin and P. Suppes, (eds.) *Mathematical Methods in the Social Sciences*, Stanford: Stanford University Press.
O'Connor, R. and Henry, E.W. (1975), *Input-Output Analysis and its Applications*, London: Charles Griffin.
Parikh, A. (1979), 'Forecasts of input-output matrices using the RAS method', *Review of Economics and Statistics*, **61**, 477-81.
Theil, H. and Tilanus, C.B. (1964), 'The demand for production factors and the price sensitivity of input-output predictions' *International Economic Review*, **5**, 258-72.

Chapter 8
APPLIED GENERAL EQUILIBRIUM MODELS

In this chapter we provide an introductory discussion of applied general equilibrium models (AGE). Space considerations preclude a detailed treatment and all we seek to do here is to indicate some of the main issues involved in constructing and subsequently making use of such models for policy purposes. The student who wishes to further his knowledge and understanding of the subject is referred to Piggott and Whalley (1985), Scarf and Shoven (1984), Shoven and Whalley (1984) and Whalley (1985), for a much more comprehensive discussion of the techniques of AGE modelling and of policy simulation utilising such models.

In Section 8.1 we outline the main features of a simple model of general equilibrium. A numerical example of a two-sector general equilibrium model is provided and this numerical model is then used as the basis for a simulation exercise. We seek to ascertain the effects of imposing a discretionary tax on the income earned by capital in one of the two industries of the model. The gainers and losers from the postulated tax changes are identified and the overall social welfare implications of the changes are assessed. In Section 8.2 we discuss some of the issues relating to the construction of an actual AGE model, paying particular attention to the question of calibrating the model to some benchmark equilibrium. In Section 8.3 we provide a brief summary of a small selection of AGE models. The appendix to the chapter contains an outline of the social accounting matrix (SAM), a method of organising information on the flows of payments and receipts between various sectors of the economy. Use of the SAM ensures the absence of inconsistencies in the data for the base period and is helpful in calibrating the model to the benchmark equilibrium.

8.1 A MODEL OF GENERAL EQUILIBRIUM

In a model of general equilibrium, consumers are assumed to be utility maximisers and firms to be profit maximisers. Given a utility function to represent an agent's preference ordering, a set of commodity demand functions for each agent can be obtained by maximising the utility function subject to the budget constraint. Furthermore, if one allows for endogenously determined factor supplies, an additional outcome of the utility-maximising procedure will be a set of factor supply functions for each agent. The market demand function for each commodity can then be obtained by adding up the demand functions of all the agents for that particular commodity; in a similar way, the market supply function for each factor of production can also be obtained.

Given the nature of the technological relationships between outputs and productive inputs, the production functions for each commodity, profit-maximising behaviour on the part of the firms in the economy leads to a set of demand functions for the factors of production and an associated set of commodity supply functions. The commodity and factor demand and supply functions are homogeneous of degree zero in prices; a doubling of all prices will have no effect on excess demands. Walras's law, the proposition that the sum of the value of excess demands is zero, holds; only relative prices are of significance and the absolute price level has no impact on the equilibrium outcome. If there are m factors of production and n commodities there will be $m + n$ equilibrium conditions that supply and demand equal each other in each market. Since, if $m + n - 1$ markets are in equilibrium, we know by Walras's law that the last market will be in equilibrium, one of the equilibrium conditions is redundant and can be dropped. We can then solve for $m + n - 1$ relative prices.

Starting from some arbitrarily chosen relative price vector the investigator can calculate the planned supplies and demands that would be desired at these prices. The price vector can then be adjusted in the light of this information on the prevailing excess demands for commodities and factors. A new set of planned supplies and demands is then calculated with adjustments being made subsequently to the price vector in the light of the new set of excess demands. This procedure is continued until the equilibrium price vector is hit upon and the markets for all the commodities and factors clear, with supply being equal to demand throughout the economy.

A numerical example of a two-sector model

We consider here a simple two-sector model of general equilibrium. In this model there are two industries, each producing a single good whose production depends upon inputs of two primary factors of production: capital services and labour services which are both in completely inelastic supply. We assume there exist two consumers/suppliers of factor services; all the labour is supplied by the worker consumer and all the capital by the capitalist consumer. Both agents treat prices parametrically.

The production functions for the two goods are given by

$$X_1 = K_1^{1/2} L_1^{1/2} \tag{8.1}$$

$$X_2 = K_2^{1/4} L_2^{3/4} \tag{8.2}$$

where X represents output, K capital services and L labour services, the subscript refers to the industry. We let r represent the price of capital services, w the wage rate and p_1 and p_2 the respective product prices. Production functions homogeneous of degree 1 are used often and meaningfully in economics, despite the indeterminacy regarding the size of the firm which results from such a specification of the technological opportunities facing the firm. To deal with this problem of the indeterminacy of firm size, one could assume that firm size and firm numbers are determined by some arbitrary mechanism subject to the condition that industry output satisfy industry demand. Alternatively one could assume that constant returns to scale prevail at the industry level, but that they do not apply at the level of the firm regardless of the output produced by the firm.

By maximising profits for each industry by equating the value of the marginal product of a factor input to its price, we can obtain the input demand functions (equations (8.3), (8.4), (8.6) and (8.7))

$$L_1 = 0.5 p_1 X_1 / w \tag{8.3}$$

$$L_2 = 0.75 p_2 X_2 / w \tag{8.4}$$

$$\bar{L} = L_1 + L_2 \tag{8.5}$$

$$K_1 = 0.5 p_1 X_1 / r \tag{8.6}$$

$$K_2 = 0.25 p_2 X_2 / r \tag{8.7}$$

$$\bar{K} = K_1 + K_2 \tag{8.8}$$

To derive equations (8.3) and (8.6), we write the profits function of the first industry:

$$\Pi_1 = p_1 X_1 - w L_1 - r K_1$$
$$= p_1 K_1^{1/2} L_1^{1/2} - w L_1 - r K_1$$

which we then differentiate partially with respect to L_1 and K_1 to obtain the first-order conditions for a maximum of Π_1.

$$\frac{\partial \Pi_1}{\partial L_1} = 0.5 p_1 K_1^{1/2} L_1^{-1/2} - w = 0$$

$$\frac{\partial \Pi_1}{\partial K_1} = 0.5 p_1 K_1^{-1/2} L_1^{1/2} - r = 0$$

Noting that $X_1 / L_1 = K_1^{1/2} L_1^{-1/2}$ and $X_1 / K_1 = K_1^{-1/2} L_1^{1/2}$ and rearranging, we obtain the expressions given in equations (8.3) and (8.6). The second-order conditions for a maximum are satisfied. A similar procedure enables us to obtain equations (8.4) and (8.7).

Equations (8.5) and (8.6) state that the total demand for each input must equal the exogenously given supply; a more general model would allow factor supplies to be endogenously determined.

The worker and the capitalist are assumed to possess utility functions of the following form:

$$U_w = X_{1w}^{3/4} X_{2w}^{1/4} \tag{8.9}$$

$$U_c = X_{1c}^{1/2} X_{2c}^{1/2} \tag{8.10}$$

Each consumer seeks to maximise his utility subject to his budget constraint; given our assumptions about ownership of the exogeneously given factor supplies, then the worker's income is simply $w\bar{L}$ and that of the capitalist $r\bar{K}$. We derive the commodity demand functions for each consumer by maximising utility subject to the budget constraint. These demand functions are given below in equations (8.11), (8.12), (8.14) and (8.15):

$$X_{1w} = 0.75w\bar{L}/p_1 \tag{8.11}$$

$$X_{1c} = 0.5r\bar{K}/p_1 \tag{8.12}$$

$$X_1 = X_{1w} + X_{1c} \tag{8.13}$$

$$X_{2w} = 0.25w\bar{L}/p_2 \tag{8.14}$$

$$X_{2c} = 0.5r\bar{K}/p_2 \tag{8.15}$$

$$X_2 = X_{2w} + X_{2c} \tag{8.16}$$

To derive equations (8.12) and (8.15), we first write the Lagrangean function:

$$L = X_{1c}^{1/2} X_{2c}^{1/2} + \lambda[r\bar{K} - p_1 X_{1c} - p_2 X_{2c}]$$

which we then differentiate partially with respect to X_{1c}, X_{2c} and λ to obtain the first-order conditions for a maximum of utility subject to the budget constraint:

$$\frac{\partial L}{\partial X_1} = 0.5 X_{1c}^{-1/2} X_{2c}^{1/2} - \lambda p_1 = 0$$

$$\frac{\partial L}{\partial X_2} = 0.5 X_{1c}^{1/2} X_{2c}^{-1/2} - \lambda p_2 = 0$$

$$\frac{\partial L}{\partial \lambda} = r\bar{K} - p_1 X_{1c} - p_2 X_{2c} = 0$$

The first two conditions imply that $X_{2c}/X_{1c} = p_1/p_2$ and then using the budget constraint (the third condition), we obtain the expressions given in equations (8.12) and (8.15). The second-order conditions for a maximum are satisfied. A similar procedure enables us to obtain equations (8.11) and (8.14).

Equations (8.13) and (8.16) state that the demand and supply of each commodity should be equal. There exist fourteen equations in fourteen unknowns [X_1, X_{1w}, X_{1c}, X_2, X_{2w}, X_{2c}, K_1, K_2, L_1, L_2, w, r, p_1 and p_2]. By Walras's law, however, we know that if in a model with n markets, $n-1$ markets are in equilibrium, then so is the nth market. We can only solve for relative prices, we let labour be the numeraire and set $w = 1$ and drop one of the equilibrium conditions, say equation (8.16). Letting $\bar{K} = 400$ and $\bar{L} = 200$ and using an iterative procedure, we can solve for the thirteen unknowns and their equilibrium values are given in the first column of Table 8.1.

We now wish to consider the implications of imposing a tax on capital income earned in the first industry at a rate of 50 per cent. The proceeds of this tax are then to be redistributed to consumers, with the capitalist receiving 25 per cent of the proceeds and the worker 75 per cent. Since capital is assumed to be freely mobile between industries, then the gross rate of return to capital in industry 1 must in the new equilibrium be twice as large as the rate of return to capital in industry 2. Only in these

A model of general equilibrium 199

Table 8.1 Characteristics of the three equilibria

Original equilibrium	Tax on capital employed in X_1 industry	Tax on capital employed in X_2 industry
$w = 1$	$w = 1$	$w = 1$
$p_1 = 1.183$	$p_1 = 1.312$	$p_1 = 1.124$
$p_2 = 1.350$	$p_2 = 1.333$	$p_2 = 1.565$
$r = 0.350$	$r_1 = 0.430$	$r_1 = 0.316$
	$r_2 = 0.215$	$r_2 = 0.632$
$K_1 = 314.286$	$K_1 = 270.8$	$K_1 = 353.4$
$K_2 = 85.714$	$K_2 = 129.2$	$K_2 = 46.6$
$L_1 = 110$	$L_1 = 116.573$	$L_1 = 111.659$
$L_2 = 90$	$L_2 = 83.427$	$L_2 = 88.341$
$X_1 = 185.934$	$X_1 = 177.674$	$X_1 = 198.646$
$X_{1w} = 126.773$	$X_{1w} = 139.353$	$X_{1w} = 140.781$
$X_{1c} = 59.161$	$X_{1c} = 38.321$	$X_{1c} = 57.865$
$X_2 = 88.909$	$X_2 = 83.427$	$X_2 = 75.287$
$X_{2w} = 37.045$	$X_{2w} = 45.709$	$X_{2w} = 33.727$
$X_{2c} = 51.864$	$X_{2c} = 37.718$	$X_{2c} = 41.560$
$U_w = 93.208$	$U_w = 105.419$	$U_w = 98.503$
$I_w = 200$	$I_w = 243.6665$	$I_w = 211.0442$
$U_c = 55.392$	$U_c = 38.018$	$U_c = 49.039$
$I_c = 140$	$I_c = 100.5555$	$I_c = 130.3814$

circumstances where net returns are equalised across industries will there no longer be any incentive to reallocate capital services between industries. For this specific case the following additional condition must be satisfied:

$$r_1 = 2r_2$$

or, more generally, we would have

$$r_1(1 - t_1) = r_2(1 - t_2)$$

where r_i is the gross rate of return and t_i the rate of tax levied on capital income in industry i.

The new equilibrium values of the variables of the model when capital income earned in the first industry is taxed at a rate of 50 per cent and the proceeds are redistributed in the specified way given in column 2 of Table 8.1. The corresponding equilibrium values of the variables of the model when it is capital income earned in the second industry which is taxed at a rate of 50 per cent are given in column 3 of the same table. It will be noted that in both cases it is the worker who gains and the capitalist who loses from the change.

Evaluation of welfare gains and losses

In order to consider the welfare implications of the introduction of the tax/transfer system we may ask the following question: how much would an agent be prepared to pay in order to receive some share of the tax proceeds obtained from taxing the income of capital employed in a particular industry? The maximum amount an agent would be prepared to pay is the amount that would leave him just as well off as he was before the postulated change was introduced. This amount is known as the compensating variation (CV). As we have seen, the tax/transfer system changes the equilibrium set of prices; when faced with these new equilibrium prices, how large must the income of the agent be for him to obtain the same level of utility as previously? If we subtract this hypothetical income from his original income, we will obtain his compensating variation. If an agent's CV is positive, then he has gained from the change and, conversely, if it is negative he had become worse off. From the perspective of society as a whole, we may give a monetary value to the welfare change stemming from the policy change by adding the CVs of all the agents in the economy. If this sum is positive, then society has benefited from the change, though some individual agents may well be worse off. On the other hand, if the sum is negative, then society is worse off as a result of the change. Note that we are not weighting differentially the gains or losses to particular agents.

An alternative approach to measurement of the welfare gain or loss would be to ask the agent how large an income transfer he would require for him to be as well off as he is following the change if he were faced with the original equilibrium price vector. This is the equivalent variation and again is clearly positive for an agent who gains and negative for an agent who loses from the change. Summing the EVs of all the agents will provide a monetary measure of the change in social welfare.

The following formulae may be utilised in order to obtain numerical values for an agent's CV and EV:

$$CV = \frac{U^N - U^O}{U^N} \cdot I^N \qquad (8.17)$$

$$EV = \frac{U^N - U^O}{U^O} \cdot I^O \qquad (8.18)$$

where U^N and U^O represent, respectively, the new and original utility levels of the agent and I^N and I^O the new and original levels of income of the said agent. The above formulae are valid whenever the utility functions are linear homogeneous.

Using the data provided in Table 8.2 we may calculate these measures for the two postulated changes for both the worker and the capitalist as well as for society as a whole. Regardless of whether the tax is imposed on the use of capital in the first or second industry, the worker gains and the capitalist loses from the change, though the gains and losses are greater in the first case then the second. When the tax is imposed on the income of capital in the first industry, the welfare loss as a percentage of

Table 8.2 Welfare gains and losses due to tax changes

	CV			EV		
	Worker	Capitalist	Society	Worker	Capitalist	Society
Tax on capital in first industry	28.2246	−45.953	−17.7284	26.2016	−43.912	−17.7104
Tax on capital in second industry	11.345	−16.891	−5.507	11.362	−16.057	−4.695

national income is 5.21 per cent with the CV measure and 5.15 per cent with the EV measure. The corresponding figures for the second case are 1.62 per cent with the CV measure and 1.38 per cent with the EV measure. If we measure the welfare loss as a percentage of the tax revenues, the figures are correspondingly higher. In the first case, the figure is in the region of 30.4 per cent for both the CV and EV measure, whereas in the second case, the corresponding figures are 37.4 per cent for the CV measure and 31.9 per cent for the EV measure. These high average figures suggest that to raise revenue with this discriminatory tax system is highly inefficient. Furthermore for an additional pound of revenue, the marginal welfare loss would be significantly higher than the average welfare loss per pound of revenue raised.

8.2 THE CONSTRUCTION OF AN AGE MODEL

In constructing an AGE model, the analyst must decide upon the appropriate level of disaggregation which will be influenced, in part, by the purpose for which the model is to be utilised and, in part, by the availability of data from such sources as censuses of production, household expenditure surveys, input–output tables, tax revenue statistics and national income accounts. Choice must be made regarding the functional form of the utility and production functions. In the simple numerical example we worked through above, both the utility and production functions were of the Cobb–Douglas form. This makes for ease of computation but is unnecessarily restrictive; and the implied unitary own-price and income elasticities of demand and zero cross-elasticities of demand are obviously inconsistent with econometric evidence on demand elasticities. A less restrictive assumption would be to allow for constant elasticity of substitution (CES) utility and production functions. Alternatively, on the production side, intermediate inputs could be incorporated into the model through the input–output framework by assuming fixed production coefficients, but with substitution possibilities being allowed for between the primary inputs, labour and capital, by using a standard neo-classical value added production framework at this level.

In an AGE model, it is assumed that the initial position is one of equilibrium. This is known as the benchmark equilibrium and, typically, the AGE modeller will adjust the available data in order to ensure that certain equilibrium conditions are met by the benchmark equilibrium data set. These are as follows:

1. The markets for the commodities and factors clear, with demand equalling supply in all markets. The possibility that some goods are free with negative excess demands can be tackled through an assumption of free disposal. Such an assumption rules out negative prices.
2. The profits earned in each industry are nonpositive; in other words, the modeller treats the residual income received by the equity holders as if it were a contractual payment.
3. The consumption choices of each domestic agent lie on his or her budget

constraint. This condition is assumed to hold not only for all private agents but also for the goverment.
4. The external accounts of the economy are in balance.

A major task in the construction of every AGE model is to achieve an initial calibration of the model. Data collected from a variety of governmental and other sources will invariably not be internally consistent and adjustments will have to be made to the data in order to eliminate such discrepancies. The social accounting matrix (SAM), a brief discussion of which is provided in the appendix to this chapter, is often utilised by the investigator in single-economy studies to ensure consistency. Having eliminated these inconsistencies, parameter values must then be assigned such that they are consistent with the economy being in a state of equilibrium in the benchmark year. There will not normally be a unique set of such parameter values, nor will it be possible to obtain econometric estimates of these parameters from the data available, which usually relate to one year only. The model builder must therefore necessarily engage in a search of the literature for estimates that have previously been made of such key parameters as demand elasticities for particular commodities, for exports and imports, elasticities of substitution between factor inputs, etc.

The choice of the explicit functional forms for the utility and production functions and the exogenous information utilised on the elasticity values must thus be such that the utility and profit-maximising choices of the households and firms give rise to the actual outcomes observed in the base year. Once this condition has been met, the model has been calibrated to the benchmark equilibrium and the stage is then set for the model builder to investigate the consequences for output, prices and the distribution of income of some postulated policy change.

The following examples will help to illuminate the calibration procedure. Assume the production technology for a particular commodity X_1 can be represented by the following CES production function:

$$X_1 = [\delta K_1^{-\rho} + (1-\delta) L_1 - \rho]^{-1/\rho} \tag{8.19}$$

where K_1 and L_1 are, respectively, the amounts of capital and labour services employed in the production of X_1, δ is a weighting parameter and the elasticity of substitution, σ, is equal to $1/1 + \rho$.

Profit-maximising behaviour on the part of the firm will ensure that relative factor prices are equated with the marginal rate of substitution between the two factors:

$$MRS_{KL}^1 = \frac{\text{marginal product of labour in industry 1}}{\text{marginal product of capital in industry 1}}$$

$$= \frac{\delta}{1-\delta} \left(\frac{K_1}{L_1}\right)^{1+\rho} = \frac{w}{r} \tag{8.20}$$

Given an exogenous estimate of the elasticity of substitution between the two inputs and data on prices and quantities for the benchmark year, we may obtain an estimate of the parameter δ.

On the demand side, econometric estimates of price and income elasticities are available and these can be utilised to fix the parameters of the utility function. Assume a household's preferences over two commodities, X_1 and X_2, can be represented by the following CES utility function:

$$U = [\alpha X_1^{-\rho} + (1-\alpha) X_2^{-\rho}]^{-1/\rho} \qquad (8.21)$$

where α is the weighting parameter and, as before, the elasticity of substitution is given by $1/1 + \rho$.

Letting I represent household income and p_1 and p_2 the prices of the two commodities, maximisation of equation (8.21) subject to the household's budget constraint yields the following commodity demand functions:

$$X_1 = \frac{\alpha I}{(1-\alpha) p_1^\sigma p_2^{1-\sigma}} \qquad (8.22)$$

$$X_2 = \frac{(1-\alpha) I}{\alpha p_1^{1-\sigma} p_2^\sigma} \qquad (8.23)$$

The associated uncompensated own-price elasticities of demand are then given by

$$\frac{\partial X_1}{\partial p_1} \cdot \frac{p_1}{X_1} = -\sigma - \frac{\alpha(1-\sigma)}{(1-\alpha) p_1^{\sigma-1} p_2^{1-\sigma}} \qquad (8.24)$$

$$\frac{\partial X_2}{\partial p_2} \cdot \frac{p_2}{X_2} = -\sigma - \frac{(1-\alpha)(1-\sigma)}{\alpha p_1^{1-\sigma} p_2^{\sigma-1}} \qquad (8.25)$$

Extraneous estimates of the own-price elasticities of demand may then be utilised to obtain estimates of the parameters of the utility function, σ and α.

Another functional form which is sometimes adopted on the demand side is the linear expenditure system (LES). In this case the associated utility function for the two-commodity case is given by

$$U = (X_1 - A_1) \alpha_1 (X_2 - A_2) \alpha_2 \qquad (8.26)$$

where A_1 and A_2 are the subsistence quantities or minimum requirements of the two goods, and α_1 and α_2 are the marginal propensities to consume out of discretionary income, these propensities summing to unity. Maximisation of this utility function subject to the household's income constraint then yields the following demand functions:

$$X_1 = A_1 + \frac{\alpha_1 [I - (p_1 A_1 + p_2 A_2)]}{p_1} \qquad (8.27)$$

$$X_2 = a_2 + \frac{\alpha_2 [I - (p_1 A_1 + p_2 A_2)]}{p_2} \qquad (8.28)$$

The associated income elasticities of demand are given by

$$\epsilon_1^i = \frac{\alpha_1}{p_1} \left\{ \frac{I}{A_1 + (\alpha_1/p_1)[I - (p_1 A_1 + p_2 A_2)]} \right\} \qquad (8.29)$$

$$\epsilon_2^I = \frac{\alpha_2}{p_2} \left\{ \frac{I}{A_2 + (\alpha_2/p_2)[I - (p_1 A_1 + p_2 A_2)]} \right\} \qquad (8.30)$$

In this case, exogenously given measures of the income elasticities of demand can be utilised to fix values for the origin displacement parameters A_1 and A_2.

The calibration procedure for an actual model is naturally much more complex but the above simple illustrations do help to bring out the essence of the procedure. Successful calibration of the model implies that with this setting of parameter values in the utility and production functions, the utility-maximising choices of households and the profit-maximising choices of firms generate the actual outcomes that are observed in the base year. Hence, we have our benchmark equilibrium.

Having established the benchmark equilibrium, the stage is then set for simulating the effects of policy change. Applied general equilibrium analysis throws no light on the dynamic path that the economy will take as it moves towards the new equilibrium position following some policy change. No specification is given of the precise adjustment that will occur since the model is essentially timeless. Where an AGE model can be used to great effect is in comparative static analysis. A clear comparison of the properties of the alternative equilibria which follow upon the adoption of different sets of policies can be effected. The greater the degree of disaggregation of the model on the demand side the greater will be the degree of information obtained on the implications for the distribution of income of any postulated change.

8.3 SOME RECENT AGE MODELS

Over the last 30 years economists have devoted increasing attention to the construction of AGE models. The main focus of this intellectual effort has been on matters pertaining to public finance and international trade. A motivation for many of these studies has been provided by a desire to estimate the likely effects on social welfare of replacing one type of policy regime with another. In the public finance field, for example, the pioneering study by Harberger (1962) was concerned with estimating the implications for the allocation of resources and the distribution of income of the US corporation tax: how would the outcome differ from that under a tax system in which capital income in the corporate sector was taxed no differently than capital income in the noncorporate sector? Using a simple, static, two-sector, two-factor model of general equilibrium, Harberger was able to show that the incidence of the US corporation tax fell wholly on the suppliers of capital in that the reduction in the net income of capital was roughly equal to the revenue raised by the tax.

An early example of an AGE model in the international trade arena was the study undertaken by Miller and Spencer (1977) who sought to estimate the effects on the United Kingdom of her joining the European Economic Community (EEC): UK membership of the EEC involved the removal of tariffs on trade between the United Kingdom and the original six members and, in addition, the dismantling of the preferential system of trade with members of the Commonwealth. Furthermore, the operation of the Common Agricultural Policy (CAP) of the EEC had implications for resource transfers between the United Kingdom and the Community. On the production side, the Community model contained two sectors: agriculture and nonagriculture. On the demand side the analysis allowed for the existence of four groups: the United Kingdom, the six original members of the EEC, Australia and New Zealand combined, and the rest of the world. The overall findings of the study were: a massive 50 per cent increase in UK imports of manufactures from the EEC; only a small increase in UK income but, as a result of the net transfers associated with the CAP, the United Kingdom would suffer a net loss from membership equal to 1.8 per cent of national income.

In recent years, AGE models have become much less aggregative; gone are the days of simple two-sector models of the Harberger type. Piggott and Whalley (1985) analyse the extent of the distortionary losses imposed by the UK tax system as it existed in 1973 in a model which on the demand side includes 100 socio-economic household groups in addition to three aggregate sectors: government, capital formation, and the rest of the world. On the supply side, their model contains thirty-three different industries. They concluded that the 1973 tax system imposed losses of somewhere between 6 and 9 per cent of net national product, with the main losses resulting from the provision of public sector housing subsidies, the fact that excise duties were levied on a narrow range of commodities, and from the way in which the income from capital was taxed. They estimated that moving to a neutral sales tax regime in which the same amount of revenue was raised would have a significant impact on the distribution of income, with substantial gains being conferred on the richest 10 per cent of households and substantial losses on the poorest 10 per cent.

Similarly, increasingly sophisticated AGE models have been estimated and used for predictive purposes in the area of international trade. In looking at the likely implications of a 25 per cent across-the-board increase in the Australian import tariff, Dixon et al. (1982) deal with 114 different commodities on the supply side, though they have no disaggregation on the demand side. They trace through the effects of the postulated change on Australian employment, balance of trade and prices. In a massive recent study, Whalley (1985) examined the implications of the abolition of all trade barriers, both tariff and nontariff, in an AGE model with seven trade blocs and six commodities in each bloc. He considered three policy options: the abolition of all barriers by the North; the abolition of all barriers by the South; and the simultaneous abolition of all barriers throughout the world. Annual welfare gains at the world level are positive in all three cases, but with the bulk of the gains accruing to the South in the first case and with actual losses being incurred by the South in the latter two cases.

Brown and Stern (1988) constructed a computable general equilibrium model to study the economic effects of the bilateral tariff reductions in the United States–Canadian Free Trade Agreement (FTA). Their model included the United States, Canada, thirty-two other countries treated together and the rest of the world. For each country or region there were twenty-two tradable sectors and seven nontradable sectors, with each sector in the model being characterised by one of five market structures: (a) perfect competition; (b) monopolistic competition with free entry; (c) monopolistic competition without free entry; (d) market segmentation with free entry; and (e) market segmentation without free entry.

Canadian bilateral tariffs and nontariff barriers are noticeably higher for more sectors than the corresponding tariffs and barriers in the United States. Brown and Stern studied the impact of the removal of these barriers using an applied general equilibrium model and identified three main channels through which this liberalisation might be expected to increase welfare in the two economies. These three separate factors were: (i) intersectoral specialisation; (ii) rationalisation; and (iii) macroeconomic. As a result of the tariff reduction, one would expect resources to be allocated more in line with each country's comparative advantage. Welfare gains would then be expected to flow from this increased intersectoral specialisation. The increased competition and rationalisation of production resulting from lowering trade barriers and the scope for further reduction of unit costs by realising economies of scale further add to the gains. Consumers can also be expected to benefit from the greater variety of products resulting from the increased integration of the two economies. There may also be some macroeconomic benefits to be reaped as lower prices stimulate an increase in consumer spending and a consequent increase in aggregate output and employment.

The study concluded that considerable welfare gains are likely to flow from FTA. Taking as their baseline the 1976 pattern of trade, Brown and Stern calculated that the welfare gains to the United States would be of the order of $1.5 billion, which is equal to 0.1 per cent of the 1976 US GDP. The anticipated gains to the Canadians were estimated to be as high as $2 billion, which is equal to 1.1 per cent of the 1976 Canadian GDP. The main impact in proportionate terms is, therefore, on the Canadian economy and at a sectoral level in Canada quite significant changes in both output and employment are likely to result from the agreement.

APPENDIX: SOCIAL ACCOUNTING MATRIX (SAM)

The origin of social accounting matrices can be traced back to Quesnay's *Tableau Economique* (1758) but it is more useful to consider them as deriving from Stone's (1966) work in the 1960s on the Cambridge Growth Project, and the matrix formulation of the United Nations (1968). Conventional input–output tables can be considered to be a special case of the UN national accounting matrix but they were found to be inadequate in that they concentrate on the detail of industry transactions and pay scant regard to details of factor incomes, transfer payments, household expenditures, etc. For many countries, particularly developing ones, industrial structure is limited, but the evolution of household incomes is all-important. Some new tool was needed, and this was provided by SAMs, first used by Stone and then elaborated by Pyatt and Round (1985), etc.

A SAM is a square matrix statement of accounts that differs from input–output tables in that it includes factors (labour, etc.) and institutions (households, firms, government, etc.) as separate sectors, along with production activities (Table 8.3). Row entries represent receipts, column entries represent payments, and the total receipts and payments of corresponding rows/columns are equal. By dividing column entries by the corresponding column totals coefficients may be obtained that are equivalent to conventional input–output coefficients. The simplified SAM shown in Table 8.3 details the economic nature of most of the major blocks of transactions between sectors, with the input–output matrix appearing as $(T_{3,3})$.

In a sense, a SAM may be said to describe the circular nature of economic activity in an economy. Factors receive payments from production activities $(T_{1,3})$, and pass these incomes on to institutions via $(T_{2,1})$. Institutions also acquire income from internal transfers between themselves $(T_{2,2})$, and spend their incomes on the products of production activities $(T_{3,2})$, as well as imports, leaving some income as savings. Production activities also engage in interindustry sales $(T_{3,3})$, as well as producing for export and gross capital formation. Beyond this, SAMs provide a full and balanced data set for an economy, including the balance of payments, savings and investment accounts, and the finance and expenditure of government.

Inasmuch as SAMs have yet to achieve official UN status, with a consequential rigidly prescribed outline, there is considerable scope for free choice in their design and detail. Production activities and commodity production may be considered as separate sectors, institutions' capital accounts may be brought in alongside their current account receipts and expenditures, and detailed breakdowns may be provided for factors (labour force by occupation or skill level), households (rural/urban, by overall income levels, by race), or companies (state, public joint-stock, private, etc.). The design may be determined by the objectives of the practitioner and the availability of data.

Mathematically, SAMs may be treated in a way analagous to that used with input–output tables and a multiplier system may be derived. For SAMs the multipliers are considerably richer than those emanating from input–output analysis, and provide scope for considerably more detailed analysis of the effects of an external disturbance (Pyatt and Round, 1979). Effectively, some of the exogenous sectors of input–output analysis have been endogenised. However, such analysis is even more hampered by the assumption of the fixity of coefficients than is the case with input–output tables. A fixed allocation of household expenditure does not make much sense when one considers the wide variety of income elasticities of demand that are found.

Beyond this linear analysis the SAM framework may be used as the basis for general equilibrium models, and some computable general equilibrium (CGE) models may be said to be based implicitly upon SAMs (Thorbecke, 1985). Such models may use many behavioural and technical relations that are nonlinear, and software packages now exist that can take a given SAM, allow a variety of functional forms to be specified, impose closure rules, and generate new SAMs for any altered external scenario that the researcher may determine (Pyatt, 1987). In this context the advantage of SAMs is that they start from a consistent and balanced accounting

Table 8.3 A simplified social accounting matrix

		Expenditures					
		1	2	3	4 Other accounts		Total
		Factors	Institutions including households	Production activities	Combined capital	Rest of world	
1	Factors			Factorial income distribution ($T_{1,3}$)			Income of factors
2	Institutions including households	Income distribution to households and other institutions ($T_{2,1}$)	Transfers, taxes, and subsidies ($T_{2,2}$)			Receipts of institutions, from rest of the world	Income of institutions
3	Production activities		Institutional demand (households and others) for goods and services ($T_{3,2}$)	Interindustry demand ($T_{3,3}$)	Gross capital formation	Exports	Gross demand = gross output
4	Combined capital		Domestic savings			Balance of payments current account deficit	Aggregate savings
	Rest of world		Imports of competitive goods	Imports of complementary goods			Total foreign exchange outflow
	Total	Outlay (= income) of factors	Expenditures of institutions	Gross output	Aggregate investment	Total foreign exchange inflow	

Receipts

framework that presents the structure of an economy in a format disaggregated to a degree that is meaningful for the given economy. The CGE model based on that SAM then produces results that may be directly related to that economy.

References

Brown, D.K. and Stern, R.M. (1988), 'Computable general equilibrium estimates of the gains from US–Canadian trade liberalisation', Paper presented at Lehigh University Conference on Economic Aspects of Regional Trading Arrangements, Bethlehem Pa.

Dixon, P.B., Parmenter, B., Sutton, J. and Vincent D., (1982) *ORANI: a multi-sectoral model of the Australian economy*, Amsterdam: North-Holland.

Harberger, A.C. (1962), 'The incidence of the corporation income tax', *Journal of Political Economy*, **70**, 215–240.

Miller, M.H. and Spencer, J.F., (1977), 'The static economic effects of the UK joining the EEC: a general equilibrium approach', *Review of Economic Studies*, **44**, 71–93.

Piggott, J.R. and Whalley, J. (1985), *Applied General Equilibrium Analysis: An Application to UK Tax Policy*, Cambridge: Cambridge University Press.

Pyatt, G. (1987), 'The SAM approach in retrospect and prospect', *University of Warwick Economics Discussion Paper, no. 290*, Warwick.

Pyatt, G. and Round J.I. (1979). 'Accounting and fixed-price multipliers in a social accounting matrix framework', *Economic Journal*, **89**, 850–73.

Pyatt, G. and Round, J.I. (eds.) (1985), *The Social Accounting Matrices*, A World Bank Symposium, Washington D.C.

Quesnay, F. (1758), *Tableau Economique*, reproduced in facsimile, with an introduction by H. Higgs, by the British Economic Society, 1895.

Scarf, H. and Shoven, J.B. (eds.) (1984), *Applied General Equilibrium Analysis*, New York: Cambridge University Press.

Shoven, J.B. and Whalley J., (1984), 'Applied general equilibrium models of taxation and international trade: an introduction and survey', *Journal of Economic Literature*, **22**, 1007–51.

Stone, J.R.N. (1966) 'The social accounts from a consumer point of view', *Review of income and wealth*, Series 12, pp. 1–33.

Thorbecke, E. (1985), 'The social accounting matrix and consistency-type planning models', in G. Pyatt and J.I. Round (eds.), *Social Accounting Matrices: a basis for planning*, Washington: World Bank.

United Nations Statistical Office (1968), *A System of National Accounts*, Series F., no. 2, Rev. 3, New York: United Nations.

Whalley, J. (1985) *Trade Liberalization Among Major World Trading Areas*, Cambridge, Mass.: The M.I.T. Press.

Chapter 9

LINEAR PROGRAMMING

In this chapter we explain the basic principles of linear programming (LP). In section 9.1 we outline the main features of this optimisation technique and provide a diagrammatic analysis for the simple case of a linear program with two choice variables. The discussion is generalised in Section 9.2 where we outline the simplex method, derive the optimality and feasibility criteria and comment on the economic significance of the procedures. In the third, and most important, section of the chapter we discuss the dual of a linear program, showing the connections between the original problem, the primal, and its dual. Throughout our analysis we emphasise the economic significance of our results. The dual simplex method is presented in Section 9.4 and its usefulness in sensitivity analysis is explored. Finally, in Section 9.5 a special kind of linear programming problem – the transportation problem – is analysed. Throughout the chapter numerical examples employing the various techniques discussed are presented as an aid to the reader's understanding of the procedures.

9.1. AN INTRODUCTION TO LINEAR PROGRAMMING

In this chapter we consider a special type of optimisation problem in which we seek to optimise a linear objective function subject to a set of linear inequalities and non-negativity requirements on the variables entering the objective function. Such problems are known as linear programming problems and the methods for solving them were developed by Dantzig and others during and following the Second World War. For a discussion of the historical development of linear programming see Dantzig (1982) and Dorfman (1984).

Consider the case of a firm faced with fixed prices for the products it can produce and subject to a linear production technology and constraints on the availability of productive inputs. If the aim of the firm is to maximise the value of its output, then we may formulate the problem as follows:

$$\text{Max } Z = c_1 x_1 + c_2 x_2 + \ldots + c_n x_n$$

subject to

$$\begin{aligned} a_{11}x_1 + a_{12}x_2 + \ldots + a_{1n}x_n &\leq b_1 \\ a_{21}x_1 + a_{22}x_2 + \ldots + a_{2n}x_n &\leq b_2 \\ &\vdots \\ a_{m1}x_1 + a_{m2}x_2 + \ldots + a_{mn}x_n &\leq b_m \\ x_1, x_2, \ldots, x_n &\geq 0 \end{aligned} \tag{9.1}$$

More compactly we have in matrix notation:

$$\begin{aligned} \text{Max } & cx \\ \text{st } & Ax \leq b \\ & x \geq 0 \end{aligned} \tag{9.2}$$

where c is a row vector of prices, x is a column vector of outputs, A is a matrix of technical input–output coefficients in which a typical component a_{ij} signifies the amount of the ith input necessary to produce a unit of the jth output, and b is a column vector of available inputs. First we provide a diagrammatic treatment of the solution to a simple LP problem, before going on to discuss a general method of solution. Consider the following problem:

$$\begin{aligned} \text{Max} \quad & x_1 + x_2 \\ \text{st} \quad & x_1 \leq 12 \\ & 2x_1 + x_2 \leq 28 \\ & x_1 + 2x_2 \leq 26 \\ & x_2 \leq 11 \\ & x_1, x_2 \geq 0 \end{aligned} \tag{9.3}$$

Plotting the constraints in Figure 9.1 we obtain the convex feasible region $OABCDE$. In fact, whenever feasible solutions exist to a LP problem, the set of feasible points is convex. The firm, in seeking to maximise the value of its output, must choose a combination of the two products which lie in this region, including its boundaries. The objective function gives rise to a set of downward sloping iso-revenue lines with a slope of -1. The highest such iso-revenue line that the firm can attain is the line that just touches the feasible region at the vertex C. Combinations of the two products which lie on iso-revenue lines to the right of this one are unattainable since they lie outside the feasible region; some combinations of the two products which lie on iso-revenue lines to the left of the one through C are attainable but yield less revenue. The coordinates of the point C yield the revenue-maximising combination of the two products: the firm produces ten units of x_1 and eight units of x_2, receiving a revenue of eighteen units in total.

In the case where the objective function contains three unknowns, we will have a set of iso-revenue planes in three-dimensional Euclidian space. For the general

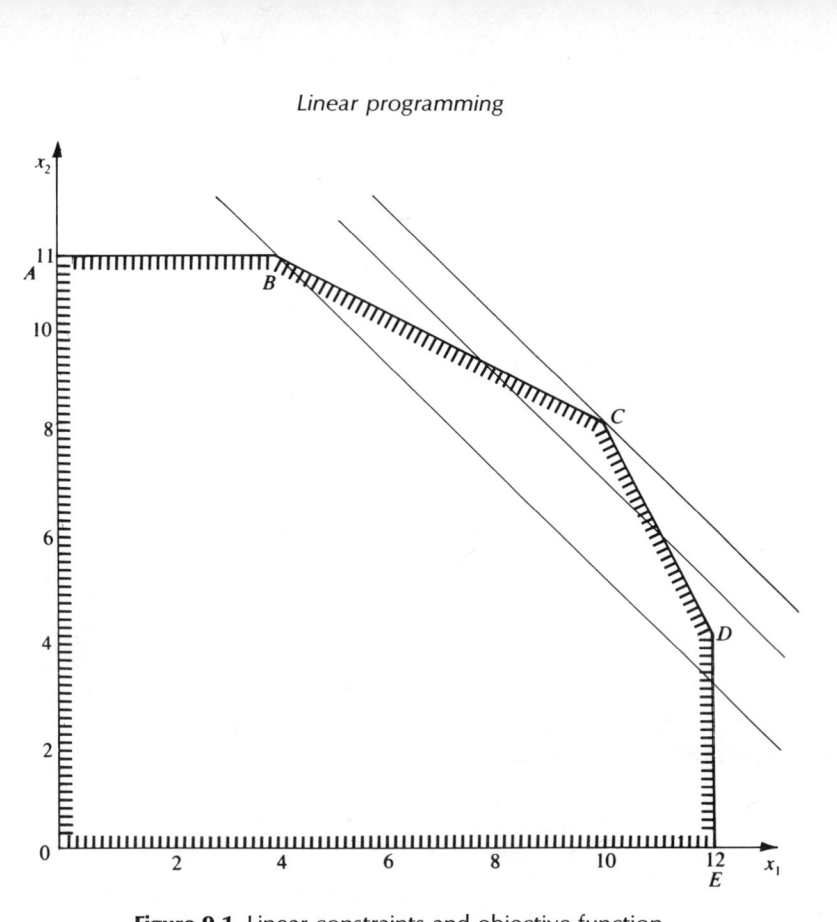

Figure 9.1 Linear constraints and objective function.

problem with n unknowns, the objective function gives rise to a set of hyperplanes in n-dimensional Euclidian space E^n). The hyperplane associated with the maximum value of this function is a supporting hyperplane to the convex polyhedron formed from the constraints and the non-negativity requirements of the problem. A supporting hyperplane possesses the following property: it passes through a boundary point of the convex polyhedron such that the convex set lies in one closed half-space produced by the hyperplane. In the two-dimensional case shown in Figure 9.2 the line z_0 is a supporting hyperplane to the convex feasible region $OABCDE$. The feasible region lies wholly to the left of this line other than along the line segment BC where the line z_0 coincides with a boundary of the feasible region; z_1 is also a supporting hyperplane, just touching the feasible region at the point C.

The optimal solution to a LP problem, if it exists, will always include an extreme point of the convex set of feasible solutions. An extreme point of the set is one which cannot be expressed as a convex combination of other points in the set. All other points can be expressed as convex combinations of extreme points. If there exists a nonunique solution to the problem, then points other than extreme points will be optimal but, nevertheless, at least one extreme point will be optimal. Since there exist a finite number of such points, the general procedure for solving these problems

An introduction to linear programming

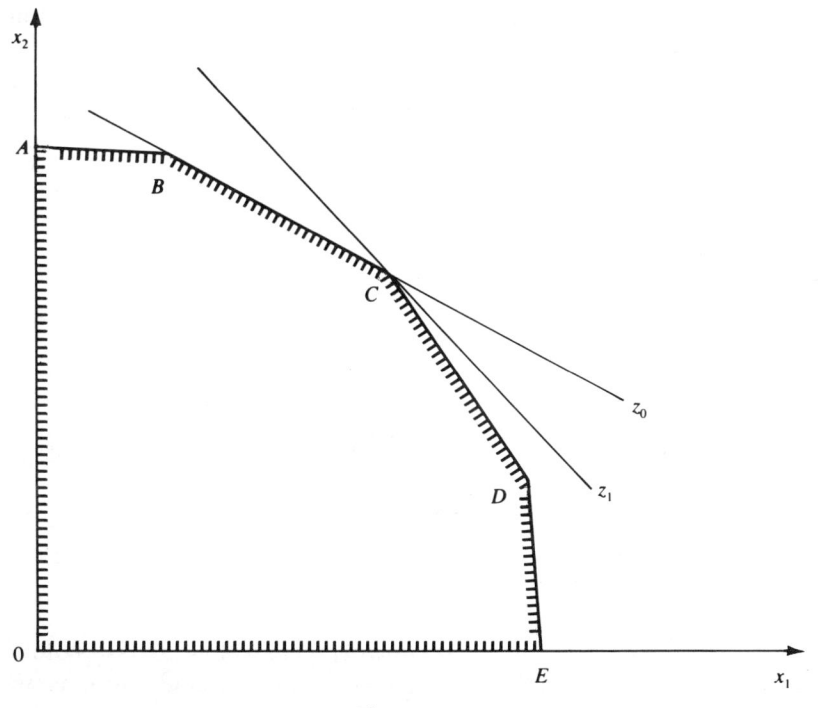

Figure 9.2

involves finding an extreme point and then moving to another such point as long as the objective function continues to increase in value.

The constraints of the problem have been written in the form $Ax \leq b$; it is now more useful to convert the constraints into equalities by the addition of slack variables (s_i, $i = 1, 2, \ldots, m$). In the example of a firm seeking to maximise the value of its output, then s_i will represent the amount of the ith resource which remains unutilised; naturally $s_i \geq 0$. We now have a set of m equations in $m + n$ unknowns. In matrix notation, we have

$$[A \quad I] \begin{bmatrix} x \\ s \end{bmatrix} = b \qquad (9.4)$$

where I is an identity matrix of order $m \times m$ and s is a column vector of m slack variables.

A basic solution to the set of m equations is obtained by setting n of the $m + n$ unknowns equal to zero and then solving for the remaining m unknowns, always assuming that the m equations so obtained are linearly independent. The variables entering these equations are known as basic variables. The total number of such basic solutions is $(m + n)!/m!n!$. A basic solution is feasible provided that all the basic variables take on non-negative values. It will be a degenerate basic feasible solution if one or more of the basic variables is zero. Furthermore, a basic feasible solution (BFS) is an extreme point of the convex set of feasible solutions and the optimal solution to the problem will accordingly be, for the case of a unique solution, one of the set of basic feasible solutions.

Consider the following problem of a firm seeking to maximise the value of its output; it can choose to produce three different products if it wishes and is subject to constraints on the availability of three different inputs:

$$\begin{aligned} \text{Max } Z = 14x_1 + 17x_2 + 7x_3 & \\ \text{st} \quad 4x_1 + 3x_2 + 2x_3 &\leq 60 \\ x_1 + 0.5x_2 + 1.5x_3 &\leq 24 \\ x_1 + 4x_2 + x_3 &\leq 36 \\ x_1, x_2, x_3 &\geq 0 \end{aligned} \quad (9.5)$$

Converting the constraints of the problem into equalities by the addition of three slack variables, we obtain

$$\begin{aligned} 4x_1 + 3x_2 + 2x_3 + s_1 &= 60 \\ x_1 + 0.5x_2 + 1.5x_3 + s_2 &= 24 \\ x_1 + 4x_2 + x_3 + s_3 &= 36 \end{aligned} \quad (9.6)$$

Since there are three equations in six unknowns, there will be 20 basic solutions, not all of which will be feasible. Solving for the set of basic feasible solutions, we obtain the following results which we present in Table 9.1. We label each BFS with a letter which corresponds to the extreme point of the feasible region given in Figure 9.3 and provide the associated value of the objective function at that extreme point. The objective function is maximised by choosing the output combination associated with the extreme point B with the supporting plane just touching the feasible region at this point.

Table 9.1 The set of basic feasible solutions

			Point	Z
$s_1 = 60$	$s_2 = 24$	$s_3 = 36$	0	0
$x_1 = 15$	$s_2 = 9$	$s_3 = 21$	A	210
$x_1 = 132/13$	$x_2 = 84/13$	$s_2 = 138/13$	B	252
$x_2 = 9$	$s_1 = 33$	$s_2 = 39/2$	C	153
$x_2 = 60/11$	$x_3 = 156/11$	$s_1 = 168/11$	D	192
$x_3 = 16$	$s_1 = 28$	$s_3 = 20$	E	112
$x_1 = 21/2$	$x_3 = 9$	$s_3 = 33/2$	F	210
$x_1 = 56/9$	$x_2 = 44/9$	$x_3 = 92/9$	G	241.77 ...

9.2 THE SIMPLEX METHOD

The number of basic solutions increases very rapidly with the number of choice variables and constraints: for example, for $m = 10$ and $n = 15$, the number of basic

The simplex method 215

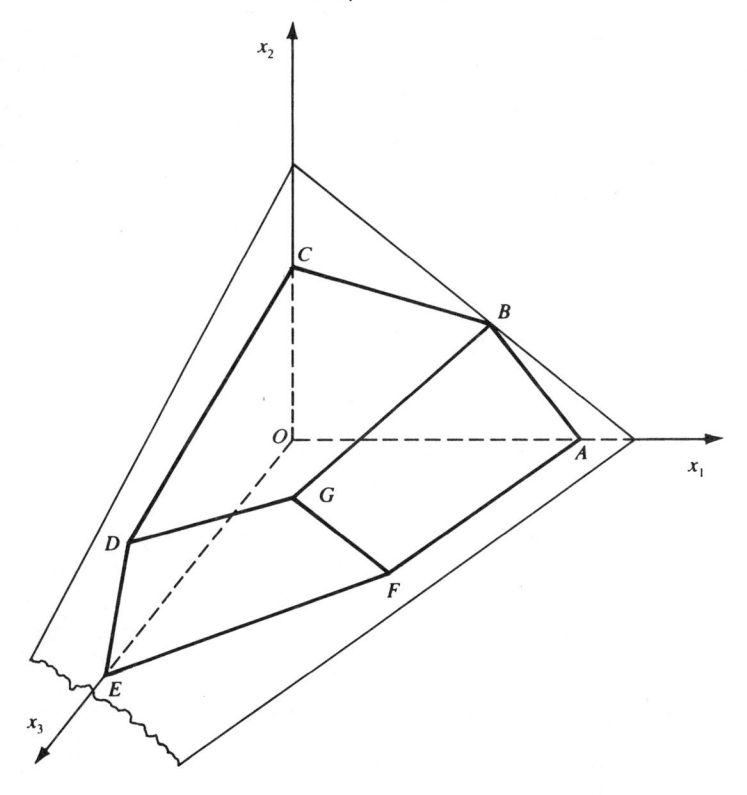

Figure 9.3 Optimal solution.

solutions is 25!/10!15! = 3 268 760. Hence, it is highly inefficient, if not impossible, to obtain all the basic solutions, check for feasibility and obtain the associated value of the objective function. An iterative technique which converges rapidly on the optimal solution was first formulated by Dantzig (1951a). With this technique, known as the simplex method, we start off from an initial BFS (an initial extreme point) and move on to an adjacent extreme point. Of the adjacent extreme points, we move to the one which gives us the largest increase in the value of the objective function. The method provides us with information on whether the extreme point we have reached is the optimal one or not. If it is not optimal, we move onto another adjacent extreme point until the optimal point is reached.

We may find that the objective function can be increased without bound, in which case we cannot obtain a finite solution. The simplex method is able to identify the case where there is no finite solution.

In explaining the simplex method, we shall write the general problem in canonical form where inequalities have been converted into equalities by adding slack variables:

$$\text{Max } cx \quad \text{st } Ax = b \\ x \geqslant 0 \tag{9.7}$$

where the matrix A now includes columns relating to the slack variables, with the latter also appearing in the vector x. The coefficients on the slack variables in the new c vector are naturally all equal to zero. We shall assume that the rank of the matrix A is m and that the rank of any matrix B made up of any m columns of A is also m.

Consider some initial BFS. Let the variables entering the basis be given by the vector x^B and let the matrix B be made up of columns of A relevant to the vector x^B; c^B is the vector of coefficients in the objective function on the basic variables. Then

$$Bx^B = b \tag{9.8}$$

and premultiplying by B^{-1} we have

$$x^B = B^{-1}b \tag{9.9}$$

and the value of the objective function is given by

$$Z^B = c^B x^B = c^B B^{-1} b \tag{9.10}$$

Naturally, feasibility requires $x^B \geq 0$.

Let us consider whether introducing a nonbasic variable x_j into the basis at some level t will increase the value of the objective function. When x_j is introduced into the basis the constraints of the problem must continue to hold as equalities. Hence we must have

$$Bx^B(t) + A_j x_j(t) = b \tag{9.11}$$

where x^B and x_j have both been written as functions of t and A_j is the column of A referring to the variable x_j.

Premultiplying equation (9.11) by B^{-1} and rearranging, we have

$$x^B(t) = B^{-1}b - B^{-1}A_j x_j(t) \tag{9.12}$$

Hence, if x_j is introduced into the basis, the new value of the objective function will be given by

$$\begin{aligned} Z(t) &= c^B x^B(t) + c_j x_j \\ &= c^B B^{-1} b - (c^B B^{-1} A_j - c_j) x_j(t) \end{aligned} \tag{9.13}$$

Introducing x_j into the basis will increase the value of the objective function provided that

$$c^B B^{-1} A_j - c_j < 0 \tag{9.14}$$

Assume that the above condition holds for some nonbasic variable x_j. Then in order to make way for this variable an existing basic variable must be removed from the basis. We wish to introduce x_j at as large a level as possible subject to the solution still remaining feasible. None of the original basic variables can be reduced below zero when x_j is introduced into the basis. We must have

$$x^B(t) = B^{-1}b - B^{-1}A_j x_j(t) \geq 0 \tag{9.15}$$

For this to be the case,

$$\frac{(B^{-1}b)_i}{(B^{-1}A_j)_i} \geq x_j(t) \geq 0 \text{ (for all } i\text{)} \tag{9.16}$$

where $(B^{-1}b)_i$ and $(B^{-1}A_j)_i$ are the ith elements in the column vectors $B^{-1}b$ and $B^{-1}A_j$ respectively.

Thus the variable to be removed from the basis is the one with the smallest positive ratio of $(B^{-1}b)_i/(B^{-1}A_j)_i$. If, for some particular basic variable $(B^{-1}A_j)_i$ is nonpositive, no limit is imposed by this basic variable upon the level t at which the variable x_j can be introduced into the basis. If all the elements in the vector $B^{-1}A_j$ are nonpositive, there is no restriction on the level at which x_j can be introduced into the basis. In this case, the solution to the problem does not exist as the objective function is unbounded.

In summary, the optimal solution to the problem has been reached if there is no nonbasic variable for which

$$c^B B^{-1} A_j - c_j < 0 \tag{9.17}$$

If there does exist a nonbasic variable for which the above condition holds, then the leaving variable is the one with the smallest positive values of

$$\frac{(B^{-1}b)_i}{(B^{-1}A_j)_i} \tag{9.18}$$

Let us provide an economic interpretation of the optimality criterion. Define $y^B = c^B B^{-1}$ and assume the nonbasic variable x_j is the slack variable corresponding to the first constraint of the problem; then

$$A_j = \begin{bmatrix} 1 \\ 0 \\ \vdots \\ 0 \end{bmatrix} \text{ and } c_j = 0 \tag{9.19}$$

Hence, for this particular case, $c^B B^{-1} A_j - c_j = y_1^B$. If the first slack variable is introduced into the new basis at the unit level, as can be seen from equation (9.13), the value of the objective function will fall by y_1^B. We may therefore interpret y_1^B as a measure of the value to the firm of a unit of this particular input when the activities to which the firm's inputs can be put are confined to those in the basis. Thus y^B is a vector of the unit values of the firm's inputs, with y_i^B being a measure of the opportunity cost or shadow price of a unit of the ith input.

Let us now consider the case of a nonbasic variable which is not a slack variable. In this case, the column A_j contains the quantities of each input necessary to produce a unit of x_j and the product $y^B A_j$ measures the opportunity cost of the resources necessary to produce a unit of x_j. If this opportunity cost falls short of the market value of the good c_j, then x_j should be produced. Hence the rationale for introducing x_j into the basis is clear.

Let us return to the problem for which we provided a three-dimensional

218   Linear programming

diagrammatic analysis and show how to solve such a problem using the simplex method:

$$\text{Max } Z = 14x_1 + 17x_2 + 7x_3$$
$$\text{st} \quad 4x_1 + 3x_2 + 2x_3 \leqslant 60$$
$$x_1 + 0.5x_2 + 1.5x_2 \leqslant 24 \qquad (9.20)$$
$$x_1 + 4x_2 + x_3 \leqslant 36$$
$$x_1, x_2, x_3 \geqslant 0$$

Converting the problem into a canonical one by introducing slack variables, we obtain the following extended A matrix and c vector:

$$A = \begin{bmatrix} 4 & 3 & 2 & 1 & 0 & 0 \\ 1 & 0.5 & 1.5 & 0 & 1 & 0 \\ 1 & 4 & 1 & 0 & 0 & 1 \end{bmatrix}$$

$$c = \begin{bmatrix} 14 & 17 & 7 & 0 & 0 & 0 \end{bmatrix}$$

The origin is available as an initial basic feasible solution (BFS):

$$x^{B_1} = B_1^{-1}b = \begin{bmatrix} 1 & 0 & 0 \\ 0 & 1 & 0 \\ 0 & 0 & 1 \end{bmatrix} \begin{bmatrix} 60 \\ 24 \\ 36 \end{bmatrix} = \begin{bmatrix} 60 \\ 24 \\ 36 \end{bmatrix}$$

$$c^{B_1}B_1^{-1} = \begin{bmatrix} 0 & 0 & 0 \end{bmatrix}$$

Letting $z^{NB_1} = c^{B_1}B_1^{-1}A_{NB_1}$ where A_{NB_1} is a matrix of columns of A not in B_1, then

$$z^{NB_1} - c^{NB_1} = \begin{bmatrix} -14 & -17 & -7 \end{bmatrix}$$

The largest negative value of $z_j - c_j$ is -17 and this refers to the nonbasic variable x_2, for which we calculate $B_1^{-1}A_2$ and then obtain the ratios $(B_1^{-1}b)_i/(B_1^{-1}A_2)_i$ (for $i = 1, \ldots, 3$):

$$B_1^{-1}A_2 = \begin{bmatrix} 3 \\ 0.5 \\ 4 \end{bmatrix} \text{ and the ratios} = \begin{bmatrix} 20 \\ 48 \\ 9 \end{bmatrix}$$

The smallest one, 9, refers to the basic variable $s_3 = x_6$; we therefore eliminate $s_3 = x_6$ to make way for x_2. The new B matrix is B_2:

$$B_2 = \begin{bmatrix} 1 & 0 & 3 \\ 1 & 0 & 0.5 \\ 0 & 0 & 4 \end{bmatrix} \text{ and } B_2^{-1} = \begin{bmatrix} 1 & 0 & -3/4 \\ 0 & 1 & -1/8 \\ 0 & 0 & 1/4 \end{bmatrix}$$

and

$$x^{B_2} = B_2^{-1}b = \begin{bmatrix} 33 \\ 39/2 \\ 9 \end{bmatrix} \text{ and } c^{B_2} = [0 \quad 0 \quad 17]$$

$$c^{B_2}B_2^{-1} = [0 \quad 0 \quad 17/4]$$

For the nonbasic variables:

$$z^{NB_2} - c^{NB_2} = [-39/4 \quad -11/4 \quad 17/4]$$

The largest negative value of $z_j - c_j$ is $-39/4$ and this refers to the nonbasic variable x_1. We now find which variable must leave the basis:

$$B_2^{-1}A_1 = \begin{bmatrix} 13/4 \\ 7/8 \\ 1/4 \end{bmatrix} \text{ and the ratios } = \begin{bmatrix} 132/13 \\ 156/7 \\ 36 \end{bmatrix}$$

The smallest ratio, 132/13, refers to the basic variable $x_4 = s_1$: hence $x_4 = s_1$ is eliminated to make way for x_1. The new B matrix is B_3:

$$B_3 = \begin{bmatrix} 4 & 0 & 3 \\ 1 & 1 & 0.5 \\ 1 & 0 & 4 \end{bmatrix} \text{ and } B_3^{-1} = \begin{bmatrix} 4/13 & 0 & -3/13 \\ -7/26 & 1 & 1/13 \\ -1/13 & 0 & 4/13 \end{bmatrix}$$

and

$$x^{B_3} = B_3^{-1}b = \begin{bmatrix} 132/13 \\ 138/13 \\ 84/13 \end{bmatrix}$$

$$c^{B_3}B_3^{-1} = [3 \quad 0 \quad 2]$$

For the nonbasic variables:

$$z^{NB_3} - c^{NB_3} = [1 \quad 3 \quad 2]$$

The value $z_j - c_j < 0$, does not hold for any of the variables that are not in the basis, so the optimal solution has now been reached with $x_1 = 132/13$, $x_2 = 84/13$ and $x_5 = 138/13$. The value of the objective function is 252.

For ease of calculation it is most convenient to present the material in the following tableau, which refers to the initial basic feasible solution operating only slack activities:

		x_1	x_2	x_3	$s_1 = x_4$	$s_2 = x_5$	$s_3 = x_6$	Solution
	$z_j - c_j$	-14	-17	-7	0	0	0	0
	$x_4 = s_1$	4	3	2	1	0	0	60
Basic variables	$x_5 = s_2$	1	1/2	3/2	0	1	0	24
	$x_6 = s_3$	1	4	1	0	0	1	36

For the moment ignore the last column of the tableau. In the first row we measure $z_j - c_j$ for all the variables in the problem; in the remaining rows are to be found the elements of the matrix $B^{-1}A$, where B is a matrix made up of the columns of A referring to the basic variables and in the order in which these variables appear in the basis. Note that this order need not be the same as the order in which the variables appear in the original problem, B^{-1} appears under the slack variables. Turning to the last column, in the first row we have the value of the objective function for this particular basic solution and the remaining elements in the column are the values taken by the basic variables ($B^{-1}b$). For the problem of equation (9.20), the initial basic feasible solution yields a zero value for the objective function since only slack activities are carried out.

When one variable is removed from the basis and replaced by another, the new inverse is easily obtained by simple row operations, since in the column for each basic variable x_i, we must have 1 in the ith row and 0 everywhere else. The optimality criterion points to the introduction of x_2 and the feasibility criterion to the removal of $s_3 = x_6$. In order to generate the next tableau, the following operations are performed:

1. The x_6 row is multiplied by 1/4 to form the x_2 row.
2. The x_6 row is multiplied by $-1/8$ and added to the x_5 row to form the new x_5 row.
3. The x_6 row is multiplied by $-3/4$ and added to the x_4 row to form the new x_4 row.
4. The x_6 row is multiplied by 17/4 and added to the $z_j - c_j$ row to form the new $z_j - c_j$ row.

We have a new basic feasible solution with $z = 153$. The procedure is again repeated; x_1 enters the basis in place of x_4. The following row operations are performed:

1. The x_4 row is multiplied by 4/13 to form the x_1 row.
2. The x_4 row is multiplied by $-7/26$ and added to the x_5 row to form the new x_5 row.
3. The x_4 row is multiplied by $-1/13$ and added to the x_2 row to form the new x_2 row.
4. The x_4 row is multiplied by 3 and added to the $z_j - c_j$ row to form the new $z_j - c_j$ row.

		x_1	x_2	x_3	x_4	x_5	x_6	Solution
	$z_j - c_j$	$-39/4$	0	$-11/4$	0	0	17/4	153
	x_4	13/4	0	5/4	1	0	$-3/4$	33
Basic variables	x_5	7/8	0	11/8	0	1	$-1/8$	39/2
	x_2	1/4	1	1/4	0	0	1/4	9
	$z_j - c_j$	0	0	1	3	0	2	252
	x_1	1	0	5/13	4/13	0	$-3/13$	132/13
Basic variables	x_5	0	0	27/26	$-7/26$	1	1/13	138/13
	x_2	0	1	2/13	$-1/13$	0	4/13	84/13

The optimal solution has now been reached; there are no nonbasic variables for which $z_j - c_j < 0$. The value of the objective function is 252; $x_1 = 132/13$, $x_2 = 84/13$ and

$x_5 = 138/13$. The good x_3 is not produced since the opportunity cost of the resources necessary to produce a unit of the product (yA_3) equals 8 and this exceeds the price of the good by 1.

9.3 THE DUAL OF A LINEAR PROGRAM

Consider the following LP problem:

$$\left.\begin{aligned}
\text{Max } Z = c_1x_1 + c_2x_2 + \ldots + c_nx_n & \\
\text{st } \quad a_{11}x_1 + a_{12}x_2 + \ldots + a_{1n}x_n \leq b_1 & \\
a_{21}x_1 + a_{22}x_2 + \ldots + a_{2n}x_n \leq b_2 & \\
\vdots & \\
a_{m1}x_1 + a_{m2}x_2 + \ldots + a_{mn}x_n \leq b_m & \\
x_j \geq 0 \quad (j = 1, 2, \ldots, n) &
\end{aligned}\right\} \quad (9.21)$$

This is the primal problem; associated with every LP problem of the above type is another LP problem which is known as the dual. The dual of the above primal takes the following form

$$\left.\begin{aligned}
\text{Min } C = b_1y_1 + b_2y_2 + \ldots + b_my_m & \\
\text{st } \quad a_{11}y_1 + a_{21}y_2 + \ldots + a_{m1}y_m \geq c_1 & \\
a_{12}y_1 + a_{22}y_2 + \ldots + a_{m2}y_m \geq c_2 & \\
\vdots & \\
a_{1n}y_1 + a_{2n}y_2 + \ldots + a_{mn}y_m \geq c_n & \\
y_i \geq 0 \quad i = 1, 2, \ldots, m &
\end{aligned}\right\} \quad (9.22)$$

More compactly we have in matrix notation the primal and its associated dual

$$\left.\begin{aligned} \text{Max } cx \text{ st } Ax \leq b \\ x \geq 0 \end{aligned}\right\} \quad (9.23)$$

$$\left.\begin{aligned} \text{Min } yb \text{ st } yA \geq c \\ y \geq 0 \end{aligned}\right\} \quad (9.24)$$

We may briefly summarise the links between the two problems as follows:

1. If the primal is a maximisation problem, then its dual will be a minimisation problem and vice versa.
2. The inequality signs in the primal constraints are reversed in the dual.
3. The matrix of constraint coefficients in the dual problem is the transpose of the matrix of the constraint coefficients in the primal problem.

4. The coefficients of the objective function of the primal appear on the right-hand side of the constraints in the dual; similarly for the dual.
5. The number of unknowns in the dual (m) equals the number of constraints in the primal; similarly if there are n unknowns in the primal there are n constraints in the dual.

Let x^0 and y^0 represent feasible solutions to the primal and dual problems respectively; postmultiplying the dual constraints by x^0 and premultiplying the primal constraints by y^0 and using the non-negatively requirements, it follows that:

$$y^0 b \geqslant y^0 A x^0 \geqslant c x^0 \tag{9.25}$$

If y^* represents the optimal solution to the dual it is clear that $y^* b \geqslant c x^0$ and if x^* represents the optimal solution to the primal, it is also the case that $y^0 b \geqslant c x^*$. If feasible solutions exist to both primal and dual, then there exist optimal solutions to both problems. For example, consider the following problem:

$$\begin{aligned} \text{Max } & 10x_1 - 8x_2 \\ \text{st } & x_1 - x_2 \leqslant 8 \\ & x_1 - 2x_2 \leqslant 4 \\ & x_1, x_2 \geqslant 0 \end{aligned} \tag{9.26}$$

Then its dual is:

$$\begin{aligned} \text{Min } & 8y_1 + 4y_2 \\ \text{st } & y_1 + y_2 \geqslant 10 \\ & -y_1 - 2y_2 \geqslant -8 \\ & y_1, y_2 \geqslant 0 \end{aligned} \tag{9.27}$$

The primal and dual problems are depicted in Figure 9.4. Note there does not exist a bounded solution to the primal and the dual is consequently infeasible. The feasible region for the primal is the area between the x_2 axis and *OABC* extended; there is clearly no restriction on the extent to which the value of the objective function can be kept within a bound. Turning to the dual: one can see from the diagram that the two dual constraints are mutually inconsistent and the feasible region for the two dual variables is empty.

Consider feasible solutions to the primal and dual, x^* and y^* respectively, such that $cx^* = y^* b$. Then these two feasible solutions must be optimal. The proof of this proposition is straightforward.

We have already shown that:

$$y^0 b \geqslant y^0 A x^0 \geqslant c x^0 \tag{9.28}$$

Now if $y^* b = c x^*$, then for any other basic feasible solution to the primal x^0 we must have $cx^* \geqslant cx^0$. Hence, x^* is the optimal solution to the primal. Similarly, for any other basic feasible solution to the dual y^0 we must have $y^0 b \geqslant y^* b$. Hence, y^* is the optimal solution to the dual.

The dual of a linear program

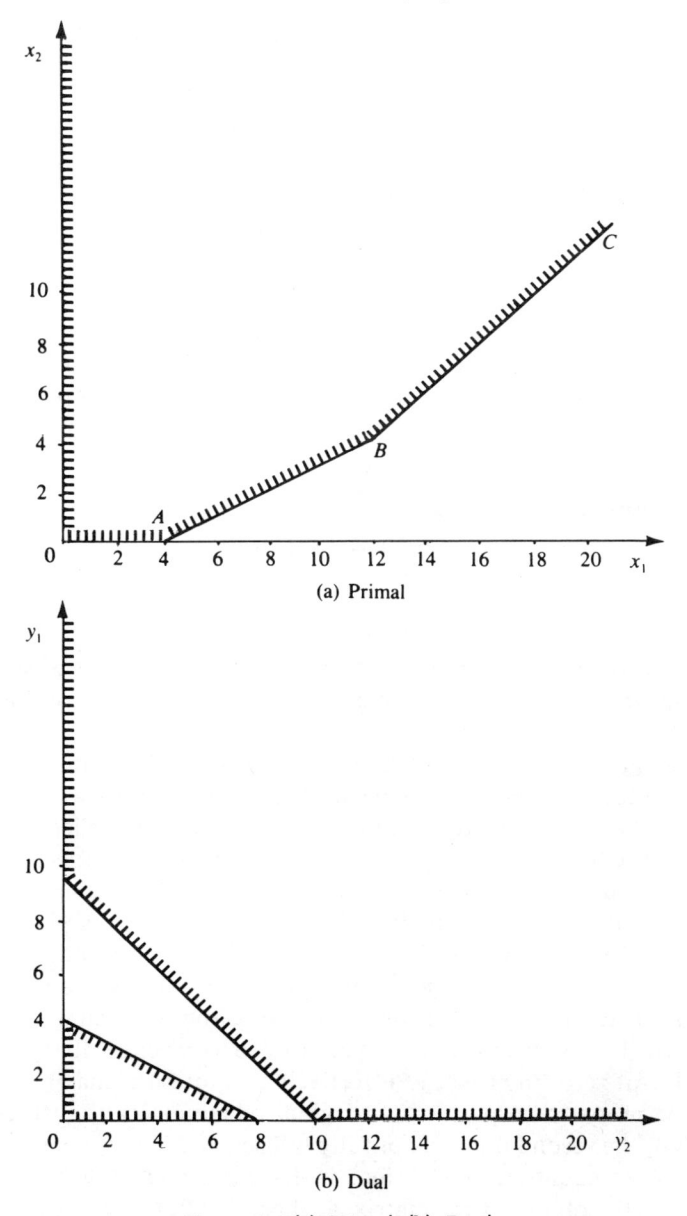

Figure 9.4 (a) Primal. (b) Dual.

A feasible vector x^* of the primal problem is optimal if and only if the dual has a feasible vector y^* such that when evaluated at these vectors the value of the primal is equal to the value of the dual. The vector y^* is then optimal for the dual.

We start out with a particular basic feasible solution to the primal and assume that this does indeed represent an optimal solution to the problem with the value of the primal being given by $c^B x^*$. For the objective function not to increase in value when a nonbasic variable is introduced, then, as demonstrated earlier in equation (9.17), we must have

$$c^B B^{-1} A_j - c_j \geq 0 \quad \text{(for all j)} \tag{9.29}$$

Define $y^* = c^B B^{-1}$, then $c^B B^{-1}$ constitute a feasible solution to the dual. For each slack variable, $c_j = 0$ and $c^B B^{-1} A_j = y_j^*$ which is clearly non-negative. But what about the optimality of y^*? Since we have defined $y^* = c^B B^{-1}$, then we must have $y^* b = c^B B^{-1} b$, but $B^{-1} b = x^*$. Hence, $y^* b = c^B x^*$ but if this is the case, then y^* is optimal.

In example (9.20) the dual variables take on the following values: $y_1 = 3$, $y_2 = 0$ and $y_3 = 2$. They appear as the coefficients on the slack variables in the $z_j - c_j$ row of the tableau. Note that the value of the dual is 252 and equal to that of the primal.

At the solution to a linear programming problem we have shown that

$$y^* b = y^* A x^* = c x^* \tag{9.30}$$

It therefore follows that

$$y^* [b - A x^*] = 0 \tag{9.31}$$

and

$$[y^* A - c] x^* = 0 \tag{9.32}$$

These results, known as the complementary slackness conditions or the equilibrium theorem of linear programming, are of great economic significance. Turning first to equation (9.31), since $y^* \geq 0$ and $b - Ax^* \geq 0$, then if $b_i - A_i x^* > 0$, where A_i is the ith row of the matrix, A, $y_i^* = 0$. If the ith constraint in the primal holds as a strict inequality, then the corresponding dual variable y_i^* must take on a value of zero. This result should not be surprising to economists; we have shown earlier that y_i^* measures the opportunity cost of the ith resource at the optimal solution to the problem. Assume that at this optimal position the ith constraint is binding (i.e. an equality without a slack) and $y_i^* > 0$. If the ith constraint were to be marginally relaxed the firm would be able to produce a slightly different bundle of outputs and increase its revenue by an amount equal to y_i^*. However, if an unutilised amount of the ith resource existed at the optimal position, relaxing the constraint would make no difference to the firm's optimal output bundle or to its revenue. In this case y_i^* would take on a value of zero. In effect, y_i^* effectively measures the maximum amount the firm would be prepared to pay for a marginal relaxation of the ith constraint. In example (9.20), the second input is not fully utilised and hence $y_2 = 0$.

Now turning to equation (9.32), since $y^* A - c \geq 0$ and $x^* \geq 0$, if $y^* A_j - c_j > 0$, where A_j is the jth column of the matrix A, then $x_j^* = 0$. If the jth constraint of the dual holds as a strict inequality, then the corresponding primal variable x_j^* must take on a value of zero. Once again, the economic rationale for this result is straightforward. The opportunity cost of the resources necessary to produce a unit of x_j is measured by $y^* A_j$ and if this opportunity cost exceeds the market price of x_j, it is not profitable to produce that product. When a commodity is produced (i.e. $x_j > 0$), then the opportunity cost of producing the commodity just equals the price ($y^* A_j - c_j = 0$).

A diagrammatic analysis may help to clarify the discussion. Consider the primal problem and its associated dual which are depicted in Figures 9.5(a) and (b) respectively:

$$\left.\begin{array}{l} \text{Max } 5x_1 + 6x_2 \\ \text{st } \quad x_1 + 2x_2 \leqslant 32 \\ \quad\quad 3x_1 + 2x_2 \leqslant 48 \\ \quad\quad x_1, x_2 \geqslant 0 \end{array}\right\} \quad (9.33)$$

$$\left.\begin{array}{l} \text{Min } 32y_1 + 48y_2 \\ \text{st } \quad y_1 + 3y_2 \geqslant 5 \\ \quad\quad 2y_1 + 2y_2 \geqslant 6 \\ \quad\quad y_1, y_2 \geqslant 0 \end{array}\right\} \quad (9.34)$$

For the primal, the feasible region is $OABC$ and the optimal position occurs at the vertex B with both constraints holding as equalities. Since both primal variables are positive, both dual slacks are zero. For the dual, the feasible region is the shaded area and the optimal position occurs at L. A relaxation of either constraint of the primal will make possible the attainment of a higher value of the objective function. If the first constraint is relaxed, the new optimal position occurs at B', whereas a relaxation of the second constraint leads to a new optimal position at B''. Regarding the dual, the effect of a relaxation of the first constraint in the primal is to increase the absolute slope of the iso-cost line, while a relaxation of the second primal constraint leads to a fall in its absolute slope; the feasible region is unchanged.

In Figure 9.6(a) we depict a primal problem which only differs from the one above in that its objective function is $5x_1 + 10x_2$. There is now no longer a unique solution to the problem; anywhere along AB is optimal. The corresponding dual is shown in Figure 9.6(b); note that y_2 is zero, even though at B, which is optimal, the second constraint holds as an equality. Note also that at A, which is also optimal, x_1 is zero, even though the first constraint in the dual holds as an equality. Relaxation of the first primal constraint will lead to an increase in the value of the objective function, but relaxing the second will make no difference.

In the final case, depicted in Figures 9.7(a) and 9.7(b), the new objective function of the primal is $5x_1 + 11x_2$. The slope of the iso-profit line is absolutely less than the slope of either constraint and the optimal solution occurs at A. The x_1 is not produced and the first dual constraint holds as a strict inequality; the second resource is not fully utilised and the corresponding dual variable y_2 is zero.

Given the primal problem:

$$\left.\begin{array}{l} \text{Max } \quad cx \\ \text{st } \quad Ax \leqslant b \\ \quad\quad x \geqslant 0 \end{array}\right\} \quad (9.35)$$

we have the associated dual

226 *Linear programming*

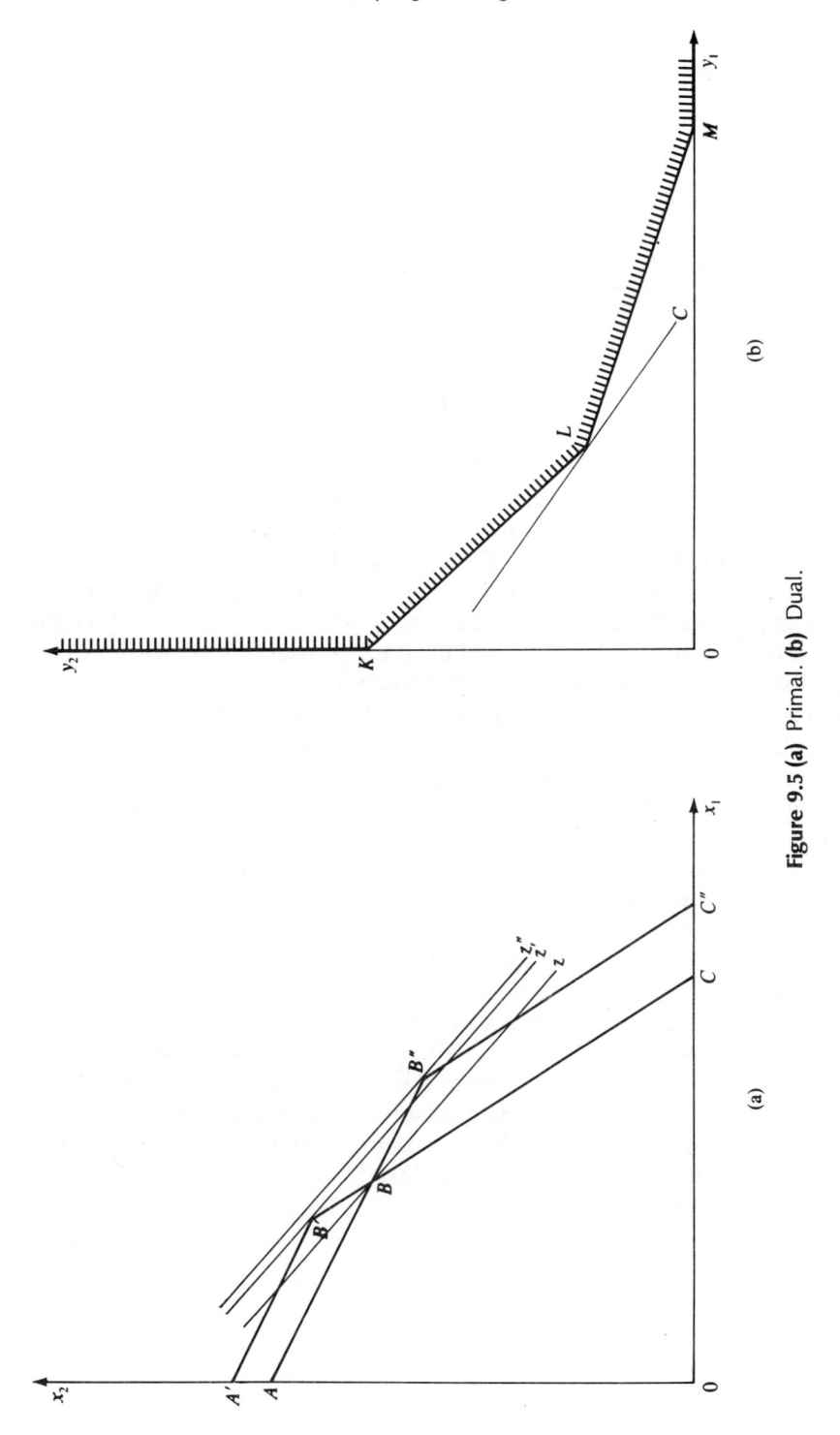

Figure 9.5 (a) Primal. (b) Dual.

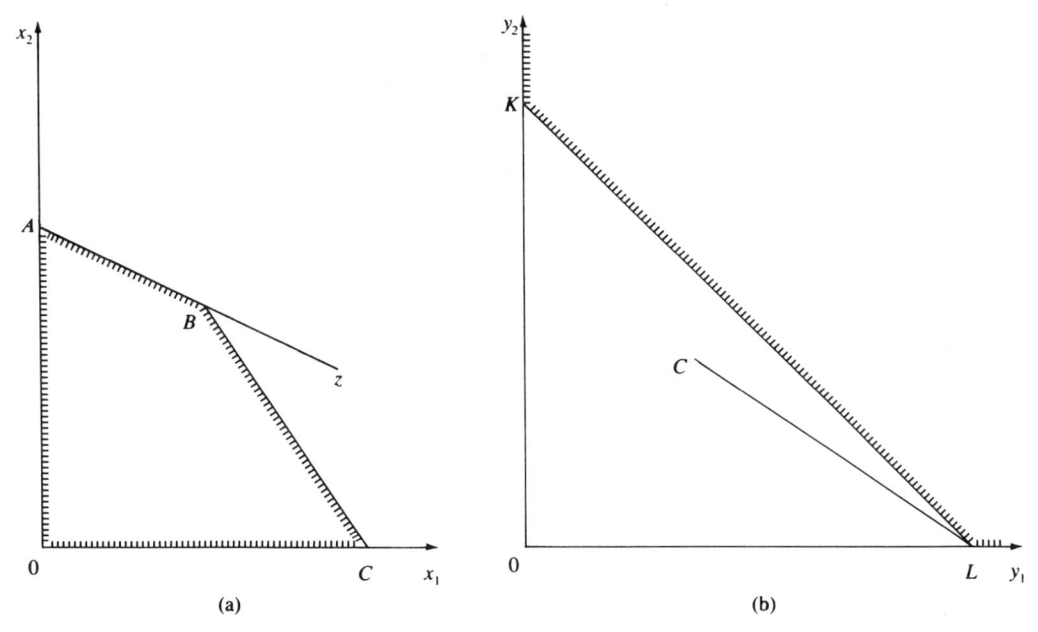

Figure 9.6 (a) Primal with changed objective function ($5x_1 + 10x_2$). **(b)** Corresponding dual.

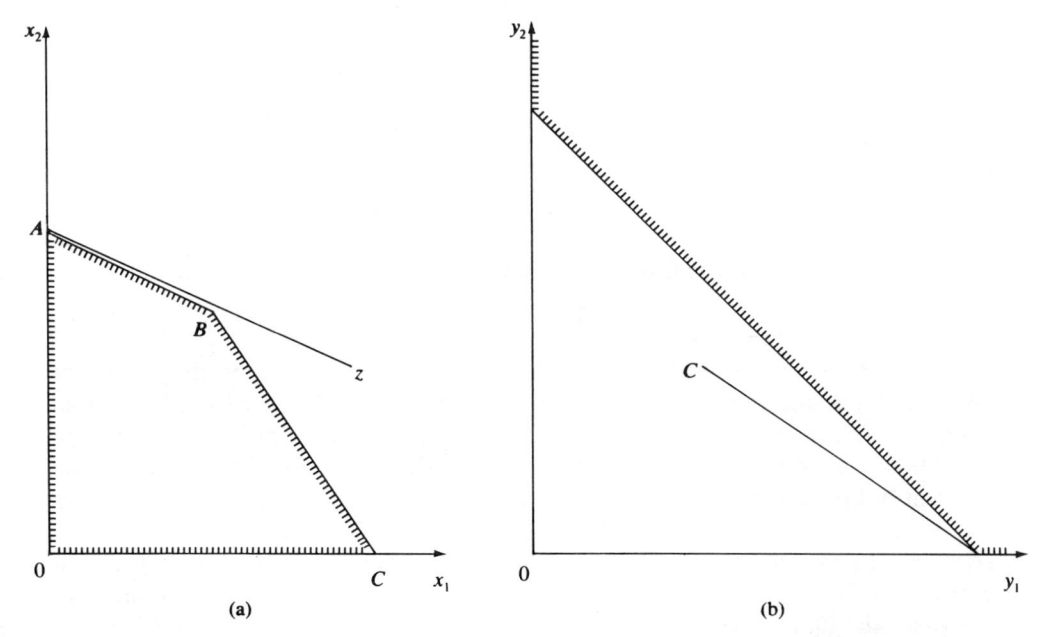

Figure 9.7 (a) Primal with further changes in objective function ($5x_1 + 11x_2$). **(b)** Corresponding dual.

$$\text{Min } yb$$
$$\text{st } yA \geq c \qquad (9.36)$$
$$y \geq 0$$

Let us convert the constraints of the dual into equalities by the introduction of slack variables and make the necessary adjustments to b and y. Let the extended matrix $\begin{bmatrix} A \\ -I \end{bmatrix}$ be symbolised by D; we now have

$$\text{Min } yb$$
$$\text{st } yD = c$$
$$y \geq 0$$

Consider a basic feasible solution to the dual y^F; we must have

$$y^F F = c$$
$$y^F \geq 0 \qquad (9.37)$$

where F is a matrix made up of rows of D. Hence $y^F = cF^{-1}$ and the value of the objective function is given by $cF^{-1}b^F$ where b^F is the subvector of elements in b relevant to the basic variables y^F.

Now introduce a nonbasic variable y_i into the basis at some level t. We must have

$$y^F(t)F + y_i(t)D^i = c \qquad (9.38)$$

where D^i is the ith row of D.

Postmultiplying by F^{-1} and rearranging, we obtain

$$y^F(t) = cF^{-1} - y_i(t)D^i F^{-1} \qquad (9.39)$$

and the new value of the objective function is given by

$$cF^{-1}b^F - y_i(t)[D^i F^{-1} b^F - b_i] \qquad (9.40)$$

This will be smaller than the old value provided that

$$b_i - D^i F^{-1} b^F < 0 \qquad (9.41)$$

The vector $F^{-1}b^F$ is the vector of primal variables consequent upon the particular dual variables appearing in the basis matrix F. Note that if one of the basic dual variables is a slack dual variable, then the corresponding element in $F^{-1}b^F$ is zero. This follows directly from the complementary-slackness conditions: if a dual constraint holds as a strict inequality, the corresponding primal variable takes on a value of zero.

Assume the nonbasic variable y_i is the slack variable associated with the first constraint of the dual; then the row vector D^i has -1 in the first column and zero everywhere else and $b_i = 0$. Hence,

$$b_i - D^i F^{-1} b^F = x_1 \qquad (9.42)$$

But if y_i is nonbasic, then x_1 must be non-negative by the complementary-slackness conditions and introducing y_i into the basis would not reduce the value of the objective function.

Assume the nonbasic variable y_i is the dual variable associated with the ith constraint of the primal. Introducing y_i into the basis will reduce the value of the objective function if

$$b_i - D^i F^{-1} b^F < 0 \tag{9.43}$$

where b_i is the available supply of the ith input and $D^i F^{-1} b^F$ is the demand for this input in order to be able to produce the vector of primal variables $F^{-1} b^F$. Economically, therefore, the condition states that y_i should be introduced into the basis if there exists an excess demand for the ith input. Since y_i is a measure of the opportunity cost of using the ith input, the rationale for introducing the variable into the basis when there is an excess demand for that input is clear. Note also that if at a particular basic feasible solution to the dual the optimal solution has not yet been reached, then the primal will be infeasible since one or more of the slack variables in the primal will be negative. Only when the dual is optimal will the primal become feasible. Note the symmetry with our findings on the optimality of the primal and feasibility of the dual.

In solving many maximisation problems, the origin is available as an initial basic feasible solution. However, this is not the case with minimisation problems. An approach which gets round the problem of the nonavailability of the origin relies on the introduction of artificial variables into the problem, with arbitrarily high values being assigned to the coefficients on these variables in the objective function to ensure that these variables will not appear in the final solution to the problem. An artificial variable will appear with a coefficient of unity in each constraint of the form $yA_j > c_j$. If all constraints of a problem are of this form, the initial basic feasible solution will be made up solely of artificial variables. If the constraints are mixed (i.e. greater than and less than), then the initial basic solution will be a combination of artificial and slack variables.

By applying the optimality criterion, we move from one basic feasible solution to another associated with a lower value of the objective function. Feasibility must be maintained when a new variable is introduced into the basis. The feasibility condition is the same as for the primal problem. When y_i is introduced into the basis at some level t, the vector $y^F(t)$ must be non-negative. For this to be the case:

$$\frac{(cF^{-1})_j}{(D^i F^{-1})_j} \geq y_i(t) \geq 0 \quad \text{(given } (D^i F^{-1})_j \geq 0\text{)} \tag{9.44}$$

The leaving variable is the one which gives rise to the smallest positive ratio of $(cF^{-1})_j/(D^i F^{-1})_j$. If $(D^i F^{-1})_j \leq 0$ for all j, then there is no bounded solution to the dual.

Consider the following example:

$$\left. \begin{array}{rl} \text{Min} & 2x_1 + 7x_2 \\ \text{st} & x_1 + 2x_2 \geq 8 \\ & x_2 \geq 3 \\ & x_1, x_2 \geq 0 \end{array} \right\} \tag{9.45}$$

Given the nature of the constraints, the origin is not available as a basic feasible solution and we must introduce both artificial variables (r_1 and r_2), as well as slack variables (S_1 and S_2). In the objective function, r_1 and r_2 both appear with a large positive coefficient (m); this ensures that they will not appear in the optimal basis. The original problem is, therefore, reformulated as follows:

$$\left. \begin{array}{rl} \text{Min} & 2x_1 + 7x_2 + mr_1 + mr_2 \\ \text{st} & x_1 + 2x_2 + r_1 - S_1 = 8 \\ & x_2 + r_2 - S_2 = 3 \\ & x_1, x_2, r_1, r_2, S_1, S_2 > 0 \end{array} \right\} \quad (9.46)$$

In tableau form, we have

	x_1	x_2	r_1	r_2	S_1	S_2	Solution
$z_j - c_j$	-2	-7	$-m$	$-m$	0	0	0
r_1	1	2	1	0	-1	0	8
r_2	0	1	0	1	0	-1	3

Multiply both the r_1 and r_2 rows by m and add to the $z_j - c_j$ row to form the new $z_j - c_j$ row:

	x_1	x_2	r_1	r_2	S_1	S_2	Solution
$z_j - c_j$	$-2 + m$	$-7 + 3m$	0	0	$-m$	$-m$	$11m$
r_1	1	2	1	0	-1	0	8
r_2	0	1	0	1	0	-1	3

The entering variable is x_2 and the leaving variable r_2. Carry out the following row operations: (i) multiply the r_2 row by -2 and add to the r_1 row to form the new r_1 row; (ii) multiply the r_2 row by $7 - 3m$ and add to the $z_j - c_j$ row to form the new $z_j - c_j$ row:

	x_1	x_2	r_1	r_2	S_1	S_2	Solution
$z_j - c_j$	$-2 + m$	0	0	$7 - 3m$	$-m$	$2m - 7$	$21 + 2m$
r_1	1	0	1	-2	-1	2	2
x_2	0	1	0	1	0	-1	3

The new entering variable is S_2 instead of r_1. The row operations are: (i) multiply the r_1 row by 0.5 to form the S_2 row; (ii) multiply the r_1 row by 0.5 and add to the x_2 row to form the new x_2 row; (iii) multiply the r_1 row by $(7 - 2m)/2$ and add to the $z_j - c_j$ row to form the new $z_j - c_j$ row:

	x_1	x_2	r_1	r_2	S_1	S_2	Solution
$z_j - c_j$	$\frac{3}{2}$	0	$\frac{7-2m}{2}$	$-m$	$-\frac{7}{2}$	0	28
S_2	$\frac{1}{2}$	0	$\frac{1}{2}$	-1	$-\frac{1}{2}$	1	1
x_2	$\frac{1}{2}$	1	$\frac{1}{2}$	0	$-\frac{1}{2}$	0	4

Now introduce x_1 instead of S_2. The row operations are: (i) multiply the S_2 row by 2 to form the x_1 row; (ii) multiply the S_2 by -1 and add to the x_2 row to form the new x_2 row; (iii) multiply the S_2 row by -3 and add to the $z_j - c_j$ row to form the new $z_j - c_j$ row:

z_j-c_j	0	0	$2-m$	$3-m$	-2	-3	25
x_1	1	0	1	-2	-1	2	2
x_2	0	1	0	1	0	-1	3

The optimal solution has now been reached with $x_1 = 2$, $x_2 = 3$ and the value of the objective function is 25.

9.4 THE DUAL SIMPLEX METHOD

In certain circumstances, an alternative method is available for the solution of minimisation problems. This approach, known as the dual simplex method and due to Lemke (1954), is to be utilised for the solution of a problem for which the current basis is optimal but infeasible in that the non-negativity requirement is violated for one or more of the basic variables. In general, this approach can be utilised for the solution of either maximisation or minimisation problems whenever the current basis is optimal but infeasible.

Consider the simplex minimisation problem we solved in th preceding section:

$$\begin{aligned} \text{Min} \quad & C = 2x_1 + 7x_2 \\ \text{st} \quad & x_1 + 2x_2 \geq 8 \\ & x_2 \geq 3 \\ & x_1, x_2 \geq 0 \end{aligned} \qquad (9.47)$$

This problem can be converted into the standard form for a maximisation problem by multiplying the objective function and the two constraints by -1 to yield

$$\begin{aligned} \text{Max} \quad & Z = -2x_1 - 7x_2 \\ \text{st} \quad & -x_1 - 2x_2 \leq -8 \\ & -x_2 \leq -3 \\ & x_1, x_2 \geq 0 \end{aligned} \qquad (9.48)$$

The first tableau for the problem is

	x_1	x_2	S_1	S_2	Solution
z_j-c_j	2	7	0	0	0
S_1	-1	-2	1	0	-8
S_2	0	-1	0	1	-3

Since $z_j - c_j$ is non-negative for both nonbasic variables, the current basis is clearly optimal but infeasible since the two slack variables both take on negative values. These are precisely the circumstances in which the dual simplex method can be applied.

We first outline the dual simplex method, deriving the rules for eliminating existing basic variables and replacing them with nonbasic variables. We then illustrate its usefulness in sensitivity analysis, where we analyse the implications of parametric changes in the model. We consider the implications of such factors as tightening a constraint or changing the value of a parameter in the objective function.

Write the primal problem in canonical form:

$$\left. \begin{array}{l} \text{Max } Z = cx \quad \text{st } Ax = b \\ \phantom{\text{Max } Z = cx \quad \text{st }} x \geqslant 0 \end{array} \right\} \tag{9.49}$$

Then its associated dual is given by

$$\text{Min } C = yb \quad \text{st } yA \geqslant c \tag{9.50}$$

with y being unrestricted in sign because of the equality constraints in the primal.

Now consider a solution to the dual

$$y = c^B B^{-1} \tag{9.51}$$

where B is a matrix made up of m columns of A and B^{-1} is its inverse. Naturally, we have

$$yB_i = c_i^B \quad (i = 1, 2, \ldots, m) \tag{9.52}$$

where B_i is the ith column of B. In addition, we will assume that for all the columns of A not included in B

$$yA_j \geqslant c_j \tag{9.53}$$

In other words, the optimality criterion is satisfied for the primal; $z_j - c_j \geqslant 0$ for all x_j not in the basis. Hence, the solution to the dual can only be nonoptimal if one or more of the xs in the basis is negative.

Let the jth row of B^{-1}, be given by β^j, then we must obviously have

$$\beta^j B_i = 0 \quad (\text{for } i \neq j) \tag{9.54}$$
$$ = 1 \quad (\text{for } i = j)$$

Note also that

$$x_k^B = \beta^k b \tag{9.55}$$

and assume that this basic variable is negative. Define a new vector

$$\hat{y} = y - t\beta^k \tag{9.56}$$

where t is a scalar. Postmultiplying equation (9.56) by b, we have

$$\hat{C} = \hat{y}b = yb - t\beta^k b$$
$$\phantom{\hat{C} = \hat{y}b} = yb - tx_k^B \tag{9.57}$$

The dual simplex method

If $t < 0$ and with $x_k^B < 0$, then $\hat{C} < C$ and if $\hat{y}$ satisfies the dual constraints, then we have a new solution to the dual with $\hat{C} < C$.

Postmultiply the new vector $\hat{y}$ by B_i to obtain

$$\hat{y}B_i = yB_i - t\beta^k B_i$$
$$= c_i^B \quad (\text{for } i \neq k)$$
$$= c_k^B - t \quad (\text{for } i = k) \qquad (9.58)$$

with $t \leq 0$, then $c_k^B - t \geq c_k^B$.

For all the columns of A not in the primal basis

$$\hat{y}A_j = yA_j - t\beta^k A_j \qquad (9.59)$$

Since $yA_j \geq c_j$, then if $\beta^k A_j \geq 0$ for all the columns of A not in B, for $t \leq 0$, $\hat{y}A_j \geq c_j$. In these circumstances, t can be made an arbitrarily large negative number with the obvious implication that the solution to the dual is unbounded. Correspondingly, there exists no feasible solution to the primal. Accordingly for the dual to have a bounded solution and its primal to be feasible, there must be at least one $\beta^k A_j$ which is negative. Let us assume that this is indeed the case and define

$$\beta^k A_j = w_{kj} \qquad (9.60)$$

where w_{kj} is the kth component of $B^{-1}A_j$. Now for all $w_{kj} < 0$, in order to have $\hat{y}A_j \geq c_j$, the following condition must be satisfied:

$$t \geq \frac{yA_j - c_j}{w_{kj}} = \frac{z_j - c_j}{w_{kj}} \qquad (9.61)$$

To decrease the value of the dual by as much as possible, we must have t taking as large as possible an absolute value subject to the above condition being satisfied.

We may, therefore, state the elimination and introduction rules of the dual simplex. The primal variable to be removed from the basis is that variable which has the largest negative value. If all primal basic variables are non-negative, then the solution is optimal. The nonbasic variable to be introduced into the basis is the one for which

$$\frac{z_j - c_j}{w_{kj}} \text{ is maximised with } w_{kj} < 0 \qquad (9.62)$$

If the primal problem is a maximisation problem, then the entering variable is the one with the smallest absolute ratio of the entry in the $z_j - c_j$ row to the corresponding entry in the row of the leaving variable, since with the solution remaining optimal (but not feasible until the final iteration) $z_j - c_j \geq 0$. On the other hand, for a minimisation problem in the primal, the entering variable is the one with the smallest ratio since $z_j - c_j \leq 0$ in this case.

Returning to the opening tableau of the simple example (9.48) given in the start of this section, we have

234   Linear programming

		x_1	x_2	S_1	S_2	Solution
	$z_j - c_j$	2	7	0	0	0
Basic variables	S_1	−1	−2	1	0	−8
	S_2	0	−1	0	1	−3

The basic variable with the larger negative value is S_1, hence S_1 leaves the basis and x_1 enters in its place since -2 is larger than -3.5. We then perform the following row operations to obtain the following new basic solution:

1. Multiply the S_1 row by -1 to form the x_1 row.
2. Multiply the S_1 row by 2 and add to the $z_j - c_j$ row to form the new $z_j - c_j$ row.

		x_1	x_2	S_1	S_2	Solution
	$z_j - c_j$	0	3	2	0	−16
Basic variables	x_1	−1	2	−1	0	8
	S_2	0	−1	0	1	−3

We now eliminate S_2 from the basis and introduce x_2 in its place. The new basic solution is obtained in the following way:

1. Multiply the S_2 row by -1 to form the x_2 row.
2. Multiply the S_2 row by 2 and add to the x_1 row to form the new x_1 row.
3. Multiply the S_2 row by 3 and add to the $z_j - c_j$ row to form the new $z_j - c_j$ row.

		x_1	x_2	S_1	S_2	Solution
	$z_j - c_j$	0	0	2	3	−25
Basic variables	x_1	1	0	−1	2	2
	x_2	0	1	0	1	3

The optimal solution to the minimisation problem has now been reached with $x_1 = 2$, $x_2 = 3$, and $C = 25$.

As we saw earlier at the optimal solution to the primal, we have

$$x^B = B^{-1}b \geq 0 \text{ and } c^B B^{-1} A_j - c_j \geq 0 \tag{9.63}$$

Hence it is clear that changes in the b vector can, at most, affect the feasibility of the particular primal basis; such changes do not affect its optimality. On the other hand, changes in the c vector can, at most, affect the optimality of the particular primal basis; they do not influence its feasibility. Furthermore, changes in the technological coefficients on nonbasic variables leave the feasibility of the primal basis unaffected but can potentially influence its optimality as a result of the consequent change in A_j.

The dual simplex method

Turning to the dual, at its optimal solution we have
$$y^F = cF^{-1} \geq 0 \text{ and } D^iF^{-1}b^F - b_i \leq 0 \tag{9.64}$$

Changes in the *b* vector may therefore affect the optimality of the dual, while leaving unaltered its feasibility, whereas changes in the *c* vector have no impact on the optimality of the dual but may affect its feasibility. Similarly as for the primal, changes in the technological coefficients on nonbasic variables of the dual do not change the feasibility of the current dual basis but can affect its optimality.

Given that the dual only becomes feasible when the primal solution is reached, and similarly for the primal, any change which affects the optimality of the primal must necessarily affect the feasibility of the dual and vice versa.

Consider the following problem:

$$\begin{aligned} \text{Max } Z = {} & x_1 + x_2 + \tfrac{3}{4}x_3 \\ \text{st} \quad & 2x_1 + 3x_2 + 4x_3 \leq 24 \\ & 4x_1 + 2x_2 + 2x_3 \leq 20 \\ & x_1, x_2, x_3 \geq 0 \end{aligned} \tag{9.65}$$

The optimal tableau for the above problem is as follows:

		x_1	x_2	x_3	S_1	S_2	Solution
	$z_j - c_j$	0	0	1/2	1/4	1/8	17/2
Basic variables	x_1	1	0	-1/4	-1/4	3/8	3/2
	x_2	0	1	3/2	1/2	-1/4	7

Let us change the *b* vector from $\begin{bmatrix} 24 \\ 20 \end{bmatrix}$ to $\begin{bmatrix} 8 \\ 20 \end{bmatrix}$. Then

$$x = \begin{bmatrix} -1/4 & 3/8 \\ 1/2 & -1/4 \end{bmatrix} \begin{bmatrix} 8 \\ 20 \end{bmatrix} = \begin{bmatrix} 11/2 \\ -1 \end{bmatrix}$$

Hence, the original basis, though still optimal, is now infeasible and we make use of the dual simplex method to clear the infeasibility:

		x_1	x_2	x_3	S_1	S_2	Solution
	$z_j - c_j$	0	0	1/2	1/4	1/8	9/2
Basic variables	x_1	1	0	-1/4	-1/4	3/8	11/2
	x_2	0	1	3/2	1/2	-1/4	-1

We eliminate x_2 and introduce S_2; having carried out elementary row operations, we obtain the following optimal tableau:

	x_1	x_2	x_3	S_1	S_2	Solution
$z_j - c_j$	0	1/2	5/4	1/2	0	4
Basic variables x_1	1	3/2	2	1/2	0	4
S_2	0	−4	−6	−2	1	4

The optimal solution is $x_1 = 4$, $x_2 = 0$, $x_3 = 0$ and $Z = 4$.

Returning to the original problem, let us now change the c vector from [1 1 3/4] to [3 1 3/4]. The result of this change is that for the original optimal basis we have new dual variables given by

$$[3 \ 1] \begin{bmatrix} -1/4 & 3/8 \\ 1/2 & -1/4 \end{bmatrix} = [-1/4 \ \ 7/8]$$

The dual is no longer feasible since the first dual variable is now negative and the primal basis is no longer optimal. The coefficient of S_1 in the $z_j - c_j$ row is now $-1/4$. We thus introduce S_1 into the basis and eliminate x_2. Having carried out the elementary row operations, we obtain the optimal solution to the new problem:

	x_1	x_2	x_3	S_1	S_2	Solution
$z_j - c_j$	0	1/2	3/4	0	3/4	15
Basic variables x_1	1	1/2	1/2	0	1/4	5
S_1	0	2	3	1	−1/2	14

The optimal solution is $x_1 = 5$, $x_2 = 0$, $x_3 = 0$; the associated dual solution is $y_1 = 0$, $y_2 = 3/4$ and the value of the objective function is 15.

Finally, returning to the original problem and changing the A_3 vector from $\begin{bmatrix} 4 \\ 2 \end{bmatrix}$ to $\begin{bmatrix} 1 \\ 1 \end{bmatrix}$, we now have

$$B^{-1}A_3 = \begin{bmatrix} -1/4 & 3/8 \\ 1/2 & -1/4 \end{bmatrix} \begin{bmatrix} 1 \\ 1 \end{bmatrix} = \begin{bmatrix} 1/8 \\ 1/4 \end{bmatrix}$$

and

$$z_3 - c_3 = [1/4 \ \ 1/8] \begin{bmatrix} 1 \\ 1 \end{bmatrix} - 3/4 = -3/8$$

Hence, the existing primal basis is no longer optimal and the dual is infeasible. We have the following new tableau:

	x_1	x_2	x_3	S_1	S_2	Solution
$z_j - c_j$	0	0	−3/8	1/4	1/8	17/2
Basic variables x_1	1	0	1/8	−1/4	3/8	3/2
x_2	0	1	1/4	1/2	−1/4	7

Introduce x_3 and eliminate x_1:

		x_1	x_2	x_3	S_1	S_2	Solution
	$z_j - c_j$	3	0	0	$-1/2$	$5/4$	13
Basic variables	x_3	8	0	1	-2	3	12
	x_2	-2	1	0	1	-1	4

Introduce S_1 and eliminate x_2:

		x_1	x_2	x_3	S_1	S_2	Solution
	$z_j - c_j$	2	$1/2$	0	0	$3/4$	15
Basic variables	x_3	4	2	1	0	1	20
	S_1	-2	1	0	1	-1	4

The optimal solution to the problem is now reached with $x_1 = 0$, $x_2 = 0$ and $x_3 = 20$. The associated value of the objective function is 15.

9.5 THE TRANSPORTATION PROBLEM

A special kind of LP problem is the transportation problem which was first analysed by Hitchcock (1941), Koopmans (1949) and Dantzig (1951 a,b).

An enterprise wishes to ship goods from certain sources to certain destinations at minimum cost. Let x_{ij} represent the amount shipped from source i to destination j at a cost per unit of c_{ij}. Assume there are m sources and n destinations with the quantity of the good available at source i represented by s_i and the quantity of the good required at destination j represented by d_j. Then our problem is the following one:

$$\text{Min} \sum_{i=1}^{m} \sum_{j=1}^{n} c_{ij} x_{ij}$$

$$\text{st} \sum_{j=1}^{n} x_{ij} \leqslant s_i \quad (i = 1, 2, \ldots, m)$$

$$\sum_{i=1}^{m} x_{ij} \geqslant d_j \quad (j = 1, 2, \ldots, n) \tag{9.66}$$

$$\sum_{i=1}^{m} s_i = \sum_{j=1}^{n} d_j$$

$$x_{ij} \geqslant 0 \quad \text{(for all } i, j\text{)}$$

The first m constraints are of the form that the amount shipped from source i must not exceed the amount available at that source. In the second set of constraints we impose the condition that the amount shipped to destination j must be at least as great as the requirements at that destination. Our transportation problem is a balanced one in that the total available at the sources equals the total required at the destinations. When this is not the case it is called an unbalanced problem. An unbalanced problem can always be converted into a balanced one by the inclusion of a fictititous source if total requirements exceed total availabilities and a fictititous destination if total availabilities exceed total requirements. Given the balanced nature of the problem, the first $m + n$ constraints will in fact all hold as equalities, and only $m + n - 1$ of these constraints are independent. The implication of this is that not more than $m + n - 1$ of the x_{ij}'s will be different from zero, i.e. no more than $m + n - 1$ routes will be utilised in the cost-minimising shipment plan.

It is convenient for us to specify the first $m + n$ constraints of the primal problem in the form we have when we turn to consider the dual of the transportation problem. The associated dual takes the following form:

$$\text{Max} \sum_{j=1}^{n} v_j d_j - \sum_{i=1}^{m} u_i s_i$$

$$\left. \begin{array}{l} \text{st } v_j - u_i \leqslant c_{ij} \quad (i = 1, 2, \ldots, m \quad j = 1, 2, \ldots, n) \\ u_i, v_j \geqslant 0 \end{array} \right\} \quad (9.67)$$

We may give the following economic interpretation to the dual variables of the transportation problem: v_j refers to the imputed value of a unit of the good at destination j and u_i refers to the imputed value of the good at source i. If the cost of shipping a unit of the good from source i to destination j exceeds the difference in imputed values at destination and source, then that particular route should not be utilised. This follows from the equilibrium theorem of linear programming; in the context of the transportation problem, we have

$$\left. \begin{array}{l} [c_{ij} - (v_j - u_i)] x_{ij} = 0 \\ x_{ij} \geqslant 0, c_{ij} \geqslant v_j - u_i \end{array} \right\} \quad (9.68)$$

If a route is utilised, then the difference between the imputed values just equals the unit transport cost. The application of this result enables transportation problems to be solved with ease.

As we have stated above, in solving transportation problems we will find no more than $m + n - 1$ routes utilised. Hence we cannot solve for $m + n$ dual variables, we can only solve for $m + n - 1$. This we do by setting an arbitrary value for one of the dual variables and then solving for the remainder. In our computational work we will invariably adopt the convention of setting u_1 equal to zero. By adopting this convention it will not necessarily be the case that the non-negativity requirements for the dual will be satisfied. However, by a suitable rescaling we could ensure if we wished that these non-negativity requirements were not broken. This point will become clearer as we work through a numerical example.

A method of solution for the transportation problem involves obtaining a BFS to the primal, calculating the dual variables associated with this BFS and then checking whether the dual is feasible. If the dual is feasible, i.e. $c_{ij} \geq v_j - u_i$ for all i, j, then the current basis yields the cost-minimising shipment plan. However, if one or more of the constraints of the dual are not satisfied, then we introduce into the basis that route of the previously unutilised routes for which the difference between the increase in the imputed value of the good and the unit transport cost is the greatest. In order to make way for the new route, shipments over some of the currently utilised routes will have to be reduced. In order to maintain the feasibility of the primal, the route to be eliminated from the basis is that route of this particular set over which the smallest quantity is currently being shipped. This amount determines the maximum level at which the new route can be introduced while maintaining the feasibility of the primal.

We now provide an illustration to clarify the above discussion. A good is available at three sources in the following quantities:

$$[150 \quad 240 \quad 110]$$

and is required at four destinations in the following quantities:

$$[120 \quad 80 \quad 200 \quad 100]$$

The matrix of unit shipment costs from the ith source to the jth destination is given by

$$C = \begin{bmatrix} 6 & 3 & 4 & 2 \\ 4 & 8 & 6 & 5 \\ 8 & 5 & 7 & 9 \end{bmatrix}$$

In order to derive the cost-minimising shipment plan we must first arrive at an initial BFS. There are a number of alternative methods available for finding such a basis; we shall deal with the least cost method, by which an initial BFS can be easily obtained. Although this method will not necessarily minimise the number of subsequent iterations required, it is reasonably efficient. The basic procedure is to introduce the lowest cost route first and ship the maximum amount possible over this route. We then move on to the next lowest cost route of those still available and ship the maximum amount possible over this route given the allocation already made. The procedure is then repeated until the whole plan has been met.

For the particular example under consideration, we have the following initial BFS:

1. The lowest cost route is (1,4), the maximum that can be shipped is 100.
2. The next lowest cost route is (1,2), the maximum that can be shipped is 50.
3. The next lowest cost route is (2,1), the maximum that can be shipped is 120.
4. The next lowest cost route is (3,2), the maximum that can be shipped is 30.
5. The next lowest cost route is (2,3), the maximum that can be shipped is 120.
6. 80 units remain to be shipped over route (3,3).

Note that six routes are utilised; for each of these routes we must have $c_{ij} = v_j - u_i$. Hence

$$v_2 - u_1 = 3$$
$$v_4 - u_1 = 2$$
$$v_1 - u_2 = 4$$
$$v_3 - u_2 = 6$$
$$v_2 - u_3 = 5$$
$$v_3 - u_3 = 7$$

Setting $u_1 = 0$, we can easily solve for the remaining six dual variables; $u_2 = -1$, $u_3 = -2$, $v_1 = 3$, $v_2 = 3$, $v_3 = 5$, $v_4 = 2$. The cost of this shipment plan is 2260. u_2 and u_3 are negative; however, by adding 2 to each dual variable we would ensure that the non-negativity requirements were satisfied. This rescaling, however, would have no implications for the way the problem is solved and we do not perform it.

In order to ascertain whether costs can be further reduced by introducing a nonutilised route into the basis, we check whether the above solution to the dual is in fact feasible, i.e. whether $c_{ij} \geq v_j - u_i$ for each nonutilised route:

route	c_{ij}	$v_j - u_i$
(1,1)	6	3
(1,3)	4	5
(2,2)	8	4
(2,4)	5	3
(3,1)	8	5
(3,4)	9	4

There is one nonutilised route for which the dual constraint does not hold; this is route (1,3). In order to introduce route (1,3) into the basis and for the new shipment plan to remain feasible, then shipments over routes (1,2) and (3,3) must be reduced and shipments over route (3,2) must be increased. Currently, fifty units are being shipped over route (1,2) and eighty units over route (3,3); the maximum level at which the new route can thus be introduced is fifty. In shipping fifty units over this new route, we increase shipments over route (3,2) by fifty units to eighty units and reduce shipments over routes (1,2) and (3,3) by fifty units to zero and thirty units respectively. The new shipment plan is

$$x_{13} = 50, \ x_{14} = 100, \ x_{21} = 120, \ x_{23} = 120, \ x_{32} = 80, \ x_{33} = 30$$

To test for the optimality of this new basis, we again set $u_1 = 0$ and, using the condition that for each utilised route $c_{ij} = v_j - u_i$, we can solve for the remaining dual variables. We have

$$v_3 - u_1 = 4$$
$$v_4 - u_1 = 2$$
$$v_1 - u_2 = 4$$
$$v_3 - u_2 = 6$$

The transportation problem 241

$$v_2 - u_3 = 5$$
$$v_3 - u_3 = 7$$

from which it follows that $u_2 = -2$, $u_3 = -3$, $v_1 = 2$, $v_2 = 2$, $v_3 = 4$, $v_4 = 2$. Checking for the optimality of this plan we again calculate $v_j - u_i$ for the nonutilised routes and compare with c_{ij}:

route	c_{ij}	$v_j - u_i$
(1,1)	6	2
(1,2)	3	2
(2,2)	8	4
(2,4)	5	4
(3,1)	8	5
(3,4)	9	5

There is no route for which $v_j - u_i > c_{ij}$; hence the current shipment plan is the optimal one with total costs being 2210.

In our discussions of the dual of the transportation problem we interpreted $v_j - u_i$ as measuring the difference in the imputed value of a unit of the good at destination j and source i. If for a nonutilised route $v_j - u_i > c_{ij}$, then that route should be introduced into the basis. Alternatively, we may consider the change in total cost which will result from shipping one unit over this route, having made the consequential changes in shipments over the other routes in the basis for feasibility to be maintained. Shipping one unit over route (1,3) requires one less unit shipped over route (3,3), one more unit shipped over route (3,2) and one less unit shipped over route (1,2). The resultant change in cost is given by

$$c_{13} - c_{33} + c_{23} - c_{12}$$

this equals -1 and is the same as $c_{13} - (v_3 - u_1)$. For every unit shipped over this new route we will reduce costs by one. We wish to ship as much as possible subject to the plan being feasible: as we have seen, the maximum we can ship is fifty units.

In arriving at an initial BFS, there may be occasions upon which a decision to use a particular route at the maximum level possible simultaneously exhausts supplies at the source and fulfils requirements at the destination. It is necessary in these circumstances to ship a zero quantity over an adjacent route (either the route appearing in the same row and adjacent column or same column and adjacent row). The current basis will thus be degenerate and if we fail to make the above adjustment we will have too few routes utilised to solve for the dual variables.

If a transportation problem is unbalanced, then it can be balanced by the introduction of a fictitious source if $\Sigma_{j=1}^{n} d_j > \Sigma_{i=1}^{m} s_i$, or a fictitious destination if $\Sigma_{j=1}^{n} d_j < \Sigma_{i=1}^{m} s_i$. The associated unit transport costs from the fictitious source to the destinations or from the sources to the fictitious destinations will normally be zero. However, circumstances may arise in which, in the case of excess demand, demand must be satisfied at one particular destination. This condition can be ensured by assigning a very high value to the shipment cost from the fictitious source to this particular destination. Now consider the case of excess supply but assume that all the

242   Linear programming

goods at one source must be removed; to ensure this we assign a high value to the shipment cost from this source to the fictitious destination. More generally, penalties may be assigned for failure to deliver to destinations in the presence of excess demand or failure to clear stocks from particular locations in the presence of excess supply; these penalties can differ by source/destination and are then reflected in the unit costs associated with the routes involving the fictitious source/destination.

The literature on linear programming is enormous and the student who wishes to read more extensively in the subject is faced with an embarrassment of riches. Classic texts include Beale (1968), Charnes and Cooper (1961), Dantzig (1963), Gale (1960), Gass (1975), Hadley (1962). Economists will find a particularly stimulating discussion in Dorfman, Samuelson and Solow (1958), and a clear, informal review of duality and linear programming is provided in Baumol and Quandt (1963).

Exercises

1. Solve the following linear programming problems graphically:

    (a) Max $Z = x_1 + 1.5x_2$
         st $2x_1 + 3x_2 \leqslant 6$
              $x_1 + 4x_2 \leqslant 4$
              $x_1, x_2 \geqslant 0$

    (b) Min $C = 6x_1 + 4x_2$
         st $2x_1 + x_2 \geqslant 1$
              $3x_1 + 4x_2 \geqslant 1.5$
              $x_1, x_2 \geqslant 0$

    (c) Max $Z = 40x_1 + 30x_2$
         st $x_1 \leqslant 16$
              $x_2 \leqslant 8$
              $x_1 + 2x_2 \leqslant 24$
              $x_1, x_2 \geqslant 0$

2. Find all the basic solutions to the following simultaneous equations:

$$x_1 + 3x_2 + x_3 + x_4 = 12$$
$$2x_1 + 5x_2 + 4x_3 + x_5 = 20$$

    Indicate whether they are (i) degenerate; and (ii) feasible.

3. (a) Show that the solution to the following problem is unbounded:

    Max $Z = x_1 + x_2$
    st $-3x_1 + 2x_2 \leqslant -1$
         $x_1 - x_2 \leqslant 2$
         $x_1, x_2 \geqslant 0$

(b) Write out the dual of the above problem and indicate its features in the light of the characteristics of the primal problem.

4. An enterprise in a centrally planned economy can produce three goods: X_1, X_2 and X_3; the prices of these goods are respectively 7, 6 and 5. The planners have allocated the following quantities of three inputs to the firm: $n_1 = 16$, $n_2 = 34$, $n_3 = 50$. In order to produce a unit of X_1 the firm requires 2 units of n_1, 3 units of n_2 and 5 units of n_3. The per unit requirements for x_2 are 1 unit of n_1, 4 units of n_2 and 2 units of n_3; and for X_3 are 5 units of n_1, 2 units of n_2 and 1 unit of n_3. The enterprise is instructed to maximise the value of its output.
   (a) How much should it produce of each good?
   (b) What values are taken by the dual variables?
   (c) Would the optimal solution change if the planners increased the price of x_3 from 5 to 12?

5. Suppose that the basis B is proposed as the optimal basis, where the problem is to maximise cx subject to $Ax = b$ $(x \geqslant 0)$, and we have

$$B = \begin{bmatrix} 2 & 1 & 0 \\ 1 & 2 & 1 \\ 4 & 3 & 0 \end{bmatrix}$$

$$c = [28 \quad 17 \quad 21 \quad 0 \quad 0 \quad 0]$$

$$A = \begin{bmatrix} 2 & 1 & 1 & 1 & 0 & 0 \\ 1 & 4 & 2 & 0 & 1 & 0 \\ 4 & 1 & 3 & 0 & 0 & 1 \end{bmatrix}$$

$$b = \begin{bmatrix} 44 \\ 60 \\ 100 \end{bmatrix}$$

Given that

$$B^{-1} = \begin{bmatrix} 3/2 & 0 & -1/2 \\ -2 & 0 & 1 \\ 5/2 & 1 & -3/2 \end{bmatrix}$$

determine whether the basis is indeed optimal. If it is not proceed to find the optimal solution to the problem.

6. Three foodstuffs, each containing three nutrients, are available to meet the nutritional requirements of an individual. The individual's diet must contain at least 38 units of the first nutrient, 60 units of the second and 50 units of the third. A unit of the first foodstuff contains 3, 4 and 1 units, respectively, of the three nutrients and costs 10p. A unit of the second foodstuff contains 1, 3 and 5 units, respectively, of the nutrients and costs 8p.

Finally, a unit of the third foodstuff contains 2, 1 and 4 units, respectively, of the nutrients and costs 12p. Suppose that the individual seeks to minimise the cost of satisfying the dietary requirements. Then answer the following:

(a) Solve the dual of the minimisation problem. What interpretation can be given to the dual variables?

(b) What are the quantities of the three foodstuffs consumed in the cost-minimising diet?

(c) If the price of the second foodstuff rises to 10p, will this affect the cost-minimising diet?

7. (a) Solve the following problem using the simplex method:

$$\text{Max } Z = 14x_1 + 5x_2 + 8x_3$$
$$\text{st} \quad 2x_1 + x_2 + x_3 \leq 18$$
$$3x_1 + 2x_2 + 2x_3 \leq 31$$
$$x_1, x_2, x_3 \geq 0$$

(b) Does it make any difference to the solution to the above problem if the coefficient on x_2 in the objective function is increased from 5 to 8? What would happen if x_2 did not appear in the first constraint?

(c) If the following constraint is introduced into the original problem:

$$4x_1 + x_2 + x_3 \leq 24$$

use the dual simplex method to obtain the new optimal solution.

8. Solve the following by the simplex method:

(a) $\text{Min } C = 2x_1 + 7x_2$
$$\text{st} \quad x_1 + 2x_2 \geq 8$$
$$x_2 \geq 3$$
$$x_1, x_2 \geq 0$$

(b) $\text{Min } C = 8x_1 + 6x_2 - 11x_3$
$$\text{st} \quad x_1 - x_2 - 2x_3 \geq 6$$
$$2x_1 + x_2 - 3x_3 \geq 5$$
$$x_1, x_2, x_3 \geq 0$$

9. (a) If you are told that at the optimum to the dual of the following problem the first and second dual variables are positive, find the solution to the primal problem without using the simplex method or graphical techniques:

$$\text{Max } Z = 6x_1 + 4x_2$$
$$\text{st} \quad 4x_1 + 2x_2 \leq 10$$
$$2x_1 + 2x_2 \leq 6$$
$$3x_1 + 4x_2 \leq 12$$
$$x_1, x_2 \geq 0$$

The transportation problem

(b) Explain why the dual variable associated with an equality constraint in the primal is unrestricted in sign.

10. A firm has stocks of a particular good available at each of three factories in the following quantities: 150 units at the first factory, 60 units at the second and 190 units at the third. The firm is required to ship the following quantities from its factories to four different warehouses: 100 units to the first warehouse, 75 units to the second, 160 units to the third and 65 units to the fourth. The matrix of per unit shipment costs from the ith factory to the jth warehouse is given by

$$C = \begin{bmatrix} 5 & 3 & 8 & 2 \\ 9 & 10 & 5 & 4 \\ 8 & 4 & 7 & 1 \end{bmatrix}$$

Obtain the cost-minimising shipment plan.

11. A good is available at four factories in the following quantities:

$$[100 \quad 150 \quad 50 \quad 50]$$

and is required at three warehouses in the following quantities:

$$[75 \quad 120 \quad 105]$$

The matrix of per unit shipment costs from the ith factory to the jth warehouse is given by

$$C = \begin{bmatrix} 4 & 6 & 5 \\ 10 & 5 & 8 \\ 6 & 3 & 2 \\ 3 & 2 & 5 \end{bmatrix}$$

It is not permissible to ship to a warehouse more of a good than is actually required there. Output which is not shipped must be stored at the factory where it is produced; there are no storage facilities at the second factory. Derive the cost-minimising shipment plan.

References

Baumol, W.J. and Quandt, R.E. (1963), 'Dual prices and Competition', in A.R. Oxenfeldt, (ed.), *Models of Markets*, pp. 237–64, New York: Columbia University Press. Reprinted in G.C. Archibald, (ed.) (1971), *The Theory of the Firm*, Harmondsworth: Penguin Books.

Beale, E.M.L. (1968), *Mathematical Programming in Practice*, London: Pitman.

Charnes, A. and Cooper, W.W. (1961), *Management Models and Industrial Applications of Linear Programming*, New York: Wiley.

Dantzig, G.B. (1951a), 'Maximisation of a linear function of variables subject to linear inequalities', in T.C. Koopmans (ed.) *Activity Analysis of Production and Allocation*, New York: Wiley.

Dantzig, G.B. (1951b), Application of the simplex method to a transportation problem', in T.C. Koopmans (ed.) *op. cit.*

Dantzig, G.B. (1963), *Linear Programming and Extensions*, Princeton, NJ: Princeton University Press.

Dantzig, G.B. (1982), 'Reminiscences about the origins of linear programming', *Operations Research Letters*, **1**, 43–8.

Dorfman, R. (1984), 'The discovery of linear programming', *Annals of the History of Computing*, **6**, 283–95.

Dorfman, R., Samuelson, P.A. and Solow R.M. (1958), *Linear Programming and Economic Analysis*, New York: McGraw-Hill.

Gale, D. (1960), *The Theory of Linear Economic Models*, New York: McGraw-Hill.

Gass, S.I. (1975), *Linear Programming: methods and applications*, New York: McGraw Hill.

Hadley, G. (1962), *Linear Programming*, New York: McGraw-Hill.

Hitchcock, F.L. (1941), 'The distribution of a product from several sources to numerous localities', *Journal of Mathematics and Physics*, **20**, 224–30.

Koopmans, T.C. (1949), 'Optimum utilization of the transportation system', *Econometrica*, **17** (Supplement, July), 136–46.

Lemke, C.E. (1954), 'The dual method of solving the linear programming problem', *Naval Research Logistics Quarterly*, **1**, 36–47.

Chapter 10
INTEGER AND NONLINEAR PROGRAMMING

In this chapter we introduce the topics of integer and nonlinear programming. We firstly modify the linear programming framework to deal with the case where the choice variables are restricted to taking integer values. Other than for this requirement, the structure of the integer program is similar to that of a linear program; the objective function and the constraints are both linear. In principle, there is no good reason why integer programming should not allow for nonlinearities in the objective function and/or the constraints; but, in practice, analysis has concentrated on the linear case. In Section 10.1 we outline the main features of the cutting method approach to integer programming, first in the context of the all-integer problem and second for the mixed case. Duality and integer programming is discussed in Section 10.2. The problems which can arise in the interpretation of dual variables in integer programming are considered, along with a treatment of the recomputed dual variables proposed by Gomory and Baumol (1960). Examples are given throughout the two sections.

In Section 10.3 we provide an introduction to nonlinear programming. After briefly reviewing the classical optimisation problem we consider the significance of non-negativity requirements and inequality constraints for the problem in which nonlinearities are present in the objective function and/or the constraints. The economic significance of the Kuhn–Tucker (K–T) conditions is made clear and the Kuhn–Tucker sufficiency theorem is outlined. A further extensive discussion of the economic significance of the K–T conditions is given in Section 10.4, where optimal pricing and capacity decisions are presented for a public enterprise producing, first a nonstorable output and second, a storable output.

10.1 INTEGER PROGRAMMING

We present first a diagrammatic treatment of the following problem:

$$\text{Max } 3x_1 + 2x_2$$
$$\text{st } 4x_1 + 2x_2 \leq 18$$

$$2x_1 + 3x_2 \leq 12$$

x_1, x_2 non-negative integers

In Figure 10.1, we depict the feasible region assuming the problem was a continuous, ordinary linear programming one. The feasible region would have been the convex area $OABC$, with the optimal position occurring at the vertex B. For the all-integer problem, however, the feasible set is no longer convex and consists simply of a finite number of all-integer points, marked with a cross in Figure 10.1. The optimal solution to the integer programming problem is obtained by shifting the iso-revenue line to the left parallel to itself until it passes through the first all-integer point. This occurs at the point E where $x_1 = 4$, $x_2 = 1$ and the value of the objective function is 14. We may contrast this with the solution to the ordinary LP problem, where $x_1 = 15/4$, $x_2 = 3/2$ and the value of the objective function is 57/4.

For solving integer programming problems, there exist two methods of solution: cutting methods and search methods. In the former, the problem is initially solved as a continuous ordinary LP problem and then one or more additional constraints are introduced into the problem. The role of these additional constraints is to eliminate from the solution space areas that do not contain feasible integer points. If, following the introduction of an additional constraint, the solution to the continuous problem is all-integer, then the optimal solution has been reached. In our diagrammatic

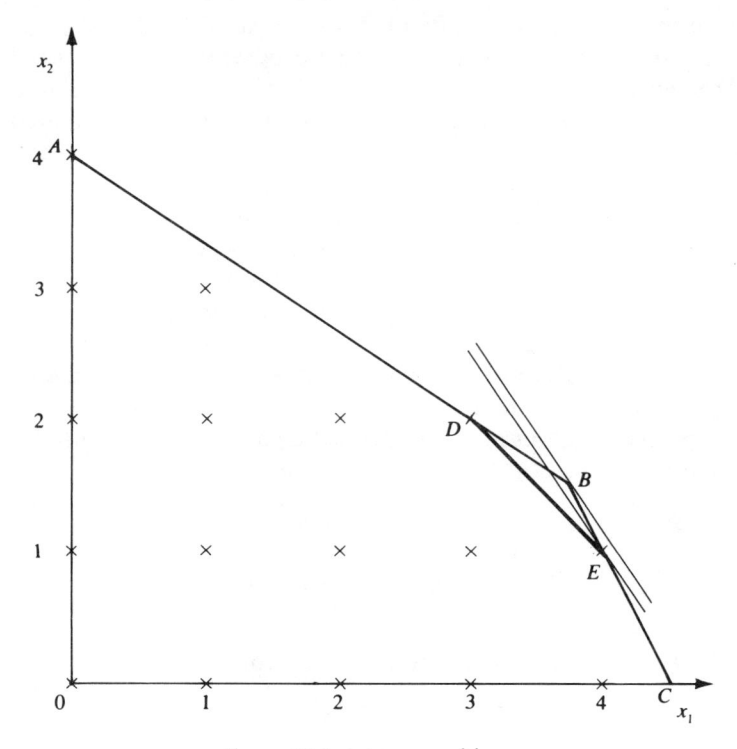

Figure 10.1 Integer problem.

example, the additional constraint eliminates that segment of the original feasible region lying to the right of the line *DE*. If, however, the integrality conditions are not satisfied, a further subset of the solution space must be sliced off. The procedure continues with additional constraints being introduced into the problem until the first all-integer solution is attained (Gomory, 1958).

In the second approach, one searches over the feasible integer solutions, employing an algorithm which considers explicitly only a small subset of the feasible set of solutions, with implicit consideration being given to the remaining possibilities. In this chapter we shall consider the first method of solution only in that it is of more interest to the economist, particularly when we come to provide an interpretation of the dual in integer programming. For a discussion of the search approach as exemplified by the branch and bound technique, the interested reader is referred to Taha (1975).

The all integer problem

Consider the following problem:

$$\text{Max } cx$$
$$\text{st } Ax = b \tag{10.1}$$
$$x \text{ a vector of non-negative integers}$$

where c and x are, respectively, a row and a column vector, each containing $m + n$ elements, A is a matrix of order $m \times m + n$ and b is a column vector containing m elements; all the elements of both A and b take on integer values.

Assume $x^B = B^{-1}b$ represents the solution to the ordinary linear programming problem but that the integrality condition is not satisfied. Note that, as before, B is a square matrix made up of m columns of A. Let

$$\beta_i = (B^{-1}b)_i \tag{10.2}$$

where $(B^{-1}b)_i$ is the ith element in the solution column. Hence β_i is the value taken by the basic variable x_i^B. Assume that β_i is noninteger and let

$$\beta_i = [\beta_i] + f_i \tag{10.3}$$

where $[\beta_i]$ is the largest integer such that $[\beta_i] < \beta_i$. Hence, we must have

$$0 < f_i < 1 \tag{10.4}$$

Furthermore let

$$\gamma_{ij} = (B^{-1}A_j)_i \tag{10.5}$$

where $(B^{-1}A_j)_i$ is the ith element in the column for the jth nonbasic variable (x_j^{NB}). Let

$$\gamma_{ij} = [\gamma_{ij}] + f_{ij} \tag{10.6}$$

where $[\gamma_{ij}]$ is the largest integer such that $[\gamma_{ij}] < \gamma_{ij}$. Hence, we must have

$$0 \leqslant f_{ij} < 1 \quad \text{(for } j = 1, 2, \ldots, n\text{)} \tag{10.7}$$

We may now write the following equation which defines the basic variable which violates the integrality condition in terms of the nonbasic variables:

$$x_i^B = \beta_i - \sum_{j=1}^{n} \gamma_{ij} x_j^{NB} \tag{10.8}$$

This is known as the source row. Substituting equations (10.3) and (10.6) into (10.8), we obtain

$$x_i^B = [\beta_i] + f_i - \sum_{j=1}^{n} [\gamma_{ij}] x_j^{NB} - \sum_{j=1}^{n} f_{ij} x_j^{NB} \tag{10.9}$$

Rearranging we have

$$f_i - \sum_{j=1}^{n} f_{ij} x_j^{NB} = x_i^B - [\beta_i] + \sum_{j=1}^{n} [\gamma_{ij}] x_j^{NB} \tag{10.10}$$

For the basic variable, x_i^B, and all the nonbasic variables to be integer, the right-hand side of equation (10.10) must be integer and, clearly, so must the left-hand side. Since each nonbasic variable must be non-negative and, given the inequality expressed in equation (10.7), then

$$\sum_{j=1}^{n} f_{ij} x_j^{NB} \geqslant 0 \tag{10.11}$$

Hence

$$f_i - \sum_{j=1}^{n} f_{ij} x_j^{NB} \leqslant f_i < 1 \tag{10.12}$$

since $0 < f_i < 1$. Given that the left-hand of equation (10.10) must take on an integer value, a necessary condition for this to be so is that

$$f_i - \sum_{j=1}^{n} f_{ij} x_j^{NB} \leqslant 0 \tag{10.13}$$

This constraint can be converted into the following equality:

$$T_i = \sum_{j=1}^{n} f_{ij} x_j^{NB} - f_i \tag{10.14}$$

where T_i is a slack variable which must be a non-negative integer. The new constraint defines the fractional cut and since all the nonbasic variables are zero, the problem starts out optimal with $z_j - c_j > 0$ for all the nonbasic variables, but infeasible since

Integer programming

$T_i = -f_i$. These are precisely the circumstances under which the dual simplex algorithm can be applied to clear the infeasibility. If we obtain a non-negative all-integer solution, the problem is then solved. Otherwise, we repeat the procedure until a non-negative all-integer solution is reached. However, if the dual simplex algorithm indicates that no feasible solution exists (i.e. there are no negative entries in the source row) the problem has no feasible integer solution. A further factor to be noted is that the elements of both A and b should all be integer; if this condition is not met in the original formulation of the problem, an appropriate rescaling of the coefficients must be undertaken.

We now utilise the above procedure to solve the example for which we have previously provided a diagrammatic treatment:

$$\text{Max } 3x_1 + 2x_2$$

$$\text{st } 4x_1 + 2x_2 \leq 18$$

$$2x_1 + 3x_2 \leq 12$$

x_1, x_2 non-negative integers

We first solve this problem as an ordinary LP problem; it is a straightforward matter to obtain the optimal tableau for this problem and we simply present it here:

		x_1	x_2	S_1	S_2	Solution
	$z_j - c_j$	0	0	5/8	1/4	57/4
Basic variables	x_1	1	0	3/8	-1/4	15/4
	x_2	0	1	-1/4	1/2	3/2

Since neither of the basic variables is integer, we have a choice of source row. One option is to choose as the source row the row with the larger (or, in the general case, the largest) value of f_i. An alternative criterion is to select as the source row the row with the largest value of $f_i / \Sigma_{j=1}^{n} f_{ij}$; it is this second criterion which is usually recommended as the one to employ. For the above problem, we have

$$f_1 = 3/4, \ f_2 = 1/2$$

$$f_{11} = 3/8, \ f_{12} = 3/4$$

$$f_{21} = 3/4, \ f_{22} = 1/2$$

Employing the second criterion, we therefore take the first row as the source row and the equation for the fractional cut is accordingly given by

$$T_1 - 3/8 \ S_1 - 3/4 \ S_2 = -3/4$$

Our extended tableau now becomes

	x_1	x_2	S_1	S_2	T_1	Solution
$z_j - c_j$	0	0	5/8	1/4	0	57/4
x_1	1	0	3/8	-1/4	0	15/4
x_2	0	1	-1/4	1/2	0	3/2
T_1	0	0	-3/8	-3/4	1	-3/4

Basic variables

In line with the dual simplex algorithm, we introduce S_2 in place of T_1. Carrying out the row operations we immediately obtain the optimal tableau:

	x_1	x_2	S_1	S_2	T_1	Solution
$z_j - c_j$	0	0	1/2	0	1/3	14
x_1	1	0	1/2	0	-1/3	4
x_2	0	1	-1/2	0	2/3	1
S_2	0	0	1/2	1	-4/3	1

Basic variables

At the optimal solution, $x_1 = 4$, $x_2 = 1$ and the value of the objective function is 14. The equation of the fractional cut we introduced is given by

$$T_1 - 3/8 \; S_1 - 3/4 \; S_2 = -3/4$$

However, we may eliminate S_1 and S_2 from the above equation by substituting

$$S_1 = 18 - 4x_1 - 2x_2$$
$$S_2 = 12 - 2x_1 - 3x_2$$

After some manipulation we obtain

$$T_1 + 3x_1 + 3x_2 = 15$$

Hence, the additional constraint (the fractional cut) takes the form

$$3x_1 + 3x_2 \leqslant 15$$

The mixed problem

We now turn to consideration of how to solve mixed problems in which only a subset of the variables is constrained to be integer. In these circumstances, the cut we have derived for the all-integer problem is no longer appropriate and it is necessary to derive an alternative cut for the mixed problem.

Assume that we require the basic variable x_i^B to be integer. From the equation of the source row, we have

$$x_i^B - [\beta_i] = f_i - \sum_{j=1}^{n} \gamma_{ij} x_j^{NB} \tag{10.15}$$

Note that in this case we have not decomposed the term containing the nonbasic variables into an integral and nonintegral component. A necessary condition for x_i to be integer is that

$$\text{either } x_i \leqslant [\beta_i] \text{ or } x_i \geqslant [\beta_i] + 1 \tag{10.16}$$

Using the source row, the above condition may alternatively be expressed as

either $$\sum_{j=1}^{n} \gamma_{ij} x_j^{NB} \geqslant f_i \text{ or } \sum_{j=1}^{n} \gamma_{ij} x_j^{NB} \leqslant f_i - 1 \tag{10.17}$$

If we now let J^+ and J^- represent the set of subscripts j for which the coefficients in the source row, the γ_{ij}s, are non-negative and negative, respectively, then it is clear that a necessary condition for x_i to be integer is

either $$\sum_{j \in J^+} \gamma_{ij} x_j^{NB} \geqslant f_i \text{ or } \frac{f_i}{f_i - 1} \sum_{j \in J^-} \gamma_{ij} x_j^{NB} \geqslant f_i \tag{10.18}$$

The reversal of sign in the second inequality results from the fact that we have multiplied by a negative scalar,

$$f_i / f_i - 1.$$

Combining the two constraints in equation (10.18), which is permissible since they cannot both occur simultaneously, we obtain the following constraint which is a necessary condition for x_i to be integer:

$$T_i - \left[\sum_{j \in J^+} \gamma_{ij} x_j^{NB} + \frac{f_i}{f_i - 1} \sum_{j \in J^-} \gamma_{ij} x_j^{NB} \right] = -f_i \tag{10.19}$$

where T_i is a non-negative slack variable.

If some of the nonbasic variables are restricted to be integer and others just to be non-negative a more complicated cut results. For a comprehensive discussion of this and many other issues relating to integer programming, see Taha (1975).

To illustrate the method of solving mixed problems we shall consider the following problem:

$$\text{Max } 100x_1 + 120x_2$$
$$\text{st } 5x_1 + 3x_2 \leqslant 40$$
$$2x_1 + 6x_2 \leqslant 60$$
$$x_1 \text{ non-negative integer, } x_2 \geqslant 0$$

The final tableau of the ordinary simplex is as follows

		x_1	x_2	S_1	S_2	Solution
	$z_j - c_j$	0	0	15	25/2	1350
Basic variables	x_1	1	0	1/4	$-1/8$	5/2
	x_2	0	1	$-1/12$	5/24	55/6

Given that x_1 must be a non-negative integer, we calculate the mixed cut using the x_1 row as the source row. Since

$$f_1 = 1/2, \quad \frac{f_1}{f_1 - 1} = -1, \quad \gamma_{11} = 1/4 \text{ and } \gamma_{12} = -1/8$$

the mixed cut is

$$T_1 - 1/4 \; S_1 - 1/8 \; S_2 = -1/2$$

We add this row to the tableau and utilise the dual simplex algorithm:

		x_1	x_2	S_1	S_2	T_1	Solution
	$z_j - c_j$	0	0	15	25/2	0	1350
Basic variables	x_1	1	0	1/4	$-1/8$	0	5/2
	x_2	0	1	$-1/12$	5/24	0	55/6
	T_1	0	0	$-1/4$	$-1/8$	1	$-1/2$

We eliminate T_1 and introduce S_1. Having carried out elementary row operations we arrive at the optimal solution

	x_1	x_2	S_1	S_2	T_1	Solution
$z_j - c_j$	0	0	0	5	60	1320
x_1	1	0	0	$-1/4$	1	2
x_2	0	1	0	1/4	$-1/3$	28/3
S_1	0	0	1	1/2	-4	2

At the optimal solution, $x_1 = 2$, $x_2 = 28/3$ and the value of the objective function is 1320.

Alternatively, we could have required x_1 to be non-negative and x_2 to be a non-negative integer. The solution to this problem is left as an exercise for the reader.

10.2 DUALITY AND INTEGER PROGRAMMING

Assume the integer programming problem we are concerned with relates to the maximisation of the value of output by a subordinate authority which is subject to constraints on the availability of various productive inputs. We have seen that problems of this nature can be solved by introducing additional artificial constraints into the problem, these artificial constraints being nothing more than weighted averages of the original constraints of the problem with weights equal to the f_{ij}s. Attached to both the original and additional sets of constraints are dual variables. We continue to interpret the dual variables attached to the original set of constraints as the shadow prices or opportunity costs of those productive inputs which are limited in supply, while the dual variables associated with the additional constraints can be interpreted as the shadow prices of these artificial capacities,

> a measure of the opportunity cost of indivisibility – e.g. the loss imposed on the businessman by a unit of the artificial capacity constraint which prevents him from seeking to stuff that last four tenths of a case into his warehouse. (Gomory and Baumol, 1960, p. 530.)

One should note, however, that the opportunity cost or marginal revenue productivity of an indivisible input is a slippery concept in the context of integer programming, since it is not permissible to vary the availability of such an input by an infinitesimally small amount. Letting b_i represent the available quantity of the ith input, then with indivisibilities it will no longer necessarily be the case that $\Delta Z / \Delta b_i$ will be the same for unit increases or decreases in b_i, or that either will equal $\partial Z / \partial b_i$.

The effects on the original dual variables of introducing the integrality condition into a linear programming problem are quite complex; it is likely that some dual variables will fall in value and that others will increase in value. A diagrammatic exposition of the following problem will help to clarify the point:

$$\text{Max} \quad x_1 + 5x_2$$
$$\text{st} \quad 4x_2 \leqslant 11$$
$$2x_1 + 5x_2 \leqslant 18$$
$$2x_1 + x_2 \leqslant 8$$

x_1, x_2 non-negative integers

The solution to the ordinary linear programming problem occurs at the vertex B in Figure 10.2 where the first two constraints hold as strict equalities and the corresponding dual variables will both be positive. There is slack in the third constraint and the third dual variable will, accordingly, be zero by the complementary-slackness conditions. The solution, however, to the integer programming problem occurs at the point E; the third constraint holds as a strict equality, while there is slack in the first two constraints. In this example, therefore, the introduction of the integrality condition leads to a fall to zero in the first two dual variables, while the third dual variable now becomes positive.

What we can say is that the arithmetic mean shadow price of the original productive inputs cannot be greater in the integer solution than in the noninteger solution. Let y_i and y_i^* represent the ith dual variable in the noninteger and integer solutions, respectively and b_i the right-hand side of the ith primal constraint. The value of the dual in the noninteger solution with m original constraints is given by

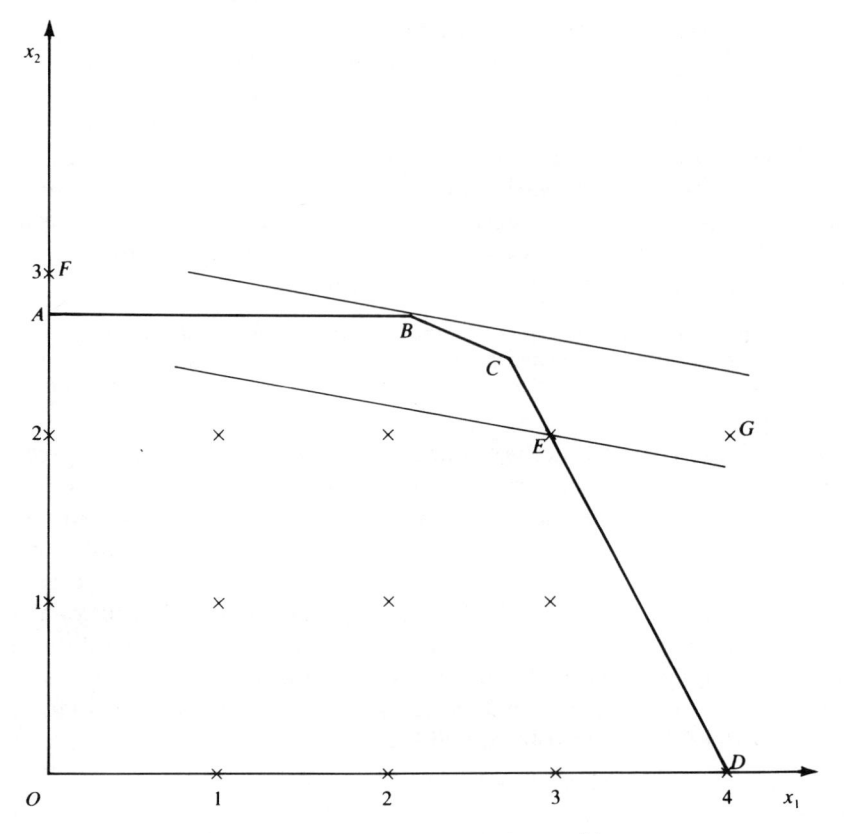

Figure 10.2 Integer programming problem.

$$\sum_{i=1}^{m} y_i b_i \qquad (10.20)$$

The value of the dual in the integer solution is given by

$$\sum_{i=1}^{m+p} y_i^* b_i \qquad (10.21)$$

where there are p additional constraints in the integer problem.

Naturally, the value of the dual in the integer solution cannot exceed the value of the dual in the noninteger solution. Hence,

$$\sum_{i=1}^{m} y_i b_i \geqslant \sum_{i=1}^{m+p} y_i^* b_i \qquad (10.22)$$

Provided that b_i is non-negative in all the constraints, both original and artificial, we must have

Duality and integer programming 257

$$\sum_{i=1}^{m} y_i b_i \geqslant \sum_{i=1}^{m} y_i^* b_i \qquad (10.23)$$

Gomory and Baumol (1960) have shown that the non-negativity requirement does in fact hold for all the artificial constraints, while the original inputs can all reasonably be assumed to be positive. Hence, it will be the case that

$$\frac{\sum_{i=1}^{m} y_i b_i}{\sum_{i=1}^{m} b_i} \geqslant \frac{\sum_{i=1}^{m} y_i^* b_i}{\sum_{i=1}^{m} b_i} \qquad (10.24)$$

which proves our statement about the arithmetic mean shadow price.

Returning to our simple example, even though the first dual variable takes on a zero value in the integer solution, the authority could still benefit from a relaxation of the first constraint. A sufficiently large relaxation would enable the point F in the diagram to be attained. The second dual variable in the integer solution is also zero, but in this case no relaxation of the second constraint would, *ceteris paribus*, enable the authority to produce an all-integer bundle of goods with a higher value than the one it is currently producing. The third dual variable is positive and a sufficiently large relaxation of the associated constraint would permit the attainment of point G in the diagram. However, even though a dual variable is positive in the integer solution, it does not necessarily follow that a relaxation of the corresponding constraint will be associated with an increase in the value of the objective function. Had the second constraint in our example been $22x_1 + 12x_2 \leqslant 99$, E would still have been the optimal position, the third dual variable would have been positive, but any relaxation of the third constraint would not have enlarged the feasible set of integer points.

In their influential paper Gomory and Baumol introduce the concept of recomputed prices for the original productive inputs. These recomputed dual prices are defined as follows:

$$\left. \begin{array}{l} y_j' = y_j + \sum_{i=1}^{p} f_{ij} y_i \quad (j = 1, 2, \ldots, m) \\ y_i' = 0 \quad (i = 1, 2, \ldots, p) \end{array} \right\} \qquad (10.25)$$

The recomputed dual variable for the jth original input is equal to the value of the dual variable attached to the jth original constraint in the original solution plus the sum of the products of the ith artificial dual variable and the corresponding element in the ith artificial constraint. In this recomputation, y_i is to be interpreted as the shadow price attached to the ith artificial constraint in the iteration following the first introduction of that particular constraint into the problem. The recomputed dual variable for an artificial input is assigned a value of zero. Note that if we were dealing with a mixed problem we would utilise the corresponding elements in the artificial constraints for that problem (i.e. the γ_{ij}s) rather than the f_{ij}s.

These recomputed dual prices do, in fact, possess certain desirable properties.

First, when a particular good is produced the opportunity cost of producing this good evaluated at these prices will just equal the price of the good. If the opportunity cost exceeds the price, the good will not be produced. This is simply an analogue, in an integer programming setting, of the equilibrium theorem of linear programming. Second, if a recomputed dual variable takes on a zero value, then no increase in the associated original input will enable a more valuable all-integer bundle of goods to be produced. Such an input is therefore a free good in the true economic sense.

Only under a special set of circumstances, however, will the dual variables so recomputed be unique. For the uniqueness property to hold, it must be the case that there exists a unique subset of the original inequalities which gives rise to the same integer solution as the full set of inequalities. If this condition is met then by dropping the redundant inequalities and solving the integer programming problem employing the unique subset of the original inequalities, the recomputed dual prices which so emerge will be unique and will equal the dual prices which would have resulted from solving the scaled-down problem as an ordinary linear programming problem. An important result follows from the fact that the recomputed prices will not necessarily be unique: one cannot guarantee that an input whose recomputed dual price is positive is not a free good. Assume there are two subsets of the original constraints which give rise to the same all-integer solution; then at least one constraint appearing in the first subset must be absent from the second and vice versa. Consider a constraint which appears in the first subset but is absent from the second. In the first set of recomputed prices, its price will be positive, but in the second case it will be zero since the constraint has been dropped without affecting the actual solution. The corresponding original input is therefore a free good, even though in one solution to the problem its recomputed price is in fact positive.

In the light of the above discussion on dual variables in integer programming, let us consider the following problem:

$$\text{Max} \quad x_1 + 2x_2$$
$$\text{st} \quad 5x_2 \leq 12$$
$$4x_1 + 3x_2 \leq 12$$
$$-x_1 + x_2 \leq 2$$

x_1, x_2 non-negative integers

We first solve the problem as an ordinary linear programming problem and after three iterations we obtain the optimal solution to this problem. We present the optimal tableau:

		x_1	x_2	S_1	S_2	S_3	Solution
	$z_j - c_j$	0	0	1/4	1/4	0	6
	x_1	1	0	-3/20	1/4	0	6/5
Basic variables	S_3	0	0	-7/20	1/4	1	4/5
	x_2	0	1	1/5	0	0	12/5

Duality and integer programming

Since the integrality condition is not met we employ Gomory's fractional cut algorithm. The x_2 row is the source row and the equation for the fractional cut is given by

$$T_1 - 1/5 \ S_1 = -2/5$$

Our extended tableau now becomes

		x_1	x_2	S_1	S_2	S_3	T_1	Solution
	$z_j - c_j$	0	0	1/4	1/4	0	0	6
	x_1	1	0	-3/20	1/4	0	0	6/5
Basic variables	S_3	0	0	-7/20	1/4	1	0	4/5
	x_2	0	1	1/5	0	0	0	12/5
	T_1	0	0	-1/5	0	0	1	-2/5

We introduce S_1 in place of T_1 and carry out the necessary row operations to obtain the new basic solution:

		x_1	x_2	S_1	S_2	S_3	T_1	Solution
	$z_j - c_j$	0	0	0	1/4	0	5/4	11/2
	x_1	1	0	0	1/4	0	-3/4	3/2
Basic variables	S_3	0	0	0	1/4	1	-7/4	3/2
	x_2	0	1	0	0	0	1	2
	S_1	0	0	1	0	0	-5	2

The integrality condition is still not satisfied; using our criterion for choosing the source row, we may choose either the x_1 row or the S_3 row since the value of $f_i / \Sigma f_{ij}$ is the same for both. In fact, whether we choose the x_1 row or the S_3 row as the source row, the equation for the new fractional cut is given by

$$T_2 - 1/4 \ S_2 - 1/4 \ T_1 = -1/2$$

The extended tableau is given below:

		x_1	x_2	S_1	S_2	S_3	T_1	T_2	Solution
	$z_j - c_j$	0	0	0	1/4	0	5/4	0	11/2
	x_1	1	0	0	1/4	0	-3/4	0	3/2
	S_3	0	0	0	1/4	1	-7/4	0	3/2
Basic variables	x_2	0	1	0	0	0	1	0	2
	S_1	0	0	1	0	0	-5	0	2
	T_2	0	0	0	-1/4	0	-1/4	1	-1/2

We introduce S_2 in place of T_2 and carry out the necessary row operations to obtain the new basic solution which does, in fact, satisfy the integrality condition:

		x_1	x_2	S_1	S_2	S_3	T_1	T_2	Solution
	$z_j - c_j$	0	0	0	0	0	1	1	5
	x_1	1	0	0	0	0	-1	1	1
	S_3	0	0	0	0	1	-2	1	1
Basic variables	x_2	0	1	0	0	0	1	0	2
	S_1	0	0	1	0	0	-5	0	2
	S_2	0	0	0	1	0	1	$-1/4$	2

In the optimal solution to the integer programming problem we have $x_1 = 1$, $x_2 = 2$ and the value of the objective function is 5. The dual variables attached to the three original constraints are all zero, while the dual variables attached to the two artificial constraints are both unity. Using the formula for the recomputed dual variables for the original constraints, we have

$$y_1' = 0 + 0(1) + 1/5(5/4) = 1/4$$

$$y_2' = 0 + 1/4(1) + 0(5/4) = 1/4$$

$$y_3' = 0 + 0(1) + 0(5/4) = 0$$

Note that these dual variables take on the same value as the dual variables in the solution to the ordinary linear programming problem. However, they are not unique; by considering Figure 10.3 we can see that this will indeed be the case. The optimal position for the linear programming problem occurs at the vertex C, while the optimal position for the integer programming problem occurs at the vertex E where the two artificial constraints intersect. If we drop the third constraint from the problem, then this will have no effect on the solution to either problem: in particular, the solution to the integer programming problem will remain at E. Consider what now happens if we drop the first constraint from the problem. The vertex F, where the second and third constraints intersect each other, now becomes the solution to the linear programming problem; but the solution to the integer programming problem remains at E. There does not, therefore, exist a unique subset of constraints which gives rise to the same integer solution as the full set of constraints, and hence the recomputed dual variables are not unique. Note, in particular, that in our solution to the problem y_1' is assigned a positive value despite the fact that no relaxation, however large, of the first constraint will change the optimal position. The reader should check for himself that the other solution vector for the recomputed dual variables is given by

$$[0, 3/7, 5/7]$$

and in this case the third dual variable takes on a positive value despite the fact that no relaxation, however large, of the third constraint will change the optimal position.

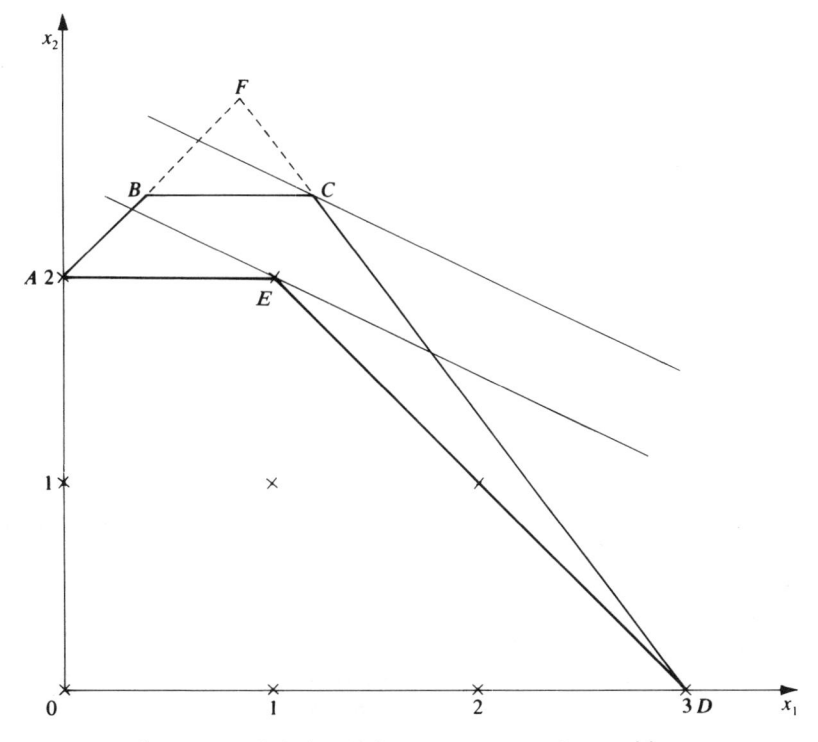

Figure 10.3 Solution to integer programming problem.

10.3 AN INTRODUCTION TO NON-LINEAR PROGRAMMING

In Chapter 9 we outlined the procedures for solving a particular category of programming problems: that in which both the objective function and the constraints are linear functions of the choice variables. Modifications to the basic linear problem were made in the first section of this chapter where we constrained some or all of the choice variables to take on integer values, but otherwise the framework remained that of linear programming. We now turn to a general class of optimisation problems in which nonlinearities are present in the objective function and/or the constraints. We shall be assuming throughout that these functions are differentiable.

Classical optimisation

We commence our discussion by briefly reviewing a simple classical optimisation problem in which we seek to find values for the choice variables $x_1, x_2, \ldots, x_n$, which give rise to a maximum of some function subject to an equality constraint involving the above choice variables. For the moment, we impose no restriction on the values that can be taken by the choice variables. In order to maximise

$$Z = f(x_1, x_2, \ldots, x_n)$$
$$\text{st } c = g(x_1, x_2, \ldots, x_n) \tag{10.26}$$

we form the Lagrangean function

$$l = f(x_1, x_2, \ldots, x_n) + y[c - g(x_1, x_2, \ldots, x_n)] \tag{10.27}$$

where y is a Lagrangean multiplier, the interpretation of which we shall consider below. Differentiating the Lagrangean function partially with respect to x_j and y and setting these partial derivatives equal to zero, we obtain the following set of first-order conditions:

$$\frac{\partial l}{\partial x_j} = f_j - y g_j = 0 \quad (j = 1, 2, \ldots, n) \tag{10.28}$$

$$\frac{\partial l}{\partial y} = c - g(x_1, x_2, \ldots, x_n) = 0 \tag{10.29}$$

where f_j and g_j are, respectively, the partial derivatives of the objective function and the constraint with respect to x_j. The last equation ensures that the constraint is satisfied and that the maximum value of l is also the maximum value of Z. Solving equations (10.28) and (10.29) we obtain the values of $x_j, j = 1, 2, \ldots, n$ and y, which yield a constrained maximum of Z, always assuming that the second-order conditions for a maximum are satisfied at this point. The nature of these latter conditions and the more specific matter of whether a local or global optimum has been identified are discussed below in the context of the general nonlinear programming problem.

For given specifications of the objective function and the constraint, the optimising values of the set of choice variables and the Lagrangean multiplier, which we shall label $x_j^*, j = 1, 2, \ldots, n$ and y^*, will depend upon the c parameter of the constraint. Relaxing the constraint by increasing the value of c will enable a different set of points to be attained and will lead to a change in the value of the objective function. Writing the first-order conditions of equations (10.28) and (10.29) in the following form:

$$\frac{\partial l}{\partial x_j}[x_1, x_2, \ldots, x_n, y : c] = 0 \quad (j = 1, 2, \ldots, n) \tag{10.30}$$

$$\frac{\partial l}{\partial y}[x_1, x_2, \ldots, x_n, y : c] = 0 \tag{10.31}$$

and assuming that they all have continuous partial derivatives, then, provided the Jacobian:

$$|J| = \begin{vmatrix} \dfrac{\partial^2 l}{\partial x_1^2} & \dfrac{\partial^2 l}{\partial x_1 \partial x_2} & \cdots & \dfrac{\partial^2 l}{\partial x_1 \partial x_n} & \dfrac{\partial^2 l}{\partial x_1 \partial y} \\ \dfrac{\partial^2 l}{\partial x_2 \partial x_1} & \dfrac{\partial^2 l}{\partial x_2^2} & & \dfrac{\partial^2 l}{\partial x_2 \partial x_n} & \dfrac{\partial^2 l}{\partial x_2 \partial y} \\ \vdots & & & & \\ \dfrac{\partial^2 l}{\partial y \partial x_1} & \dfrac{\partial^2 l}{\partial y \partial x_2} & & \dfrac{\partial^2 l}{\partial y \partial x_n} & \dfrac{\partial^2 l}{\partial y^2} \end{vmatrix} \tag{10.32}$$

does not vanish, we have by the implicit function theorem

$$x_j^* = x_j^*(c) \quad (j = 1, 2, \ldots, n) \qquad (10.33)$$

$$y^* = y^*(c) \qquad (10.34)$$

The optimal value of the Lagrangean function (l^*) depends upon x_j^*, $j = 1, 2, \ldots, n$ and y^*; however, they in turn depend upon c. Hence the optimal value of the Lagrangean function depends upon c. Differentiating l^* totally with respect to c, we obtain

$$\frac{dl^*}{dc} = \sum_{j=1}^{n}(f_j - y^* g_j)\frac{dx_j^*}{dc} + [c - g(x_1^*, x_2^*, \ldots, x_n^*)]\frac{dy^*}{dc} + y^* \qquad (10.35)$$

where the partial derivatives of the objective function and the constraint are to be evaluated at the optimal point. Hence, equation (10.35) collapses to

$$\frac{dl^*}{dc} = y^* \qquad (10.36)$$

In other words, the Lagrangean multiplier y^* measures the effect a marginal relaxation of the constraint has on the value of the Lagrangean (l) and objective function (Z) since as we have seen $l^* = Z^*$.

Example

A representative consumer derives utility (U) from consuming two commodities x_1 and x_2 such that $U = U(x_1, x_2) = x_1 x_2$. The prices of these two goods are £4 and £2 per unit, respectively, and the consumer has an income of £200. What is the consumer's utility-maximising consumption bundle? The Lagrangean function is

$$l = x_1 x_2 + y [200 - 4x_1 - 2x_2]$$

Differentiating the Lagrangean function partially with respect to x_1, x_2 and y and setting these derivatives equal to zero, we obtain

$$\frac{\partial l}{\partial x_1} = x_2 - 4y = 0$$

$$\frac{\partial l}{\partial x_2} = x_1 - 2y = 0$$

$$\frac{\partial l}{\partial y} = 200 - 4x_1 - 2x_2 = 0$$

Solving the above three equations, we have

$$x_1^* = 25, \ x_2^* = 50, \ y^* = 12.5$$

Given that the utility function gives rise to a set of indifference curves which possess the usual property of a diminishing marginal rate of substitution and the budget constraint is linear, one can easily check that the point we have found is indeed a maximum and a global one at that. The marginal utility of income is measured by y^*, since, as we have shown above, the Lagrangean multiplier shows the effect on the objective function (in this case utility) of a relaxation of the constraint (a very small increase in income).

Non-negativity requirements

In our discussion of classical constrained optimisation, we did not restrict the values that could be taken by the choice variables. In very many problems in economics, however, negative values of variables are economically nonsensical. Let us consider the effect, first, of introducing non-negativity requirements into a simple optimisation problem. Say we wish to find the value of x which maximises some function $f(x)$, subject to the requirement that x be non-negative. Intuitively we can see from Figure 10.4 that there are three possible solutions to this type of problem. In the first case, $f(x)$ reaches a maximum at the point $x = x^*$ where $f'(x^*) = 0$ and $x^* > 0$ (Figure 10.4(a)). In the second case, $f(x)$ is a monotonically decreasing function of x, i.e. $f'(x) < 0$ for all x and, given the non-negativity requirement, the function reaches a maximum at $x = 0$ (Figure 10.4(b)). In the third, rather special case we have $f'(0) = 0$ (Figure 10.4(c)).

We may therefore conveniently express the first-order condition for a maximum of a function of a single variable subject to a non-negativity requirement as follows:

$$f'(x) < 0, \; x > 0, \; xf'(x) = 0 \qquad (10.37)$$

This statement encompasses the three possibilities we have outlined in Figure 10.4. By analogy, the first-order condition for a minimum of a function of a single variable subject to a non-negativity requirement is

$$f'(x) \geqslant 0, \; x \geqslant 0, \; xf'(x) = 0 \qquad (10.38)$$

For a function of many variables which we seek to maximise subject to the requirement that x_j be non-negative, the condition takes the form

$$f_j \leqslant 0, \; x_j \geqslant 0, \; x_j f_j = 0 \qquad (10.39)$$

An analogous modification to the first-order conditions in the minimisation problem must also be made:

$$f_j \geqslant 0, \; x_j \geqslant 0, \; x_j f_j = 0 \qquad (10.40)$$

The Kuhn–Tucker conditions

The other obvious change to make to the classical optimisation problem is to drop the requirement that the constraint hold as a strict equality and allow for slack. Consider the case of a firm seeking to maximise the profits it obtains from producing two goods subject to a capacity constraint. With the nonlinear profits function giving rise to elliptical profit contours, it is quite possible that the profit-maximising combination of outputs lies inside the constraint. Under these circumstances, the entrepreneur will be happy to leave idle some of his capacity. Even if the objective

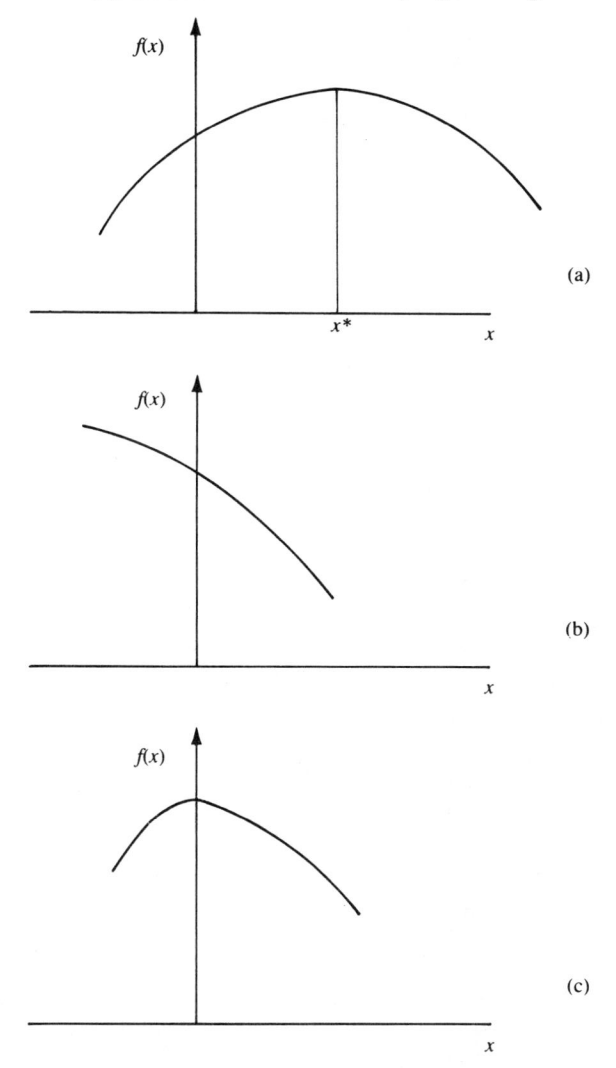

Figure 10.4 Concave functions.

function has no finite maximum, in a problem with more than one constraint one would not necessarily expect all the constraints to hold as equalities. What are the implications for the first-order conditions of introducing inequality constraints as well as non-negativity requirements into an optimisation problem? Consider the following problem:

$$\left.\begin{array}{l} \text{Max } f(x_1, x_2, \ldots, x_n) \\ \text{st } g^i(x_1 x_2, \ldots, x_n) \leqslant c_i \quad (i = 1, 2, \ldots, m) \\ \phantom{\text{st }} x_j \geqslant 0 \quad\quad\quad\quad\quad\ (j = 1, 2, \ldots, n) \end{array}\right\} \quad (10.41)$$

For the moment, let us convert the inequality constraints into equality constraints through introducing non-negative slack variables s_i. Hence, we have

$$g^i(x_1, x_2, \ldots, x_n) + s_i = c_i \quad (i = 1, 2, \ldots, m) \tag{10.42}$$

Now form the Lagrangean function

$$l = f(x_1, x_2, \ldots, x_n) + \sum_{i=1}^{m} y_i[c_i - g^i(x_1, x_2, \ldots, x_n) - s_i] \tag{10.43}$$

Differentiating the Lagrangean function partially with respect to x_j, s_i and y_i, we obtain the following first-order conditions:

$$\frac{\partial l}{\partial x_j} = f_j - \sum_{i=1}^{m} y_i g_j^i \leq 0, \; x_j \geq 0, \; x_j \frac{\partial l}{\partial x_j} = 0 \quad (j = 1, 2, \ldots, n) \tag{10.44}$$

$$\frac{\partial l}{\partial s_i} = -y_i \leq 0, \; s_i \geq 0, \; s_i \frac{\partial l}{\partial s_i} = 0 \quad (i = 1, 2, \ldots, m) \tag{10.45}$$

$$\frac{\partial l}{\partial y_i} = c_i - g^i(x_1, x_2, \ldots, x_n) - s_i = 0 \quad (i = 1, 2, \ldots, m) \tag{10.46}$$

where g_j^i represents the partial derivative of the ith constraint function with respect to x_j. Note that in equation (10.46) y_i is unrestricted in sign since the constraints have been converted into equalities. However, we see from equation, (10.45) that y_i must be non-negative and that it will take on a zero value whenever there is slack in the ith constraint. If y_i is positive, then correspondingly s_i must take on a value of zero. This is the nonlinear programming analogue of the equilibrium theorem of linear programming.

Since both s_i and y_i must be non-negative for all i, the second and third parts of the conditions for a maximum can be consolidated into one single condition and the slack variables can be suppressed. The Lagrangean function becomes

$$l = f(x_1, x_2, \ldots, x_n) + \sum_{i=1}^{m} y_i[c_i - g^i(x_1, x_2, \ldots, x_n)] \tag{10.47}$$

Great care should be taken when formulating the Lagrangean function for a maximum by ensuring that all the nonzero elements in the constraint appear on the left-hand side and that the left-hand side be non-negative. The first-order conditions, which are known as the Kuhn–Tucker conditions, are then as follows:

$$\frac{\partial l}{\partial x_j} \leq 0, \; x_j \geq 0, \; x_j \frac{\partial l}{\partial x_j} = 0 \quad (j = 1, 2, \ldots, n) \tag{10.48}$$

$$\frac{\partial l}{\partial y_i} \geq 0, \; y_i \geq 0, \; y_i \frac{\partial l}{\partial y_i} = 0 \quad (i = , 2, \ldots, m) \tag{10.49}$$

If the problem we are dealing with is a minimisation problem, then the Lagrangean function should be formulated such that all the nonzero elements in the constraint appear on the left-hand side and that the left-hand side be nonpositive. The Kuhn–Tucker conditions for the minimisation problem are thus

$$\frac{\partial l}{\partial x_j} \geq 0, \ x_j \geq 0, \ x_j \frac{\partial l}{\partial x_j} = 0 \quad (j = 1, 2, \ldots, n) \tag{10.50}$$

$$\frac{\partial l}{\partial y_i} \leq 0, \ y_i \geq 0, \ y_i \frac{\partial l}{\partial y_i} = 0 \quad (i = 1, 2, \ldots, m) \tag{10.51}$$

Let us recapitulate briefly. Consider the conditions for a maximum. The first part states that x_j will be zero if $\partial l/\partial x_j < 0$; otherwise x_j will be non-negative. Refer back to our earlier discussion and diagrams. Regarding the second part of the conditions, the requirement that $\partial l/\partial y_i$ be non-negative ensures that the ith constraint is satisfied (note the importance of writing the constraints in the way we specified) and if the ith constraint holds as a strict equality, then the corresponding Lagrangean multiplier (dual variable) takes on a non-negative value, otherwise it is zero. The reader should provide his own rationale for the Kuhn–Tucker minimum conditions.

Example

Consider a firm which can produce two outputs, x_1 and x_2, and whose profits function is given by

$$\Pi = 24x_1 - x_1^2 + 21x_2 - 0.5x_2^2$$

To produce each good requires inputs of two scarce resources and the output bundle which the firm produces must satisfy the following two constraints:

$$2x_1 + 3x_2 \leq 28$$

$$x_1 + 4x_2 \leq 24$$

Naturally, both x_1 and x_2 are constrained to be non-negative. The firm seeks to maximise its profits.

The Lagrangean function takes the following form:

$$l = 24x_1 - x_1^2 + 21x_2 - 0.5x_2^2 + y_1[28 - 2x_1 - 3x_2] + y_2[24 - x_1 - 4x_2]$$

The Kuhn–Tucker conditions for a maximum are

$$\frac{\partial l}{\partial x_1} = 24 - 2x_1 - 2y_1 - y_2 \leq 0, \ x_1 \geq 0, \ x_1 \frac{\partial l}{\partial x_1} = 0$$

$$\frac{\partial l}{\partial x_2} = 21 - x_2 - 3y_1 - 4y_2 \leq 0, \ x_2 \geq 0, \ x_2 \frac{\partial l}{\partial x_2} = 0$$

$$\frac{\partial l}{\partial y_1} = 28 - 2x_1 - 3x_2 \geq 0, \ y_1 \geq 0, \ y_1 \frac{\partial l}{\partial x_1} = 0$$

$$\frac{\partial l}{\partial y_2} = 24 - x_1 - 4x_2 \geq 0, \ y_2 \geq 0, \ y_2 \frac{\partial l}{\partial x_2} = 0$$

268   *Integer and nonlinear programming*

We depict the problem diagrammatically in Figure 10.5. The feasible region is $OABC$ and the objective function gives rise to a set of iso-profit contours which are circular with centre at $x_1 = 12$, $x_2 = 21$; this latter point is the unconstrained maximum which lies outside the feasible region. In principle, the solution to a nonlinear programming problem can lie at a vertex, at a tangency position between an iso-profit contour and a boundary of the feasible region or at an interior point with none of the constraints binding.

Let us consider each of these possible solutions, seeing which satisfies the K–T maximum conditions, as follows:

1. We can immediately rule out the point $x_1 = 0$, $x_2 = 0$. With neither constraint binding, both y_1 and y_2 must equal zero, but then both $\partial l/\partial x_1$ and $\partial l/\partial x_2$ would be positive.
2. We can rule out the unconstrained maximum, $x_1 = 12$, $x_2 = 21$, since it lies outside the feasible region.
3. Re: the vertex A at which $x_1 = 0$, $x_2 = 6$, the condition that $\partial l/\partial x_2 = 0$ and the

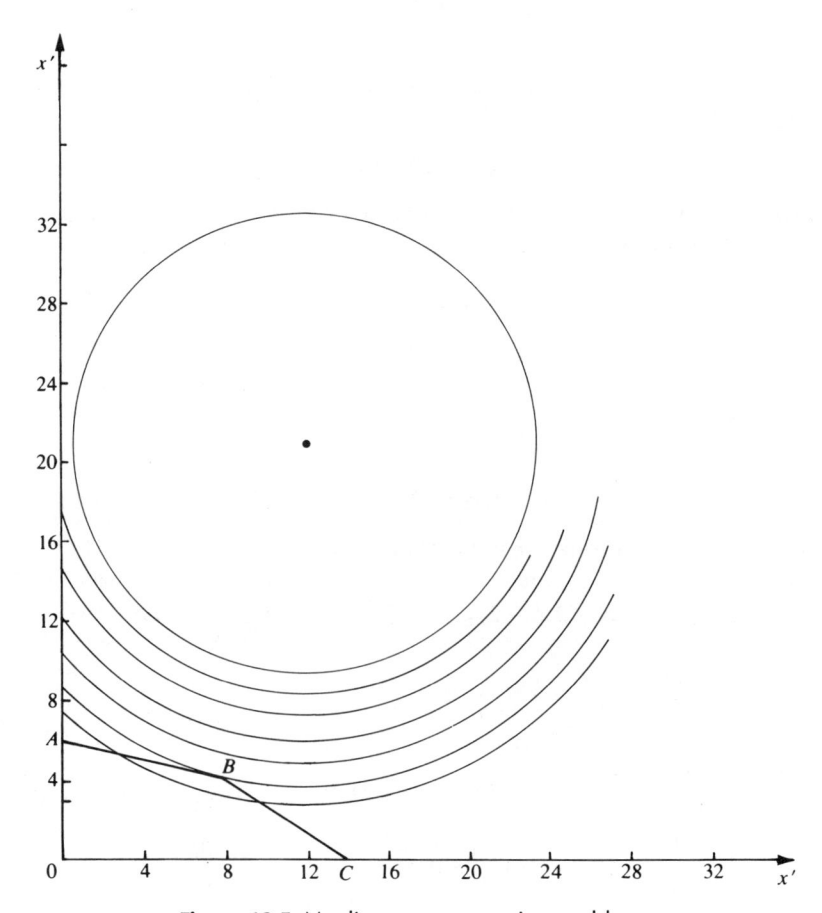

Figure 10.5 Nonlinear programming problem.

fact that there is slack in the first constraint (i.e. y_1 must be zero) implies that $y_2 = 15/4$ but then $\partial l/\partial x_1 > 0$.
4. Re: the vertex C at which $x_1 = 14$, $x_2 = 0$, the condition that $\partial l/\partial x_1 = 0$ and the fact that there is slack in the second constraint implies that $y_1 = -2$.
5. The outcome where x_1, x_2 and y_1 are all positive and $y_2 = 0$ (i.e. $x_1 = 73/11$, $x_2 = 54/11$, $y_1 = 59/11$) violates the second constraint and hence is not feasible.
6. The outcome where x_1, x_2 and y_2 are all positive and $y_1 = 0$ ($x_1 = 108/11$, $x_2 = 39/11$, $y_2 = 48/11$) violates the first constraint and hence is not feasible.
7. The K–T maximum conditions, however, are satisfied at the vertex B where $x_1 = 8$, $x_2 = 4$; both constraints hold as equalities with $y_1 = 3$, $y_2 = 2$. The optimal solution can be easily seen in Figure 10.5.

The Kuhn–Tucker sufficiency theorem

Assume that a particular point satisfies the K–T maximum conditions. What further conditions must be satisfied to guarantee that this point does, in fact, give rise to a global maximum of the Lagrangean function and hence of the objective function subject to all the constraints of the problem? The Kuhn–Tucker sufficiency theorem states that, for the standard nonlinear programming problem of equation (10.41):

A point which satisfies the K–T maximum conditions will give a global maximum of the objective function provided that the objective function is differentiable and concave in the non-negative orthant and that each constraint function is differentiable and convex in the non-negative orthant.

When applied to a minimisation problem, the requirement becomes that

A point which satisfies the K–T minimum conditions will give a global minimum of the objective function provided that the objective function is differentiable and convex in the non-negative orthant and that each constraint function is differentiable and concave in the non-negative orthant.

The above two sets of sufficient conditions can be converted into necessary and sufficient conditions by the inclusion of a constraint qualification which rules out certain irregularities on the boundary of the feasible region. This is purely a mathematical requirement and has no economic significance; for an accessible discussion of the constraint qualification, see Chiang (1984). It should, however, be noted that the constraint qualification will always be satisfied when the constraints of the problem are linear.

A differentiable function of several variables:

$$f(x) = f(x_1, x_2, \ldots, x_n) \tag{10.52}$$

is concave if and only if

$$f(x) \leq f(\bar{x}) + \sum_{j=1}^{n} f_j(\bar{x})(x_j - \bar{x}_j) \tag{10.53}$$

whereas a differentiable function of several variables is convex if

$$f(x) \geq f(\bar{x}) + \sum_{j=1}^{n} f_j(\bar{x})(x_j - \bar{x}_j) \tag{10.54}$$

where $f_j(\bar{x})$ is the partial derivative of the function with respect to x_j evaluated at the point $\bar{x}$. Furthermore, a function which is the sum of two concave (convex) functions is itself also a concave (convex) function.

Returning to the Lagrangean function for a nonlinear programming maximisation problem with m constraints and having assigned specific values of the dual variables, say $\bar{y}_i$, $i = 1, 2, \ldots, m$, l becomes a function simply of the x_j variables:

$$l(x) = f(x) + \sum_{i=1}^{m} \bar{y}_i [c_i - g^i(x)] \tag{10.55}$$

If the objective function is concave and each of the constraint functions convex, then $-g^i(x)$ is concave for all i and $l(x)$ is therefore a concave function. Accordingly, we have

$$l(x) \leq l(\bar{x}) + \sum_{j=1}^{n} \frac{\partial l}{\partial x_j}(x_j - \bar{x}_j) \tag{10.56}$$

Let

$$P_1 = \sum_{j=1}^{n} \frac{\partial l}{\partial \bar{x}_j} \cdot x_j \text{ and } P_2 = -\sum_{j=1}^{n} \frac{\partial l}{\partial \bar{x}_j} \cdot \bar{x}_j \tag{10.57}$$

It is clear from the K-T conditions that P_2 must be zero and P_1 must be nonpositive. Assume the vectors $\bar{x}$ and $\bar{y}$ satisfy the K-T maximum conditions. Hence it follows for a given vector $\bar{y}$ that

$$l(x, \bar{y}) \leq l(\bar{x}, \bar{y}) \tag{10.58}$$

In other words, $\bar{x}$ gives rise to a global maximum of $f(x)$, if $y = \bar{y}$.

Now return to the Lagrangean function, in this instance having assigned specific values to the primal variables, say $\bar{x}_j$, $j = 1, 2, \ldots, n$.

$$l(y) = f(\bar{x}) + \sum_{i=1}^{m} y_i [c_i - g^i(\bar{x})] \tag{10.59}$$

which is linear in the variables y_i and hence is convex in y_i. The following inequality must, therefore, hold:

$$l(y) \geq l(\bar{y}) + \sum_{i=1}^{m} \frac{\partial l}{\partial \bar{y}_i}(y_i - \bar{y}_i) \tag{10.60}$$

Let

$$Q_1 = \sum_{i=1}^{m} \frac{\partial l}{\partial \bar{y}_i} \cdot y_i \text{ and } Q_2 = -\sum_{i=1}^{m} \frac{\partial l}{\partial \bar{y}_i} \cdot \bar{y}_i \tag{10.61}$$

It is clear from the K-T conditions that Q_2 must be zero and Q_1 must be non-negative. Continue to assume that the K-T maximum conditions hold at $\bar{x}, \bar{y}$. Thus it follows for a given vector $\bar{x}$ that

$$l(\bar{x}, y) \geqslant l(\bar{x}, \bar{y}) \tag{10.62}$$

Putting the two inequalities (10.58) and (10.62), together we have

$$l(x, \bar{y}) \leqslant l(\bar{x}, \bar{y}) \leqslant l(\bar{x}, y) \tag{10.63}$$

The point $\bar{x}, \bar{y}$ which satisfies the K-T maximum conditions is a saddle-point with the Lagrangean function reaching a maximum with respect to x at $x = \bar{x}$ given that y is fixed at $\bar{y}$, and a minimum with respect to y at $y = \bar{y}$ given that x is fixed at $\bar{x}$.

The concavity conditions which must be imposed on the objective function and on the negative of the constraint functions in order for it to be sufficient for the K-T maximum conditions to give rise to a global maximum are somewhat restrictive. Arrow and Enthoven (1961), however, have shown that in certain circumstances the marginally less restrictive condition of quasi-concavity for the above functions will yield the same result.

10.4 QUADRATIC PROGRAMMING

In general, nonlinear programming problems are much more difficult to solve than linear programming ones. As we have seen, the solution to the latter will always include an extreme point of the feasible region, whereas in the solution to the former, a much more extensive range of possibilities needs to be considered. The usual computational approach to solving nonlinear problems is to employ an iterative procedure which involves moving from one point to a new one, the direction of movement being determined by the gradient of the objective function at the previous point. The steepest line of ascent is chosen, subject to the constraints and the non-negativity requirements of the problem not being violated. With a concave objective function, the iterative procedure guarantees that a point sufficiently close to the optimal position will be reached, though the convergence will not be perfectly exact.

For a certain class of problem, however, the simplex method can be utilised to obtain the solution. This method can be applied to solve problems where the objective function is quadratic and the constraints are linear. Such problems are known as quadratic programming problems. To illustrate the procedure for solving these problems, we will consider the following simple numerical example:

$$\text{Max } 20x_1 - x_1^2 + 32x_2 - 2x_2^2$$
$$\text{st } 5x_1 + 6x_2 \leqslant 55$$
$$x_1, x_2 \geqslant 0$$

The procedure is to include explicitly in the Lagrangean function the non-negativity requirements of the problem and then to write out the K-T conditions. For the above problem, we have

$$l = 20x_1 - x_1^2 + 32x_2 - 2x_2^2 + y_1[55 - 5x_1 - 6x_2] + \mu_1 x_1 + \mu_2 x_2$$

and the corresponding K-T conditions are

$$\frac{\partial l}{\partial x_1} = 20 - 2x_1 - 5y_1 + \mu_1 = 0$$

$$\frac{\partial l}{\partial x_2} = 32 - 4x_2 - 6y_1 + \mu_2 = 0$$

$$\frac{\partial l}{\partial y_1} = 55 - 5x_1 - 6x_2 \geqslant 0, \; y_1 \geqslant 0, \; y_1 \frac{\partial l}{\partial y_1} = 0$$

$$\frac{\partial l}{\partial \mu_1} = x_1 \geqslant 0, \qquad \mu_1 \geqslant 0, \; \mu_1 \frac{\partial l}{\partial \mu_1} = 0$$

$$\frac{\partial l}{\partial \mu_2} = x_2 \geqslant 0, \qquad \mu_2 \geqslant 0, \; \mu_2 \frac{\partial l}{\partial \mu_2} = 0$$

Note that, unlike our previous cases, we have $\partial l/\partial x_j = 0$ rather than $\leqslant 0$. This arises from the fact that we have included the non-negativity constraints in the Lagrangean function. If x_j is positive, then the corresponding dual variable, μ_j, will be zero; on the other hand, if μ_j is positive, then x_j will be zero.

The K-T conditions may, then, be utilised as the constraints in a new auxiliary linear programming problem whose objective function contains two artificial variables, r_1 and r_2. In order for there to be an initial BFS, r_1 and r_2 will appear in the first and second constraints, respectively, while a slack variable, S_1, will be added to the third constraint to convert it into an equality. If there exists a feasible solution to the nonlinear programming problem, the artificial variables will not appear in the optimal basis for the new LP problem. Moreover, at this optimal basis, the K-T maximum conditions will be satisfied and the value of the original objective function can then be calculated.

The new problem is

$$\text{Max} \quad -r_1 - r_2$$
$$\text{st} \; 2x_1 + 5y_1 - \mu_1 + r_1 \quad = 20$$
$$4x_2 + 6y_1 - \mu_2 + r_2 \quad = 32$$
$$5x_1 + 6x_2 + S_1 \quad = 55$$
$$x_j \geqslant 0, \; \mu_j \geqslant 0, \; \mu_j x_j = 0 \quad (j = 1, 2)$$
$$S_1 \geqslant 0, \; y_1 \geqslant 0, \; y_1 S_1 = 0$$

The significance of the last two constraints is to prevent both x_j and μ_j from being basic, and similarly for y_1 and S_1.

The iterations necessary to obtain the optimal solution are given below:

		x_1	x_2	S_1	y_1	μ_1	μ_2	r_1	r_2	Solution
	$z_j - c_j$	-2	-4	0	-11	1	1	0	0	-52
	r_1	2	0	0	5	-1	0	1	0	20
Basic variables	r_2	0	4	0	6	0	-1	0	1	32
	S_1	5	6	1	0	0	0	0	0	55
	$z_j - c_j$	-2	0	0	-5	1	0	0	1	-20
	r_1	2	0	0	5	-1	0	1	0	20
Basic variables	x_2	0	1	0	3/2	0	$-1/4$	0	1/4	8
	S_1	5	0	1	-9	0	3/2	0	$-3/2$	7
	$z_j - c_j$	0	0	2/5	$-43/5$	1	3/5	0	2/5	$-86/5$
	r_1	0	0	$-2/5$	43/5	-1	$-3/5$	1	3/5	86/5
Basic variables	x_2	0	1	0	3/2	0	$-1/4$	0	1/4	8
	x_1	1	0	1/5	$-9/5$	0	3/10	0	$-3/10$	7/5
	$z_j - c_j$	0	0	0	0	0	0	1	1	0
	y_1	0	0	$-2/43$	1	$-5/43$	$-3/43$	5/43	3/43	2
Basic variables	x_2	0	1	3/43	0	15/86	$-25/172$	$-15/86$	25/172	5
	x_1	1	0	5/43	0	$-9/43$	15/86	9/43	$-15/86$	5

Despite the fact that the largest negative entry in the $z_j - c_j$ row of the initial BFS refers to y_1, this variable cannot be introduced into the basis since S_1 is already basic and to introduce y_1 would violate the condition that $y_1 S_1 = 0$. Since μ_2 is a nonbasic variable, it is permissible to introduce x_2 in place of r_2. At the next iteration, we are still not able to introduce y_1; x_1 must therefore be introduced in place of S_1, this being permissible since μ_1 is nonbasic. At the final iteration, y_1 can now be introduced since S_1 is now nonbasic. Both artificial variables have been eliminated from the basis, the K-T maximum conditions are satisfied at $x_1 = 5$, $x_2 = 5$, $y_1 = 2$, and the value of the objective function is 185.

10.5 THE PEAK LOAD PRICING PROBLEM

An interesting application of the usefulness of the K-T maximum conditions in economic analysis arises in the economics of public enterprise. Let us consider the derivation of optimal pricing and capacity decision rules for a public enterprise which produces a nonstorable output (x), the demand for which varies in some systematic way over the course of the day. We shall later relax the assumption of nonstorability. In order to keep the discussion simple, let us assume that the day can be divided into an off-peak period (period 1) and a peak period (period 2), and that these periods are of equal duration. Let the inverse demand function for the good in period i be given by $p_i = f_i(x_i)$ where p_i is price in period i. The social benefit from consuming x_i units of the good in period i is given by the total area under the demand curve, i.e. by

$$B_i(x_i) = \int_0^{x_i} f_i(x_i) \, dx_i \qquad (i = 1, 2) \tag{10.64}$$

On the cost side, we assume that unit operating costs are constant and equal to c, being invariant both to the scale of output per period and the period in which the output is produced. A unit of capacity can produce a unit of output per half-day and its cost on a daily basis (the daily interest on a permanent loan) is constant and equal to d. The installed level of capacity is sufficient to produce an output level of $\bar{x}$ per half-day. In the short run when it is not possible to change the level of capacity, the public enterprise, in choosing the prices to charge for its output in the two periods in order to maximise net social benefit, must ensure that demand does not exceed capacity. The public enterprise's problem is

$$\left. \begin{array}{l} \text{Max } B_1(x_1) + B_2(x_2) - c(x_1 + x_2) - d\bar{x} \\ \text{st } x_1 \leqslant \bar{x} \\ \phantom{\text{st }} x_2 \leqslant \bar{x} \\ \phantom{\text{st }} x_1, x_2 \geqslant 0 \end{array} \right\} \tag{10.65}$$

The associated Lagrangean function is

$$l = B_1(x_1) + B_2(x_2) - c(x_1 + x_2) - d\bar{x} + y_1[\bar{x} - x_1] + y_2[\bar{x} - x_2] \tag{10.66}$$

The Kuhn–Tucker maximum conditions are

$$\frac{\partial l}{\partial x_1} = p_1 - c - y_1 \leqslant 0, \; x_1 \geqslant 0, \; x_1 \frac{\partial l}{\partial x_1} = 0 \tag{10.67a}$$

$$\frac{\partial l}{\partial x_2} = p_2 - c - y_2 \leqslant 0, \; x_2 \geqslant 0, \; x_2 \frac{\partial l}{\partial x_2} = 0 \tag{10.67b}$$

$$\frac{\partial l}{\partial y_1} = \bar{x} - x_1 \geqslant 0, \qquad y_1 \geqslant 0, \; y_1 \frac{\partial l}{\partial y_1} = 0 \tag{10.68a}$$

$$\frac{\partial l}{\partial y_2} = \bar{x} - x_2 \geqslant 0, \qquad y_2 \geqslant 0, \; y_2 \frac{\partial l}{\partial y_2} = 0 \tag{10.68b}$$

In the long run when the installed level of capacity becomes a variable, it is necessary to add the following condition to the above:

$$\frac{\partial l}{\partial \bar{x}} = -d + y_1 + y_2 \leqslant 0, \; \bar{x} \geqslant 0, \; \bar{x} \frac{\partial l}{\partial \bar{x}} = 0 \tag{10.69}$$

If demand is such that in the off-peak period capacity is not fully utilised, then y_1^* will equal zero and the price charged will simply equal unit operating cost. If y_2^* is positive, then capacity in the peak period will be fully utilised and a price higher than unit operating cost will be charged. If capacity is increased, then output can be higher in both periods; y_i^*, in fact, measures the marginal social benefit of expanding capacity for consumers of the product in period i. In other words, y_i^* is a measure of the valuation consumers in period *i* would place on a marginal expansion of capacity which enabled them to increase their consumption of the good and, correspondingly, it is the maximum amount they would be prepared to pay for a relaxation of the capacity constraint. If capacity is not being fully utilised in some period, then an expansion of capacity brings no benefit to the consumers of the good in that period and their willingness to pay for such an expansion is obviously zero. For a positive amount of the good to be produced in a particular period in the short run, it is necessary that the price of the good be at least as large as the unit operating cost.

Assume there exists a long run equilibrium with a positive amount of the good being produced at least in the peak period. From the last part of the K–T maximum conditions we see that the optimal level of capacity is the level at which

$$y_1^* + y_2^* = d \tag{10.70}$$

The marginal social benefit of expanding capacity should just equal the marginal social cost of so doing. If the sum of the Lagrangean multipliers exceeds the marginal capacity cost in the short-run equlibrium, this is a sign that capacity should be expanded since willingness to pay for such an expansion is greater than the costs of that expansion. Conversely, if $y_1^* + y_2^*$ falls short of d, then, in the longer term, capacity should be reduced.

There are two forms which the long-run equilibrium can take. The first case, known as the firm peak case, involves full utilisation in the peak period but excess capacity in the off-peak period. The off-peak price simply covers operating costs and the capacity costs fall solely on the peak period consumers with

$$p_2^* - c = y_2^* = d \tag{10.71}$$

In the second case, that of the shifting peak, capacity is fully utilised in both periods and capacity costs are shared. The characteristics of the equilibrium are

$$p_1^* = c + y_1^* \tag{10.72}$$

$$p_2^* = c + y_2^* \tag{10.73}$$

$$y_1^* + y_2^* = d \tag{10.74}$$

Figure 10.6 provides a diagrammatic illustration of the firm and shifting peak cases.

Let us drop the assumption of nonstorability of the public enterprise's output but retain all the other features of our simple model. Assume that the installed level of storage capacity is $\bar{s}$ and the amount produced and then stored during the off-peak period for sale in the peak period is s. Let the operating cost of storing a unit of output be e and the daily capacity cost to store a unit of output be f. The maximand now becomes

$$B_1(x_1) + B_2(x_2) - c(x_1 + x_2) - d\bar{x} - es - f\bar{s} \tag{10.75}$$

Since we are allowing for storage, a distinction must be made between production and sales, with x_i now representing the volume of sales in period *i*. Off-peak period sales cannot exceed capacity output less that part of current production that is stored, while peak period sales cannot be greater than capacity output plus the amount stored

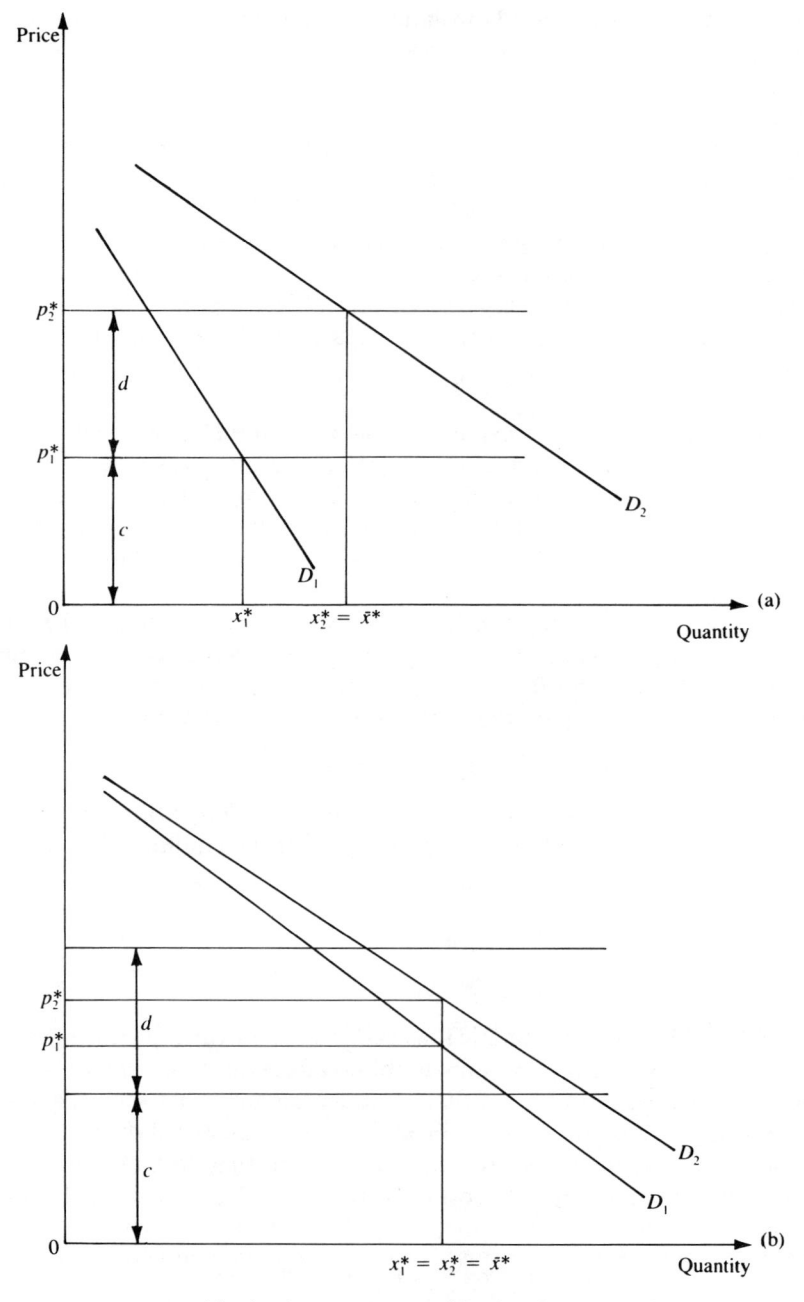

Figure 10.6 (a) The firm peak case. **(b)** The shifting peak case.

during the off-peak period, nor can storage capacity be exceeded. In the short run, we must therefore find non-negative values of x_1, x_2 and s which give rise to a maximum given in equation (10.75) subject to the following three constraints:

$$x_1 + s \leqslant \bar{x} \tag{10.76}$$

$$x_2 - s \leqslant \bar{x} \tag{10.77}$$

$$s \leqslant \bar{s} \tag{10.78}$$

The Lagrangean function is, therefore,

$$l = B_1(x_1) + B_2(x_2) - c(x_1 + x_2) - d\bar{x} - es - f\bar{s} + y_1[\bar{x} - x_1 - s] \\ + y_2[\bar{x} - x_2 + s] + y_s[\bar{s} - s] \tag{10.79}$$

The Kuhn–Tucker maximum conditions are

$$\frac{\partial l}{\partial x_1} = p_1 - c - y_1 \leqslant 0, \qquad x_1 \geqslant 0, \ x_1 \frac{\partial l}{\partial x_1} = 0 \tag{10.80a}$$

$$\frac{\partial l}{\partial x_2} = p_2 - c - y_2 \leqslant 0, \qquad x_2 \geqslant 0, \ x_2 \frac{\partial l}{\partial x_2} = 0 \tag{10.80b}$$

$$\frac{\partial l}{\partial s} = -e - y_1 + y_2 - y_s \leqslant 0, \qquad s \geqslant 0, \ s \frac{\partial l}{\partial s} = 0 \tag{10.81}$$

$$\frac{\partial l}{\partial y_1} = \bar{x} - x_1 - s \geqslant 0, \qquad y_1 \geqslant 0, \ y_1 \frac{\partial l}{\partial y_1} = 0 \tag{10.82a}$$

$$\frac{\partial l}{\partial y_2} = \bar{x} - x_2 + s \geqslant 0, \qquad y_2 \geqslant 0, \ y_2 \frac{\partial l}{\partial y_2} = 0 \tag{10.82b}$$

$$\frac{\partial l}{\partial y_s} = \bar{s} - s \geqslant 0, \qquad y_s \geqslant 0, \ y_s \frac{\partial l}{\partial y_s} = 0 \tag{10.83}$$

In the long run when both productive and storage capacity can be varied, the following conditions must be added to those above:

$$\frac{\partial l}{\partial \bar{x}} = -d + y_1 + y_2 \leqslant 0, \quad \bar{x} \geqslant 0, \ \bar{x} \frac{\partial l}{\partial \bar{x}} = 0 \tag{10.84}$$

$$\frac{\partial l}{\partial \bar{s}} = -f + y_s \leqslant 0, \qquad \bar{s} \geqslant 0, \ \bar{s} \frac{\partial l}{\partial \bar{s}} = 0 \tag{10.85}$$

In the short run, with given levels of productive and storage capacity, the equilibrium will take one of many possible forms. Since a taxonomic treatment of all the possibilities would be tedious in the extreme, we restrict our discussion of the possible short-run equilibria to a few general points of interest. As in our previous discussion of the nonstorable output case, the available productive capacity may or may not be fully utilised in the off-peak period; in the later case the off-peak price would simply equal unit operating cost of production. We can rule out the case where there is excess capacity in the peak period as being of no interest in the storage case, since it is necessary, though not a sufficient condition, that productive capacity be fully utilised in the peak for some storage to take place. Assume productive capacity was never fully utilised; then price would be invariant across the two periods and equal to c. There would be no incentive to incur operating costs of storage since there would be no way in which they could be recouped. For storage to take place, the difference between peak period price and off-peak period price must at least cover the unit operating cost of storage and this difference will only be positive if productive capacity is fully utilised in the peak. If this difference in price exceeds the unit operating cost of storage, then the available storage capacity will be fully utilised. If some storage takes place but there is not full utilisation of the capacity, then the price difference will just equal e. By referring to the K–T maximum conditions the reader can verify the truthfulness of the above statements.

We now turn to consider the possible long-run equilibrium outcomes. The first case to be considered is that where storage takes place and productive capacity is fully utilised in both periods. The equilibrium is characterised by $s^* = \bar{s}^* \geqslant 0$, $y_1^* \geqslant 0$, and $y_2^* > 0$. Since the optimal amount of storage capacity is positive, we must have

$$y_s^* = f \text{ and } y_2^* - y_1^* = e + f \qquad (10.86)$$

The optimal prices for the two periods are

$$p_1^* = c + y_1^* \qquad (10.87)$$

$$p_2^* = c + y_2^* \qquad (10.88)$$

Hence,

$$p_2^* - p_1^* = y_2^* - y_1^* \qquad (10.89)$$

The requirement that productive capacity be optimal yields the condition

$$y_1^* + y_2^* = d \qquad (10.90)$$

which in association with equation (10.86) yields

$$d = 2y_1^* + e + f \qquad (10.91)$$

Since $y_1^* \geqslant 0$, then

$$d \geqslant e + f \qquad (10.92)$$

The cost of expanding productive capacity by one unit is at least as large as the marginal operating and capacity costs of storing one unit. If $y_1^* > 0$, which we would expect to be the normal case in these circumstances, then $d > e + f$.

In the second case, storage takes place but productive capacity is only fully utilised in the peak period. In this case y_1^* is definitely zero and building upon the analysis of the previous case one finds that for the equilibrium to take this particular form it must be the case that

$$d = e + f$$

The management of the public enterprise will be indifferent between expanding productive or storage capacity. Whichever option is chosen, the additional costs are the same.

The final case of interest to consider is where there is no storage and there is surplus productive capacity in the off-peak period. Given that $s^* = \bar{s}^* = 0$, $y_1^* = 0$ and $y_2^* > 0$, the following must also hold:

$$y_s^* \leqslant f \tag{10.93}$$

$$y_2^* \leqslant e + y_s^* \tag{10.94}$$

$$y_2^* = d \tag{10.95}$$

Hence,

$$d \leqslant e + f \tag{10.96}$$

Expanding productive capacity by one unit will not cost more than the marginal operating and capacity costs of storage. Once again, in these circumstances we would normally expect the marginal valuation of a unit of storage capacity to fall short of its cost with the strong inequality therefore holding.

The reader who is interested in a more extensive treatment of these issues in the economics of public enterprise is referred to Crew and Kleindorfer (1979), Littlechild (1970) and Rees (1984).

Exercises

1. Use the fractional cut algorithm to solve the following integer programming problem:

$$\text{Max } Z = 3x_1 + 2x_2$$
$$\text{st} \quad 4x_1 + 2x_2 \leqslant 23$$
$$x_1 + x_2 \leqslant 8$$
$$x_1, x_2 \text{ non-negative integers}$$

What artificial constraints do the fractional cut give rise to?

2.
$$\text{Max } Z = 18x_1 + 15x_2 + 8x_3$$
$$\text{st} \quad 8x_1 + 6x_2 + 2x_3 \leqslant 50$$
$$2x_1 + 3x_2 + 5x_3 \leqslant 18$$
$$x_1, x_2, x_3 \text{ non-negative integers}$$

3. How is the solution to question 1 changed if x_1 is simply required to be non-negative with x_2 remaining a non-negative integer.

4. Solve the following problem using the mixed cut algorithm:

$$\text{Max } Z = x_1 + x_2$$
$$\text{st} \quad 2x_1 + 5x_2 \leqslant 16$$
$$6x_1 + 3x_2 \leqslant 30$$
$$x_1 \geqslant 0, x_2 \text{ non-negative integer}$$

5. Show that the recomputed dual variables for the following problem are not unique:

$$\text{Max } Z = 2x_1 + 5x_2$$
$$\text{st} \quad 6x_2 \leqslant 15$$
$$6x_1 + 5x_2 \leqslant 20$$
$$-x_1 + x_2 \leqslant 2$$
$$x_1, x_2 \text{ non-negative integers}$$

6. A firm can produce two goods x_1 and x_2 and its profit function is given by

$$\Pi = 200x_1 + 150x_2 - 2x_1^2 - 3x_2^2 - 2x_1 x_2$$

It is also subject to constraints on the availability of resources with

$$2x_1 + 5x_2 \leqslant 120$$
$$4x_1 + 2x_2 \leqslant 160$$

and

$$x_1, x_2 \geqslant 0$$

(a) Write out the Kuhn–Tucker conditions for a maximum.
(b) Derive the profit-maximising output bundle and the associated shadow prices of the resources.
(c) Is the Kuhn–Tucker sufficiency theorem satisfied?

7. A consumer's utility function is given by

$$U = x_1 x_2$$

To purchase a unit of x_1, the consumer must pay a price of £3 and also hand over one ration coupon, whereas the price per unit of x_2 is £2 and two ration coupons are required. The consumer had an initial money income of £230 and is allocated 130 ration coupons by the Ministry of Food:

(a) Derive the consumer's utility-maximising consumption bundle.
(b) What is the marginal utility of a ration coupon and the marginal utility of income? Calculate thereby the shadow price of a ration coupon.
(c) If ration coupons are tradable at an exogenously given price of £2 per coupon, would the consumer buy or sell coupons? How would the composition of his utility-maximising bundle change?

8. Consider the problem:

$$\text{Max } Z = ax_1 - bx_1^2 + cx_2 - dx_2^2$$
$$\text{st} \quad 4x_1 + x_2 \leqslant 20$$
$$x_1^2 + 4x_2 \leqslant 36$$
$$x_1, x_2 \geqslant 0$$

where a, b, c and d are all positive parameters:

(a) What restrictions would have to be imposed on the parameters for the optimal solution to the problem to occur at $x_1 = 5$, $x_2 = 0$?
(b) Is it possible to have an optimal solution at $x_1 = 0$, $x_2 = 9$?

9. The demand for electricity depends upon the time of day. Peak period demand price is given by $p_1 = 100 - q_1$, whereas in the off-peak period of equal duration we have $p_2 = 50 - q_2$. Marginal operating costs are constant and equal to 10, unit capital cost per day is 50 and to produce a unit of output per half-day requires a unit of capital. Installed capacity is sufficient to produce 40 units of output per half-day:
   (a) Calculate the optimal prices for the peak and off-peak periods.
   (b) Should capacity be expanded or contracted?
   (c) If off-peak demand increased so that $p_2 = 80 - 1.5q_2$, find the new long-run equilibrium capacity of the industry and the optimal prices to be charged in the peak and off-peak periods.

10. Use the quadratic programming algorithm to solve the following problems:
    (a)
    $$\text{Max } 16x_1 - x_1^2 + 24x_2 - x_2^2$$
    $$\text{st } 2x_1 + 4x_2 \leqslant 34$$
    $$x_1, x_2 \geqslant 0$$
    (b)
    $$\text{Min } x_1^2 - 12x_1 + 2x_2^2 - 20x_2$$
    $$\text{st } x_1 + 2x_2 \geqslant 20$$
    $$x_1, x_2 \geqslant 0$$

References

Arrow, K.J. and Enthoven, A.C. (1961), 'Quasi-concave Programming', *Econometrica*, 29, 779–800.

Chiang, A.C. (1984), *Fundamental Methods of Mathematical Economics*, 3rd edn, New York: McGraw-Hill.

Crew, M.A. and Kleindorfer, P.R. (1979), *Public Utility Economics*, London: MacMillan.

Gomory, R.E. (1958), 'Outline of an algorithm for integer solutions to linear programs', *Bulletin of the American Mathematical Society*, 64, 275–8.

Gomory, R.E. and Baumol, W.J. (1960), 'Integer programming and pricing', *Econometrica*, 28, 521–50.

Kuhn, H.W. and Tucker, A.W. (1951), 'Nonlinear programming', in J. Neyman (ed.), *Proceedings of the Second Berkeley Symposium on Mathematical Statistics and Probability*, Berkeley: University of California Press.

Littlechild, S.C. (1970), 'Peak-load pricing of telephone calls', *The Bell Journal of Economics and Management Science*, 1, 191–210.

Rees, R. (1984), *Public Enterprise Economics*, 2nd edn, London: Weidenfeld and Nicolson.

Taha, H. (1975), *Integer Programming: theory, applications and computations*, New York: Academic Press.

Chapter 11
AN INTRODUCTION TO DYNAMIC OPTIMISATION

Whereas in the preceding two chapters we have discussed a variety of static optimisation problems, we now provide an introductory treatment of dynamic optimisation. In dynamic optimisation, time may be treated as either a continuous or a discrete variable, while the time horizon over which decisions are taken by economic agents may be finite or infinite. We shall first treat time as a continuous variable and outline the main elements of optimal control theory in Section 11.1. We then proceed in Section 11.2 to a discussion of some important economic applications of the technique by looking at the following:

1. The determination of an optimal consumption plan for an individual consumer.
2. The determination of the optimal depletion path for an exhaustible resource. We also compare and contrast the depletion path of a resource under perfect competition with that under monopoly.

In Section 11.3 we provide an introduction to dynamic programming, first in the context of continuous time and then using discrete time. For discrete time problems, in fact, dynamic programming is the only available solution technique. We state Bellman's optimality principle and show that associated with each dynamic programming problem is a fundamental recurrence relation which can be utilised to solve the problem. An important advantage of dynamic programming is that the usefulness of the technique is not simply confined to problems with a time dimension. Whenever a problem requires sequential decision-making, whether the nature of the sequence be temporal, spatial or neither, use can be made of the optimality principle and the appropriate fundamental recurrence relation. In the final section we provide some economic examples which can be solved using this technique.

11.1 OPTIMAL CONTROL THEORY

We first outline the characteristics possessed by a dynamic optimisation problem. For the continuous time case, we typically have a problem of the following form:

$$\text{Max} \int_0^T f(x(t), z(t), t) \mathrm{d}t \tag{11.1}$$

$$\text{st } \dot{z}(t) \leq g(x(t), z(t), t) \tag{11.2}$$

$$z(0) = z_0, \ z(T) \text{ some condition} \tag{11.3}$$

A time path for the flow variable $x(t)$ must be chosen so as to maximise the value of the objective function. In the terminology of optimal control theory, the flow variable is known as the control variable. Consider the case of a consumer seeking to derive an optimal consumption plan which maximises a present value integral of the utilities derived from that plan: the control variable for this problem would be consumption expenditure. The relevant time horizon for the control variable may be finite or infinite. The choice of T will obviously be influenced by the problem under consideration. In the optimal consumption plan case, the economic agent would choose a time horizon on the basis of his life expectation at that point in time when the plan is formed. An economic planner, on the other hand, concerned with the optimal depletion path for an exhaustible resource (the control variable in this case being the amount of the resource extracted) would be mindful of the interests of future generations and, in the absence of an alternative backstop technology becoming available in the future, may well choose an infinite time horizon.

The initial value of the state variable, z, is given and its evolution through time is given by the constraint which takes the form of a first-order differential equation in the state variable. For the consumption problem, the state variable is the nonhuman wealth of the consumer. It will be rising (falling) through time if the consumer consumes less (more) than his income. We must naturally impose a terminal constraint on the state variable. In the consumption case, we might permit him to have consumed all his wealth by time T or, alternatively, to make a bequest of a specified amount at time T. What we clearly cannot realistically do in this case is to impose no end constraint at all, since this would permit him to go to his grave heavily in debt after having experienced a veritable consumption binge. In the exhaustible resource case, the state variable is the stock of the resource remaining unexploited: in the absence of new discoveries its rate of change is simply equal to the negative of the amount currently extracted (i.e. the control variable). The economy starts out with a known endowment at time zero and the remaining stock must be non-negative at the end of the relevant time horizon.

The Lagrangean function for the dynamic optimisation problem is given by

$$l = \int_0^T [f(x(t), z(t), t) + y(t)(g(x(t), z(t) t) - \dot{z}(t))] \mathrm{d}t \tag{11.4}$$

where $y(t)$ is a Lagrangean multiplier, which in this context is referred to as a costate variable. For the moment, we ignore the end-point constraints. It is important to note that the Lagrangean function is not separable over time in the control and state variables. From the constraint it is clear that the value of the state variable at time t depends not simply on decisions taken at that time but also on decisions made earlier. The objective function itself may or may not be separable in the control variable; it depends on the particular problem under consideration. Separability of the objective function applies in the consumption problem since f takes the form $u(c(t))e^{-\rho t}$ where utility (u) is a function of consumption at time $t(c(t))$ and ρ is the rate of time preference; but this will not necessarily always be the case. If the Lagrangean function were separable over time in the control and state variables, the solution to the problem would be obtained using the standard static optimisation procedure outlined in the preceding chapter.

How do we find the solution to the problem whose Lagrangean function is given by equation (11.4)? The presence of $\dot{z}(t)$ in this function is a potential source of difficulty, but this difficulty can be surmounted by noticing that, by integration by parts,

$$\int y(t)\dot{z}(t)dt = \int y(t)dz(t) = y(t)z(t) - \int z(t)dy(t) \tag{11.5}$$

and

$$\int_0^T -y(t)\dot{z}(t)dt = -y(T)z(T) + y(0)z(0) + \int_0^T \dot{y}(t)z(t)dt \tag{11.6}$$

Substituting equation (11.6) in (11.4), we eliminate the troublesome term $\dot{z}(t)$ from the Lagrangean function. For convenience we drop the time arguments from the control, state and costate variables and write the new Lagrangean function which is separable across time in the control and state variables:

$$l = \int_0^T [f(x, z, t) + yg(x, z, t) + \dot{y}z]dt - [y(T)z(T) - y(0)z(0)] \tag{11.7}$$

We now define a new function, known as the Hamiltonian of the problem:

$$H(x, z, t, y) = f(x, z, t) + yg(x, z, t) \tag{11.8}$$

Substituting equation (11.8) in (11.7), we obtain

$$l = \int_0^T (H + \dot{y}z)dt - [y(T)z(T) - y(0)z(0)] \tag{11.9}$$

In order to solve the dynamic optimisation problem, we make use of Pontryagin's maximum principle, which states that if there exists a time path for the control variable (x^*) which does in fact lead to a maximum of the Lagrangean function, this maximum being equal to the maximum value function V where

$$V = \int_0^T f(x^*, z^*, t) dt \tag{11.10}$$

then there exists a time path for the costate variable such that x^* and z^* yield a maximum of $H + \dot{y}z$.

Necessary conditions for the solution to the dynamic optimisation problem may thus be formulated in terms of the Hamiltonian. These are

$$\frac{\partial H}{\partial x} = 0 \tag{11.11}$$

$$\frac{\partial H}{\partial z} + \dot{y} = 0 \tag{11.12}$$

In addition, in order to ensure that the constraint is satisfied, we must also have

$$\frac{\partial H}{\partial y} = \dot{z} \tag{11.13}$$

In conjunction with the transversality condition to be discussed below when we turn to explicit consideration of the end-point constraints, these Hamiltonian conditions are necessary but not sufficient for the solution to our problem. They will, however, be necessary and sufficient if

(a) $f(x, z, t)$ is concave in x and z and $g(x, z, t)$ is linear in x and z, or (11.14)
(b) H is concave in z, which will be the case if (i) is true or if both f and g are concave in x and z. (11.15)

To date we have neglected the end-point constraints of the problem; it is now time to rectify this omission. Let us assume that these constraints take the following form:

$$z(0) = z_0 \text{ and } z(T) \geqslant z_T \tag{11.16}$$

The initial constraint is easily dealt with; one simply substitutes $z(0) = z_0$ in equation (11.9). As far as the terminal constraint is concerned, we need to add the following term: $y_E[z(T) - z_T]$, to the Lagrangean function. Making these two changes, we obtain

$$l = \int_0^T (H + \dot{y}z) dt - [y(T)z(T) - y(0)z_0] + y_E[z(T) - z_T] \tag{11.17}$$

Differentiating equation (11.17) partially with respect to $z(T)$ and y_E, we obtain the following results which must be satisfied for l to be maximised:

$$\frac{\partial l}{\partial z(T)} = y_E - y(T) = 0 \tag{11.18}$$

$$\frac{\partial l}{\partial y_E} = z(T) - z_T \geqslant 0, \; y_E \geqslant 0, \; y_E \frac{\partial l}{\partial y_E} = 0 \tag{11.19}$$

Equation (11.18) requires that a small change in the terminal value of the state variable should not change the value of the integral we are seeking to maximise, while in equation (11.19) we have the usual complementary–slackness conditions. Combining the two results we obtain the following transversality condition for the terminal constraint $z(T) > z_T$:

$$y(T) \geqslant 0, y(T)[z(T) - z_T] = 0 \qquad (11.20)$$

For these particular end-point constraints, the Lagrangean function simplifies to

$$l = \int_0^T (H + \dot{y}z)dt - [y(T)z_T - y(0)z_0] \qquad (11.21)$$

Letting the optimal paths for the control and state variables be represented by x^* and z^*, respectively, then the Lagrangean function and the maximum value function, when evaluated along these paths, are equal:

$$V = \int_0^T f(x^*, z^*, t)dt = \int_0^T H(x^*, z^*, t, y)dt - [y(T)z_T - y(0)z_0] \qquad (11.22)$$

Hence

$$\frac{\partial V}{\partial z_T} = -y(T) \qquad (11.23)$$

$$\frac{\partial V}{\partial z_0} = y(0) \qquad (11.24)$$

The costate variable at time $t = 0$ measures the impact on the maximum value function of a slight increase in the initial stock. In the consumption problem, it would measure the change in the discounted utility integral resulting from a small change in initial nonhuman wealth. A similar interpretation can be given to the costate variable $y(T)$; if nonhuman wealth at the end of the consumption plan must be marginally higher, then a small adjustment to the optimal consumption plan may be necessary. It certainly would be if $y(T)$ were positive and, in terms of discounted utility, the consumer would be worse off by the amount $y(T)$. If the terminal constraint was not binding, then $y(T)$ would be zero and a marginal tightening would in these circumstances make no difference to the optimal consumption plan.

More generally we may state that $y(s)$ measures the impact on the maximum value function of an exogenous change in $z^*(s)$. Consider the exhaustible resource problem: if at time s a small increment to the unexploited stock is discovered, then the previous optimal time path z^* from s to T can now be improved upon. By making a slight adjustment to the time path from s onwards, a higher value for discounted net social benefits can be attained and this increase in value is given by $y(s)$.

It is a straightforward matter to obtain the transversality conditions for some alternative simple terminal conditions for the state variable. The reader should check his understanding of the following conditions:

Some economic applications

1. If $z(T) = z_T$, the corresponding transversality condition is that $y(T)$ be unrestricted in sign.
2. If no condition is imposed on the terminal value of the state variable, then $y(T) = 0$.

In case (i) a small increase in the terminal value of the state variable will have an indeterminate effect on the maximum value. Compare this result with the discussion of the Lagrangean multiplier in the classical optimisation problem or of the dual variable attached to an equality constraint in linear programming. In case (ii) since there is no restriction on the value which can be taken by $z(T)$, $z^*(T)$ is chosen so as to yield the largest possible value of V and a small change in $z^*(T)$ would thus have no effect on V.

11.2 SOME ECONOMIC APPLICATIONS OF OPTIMAL CONTROL THEORY

Optimal consumption plan

The preferences of an economic agent can be represented by the following utility function which is assumed to be increasing and concave in consumption (c):

$$U(t) = U(c(t)) \tag{11.25}$$

His objective is to choose a consumption plan over a finite time horizon T which is optimal in the sense of maximising the present value of the utility derived from this consumption, the discount factor being his rate of time preference (ρ). He receives earned income as a continuous flow at a rate of w per period and unearned income at a rate of $rk(t)$ per period, where r is the rate of interest and $k(t)$ the value of his non-human wealth at time t. There exists a perfect capital market in which he can lend or borrow as much as he likes at the above interest rate r, though he is subject to certain end-point constraints. We assume he starts out with zero nonhuman wealth and we impose the further constraint that his nonhuman wealth should also be zero at time T.

Our problem thus takes the following form:

$$\text{Max} \int_0^T U(c(t)) e^{-\rho t} dt \tag{11.26}$$

$$\text{st} \quad \dot{k}(t) = w + rk(t) - c(t) \tag{11.27}$$

$$k(0) = 0 \tag{11.28}$$

$$k(T) = 0 \tag{11.29}$$

The Hamiltonian for the above problem is

$$H = U(c(t)) e^{-\rho t} + y(t)[w + rk(t) - c(t)] \tag{11.30}$$

and the corresponding Hamiltonian conditions are

$$\frac{\partial H}{\partial c} = U'(c(t))e^{-\rho t} - y(t) = 0 \tag{11.31}$$

$$\frac{\partial H}{\partial k} = ry(t) = -\dot{y}(t) \tag{11.32}$$

$$\frac{\partial H}{\partial y} = w + rk(t) - c(t) = \dot{k} \tag{11.33}$$

Solving the differential equation in equation (11.32), we obtain

$$y(t) = y(0)e^{-rt} \tag{11.34}$$

Substituting equation (11.34) in (11.31), we have, after a little manipulation,

$$U'(c(t)) = y(0)e^{(\rho - r)t} \tag{11.35}$$

Differentiating equation (11.35) with respect to time, we obtain

$$\frac{dU'(c(t))}{dt} = (\rho - r)U'(c(t)) \tag{11.36}$$

If the rate of time preference exceeds the rate of interest, then the right-hand side of equation (11.36) is positive and the marginal utility of consumption must be increasing through time. Since we have assumed a concave utility function (i.e. $U''(c) < 0$), then with $\rho > r$, consumption will be falling through time along the optimal path. The consumer will initially consume more than his earnings, financing the deficit through borrowing; after an elapse of time, maximum indebtedness will be reached and subsequently the debt will be repaid, being completely extinguished at time T. Conversely, if $r > \rho$, consumption will rise along the optimal path with nonhuman wealth increasing initially, reaching a maximum and then falling to zero as the consumer reaches time T. In the special case where $r = \rho$, optimal consumption will be constant through time.

We can say no more without specifying the form of the utility function. Let us assume that

$$U(c(t)) = \log_e c(t) \tag{11.37}$$

Then

$$U'(c(t)) = \frac{1}{c(t)} = y(0)e^{(\rho - r)t} \tag{11.38}$$

Hence

$$c(t) = y(0)^{-1}e^{(r - \rho)t} = c(0)e^{(r - \rho)t} \tag{11.39}$$

Substituting equation (11.39) in (11.33), we obtain

$$\dot{k}(t) = w + rk(t) - c(0)e^{(r - \rho)t} \tag{11.40}$$

In this particular case, the above differential equation can be solved without too much difficulty. It has the following solution:

Some economic applications

$$k(t) = e^{rt}\left[(1-e^{-rt})\frac{w}{r} - (1-e^{-\rho t})\frac{c(0)}{\rho}\right] \quad (11.41)$$

Note that the initial condition that $k(0) = 0$ is satisfied; however, we must also ensure that the other end-point constraint (i.e. $k(T) = 0$) also holds. The requirement that $k(T) = 0$ enables us to fix $c(0)$, the initial consumption rate. We must have

$$c(0) = \frac{\rho}{r}\left[\frac{1-e^{-rT}}{1-e^{-\rho T}}\right]w \quad (11.42)$$

Substituting equation (11.42) in (11.41) the optimal time path for nonhuman wealth is obtained:

$$k(T) = \frac{we^{rt}}{r}\left[(1-e^{-rt}) - (1-e^{-\rho t})\left[\frac{1-e^{-rT}}{1-e^{-\rho T}}\right]\right] \quad (11.43)$$

Given that the terminal constraint took the form $k(T) = 0$, the transversality condition imposes no restriction on the sign of $y(T)$. However, for this particular problem, $y(T)$ will be definitely positive. From equation (11.34) we must have

$$y(T) = y(0)e^{-rT} \quad (11.44)$$

but from equation (11.39)

$$y(0) = c(0)^{-1} \quad (11.45)$$

and from equation (11.42)

$$c(0) > 0 \quad (11.46)$$

Hence,

$$y(T) > 0 \quad (11.47)$$

The adjustments to the optimal consumption plan which would be necessary were a bequest to be made at time T would definitely make the agent worse off.

We now work through a numerical example in which the following values have been assigned to the parameters of the model:

$$w = 10\,000,\ T = 40,\ r = 0.05,\ \rho = 0.04$$
$$k(0) = 0,\ k(T) = 0$$

Substituting in equation (11.42) we find

$$c(0) = 8667.2021 \quad (11.48)$$

Along the optimal path consumption rises at an exponential rate of 0.01 per period and by the end-point:

$$c(40) = 12\,929.905$$

Nonhuman wealth rises to reach a maximum value of 20 075.86 at $T = 23.87$ years and then declines to reach zero at $T = 40$. The discounted utility integral is given by

$$\int_0^{40} \log_e[c(0)e^{0.01t}]e^{-0.04t}dt = 6925.32 \tag{11.49}$$

Dynamic optimisation and the calculus of variations

For that set of dynamic optimisation problems for which the maximand can be expressed as a function of the state variable and its rate of change as well as time, and end-point constraints are imposed on the state variable, an alternative method of solution employing the calculus of variations is available. Mathematically, this technique predates optimal control theory and space considerations preclude other than a brief comment on the approach. The interested reader is referred to Hadley and Kemp (1971) and Kamien and Schwarz (1981) for a detailed discussion of the calculus of variations. A more introductory treatment is provided in Dixit (1976) and Intriligator (1971).

Consider the following problem:

$$\text{Max} \int_0^T f(t, z, \dot{z})dt \quad st\ z(0) = z_0 \text{ and } z(T) = z_T \tag{11.50}$$

Then it can be shown that a necessary condition for $z^*(t)$ to be the optimal time path for the state variable is that the following equation, known as the Euler–Lagrange equation, be satisfied:

$$\frac{\partial f}{\partial z} = \frac{d(\partial f/\partial \dot{z})}{dt} \tag{11.51}$$

In the general case, the above equation gives rise to a second-order differential equation in the state variable which can, in principle, be solved with the necessary adjustments being made to the solution to ensure the satisfaction of the end-point constraints.

The optimal consumption problem can be written in a form suitable for the application of the Euler–Lagrange equation by noting that since from the constraint,

$$c = w + rk - \dot{k} \tag{11.52}$$

the maximand can be written in the form

$$\text{Max} \int_0^T U(w + rk - \dot{k})e^{-\rho t}dt \tag{11.53}$$

The end-point constraints are

$$k(0) = 0 \text{ and } k(T) = 0 \tag{11.54}$$

Since

$$f(t, k, \dot{k}) = U(c)e^{-\rho t} = U(w + rk - \dot{k})e^{-\rho t} \tag{11.55}$$

we have

$$\frac{\partial f}{\partial k} = re^{-\rho t}U'(c) \qquad (11.56)$$

$$\frac{\partial f}{\partial \dot{k}} = -e^{-\rho t}U'(c) \qquad (11.57)$$

and

$$\frac{d(\partial f/\partial \dot{k})}{dt} = \rho e^{-\rho t}U'(c) - e^{-\rho t}\frac{dU'(c)}{dt} \qquad (11.58)$$

From the Euler–Lagrange equation, we then have, after some manipulation,

$$(\rho - r)U'(c) = \frac{dU'(c)}{dt} \qquad (11.59)$$

with the obvious implication that

$$\frac{dU'(c)}{dt} \lesseqgtr 0 \text{ for } \rho \lesseqgtr r \qquad (11.60)$$

The marginal utility of consumption will be rising and consumption correspondingly falling through time if the rate of time preference exceeds the rate of interest, etc. This is exactly the same result as we earlier derived using optimal control theory. The great advantage, however, of the latter approach over the former, particularly from the perspective of the economist, is the important information contained in the costate variables which is absent in the calculus of variations.

Exhaustible resource problem

We now turn to consider the case of a planner seeking to set the depletion path for an exhaustible resource so as to maximise net social benefits over an infinite time horizon. The maximand is thus

$$\int_0^\infty [B(x(t)) - c(x(t), S(t))]e^{-rt}dt \qquad (11.61)$$

where B is the benefit function, $x(t)$ the amount extracted at time t, c is the cost function assumed to depend upon both the currrent rate of extraction and the amount of the stock remaining at time t ($S(t)$), and r is the rate of interest assumed equal to the rate of social time preference.

The constraints of the problem are

$$x(t) = -\dot{S}(t) \qquad (11.62)$$

$$S(0) = S_0 \qquad (11.63)$$

$$\lim_{T\to\infty} S(T) \geq 0 \qquad (11.64)$$

The rate of extraction at time t is equal to the rate of change of the stock; the initial stock of the resource is S_0 and in the limit as we approach the time horizon, the amount remaining must be non-negative.

The Hamiltonian for this problem is

$$H = [B(x(t)) - c(x(t), S(t))]e^{-rt} + y(t)(-x(t)) \tag{11.65}$$

and the associated Hamiltonian conditions are

$$\frac{\partial H}{\partial x(t)} = \left[p(t) - \frac{\partial c}{\partial x(t)} \right] e^{-rt} - y(t) = 0 \tag{11.66}$$

where $p(t)$ is the price of a unit of the extracted resource at time t. Note that the benefit to society from the last unit extracted at time t is equal to the price of a unit of the extracted resource at time t:

$$\frac{\partial H}{\partial S(t)} = -\dot{y}(t) \tag{11.67}$$

which implies

$$\dot{y}(t) = \frac{\partial c}{\partial S(t)} e^{-rt} \tag{11.68}$$

Finally, to ensure the constraint is satisfied we have

$$\frac{\partial H}{\partial y(t)} = -x(t) = \dot{S}(t) \tag{11.69}$$

while the transversality condition requires

$$\lim_{T \to \infty} y(T) \geq 0, \quad \lim_{T \to \infty} S(T) \geq 0, \quad \lim_{T \to \infty} y(T)S(T) = 0 \tag{11.70}$$

In the exhaustible resource problem, $y(t)$ measures the impact on discounted profits, discounted to time $t = 0$, of a marginal change in the unexploited stock at time t. We may call $y(t)$ the discounted royalty of the resource. Note from the transversality condition that, if at the end of the time horizon some of the resource is not utilised, then the corresponding costate variable (Lagrangean multiplier) will be zero. Furthermore, in the special case where extraction costs are invariant to the amount of stock remaining, the rate of change of the costate variable is zero; the more likely case, however, will be for extraction costs to increase as the amount of unexploited stock becomes smaller (i.e. $\partial c / \partial S(t) < 0$), with the more accessible and productive deposits being exploited earlier in time.

For the economic interpretation of the Hamiltonian conditions it is more useful to work in terms of an undiscounted costate variable. Let $m(t)$ represent such a variable:

$$m(t) = y(t)e^{rt} \tag{11.71}$$

from which it follows that

$$\dot{m}(t) = rm(t) + \dot{y}(t) e^{rt} \tag{11.72}$$

Under the special circumstances previously mentioned, where $\partial c/\partial S(t) = 0$, the undiscounted royalty will rise at a rate equal to the rate of interest. By keeping a unit of the resource in the ground at time t, the resource owner incurs an opportunity cost in the form of the interest foregone on the net proceeds he would have earned had he exploited this additional unit, but he is compensated for failure to exploit now by the fact that the royalty is rising at a rate equal to the rate of interest. For the more likely case where $\partial c/\partial S(t) < 0$ and hence where $\dot{y}(t)$ is also negative, the undiscounted royalty rises less rapidly than the rate of interest. The rationale for this result is that by failing to extract an additional unit at time t, part of the opportunity cost of the interest foregone on the royalty is offset by the fact that next period extraction costs are now lower than they would otherise have been since the opening stock in that period is higher than it would otherwise have been.

What can we say about the time path of the price of the resource? Returning to equation (11.66) and using equation (11.71) to eliminate $y(t)$, we have

$$p(t) = \frac{\partial c}{\partial x(t)} + m(t) \tag{11.73}$$

In the limiting case where marginal extraction costs are zero (the resource is manna from heaven which can be costlessly collected), then the time paths of the price and the undiscounted royalty are the same, with both rising at a rate equal to the rate of interest. However, with a more plausible cost function in which we not only allow the current rate of extraction and the current stock to be arguments but also allow for changing input prices and technological progress in the extraction process, the time path for both the royalty and the price of the extracted resource will be very complex. The basic model can be further extended by allowing for exploration activity to increase the known stock at time t. This path is not followed here but the interested reader is referred to Fisher (1981) for a discussion of such issues.

In a decentralised, perfectly competitive economy, the aggregate decisions of a set of profit-maximising resource owners would give rise to the same depletion path as that chosen by the planner. What would happen, however, if the resource was controlled by a profit-maximising monopolist? The maximand now becomes

$$\int_0^\infty [R(x(t)) - c(x(t), S(t))]e^{-rt} dt \tag{11.74}$$

where $R(x(t))$ is the total revenue function. The constraints of the problem are unchanged.

The Hamiltonian for this problem is

$$H = [R(x(t)) - c(x(t), S(t))]e^{-rt} + y(t)(-x(t)) \tag{11.75}$$

which yields the same Hamiltonian conditions as before, except that we now have

$$\frac{\partial H}{\partial x(t)} = \left[R'(x(t)) - \frac{\partial c}{\partial x(t)}\right]e^{-rt} - y(t) = 0 \tag{11.76}$$

In terms of the undiscounted royalty, the condition now becomes

$$m(t) = R'(x(t)) - \frac{\partial c}{\partial x(t)} \qquad (11.77)$$

Let us consider the extreme case of costless extraction. Under monopoly it is marginal revenue that would rise through time at a rate equal to the rate of interest. What would be happening to price under the circumstances? Remembering that

$$R'(x(t)) = p(t)\left[1 - \frac{1}{ed(t)}\right] \qquad (11.78)$$

where $ed(t)$ is the absolute value of the own price elasticity of demand at time t and which must be greater than unity for an equilibrium to exist under monopoly, it follows that

$$\frac{dp}{dt}\frac{1}{p} \gtreqless \frac{dR'(x)}{dt}\frac{1}{R'(x)} = r \text{ for } \frac{ded}{dt}\frac{1}{ed} \lesseqgtr 0 \qquad (11.79)$$

Hence, if the elasticity of demand is constant through time, both price and marginal revenue will rise at the same rate and the monopolistic and competitive depletion paths would coincide. However, if the elasticity of demand was rising through time, as would be the case with a linear demand schedule, monopoly price would rise less rapidly than marginal revenue and hence less rapidly than price under perfect competition. If price is to rise less rapidly under monopoly than under perfect competition, then its initial value must be higher under the former than under the latter for the resource to be completely depleted over an infinite time horizon in both cases. Hence, in comparing the two depletion paths, monopoly will be a conserving force in the sense that exploitation will proceed less rapidly in the early years than under perfect competition. However, as far as the social optimum is concerned, this will coincide with the perfectly competitive outcome provided that there is equality between the social rate of time preference and the rate at which firms discount their profits. If firms are myopic and insufficiently sensitive to the interests of future generations, then there may be something to be said for the presence of monopoly in nonrenewable resource markets. If the elasticity of demand is falling through time, then price will rise more rapidly under monopoly and exploitation of the resource would be pushed into the present more than under perfect competition.

11.3 DYNAMIC PROGRAMMING

An alternative approach to the solution of dynamic optimisation problems is the method of dynamic programming. This method is particularly well suited to the solution of discrete time problems and we will have more to say on this later in the section. Initially, however, we continue to treat time as a continuous variable.

Given the standard dynamic optimisation problem of equation (11.1) for which the optimal time paths for the control and state variables are, respectively, x_t^* and z_t^*, $t = 0, \ldots, T$, let us subdivide the problem into two parts so that we now have

$$\text{Max} \int_0^s f(t, x, z) dt$$

$$\text{st} \quad \dot{z} = g(t, x, z) \tag{11.80}$$

$$z(0) = z_0$$

$$z(s) = z^*(s)$$

and

$$\text{Max} \int_s^T f(t, x, z) dt$$

$$\text{st} \quad \dot{z} = g(t, x, z) \tag{11.81}$$

$$z(s) = z^*(s)$$

$$z(T) = z_T$$

The terminal constraint for the first part of the problem and the beginning constraint for the second part of the problem are both equal to the optimal value of the state variable at time s for the original problem. Hence it follows that

$$\int_0^T f(t, x^*, z^*) dt = \int_0^s f(t, x^*, z^*) dt + \int_s^T f(t, x^*, z^*) dt \tag{11.82}$$

or, more succinctly,

$$V = V_1 + V_2 \tag{11.83}$$

Given that the value which must be taken by the state variable at time s in the two subproblems is in fact the optimal value taken by the state variable at time s in the original problem, the maximum value of the original problem (V) is just equal to the sum of the maximum values of the two subproblems ($V_1 + V_2$). This follows from Bellman's optimality principle which states:

> An optimal policy has the property that whatever the initial state and initial decisions are, the remaining decisions must constitute an optimal decision with regard to the state resulting from the first decision. (Bellman 1957, p. 83.)

The legitimacy of the above claim is clear. The value of the state variable at time s results from earlier decisions regarding the control variable. However, the decisions to be taken at time s and in the future regarding the control variable, which together determine the future values of the state variable over the remaining time, must be optimal. If such decisions are not optimal for the remaining interval (s, T) there is no way that the whole plan can be optimal.

In order to proceed further, it is convenient to define the maximum value function for the following dynamic optimisation problem:

$$\left. \begin{array}{c} \text{Max} \int_0^T f(t, x, z) dt \\ \text{st} \quad z = g(t, x, z) \\ z(s) = p \\ z(T) = q \end{array} \right\} \quad (11.84)$$

as

$$V[s, p \mid T, q] \quad (11.85)$$

Using this notation, equation (11.82) can be written as

$$V[0, z_0 \mid T, z_T] = V[0, z_0 \mid s, z^*(s)] + V[s, z^*(s) \mid T, z_T] \quad (11.86)$$

Furthermore, Bellman's optimality principle can be utilised in the context of dividing the interval (s, T) into two subintervals $(s, s + ds)$ and $(s + ds, T)$. Hence,

$$V[s, z^*(s) \mid T, z_T] = V[s, z^*(s) \mid s + ds, z^*(s + ds)] + V[s + ds, z^*(s + ds)T, z_T] \quad (11.87)$$

Now since the first term on the right-hand side of equation (11.87) is

$$V[s, z^*(s), \quad s + ds, z^*(s + ds)] = \int_s^{s+ds} f(t, x^*, z^*) dt \quad (11.88)$$

and since we assume that the subinterval $(s, s + ds)$ is very small then

$$\int_s^{s+ds} f(t, x^*, z^*) dt \simeq f(s, x^*(s), z^*(s)) \, ds \quad (11.89)$$

Hence, to a close approximation we have

$$V[s, z^*(s) \mid T, z_T] = f(s, x^*(s), z^*(s)) ds + V[s + ds, z^*(s + ds) \mid T, z_T] \quad (11.90)$$

If we now assume that during the period $(s, s + ds)$, the value chosen for the control variable was x rather than x^*, then the state variable at time $s + ds$ $(z(s + ds))$ would not equal $z^*(s + ds)$. As an approximation we would have instead,

$$z(s + ds) = z^*(s) + g[t, x, z^*(s)] = z^* + dz$$

Hence, we may express equation (11.90) in the following way:

$$V[s, z^*(s) \mid T, z_T] = \max_x \{ f(s, x, z^*(s)) ds + V[s + ds, z^* + dz \mid T, z_T] \}$$

$$(11.91)$$

Equation (11.91) is known as the fundamental recurrence relation of dynamic programming. Such a relation applies in all DP problems and is of crucial significance for the solution of the problem.

Taking a first-order Taylor series expansion of $V[s + ds, z^* + dz \mid T, z_T]$ around $V[s, z^* \mid T, z_T]$, we obtain, after having suppressed the terms T and z_T for reasons of notational simplicity,

$$V[s + ds, z^* + dz] = V[s, z^*] + \frac{\partial V}{\partial s}(s, z^*)ds + \frac{\partial V}{\partial z}(s, z^*)dz$$

$$= V[s, z^*] + \frac{\partial V}{\partial s}(s, z^*)ds + \frac{\partial V}{\partial z}(s, z^*)g(t, x, z^*)ds \quad (11.92)$$

since $dz = g(t, x, z^*)ds$. Substituting equation (11.92) into (11.91) we obtain, after some manipulation, the following differential equation:

$$\frac{\partial V}{\partial s}(s, z^*) + \max_x \left\{ f(t, x, z^*) + \frac{\partial V}{\partial z}(s, z^*)g(t, x, z^*) \right\} = 0 \quad (11.93)$$

This is known as Bellman's equation and its solution gives the maximum value function V. For solving problems in continuous time, DP is a much more difficult technique to utilise than optimal control theory and its use is not recommended. However, for problems in discrete time, the technique comes into its own.

Consider the following problem:

$$\left. \begin{array}{c} \text{Max} \displaystyle\sum_{t=0}^{T} f_t(x_t, z_t) \\[2mm] \text{st } z_{t+1} = g_t(x_t, z_t) \\[2mm] z_0 = \bar{z}_0, \; z_T = \bar{z}_T \end{array} \right\} \quad (11.94)$$

With discrete time, the fundamental recurrence relation takes the following form:

$$V[s, z_s] = \max_{x_s} \{ f_s(x_s, z_s) + V[s+1, z_{s+1}] \} \quad (11.95)$$

The maximum value from s onwards is the maximised sum of the maximum value obtainable from the optimal plan from $s + 1$ onwards and the value of the function at s. Note that we do not seek to maximise $f_s(\ )$ *per se*; we must take into account the implications of choosing a particular value of the control variable, x, in period s for the evolution of the state variable in the subsequent period and hence for the maximum value obtainable from $s + 1$.

Dynamic programming is a powerful tool for the solution not only of discrete time problems but also of any problems involving sequential decision making at discrete stages. The sequential nature of the decision making process can be temporal, spatial or it may be of no significance as to the order in which the decisions are taken. The standard DP problem with the sequential decision making process taking a spatial form is the shortest route problem. An agent seeks to minimise the distance travelled from one town to another. En route, he will pass through a number of junctions or nodes where the road divides. As he reaches each node he must make a decision as to

298   *An introduction to dynamic optimisation*

which one of the set of alternative routes he should take. The optimality principle tells us in this context that at whatever node the agent finds himself the remaining decisions he makes regarding the route to be taken must be optimal in the sense of minimising the distance from this particular node to his destination. An example of the third category of problem in which the order in which the decisions are taken is irrelevant would be a situation where a firm wished to allocate a limited quantity of a good over a number of markets in order to maximise its profits. Depending on the nature of the profits function it may be possible to solve this problem using techniques described earlier in the book. If the profits function is a nonlinear differentiable function of the amounts allocated to each market, it can be solved as a nonlinear programming problem. However, whether or not the profits function is differentiable, such a problem can be treated as a dynamic programming problem with a fundamental recurrence relation lying at the centre of the solution to the problem. The control variable at some stage would be the amount allocated to the particular market under consideration, while the state variable would be the amount remaining to be allocated to those markets not yet considered. In the next section we will solve an example of this kind.

11.4 SOME ECONOMIC APPLICATIONS OF DYNAMIC PROGRAMMING

Consider the following model of an economy. Output during a particular period depends upon the input of capital services during that period, these capital services being assumed to be proportional to the capital stock. Output can be allocated to either consumption or investment purposes. Social welfare in period t depends upon consumption in that period. The planners wish to maximise the present value of social welfare over some finite time horizon T subject to the capital stock being at a particular level in period T. The initial value of the capital stock is known.

In symbols, we have

$$\text{Max} \sum_{t=0}^{T-1} \frac{W(C_t)}{(1+\rho)^t} \qquad (11.96)$$

$$\text{st} \quad Q_t = f(K_t) \qquad (11.97)$$

$$Q_t = C_t + I_t \qquad (11.98)$$

$$K_{t+1} = (1-\delta)K_t + I_t \qquad (11.99)$$

$$K_0 = \bar{K}_0, K_T = \bar{K}_T \qquad (11.100)$$

where $W(\ )$ is the social welfare function, C is consumption, ρ is the rate of time preference, Q is output, $f(\ )$ is the production function, I is gross investment, K is the capital stock and δ the depreciation rate.

The above problem, though highly stylised, can be utilised to provide a clear illustration of the use of the optimality principle of dynamic programming. Whatever the current value of the state variable (in this case the capital stock), the remaining decisions taken regarding the value of the control variable (consumption), and hence the evolution of the state variable, must be optimal. The requirement that the capital stock take a particular value in period T enables us to define the optimal control for period $T-1$ in terms of the capital stock of the same period:

$$C_{T-1} = f(K_{T-1}) + (1-\delta)K_{T-1} - \bar{K}_T \tag{11.101}$$

Given the value of the capital stock in period $T-2$, it is then possible to obtain the value of K_{T-1} which maximises the sum of the social welfare, appropriately discounted, of the remaining two periods. Then, given the value of the capital stock in period $T-3$, it is possible to obtain the value of K_{T-2} which maximises the sum of the discounted social welfare of the remaining three periods, and so on. At each stage of this recursive procedure we obtain a relationship of the form

$$K_{T-i} = f_i(K_{T-i-1}) \quad (i = 1, 2, \ldots, T-1) \tag{11.102}$$

In particular, we will end up with

$$K_1 = f_{T-1}(K_0)$$

but K_0 is the initial value of the state variable, which is known. The optimal path for the capital stock and the associated path for consumption can now be obtained. Naturally, this solution method by backward induction can only be applied to problems with finite time horizons.

Let us obtain the numerical solution to the following problem, in which both the depreciation rate and the rate of time preference are assumed to be zero. The social welfare and production functions take the following forms:

$$W_t = \log_e C_t \tag{11.103}$$

$$Q_t = 0.2 K_t \tag{11.104}$$

The end-point constraints are

$$K_0 = 10\,000 \quad K_3 = 12\,000 \tag{11.105}$$

The planners wish to choose a time path for the capital stock satisfying the end-point constraints which maximises

$$\sum_{t=0}^{2} \log_e C_t \tag{11.106}$$

Given the assumptions we have made we must have

$$C_t = 1.2 K_t - K_{t+1} \tag{11.107}$$

and, more particularly, for the terminal constraint to be satisfied we must have

$$C_2 = 1.2 K_2 - 12\,000 \tag{11.108}$$

Given the installed stock at time 1, the planners must choose the level for the capital stock of period 2 so as to maximise the welfare of society over the remaining two periods. Hence, we have

$$\underset{K_1 \leqslant K_2 \leqslant 12\,000}{\text{Max}} [\log_e(1.2K_1 - K_2) + \log_e(1.2K_2 - 12\,000)] \qquad (11.109)$$

Since we have assumed a zero rate of depreciation and investment is non-negative, the capital stock will be nondecreasing through time. A necessary condition for a maximum of equation (11.109), assuming an interior solution, is that

$$-\frac{1}{1.2K_1 - K_2} + \frac{1.2}{1.2K_2 - 12\,000} = 0 \qquad (11.110)$$

Hence

$$K_2 = 0.6K_1 + 5000 \qquad (11.111)$$

Given the installed stock at time 0, the planners must choose the level for the capital stock of period 1 so as to maximise the welfare of society over the remaining three periods. Hence we have

$$\underset{10\,000 \leqslant K_1}{\text{Max}} [\log_e(12\,000 - K_1) + \log_e(1.2K_1 - K_2) + \log_e(1.2K_2 - 12\,000)] \qquad (11.112)$$

Eliminating K_2 by using equation (11.111), we obtain

$$\underset{10\,000 \leqslant K_1}{\text{Max}} [\log_e(12\,000 - K_1) + \log_e(0.6K_1 - 5000) + \log_e(0.72K_1 - 6000)] \qquad (11.113)$$

Differentiating with respect to K_1 we have the following necessary condition for an interior solution:

$$-\frac{1}{12\,000 - K_1} + \frac{0.6}{0.6K_1 - 5000} + \frac{0.72}{0.72K_1 - 6000} = 0 \qquad (11.114)$$

Solving equation (11.114) for K_1, we find

$$K_1 = 10\,777.777$$

and, from equation (11.111),

$$K_2 = 11\,466.666$$

The values taken by the different variables along the optimal path are tabulated below

Period	Y	C	I	K
0	2000	1222.223	777.777	10 000
1	2155.5554	1466.6664	688.889	10 777.777
2	2293.3332	1759.9992	533.334	11 466.666
3	2400			12 000

The particular numerical example is extremely simple with no allowance made for

Some economic applications of dynamic programming

depreciation of the capital stock and a zero discount factor being assumed. The effect of allowing for a positive rate of time preference would be to increase consumption and reduce investment in the early periods, with the converse applying at the end of the transitional period, as compared to the above case. The higher the rate of time preference, the lower would be the rate of increase of consumption during the adjustment period; at the very high rates of discount, it could even be negative.

We return to the problem of the firm seeking to allocate a limited amount of a good to a number of different markets in order to maximise its profits. Only non-negative integer amounts can be allocated. We make use of the following notation:

1. $V_j(x)$ represents profits when x units are allocated in an optimal fashion to the markets $1, 2, \ldots, j$.
2. $x_j(x)$ represents the amount allocated to market j that yields total profit $V_j(x)$.

The dynamic programming recurrence relation for this particular problem is

$$V_j(x) = \max_{x_j} \, [\Pi_j(x_j) + V_{j-1}(x - x_j)] \quad (j = 1, 2, \ldots, n) \tag{11.115}$$

where $\Pi_j(x_j)$ represents profits from selling x_j units in market j, and $V_{j-1}(x - x_j)$ represents profits when $x - x_j$ units are allocated optimally in the markets $1, 2, \ldots, j-1$. Obviously, if there are no fixed costs or costs of disposal, $V_0(x) = 0$. The firm has five units of the good to allocate across three markets. The data for the problem are contained in the following table:

	Profitability		
Units sold	Market 1	Market 2	Market 3
0	0	0	0
1	9	12	13
2	16	21	23
3	21	28	31
4	24	33	37
5	25	36	42

The order in which the markets are considered is irrelevant. We shall start with market 1. It is a straightforward matter to obtain $V_1(x)$ and $x_1(x)$; at the first stage, $x_1(x) = x$.

$V_1(x)$	$x_1(x)$
0	0
9	1
16	2
21	3
24	4
25	5

In order to derive $V_2(x)$, construct a profitability matrix Π_2 whose elements – the π_{ij}s –

refer to total profit obtainable when i units are allocated to the first market and j units to the second market, where $i, j = 0, 1, \ldots, 5$ and $i + j \leqslant 5$. From this profitability matrix, $V_2(x)$ is easily obtained, since $V_2(x) = \underset{i+j=x}{\text{Max}} \pi_{ij}$.

Since

$$\Pi_2 = \begin{bmatrix} 0 & 12 & 21 & 28 & 33 & 36 \\ 9 & 21 & 30 & 37 & 42 \\ 16 & 28 & 37 & 44 \\ 21 & 33 & 42 \\ 24 & 36 \\ 25 \end{bmatrix}$$

we have

x	$V_2(x)$	$x_2(x)$
0	0	0
1	12	1
2	21	1 or 2
3	30	2
4	37	2 or 3
5	44	3

Then $V_3(x)$ is obtained in a similar way from the profitability matrix Π_3 whose elements in this case refer to the total profit obtainable when i units are allocated optimally between the first two markets and j units to the third market. Since

$$\Pi_3 = \begin{bmatrix} 0 & 13 & 23 & 31 & 37 & 42 \\ 12 & 25 & 35 & 43 & 49 \\ 21 & 34 & 44 & 52 \\ 30 & 43 & 53 \\ 37 & 50 \\ 44 \end{bmatrix}$$

we have

x	$V_3(x)$	$x_3(x)$
0	0	0
1	13	1
2	25	1
3	35	2
4	44	2
5	53	2

Some economic applications of dynamic programming 303

From the above, we see that $V_3(5) = 53$ and $x_3(5) = 2$. Hence, total profits are 53, with two units being allocated to the third market. The remaining three units must now be optimally allocated between the first two markets. We see from the above that the values taken by $V_2(3)$ and $x_2(3)$ are 30 and 2 respectively. Hence, two units are also allocated to the second market with the remaining unit allocated to the first market.

Our discussion of dynamic optimisation techniques has been of a brief, introductory nature. For the reader interested in developing his knowledge further, a firstclass treatment of optimal control theory is provided by Kamien and Schwartz (1981), while for an excellent discussion of the theory from the perspective of an economist, the reader is referred to an important paper by Dorfman (1969). Beckmann (1968) provides a useful discussion of many economic applications of dynamic programming, while an extensive analysis of the techniques of dynamic programming is to be found in Bellman (1957), Bellman and Dreyfus (1962) and Larson and Casti (1982).

Exercises

1. Use the model and data given in Section (11.2) to show how the optimal consumption path would change if:
   (a) the agent were endowed with an initial nonhuman wealth of 50 000;
   (b) the agent wished to leave a bequest of 20 000;
   (c) the rate of interest were to fall from 0.05 to 0.03.

2. The demand for a nonrenewable resource at time t is given by

$$x(t) = 100 p(t)^{-1}$$

   The initial known stock of the resource is 500 and there are zero costs of extraction; the market rate of interest, assumed equal to the social rate of time preference, is 0.05.
   (a) Show that if the resource is to be optimally depleted over an infinite time horizon the resource royalty and the price must be both equal to 4 at time $t = 0$.
   (b) Derive a general expression for the present value of the royalty if the resource is to be optimally depleted over T years.
   (c) What is the optimal price at time $t = 0$ if the resource is to be optimally depleted over a twenty year period?
   (d) What will be the present value of the royalty if the marginal extraction cost is unity and the resource is to be optimally depleted over an infinite time horizon?

3. In question 2 we dealt with a continuous time model, now consider a discrete two period depletion model. The demand for a nonrenewable resource is invariant between the two periods and is given by

$$q_t = 1000 - p_t \quad (t = 1, 2)$$

The unit cost of extraction is constant and equal to 100. The known initial stock of

the resource is 500. The market rate of interest, assumed equal to the social rate of time preference, is equal to 10 per cent:
  (a) Derive the optimal depletion path of the resource. What are the equilibrium prices and resource royalties in the two periods?
  (b) How would the amounts extracted and the prices charged in the two periods change if the resource were under the control of a profit-maximising monopolist?
  (c) What would be the effect on the optimal depletion path and the prices charged in the two periods of:
    (i) a fall in the rate of interest to 5%?
    (ii) an expected increase in the demand for the resource in the second period such that $q_2 = 1200 - p_2$?
    (iii) the announcement at the beginning of the first period of the discovery of new reserves of 50 available to be extracted at the same constant unit cost in the second period?
  (d) How large an increase in the initial stock of the resource can occur before the royalty will fall to zero?
  (e) Now assume that extraction costs are an increasing function of cumulative output extracted: the total costs of extracting q_1 units of output in period 1 are $\int_0^{q_1} 0.5q\,dq$ and the total costs of extracting q_2 units of output in period 2, given that q_1 units have already been extracted in period 1 are $\int_{q_1}^{q_2} 0.5q\,dq$. Derive the optimal depletion path.

4. On the following diagram are depicted routes for travelling from London (labelled 0) to Edinburgh (labelled 12). The cost associated with each subsection of a route is given on the line joining the respective pair of nodes:

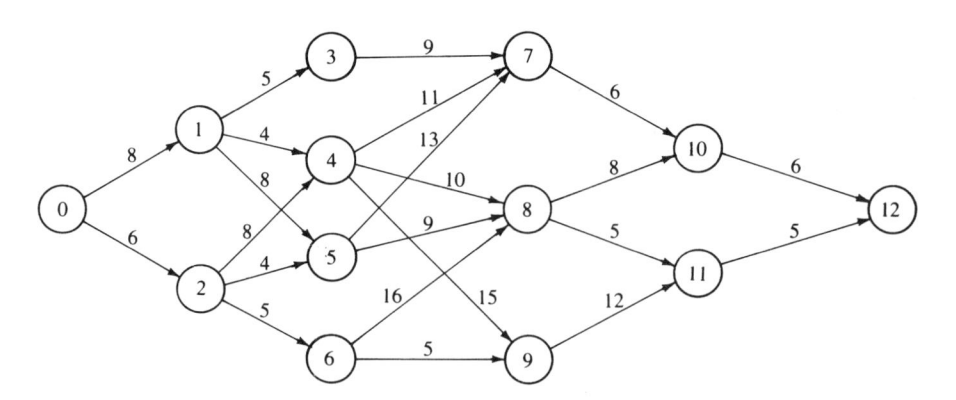

  (a) Find the cheapest route from London to Edinburgh.
  (b) Find the cheapest route from London to Edinburgh that passes through node 4.
  (c) Find the cheapest route from London to Edinburgh that passes through nodes 2 and 7.
  (d) Find the most expensive route from London to Edinburgh.

References

Beckmann, M. (1968), *Dynamic Programming of Economic Decisions*, Berlin: Springer-Verlag.
Bellman, R (1957), *Dynamic Programming*, Princeton, NJ: Princeton University Press.
Bellman, R. and Dreyfus, S. (1962), *Applied Dynamic Programming*, Princeton, NJ: Princeton University Press.
Dixit, A.K. (1976), *Optimization in Economic Theory*, Oxford: Oxford University Press.
Dorfman, R. (1969), 'An economic interpretation of optimal control theory', *American Economic Review*, **LIX**, (5), 817–31.
Fisher, A.C. (1981), *Resource and Environmental Economics*, Cambridge: Cambridge University Press.
Hadley, G. and Kemp, M.C. (1971), *Variational Methods in Economics*, New York: North-Holland.
Intriligator, M.D. (1971), *Mathematical Optimization and Economic Theory*, Englewood Cliffs, NJ: Prentice-Hall.
Kamien, M.I. and Schwartz, N.L., (1981), *Dynamic Optimization: the calculus of variations and optimal control in economics and management*, New York: North Holland.
Larson, R.E. and Casti, J.L. (1982), *Principles of Dynamic Programming*, New York: Dekker.
Pontryagin, L.S., Bol'tanskii, V.G., Gamkrelidze, R.V. and Mishchenko, E.F. (1962) *The Mathematical Theory of Optimal Processes*, trans. by K.N. Trirogoff, New York: Wiley.

Appendix 1:
SUMMARY OF MATRIX ALGEBRA

The purpose of this mathematical appendix is to provide a summary of the main results of matrix algebra. There are a number of excellent texts available on matrix algebra and readers who are interested in proofs of propositions are referred to: Hadley (1961), *Linear Algebra*, and Gantmacher (1959), *Theory of Matrices*.

DEFINITION OF A MATRIX AND OPERATIONS

1. A $m \times n$ matrix is a rectangular array of mn real numbers arranged in m rows and n columns:

$$A = \begin{bmatrix} a_{11} & a_{12} & \ldots & a_{1n} \\ a_{21} & a_{22} & & a_{2n} \\ \vdots & & & \\ a_{m1} & a_{m2} & & a_{mn} \end{bmatrix}$$

2. A matrix of dimension $m \times 1$ is a column vector while a matrix of dimension $1 \times m$ is called a row vector:

$$a = \begin{bmatrix} a_{11} \\ \vdots \\ a_{1m} \end{bmatrix} \qquad a' = [a_{11} \ldots a_{1m}]$$

3. Two matrices are equivalent if they are equal element-by-element. $A = B$ if and only if $a_{ij} = b_{ij}$.

4. To add two matrices, add their corresponding elements. Thus $C = A + B$ if and only if $c_{ij} = a_{ij} + b_{ij}$ $(i = 1, \ldots, m, j = 1, \ldots, n)$.

5. To multiply a matrix by a scalar, multiply each element of the matrix by a scalar:

$$B = cA, \text{ i.e. } b_{ij} = ca_{ij} \text{ where } c \text{ is a scalar}$$

6. Additions of two matrices are: $A + B = B + A$.

7. For two matrices to be conformable for multiplication such that the matrix $C = AB$ is defined, then A must have as many columns as B has rows. If A is of dimension $m \times n$ and B of dimension $n \times p$, then C is defined and is of dimension $m \times p$, with a typical element of the C matrix being given by

$$c_{ij} = a_{i1}b_{1j} + a_{i2}b_{2j} + \ldots + a_{in}b_{nj} = \sum_{k=1}^{n} a_{ik}b_{kj}$$

Note that BA will only be defined if $p = m$, in which case $D = BA$ will be of dimension $n \times m$.

8. (a) $(AB)(C) = A(BC)$;
   (b) $A(B + C) = AB + AC$;
   (c) $BA \neq AB$.

9. The transpose of a matrix, denoted by a prime, is the matrix obtained by interchanging the rows and columns. Thus the transpose of the $m \times n$ matrix A is

$$A' = \begin{bmatrix} a_{11} & a_{21} \ldots & a_{m1} \\ a_{1n} & a_{2n} & a_{mn} \end{bmatrix}$$

10. (a) $(A')' = A$;
    (b) $(A + B)' = A' + B'$;
    (c) $(AB)' = B'A'$.

11. A matrix is called a square matrix if it has as many rows as it has columns, i.e. if $m = n$. The diagonal of a square matrix ($n \times n$) of A consists of $a_{11}, \ldots, a_{nn}$.

12. The trace of a square matrix is the sum of its diagonal elements:

$$\text{tr}(A) = a_{11} + \ldots + a_{nn} = \sum_{i=1}^{n} a_{ii}$$

$$\text{tr}(A + B) = \text{tr}(A) + \text{tr}(B)$$

$$\text{tr}(A') = \text{tr}(A)$$

$$\text{tr}(cA) = c\,\text{tr}(A)$$

$$\text{tr}(AB) = \text{tr}(BA)$$

13. If A is a square matrix and $A = A'$, then A is symmetric.

14. A square matrix whose diagonal elements are all 1 and off-diagonal elements are zero is called the identity matrix and is written I:

$$I = \begin{bmatrix} 1 & 0 \ldots & 0 \\ 0 & 1 & 0 \\ \vdots & & \\ 0 & 0 & 1 \end{bmatrix}$$

15. Partitioned matrix: it is often convenient to partition a matrix into submatrices. An $m \times n$ matrix may be partitioned as

$$A = (A_1 | A_2) \text{ where } A_1 \text{ is } m \times n_1, A_2 \text{ is } m \times n_2 \text{ and } n_1 + n_2 = n$$

(a) $A' = (A_1 | A_2)' = (A_1'/A_2')$;
(b) Let B be partitioned as (B_1/B_2) where B_1 is $n_1 \times p$ and B_2 is $n_2 \times p$. Then

$$C = AB = (A_1 | A_2) \begin{pmatrix} B_1 \\ B_2 \end{pmatrix} = (A_1 B_1 + A_2 B_2).$$

16. The inverse of a square matrix $(n \times n)$ written as A^{-1} has the property that $AA^{-1} = A^{-1}A = I$:
(a) $(AB)^{-1} = B^{-1}A^{-1}$;
(b) $(ABC)^{-1} = C^{-1}B^{-1}A^{-1}$.

DETERMINANTS

17. For every square matrix, there exists a number (scalar) known as the determinant of the matrix denoted by the symbol $|A|$. A matrix has no numerical value but the determinant of a matrix is a number.

A 2×2 determinant is evaluated by cross-multiplying the elements on the main diagonal and subtracting from it the cross multiplication of the elements of the other diagonal of the matrix A:

$$|A| = \begin{vmatrix} a_{11} & a_{12} \\ a_{21} & a_{22} \end{vmatrix} = a_{11}a_{22} - a_{12}a_{21}$$

Properties of determinants

(a) A matrix whose determinant is zero is called a singular matrix.
(b) If all elements of any row of A are zero, its determinant is zero.
(c) $|A'| = |A|$, i.e. the determinant of A and A transpose are the same.
(d) Interchanging any two rows or any two columns of a matrix A changes the sign of A.
(e) If every element of a row or a column of A is multiplied by a scalar λ, then A is multiplied by λ.
(f) If two rows or two columns of a matrix are identical, its determinant is zero.
(g) If one row or a column of a matrix is a multiple of another row or column of that matrix, its determinant is zero.
(h) $|AB| = |A| |B|$, i.e. the determinant of the product of two matrices is the product of their individual determinants.

18. The rank of a matrix is the order of the largest square submatrix whose determinant is nonzero.

19. The rank of the product of two matrices is

$$\rho(AB) \leq \text{Min}\,[\rho(A), \rho(B)]$$

The rank of the product AB cannot exceed the smaller of the ranks A, B. Also, if A and C are nonsingular matrices, then

$$\rho(AB) = \rho(BC) = \rho(B)$$

20. If $a' = [a_1, \ldots, a_n]$ is a row vector of numbers and

$$x = \begin{bmatrix} x_1 \\ \vdots \\ x_n \end{bmatrix}$$

is a column vector of the variables $x_1, x_2, \ldots, x_n$, then

$$\frac{\partial a'x}{\partial x} = \underset{\sim}{a} = \begin{bmatrix} a_1 \\ a_2 \\ \vdots \\ a_n \end{bmatrix}$$

21. Consider the matrix $x'Ax$ such that

$$x'Ax = [x_1, \ldots, x_n] \begin{bmatrix} a_{11} & a_{12} & \cdots & a_{1n} \\ a_{21} & a_{22} & & a_{2n} \\ \vdots & & & \\ a_{n1} & a_{n2} & & a_{nn} \end{bmatrix} \begin{bmatrix} x_1 \\ x_2 \\ \vdots \\ x_n \end{bmatrix}$$

then $\partial x'Ax/\partial x = 2Ax$ which is a column vector of n elements or

$$\frac{\partial x'Ax}{\partial x} = 2x'A$$

which is a row vector of n elements.

CHARACTERISTIC ROOTS AND VECTORS

22. The characteristic value problem is defined as that of finding values of a scalar λ and an associated vector $x \neq 0$ which satisfy $Ax = \lambda x$ where A is a given $n \times n$ matrix, λ is called a characteristic root of A, and x is a characteristic vector. In matrix form:

$$(A - \lambda I)x = 0$$

There will be a solution $x \neq 0$ only if $A - \lambda I$ is singular, i.e. $|A - \lambda I| = 0$:
  (a) For any symmetric matrix, all characteristic roots are real.

(b) All characteristic vectors of a symmetric matrix are orthogonal.
(c) Two vectors are said to be orthogonal if $x'y = y'x = 0$.
(d) If a characteristic root has multiplicty k (i.e. repeated k times) there will be exactly k orthogonal characteristic vectors corresponding to this root.
(e) Orthogonal vectors of a symmetric matrix, when normalised, yield a set of orthonormal vectors. A matrix is orthogonal if its transpose is equivalent to its inverse, i.e. $Q' = Q^{-1}$.
(f) A matrix can be diagonalised by using an orthogonal matrix: $Q'AQ = D$ where D is a diagonal matrix of characteristic roots of A.
(g) If x is a characteristic vector of the symmetric matrix A, corresponding to root λ, so is $-x$.
(h) If A is non-singular, the characteristic roots of A^{-1} are the reciprocals of those of A and the characteristic vectors are the same as those of A.
(i) The characteristic roots of a positive definite (semidefinite) matrix are all positive (non-negative).
(j) The number of nonzero roots of a symmetric matrix is equal to the rank of A. This, however, does not always hold true for nonsymmetric square matrices.
(k) If all roots of a symmetric matrix are positive (non-negative) the diagonal elements of this matrix are all positive (non-negative). But if this matrix is nonsymmetric, we can have negative diagonal elements despite positive roots.
(l) The roots of AA' and $A'A$ are equal except for an additional set of zero roots of the matrix of larger order.
(m) If $x_1, x_2, \ldots, x_n$ are characteristic vectors of AA' corresponding to the roots $\lambda_1 \lambda_2, \ldots, \lambda_n$, and if these vectors are pairwise orthogonal and have unit length, then corresponding characteristic vectors $A'x_1, A'x_2, \ldots,$ of $A'A$ are orthogonal but they do not have unit length unless the corresponding root is equal to 1.

IDEMPOTENT MATRIX

23. (a) If $A = A^{-1}$ and $A^2 = A$, the matrix is a symmetric idempotent matrix.
(b) Characteristic roots of such a matrix are either zero or one.
(c) When an idempotent matrix of order n and rank $n - k$ is diagonalised, there will be $n - k$ units in the principal diagonal and k zeros.

QUADRATIC FORMS

24. A quadratic form is defined as a square matrix postmultiplied by a column vector and premultiplied by the transpose of that vector:

$$x'Ax = \sum_{i=1}^{n} \sum_{j=1}^{n} a_{ij} x_i x_j$$

Some quadratic forms are always positive for any vector $x \neq 0$. Let us define a nonsingular transformation

(a) $x = Qy$ where Q is an orthogonal matrix. Then it follows that

$$x'Ax = y'Q'AQy$$

The right-hand side of the above expression is a quadratic form in y and the matrix $Q'AQ$ is a diagonal matrix containing the characteristic roots of A along its principal diagonal. Hence

$$x'Ax = \lambda_1 y_1^2 + \ldots + \lambda_n y_n^2$$

(b) The quadratic form $x'Ax$ and associated symmetric matrix are said to be positive definite if $x'Ax > 0$ holds for any $x \neq 0$ and they are called positive semidefinite if $x'Ax > 0$ holds for any x. We also have negative definite, negative semidefinite and indefinite matrices and quadratic forms:
  (i) $x'Ax < 0$ for any $x \neq 0$, negative definite;
  (ii) $x'Ax \leqslant 0$ for any x without restriction, negative semidefinite; and
  (iii) $x'Ax < 0$ and $y'Ay > 0$ for two obviously different vectors x and y (indefinite matrix).

(c) If x and y are related by $x = Py$, the quadratic form $x'Ax$ is identical with a quadratic form in y with $P'AP$ as matrix.

(d) If A is a positive definite matrix, then it is non-singular.

(e) If P is a nonsingular matrix and A is positive definite, then $P'AP$ is positive definite.

(f) A necessary and sufficient condition for A to be positive definite is

$$a_{11} > 0 \quad \begin{vmatrix} a_{11} & a_{12} \\ a_{21} & a_{22} \end{vmatrix} > 0 \ldots \begin{vmatrix} a_{11} & a_{12} & \ldots & a_{1n} \\ a_{21} & a_{22} & & a_{2n} \\ a_{n1} & a_{n2} & & a_{nn} \end{vmatrix} > 0$$

(g) If A is a $m \times n$ matrix of rank $m < n$, then AA' is positive definite and $A'A$ is positive semidefinite but not positive definite.

(h) If A is an $m \times n$ matrix of rank r and if $r < m$ and $r < n$, then AA' and $A'A$ are both positive semidefinite and neither is positive definite.

SEMIPOSITIVE MATRIX

25. An important property of semipositive vectors is that the product of a semipositive vector and a positive vector is always positive. A matrix is semipositive if all its rows are semipositive vectors and all its columns are semipositive vectors:

  (a) A square matrix A of order $n \times n$ has a dominant diagonal if there exist n positive numbers d_j such that

$$d_j|a_{jj}| > \sum_{i \neq j} d_i|a_{ij}| \quad (j=1,\ldots,n)$$

This is more general than the usual definition of a dominant diagonal in which the absolute value of every diagonal element exceeds the simple sum of the absolute values of the off-diagonal elements in the same column (or row).

(b) The square matrix is said to be decomposable if it can be reduced to

$$\begin{bmatrix} A_{11} & A_{12} \\ 0 & A_{22} \end{bmatrix}$$

where A_{11} and A_{22} are square but not necessarily of the same order. The square matrix A which can be decomposed finally into a form

$$A = \begin{bmatrix} A_{11} & 0 & 0 \\ & \ddots & \\ 0 & 0 & A_{kk} \end{bmatrix}$$

in which $A_{11}, \ldots, A_{kk}$ are square and indecomposable, not necessarily of the same order, is called a completely decomposable matrix.

(c) If A is a semipositive matrix, it has among its characteristic roots, one particular root λ^*, with an associated characteristic vector x^*, such that
  (i) λ^* is real and non-negative
  (ii) No other characteristic root has a modulus exceeding λ^*.
  (iii) x^* is a non-negative vector
  (iv) For all $\mu > \lambda^*$, $\mu I - A$ is nonsingular and $(\mu I - A)^{-1}$ is a semipositive matrix.

If A is indecomposable, the following will apply:
  (v) λ^* is positive and is not a repeated root.
  (vi) x^* is a strictly positive vector.
  (vii) $(\mu I - A)^{-1}$ is a strictly positive matrix.
  (viii) If A is a strictly positive matrix, λ^* exceeds the modulus of every other root.

Other results are summarised in Lancaster (1968), *Mathematical Economics*.

CONVEX AND CONCAVE FUNCTIONS

26. (a) A function is said to be convex if for any two points x^1, x^2 belonging to the set

$$f[\lambda x^1 + (1-\lambda)x^2] \leq \lambda f(x^1) + (1-\lambda)f(x^2) \quad (0 \leq \lambda \leq 1)$$

It is strictly convex if the strict equality holds for all λ, such that $0 < \lambda < 1$ and $x^1 \neq x^2$.

(b) A function $f(x)$ is concave or strictly concave if $[-f(x)]$ is convex or strictly convex. Explicitly,

$$f[\lambda x^1 + (1-\lambda)x^2] \geq \lambda f(x^1) + (1-\lambda)f(x^2) \quad (0 \leq \lambda \leq 1)$$

and strict inequality for strictly concave functions.

(c) A linear function is both convex and concave, but not strictly convex or concave.

(d) The sum of convex functions is convex and the sum of concave functions is concave.

(e) If $f(x)$ is convex, the set $V = \{x \mid f(x) \leq f(x^*)\}$ is convex. If $f(x)$ is concave, the set $V = \{x \mid f(x) \geq f(x^*)\}$ is convex where x^* is any point in the set S.

(f) If $f(x)$ is convex (concave), the second-order partial derivative matrix (Hessian) is positive (negative) semidefinite. If $f(x)$ is strictly convex (concave), its Hessian is positive (negative) definite.

(g) If a convex (concave) function has a critical point, it has a minimum (maximum) at that point.

References

Gantmacher, F.R. (1959), *Theory of Matrices*, 2 vols, New York: Chelsea.
Hadley, G. (1961), *Linear Algebra*, Reading, Mass.: Addison Wesley.
Lancaster, K.J. (1968), *Mathematical Economics*, pp. 310–11, New York: Macmillan & Co.

Appendix 2:
STATISTICAL RESULTS

In this appendix we present a number of important statistical results. Proofs, however, are avoided; the reader who is interested in the derivation of the results should consult a good intermediate text on statistics such as Mood and Graybill (1963).

ADDITION AND MULTIPLICATION THEOREMS OF PROBABILITY

Mutually exclusive events

Two events are defined to be mutually exclusive if the occurrence of one of these events prevents the occurrence of the other.

Independent events

Two events are defined to be indepedent if the occurrence or nonoccurrence of one of these events has no effect on the probability of the occurrence of the other event. This concept of independence can be generalised to more than two events. Two events which are independent cannot be mutually exclusive. The condition for two events to be mutually exclusive can be expressed in terms of the two sets being nonintersecting, while for independent events with nonzero probability, the sets must intersect.

Addition theorem of probability

For mutually exclusive events, the probability of observing either A or B is the sum of their respective probabilities:

$$P(A \text{ or } B) = P(A) + P(B)$$

For nonmutually exclusive events, however, the probability of observing either A or B is the sum of their respective probabilities minus the probability of observing both A and B:

$$P(A \text{ or } B) = P(A) + P(B) - P(A \text{ and } B)$$

Multiplication theorem of probability

For independent events, the probability of observing both A and B is the product of their respective probabilities

$$P(A \text{ and } B) = P(A) P(B)$$

For nonindependent events, however, the probability of observing both A and B is given by the product of the probability of $A(B)$ and the probability of observing $B(A)$ given that $A(B)$ has occurred. In symbols, we have

$$P(A \text{ and } B) = P(A) P(B/A) = P(B) P(A/B)$$

Concept of random variable and expectation

A random variable is one which has a probability distribution. The expected value of a random variable X is defined by

$$E(X) = \sum_{i=1}^{N} X_i P(X_i)$$

This is the weighted average of X_i where the weights are the respective probabilities. The variance of X is a measure of dispersion of a random variable and is defined by

$$\text{Var } X = \left[\sum_{i=1}^{n} [X_i - E(X)]^2 P(X_i) \right]$$

or

$$\text{Var } X = E[(X - \mu)]^2$$

Probability density of a random variable (for a continuous variable) is defined as the probability that X lies in the range divided by the width of the range:

$$= \left[\lim_{h \to 0} \frac{P[X_0 \leqslant X \leqslant X_{0+h}]}{h} = f(X_0) \right]$$

If we know the probability density function of a random variable, then we have all the information we need in order to make probability statements about it since probabilities are given by the area under the function.

For a continuous random variable $E(X) = \int_R X f(X) dX$ and $\text{Var}(X) = \int_R [X - E(X)]^2 f(X) dX$ where $f(X)$ is the probability density function of a random variable X; R is the range over which expectation is to be determined. Also $\int_R f(X) dX$ is the area under the density function over the range, R, of random variable X. This area is the probability that the random variable X lies between X and $X + \Delta X$ (which is the range).

Appendix 2
NORMAL DISTRIBUTION AND CONFIDENCE INTERVAL

For a continuous random variable X in the range $-\infty < X < \infty$ the distribution function (of a normal variable) is given by

$$f(X) = \frac{1}{\sqrt{(2\pi)}\sigma} \exp\left[-\frac{1}{2}\left(\frac{X-\mu}{\sigma}\right)^2\right] dX$$

It is a bell-shaped continuous distribution with asymptote not touching the x-axis; the term dX indicates that we are not considering the value of $f(X)$ at one point but in some range dX around the point; $E(X) = \mu$, and variance $E[(X - \mu)]^2 = \sigma^2$; μ and σ^2 are the parameters of the normal distribution. The probability that X will fall inside some range, say $X_1 \leqslant X \leqslant X_2$ can be evaluated by integrating the function $f(X)$. This is, however, not an easy integral to work with and the possibility of tabulating relevant areas under the curve is made difficult by combinations of μ and σ^2. This problem, however, is avoided using the important properties of the normal distribution that a random variable can be converted into a standard normal variable with mean 0 and standard deviation 1. Areas under the curve for standard normal distribution are tabulated.

Use is made of symmetry in working out such areas. About 68.3 per cent of the area under the normal curve lies within ± 1 standard deviation of the mean while 95.5 per cent of the area lie within ± 2 standard deviations around the mean.

If we are dealing with samples, then there will be a distribution of the sample mean with its standard deviation which is called the standard error. This can be used for making deductive and inductive statements in statistics:

$$\bar{x} \pm 1.96\,\sigma_{\bar{x}} = \bar{x} \pm 1.96\,\frac{\sigma_x}{\sqrt{n}}$$

is a confidence interval statement. If repeated random samples of the same size were drawn from this population and the interval was constructed from each of them, then 95 per cent of the statements that the interval contains the population mean μ would be correct. Alternatively, in 95 samples out of 100 the mean μ, would lie within intervals constructed by this procedure.

SAMPLING AND CENTRAL LIMIT THEOREM

Random sample selection is made, $E(\bar{x}) = \mu$:

$$E[\bar{x} - E(\bar{x})]^2 = \frac{\sigma^2}{n}$$

Sampling from normal population $\bar{x} \sim N(\mu, \sigma^2/n)$. If a random variable X, either discrete or continuous, has a mean μ and a finite standard deviation σ_x, then the probability distribution of $z = (\bar{x} - \mu)/\sigma_{\bar{x}}$ approaches the standard normal distribution as n increases without limit.

RELATIONSHIPS AMONG DISTIRBUTIONS

χ^2 distribution

Let $x_1, \ldots, x_k$ be independent $N(0, 1)$ variables and let $w = \Sigma x_i^2$. Then w has the χ_k^2 distribution, i.e. the sum of squares of k independent standard normal variables has the χ^2 distribution with k degrees of freedom, χ^2 distribution is a one-parameter family of distributions, the parameter k is called the degrees of freedom (d.f.) of the distribution:

$$E(\chi_k^2) = k \text{ and Var } (\chi_k^2) = 2k$$

Properties of the χ^2 distribution

The χ^2 distribution is a skewed distribution, the degree of skewness depending on the d.f. The distribution is highly skewed to the right but as the d.f. increases, the distribution becomes increasingly symmetrical. For d.f. in excess of 100, the distribution of the variable $\sqrt{(2\chi_k^2)} - \sqrt{(2k-1)}$ approximates the standard normal distribution.

t distribution

Let x be distributed $N(0,1)$ and w be distributed χ_k^2 and suppose that x and w are independent. Then $x/\sqrt{(w/k)}$ has the t_k distribution, i.e. the ratio of a standard normal variable to the square root of an independent χ^2 variable divided by its degrees of freedom has the t distribution with those degrees of freedom.

A variable has the t_k distribution or is said to be distributed as t_k; t distribution is symmetric, $E_{t_k} = 0$ and Var $(t_k) = k/(k-2)$ and as $k \to \infty$, the t_k approaches the standard normal distribution $N(0,1)$.

F distribution

Let w_1 be distributed $\chi_{k_1}^2$; let w_2 be distributed $\chi_{k_2}^2$ and suppose that w_1 and w_2 are independent. Then $(w_1/k_1) + (w_2/k_2)$ has the $F_{k_2}^{k_1}$ distribution, i.e. the ratio of two independent χ^2 variables, each divided by the degrees of freedom has the F distribution with those degrees of freedom.

Properties of F distribution

1. F distribution is skewed to the right.
2. The mean value of an F distributed variable is $k_2/k_2 - 2$ which is defined for $k_2 > 2$ and its variance is

$$\frac{2k_2^2(k_1 + k_2 - 2)}{k_1(k_2 - 2)^2(k_2 - 4)} \text{ which is defined for } k_2 > 4$$

3. The square of a t distributed random variable with k degrees of freedom has an F distribution with 1 and k d.f.:

$$t_k^2 = F_{1,k}$$

For large degrees of freedom the t, chi-square and F distributions approach the normal distribution.

TESTS OF HYPOTHESES

We shall discuss the procedure for testing hypotheses regarding population means, noting that the basic procedure is the same for all hypothesis testing. Given the maintained hypothesis regarding the random variable X, for example, X is normally distributed with variance σ^2, we first state the null and alternative hypotheses:

$$H_0: \mu = \mu_0$$
$$H_A: \mu \neq \mu_0$$

The test statistic is the sample mean, $\bar{X}$, based on N observations; under the null hypothesis, the distribution of the test statistic $[(\bar{X} - \mu_0)\sqrt{n}]/\sigma$ is standard normal. We then choose the level of significance for the test and determine the acceptance and rejection regions. If we select the 5 per cent significance level, then we will not reject the null hypothesis if

$$-1.96 \leqslant \frac{(\bar{X} - \mu_0)\sqrt{n}}{\sigma} \leqslant 1.96$$

or, equivalently, if

$$\mu_0 - \frac{1.96\sigma}{\sqrt{n}} \leqslant \bar{X} \leqslant \mu_0 + \frac{1.96\sigma}{\sqrt{n}}$$

Otherwise, we will reject the null hypothesis in favour of the alternative hypothesis.

A sample of n observations on the random variable X is then drawn, the sample mean is obtained and we now consider whether there is a high probability that the observations were drawn from a parent population whose mean is equal to μ_0. Having evaluated whether or not the sample mean lies in the acceptance region, we are then able to conclude whether or not this particular sample provides evidence for or against the null hypothesis.

Using the above two-tail test we will reject the null hypothesis that the population mean is equal to μ_0 if the sample mean lies either below the lower limit or above the upper limit. Both these events are equiprobable, with probability equal to $\alpha/2$, where α is the level of significance for the test. In certain circumstances, however, a more appropriate alternative hypothesis might be

$$H_A: \mu > \mu_0$$

In this case, the investigator should perform a one-tail test, rejecting the null hypothesis in favour of the alternative if $\bar{X}$ is so much greater than μ_0 that the probability of observing a value at least as large as $\bar{X}$ if the null hypothesis were true is α. If the chosen level of significance for the test is 5 per cent, then one would reject H_0 if

$$\frac{(\bar{X} - \mu_0)\sqrt{n}}{\sigma} > 1.645$$

or alternatively, if

$$\bar{X} > \mu_0 + 1.645 \frac{\sigma}{\sqrt{n}}$$

Otherwise, one would not reject the null hypothesis.

In the testing of statistical hypotheses, cognisance must be taken of the possibility of erroneous inferences being drawn from the sample data. The errors which may be made take two forms: rejection of the null hypothesis when it is in fact true (type I error) and non-rejection of the null hypothesis when it is in fact false (type II error). The probability of the occurrence of type I error is simply the level of significance of the test, α. Assume this level is set at 5 per cent; if the null hypothesis is in fact true, on average the sample means will lie outside the acceptance region on five occasions in any 100 replications of the test and, on these occasions, the testing procedure will lead the investigator to reject the null hypothesis. The probability of committing type I error can be reduced by changing the significance level of the test from, say 5 per cent to 1 per cent. Now, if the null hypothesis is in fact true, on average in only one case in 100 will this error occur.

While the probability of committing type I error is known, this is not generally the case for type II error. We may assign a probability of β to not rejecting the null hypothesis when it is false and, correspondingly, a probability of $1 - \beta$ to rejecting the null hypothesis when it is false, this latter measure being the power of the test to discriminate between the null and alternative hypotheses. In the context of testing hypotheses regarding population means, the precise numerical value of β will depend, *inter alia*, upon the values postulated for the population mean under the null and alternative hypotheses. In addition, there exists a trade-off between the two types of error. By widening the region for acceptance of the null hypothesis, the probability of committing type I error is reduced, but at the cost of increasing the probability of not rejecting the null hypothesis if it is in fact false. The investigator does, however, have some control over the terms on which the two types of error are traded off against each other; for example, employing a two-tail test in circumstances where a one-tail test is appropriate will lead to a higher probability of type II error occurring for a given incidence of type I error.

Since the probabilities of making the two kinds of error are never zero, it is never possible to prove or disprove a hypothesis with certainty. At most, the investigator may claim that on the balance of the probabilities the null hypothesis is not rejected or that the null hypothesis is rejected in favour of the alternative hypothesis.

Appendix 2
ESTIMATORS AND THEIR PROPERTIES

Consider a random variable X whose distribution is characterised by some parameter θ. From sample observations on X, we seek to estimate θ. Let $\hat{\theta}$ represent the estimator of θ; this estimator is obtained by substituting the sample observation on X into a formula and hence we have

$$\hat{\theta} = \hat{\theta}(x_1, x_2, \ldots, x_n)$$

Regarding the distribution of $\hat{\theta}$, its mean is given by $E(\hat{\theta})$ and its variance by

$$\text{Var}(\hat{\theta}) = E[\hat{\theta} - E(\hat{\theta})]^2 = E(\hat{\theta}^2) - [E(\hat{\theta})]^2$$

The standard deviation of $\hat{\theta}$ is defined as the square root of the variance and is also known as the standard error of $\hat{\theta}$.

We may define the following important concepts: sampling error, bias and mean square error. Sampling error is the difference between the value of the estimator and the true value of the parameter we are estimating:

$$\text{Sampling error} = \hat{\theta} - \theta$$

Bias is the difference between the mean of the sampling distribution of a given parameter and the true value of the parameter:

$$\text{Bias} = E(\hat{\theta}) - \theta$$

Mean square error is a measure of the dispersion around the true value of the parameter and is given by

$$\text{Mean square error} = E(\hat{\theta} - \theta)^2$$
$$= E[\hat{\theta} - E(\hat{\theta})]^2 + [E(\hat{\theta}) - \theta]^2$$
$$= \text{variance} + \text{square bias}$$

Regarding the properties of estimators, we need to distinguish between small-sample and asymptotic or large-sample properties. Finite-sample or small-sample properties refer to the properties of the sampling distribution based on any fixed sample size, while the latter refer to the properties of the sampling distribution as the number of observations in the sample approaches infinity.

Small sample properties

A most desirable property for any sample estimator to possess is that of unbiasedness, which we define in the following way:

$$\hat{\theta} \text{ is an unbiased estimator of } \theta \text{ if } E(\hat{\theta}) = \theta$$

An estimator that is unbiased but has a large variance, however, is not very useful since many estimates of the parameter will diverge quite markedly from its true value. Even more serious problems will arise with an estimator which is biased and the direction of the bias is unknown even though it might have a low variance. Ideally, we would like an estimator which is unbiased and which has a lower variance than any other unbiased estimator: such an estimator is called a minimum variance unbiased estimator or best unbiased estimator or an efficient estimator.

In comparing two unbiased estimators we can use the concept of relative efficiency, i.e. the estimator which has the smaller variance is declared to be an efficient estimator. In some circumstances, however, we need not concern ourselves with relative efficiency and are able to make statements about absolute efficiency. This results from the fact that the Cramer-Rao inequality provides a lower bound to the variance of any unbiased estimator, θ_i, as long as the distribution of the random variable is known. This lower bound for the variance of θ_i is provided by the element in the ith row and ith column of the inverse of the information matrix, where the information matrix is the negative of the matrix made up of the expected second-order partial derivatives of the log-likelihood function for the particular sample with respect to the population parameters, $\theta_1, \theta_2, \ldots, \theta_k$. One should note, however, that it will not always be the case that the variance of an unbiased estimator will actually reach this lower bound. For a detailed discussion of these results, the reader is referred to Rao (1973).

A more straightforward case arises if the analysis is limited to estimators that are linear functions of the sample observations. There are three conditions which must be satisfied for $\hat{\theta}$ to be a best linear unbiased estimator (BLUE) of θ: (i) $\hat{\theta}$ is a linear function of the sample observations; (ii) $\hat{\theta}$ is unbiased; and (iii) Var ($\hat{\theta}$) is smaller than the variance of any other linear unbiased estimator of θ.

ASYMPTOTIC PROPERTIES

According to the central limit theorem, as the sample size increases, the distribution of the sample mean approaches the normal distribution. The normal distribution is the asymptotic or limiting distribution of the sample mean. Asymptotic distributions can be described by their moments.

The asymptotic mean is defined as

$$\lim_{n \to \infty} E(\hat{\theta})$$

The formula for the asymptotic variance is given by

$$\text{Asympt. Var } (\hat{\theta}) = \frac{1}{n} \lim_{n \to \infty} E[n^{\frac{1}{2}}(\hat{\theta} - \theta)]^2$$

An alternative and more convenient specification is defined in terms of $n^{\frac{1}{2}}(\hat{\theta} - \theta)$

$$\text{Asympt. Var } [n^{\frac{1}{2}}(\hat{\theta} - \theta)] = \lim_{n \to \infty} E[n^{\frac{1}{2}}(\hat{\theta} - \theta)]^2$$

In dealing with the desirable asymptotic properties of an estimator, we shall consider asymptotic unbiasedness, consistency and asymptotic efficiency:

(a) $\hat{\theta}$ is an asymptotically unbiased estimator of θ if $\lim_{n \to \infty} E(\hat{\theta}) = \theta$. An estimator could be asymptotically unbiased without being consistent.
(b) $\hat{\theta}$ is a consistent estimator of θ if plim $\hat{\theta} = \theta$, where plim (or probability limit) is the point on which the distribution collapses as $n \to \infty$.
(c) If $\hat{\theta}$ is an estimator of θ and if $\lim_{n \to \infty} MSE(\hat{\theta}) = 0$, then $\hat{\theta}$ is a consistent estimator.
(d) If plim $\hat{\theta} = \theta$ and $g(\hat{\theta})$ is a continuous function of θ, then plim $g(\hat{\theta}) = g(\theta)$. This maintenance of consistency following a nonlinear transformation is highly convenient; note that unbiasedness is not generally maintained following such a transformation. If $\hat{\theta}$ is a consistent estimator of θ, then $1/\hat{\theta}$ is a consistent estimator of $1/\theta$; but if $\hat{\theta}$ is an unbiased estimator of θ, it does not follow that $1/\hat{\theta}$ is an unbiased estimator of $1/\theta$.
(e) $\hat{\theta}$ is an asymptotically efficient estimator of θ if all the following conditions are satisfied: (a) $\hat{\theta}$ has an asymptotic distribution with finite mean and finite variance; (b) $\hat{\theta}$ is consistent; (c) no other consistent estimator of θ has a smaller asymptotic variance than $\hat{\theta}$.

References

Mood, A.M. and Graybill, F.A. (1963), *Introduction to the Theory of Statistics*, New York: McGraw-Hill.

Rao, C.R. (1983), *Linear Statistical Inference and its Applications*, 2nd edn, New York: Wiley.

Appendix 3:
SOLUTIONS AND HINTS

CHAPTER 2

1. Express all variables as deviations from their means in all relationships, and rewrite them with lower case letters

$$x_{2i} = \alpha_3 x_{3i} + u'_i - \bar{u}'$$

and

$$\hat{\alpha}_3 = \frac{\Sigma x_{2i} x_{3i}}{\Sigma x_{3i}^2}$$

Residuals

$$e_i = x_{2i} - \hat{\alpha}_3 x_{3i}$$

Covariance $(e_i, x_{3i}) = 0$ and hence regressing y_i on e_i and x_{3i} yields

$$b'_2 = \frac{\Sigma y_i e_i}{\Sigma e_i^2} \quad \text{and} \quad b'_3 = \frac{\Sigma x_{3i} y_i}{\Sigma x_{3i}^2}$$

$$y_i = b'_2 (x_{2i} - \alpha_3 x_{3i}) + b'_3 x_{3i} + \text{residuals}$$
$$= b'_2 x_{2i} + (b'_3 - b'_2 \alpha_3) x_{3i} + \text{residuals}$$

Hence $b'_2 = \hat{\beta}_2$ and $b'_3 - b'_2 \alpha_3 = \hat{\beta}_3$. Where $\hat{\beta}_2$ and $\hat{\beta}_3$ are the partial regression coefficients of y_i on x_{2i} and x_{3i}.

2. Using equation (2.33) from the text, we obtain

$$\Sigma e_i^2 = \Sigma (y_i - b_2 x_{2i} - b_3 x_{3i})^2$$

which yields

$$\Sigma y_i^2 = \Sigma (b_2 x_{2i} + b_3 x_{3i})^2 + \Sigma e_i^2$$

3. (a) Explained sum of squares $\hat{\beta}_2 \Sigma x_{1t} y_t$ (variables measured from their means)

$$\Sigma e^2 = \Sigma y^2 - \hat{\beta}_2 \Sigma x_{it} y_t$$

For the second equation, use Table 2.1 or equation (2.36) from the text.

(b)
$$R^2 = 1 - \frac{\Sigma e_t^2}{\Sigma y_t^2}$$

$$\bar{R}^2 = 1 - \frac{\Sigma e_t^2/n - 2}{\Sigma y_t^2/n - 1} \quad \text{(for eqn (1))}$$

$$\bar{R}^2 = 1 - \frac{\Sigma e_t^2/n - 3}{\Sigma y_t^2/n - 1} \quad \text{(for eqn (2))}$$

(c) R^2 will always be $\geqslant$ for the second equation compared to first, since the addition of an explanatory variable cannot reduce R^2, which measures goodness of fit within an equation. If R^2 is significant in the first equation, $\hat{\beta}_2$ must be significantly different from zero. In the second equation, if R^2 is significant, it does not necessarily imply that both $\hat{\theta}_1$ and $\hat{\theta}_2$ are statistically significantly different from zero. If x_{1t} and x_{2t} are highly correlated, neither $\hat{\theta}_1$ nor $\hat{\theta}_2$ may be significant and yet R^2 could be significant.

$\bar{R}^2$ can decline when an extra variable is added in the equation because an additional variable can produce too small a reduction in $1 - R^2$ to compensate for the increase in $(n-1)/(n-3)$.

4. There are three features of a sampling distribution that are crucial to the assessment of an estimator; mean, variance and mean square error of the estimator.
   (a) The greater the size of the variance of the error term, the larger will be the variance of the estimator. Estimator will be BLUE.
   (b) If the X_2 variable has a higher variance (dispersion), the variance of $\hat{\beta}_2$ will be smaller. Estimator will be BLUE.
   (c) The larger the sample size, the smaller the variance of the estimator.
   (d) The introduction of a variable, which is positively correlated with the existing explanatory variable changes the estimator, and variance. The magnitude of the existing estimator will be reduced and variance of $\hat{\beta}_2$ will be $\sigma_u^2/[\Sigma x_{2t}^2 (1 - r_{23}^2)]$ where r_{23}^2 is the square of the correlation coefficient between x_{2t} and x_{3t}.
   (e) If a variable is omitted from the regression equation, both the estimators and variances are biased:
   $$E(\hat{\beta}_2) = \beta_2 + \beta_3 d_{32} \text{ where } d_{32} = \frac{\Sigma x_{2i} x_{3i}}{\Sigma x_{2i}^2}$$

   If β_3 and d_{32} are of the same sign, the bias will be positive. Var $(\hat{\beta}_2) \neq \sigma^2/\Sigma x_{2i}^2$ but will be equivalent to equation (2.24) in the text.

5. *Hint*:
   (a) Use any computer package such as TSP, SHAZAM or MINITAB on multiple linear regression. The estimated coefficients in a log model are elasticities. Let the elasticity coefficients for irrigated and unirrigated area be $\hat{\alpha}_1$ and $\hat{\alpha}_2$:

Solutions and hints

$$H_0: \alpha_1 = \alpha_2$$
$$H_1: \alpha_1 \neq \alpha_2$$

Test statistic

$$t = \frac{|\hat{\alpha}_1 - \hat{\alpha}_2|}{\sqrt{[\text{Var}(\hat{\alpha}_1) + \text{Var}(\hat{\alpha}_2) - 2[\text{Cov}(\hat{\alpha}_1 \hat{\alpha}_2)]}}$$

(b) If fertilisers and irrigation are positively correlated, dropping the fertiliser variable yields a coefficient with respect to the irrigation which is an overestimate of its true value.

6. (a) Using a computer package, savings against personal income may be plotted. The relationship may be nonlinear and various models may be attempted.
(b) $s = a + by + cy^2$ and examine the hypothesis whether the marginal propensity to save rises with income, i.e. is $c > 0$?
(c) Derive the residuals from the various specified relationships and plot them against time. If successive values tend to be close to each other (either positive or negative successively) this suggests the presence of positive autocorrelation. If successive residuals change sign often, then negative serial correlation may be the case.

7. (a) $d = 0.7316$

$$\left.\begin{array}{l} d_L = 0.857 \\ d_U = 1.728 \end{array}\right\} \text{ for three explanatory variables from the table}$$

Since $d < d_L$, it indicates positive serial correlation.

(b) When there is a lagged dependent variable, one uses the h statistic to test for the existence of first-order serial correlation

$$h = (1 - \tfrac{1}{2}d) \sqrt{\left[\frac{n}{1 - n \, \text{Var}(b_1)}\right]}$$

where Var (b_1) is the variance of the coefficient on the lagged dependent variable; h is normally distributed. The other test is the Lagrange-multiplier test which is discussed in Chapter 4.

8. This requires the use of computer routine to perform multiple linear regression.

9. (a) $\hat{\beta}_2 = 0.2$

$SEE = 0.2182$

SE of $\hat{\beta}_2 = 0.03086$

$t = 6.4808$

(b) $y_t - 0.6 x_{3t} = \hat{\beta}_2 x_{2t}$, where all variables are measured from their means

$$\hat{\beta}_2 = \frac{\Sigma x_{2t}(y_t - 0.6 x_{3t})}{\Sigma x_{2t}^2} = -0.10$$

So
$$\hat{\beta}_2 = -0.10, \quad \hat{\beta}_3 = 0.6$$

10.
$$\frac{Y_t}{X_t} = \frac{\alpha}{X_t} + \beta + \frac{u_t}{X_t}$$

will be free of heteroscedasticity. So

$$\hat{\alpha} = 2.8332 \qquad \hat{\beta} = 1.4225$$
$$t(\hat{\alpha}) = 1.0119 \quad t(\hat{\beta}) = 4.4027$$
$$R^2 = 0.2545 \qquad \bar{R}^2 = 0.00593 \quad SEE = 0.2061$$
$$LM(\chi^2) = 0.3148 \quad \text{with one degree of freedom}$$

11. *Hint:*
Use the computer routine on multiple linear regression to estimate the four equations. DATAFIT and GIVE, which may be used on a PC, provide all diagnostic tests.

CHAPTER 3

1. (a) When disturbances are autocorrelated $E(u_t u_{t-s}) \neq 0$ $(t \neq s)$. It arises due to the omission of explanatory variables (which are autocorrelated), measurement error and misspecification.

   (b) (i) b_2 is unbiased since unbiasedness is not influenced by the variances and covariances of the disturbances.

   (ii) Var (b_2) is biased and not equal to $\sigma_u^2/\Sigma x_t^2$, which is an underestimate of the true variance.

   (iii) s^2 is biased, if x_t is first-order autocorrelated (i.e. $x_t = \lambda x_{t-1} + \epsilon_t$) in which λ is autocorrelation coefficient and u_t is autocorrelated (i.e. $u_t = \beta u_{t-1} + v_\tau$) and assume that both λ and ρ have the same signs. Then s^2 will be downward biased.

   (iv) t and F statistics are not appropriate because s^2 and the standard errors of the estimated parameters are biased.

2. Estimate β_1 and β_2 by OLS, derive the residuals and regress them on the residuals lagged one period, and obtain $\hat{\lambda}$. Rewrite equation

$$Y_t - \hat{\lambda} Y_{t-1} = \beta_1(1-\hat{\lambda}) + \beta_2(X_t - \hat{\lambda} X_{t-1}) + V_t$$

Estimate β_1 and β_2 from the above equation and use the following equation to re-estimate $\hat{\lambda}$:

$$Y_t - \hat{\beta}_1 - \hat{\beta}_2 x_t = \lambda(Y_{t-1} - \hat{\beta}_1 - \hat{\beta}_2 x_{t-1}) + V_t$$

Continue the process until the estimators $\hat{\lambda}, \hat{\beta}_1,$ and $\hat{\beta}_2$ converge and do not differ in successive iterations by more than a preassigned criterion (0.01).

3. Regress the residuals from the regression of M on P, i.e. e_t on e_{t-1},

$P_{t-1}, \ldots, P_{t-s}, M_{t-1}, \ldots, M_{t-k}$ and derive nR^2 and, similarly, e_t on e_{t-1}, $e_{t-2}, \ldots, M_{t-k}$ and derive nR^2; nR^2 is $\chi^2(p)$ distributed where p is the order of autoregression (used in equation (3.11)).

4. *Hint:*
After fitting the regression, derive the squared residuals which are then regressed on a constant, *IRGIP, HYV, INTEN, PRAM, PRAU*, and the cross-products and squares of the explanatory variables. It will not be possible to use all, so choose a subset and test for heteroscedasticity as presented on p. 43.

5. *Hint:*
See the discussion in Section 3.4.

6. The BLUE is given by OLS in a normal way as long as x_2 and x_3 are not perfectly correlated. Individually, β_2 and β_3 might not be significantly different from zero in the presence of multicollinearity:

$$Y_t = \beta_1 + \beta_2 x_{2t} + (\tau - \beta_2) x_{3t} + u_t$$

$$Y_t - \tau x_{3t} = \beta_1 + \beta_2 (x_{2t} - x_{3t}) + u_t$$

and, given knowledge of τ, β_1 and β_2 can be estimated from the above relationship.

7. Hint:
Refer to Benjamin and Kochin (1979) and use a computer package to perform the regressions. Try a dummy for 1920 and see whether it is significant.

CHAPTER 4

1. (a) The Durbin–Watson test is not recommended when there are lagged dependent variables in the model. The combination of a lagged Y variable and a positively autocorrelated disturbance term will bias the Durbin–Watson statistic upward and will yield misleading indications. The recommended test is Durbin's h statistic or LM test.
   (b) Instrumental variable estimation is the procedure recommended when the error term is correlated with the explanatory variables of the model. Instruments should be chosen in such a way that they are highly correlated with the explanatory variables of the model and uncorrelated with the stochastic disturbance term in probability limit. Instrumental variable estimation yields consistent estimates of the parameters, as the IV estimators are biased in small samples and their variances are difficult to establish in finite samples.

2. When an explanatory variable is correlated with the stochastic disturbance term, OLS yields biased estimators (see equation (4.138)). This is the case of errors in variables. The situation is similar when there is a simultaneous equation model with jointly endogenous variables (refer to Chapter 6). When there are errors in

variables or distributed lags with serial correlation or simultaneous equations model, the instrumental variable estimation is recommended.

3. (a) When $\rho = \lambda$, direct substitution of $u_t - \lambda u_{t-1} = \epsilon_t$ can be undertaken. The model does not have serial correlation and OLS estimations of the transformed equation are consistent, and asymptotically efficient.

   (b) As there is a lagged dependent variable, the matrix of explanatory variables contains a stochastic regressor. While u_t is independent of all x_t and also independent of Y_{t-s}, it is not independent of Y_t and since Y_t influences Y_{t+1}, and so on, u_t is not independent of $Y_{t+1}, Y_{t+2}, \ldots$. Because of this we can only obtain consistent estimators in a model with stochastic regressors where a regression is a lagged dependent variable.

   (c) The geometric lag model is not suitable to estimate in its original form. When the Koyck transformation is applied, we obtain a lagged dependent variable in the estimating equation and a transformed error structure. It is unreasonable to assume that the original disturbances are correlated with the same autocorrelation coefficient as the Koyck transformation would yield.

4. (a) The coefficient of adjustment $= 1 - 0.864 = 0.136$. It indicates the rate of adjustment of Y to the desired value Y^*. The coefficient enables us to determine the number of periods required to close a given proportion p of the gap between Y_t^* and Y_t. Adjustment is slow in the model and it would take 7.35 years to reach the desired stock of tractors with the current purchasing behaviour.

   (b) Short-run price elasticity $= -0.218$

   Long-run price elasticity $= -1.603$

   (c) Short-run interest elasticity $= -0.855$

   Long-run interest elasticity $= -6.2867$

5. (a) Replace x_t by z_t, an instrumental variable – see p. 90.
   (b) This is similar to the model and results discussed on pp. 91–2.

6. Use SHAZAM or TSP routine. A similar example is given in the text. As it is monthly data, use a constant, 11 seasonals, a time trend in your regressions.

7. (a) The estimation of (B) is similar to equations (4.86) and (4.87). Follow the procedure as outlined on p. 73. Estimation by normalising $\log P_t$ can be carried out in a similar way, excepting that $\log P_t$ will be a dependent variable and $\log NM_t$ will be an explanatory variable; $\Pi_t = \log P_t - \log P_{t-1}$ and it should be treated endogenously.

   (b) In equation (4.90) in the text, we used a polynomial lag of the third degree. Derive $Z_{0t}, Z_{1t}, Z_{2t}, Z_{3t}$ using twelve period lags (p.75) and thereafter regress y_t on $Z_{0t}, Z_{1t}, Z_{2t}, Z_{3t}$

$$y_t = \beta_0 Z_{0t} + \beta_1 Z_{1t} + \beta_2 Z_{2t} + \beta_3 Z_{3t} + u_t$$

where

$$Z_{0t} = \Pi_t + \Pi_{t-1} + \ldots + \Pi_{t-12}$$
$$Z_{1t} = \Pi_{t-1} + 2\Pi_{t-2} + \ldots + 12\Pi_{t-12}$$
$$Z_{2t} = \Pi_{t-1} + 4\Pi_{t-2} + \ldots + 144\Pi_{t-12}$$
$$Z_{3t} = \Pi_{t-1} + 8\Pi_{t-2} + \ldots + (12)^3\Pi_{t-12}$$

The variables $Z_{0t}, \ldots, Z_{3t}$ should be generated first.

8. Regression package or TSP may be used.

CHAPTER 5

Solutions

1. (a) To test the hypothesis where there are cross-equation restrictions, use the likelihood ratio test. The expression (5.86) can be used.
   (b) For testing $\alpha_2 = \alpha_3$, a t test can be used since there are constraints within an equation. Alternatively, the F test can be used after obtaining residuals from the restricted model versus unrestricted model.

$$F = \frac{\text{(restricted residual sum of squares} - \text{unrestricted residual sum of squares)}/1}{\text{unrestricted residual sum of squares)}/n - 3}$$

2. *Hint:*
A similar example is illustrated in the text.
   (a) Equation by equation estimation and SURE estimates for $(n-1)$ equations can be obtained.
   (b) Instrumental variable estimation.
   (c) Symmetry restrictions will yield a restricted model and test using LR test of equation (5.86).
   (d) LM involves only restricted estimates and this is its advantage over LR test.

Both SURE with and without restrictions can be obtained using SHAZAM with GLS option.

3. *Hint:*
Use SHAZAM program (OLS, GLS)
   (a) Estimate 16 OLS regression equations.
   (b) Estimate 19 OLS regression equations.
   (c) Long run relationship using mean values for each district and run OLS on a cross-section.

330   Appendix 3

(d) Requires generation of district and time dummies and pooling of data, 304 observations.
(e) SURE procedure can be used when the number of observations in each equation exceeds the number of parameters and the total number of equations is less than the number of observations in each set.
(f) This is similar to the model estimated on pp. 106–9. Use Pool option of SHAZAM program.
(g) Specification errors or misspecification due to serial correlation and heteroscedasticity is incorporated in (f) and not in (c) and (d).

CHAPTER 6

1. Order and rank condition:
   (a) Order condition: number of excluded variables (2) = number of endogenous variables less 1 (2)

   $$\text{Rank condition: Rank} \begin{bmatrix} \beta_{23} & \tau_{22} \\ 1 & 0 \end{bmatrix} = 2$$

   Equation (1) is just identified.
   (b) Order condition suggests underidentification. No need to apply rank condition since necessary condition is violated.
   (c) Order condition no. of excluded variables (3) > no. of endogenous variables less 1(2)

   $$\text{Rank condition: Rank} \begin{bmatrix} 1 & 0 & \tau_{13} \\ \beta_{21} & \tau_{22} & 0 \end{bmatrix} = 2$$

   the rank condition is satisfied and the number of restrictions is more than required, the equation is overidentified using order condition.

2. (a) (i) Order condition: no. of excluded variables (1) = no. of endogenous variables less 1(1)

   $$\text{Rank condition: rank } [\tau_{22}] = 1$$

   Equation is just identified
   (ii) Order condition: no. of excluded variables (1) = no. of endogenous variables less 1(1)

   $$\text{Rank condition: rank } [\tau_{11}] = 1$$

   Equation is just identified.
   Two-stage least squares or indirect least squares can be used.
   (b) Data show that $x_{2t} = 2x_{3t}$. So the identification should be re-examined. In the second equation of the model, substitute $x_{2t} = 2x_{3t}$, which yields

$$\tau_{23}^* = 2\tau_{22} + \tau_{23}$$

and this means that only the second equation is identified, and hence τ_{23}^* and β_{21} can be estimated; τ_{22} and τ_{23} are not separately identifiable.

3. Two-stage least squares estimates of the first equation are:

$$\hat{\beta}_{12} = -4.64 \quad \hat{\tau}_{12} = 2.98 \quad \hat{\tau}_{13} = 5.32 \quad s^2 = 0.361$$
$$se\ \hat{\beta}_{12} = 0.4162 \quad se\ \hat{\tau}_{12} = 0.5272 \quad se\ \hat{\tau}_{13} = 0.6358$$

4. Indirect least squares:

$$\alpha^* = 8.2291 \quad \beta^* = 0.5896$$

Ordinary least squares:

$$R^2 = 1.000 \quad \hat{\alpha} = 8.2277 \quad \hat{\beta} = 0.5897.$$

Since $R^2 = 1.000$, ILS do not differ from OLS.

5. Equation (6.120) is just-identified. Equation (6.121) is over-identified. Some of the answers are in the text. Use three-stage least squares and full-information maximum likelihood routine for the model using TSP routine.

6. Derive the values of Y_1 and Y_2 using X_2, X_3, X_4, X_5 from Table 6.1 and then use TSP version (4.1) or (4.2) routine to obtain estimator using different procedures. A similar example is in the text.

CHAPTER 7

1. (a)
$$x = \begin{bmatrix} 261.835\ldots \\ 257.615\ldots \\ 280.41\ldots \end{bmatrix}$$

(b) Direct and indirect labour requirements per unit of final demand for each good are

$$[0.3514 \quad 0.5879 \quad 0.5811]$$

The second good has, therefore, the most labour embodied in it.

(c) Total labour required is 239.545

2. (a)
$$x = \begin{bmatrix} 208.88\ldots \\ 433.33\ldots \\ 222.22\ldots \end{bmatrix}$$

(b)
$$p = [0.616\ldots 0.466\ldots 1.283\ldots]$$

(c) The A matrix is decomposable: the third good is not required in order for unit net output of either the first or second good to be made available.

3.
$$d = \begin{bmatrix} 118.75 \\ 103.125 \end{bmatrix}$$

4. (a) (i) £150m, (ii) £135m, (iii) Agriculture £30m, Industry £50m, Services £55m

(b)
$$[I - A]^{-1} = \frac{1}{0.938\,75} \begin{bmatrix} 0.95 & 0.05 & 0.0125 \\ 0.225 & 1 & 0.25 \\ 0.14 & 0.205 & 0.99 \end{bmatrix}$$

(c) (i) Agricultural output will rise by £5.7923m, industrial output by £17.0439m, and the output of services by £16.5646m.
(ii) Imports will rise by £3.31891m, and indirect taxes by £2.5566m.
(iii) GDP at factor cost will rise by £21.6811m.

(d) Export surplus will rise by £0.8655m as a result of £1m increase in export demand for agricultural output, but by £0.8745m as a result of £1m increase in export demand for industrial output.

5.

	bL_j	CV_j^b	fL_i	CV_i^F
Agriculture	1.1023	0.8478	1.1421	0.8738
Manufactures	1.1603	1.0023	1.0653	1.2023
Services	0.7373	1.3144	0.7926	0.6738

6. Net capital requirements (direct and indirect) per million pounds of competitive import replacements are $-0.326\,46$; net labour requirements are 1.1395. Hence imports into this hypothetical economy are labour intensive. The above calculations were done on the assumption that the balance of trade was in equilibrium. If we drop this assumption, we find that capital requirements for exports are 11.0434 and for import replacements are 9.3699, while labour requirements for exports are 1.8551 and for import replacements 2.7681.

7. (a) Indecomposable.
(b) Try to reduce it to a triangular matrix. If not, it remains indecomposable.
(c) Frobenius theorem and dominant characteristic roots will be the significance of indecomposability. Any arbitrary vector of final demands will require production of all goods in the system.

8. (a) 10.77 per cent; (b) 2.1542 per cent.

ANSWERS TO SELECTED EXERCISES IN CHAPTER 9

4. (a) $X_1 = 6$, $X_2 = 4$, $X_3 = 0$, value of objective function is 66.
(b) $y_1 = 2$, $y_2 = 1$, $y_3 = 0$, note $S_3 = 12$.

(c) $Z_3 - C_3$ would now equal 0; the solution to the problem is no longer unique. X_3 can be introduced into the basis in place of X_1 with no change in the value of the objective function; X_2 would now equal 23/3 and X_3 would equal 10/3.

5. At the proposed basis, by evaluating $B^{-1}b$ we find $x_1 = 16$, $x_3 = 12$ and x_5 (i.e. the second slack variable) = 20. The associated values of the dual variables are given by $c^B B^{-1}$, from which it follows that $y_1 = 0$, $y_2 = 0$ and $y_3 = 7$. Calculate $z_2 = yA_2$; since $z_2 = 7$ and $c_2 = 17$, $z_2 - c_2 < 0$; x_2 should therefore be introduced into the basis. By the elimination rule, x_5 leaves the basis to make way for x_2. The new basis can then be shown to be the optimal one with $x_1 = 12$, $x_2 = 4$ and $x_3 = 16$; the associated dual variables take the following values: $y_1 = 5$, $y_2 = 2$ and $y_3 = 4$.

6. (a) The dual variables (i.e. the shadow prices of the three nutrients) are 3, 0 and 1 respectively.
   (b) The individual consumes 10 units of the first foodstuff, 8 units of the second foodstuff and zero units of the third foodstuff. The cost of the diet is £1.64.
   (c) A rise in the price of the second foodstuff from 8 to 10 does not alter the feasibility of the basis; the new shadow prices are obtained by solving the following two equations:

$$3y_1 + y_3 = 10$$
$$y_1 + 5y_3 = 10$$

from which it follows that $y_1 = 20/7$ and $y_3 = 10/7$. At these shadow prices, the value of the nutrients contained in a unit of the third foodstuff $[20/7(2) + 0(1) + 10/7(4)]$ still falls short of the cost of such a unit. Hence the individual would still not wish to consume the third foodstuff.

7. (a) $x_1 = 5$, $x_2 = 0$ and $x_3 = 8$ with $Z = 134$.
   (b) At the optimal solution, we have $y_1 = 4$ and $y_2 = 2$. Hence $Z_2 = 4(1) + 2(2) = 10$. So it would make no difference to the solution if c_2 were to increase in value from 5 to 8. However, if x_2 did not appear in the first constraint, then $Z_2 = 4$ and $Z_2 - C_2$ would be negative. We would wish to enter x_2 into the basis in place of x_3. The new solution would be $x_1 = 9$, $x_2 = 2$.
   (c) $x_1 = 17/5$, $x_2 = 0$ and $x_3 = 52/5$ with $Z = 130.8$; the dual variables take on the following values:

$$y_1 = 0, y_2 = 18/5 \text{ and } y_3 = 4/5.$$

8. (a) $x_1 = 2$, $x_2 = 3$ and $C = 25$.
   (b) $x_1 = 6$, $x_2 = 0$, $x_3 = 0$ and $C = 48$.

9. (a) Given the information that both y_1 and y_2 are positive, the first two constraints of the primal hold as strict equalities from which it follows that $x_1 = 2$, $x_2 = 1$ and $Z = 16$.

10. $x_{11} = 100$, $x_{12} = 50$, $x_{23} = 60$, $x_{32} = 25$, $x_{33} = 100$ and $x_{34} = 65$. The total shipment cost is 1815.

11. $x_{11} = 25$, $x_{13} = 25$, $x_{14} = 50$, $x_{22} = 120$, $x_{23} = 30$, $x_{33} = 50$, $x_{41} = 50$. Note x_{14} represents shipments to a fictitious destination (i.e. the amount that is stored at the first factory). Total shipment costs are 1315.

CHAPTER 10

1. $x_1 = 3$, $x_2 = 5$ and $Z = 19$. The artificial constraint is $4x_1 + 2x_2 \leq 22$.

2. $x_1 = 4$, $x_2 = 3$, $x_3 = 0$, and $Z = 117$.

3. $x_1 = 15/4$, $x_2 = 4$ and $Z = 77/4$.

4. $x_1 = 9/2$, $x_2 = 1$ and $Z = 11/2$.

5. Solving the problem as an ordinary LP problem, we obtain the solution: $x_1 = 5/4$, $x_2 = 5/2$ and $Z = 15$ with $y_1 = 5/9$, $y_2 = 1/3$ and $y_3 = 0$. We would obviously obtain the same solution in the absence of the third constraint. If we drop the first constraint, the solution to the ordinary LP problem is $x_1 = 10/11$, $x_2 = 32/11$ and $Z = 180/11$ with $y_2 = 7/11$ and $y_3 = 20/11$. The subset consisting of the first and second constraints gives rise to the same all-integer solution as the subset consisting of the second and third constraints. The all-integer solution is $x_1 = 2$, $x_2 = 1$ and $Z = 12$; but the recomputed duals can be either $y_1 = 5/9$, $y_2 = 1/3$ and $y_3 = 0$ or $y_1 = 0$, $y_2 = 7/11$ and $y_3 = 20/11$.

6. (b) $x_1 = 35$, $x_2 = 10$; $y_1 = 0$, $y_2 = 10$. Note that $y_1 = 0$ despite the fact that the first constraint holds as a strict equality.
   (c) The profits function is concave and the constraints are both linear; hence the Kuhn–Tucker sufficiency theorem is satisfied.

7. (a) $x_1 = 50$, $x_2 = 40$.
   (b) The marginal utility of income is 7.5 and the marginal utility of a ration coupon is 17.5 The shadow price of a ration coupon to this consumer is 7/3.
   (c) Since the shadow price of a ration coupon is greater than 2, the consumer would wish to buy ration coupons and increase his consumption of x_2. His utility-maximising bundle would be $x_1 = 49$, $x_2 = 245/6$.

8. (a) $a - 10b \geq 4c$.
   (b) No, for $x_1 = 0$, $x_2 = 9$ to be the optimal solution would require a to be nonpositive, but it is restricted to be positive.

9. (a) $q_1 = 40$, $y_1 = 50$; $q_2 = 40$, $y_2 = 0$; optimal prices are p_1 (peak) $= 60$ and p_2 (off-peak) $= 10$.
   (b) Capacity should not be expanded; it is already at the optimal level since $\Sigma_{i=1}^{2} y_i = 50 =$ unit capital cost on a daily basis.
   (c) In the short run, we have $q_1 = q_2 = 40$, $y_1 = 50$, $y_2 = 10$. Since $\Sigma_{i=1}^{2} y_i > 50$, capacity should be expanded. In long-run equilibrium, the optimal level of

capacity is 44, $y_1 = 46$, $y_2 = 4$, $p_1 = 56$ and $p_2 = 14$. This is an example of the shifting peak case.

10. (a) $x_1 = 5$, $x_2 = 6$, $y_1 = 3$.
    (b) $x_1 = 22/3$, $x_2 = 19/3$, $y_1 = 8/3$.

CHAPTER 11

1. (a) Equation (11.41) will include an additional term of plus 50 000 on the right-hand side to ensure the initial wealth condition is met. Given that bequests are zero, we set $K(T) = 0$ and solve for $C(0)$. Consumption will rise through time at an exponential rate of 1 per cent per year: $C(0) = 17\,145.74$ and $C(40) = 25\,578.36$.
   (b) In this case when we solve for $C(0)$, we must have first set $K(T) = 20\,000$, $C(0) = 5275.79$ and $C(40) = 7870.52$.
   (c) Here the rate of interest is below the rate of time preference so, along the optimal path, consumption will be falling: $C(0) = 11\,674.45$ and $C(40) = 7825.62$.

2. (a) Given zero extraction costs and equality between the rate of interest and the social rate of time preference (both equal 0.05), the price and the undiscounted royalty at each point in time coincide and rise at an exponential rate of 5 per cent per period along the optimal depletion path. To find the initial value of the resource royalty which will yield the optimal depletion path over an infinite time horizon, we must solve for $y(0)$ in the following expression:

$$\int_0^\infty 100\,[y(0)e^{0.05t}]^{-1}\,dt = 500$$

   It is a straightforward matter to show that this requires $y(0)$ to equal 4.
   (b) For a finite time horizon, the expression is the same as the above except that the upper limit of integration is T. Carrying out the definite integration and simplifying, we obtain the following expression

$$y(0) = 4[1 - e^{-0.05T}]$$

   (c) For $T = 20$, then $y(0) = 2.5285$
   (d) With a constant marginal cost of extraction of unity, we must have

$$p(t) = 1 + y(0)e^{0.05t}$$

   and hence

$$x(t) = \frac{100}{1 + y(0)e^{0.05t}}$$

For optimal depletion over an infinite time horizon, we must have

$$\int_0^\infty \frac{100}{1+y(0)e^{0.05t}} \, dt = 500$$

Letting $Z = 1 + y(0)e^{0.05t}$, it can be shown that

$$\int_0^\infty \frac{100}{1+y(0)e^{0.05t}} \, dt = \int_{1+y(0)}^\infty \frac{2000}{Z(Z-1)} \, dZ$$

$$= \lim_{b\to\infty} \left[2000 \log_e \left(\frac{Z-1}{Z}\right) \right]_{1+y_0}^b$$

$$= -2000 \log_e \left(\frac{y(0)}{1+y(0)}\right)$$

This last expression must equal the initial stock of 500, thus enabling us to solve for $y(0)$. Hence $y(0)$ must equal 3.520755.

3. y_t represents the value of the resource royalty at time t:

   (a) $q_1 = 280.952$, $q_2 = 219.048$

   $p_1 = 719.048$, $p_2 = 780.952$

   $y_1 = 619.048$, $y_2 = 680.952$

   (b) $q_1 = 259.524$, $q_2 = 240.476$

   $p_1 = 740.476$, $p_2 = 759.524$

   (c) (i) $q_1 = 265.584$, $q_2 = 234.146$

   $p_1 = 734.146$, $p_2 = 765.854$

   (ii) $q_1 = 185.714$, $q_2 = 314.286$

   $p_1 = 814.286$, $p_2 = 885.714$

   (iii) $q_1 = 304.762$, $q_2 = 245.238$

   $p_1 = 695.238$, $p_2 = 754.762$

   (d) 1800

   (e) $q_1 = 279.070$, $q_2 = 220.930$
   $p_1 = 720.930$, $p_2 = 779.070$

   the marginal cost of producing the last unit extracted in period 1 is 139.535.

4. (a) The cheapest route from 0 to 12 passes through the following nodes: 2, 5, 8 and 11; the cost is 29.
   (b) The cheapest route from 0 to 12 that passes through node 4 passes through the following nodes: 1, 4, 8, and 11; the cost is 32.

(c) the cheapest route from 0 to 12 that passes through nodes 2 and 7 passes through the following nodes: 2, 5, 7, and 10; the cost is 35.
(d) The most expensive route from 0 to 12 passes through the following nodes: 1, 4, 9, and 11; the cost is 44.

Appendix 4:
STATISTICAL TABLES

Table A4.1 Areas of a Standard Normal Distribution

An entry in the table is the proportion under the entire curve which is between $z = 0$ and a positive value of z. Areas for negative values of z are obtained by symmetry.

z	0.00	0.01	0.02	0.03	0.04	0.05	0.06	0.07	0.08	0.09
0.0	0.0000	0.0040	0.0080	0.0120	0.0160	0.0199	0.0239	0.0279	0.0319	0.0359
0.1	0.0398	0.0438	0.0478	0.0517	0.0557	0.0596	0.0636	0.0675	0.0714	0.0753
0.2	0.0793	0.0832	0.0871	0.0910	0.0948	0.0987	0.1026	0.1064	0.1103	0.1141
0.3	0.1179	0.1217	0.1255	0.1293	0.1331	0.1368	0.1406	0.1443	0.1480	0.1517
0.4	0.1554	0.1591	0.1628	0.1664	0.1700	0.1736	0.1772	0.1808	0.1844	0.1879
0.5	0.1915	0.1950	0.1985	0.2019	0.2054	0.2088	0.2123	0.2157	0.2190	0.2224
0.6	0.2257	0.2291	0.2324	0.2357	0.2389	0.2422	0.2454	0.2486	0.2517	0.2549
0.7	0.2580	0.2611	0.2642	0.2673	0.2703	0.2734	0.2764	0.2794	0.2823	0.2852
0.8	0.2881	0.2910	0.2939	0.2967	0.2995	0.3023	0.3051	0.3078	0.3106	0.3133
0.9	0.3159	0.3186	0.3212	0.3238	0.3264	0.3289	0.3315	0.3340	0.3365	0.3389
1.0	0.3413	0.3438	0.3461	0.3485	0.3508	0.3531	0.3554	0.3577	0.3599	0.3621
1.1	0.3643	0.3665	0.3686	0.3708	0.3729	0.3749	0.3770	0.3790	0.3810	0.3830
1.2	0.3849	0.3869	0.3888	0.3907	0.3925	0.3944	0.3962	0.3980	0.3997	0.4015
1.3	0.4032	0.4049	0.4066	0.4082	0.4099	0.4115	0.4131	0.4147	0.4162	0.4177
1.4	0.4192	0.4207	0.4222	0.4236	0.4251	0.4265	0.4279	0.4292	0.4306	0.4319
1.5	0.4332	0.4345	0.4357	0.4370	0.4382	0.4394	0.4406	0.4418	0.4429	0.4441
1.6	0.4452	0.4463	0.4474	0.4484	0.4495	0.4505	0.4515	0.4525	0.4535	0.4545
1.7	0.4554	0.4564	0.4573	0.4582	0.4591	0.4599	0.4608	0.4616	0.4625	0.4633
1.8	0.4641	0.4649	0.4656	0.4664	0.4671	0.4678	0.4686	0.4693	0.4699	0.4706
1.9	0.4713	0.4719	0.4726	0.4732	0.4738	0.4744	0.4750	0.4756	0.4761	0.4767
2.0	0.4772	0.4778	0.4783	0.4788	0.4793	0.4798	0.4803	0.4808	0.4812	0.4817
2.1	0.4821	0.4826	0.4830	0.4834	0.4838	0.4842	0.4846	0.4850	0.4854	0.4857
2.2	0.4861	0.4864	0.4868	0.4871	0.4875	0.4878	0.4881	0.4884	0.4887	0.4890
2.3	0.4893	0.4896	0.4898	0.4901	0.4904	0.4906	0.4909	0.4911	0.4913	0.4916
2.4	0.4918	0.4920	0.4922	0.4925	0.4927	0.4929	0.4931	0.4932	0.4934	0.4936
2.5	0.4938	0.4940	0.4941	0.4943	0.4945	0.4946	0.4948	0.4949	0.4951	0.4952
2.6	0.4953	0.4955	0.4956	0.4957	0.4959	0.4960	0.4961	0.4962	0.4963	0.4964
2.7	0.4965	0.4966	0.4967	0.4968	0.4969	0.4970	0.4971	0.4972	0.4973	0.4974
2.8	0.4974	0.4975	0.4976	0.4977	0.4977	0.4978	0.4979	0.4979	0.4980	0.4981
2.9	0.4981	0.4982	0.4982	0.4983	0.4984	0.4984	0.4985	0.4985	0.4986	0.4986
3.0	0.4987	0.4987	0.4987	0.4988	0.4988	0.4989	0.4989	0.4989	0.4990	0.4990

Source: Paul G. Hoel (1971) *Introduction to Mathematical Statistics*, 4th edn. Reproduced by permission of John Wiley & Sons Inc. Copyright © John Wiley & Sons Inc.

Statistical tables

Table A4.2 Student's t Distribution

The first column lists the number of degrees of freedom (ν). The headings of the other columns give probabilities (P) for t to exceed the entry value. Use symmetry for negative t values.

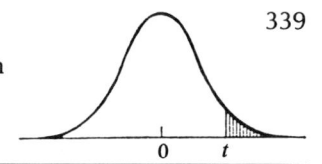

ν \ P	0.10	0.05	0.025	0.01	0.005
1	3.078	6.314	12.706	31.821	63.657
2	1.886	2.920	4.303	6.965	9.925
3	1.638	2.353	3.182	4.541	5.841
4	1.533	2.132	2.776	3.747	4.604
5	1.476	2.015	2.571	3.365	4.032
6	1.440	1.943	2.447	3.143	3.707
7	1.415	1.895	2.365	2.998	3.499
8	1.397	1.860	2.306	2.896	3.355
9	1.383	1.833	2.262	2.821	3.250
10	1.372	1.812	2.228	2.764	3.169
11	1.363	1.796	2.201	2.718	3.106
12	1.356	1.782	2.179	2.681	3.055
13	1.350	1.771	2.160	2.650	3.012
14	1.345	1.761	2.145	2.624	2.977
15	1.341	1.753	2.131	2.602	2.947
16	1.337	1.746	2.120	2.583	2.921
17	1.333	1.740	2.110	2.567	2.898
18	1.330	1.734	2.101	2.552	2.878
19	1.328	1.729	2.093	2.539	2.861
20	1.325	1.725	2.086	2.528	2.845
21	1.323	1.721	2.080	2.518	2.831
22	1.321	1.717	2.074	2.508	2.819
23	1.319	1.714	2.069	2.500	2.807
24	1.318	1.711	2.064	2.492	2.797
25	1.316	1.708	2.060	2.485	2.787
26	1.315	1.706	2.056	2.479	2.779
27	1.314	1.703	2.052	2.473	2.771
28	1.313	1.701	2.048	2.467	2.763
29	1.311	1.699	2.045	2.462	2.756
30	1.310	1.697	2.042	2.457	2.750
40	1.303	1.684	2.021	2.423	2.704
60	1.296	1.671	2.000	2.390	2.660
120	1.289	1.658	1.980	2.358	2.617
∞	1.282	1.645	1.960	2.326	2.576

Source: Paul G. Hoel (1971) *Introduction to Mathematical Statistics*, 4th edn. Reproduced by permission of John Wiley & Sons Inc. Copyright © John Wiley & Sons Inc.

Table A4.3 Values of $\chi^2_{\alpha, \nu}$

ν	$\alpha = 0.995$	$\alpha = 0.99$	$\alpha = 0.975$	$\alpha = 0.95$	$\alpha = 0.05$	$\alpha = 0.025$	$\alpha = 0.01$	$\alpha = 0.005$
1	0.0000393	0.000157	0.000982	0.00393	3.841	5.024	6.635	7.879
2	0.0100	0.0201	0.0506	0.103	5.991	7.378	9.210	10.597
3	0.0717	0.115	0.216	0.352	7.815	9.348	11.345	12.838
4	0.207	0.297	0.484	0.711	9.488	11.143	13.277	14.860
5	0.412	0.554	0.831	1.145	11.070	12.832	15.086	16.750
6	0.676	0.872	1.237	1.635	12.592	14.449	16.812	18.548
7	0.989	1.239	1.690	2.167	14.067	16.013	18.475	20.278
8	1.344	1.646	2.180	2.733	15.507	17.535	20.090	21.955
9	1.735	2.088	2.700	3.325	16.919	19.023	21.666	23.589
10	2.156	2.558	3.247	3.940	18.307	20.483	23.209	25.188
11	2.603	3.053	3.816	4.575	19.675	21.920	24.725	26.757
12	3.074	3.571	4.404	5.226	21.026	23.337	26.217	28.300
13	3.565	4.107	5.009	5.892	22.362	24.736	27.688	29.819
14	4.075	4.660	5.629	6.571	23.685	26.119	29.141	31.319
15	4.601	5.229	6.262	7.261	24.996	27.488	30.578	32.801
16	5.142	5.812	6.908	7.962	26.296	28.845	32.000	34.267
17	5.697	6.408	7.564	8.672	27.587	30.191	33.409	35.718
18	6.265	7.015	8.231	9.390	28.869	31.526	34.805	37.156
19	6.844	7.633	8.907	10.117	30.144	32.852	36.191	38.582
20	7.434	8.260	9.591	10.851	31.410	34.170	37.566	39.997
21	8.034	8.897	10.283	11.591	32.671	35.479	38.932	41.401
22	8.643	9.542	10.982	12.338	33.924	36.781	40.289	42.796
23	9.260	10.196	11.689	13.091	35.172	38.076	41.638	44.181
24	9.886	10.856	12.401	13.848	36.415	39.364	42.980	45.558
25	10.520	11.524	13.120	14.611	37.652	40.646	44.314	46.928
26	11.160	12.198	13.844	15.379	38.885	41.923	45.642	48.290
27	11.808	12.879	14.573	16.151	40.113	43.194	46.963	49.645
28	12.461	13.656	15.308	16.928	41.337	44.461	48.278	50.993
29	13.121	14.256	16.047	17.708	42.557	45.722	49.588	52.336
30	13.787	14.953	16.791	18.493	43.773	46.979	50.892	53.672

Based on Table 8 of *Biometrika Tables for Statisticians, Volume I*. By permission of the *Biometrika* trustees.

Table A4.4 Values of $F_{0.05, \nu_1, \nu_2}$

ν_1 = degrees of freedom for numerator

ν_2	1	2	3	4	5	6	7	8	9	10	12	15	20	24	30	40	60	120	∞
1	161	200	216	225	230	234	237	239	241	242	244	246	248	249	250	251	252	253	254
2	18.5	19.0	19.2	19.2	19.3	19.3	19.4	19.4	19.4	19.4	19.4	19.4	19.4	19.5	19.5	19.5	19.5	19.5	19.5
3	10.1	9.55	9.28	9.12	9.01	8.94	8.89	8.85	8.81	8.79	8.74	8.70	8.66	8.64	8.62	8.59	8.57	8.55	8.53
4	7.71	6.94	6.59	6.39	6.26	6.16	6.09	6.04	6.00	5.96	5.91	5.86	5.80	5.77	5.75	5.72	5.69	5.66	5.63
5	6.61	5.79	5.41	5.19	5.05	4.95	4.88	4.82	4.77	4.74	4.68	4.62	4.56	4.53	4.50	4.46	4.43	4.40	4.37
6	5.99	5.14	4.76	4.53	4.39	4.28	4.21	4.15	4.10	4.06	4.00	3.94	3.87	3.84	3.81	3.77	3.74	3.70	3.67
7	5.59	4.74	4.35	4.12	3.97	3.87	3.79	3.73	3.68	3.64	3.57	3.51	3.44	3.41	3.38	3.34	3.30	3.27	3.23
8	5.32	4.46	4.07	3.84	3.69	3.58	3.50	3.44	3.39	3.35	3.28	3.22	3.15	3.12	3.08	3.04	3.01	2.97	2.93
9	5.12	4.26	3.86	3.63	3.48	3.37	3.29	3.23	3.18	3.14	3.07	3.01	2.94	2.90	2.86	2.83	2.79	2.75	2.71
10	4.96	4.10	3.71	3.48	3.33	3.22	3.14	3.07	3.02	2.98	2.91	2.85	2.77	2.74	2.70	2.66	2.62	2.58	2.54
11	4.84	3.98	3.59	3.36	3.20	3.09	3.01	2.95	2.90	2.85	2.79	2.72	2.65	2.61	2.57	2.53	2.49	2.45	2.40
12	4.75	3.89	3.49	3.26	3.11	3.00	2.91	2.85	2.80	2.75	2.69	2.62	2.54	2.51	2.47	2.43	2.38	2.34	2.30
13	4.67	3.81	3.41	3.18	3.03	2.92	2.83	2.77	2.71	2.67	2.60	2.53	2.46	2.42	2.38	2.34	2.30	2.25	2.21
14	4.60	3.74	3.34	3.11	2.96	2.85	2.76	2.70	2.65	2.60	2.53	2.46	2.39	2.35	2.31	2.27	2.22	2.18	2.13
15	4.54	3.68	3.29	3.06	2.90	2.79	2.71	2.64	2.59	2.54	2.48	2.40	2.33	2.29	2.25	2.20	2.16	2.11	2.07
16	4.49	3.63	3.24	3.01	2.85	2.74	2.66	2.59	2.54	2.49	2.42	2.35	2.28	2.24	2.19	2.15	2.11	2.06	2.01
17	4.45	3.59	3.20	2.96	2.81	2.70	2.61	2.55	2.49	2.45	2.38	2.31	2.23	2.19	2.15	2.10	2.06	2.01	1.96
18	4.41	3.55	3.16	2.93	2.77	2.66	2.58	2.51	2.46	2.41	2.34	2.27	2.19	2.15	2.11	2.06	2.02	1.97	1.92
19	4.38	3.52	3.15	2.90	2.74	2.63	2.54	2.48	2.42	2.38	2.31	2.23	2.16	2.11	2.07	2.03	1.98	1.93	1.88
20	4.35	3.49	3.10	2.87	2.71	2.60	2.51	2.45	2.39	2.35	2.28	2.20	2.12	2.08	2.04	1.99	1.95	1.90	1.84
21	4.32	3.47	3.07	2.84	2.68	2.57	2.49	2.42	2.37	2.32	2.25	2.18	2.10	2.05	2.01	1.96	1.92	1.87	1.81
22	4.30	3.44	3.05	2.82	2.66	2.55	2.46	2.40	2.34	2.30	2.23	2.15	2.07	2.03	1.98	1.94	1.89	1.84	1.78
23	4.28	3.42	3.03	2.80	2.64	2.53	2.44	2.37	2.32	2.27	2.20	2.13	2.05	2.01	1.96	1.91	1.86	1.81	1.76
24	4.26	3.40	3.01	2.78	2.62	2.51	2.42	2.36	2.30	2.25	2.18	2.11	2.03	1.98	1.94	1.89	1.84	1.79	1.73
25	4.24	3.39	2.99	2.76	2.60	2.49	2.40	2.34	2.28	2.24	2.16	2.09	2.01	1.96	1.92	1.87	1.82	1.77	1.71
30	4.17	3.32	2.92	2.69	2.53	2.42	2.33	2.27	2.21	2.16	2.09	2.01	1.93	1.89	1.84	1.79	1.74	1.68	1.62
40	4.08	3.23	2.84	2.61	2.45	2.34	2.25	2.18	2.12	2.08	2.00	1.92	1.84	1.79	1.74	1.69	1.64	1.58	1.51
60	4.00	3.15	2.76	2.53	2.37	2.25	2.17	2.10	2.04	1.99	1.92	1.84	1.75	1.70	1.65	1.59	1.53	1.47	1.39
120	3.92	3.07	2.68	2.45	2.29	2.18	2.09	2.02	1.96	1.91	1.83	1.75	1.66	1.61	1.55	1.50	1.43	1.35	1.25
∞	3.84	3.00	2.60	2.37	2.21	2.10	2.01	1.94	1.88	1.83	1.75	1.67	1.57	1.52	1.46	1.39	1.32	1.22	1.00

ν_2 = degrees of freedom for denominator

Abridged from M. Merrington and C.M. Thompson, 'Tables of percentage points of the inverted beta (F) distribution', *Biometrika*, 33 (1943), 73. By permission of the *Biometrika* trustees.

Table A4.5 Values of $F_{0.01, \nu_1, \nu_2}$

ν_1 = degrees of freedom for numerator

ν_2	1	2	3	4	5	6	7	8	9	10	12	15	20	24	30	40	60	120	∞
1	4052	5000	5403	5625	5764	5859	5928	5982	6023	6056	6106	6157	6209	6235	6261	6287	6313	6339	6366
2	98.5	99.0	99.2	99.2	99.3	99.3	99.4	99.4	99.4	99.4	99.4	99.4	99.5	99.5	99.5	99.5	99.5	99.5	99.5
3	34.1	30.8	29.5	28.7	28.2	27.9	27.7	27.5	27.3	27.2	27.1	26.9	26.7	26.6	26.5	26.4	26.3	26.2	26.1
4	21.2	18.0	16.7	16.0	15.5	15.2	15.0	14.8	14.7	14.5	14.4	14.2	14.0	13.9	13.8	13.7	13.7	13.6	13.5
5	16.3	13.3	12.1	11.4	11.0	10.7	10.5	10.3	10.2	10.1	9.89	9.72	9.55	9.47	9.38	9.29	9.20	9.11	9.02
6	13.7	10.9	9.78	9.15	8.75	8.47	8.26	8.10	7.98	7.87	7.72	7.56	7.40	7.31	7.23	7.14	7.06	6.97	6.88
7	12.2	9.55	8.45	7.85	7.46	7.19	6.99	6.84	6.72	6.62	6.47	6.31	6.16	6.07	5.99	5.91	5.82	5.74	5.65
8	11.3	8.65	7.59	7.01	6.63	6.37	6.18	6.03	5.91	5.81	5.67	5.52	5.36	5.28	5.20	5.12	5.03	4.95	4.86
9	10.6	8.02	6.99	6.42	6.06	5.80	5.61	5.47	5.35	5.26	5.11	4.96	4.81	4.73	4.65	4.57	4.48	4.40	4.31
10	10.0	7.56	6.55	5.99	5.64	5.39	5.20	5.06	4.94	4.85	4.71	4.56	4.41	4.33	4.25	4.17	4.08	4.00	3.91
11	9.65	7.21	6.22	5.67	5.32	5.07	4.89	4.74	4.63	4.54	4.40	4.25	4.10	4.02	3.94	3.86	3.78	3.69	3.60
12	9.33	6.93	5.95	5.41	5.06	4.82	4.64	4.50	4.39	4.30	4.16	4.01	3.86	3.78	3.70	3.62	3.54	3.45	3.36
13	9.07	6.70	5.74	5.21	4.86	4.62	4.44	4.30	4.19	4.10	3.96	3.82	3.66	3.59	3.51	3.43	3.34	3.25	3.17
14	8.86	6.51	5.56	5.04	4.70	4.46	4.28	4.14	4.03	3.94	3.80	3.66	3.51	3.43	3.35	3.27	3.18	3.09	3.00
15	8.68	6.36	5.42	4.89	4.56	4.32	4.14	4.00	3.89	3.80	3.67	3.52	3.37	3.29	3.21	3.13	3.05	2.96	2.87
16	8.53	6.23	5.29	4.77	4.44	4.20	4.03	3.89	3.78	3.69	3.55	3.41	3.26	3.18	3.10	3.02	2.93	2.84	2.75
17	8.40	6.11	5.19	4.67	4.34	4.10	3.93	3.79	3.68	3.59	3.46	3.31	3.16	3.08	3.00	2.92	2.83	2.75	2.65
18	8.29	6.01	5.09	4.58	4.25	4.01	3.84	3.71	3.60	3.51	3.37	3.23	3.08	3.00	2.92	2.84	2.75	2.66	2.57
19	8.19	5.93	5.01	4.50	4.17	3.94	3.77	3.63	3.52	3.43	3.30	3.15	3.00	2.92	2.84	2.76	2.67	2.58	2.49
20	8.10	5.85	4.94	4.43	4.10	3.87	3.70	3.56	3.46	3.37	3.23	3.09	2.94	2.86	2.78	2.69	2.61	2.52	2.42
21	8.02	5.78	4.87	4.37	4.04	3.81	3.64	3.51	3.40	3.31	3.17	3.03	2.88	2.80	2.72	2.64	2.55	2.46	2.36
22	7.95	5.72	4.82	4.31	3.99	3.76	3.59	3.45	3.35	3.26	3.12	2.98	2.83	2.75	2.67	2.58	2.50	2.40	2.31
23	7.88	5.66	4.76	4.26	3.94	3.71	3.54	3.41	3.30	3.21	3.07	2.93	2.78	2.70	2.62	2.54	2.45	2.35	2.26
24	7.82	5.61	4.72	4.22	3.90	3.67	3.50	3.36	3.26	3.17	3.03	2.89	2.74	2.66	2.58	2.49	2.40	2.31	2.21
25	7.77	5.57	4.68	4.18	3.86	3.63	3.46	3.32	3.22	3.13	2.99	2.85	2.70	2.62	2.53	2.45	2.36	2.27	2.17
30	7.56	5.39	4.51	4.02	3.70	3.47	3.30	3.17	3.07	2.98	2.84	2.70	2.55	2.47	2.39	2.30	2.21	2.11	2.01
40	7.31	5.18	4.31	3.83	3.51	3.29	3.12	2.99	2.89	2.80	2.66	2.52	2.37	2.29	2.20	2.11	2.02	1.92	1.80
60	7.08	4.98	4.13	3.65	3.34	3.12	2.95	2.82	2.72	2.63	2.50	2.35	2.20	2.12	2.03	1.94	1.84	1.73	1.60
120	6.85	4.79	3.95	3.48	3.17	2.96	2.79	2.66	2.56	2.47	2.34	2.19	2.03	1.95	1.86	1.76	1.66	1.53	1.38
∞	6.63	4.61	3.78	3.32	3.02	2.80	2.64	2.51	2.41	2.32	2.18	2.04	1.88	1.79	1.70	1.59	1.47	1.32	1.00

ν_2 = degrees of freedom denominator

Abridged from M. Merrington and C.M. Thompson. 'Tables of percentage points of the inverted beta (F) distribution', *Biometrika*, **33** (1943), 73. By permission of the *Biometrika* trustees.

Table A4.6 Durbin–Watson statistic (Savin–White tables) 5% significance points

n	k'=1 d_L	k'=1 d_U	k'=2 d_L	k'=2 d_U	k'=3 d_L	k'=3 d_U	k'=4 d_L	k'=4 d_U	k'=5 d_L	k'=5 d_U	k'=6 d_L	k'=6 d_U	k'=7 d_L	k'=7 d_U	k'=8 d_L	k'=8 d_U	k'=9 d_L	k'=9 d_U	k'=10 d_L	k'=10 d_U
6	0.610	1.400	—	—	—	—	—	—	—	—	—	—	—	—	—	—	—	—	—	—
7	0.700	1.356	0.467	1.896	—	—	—	—	—	—	—	—	—	—	—	—	—	—	—	—
8	0.763	1.332	0.559	1.777	0.368	2.287	—	—	—	—	—	—	—	—	—	—	—	—	—	—
9	0.824	1.320	0.629	1.699	0.455	2.128	0.296	2.588	—	—	—	—	—	—	—	—	—	—	—	—
10	0.879	1.320	0.697	1.641	0.525	2.016	0.376	2.414	0.243	2.822	—	—	—	—	—	—	—	—	—	—
11	0.927	1.324	0.758	1.604	0.595	1.928	0.444	2.283	0.316	2.645	0.203	3.005	—	—	—	—	—	—	—	—
12	0.971	1.331	0.812	1.579	0.658	1.864	0.512	2.177	0.379	2.506	0.268	2.832	0.171	3.149	—	—	—	—	—	—
13	1.010	1.340	0.861	1.562	0.715	1.816	0.574	2.094	0.445	2.390	0.328	2.692	0.230	2.985	0.147	3.266	—	—	—	—
14	1.045	1.350	0.905	1.551	0.767	1.779	0.632	2.030	0.505	2.296	0.389	2.572	0.286	2.848	0.200	3.111	0.127	3.360	—	—
15	1.077	1.361	0.946	1.543	0.814	1.750	0.685	1.977	0.562	2.220	0.447	2.472	0.343	2.727	0.251	2.979	0.175	3.216	0.111	3.438
16	1.106	1.371	0.982	1.539	0.857	1.728	0.734	1.935	0.615	2.157	0.502	2.388	0.398	2.624	0.304	2.860	0.222	3.090	0.155	3.304
17	1.133	1.381	1.015	1.536	0.897	1.710	0.779	1.900	0.664	2.104	0.554	2.318	0.451	2.537	0.356	2.757	0.272	2.975	0.198	3.184
18	1.158	1.391	1.046	1.535	0.933	1.696	0.820	1.872	0.710	2.060	0.603	2.257	0.502	2.461	0.407	2.667	0.321	2.873	0.244	3.073
19	1.180	1.401	1.074	1.536	0.967	1.685	0.859	1.848	0.752	2.023	0.649	2.206	0.549	2.396	0.456	2.589	0.369	2.783	0.290	2.974
20	1.201	1.411	1.100	1.537	0.998	1.676	0.894	1.828	0.792	1.991	0.692	2.162	0.595	2.339	0.502	2.521	0.416	2.704	0.336	2.885
21	1.221	1.420	1.125	1.538	1.026	1.669	0.927	1.812	0.829	1.964	0.732	2.124	0.637	2.290	0.547	2.460	0.461	2.633	0.380	2.806
22	1.239	1.429	1.147	1.541	1.053	1.664	0.958	1.797	0.863	1.940	0.769	2.090	0.677	2.246	0.588	2.407	0.504	2.571	0.424	2.734
23	1.257	1.437	1.168	1.543	1.078	1.660	0.986	1.785	0.895	1.920	0.804	2.061	0.715	2.208	0.628	2.360	0.545	2.514	0.465	2.670
24	1.273	1.446	1.188	1.546	1.101	1.656	1.013	1.775	0.925	1.902	0.837	2.035	0.751	2.174	0.666	2.318	0.584	2.464	0.506	2.613
25	1.288	1.454	1.206	1.550	1.123	1.654	1.038	1.767	0.953	1.886	0.868	2.012	0.784	2.144	0.702	2.280	0.621	2.419	0.544	2.560
26	1.302	1.461	1.224	1.553	1.143	1.652	1.062	1.759	0.979	1.873	0.897	1.992	0.816	2.117	0.735	2.246	0.657	2.379	0.581	2.513
27	1.316	1.469	1.240	1.556	1.162	1.651	1.084	1.753	1.004	1.861	0.925	1.974	0.845	2.093	0.767	2.216	0.691	2.342	0.616	2.470
28	1.328	1.476	1.255	1.560	1.181	1.650	1.104	1.747	1.028	1.850	0.951	1.958	0.874	2.071	0.798	2.188	0.723	2.309	0.650	2.431
29	1.341	1.483	1.270	1.563	1.198	1.650	1.124	1.743	1.050	1.841	0.975	1.944	0.900	2.052	0.826	2.164	0.753	2.278	0.682	2.396
30	1.352	1.489	1.284	1.567	1.214	1.650	1.143	1.739	1.071	1.833	0.998	1.931	0.926	2.034	0.854	2.141	0.782	2.251	0.712	2.363
31	1.363	1.496	1.297	1.570	1.229	1.650	1.160	1.735	1.090	1.825	1.020	1.920	0.950	2.018	0.879	2.120	0.810	2.226	0.741	2.333
32	1.373	1.502	1.309	1.574	1.244	1.650	1.177	1.732	1.109	1.819	1.041	1.909	0.972	2.004	0.904	2.102	0.836	2.203	0.769	2.306
33	1.383	1.508	1.321	1.577	1.258	1.651	1.193	1.730	1.127	1.813	1.061	1.900	0.994	1.991	0.927	2.085	0.861	2.181	0.795	2.281
34	1.393	1.514	1.333	1.580	1.271	1.652	1.208	1.728	1.144	1.808	1.080	1.891	1.015	1.979	0.950	2.069	0.885	2.162	0.821	2.257
35	1.402	1.519	1.343	1.584	1.283	1.653	1.222	1.726	1.160	1.803	1.097	1.884	1.034	1.967	0.971	2.054	0.908	2.144	0.845	2.236
36	1.411	1.525	1.354	1.587	1.295	1.654	1.236	1.724	1.175	1.799	1.114	1.877	1.053	1.957	0.991	2.041	0.930	2.127	0.868	2.216
37	1.419	1.530	1.364	1.590	1.307	1.655	1.249	1.723	1.190	1.795	1.131	1.870	1.071	1.948	1.011	2.029	0.951	2.112	0.891	2.198
38	1.427	1.535	1.373	1.594	1.318	1.656	1.261	1.722	1.204	1.792	1.146	1.864	1.088	1.939	1.029	2.017	0.970	2.098	0.912	2.180
39	1.435	1.540	1.382	1.597	1.328	1.658	1.273	1.722	1.218	1.789	1.161	1.859	1.104	1.932	1.047	2.007	0.990	2.085	0.932	2.164
40	1.442	1.544	1.391	1.600	1.338	1.659	1.285	1.721	1.230	1.786	1.175	1.854	1.120	1.924	1.064	1.997	1.008	2.072	0.945	2.149

Table A4.6 Cont'd

n	$k'=1$ d_L	d_U	$k'=2$ d_L	d_U	$k'=3$ d_L	d_U	$k'=4$ d_L	d_U	$k'=5$ d_L	d_U	$k'=6$ d_L	d_U	$k'=7$ d_L	d_U	$k'=8$ d_L	d_U	$k'=9$ d_L	d_U	$k'=10$ d_L	d_U
45	1.475	1.566	1.430	1.615	1.383	1.666	1.336	1.720	1.287	1.776	1.238	1.835	1.189	1.895	1.139	1.958	1.089	2.002	1.038	2.088
50	1.503	1.585	1.462	1.628	1.421	1.674	1.378	1.721	1.335	1.771	1.291	1.822	1.246	1.875	1.201	1.930	1.156	1.986	1.110	2.044
55	1.528	1.601	1.490	1.641	1.452	1.681	1.414	1.724	1.374	1.768	1.334	1.814	1.294	1.861	1.253	1.909	1.212	1.959	1.170	2.010
60	1.549	1.616	1.514	1.652	1.480	1.689	1.444	1.727	1.408	1.767	1.372	1.808	1.335	1.850	1.298	1.894	1.260	1.939	1.222	1.984
65	1.567	1.629	1.536	1.662	1.503	1.696	1.471	1.731	1.438	1.767	1.404	1.805	1.370	1.843	1.336	1.882	1.301	1.923	1.266	1.964
70	1.583	1.641	1.554	1.672	1.525	1.703	1.494	1.735	1.464	1.768	1.433	1.802	1.401	1.837	1.369	1.873	1.337	1.910	1.305	1.948
75	1.598	1.652	1.571	1.680	1.543	1.709	1.515	1.739	1.487	1.770	1.458	1.801	1.428	1.834	1.399	1.867	1.369	1.901	1.339	1.935
80	1.611	1.662	1.586	1.688	1.560	1.715	1.534	1.743	1.507	1.772	1.480	1.801	1.453	1.831	1.425	1.861	1.397	1.893	1.369	1.925
85	1.624	1.671	1.600	1.696	1.575	1.721	1.550	1.747	1.525	1.774	1.500	1.801	1.474	1.829	1.448	1.857	1.422	1.886	1.396	1.916
90	1.635	1.679	1.612	1.703	1.589	1.726	1.566	1.751	1.542	1.776	1.518	1.801	1.494	1.827	1.469	1.854	1.445	1.881	1.420	1.909
95	1.645	1.687	1.623	1.709	1.602	1.732	1.579	1.755	1.557	1.778	1.535	1.802	1.512	1.827	1.489	1.852	1.465	1.877	1.442	1.903
100	1.654	1.694	1.634	1.715	1.613	1.736	1.592	1.758	1.571	1.780	1.550	1.803	1.528	1.826	1.506	1.850	1.484	1.874	1.462	1.898
150	1.720	1.746	1.706	1.760	1.693	1.774	1.679	1.788	1.665	1.802	1.651	1.817	1.637	1.832	1.622	1.847	1.608	1.862	1.594	1.877
200	1.758	1.778	1.748	1.789	1.738	1.799	1.728	1.810	1.718	1.820	1.707	1.831	1.697	1.841	1.686	1.852	1.675	1.863	1.665	1.874

Statistical tables

n	$k'=11$ d_L	d_U	$k'=12$ d_L	d_U	$k'=13$ d_L	d_U	$k'=14$ d_L	d_U	$k'=15$ d_L	d_U	$k'=16$ d_L	d_U	$k'=17$ d_L	d_U	$k'=18$ d_L	d_U	$k'=19$ d_L	d_U	$k'=20$ d_L	d_U
16	0.098	3.503	—	—	—	—	—	—	—	—	—	—	—	—	—	—	—	—	—	—
17	0.138	3.378	0.087	3.557	—	—	—	—	—	—	—	—	—	—	—	—	—	—	—	—
18	0.177	3.265	0.123	3.441	0.078	3.603	—	—	—	—	—	—	—	—	—	—	—	—	—	—
19	0.220	3.159	0.160	3.335	0.111	3.496	0.070	3.642	—	—	—	—	—	—	—	—	—	—	—	—
20	0.263	3.063	0.200	3.234	0.145	3.395	0.100	3.542	0.063	3.676	—	—	—	—	—	—	—	—	—	—
21	0.307	2.976	0.240	3.141	0.182	3.300	0.132	3.448	0.091	3.583	0.058	3.705	—	—	—	—	—	—	—	—
22	0.349	2.897	0.281	3.057	0.220	3.211	0.166	3.358	0.120	3.495	0.083	3.619	0.052	3.731	—	—	—	—	—	—
23	0.391	2.826	0.322	2.979	0.259	3.128	0.202	3.272	0.153	3.409	0.110	3.535	0.076	3.650	0.048	3.753	—	—	—	—
24	0.431	2.761	0.362	2.908	0.297	3.053	0.239	3.193	0.186	3.327	0.141	3.454	0.101	3.572	0.070	3.678	0.044	3.773	—	—
25	0.470	2.702	0.400	2.844	0.335	2.983	0.275	3.119	0.221	3.251	0.172	3.376	0.130	3.494	0.094	3.604	0.065	3.702	0.041	3.790
26	0.508	2.649	0.438	2.784	0.373	2.919	0.312	3.051	0.256	3.179	0.205	3.303	0.160	3.420	0.120	3.531	0.087	3.632	0.060	3.724
27	0.544	2.600	0.475	2.730	0.409	2.859	0.348	2.987	0.291	3.112	0.238	3.233	0.191	3.349	0.149	3.460	0.112	3.563	0.081	3.658
28	0.578	2.555	0.510	2.680	0.445	2.805	0.383	2.928	0.325	3.050	0.271	3.168	0.222	3.283	0.178	3.392	0.138	3.495	0.104	3.592
29	0.612	2.515	0.544	2.634	0.479	2.755	0.418	2.874	0.359	2.992	0.305	3.107	0.254	3.219	0.208	3.327	0.166	3.431	0.129	3.528
30	0.643	2.477	0.577	2.592	0.512	2.708	0.451	2.823	0.392	2.937	0.337	3.050	0.286	3.160	0.238	3.266	0.195	3.368	0.156	3.465
31	0.674	2.443	0.608	2.553	0.545	2.665	0.484	2.776	0.425	2.887	0.370	2.996	0.317	3.103	0.269	3.208	0.224	3.309	0.183	3.406
32	0.703	2.411	0.638	2.517	0.576	2.625	0.515	2.733	0.457	2.840	0.401	2.946	0.349	3.050	0.299	3.153	0.253	3.252	0.211	3.348
33	0.731	2.382	0.668	2.484	0.606	2.588	0.546	2.692	0.488	2.796	0.432	2.899	0.379	3.000	0.329	3.100	0.283	3.198	0.239	3.293
34	0.758	2.355	0.695	2.454	0.634	2.554	0.575	2.654	0.518	2.754	0.462	2.854	0.409	2.954	0.359	3.051	0.312	3.147	0.267	3.240
35	0.783	2.330	0.722	2.425	0.662	2.521	0.604	2.619	0.547	2.716	0.492	2.813	0.439	2.910	0.388	3.005	0.340	3.099	0.295	3.190
36	0.808	2.306	0.748	2.398	0.689	2.492	0.631	2.586	0.575	2.680	0.520	2.774	0.467	2.868	0.417	2.961	0.369	3.053	0.323	3.142
37	0.831	2.285	0.772	2.374	0.714	2.464	0.657	2.555	0.602	2.646	0.548	2.738	0.495	2.829	0.445	2.920	0.397	3.009	0.351	3.097
38	0.854	2.265	0.796	2.351	0.739	2.438	0.683	2.526	0.628	2.614	0.575	2.703	0.522	2.792	0.472	2.880	0.424	2.968	0.378	3.054
39	0.875	2.246	0.819	2.329	0.763	2.413	0.707	2.499	0.653	2.585	0.600	2.671	0.549	2.757	0.499	2.843	0.451	2.929	0.404	3.013
40	0.896	2.228	0.840	2.309	0.785	2.391	0.731	2.473	0.678	2.557	0.626	2.641	0.575	2.724	0.525	2.808	0.477	2.892	0.430	2.974
45	0.988	2.156	0.938	2.225	0.887	2.296	0.838	2.367	0.788	2.439	0.740	2.512	0.692	2.586	0.644	2.659	0.598	2.733	0.553	2.807
50	1.064	2.103	1.019	2.163	0.973	2.225	0.927	2.287	0.882	2.350	0.836	2.414	0.792	2.479	0.747	2.544	0.703	2.610	0.660	2.675
55	1.129	2.062	1.087	2.116	1.045	2.170	1.003	2.225	0.961	2.281	0.919	2.338	0.877	2.396	0.836	2.454	0.795	2.512	0.754	2.571
60	1.184	2.031	1.145	2.079	1.106	2.127	1.068	2.177	1.029	2.227	0.990	2.278	0.951	2.330	0.913	2.382	0.874	2.434	0.836	2.487
65	1.231	2.006	1.195	2.049	1.160	2.093	1.124	2.138	1.088	2.183	1.052	2.229	1.016	2.276	0.980	2.323	0.944	2.371	0.908	2.419
70	1.272	1.986	1.239	2.026	1.206	2.066	1.172	2.106	1.139	2.148	1.105	2.189	1.072	2.232	1.038	2.275	1.005	2.318	0.971	2.362
75	1.308	1.970	1.277	2.006	1.247	2.043	1.215	2.080	1.184	2.118	1.153	2.156	1.121	2.195	1.090	2.235	1.058	2.275	1.027	2.315
80	1.340	1.957	1.311	1.991	1.283	2.024	1.253	2.059	1.224	2.093	1.195	2.129	1.165	2.165	1.136	2.201	1.106	2.238	1.076	2.275
85	1.369	1.946	1.342	1.977	1.315	2.009	1.287	2.040	1.260	2.073	1.232	2.105	1.205	2.139	1.177	2.172	1.149	2.206	1.121	2.241
90	1.395	1.937	1.369	1.966	1.344	1.995	1.318	2.025	1.292	2.055	1.266	2.085	1.240	2.116	1.213	2.148	1.187	2.179	1.160	2.211
95	1.418	1.929	1.394	1.956	1.370	1.984	1.345	2.012	1.321	2.040	1.296	2.068	1.271	2.097	1.247	2.126	1.222	2.156	1.197	2.186
100	1.434	1.923	1.416	1.948	1.393	1.974	1.371	2.000	1.347	2.026	1.324	2.053	1.301	2.080	1.277	2.108	1.253	2.135	1.229	2.164
150	1.579	1.892	1.564	1.908	1.550	1.924	1.535	1.940	1.519	1.956	1.504	1.972	1.489	1.989	1.474	2.006	1.458	2.023	1.443	2.040
200	1.654	1.885	1.643	1.896	1.632	1.908	1.621	1.919	1.610	1.931	1.599	1.943	1.588	1.955	1.576	1.967	1.565	1.979	1.554	1.991

k' is the number of regressors excluding the intercept.
Reproduced by permission from *Econometrica*, **45**, no. 8, 1977, 1992–5.

Table A4.7 Durbin–Watson statistic (Savin–White tables) 1% significance points

n	$k'=1$ d_L	d_U	$k'=2$ d_L	d_U	$k'=3$ d_L	d_U	$k'=4$ d_L	d_U	$k'=5$ d_L	d_U	$k'=6$ d_L	d_U	$k'=7$ d_L	d_U	$k'=8$ d_L	d_U	$k'=9$ d_L	d_U	$k'=10$ d_L	d_U
6	0.390	1.142	—	—	—	—	—	—	—	—	—	—	—	—	—	—	—	—	—	—
7	0.435	1.036	0.294	1.676	—	—	—	—	—	—	—	—	—	—	—	—	—	—	—	—
8	0.497	1.003	0.345	1.489	0.229	2.102	—	—	—	—	—	—	—	—	—	—	—	—	—	—
9	0.554	0.998	0.408	1.389	0.279	1.875	0.183	2.433	—	—	—	—	—	—	—	—	—	—	—	—
10	0.604	1.001	0.466	1.333	0.340	1.733	0.230	2.193	0.150	2.690	—	—	—	—	—	—	—	—	—	—
11	0.653	1.010	0.519	1.297	0.396	1.640	0.286	2.030	0.193	2.453	0.124	2.892	—	—	—	—	—	—	—	—
12	0.697	1.023	0.569	1.274	0.449	1.575	0.339	1.913	0.244	2.280	0.164	2.665	0.105	3.053	—	—	—	—	—	—
13	0.738	1.038	0.616	1.261	0.499	1.526	0.391	1.826	0.294	2.150	0.211	2.490	0.140	2.838	0.090	3.182	—	—	—	—
14	0.776	1.054	0.660	1.254	0.547	1.490	0.441	1.757	0.343	2.049	0.257	2.354	0.183	2.667	0.122	2.981	0.078	3.287	—	—
15	0.811	1.070	0.700	1.252	0.591	1.464	0.488	1.704	0.391	1.967	0.303	2.244	0.226	2.530	0.161	2.817	0.107	3.101	0.068	3.374
16	0.844	1.086	0.737	1.252	0.633	1.446	0.532	1.663	0.437	1.900	0.349	2.153	0.269	2.416	0.200	2.681	0.142	2.944	0.094	3.201
17	0.874	1.102	0.772	1.255	0.672	1.432	0.574	1.630	0.480	1.847	0.393	2.078	0.313	2.319	0.241	2.566	0.179	2.811	0.127	3.053
18	0.902	1.118	0.805	1.259	0.708	1.422	0.613	1.604	0.522	1.803	0.435	2.015	0.355	2.238	0.282	2.467	0.216	2.697	0.160	2.925
19	0.928	1.132	0.835	1.265	0.742	1.415	0.650	1.584	0.561	1.767	0.476	1.963	0.396	2.169	0.322	2.381	0.255	2.597	0.196	2.813
20	0.952	1.147	0.863	1.271	0.773	1.411	0.685	1.567	0.598	1.737	0.515	1.918	0.436	2.110	0.362	2.308	0.294	2.510	0.232	2.714
21	0.975	1.161	0.890	1.277	0.803	1.408	0.718	1.554	0.633	1.712	0.552	1.881	0.474	2.059	0.400	2.244	0.331	2.434	0.268	2.625
22	0.997	1.174	0.914	1.284	0.831	1.407	0.748	1.543	0.667	1.691	0.587	1.849	0.510	2.015	0.437	2.188	0.368	2.367	0.304	2.548
23	1.018	1.187	0.938	1.291	0.858	1.407	0.777	1.534	0.698	1.673	0.620	1.821	0.545	1.977	0.473	2.140	0.404	2.308	0.340	2.479
24	1.037	1.199	0.960	1.298	0.882	1.407	0.805	1.528	0.728	1.658	0.652	1.797	0.578	1.944	0.507	2.097	0.439	2.255	0.375	2.417
25	1.055	1.211	0.981	1.305	0.906	1.409	0.831	1.523	0.756	1.645	0.682	1.766	0.610	1.915	0.540	2.059	0.473	2.209	0.409	2.362
26	1.072	1.222	1.001	1.312	0.928	1.411	0.855	1.518	0.783	1.635	0.711	1.759	0.640	1.889	0.572	2.026	0.505	2.168	0.441	2.313
27	1.089	1.233	1.019	1.319	0.949	1.413	0.878	1.515	0.808	1.626	0.738	1.743	0.669	1.867	0.602	1.997	0.536	2.131	0.473	2.269
28	1.104	1.244	1.037	1.325	0.969	1.415	0.900	1.513	0.832	1.618	0.764	1.729	0.696	1.847	0.630	1.970	0.566	2.098	0.504	2.229
29	1.119	1.254	1.054	1.332	0.988	1.418	0.921	1.512	0.855	1.611	0.788	1.718	0.723	1.830	0.658	1.947	0.595	2.068	0.533	2.193
30	1.133	1.263	1.070	1.339	1.006	1.421	0.941	1.511	0.877	1.606	0.812	1.707	0.748	1.814	0.684	1.925	0.622	2.041	0.562	2.160
31	1.147	1.273	1.085	1.345	1.023	1.425	0.960	1.510	0.897	1.601	0.834	1.698	0.772	1.800	0.710	1.906	0.649	2.017	0.589	2.131
32	1.160	1.282	1.100	1.352	1.040	1.428	0.979	1.510	0.917	1.597	0.856	1.690	0.794	1.788	0.734	1.889	0.674	1.995	0.615	2.104
33	1.172	1.291	1.114	1.358	1.055	1.432	0.996	1.510	0.936	1.594	0.876	1.683	0.816	1.776	0.757	1.874	0.698	1.975	0.641	2.080

Statistical tables

34	1.184	1.299	1.128	1.364	1.070	1.435	1.012	1.511	0.954	1.591	0.896	1.677	0.837	1.766	0.779	1.860	0.722	1.957	0.665	2.057
35	1.195	1.307	1.140	1.370	1.085	1.439	1.028	1.512	0.971	1.589	0.914	1.671	0.857	1.757	0.800	1.847	0.744	1.940	0.689	2.037
36	1.206	1.315	1.153	1.376	1.098	1.442	1.043	1.513	0.988	1.588	0.932	1.666	0.877	1.749	0.821	1.836	0.766	1.925	0.711	2.018
37	1.217	1.323	1.165	1.382	1.112	1.446	1.058	1.514	1.004	1.586	0.950	1.662	0.895	1.742	0.841	1.825	0.787	1.911	0.733	2.001
38	1.227	1.330	1.176	1.388	1.124	1.449	1.072	1.515	1.019	1.585	0.966	1.658	0.913	1.735	0.860	1.816	0.807	1.899	0.754	1.985
39	1.237	1.337	1.187	1.393	1.137	1.453	1.085	1.517	1.034	1.584	0.982	1.655	0.930	1.729	0.878	1.807	0.826	1.887	0.774	1.970
40	1.246	1.344	1.198	1.398	1.148	1.457	1.098	1.518	1.048	1.584	0.997	1.652	0.946	1.724	0.895	1.799	0.844	1.876	0.789	1.956
45	1.288	1.376	1.245	1.423	1.201	1.474	1.156	1.528	1.111	1.584	1.065	1.643	1.019	1.704	0.974	1.768	0.927	1.834	0.881	1.902
50	1.324	1.403	1.285	1.446	1.245	1.491	1.205	1.538	1.164	1.587	1.123	1.639	1.081	1.692	1.039	1.748	0.997	1.805	0.955	1.864
55	1.356	1.427	1.320	1.466	1.284	1.506	1.247	1.548	1.209	1.592	1.172	1.638	1.134	1.685	1.095	1.734	1.057	1.785	1.018	1.837
60	1.383	1.449	1.350	1.484	1.317	1.520	1.283	1.558	1.249	1.598	1.214	1.639	1.179	1.682	1.144	1.726	1.108	1.771	1.072	1.817
65	1.407	1.468	1.377	1.500	1.346	1.534	1.315	1.568	1.283	1.604	1.251	1.642	1.218	1.680	1.186	1.720	1.153	1.761	1.120	1.802
70	1.429	1.485	1.400	1.515	1.372	1.546	1.343	1.578	1.313	1.611	1.283	1.645	1.253	1.680	1.223	1.716	1.192	1.754	1.162	1.792
75	1.448	1.501	1.422	1.529	1.395	1.557	1.368	1.587	1.340	1.617	1.313	1.646	1.284	1.682	1.256	1.716	1.227	1.746	1.199	1.785
80	1.466	1.515	1.441	1.541	1.416	1.568	1.390	1.595	1.364	1.624	1.338	1.653	1.312	1.683	1.285	1.714	1.259	1.745	1.232	1.777
85	1.482	1.528	1.458	1.553	1.435	1.578	1.411	1.603	1.386	1.630	1.362	1.657	1.337	1.685	1.312	1.714	1.287	1.743	1.262	1.773
90	1.496	1.540	1.474	1.563	1.452	1.587	1.429	1.611	1.406	1.636	1.383	1.661	1.360	1.687	1.336	1.714	1.312	1.741	1.288	1.769
95	1.510	1.552	1.489	1.573	1.468	1.596	1.446	1.618	1.425	1.642	1.403	1.666	1.381	1.690	1.358	1.715	1.336	1.741	1.313	1.767
100	1.522	1.562	1.503	1.583	1.482	1.604	1.462	1.625	1.441	1.647	1.421	1.670	1.400	1.693	1.378	1.717	1.357	1.741	1.335	1.765
150	1.611	1.637	1.598	1.651	1.584	1.665	1.571	1.679	1.557	1.693	1.543	1.708	1.530	1.722	1.515	1.737	1.501	1.752	1.486	1.767
200	1.664	1.684	1.653	1.693	1.643	1.704	1.633	1.715	1.623	1.725	1.613	1.735	1.603	1.746	1.592	1.757	1.582	1.768	1.571	1.779

Table A4.7 Cont'd

n	$k'=11$ d_L	d_U	$k'=12$ d_L	d_U	$k'=13$ d_L	d_U	$k'=14$ d_L	d_U	$k'=15$ d_L	d_U	$k'=16$ d_L	d_U	$k'=17$ d_L	d_U	$k'=18$ d_L	d_U	$k'=19$ d_L	d_U	$k'=20$ d_L	d_U
16	0.060	3.446	—	—	—	—	—	—	—	—	—	—	—	—	—	—	—	—	—	—
17	0.084	3.286	0.053	3.506	—	—	—	—	—	—	—	—	—	—	—	—	—	—	—	—
18	0.113	3.146	0.075	3.358	0.047	3.557	—	—	—	—	—	—	—	—	—	—	—	—	—	—
19	0.145	3.023	0.102	3.227	0.067	3.420	0.043	3.601	—	—	—	—	—	—	—	—	—	—	—	—
20	0.178	2.914	0.131	3.109	0.092	3.297	0.061	3.474	0.038	3.639	—	—	—	—	—	—	—	—	—	—
21	0.212	2.817	0.162	3.004	0.119	3.185	0.084	3.358	0.055	3.521	0.035	3.671	—	—	—	—	—	—	—	—
22	0.246	2.729	0.194	2.909	0.148	3.084	0.109	3.252	0.077	3.412	0.050	3.562	0.032	3.700	—	—	—	—	—	—
23	0.281	2.651	0.227	2.822	0.178	2.991	0.136	3.155	0.100	3.311	0.070	3.459	0.046	3.597	0.029	3.725	—	—	—	—
24	0.315	2.580	0.260	2.744	0.209	2.906	0.165	3.065	0.125	3.218	0.092	3.363	0.065	3.501	0.043	3.629	0.027	3.744	—	—
25	0.348	2.517	0.292	2.674	0.240	2.829	0.194	2.982	0.152	3.131	0.116	3.274	0.085	3.410	0.060	3.538	0.039	3.657	0.025	3.766
26	0.381	2.460	0.324	2.610	0.272	2.758	0.224	2.906	0.180	3.050	0.141	3.191	0.107	3.325	0.079	3.452	0.055	3.572	0.036	3.682
27	0.413	2.409	0.356	2.552	0.303	2.694	0.253	2.836	0.208	2.976	0.167	3.113	0.131	3.245	0.100	3.371	0.073	3.490	0.051	3.602
28	0.444	2.363	0.387	2.499	0.333	2.635	0.283	2.772	0.237	2.907	0.194	3.040	0.156	3.169	0.122	3.294	0.093	3.412	0.068	3.524
29	0.474	2.321	0.417	2.451	0.363	2.582	0.313	2.713	0.266	2.843	0.222	2.972	0.182	3.098	0.146	3.220	0.114	3.338	0.087	3.450
30	0.503	2.283	0.447	2.407	0.393	2.533	0.342	2.659	0.294	2.785	0.249	2.909	0.208	3.032	0.171	3.152	0.137	3.267	0.107	3.379
31	0.531	2.248	0.475	2.367	0.422	2.487	0.371	2.609	0.322	2.730	0.277	2.851	0.234	2.970	0.196	3.087	0.160	3.201	0.128	3.311
32	0.558	2.216	0.503	2.330	0.450	2.446	0.399	2.563	0.350	2.680	0.304	2.797	0.261	2.912	0.221	3.026	0.184	3.137	0.151	3.246
33	0.585	2.187	0.530	2.296	0.477	2.408	0.426	2.520	0.377	2.633	0.331	2.746	0.287	2.858	0.246	2.969	0.209	3.078	0.174	3.184
34	0.610	2.160	0.556	2.266	0.503	2.373	0.452	2.481	0.404	2.590	0.357	2.699	0.313	2.808	0.272	2.915	0.233	3.022	0.197	3.126
35	0.634	2.136	0.581	2.237	0.529	2.340	0.478	2.444	0.430	2.550	0.383	2.655	0.339	2.761	0.297	2.865	0.257	2.969	0.221	3.071
36	0.658	2.113	0.605	2.210	0.554	2.310	0.504	2.410	0.455	2.512	0.409	2.614	0.364	2.717	0.322	2.818	0.282	2.919	0.244	3.019
37	0.680	2.092	0.628	2.186	0.578	2.282	0.528	2.379	0.480	2.477	0.434	2.576	0.389	2.675	0.347	2.774	0.306	2.872	0.268	2.969
38	0.702	2.073	0.651	2.164	0.601	2.256	0.552	2.350	0.504	2.445	0.458	2.540	0.414	2.637	0.371	2.733	0.330	2.828	0.291	2.923
39	0.723	2.055	0.673	2.143	0.623	2.232	0.575	2.323	0.528	2.414	0.482	2.507	0.438	2.600	0.395	2.694	0.354	2.787	0.315	2.879

Statistical tables

n	k'=1 dL	k'=1 dU	k'=2 dL	k'=2 dU	k'=3 dL	k'=3 dU	k'=4 dL	k'=4 dU	k'=5 dL	k'=5 dU	k'=6 dL	k'=6 dU	k'=7 dL	k'=7 dU	k'=8 dL	k'=8 dU	k'=9 dL	k'=9 dU	k'=10 dL	k'=10 dU
40	0.744	2.039	0.694	2.123	0.645	2.210	0.597	2.297	0.551	2.386	0.505	2.476	0.461	2.566	0.418	2.657	0.377	2.748	0.338	2.838
45	0.835	1.972	0.790	2.044	0.744	2.118	0.700	2.193	0.655	2.269	0.612	2.346	0.570	2.424	0.528	2.503	0.488	2.582	0.448	2.661
50	0.913	1.925	0.871	1.987	0.829	2.051	0.787	2.116	0.746	2.182	0.705	2.250	0.665	2.318	0.625	2.387	0.586	2.456	0.548	2.526
55	0.979	1.891	0.940	1.945	0.902	2.002	0.863	2.059	0.825	2.117	0.786	2.176	0.748	2.237	0.711	2.298	0.674	2.359	0.637	2.421
60	1.037	1.865	1.001	1.914	0.965	1.964	0.929	2.015	0.893	2.067	0.857	2.120	0.822	2.173	0.786	2.227	0.751	2.283	0.716	2.338
65	1.087	1.845	1.053	1.889	1.020	1.934	0.986	1.980	0.953	2.027	0.919	2.075	0.886	2.123	0.852	2.172	0.819	2.221	0.786	2.272
70	1.131	1.831	1.099	1.870	1.068	1.911	1.037	1.953	1.005	1.995	0.974	2.038	0.943	2.082	0.911	2.127	0.880	2.172	0.849	2.217
75	1.170	1.819	1.141	1.856	1.111	1.893	1.082	1.931	1.052	1.970	1.023	2.009	0.993	2.049	0.964	2.090	0.934	2.131	0.905	2.172
80	1.205	1.810	1.177	1.844	1.150	1.878	1.122	1.913	1.094	1.949	1.066	1.984	1.039	2.022	1.011	2.057	0.983	2.097	0.955	2.135
85	1.236	1.803	1.210	1.834	1.184	1.866	1.158	1.898	1.132	1.931	1.106	1.965	1.080	1.999	1.053	2.033	1.027	2.068	1.000	2.104
90	1.264	1.798	1.240	1.827	1.215	1.856	1.191	1.886	1.166	1.917	1.141	1.948	1.116	1.979	1.091	2.012	1.066	2.044	1.041	2.077
95	1.290	1.793	1.267	1.821	1.244	1.848	1.221	1.876	1.197	1.905	1.174	1.934	1.150	1.963	1.126	1.993	1.102	2.023	1.079	2.054
100	1.314	1.790	1.292	1.816	1.270	1.841	1.248	1.868	1.225	1.895	1.203	1.922	1.181	1.949	1.158	1.977	1.136	2.006	1.113	2.034
150	1.473	1.783	1.458	1.799	1.444	1.814	1.429	1.830	1.414	1.847	1.400	1.863	1.385	1.880	1.370	1.897	1.355	1.913	1.340	1.931
200	1.561	1.791	1.550	1.801	1.539	1.813	1.528	1.824	1.518	1.836	1.507	1.847	1.495	1.860	1.484	1.871	1.474	1.883	1.462	1.896

k' is the number of regressors excluding the intercept.
Reproduced by permission from *Econometrica*, **45**, no. 8, 1977, 1992–5.

INDEX

addition and multiplication theorems of probability, 314–15
Aitken, A.C., 102, 109, 113, 114
Allen partial elasticities in seemingly unrelated regression equations, 117, 119
Almon, S.: polynomial lag distribution, 71, 74–6
Amemiya, T., 83
Anderson, T.W., 141
applications
   in distributed lag models in maximum likelihood methods, 70–7
   economic, *see* economic applications
applied general equilibrium models, 195–209
   construction of, 201–4
   recent models, 204–6
   and social accounting matrix (SAM), 202, 206–9
   two-sector model, 204–5
      numerical example, 196–9
   welfare gains and losses, evaluation of, 199–201
Arrow, K.J., 271
Ashenfelter, O., 160
assumptions of disturbance terms in regression analysis, relaxation of, 14–25
asymptotic properties of statistical results, 321–2
Australia, imports in applied general equilibrium models, 205
autocorrelation, 17
   effect of removal, 18–19
   in heteroscedasticity, 38–9, 40

Bailey, D., 67
basic feasible solution (BFS)
   in linear programming, 213–14
      simplex method, 215–16
      transportation problem, 238–9, 241
   in quadratic programming, 272–3
Baumol, W.J., 242, 247, 255, 257
Beale, E.M.L., 242
Becker, G., 160
Beckmann, M., 303

Bellman, R., 4, 295–7, 303
benchmark equilibria in applied general equilibrium models, 201–4
Berndt, E.R., 62, 119
best linear unbiased estimators (BLUE)
   in linear regression model, 106
   and multicollinearity, 51
   in regression analysis, 8, 14, 19–20
Betancourt, R., 77
BLUE *see* best linear unbiased estimators
Boot, J.C.G., 46
Brenton, P., 63
Breusch, T.S., 39
Brown, D.K., 205–6
Bulmer-Thomas, V., 190

Cambridge Growth Project and social accounting matrix methods, 206
Canada, Free Trade Agreement, applied general equilibrium model of, 205–6
capital stock function in dynamic programming, 298–301
Casti, J.L., 303
causality
   in simultaneous equations models, 132
   tests of in maximum likelihood methods, 65–70
central limit theorem and sampling, 316
Charnes, A., 242
Chi squared distribution, 317
Chiang, A.C., 269
Christensen, L.R., 115, 119
Cobb-Douglas production function, 117
Cochrane, D., 18, 106
Cochrane-Orcutt iterative procedure
   in distributed lag model, 76–7
   in linear regression model, 106
   in regression analysis, 18
coefficient of determination, in regression analysis, 9–10
collinearity, 49, 51
Common Agricultural Policy and applied general equilibrium models, 205

compensating variation in applied general equilibrium models, 200–1
complementary slackness condition in linear programming, 224
confidence interval, and normal distribution results, 316
constant elasticity of substitution in applied general equilibrium models, 201–2
consumption
  function in dynamic programming, 298–9, 301
  in optimal control theory, 283, 286–9
convex and concave functions in matrix algebra, 312–13
Cooper, W.W., 242
covariance
  model in linear regression model, 110–12
  in regression analysis, 6, 9
  see also variance-covariance
Cramer-Rao lower bound variance, 59
Crew, M.A., 279
Cripps, T.F., 165
cross equation restrictions, estimates, 114–19
cutting method solution in integer programming, 248–9, 252–4, 259

Dantzig, G.B., 211, 215, 237, 242
Davidson, J.E.H., 63
de Wit, G.M., 46
Debreu, G., 174
determinants in matrix algebra, 308–9
distributed lag, model of, 70–7
distributions
  normal, and confidence interval, 316
  relationships among, 317–18
disturbance
  homoscedastic, 43, 45
  terms
    assumptions in regression analysis, 5–6
    in linear regression model, 101–2
    in qualitative and limited dependent model, 78, 80, 82
    in serial correlation, 41
    in simultaneous equations models, 133, 134–5
Dixit, A.K., 290
Dixon, P.B., 205
Dorfman, R., 211, 242, 303
Dreyfus, S., 303
dual problem in linear programming, 221–31
  of simplex method, 231–7
  in transportation problem, 238–9, 241
dual simplex method in integer programming, 251
duality and integer programming, 254–61
Durbin-Watson statistic
  biased variance in serial correlation, 38, 39
  in multiple linear regression, 38, 39, 48
Durbin-Watson statistic, in regression analysis, 17–18
Durbin, J., 18, 31, 39

dynamic optimisation, 282–305
  dynamic programming, 294–8
    economic applications, 298–303
  exercises, 303–4
  and optimal control theory, 282–7
    economic applications, 287–94
dynamic programming, 294–8
  economic applications, 298–303

economic applications
  dynamic programming, 298–303
  of optimal control theory, 287–94
endogenous variables in simultaneous equation models, 131–4
Engle, R.F., 132
Enthoven, A.C., 271
Episkopou, S., 42, 43
equivalent variation in applied general equilibrium models, 200–1
error component model in linear regression model, 110–12
estimates, cross equation restrictions, 114–19
estimators
  of coefficients in regression analysis, 7–8
  and their properties, 320–1
Euler-Lagrange equation in dynamic programming, 290–1
European Community, effect of UK joining in applied general equilibrium models, 204–5
exogeneity in simultaneous equations models, 132
exogenous variables in simultaneous equation models, 132–4

F distribution/test statistics, 317
  in seemingly unrelated regression equations, 114
F test
  and heteroscedasticity, 42
  in maximum likelihood methods, 62, 66
  and multicollinearity, 50
  in polynomial lag distribution, 75–6
  in regression analysis, 10–11
  and specification error, 48
feasible solution
  in integer programming, 248
  in linear programming, 211, 213–14
    in dual problems 222–3, 225, 228–9
    dual simplex methods, 233, 236
    in transportation problem, 239, 241
Finney, D.J., 83
Fisher, A.C., 293
Fomby, T.B., 111
foreign trade and input-output analysis, 179–82
Friedman, M., 36, 93
full information maximum likelihood estimation in system methods of estimation, 156–60

Gale, D., 242
Gantmacher, F.R., 306

Gass, S.I., 242
Gauss-Markov theorem of variance in regression analysis, 27
Geisel, M.S., 74
generalised least squares approach and multiple linear regression model, 106-10
geometric lag distribution, 71-4
Geweke, J., 67, 69, 70
Godfrey, L.G., 39
Gomory, R.E., 247, 249, 255, 257, 259
Granger, C.W.J., causality, 65-70, 132
Graybill, F.A., 314
Greene, W.H., 87
Griliches, Z., 162

Hadley, G., 242, 290, 306
Hamiltonian function
 in exhaustible resource problem, 292-3
 in optimal control theory, 284-5, 286-7
Harberger, A.C., 204
Hausman, J.A., 48, 91, 92-3
Hawkins, D., 171-2
Hawkins-Simon condition in input-output analysis, 171-3
Hecksher-Ohlin theorem in input-output analysis of foreign trade, 181
Heckman, J.J, 85
Hendry, D.F., 42, 63, 132, 157
Henry, E.W., 188
Herfindahl index, and heteroscedasticity, 42
Herstein, I.N., 174
heteroscedasticity
 distribution and errors in variables, 88
 and multiple linear regression, 42-5
 in regression analysis, 19-22
Hill, R.C., 111
Hitchcock, F.L., 237
Hood, W.C., 136, 154
Hsiao, C., 66
hypotheses, tests of 318-19
 see also null hypotheses

idempotent matrix, in algebra, 310
identification of structural coefficients in simultaneous equation models, 135-41
indirect least squares methods in simultaneous equation models, 142-3
input-output analysis, 167-94
 backward and forward linkages, 176-9
 dynamic Leontief model, 182-7
 exercises, 191-3
 and foreign trade, 179-82
 and social accounting matrices, 207
 static Leontief model, 168-76
 updating matrices, procedures for, 188-90
instrumental variable estimation in simultaneous equation models, 144-6
integer programming, 245-61
 all integer problem, 249-52

duality and, 254-61
exercises, 279-81
mixed problem, 252-4
Intriligator, M.D., 162, 290

Jacobian function in nonlinear programming, 262
Johnson, G.E., 160
Johnson, S.R., 111
Johnston, J., 19
Jorgenson, D.W., 115
Judge, G., 162

Kaldor, N., 161
Kamien, M.I., 290, 303
Kelejian, H., 77
Kemp, M.C., 290
Kendrick, D., 184
Kleindorfer, P.R., 279
Kmenta, J., 6, 19, 162
Koopmans, T.C., 136, 154, 237
Kuhn, H.W., 247, 264-71
Kuhn-Tucker conditions in nonlinear programming, 264-9
 and peak load pricing problem, 273-9
 and quadratic programming, 271-3
 sufficiency theorem, 269-71

lagged endogenous variables, 132-4
Lagrange multiplier test in maximum likelihood methods, 59, 61, 62, 64-5, 67
Lagrangean function
 in exhaustible resource problem, 292
 in nonlinear programming, 262-3
 and Kuhn-Tucker conditions in nonlinear programming, 266-7
 in optimal control theory, 283-7
 in peak load pricing problem, 274-5
 in quadratic programming, 271
 and sufficiency theorem in Kuhn-Tucker conditions in nonlinear programming, 269-71
Larson, R.E., 303
Lau, L.M., 115
least squares estimates of regression coefficients, 7-8, 13-14
least squares approach in linear regression model, 102-6
Lemke, C.E., 231
Leontief, W.W., input-output model
 dynamic, 182-7
 static, 168-76
likelihood ratio test in maximum likelihood methods, 59-60, 62, 64-5
limited dependent variables in maximum likelihood methods, 77-87
limited information maximum likelihood in simultaneous equation models, 151-4, 157-9

linear analysis and social accounting matrices, 207
linear expenditure system in applied general equilibrium models, 203
linear probability model in maximum likelihood methods, 78–9
linear programming, 210–46
  dual of, 221–31
    simplex methods, 231–7
  exercises, 242–5
  introduction to, 210–14
  simplex method, 214–21
    dual of, 231–7
  transportation problem, 237–42
  see also nonlinear programming
linear regression model, generalised, 101–12
  cross equation restrictions, estimates, 114–19
  error component and covariance models, 110–12
  exercises, 119–29
  and seemingly unrelated regressions, 112–19
linkages, backward and forward in input-output analysis, 176–9
Littlechild, S.C., 279
logit model in maximum likelihood methods, 79–80
Lynch, R., 189

McCallum, B.T., 51
McElroy, M.B., 113
McKenzie, L., 174
Maddala, G.S., 80
matrices
  input-output
    and price changes, 189–90
    procedures for updating, 188–90
    RAS method, 188–9
  in Leontief input-output model, 170–1, 173–6, 182, 185
  limited information maximum likelihood models, 152–3
  notation for linear regression model, 102–5
  social accounting methods, 206–9
  of structural coefficients in simultaneous equation models, 135–8
matrix algebra, summary, 306–13
  characteristic roots and vectors, 309–10
  convex and concave functions, 312–13
  definitions of operations, 306–8
  determinants, 308–9
  idempotent, 310
  quadratic forms, 310–11
  semipositive, 311–12
maximisation problems in linear programming, 229
maximum conditions, Kuhn-Tucker, 269–71
maximum likelihood methods, 56–100
  applications in distributed lag models, 70–7
  concept, 56–70

  and errors in variables, 88–94
  exercises, 94–9
  qualitative and limited dependent variables, 77–87
  and tests of causality, 65–70
  validity, tests of, 59–63, 64–5
maximum value principle in optimal control theory, 284, 286–7
Miller, E.H., 204
minimisation problems in linear programming, 231
minimum conditions, Kuhn-Tucker, 269
minimum variance bound estimator, in maximum likelihood methods, 59
models
  applied general equilibrium, 195–209
  of covariance, 110–12
  distributed lag, 70–7
  error component, 110–12
  Leontief input-output
    dynamic, 182–7
    static, 168–76
  linear regression, generalised, 101–30
  in maximum likelihood methods, 57–8, 78–87
  multiple linear regression, 106–10
  of regression analysis, 25–8
  with serial correlation, 40–1
  of simultaneous equations, 131–66
Mood, A.M., 314
multicollinearity
  and multiple linear regression, 48–52
  in polynomial lag distribution, 76
  in regression analysis, 22–3
multiple linear regression model, 35–55
  exercises, 52–4
  and generalised least squares approach, 106–10
  and heterscedasticity, 42–5
  and multicollinearity, 48–52
  and serial correlation, 35–42
  and specification error, 45–8
Mundlak, Y., 50–1, 112

nonlinear programming, 261–71
  classical optimisation, 261–4
  Kuhn-Tucker conditions, 264–9
    sufficiency theorem, 269–71
  non-negativity requirements, 264
  and quadratic programming, 271–3
non-negativity requirements in nonlinear programming, 264
non-linearity as specification error in regression analysis, 25
normal distribution and confidence interval, results, 316
null hypothesis
  of homoscedastic disturbances, 43
  in maximum likelihood methods, 64, 66
  in serial correlation, 39, 40
  and specification error, 45
  tests in regression analysis, 9, 13

O'Connor, R., 188
optimal control theory, 282-7
   economic applications, 287-94
   and calculus of variations, 290-1
   exhaustible resource problem, 291-4
   optimal consumption plan, 287-90
optimal solutions in linear programming, 212
optimality principle, Bellman's, 295-7
optimisation
   classical, 261-4
   Kuhn-Tucker conditions, 264-9
   in linear programming, 210
Orcutt, G.H., 106
ordinary least squares (OLS) approach
   biased variance in serial correlation, 35-6, 39
   as BLUE in general model of regression analysis, 26-7
   and errors in variables, 88-9
   in geometric lag distribution, 72-3
   and heteroscedasticity, 19, 43
   and indirect least squares methods, 143
   in limited dependent variable model, 87
   limited information maximum likelihood models, 151
   in linear regression model, 102-4
   and maximum likelihood methods, 58
   and multicollinearity, 49-50, 51
   and multiple linear regression model, 108
   and qualitative variable model, 78, 82
   in regression analysis, 16-17, 21
   in seemingly unrelated regression equations, 113-14
   in simultaneous equations models, 133, 135
   and specification error, 45
   in system methods of estimation, 159
   and two-stage least squares methods, 149-50

Pagan, A.R., 39
Parikh, A., 49, 51, 63, 75-6, 86, 109, 116, 161, 189
Parsley, C.J., 159
peak load pricing problem and Kuhn-Tucker conditions in nonlinear programming, 273-9
Piggott, J.R., 195, 205
polynomial (Almon) lag distribution, 71, 74-6
Pontryagin, L.S., 284
Prais, S.J., 106, 108
principal component estimation in multicollinearity, 50-1
probability, addition and multiplication theorems of, 314-15
probit model in maximum likelihood methods, 80-3
production functions in applied general equilibrium models, 195-7, 202
Pyatt, G., 206-7

quadratic forms in matrix algebra, 310-11
quadratic programming, 271-3

qualitative variables in maximum likelihood methods, 77-87
Quesnay, F., 206

Ramsey, J.D., 45, 48
random variable and expectation, concept of, 315
Rao, C.R., 321
recomputed dual prices in integer programming, 257-8
Rees, R., 279
regression
   linear, generalised model, 101-2
   residuals in serial correlation, 38, 39
   seemingly unrelated, 112-19
   specification error test (RESET), 46, 48
regression analysis, 5-34
   disturbance terms, relaxation of assumptions, 14-25
   exercises, 28-33
   general model of, 25-8
   and multiple linear regression, 5-14
residual sum of squares in regression analysis, 6-7
Richard, J.F., 132
roots, characteristic in matrix algebra, 309-10
Round, J.I., 206-7

sampling and central limit theorem, 316
Samuelson, P.A., 242
Sargent, T.J., 132
Savin, N.E., 62
Scarf, H., 195
Schmidt, P., 46
Schwartz, N.L., 290, 303
Schwartz, A., 36
search method solution in integer programming, 248, 249
seemingly unrelated regressions estimators (SURE), 112-19
   and cross equation restrictions, estimates, 114-19
semipositive matrix, 311-12
serial correlation, 15-19
   in distributed lag model, 76-7
   and multiple linear regression, 35-42
   in tests of causality, 66
Shephard, R., 115
Shoven, J.B., 195
Simon, H.A., 171-2
simple linear regression model and maximum likelihood methods, 57-8
simplex method
   in linear programming, 214-21
      dual problem, 231-7
   in quadratic programming, 271
Sims, C.A., 66, 69, 70
simultaneous equation models, 131-66
   exercises, 162-6
   identification problem, 135-41
   single equation methods, 141-54

simultaneous equation models – *contd*
  system methods of estimation, 154–60
single equation methods in simultaneous equation models, 141–54
  indirect least squares, 142–3
  instrumental variable estimation, 144–6
  limited information maximum likelihood, 151–4, 157–9
  two-stage least squares, 146–50, 157–60
small sample properties, 320–1
social welfare function in dynamic programming, 298–9
Solow, R.M., 242
specification error
  and multiple linear regression, 45–8
  in regression analysis, 23–5
Spencer, J.F., 204
Srba, F., 63
standard error of regression coefficient, 13
  and multicollinearity, 23
statistical results, 314–22
  addition and multiplication theorems of probability, 314–15
  asymptotic properties, 321–2
  estimators and their properties, 320–1
  normal distribution and confidence interval, 316
  relationships among distributions, 317–18
  sampling and central limit theorem, 316
  tests of hypotheses, 318–19
Stern, R.M., 205–6
stochastic disturbance term in regression analysis, 6
structural coefficients
  identification problem in simultaneous equation models, 135–41
  in indirect least squares methods, 142–3
  in instrumental variable estimation, 144
  in two-stage least squares models, 146–7, 153
sufficiency theorem of Kuhn-Tucker conditions in nonlinear programming, 269–71
SURE *see* seemingly unrelated
system methods of estimation in simultaneous equation models, 154–60
  full information maximum likelihood estimation, 156–60
  three-stage least squares estimation, 154–6

t statistic
  distribution, 9, 13, 317
  in heteroscedasticity, 38
  in limited dependent variable model, 84
  in maximum likelihood methods, 64
  and multicollinearity, 50
  and serial correlation, 38
  in system methods of estimation, 159
Taha, H., 249, 253
Tarling, R.J., 165
tax changes and welfare gains and losses, 200–1
Taylor series in dynamic programming, 297

Theil, H., 154, 188
Thorbecke, E., 207
three-stage least squares estimation in system methods of estimation, 154–6
Thursby, J.G., 46
Tilanus, C.B., 188
time
  discrete and dynamic programming problems, 294–7
  path
    in exhaustible resource problem, 292–4
    in optimal control theory, 283–4, 286–9, 291
Tobin, J., 85
tobit model in maximum likelihood methods, 83–7
transportation problem in linear programming, 237–42
  dual problem in, 238–9, 241
Tucker, A.W., 247, 264–71
two-sector model of applied general equilibrium models, 204–5
  numerical example, 196–9
two-stage least squares in simultaneous equation models, 146–50, 157–60

United Kingdom
  effect of joining EEC in applied general equilibrium models, 204–5
  tax system in applied general equilibrium models, 204–5
United Nations, 206
United States-Canada Free Trade Agreement, applied general equilibrium model of, 205–6
utility functions in applied general equilibrium models, 195–6, 202

variable
  absence of relevant and specification error, 23–4
  endogenous and exogenous, 131–4
  errors in and maximum likelihood methods, 88–94
  irrelevant, presence of and specification error, 24–5
  qualitative and limited dependent, 77–87
  in regression analysis, 5–6
variance
  analysis of in regression analysis, 11–12, 14
  in qualitative and limited dependent model, 78, 82
  in regression analysis, 7–9, 17
variance-covariance matrices
  in error component model, 111
  in instrumental variable estimation, 146
  for linear regression model, 102–5, 107
  and multiple linear regression model, 109
  in seemingly unrelated regression equations, 113
  in simultaneous equations models, 134–5

variance-covariance matrices – *contd*
   in three-stage least squares estimation, 155–6
   in two-stage least squares models, 150
vectors, characteristic in matrix algebra, 309–10

Wald test in maximum likelihood methods, 59, 60–2, 64–5, 67, 69
Walras's law in applied general equilibrium models, 196, 198
Watson, G.S., 18, 31

welfare gains and losses, evaluation of in applied general equilibrium models, 199–201
Whalley, J., 195, 205
White, H., 19, 43
Winsten, C.B., 106, 108

Yeo, S., 63

Zellner, A., 3, 74, 101, 113, 116–17, 154